Ghana During the First World War

CAROLINA ACADEMIC PRESS AFRICAN WORLD SERIES
Toyin Falola, Series Editor

Africa, Empire and Globalization: Essays in Honor of A. G. Hopkins
Toyin Falola, editor, and Emily Brownell, editor

African Entrepreneurship in Jos, Central Nigeria, 1902–1985
S.U. Fwatshak

An African Music and Dance Curriculum Model: Performing Arts in Education
Modesto Amegago

Authority Stealing: Anti-Corruption War and Democratic Politics in Post-Military Nigeria
Wale Adebanwi

The Bukusu of Kenya: Folktales, Culture and Social Identities
Namulundah Florence

Contemporary African Literature: New Approaches
Tanure Ojaide

Contesting Islam in Africa: Homegrown Wahhabism and Muslim Identity in Northern Ghana, 1920–2010
Abdulai Iddrisu

Converging Identities: Blackness in the Modern African Diaspora
Julius Adekunle and Hettie V. Williams

Democracy in Africa: Political Changes and Challenges
Saliba Sarsar, editor, and Julius O. Adekunle, editor

Diaspora and Imagined Nationality: USA-Africa Dialogue *and Cyberframing Nigerian Nationhood*
Koleade Odutola

Food Crop Production, Hunger, and Rural Poverty in Nigeria's Benue Area, 1920–1995
Mike Odugbo Odey

Esu: Yoruba God, Power, and the Imaginative Frontiers
Toyin Falola

Ghana During the First World War: The Colonial Administration of Sir Hugh Clifford
Elizabeth Wrangham

Globalization: The Politics of Global Economic Relations and International Business
N. Oluwafemi Mimiko

A History of Class Formation in the Plateau Province of Nigeria, 1902–1960: The Genesis of a Ruling Class
Monday Yakiban Mangvwat

Horror in Paradise: Frameworks for Understanding the Crises of the Niger Delta Region of Nigeria
Christopher LaMonica and J. Shola Omotola

Imperialism, Economic Development and Social Change in Africa
Raymond Dumett

In Search of African Diasporas: Testimonies and Encounters
Paul Tiyambe Zeleza

Intercourse and Crosscurrents in the Atlantic World: Calabar-British Experience, 17th–20th Centuries
David Lishilinimle Imbua

Julius Nyerere, Africa's Titan on a Global Stage: Perspectives from Arusha to Obama
Ali A. Mazrui and Lindah L. Mhando

Local Government in South Africa Since 1994: Leadership, Democracy, Development, and Service Delivery in a Post-Apartheid Era
Alexius Amtaika

Narratives of Struggle: The Philosophy and Politics of Development in Africa
John Ayotunde Bewaji

Perspectives on Feminism in Africa
'Lai Olurode, editor

Pioneer, Patriot, and Nigerian Nationalist: A Biography of the Reverend M. D. Opara, 1915–1965
Felix Ekechi

Satires of Power in Yoruba Visual Culture
Yomi Ola

The Tiv and Their Southern Neighbours, 1890–1990
Emmanuel Chiahemba Ayangaôr

The Vile Trade: Slavery and the Slave Trade in Africa
Abi Alabo Derefaka, Wole Ogundele, Akin Alao, and Agustus Ajibola

The Women's War of 1929: A History of Anti-Colonial Resistance in Eastern Nigeria
Toyin Falola and Adam Paddock

The Yoruba Frontier: A Regional History of Community Formation, Experience, and Changes in West Africa
Aribidesi Usman

Women, Gender, and Sexualities in Africa
Toyin Falola and Nana Akua Amponsah, editors

Ghana During the First World War

The Colonial Administration of Sir Hugh Clifford

Elizabeth Wrangham

Carolina Academic Press
Durham, North Carolina

Library of Congress Cataloging-in-Publication Data

Wrangham, Elizabeth.

Ghana during the First World War : the Colonial Administration of Sir Hugh Clifford / Elizabeth Wrangham.

p. cm. -- (African world series)

Includes bibliographical references and index.

ISBN 978-1-61163-360-3 (alk. paper)

1. Ghana--Economic conditions--To 1957. 2. Ghana--History--To 1957. 3. World War, 1914-1918--Economic aspects--Ghana. 4. Great Britain--Colonies--Africa--Administration. 5. Colonial administrators--Ghana. I. Title.

HC1060.W73 2013

966.703--dc23

2013000944

Carolina Academic Press
700 Kent Street
Durham, North Carolina 27701
Telephone (919) 489–7486
Fax (919) 493–5668
www.cap-press.com

Printed in the United States of America

Contents

Foreword

The past
Is but the cinders
Of the present;
The future
The smoke
That escaped
Into the cloud-bound sky.

Be gentle, be kind my beloved,
For words become memories,
And memories, tools
In the hands of jesters . . .

Kwesi Brew, "The Search," in G. Moore & U. Beier (eds.), *Modern Poetry from Africa*, (London, 1968), p. 96.

My introduction to Ghana came after studying history at Cambridge, when I went to teach at the Women's Teacher Training College in Tamale. During that year, 1965–1966, Kwame Nkrumah was overthrown; within the college, the Basel principal, Miss Mischler, retired and was succeeded by a Ghanaian, Miss Victoria Sackey. This research, undertaken many years later, arose out of my very happy experience of living in Ghana and working with staff and students of the college, including my fellow tutor and friend, Sue Trevelyan, and my own class, T4.

I am particularly indebted to Richard Rathbone (now professor emeritus of modern history at the University of Wales, Aberystwyth) for his judgment and constant support. I thank Toyin Falola (professor of history, University of Texas at Austin) for his constructive criticism and advice. I should also like to thank Dr. John Parker (senior lecturer in history, School of Oriental and African Studies, London University) for his encouragement; and Andrew Porter (professor emeritus, department of history, King's College, London University) and David Killingray (emeritus professor of modern history, Goldsmiths, London University) for their advice. Finally, I remember with gratitude and affection the kindness of the late Dr. Martin Lynn (Queen's University, Belfast).

Periods of study leave from Roehampton University have been essential for the completion of this book. I would also like to give special thanks for the kind help of Augustine Mensah of the Public Records and Archives Department of Ghana (PRAAD), and to Mrs. Asiedu for her kind hospitality in Accra during my research in Ghana. I must also thank the helpful staff of the UK National Archive; the British Museum newspaper library at Colindale; Rhodes House, at Oxford; the Guildhall Library; the Royal Geographical Society; the archive of the Royal Botanic Gardens at Kew; and the libraries of SOAS and the Royal Commonwealth Society. Special thanks are due, too, to Mrs. Clifford Holmes, for access to her collection of Sir Hugh Clifford's papers. I would like to record the help and efficiency of the editorial and production team at Carolina Academic Press.

I am grateful to London University's Thornley Fund for its support.

Finally, I dedicate this book to my beloved family, Gardner and Edward, in gratitude for their endless patience and unfailing support. It was, above all, Gardner's wise advice that made possible the completion of this work.

Elizabeth Wrangham

Introduction

In the Gold Coast colony (now independent Ghana), the First World War (1914–1918) happened to coincide with the relatively liberal governorship of Sir Hugh Clifford (1912–1919). The disruption brought about by the war, and the extent to which it was mediated through Clifford's administration, were to have both an immediate and lasting impact on this British West African colony.

The First World War has been a largely neglected period in the history of the Gold Coast—often seen then as Britain's "model" African colony. But though most of the fighting was remote, the war was in fact to prove central to its history. Indeed, this period would lie at the halfway point, chronologically, of colonial rule. The original coastal colony of the Gold Coast was proclaimed in 1874, and had therefore been established for forty years by the time of the First World War; independence came forty years later, in 1957. More importantly, the war was central in marking a lasting turn in the fortunes of the colony. The severe economic dislocation of the war appears to have played a part in changing the attitude of the colonized towards colonial rule in the Gold Coast. The timing is significant. The cumulative economic effects, within thirty years, of the First World War followed by the Depression and the Second World War were also to make for crucial social and political change—largely beyond the scope of this study—and made an important contribution to the process that ultimately led to ending British rule in this region.

The intention here is to examine and interpret what Karl Popper called "actual, singular or specific events"—and to only accept generalizations or "theoretical constructions" if backed by specific evidence.[1] But at the same time, the aim will be to contribute to a wider debate concerning the nature of British colonialism in Africa—and especially, on the *extent* of colonial power in a remote equatorial territory such as this. In view of such aims, previously neglected official sources provide particularly valuable evidence. As David Henige observes, "no one of us is without an ideology ... an ensemble of beliefs, attitudes and aims"; these "underpin the way we argue, the evidence we use and how we use it, and the ways we hope to influence others."[2]

This study rests on a range of sources, many of which—African as well as European—offer alternative, unofficial perceptions of life in the colony in this period. They will inform our understanding of the actual (as distinct from the supposed) consequences of colonialism. All colonial rule was, of course, intrusive and (ultimately) based on coercion. Yet the sources for the Gold Coast in this period will indicate that, while inequitable and disruptive, British colonial rule here was not consistently or universally damaging—in part because it had neither the intention nor the capacity to be so.

Insofar as it uses British colonial records as evidence, this study attempts to make sense of the ways in which officials took initiatives and, more often, reacted to circum-

1. K. Popper, *The Poverty of Historicism,* (London, 1957), p. 143.
2. D. Henige, *Historical Evidence and Argument,* (Wisconsin, 2005), p. 5.

stances—in short, what they thought they were doing. It is worth noting that documents produced at the time were, of course, for immediate, practical, internal use; they were not produced for the subsequent benefit of historians, of whatever "ideology." British colonial thinking is not ours, but in seeking to make sense of this central episode of British colonial rule in the Gold Coast, we must try to understand it. As David Henige advocates, we need to "combine the use of evidence and argument (inseparably intertwined) to present a case."[3] And in the light of his advice it is, of course, just as important for readers as for writers of history that they should "maintain open minds not suffocated by a set of beliefs."[4]

Unlike most of what has been written on the Gold Coast in the period of the First World War, this is not a military history. Studies of Britain's African empire in this period have largely concentrated on a general picture of military recruitment and campaigns, and how, very broadly, the Great War affected the West African region, or even the whole African continent.[5] For the Gold Coast, soldiers (approximately 10,000) and carriers (approximately 5,500), out of an African population of about two million, participated in the campaigns in West Africa.[6] They fought in Togo in August 1914, in Cameroon between 1914 and 1916, and in the East Africa campaign that continued for the duration of the war.[7]

The study fills an important gap concerning both the impact of the First World War on one British colony and, more widely, the impact of the war on Britain's West African empire, in what remained a nonsettler region of the continent. David Kimble provided a valuable, now classic, political study of the Gold Coast colony up to 1928, but with his strong political focus, he included less on colonial economic policy.[8] Osuntokun's book on Nigeria and Festus Cole's work on Sierra Leone provide some comparisons with conditions elsewhere in British West Africa.[9] There are also a few useful articles on the effect of the war on the Gold Coast colony: for example, those by Roger Thomas and David Killingray, and more recently, and especially on recruitment of labor, by Kwabena Akurang-Parry.[10]

The value of colonial history remains beyond doubt. Antony Hopkins argues a powerful defense: "Regional specialists writing indigenous history have nothing to fear from a revival of colonial history: the two are complementary." He goes on to warn: "A greater cause for concern arises from the widespread adoption of stereotypes that reduce colonial policies and the colonial presence in general to acts of oppression … and imply that

3. *Ibid.*, p. 7.

4. *Ibid.*, p. 6.

5. Studies which largely concentrate on military aspects, in Southern and Eastern Africa as well as West Africa, include H. Strachan, *The First World War in Africa*, (Oxford, 2004); B. Farwell, *The Great War in Africa 1914–1918*, (London, 1987); M. Page (ed.), *Africa and the First World War*, (London, 1987); and K. Akurang-Parry, "Africa and World War I" in T. Falola (ed.), *Colonial Africa 1885–1939*, Vol. 3, (Carolina, 2002).

6. "Report on the Combatant Manpower of the Native Races of British West Africa 1923," CO879/121/1098.

7. This study does not incorporate the Gold Coast's administration of (German) Togoland during the war.

8. D. Kimble, *A Political History of Ghana, 1850–1928*, (Oxford, 1963). A more recent study of the political history of Ghana concentrates on the period since independence: R. S. Gocking, *The History of Ghana*, (Westport, 2005).

9. A. Osuntokun, *Nigeria in the First World War*, (London, 1979); F. Cole, "Sierra Leone and World War I," unpublished PhD thesis, (London, 1994).

10. See listings in Bibliography, below, pp. 274, 271, 264, respectively.

colonial subjects were helpless victims."[11] Among such stereotypes, this study reconsiders the extent to which "exploitation rather than development" was the colonial aim.[12] For men such as Governor Sir Hugh Clifford, "development" entailed the utilization of the Gold Coast's natural resources—for Britain's benefit, of course, yet, as he and others of his time saw it, for the benefit of Africans too.[13] But the sources suggest that the colonial administration at this time was not capable of undertaking such economic tasks itself, especially in wartime, while its primary aim was simply retention of control, at minimum cost. It therefore seems an exaggeration to say that colonialism was at all times "bent on forcefully reshaping the values and ideas of colonial subjects."[14] Such changes as did occur appear to have been as much unforeseen results as intended consequences.

The aim in this study is therefore to follow an empirical approach to achieve a wider knowledge of the financial and economic basis of imperialism, as seen in one particular British African colony at one particular time. The study does not adopt the postmodernist concentration on cultural history; rather, it challenges the sometimes distorted picture produced by postcolonialists "in which cultural effects have been inflated *at the expense of economic and political institutions*."[15] As Richard Rathbone has argued, what is needed is "evidence rather than assertion" and "recognition of the diversity of experience rather than essentialism and generalisation."[16] Studies based on the colonial record have been dismissed too readily as merely "colonial bureaucratic accounts" that "overlook African perspectives and responses."[17] Historians of this period, as of any other, need to be grateful for any sources which have survived. While using a range of alternative sources including, for example, Africans' speeches in the legislative council and independent African newspapers (*The Gold Coast Nation* and the *Gold Coast Leader*), we may acknowledge the difficulties where there are groups whose "voices" have not been heard and in many cases may never have been recorded. Meanwhile, for an understanding of what the British were trying to do (and why), of the challenges they faced, and of the degree to which they succeeded (or thought they were succeeding), what is required is a careful, detailed, scrutiny of the documents. Fortunately, colonial officials created a mass of documents at that time—reports and correspondence, for example—and unknowingly bequeathed them to scholars of a later age.[18] This body of material helps us, moreover, to test general theories and general assumptions about the character of British colonial rule.

One such general assumption is that of universal African resistance. Barbara Bush, for example, gives primacy to resistance as having "always been a feature of the colonial relationship."[19] Indeed, she implies it was always *the* feature, using the term to cover any action which is "critical of, opposes, upsets or challenges the smooth running of colonial

---

11. A.G. Hopkins, "Back to the Future: From National History to Imperial History," *Past and Present*, 164, August 1999, pp. 229–230.

12. T. Falola (ed.), *The Dark Webs: Perspectives on Colonialism in Africa,* (Carolina, 2005), p. 12.

13. The benefits were to be unequal, though, one could argue, no more unequal than in any essentially capitalist enterprise.

14. T. Falola, *The Dark Webs*, p. 12.

15. A. Loomba, *Colonialism/PostColonialism,* (London, 2nd edition, 2005), p. 51. My italics.

16. R Rathbone, "Review," *Journal of African History*, 48, 1, 2007, pp. 152–153.

17. K. Akurang-Parry, "African Agency and Cultural Initiatives in the British Imperial Military and Labor Recruitment Drives in the Gold Coast (Colonial Ghana) during the First World War," *African Identities*, 4, 2, 2006, pp. 213 and 214–234 *passim*.

18. See, e.g., Colonial Office (CO96) for wide-ranging detailed correspondence between London and Accra.

19. B. Bush, *Imperialism, Race and Resistance*, (London, 1999), p. 16.

rule."[20] Seemingly unwilling to accept the possibility that some of the colonized may have acquiesced, for at least some of the time, she paints a picture of a constant low-level guerrilla warfare against the colonizers—even, or especially, during those times when there was no *overt* resistance. Such a picture does not represent what the sources reveal across the Gold Coast in the first couple of decades of the twentieth century. While Bush subsequently—inconsistently, reluctantly—does acknowledge collaboration and even accommodation, she still appears to rule out a different type of response: that of Africans who did not see themselves primarily as victims of colonialism but as actors, as entrepreneurs, both willing and able to take advantage of the new context in which they found themselves. Was every cocoa farmer during the boom years prior to the outbreak of the First World War "always" engaged in acts of resistance? Was every "criticism" in an African newspaper a call for the end of colonial rule, and was every positive comment evidence of "the exercise of domination"? Such conclusions would be ungrounded and condescending.

Even when Bush approves of the notion of interdependency—which surely challenges her preferred notion of "domination" and its counterpart "liberation"—she has to see colonizers "collide" with the colonized.[21] All is violence, confrontation, and oppression: surely far too simple and generalized a way to describe the shifting colonial relationship at all times and in all places. The British did "collide" with the Ashanti at the end of the nineteenth century. It is fiction, however, to describe the relationship between the Ashanti and the British as one of perpetual collision thereafter—though British officials were themselves surprised by how easy relations were with this people just before, and even during, the First World War. In short, notwithstanding her inconsistencies, Bush emphasizes just one theme, resistance (which was of course evident, in certain times and places, as we shall see later in this study), over all others, in what was a far more complex and variegated colonial relationship than she describes. As their own records clearly demonstrate, colonial administrators were "frustrated."[22] But they were constantly frustrated, not by daily acts of resistance, but by shortages of personnel and money and by a near-complete failure to understand the workings of the African societies they sought to administer.

In order to understand the impact of the war and its significance for the history of the Gold Coast, and the importance of Clifford's administration, we need to look briefly at how this British colony came into being; how it was run; and what its purpose was, as far as London was concerned. In particular, we need to look at the mindset of the British colonial administration—what its original goals were—and at the nature of the obstacles it faced.

From his arrival in the Gold Coast in 1912, Clifford's administration was made more difficult by the territory's piecemeal origins.[23] Situated on the West African coast between the French territory of the Ivory Coast to the west and German Togoland to the east, it had been formed by joining together the original coastal colony and two inland dependencies, or protectorates, Ashanti and the Northern Territories. The original (coastal) colony, proclaimed in 1874 after the Ashanti war, had been divided into three administrative units: the eastern, central, and western provinces. In 1902, following the Ashanti revolt,

20. *Ibid.*
21. *Ibid.*, pp. 15, 17.
22. *Ibid.*, p. 16.
23 See Appendix I, "The Gold Coast in 1916," page 279.

Orders in Council formally annexed the Ashanti kingdom to the north as a protectorate of the Gold Coast Colony. Ashanti's former tributary states further north were then added as the Northern Territories Protectorate.[23]

Conforming to a typical model of the time, the colonial government in the Gold Coast consisted of British political officers attempting to direct the African population through their chiefs and elders in what was called "indirect rule." This was the context before the First World War: a colony run by a local British colonial administration, under a governor based on the coast (in the capital, Accra), where were located, too, the secretariat, the treasury, and all local government departments. As in the other colonies of British West Africa, a small number of political staff were directly responsible to the governor: chief commissioners (CCs), provincial commissioners (PCs), district commissioners (DCs), and assistants (ADCs). These were the main official contact between the local British colonial government on the coast and African chiefs and, through the chiefs and elders, their African subjects across the colony.[24]

As with the other British West African colonies just before the First World War, British Crown Colony government in the Gold Coast was paternalist and authoritarian rather than democratic or representative. The governor headed the administration and, with the advice of his senior British officials in an executive council, reported back to the secretary of state for the colonies, a member of the cabinet, in the Colonial Office in London. The Gold Coast legislative council was also (like the Gold Coast executive council) simply an advisory forum concerned with issues such as legal bills and annual government financial estimates. Political reforms, for example increasing African representation on the legislative council, were to be introduced slowly and only when, according to the British paternalism of the time, members of the African population had reached the necessary educational and cultural level.

The representation on the legislative council tells us much about British colonial attitudes and priorities at this time. Apart from senior British officials, there were four "unofficials" nominated by the governor. The two British unofficials (W. H. Grey, a manager of the trading company Swanzy and Millers; and D. Hunt, representing the mines companies) between them spoke for the expatriate trading and mining interests. Their position reveals the typically close, if not always harmonious, ties between British commercial interests and the local colonial government in such a colony. The two African unofficials (both from Eastern Province: Mate Kole, the *konyor*, or head chief, of Manya Krobo; and the Accra barrister, Thomas Hutton Mills) were nominated by the governor for the (absurd, impossible) task of speaking for the whole African population on administrative affairs. The African subjects of the Gold Coast colony were thus given almost no say in the higher echelons of colonial government. These included the Western-educated Africans living mostly in the coastal towns.

The expectations of London for an African equatorial colony were few and limited: to keep possession, keep order, and keep the books balanced. British officials, including, and especially, Governor Clifford, believed that, in addition, there would be both political and economic progress in the Gold Coast—but that this would take a long time to achieve.

---

23. Following usual practice, the whole Gold Coast territory including Ashanti and the NT (Northern Territories) will be referred to in this study as "the colony," whereas the original southern coastal strip (formally established in 1874) will be referred to as "the Colony." Modern spellings of place names will normally be used in the text.

24. For details and background, see D. Kimble, *A Political History,* especially chapters 8 and 11.

As late as 1931, years after Clifford's departure in 1919, Sir Charles Jeffries in the Colonial Office was to restate that independent government for the Gold Coast remained the British goal, even though still "far away in the dim and distant future."[25] It was not foreseen that, by the time of independence in the mid-twentieth century, the infrastructure of such British colonies would still be in a rudimentary state.

Above all, British imperial officials in the early twentieth century continued to support the view that colonies should be financially self-sufficient and not a drain on the resources of the metropolitan country (even in wartime). Government revenue in the Gold Coast was largely dependent on indirect taxation in the form of customs duties on imports; meanwhile, colonial officials under Treasury scrutiny were required to keep down expenditures. Even so, official and unofficial sources in Ghana and in Britain reveal that the history of the Gold Coast in this period, when placed under a microscope, was more complex than has been suggested. Official colonial records of economic data and financial policy remain useful and underused. Economic issues cast light on the preoccupations—and in many cases, the ignorance—of British colonial administrators in this period.

In addition, contemporary material used for this study reflects the arrogance, paternalism, and often the unwitting racism, of the British and wider European society. But Governor Clifford's colonial rule remained makeshift rather than malevolent. It reflected British officers' minimal understanding of local African societies, as well as the few resources available to them. As emphasized by Cain and Hopkins, this was "colonial rule with limited supplies of capital."[26] In short, we will see how little British officials of this equatorial African colony could achieve at this time. They faced a range of obstacles, and none was to be greater than the fluctuating global economic conditions of a world war. Globalization was then, as it has remained, the interaction of the universal and the local: not so much a theory as "a set of processes."[27]

The number of British officers in the colony in this period dictated that colonial rule would be relatively light. According to the 1911 census, the total African population was just over one million—though this was clearly an underestimate. The figure just before the war is now thought to have been over two million: the 1911 census left out much of the population of the northeast province of the Northern Territories, and undercounted elsewhere.[28] These African subjects of the Gold Coast colony were governed at that time by a total British establishment of just 510 officials. The colonial administration in the Gold Coast was run on a shoestring with very few personnel (and fewer still during the war).

Nor did environmental features provide easy conditions for either trade or colonial administration. For example, there were no natural harbors for ships to bypass the heavy surf on the coast. Oceangoing ships had to anchor about half a mile out to sea in open roadsteads. Apart from the Accra plain in the southeast, tropical forest covered most of the Colony and most of Ashanti, giving way to savannah thinning to scrub in much of the Northern Territories. The northern boundary with what was then known as French

25. Sir Charles Jeffries, June 1931, quoted in D. Morgan, *The Official History of Colonial Development*, (London, 1980), p. 41.

26. P. J. Cain and A. G. Hopkins, *British Imperialism: Crisis and Deconstruction 1914–1990*, (London, 1993).

27. A. G. Hopkins (ed.), *Global History*, (London, 2006), p. 4.

28. See, e.g., K. D. Patterson, *Health in Colonial Ghana: Disease, Medicine, and Socio-Economic change 1900–1955* (Brandeis, MA, 1981), pp. 86–87.

Soudan (later Upper Volta, now Burkina Faso) was approximately 420 miles away from the sea and from the seat of the local colonial government on the coast.[29] Laissez-faire remained the official British approach to trade—but there was little possibility of any alternative, even before the war (though especially during it). Overall, the colonial government was largely a spectator of an export trade conducted by European trading, shipping, and mining companies, in association with African farmers, traders, and brokers. British and African merchants managed the exchange of cocoa and other raw material exports from the Gold Coast for a range of manufactured imports from Europe and beyond.

In this context of limited goals and limited capacity, one of the most significant continuing failures of British colonial rule in the Gold Coast at this time was its inability to deliver either "development" or "welfare" adequately. For British colonialism, "development" had a narrow definition. Indeed, its restriction largely to the building of an infrastructure that would further the export of commodities and the import and sale of foreign manufactures has long been labelled "underdevelopment"—notably in Walter Rodney's classic 1972 polemic.[30] The point to stress here, however, is that even if the British had wanted to develop the economy of the territory itself (though they did not), it would have proved quite impracticable at this time: before the war, during it, or in its aftermath. Critics have understandably emphasized an economic imbalance in colonial rule that worked to the detriment of colonial subjects, but regarding underdevelopment, they have failed to fully account for the similarities between colonial and postcolonial African experience or for the general lack of capitalist development in sub-Saharan Africa in the first fifty years of independence.

In trying to explain the absence of more efficient capitalist development in British Africa, Geoffrey Kay argued that there was a British conspiracy to hold these colonies back in order to avoid political unrest.[31] But there is no evidence of a British colonial "conspiracy" at this time against African producers. It is not hard to see why both the major expatriate commercial firms and the British colonial governments across British West Africa, including the Gold Coast, concentrated on trade rather than investing in manufacturing. It was not interest that was lacking so much as capital for investment, skilled manpower, and potential markets in the Gold Coast or overseas. Before the war, a cautious policy minimized the effects of market instability and risk—and required very little by way of capital investment. And from 1914, the problems of trying to counter the shortage of capital and skilled labor were made much more difficult by war conditions.

Though the *Gold Coast Leader* called for "factories and scientific knowledge" from Britain—and called on fellow Africans to start their own businesses—British officials chose to be, and had to be, onlookers.[32] At the same time, European companies were made even more conservative by sharp wartime fluctuations in the price of African commodities. Not surprisingly, as Ralph Austen has pointed out, they continued to prefer liquid assets in trade rather than fixed assets in manufacturing plants.[33] Improved rail and

29. See Map, Appendix I, "The Gold Coast in 1916."

30. W. Rodney, *How Europe Underdeveloped Africa,* (London, 1972). "Welfare," too, had a narrow definition for colonial officials, comprising, primarily, health and education: see below, especially Chapter 7.

31. G. B. Kay, *The Political Economy of Colonialism in Ghana,* (Cambridge, 1972).

32. *Gold Coast Leader*, editorial, 29/9/14.

33. See R. Austen, *African Economic History. Internal Development & External Dependency,* (London, 1987). And see Appendix III 4 for trade fluctuations.

road transport from the hinterland to the coast, alongside the continuing demand for European and American manufactured goods (despite high wartime prices), provided little incentive for companies to change their practices. The African press were to complain that the cost of rice and sugar doubled in the last months of 1914 alone, and "rich European firms" were accused of raising prices at the expense of "poor peoples" food necessities.[34] But expatriate trading firms continued to show no interest in investing private capital in production when African farmers were already there with raw materials to sell.[35]

In the context of little private capital investment being available in Britain's West African colonies, before and during the war, British officials in the Gold Coast did accept temporarily a limited government role. They provided a basic transport and communications infra structure and a government-backed currency. But neither officials on the coast nor officials in London accepted government involvement in manufacture as either desirable or practical in the colonies (or even, of course, at that time, in Britain). It is thus hard to support Rhoda Howard's assumption that a capitalist plot of "underdevelopment" existed to keep British colonies such as the Gold Coast in a state of "peripheral capitalism."[36] The lack of capitalist development is presented anachronistically as a failure of the colonial government: in such studies as these, the British are damned for introducing capitalism, and also damned for introducing too little. As Jean Bayart observed in his powerful plea for recognition of complexity, the application of dependency theories to Africa led to "an increase in dogma" rather than "a careful study of political dynamics."[37]

The search for an explanation of the "enigma" of inefficient colonial capitalism led Anne Phillips to attempt an alternative analysis of "underdevelopment" in British West Africa. She perceived the weakness of British control of its West African colonies, but then blamed this on Britain's "West African policy" of accepting the "peasant model" rather than the "plantation model" as the economic base for the region.[38] But there is no evidence for colonial governments having made a choice in this matter—or that a single British "model" policy ever existed in West Africa. The "plantation model" was never viable in the Gold Coast or elsewhere in British West Africa as an alternative to agricultural production undertaken by African farmers. The constraints faced by both African producers and British colonial officials need to be better understood; they form a major theme of this study.

While the British colonial government in the Gold Coast was authoritarian, it was certainly not all-powerful. For example, Africans continued to give short shrift to any challenges to their control over, or use of, their land. Africans, in this context, were for the most part not passive observers, let alone victims, but rather active players in a complex, interdependent relationship. British officers on the coast could do no more than continue to attempt to persuade African farmers to take the best advice, as they saw it, both to protect existing crops and to diversify production. They could not compel. Meanwhile,

34. Editorial, *Gold Coast Leader*, 22/8/14.

35. See, for example, A. G. Hopkins, *An Economic History of West Africa* (London, 1973), p. 213; and M. Havinden & D. Meredith, *Colonialism and Development: Britain and Its Tropical Colonies 1850–1960* (London & New York, 1993), pp. 19–21. Lever Brothers' interest in palm oil plantations and processing was the exception. See Chapter 1.

36. R. Howard, *Colonialism and Underdevelopment in Ghana*, (London, 1978), p. 23.

37. J-F. Bayart, *The State in Africa. The Politics of the Belly*, (Paris, 1989. English edition: London/ New York, 1993), pp. ix, 5, 270.

38. A. Phillips, *The Enigma of Colonialism. British Policy in West Africa*, (London, 1989), p. 106.

the prewar boom in cocoa exports from the Gold Coast benefited all Africans and Europeans involved in the colonial economy.

This trade was a "collaborative" or "cooperative" venture between African producers and largely British traders, and it was, as Havinden and Meredith argue, "a rational way for the undeveloped tropical colonies to be integrated into the world economy."[39] The term "collaboration" does not need to carry the pejorative overtones adopted by, for example, A. Isaacman and B. Isaacman, even though the colonial relationship in the Gold Coast, as in the other territories of Britain's worldwide empire at the time, remained unequal.[40] Instead, the term can remind us that the relationship is better described as *interdependent* rather than simply *dependent.* British dependence on African producers in the Gold Coast will be further discussed in this study—involving, for example, taxes on imports that were bought by the African population and thus paid for the colonial administration. For British officials, there was no alternative to Africans retaining control of agricultural production. This was the basis of the colony's trade and viability.

Meanwhile, Governor Clifford, and later his successor Guggisberg (governor, 1919 to 1927), both liberal "proconsuls," attempted to nurture the political relationship with Africans in what today appears as contradictory directions. On the one hand, they tried to reinforce the structures of indirect rule by bolstering the authority of chiefs. On the other hand, and at the same time, they encouraged the aspirations of Western-educated Africans by promoting Africanization, including, in time, increasing the number of African representatives on the legislative council. There is little evidence that either paternalistic governor saw this dual policy as contradictory or as following a deliberate plan of "divide and rule." The continuation of existing divisions among Africans through indirect rule was the outcome of an approach that owed little to guile and much to practicality: it was simply the least disruptive, most convenient, and above all, cheapest, way of establishing colonial rule. As for contradiction, both Clifford and Guggisberg appear to have considered their policies to be complementary: that in the fullness of time harmonious relations with the local African population could be more widely achieved—though the effects of war were to do little for the cause of harmony.

Colonial rule continued to exploit cheap African labor. Relentless cost-cutting contributed to the government policy, parallel with that of expatriate trading and mining companies, of keeping labor costs as low as possible.[41] Yet here we should note a tendency, in the limited literature that exists on the colony in this period, to gloss over the contrast between the priorities of colonial government and those of private capital. In trying circumstances, there could in fact be difference and tension between them. Although the colonial administration's overall raison d'être was to provide a framework for international trade, its day-to-day preoccupation was much more narrowly financial: the need to balance the books. The pervading laissez-faire policy of British colonial government towards international trade was, in a sense, an economic "nonpolicy." On the other hand, entrepreneurs and private companies, African as well as British, were above all concerned with how economic conditions of trade and production affected their own profit and

---

39. M. Havinden & D. Meredith, *Colonialism and Development,* pp. 1–7.

40. A. Isaacman and B. Isaacman, "Resistance and Collaboration in Southern and Central Ghana c.1850–1920," *The Journal of African Historical Studies,* X, I, 1977.

41. A similar policy of cost-cutting was followed elsewhere in the empire, for example, in Kenya. See J. Lonsdale and B. Berman, "Coping with the Contradictions: The Development of the Colonial State in Kenya, 1895–1914," *Journal of African History,* 20, 1979, p. 501.

loss. Though it was of course through imperial agency that the region became firmly linked to the emerging global capitalist economy, such "capitalist relationships" should at times be distinguished from—and could be more significant than—the more narrowly defined "colonial relationship" in the Gold Coast between rulers and ruled.

And capitalism was not in crisis here. There have always been problems when attempts have been made to fit African conditions into a theoretical "grand narrative" such as Marxism: Gareth Austin's research on the Ashanti shows that the Marxist model does not easily fit with the economic conditions of African land use there, such as relatively little wage labor and the spread of sharecropping.[42] Meanwhile, Lenin's description of imperialism in 1916 as "moribund capitalism" was to prove far from reality. Capitalism and imperialism were anything but moribund.

From several points of view, African as well as European, the situation in the Gold Coast colony by 1914, just before the war, was satisfactory, even promising. From the time of his arrival in the Gold Coast in 1912, Governor Clifford's energy and sense of urgency raised hopes, at least among the Western-educated of the African population of the colony, as to what he would achieve during his period of office.[43] Indeed, just before the outbreak of the Great War, when Clifford held the final sitting of the legislative council before going home on leave in May 1914, he was thanked by the African unofficials for "his determination to advance the prosperity of the colony," his "interest" in "native affairs," his "recognition of the value of education," and his efforts to advance "Africanization" by promoting "native" lawyers and "native" medical practitioners.[44]

Clifford also received some praise from elsewhere: in the press, as "an able administrator ... among the natives he is considered the most humane, best loved governor (beside Leslie Probyn) that any West African colony has ever known."[45] From the perspective of the Colonial Office in London too, and the local British colonial government in Accra, this was a successful and prosperous small colony. A flourishing export trade depended on the rapidly rising production of cocoa grown by the African population in the forest regions of the Gold Coast. By 1913, cocoa production exceeded gold as the main export of the colony. African farmers were developing cocoa as the major cash crop in order to trade it for European and American manufactured imported goods—a fruitful exchange, which helps to explain their conditional acquiescence in colonial rule at this time.

The war brought a sudden end to the Gold Coast cocoa boom. As this study will show, the unprecedented fluctuations in the international demand for cocoa exports during, and immediately after, the war bore hard on the population of the colony, badly affecting African livelihoods as well as the finances of the colonial government.[46] British administrative

---

42. G. Austin, "The Emergence of Capitalist Relations in South Asante Cocoa Farming c.1916–1933," *Journal of African History*, 28, 1987. See also G. Austin, *Labor, Land and Capital in Ghana: from Slavery to Free Labor in Asante, 1807–1956*, (Rochester, 2005).

43. Sir Hugh Clifford (1866–1941). Joined the civil service of the Malay States, 1883; British resident, Pahang, 1896–1899; governor, N. Borneo and Laban, 1899–1901; colonial secretary, Trinidad and Tobago, 1903–1907; colonial secretary, Ceylon, 1907–1912; governor, the Gold Coast, 1912–1919; governor, Nigeria, 1919–1925; governor, Ceylon, 1925–1927. Novelist; friend of Conrad and Kipling.

44. *LegCo* 1/5/14, *Gazette* 13/6/14, CO 99/55. The term "native" was used at this time not only by British officials but also, as here, by Africans of Africans.

45. *The African Telegraph and Gold Coast Mirror*, 14/11/14. (Published between 14/11/14 and 25/02/15 and then not for the rest of the war). Leslie Probyn was governor of Sierra Leone, 1904–1910.

46. See Appendix III, for fluctuations in wartime trade.

countermeasures to raise revenue and to cut spending were replicated in other British African colonies. But the Gold Coast colony's heavy dependence on the export of one (inessential) cash crop, cocoa, was to prove uniquely problematic during the war. And as we shall see, adverse wartime economic conditions made Africans far more critical than previously of colonial rule in this colony. The reaction of African subjects, first to Britain's prewar promise of improving living standards and then to its wartime agenda and record, was not static but responded to an ever-changing context. Kwabena Akurang-Parry has argued that the First World War "redefined the relationship between African communities and colonial rulers"; the ways in which this redefinition occurred in the Gold Coast will be reassessed here.[47]

The fluctuations in trade, with a brief revival in demand for cocoa and a short-lived boom in 1916, have led some historians, such as N. A. Cox-George, to conclude that the war brought prosperity to the Gold Coast; Rathbone's surer judgment is that even the apparent boom of 1916 could not counter, in real terms, the depression in the export sector.[48] Africans suffered. Beneath what Martin Kilson has called the "upper-echelon elite" of Western-educated Africans, there existed a growing number of an African "sub-elite."[49] Clerks, skilled workers (including foremen and mechanics), teachers, transport owners, traders, brokers, and cash-crop farmers were all badly hit by the war and disruption to trade; many were to participate in the formation of unions and in the strikes of the postwar slump.[50] Indeed, the barter terms of trade were never to be so favorable in the colony after the First World War. The 1918 influenza epidemic and the postwar slump added to the depressive effect at the time. Not surprisingly, economic hardship produced a more critical African response to colonial rule.

British colonial officials did what they could to keep the colony solvent, although war conditions led to a greatly increased burden of impositions on the local African population. More government intervention in the war came in the form of much higher taxation (as well as recruitment) and numerous, albeit temporary, restrictive trading regulations. In this sense, the formerly light touch of colonial rule in the Gold Coast became considerably heavier during the war, notwithstanding the diminishing number of British personnel. New wartime export taxes and trade restrictions such as the imposition of limited numbers of licenses to ship appear to mark at least a temporary modification of laissez-faire. Yet war conditions were to encourage the ever-larger expatriate shipping and commercial companies (such as the British shippers, Elder Dempster; the trading companies, Swanzy and Millers; and the Ashanti Gold mining company) to dominate further the international trade in cash crops and mining—at the expense of smaller, often African, producers.

---

47. K. Akurang-Parry, "Africa and World War I," in T. Falola (ed.), *Colonial Africa 1885–1939,* p. 53.

48. N. A. Cox-George, quoted in R. Rathbone, "World War I and Africa: Introduction," *JAH,* XIX, 1978, p. 7.

49. M. Kilson, "The Emergent Elites of Black Africa 1900–1960," in P. Duignan & L. Gann (eds.), *Colonialism in Africa 1870–1960, 2* (Cambridge, 1970), p. 355.

50. African occupational groups were largely male, including teachers. Gender is not usually specified in either the official or the unofficial records of the African population of the colony in this period. Pawnship labor, in which individuals were held in debt bondage, was predominantly female: see P.A. Lovejoy and T. Falola (eds.), *Pawnship, Slavery and Colonialism in Africa,* (Trenton, NJ, 2003), Introduction, pp. 1–6. Regarding agricultural production, there are occasional references in sources used for this study to "family labor" and to "market women traders." For a discussion of this theme, see C. Coquery-Vidrovitch, *African Women. A Modern History* (Boulder, CO, 1997).

The trend toward monopoly among commercial companies was resented by the African public and deplored by British officials. But by 1917 and 1918, war conditions in the Gold Coast were far beyond the competence of the British imperial government, let alone the local colonial British administration, to control.

In complaining, as the war progressed, about the deterioration in their standard of living, Africans were in fact criticizing, not the apparent strength of wartime colonial government in the Gold Coast, but its essential weaknesses. This was Britain's war—but the British could not protect their African subjects from its harsh economic effects. As will be shown, unprecedented sharp fluctuations in overseas demand for exports and increasingly high prices of foreign imports led to a sustained rise in the cost of living for a wide spectrum of African society across the colony.[51] At the same time, government intervention took the form of higher taxation, as mentioned above, rather than the provision of services, so Africans were squeezed and left to adapt as well as they could. Most planned construction work was brought to a halt during the war, and the small expenditure on welfare was severely reduced. Only modest public works, along with some spending on education and health—financed from a local and very narrow tax base—could be sustained in peacetime; little could be sustained in war at all.

During the war and in its immediate aftermath, expectations of what the colonial power should and would deliver changed. In particular, a new and wider spectrum of Africans in the Gold Coast protested against the deterioration in their standard of living. The result was an unprecedented African assertiveness and organized protest. In the event, the First World War's huge and durable impact served to disillusion those Africans who had looked forward to benefits from colonial rule. Clifford's prewar public plans proved to be in sharp contrast to subsequent burdens and policy postponements forced by the First World War. An interesting range of African "voices" penetrate both the official and unofficial records of this period. They filter through in a "history from below." Here are the Italian Marxist Gramsci's "subalterns"—in, for example, the organized protest of clerks' and traders' petitions, market women's complaints, demands of striking workers and artisans, and farmers' cocoa hold-ups. Apart from the cash crop farmers, most of these groups were concentrated in the coastal towns or in towns sited just inland. They had already been affected by a form of modernization in the period before the Great War with the provision of a whole range of "luxury" imports that had come to be regarded as necessities.[52] When necessities became costly or even unattainable, African criticisms of the local British administration inevitably grew.

However, secondary literature for the Gold Coast is limited in this period, and what remains of contemporary sources concerning African and British administration needs to be reviewed with care. Western-educated African voices can also be "heard" in the speeches of African unofficials in the Legislative Council and in local African newspapers such as the *Gold Coast Leader* and *The Gold Coast Nation* that reflected the concerns of Western-educated Africans in the colony and the views of some chiefs.[53] However, sadly, much of this African "voice" was not recorded. Official and unofficial sources that do remain need to be studied together in order to achieve a better understanding of how colonial rule operated at this time.

51. See Chapter 6, below.

52. M. Howard, "Structure and Process in History," *Times Literary Supplement*, 23–29/6/89.

53. The term "Western-educated" was used at the time and is adopted here, neutrally, to incorporate the stratum of Africans referred to elsewhere in the literature as, e.g., "intelligentsia" or "intellectual elite" or even "educated natives." (Gocking, *History*, *passim*).

The essential economic purposes of empire were never in dispute. They were to deny territory to commercial rivals and to provide stable conditions for Britain's own international trade—while balancing the colonial books so that no territory became a drain on the British taxpayer. Yet British colonial rule could be more muddled than monolithic. There were disagreements and tensions between the Gold Coast and London—not to mention disagreements in London and tensions among British officials in the Gold Coast. Thus a further constraint on effective government in the territory was that imperial Britain did not speak with one voice. It seems that this diversity on the British side of the colonial relationship has not been as widely recognized as the diversity of the African population—yet it helps explain the way the colony was run at this time.[54] Indeed, on a range of issues during this period, as we shall see, the local British colonial government under Clifford was to sympathize with African opinion rather than with Whitehall.

Ambitious "men on the spot" such as Clifford often struggled to obtain agreement from the Colonial Office that, like Treasury officials, favored caution and continuity, and especially balanced budgets, over change and expense.[55] In addition, the Colonial Office itself sometimes fought running battles with other imperial British departments of state in the metropolis, such as the Foreign Office and the Treasury. During the war, authority over such colonies was spread more widely across a number of government departments in London, including the Ministries of War and Food and the Board of Trade. Meanwhile, alongside imperial officialdom, war conditions favored unofficial British economic agents, in the shape of the major expatriate commercial companies with their own agenda and the opportunities presented by the war to strengthen their influence on government. From the British colonial perspective, none of this made the colony easier to govern. Moreover, the particular interests and perceptions of the local British colonial government on the West African coast and officials up-country could—and did—vary widely. Within the Gold Coast colony, as will be shown in this study, there were, for example, occasional resounding clashes between Armitage, chief commissioner of the Northern Territories, and his northern officers with "the men from the ministry," both in the secretariat in Accra and in the governor's residence on the coast.[56]

It is remarkable that in this most unfavorable context—a disruptive global war and a government apparatus under strain—a dynamic colonial governor could have some personal impact. Yet just as not all European colonies in Africa—and not all the British ones—were the same, neither were all colonial governors alike. Sir Hugh Clifford's reputation needs to be reappraised—partly to qualify Gailey's uncritical judgment.[57] He was determined to set in hand a program of reform and development. This was his first governorship, but his already long and varied experience in the colonial service, in the Far East and in the West Indies, had given him a valuable perspective on the workings of the Colonial Office in Whitehall, as well as the confidence to stand up to London officials and argue his case—if necessary, at length. Colonial administration partly reflected a

---

54. Compare with French Africa. See C. M. Andrew & A. S. Kanya-Forstner, "France, Africa and the First World War," *JAH,* XIX, 1, 1978, pp. 11–14, for the "fragmented ... official mind of French imperialism."

55. See discussion in S. Constantine, *The Making of British Colonial Development Policy 1914–1940,* (London, 1984), p. 18.

56. See Chapter 8 below.

57. H. A. Gailey, *Clifford: Imperial Proconsul,* (London, 1982).

governor's personal style and temperament: Clifford was to have a discernible influence on the Gold Coast colony.

While modernization *theory* has long been rejected by historians as unconvincingly sweeping, overoptimistic, and Eurocentric, modernization *in practice*—bringing with it everything from Western medicine to motor vehicles—was precisely what Governor Clifford and his colonial staff sought. Such goods were sought, too, by both Western-educated and other Africans in pursuit of a higher standard of living. As Falola observes, "... as far as many colonial officials were concerned, they were modernisers"—regarding, for example, modern technology applied to transport and communications.[58] This "modernisation," or the quest for modernity, remained an important shared aspiration in British colonial Africa, and it was to prove a demanding measure of the effectiveness of alien governance throughout the colonial period.[59] We shall later encounter Clifford's modernizing—though frustrated—agenda.

Modernization was particularly in demand during the time of Clifford's governorship, and as a result, his historical significance is complex, even somewhat contradictory. On the one hand, his positive proposals for improvements in the Gold Coast survived his departure from the colony in 1919. He had only just won a number of financial battles with the Colonial Office when the greater battles of the First World War had intervened—yet wartime disruption and economies simply postponed Clifford's development program until the 1920s. His successor, Guggisberg, has been given the credit for development in the Gold Coast in the interwar period, before the onset of the Depression.[60] Too little attention has been given to the extent to which his policies were Clifford's legacy. It may be true that, as a result of the 1914–1918 war, "the liberal conscience" within the British imperial government "abdicated in favour of more imperially minded figures" such as Curzon and Milner.[61] But this was not true of humane proconsuls in the field such as Clifford and subsequently Guggisberg in the Gold Coast. The impact on the colony of these two particular governors in the fifteen years between 1912 and 1927 appears to have smoothed the path of British and African relations in the Gold Coast in the difficult period that followed. On the other hand, as already indicated, in the war period the balance of economic advantage shifted unfavorably for the local population. Ironically, the contrast between what Clifford had publicly sought at the outset, and what he was able to deliver during his governorship, fed disillusionment. Largely as a result of the disruptions of war, many Africans now concluded in increasing numbers that any benefits of the colonial presence, such as opening up international and subsequently global trade, were outweighed by its demands—or ineffectiveness.

British colonial rule was not the same across the various regions of the Gold Coast. In no area was it less beneficent or less effective than in the north, and another theme of this study is the tendency towards *unevenness* in the colonial impact—"uneven develop-

---

58. T. Falola, *Economic Reform and Modernization in Nigeria, 1945–1965*, (Kent State University Press, 2004), p. 10.

59. *Ibid.* Also see T. Falola, *The Power of African Cultures*, (Rochester, NY, 2003), pp. 6, 24, 71–73.

60. See, e.g., W. E. F. Ward, *A History of Ghana*, (London, 1958); F. Agbodeka, *Ghana in the Twentieth Century*, (Accra, 1972); and A. Boahen, *Ghana: Evolution and Change in the Nineteenth and Twentieth Centuries*, (London, 1975).

61. R. Rathbone, "World War I and Africa. Introduction," *Journal of African History*, xix, 1, 1978, p. 3.

ment"—as between the south and the north of the colony. A country which had come into being arbitrarily and piecemeal became even more lacking in homogeneity, and this was to prove part of the enduring legacy of colonial rule in 1957. Although officially a unitary state, the colony remained divided between the original coastal colony and the two inland protectorates, Ashanti and the Northern Territories. An existing imbalance between the three regions of the Gold Coast colony now grew. As illustrated by Jean Allman and John Parker, the northern region in particular had a very different experience of colonial rule both before and during the war: "A degree of confusion, division, and ineffectiveness characterised British rule in this area right up to the 1930s."[62] Here is an example, in one colony, of considerable regional disparity, with "patchy and differentiated modes of imperial and colonial penetration."[63]

While general theories concerning colonialism have tended to ignore such diversity, the war revealed the sharp difference between the two protectorates, Ashanti and the Northern Territories. Ashanti, recently conquered (after the "revolt" in 1901), was in due course believed by the government to be consenting to, because of prospering under, colonial rule. This was an ironic feature of the period: a colonial government which had hitherto been uncertain of the "loyalty" of the Ashanti kingdom now came to accept that there was nothing to fear. Ashanti farmers were now peacefully exploiting the economic opportunities provided by exceptionally successful cash crop production. However, the war period also saw the contrast intensified between the Colony and Ashanti on the one hand, and the north on the other. The Northern Territories had also, like Ashanti, been recently conquered by the military—a civilian administration had only been established in 1907—but in this region, the war made for further unwelcome government intervention and coercion, without the prospect of economic opportunity. There were many signs in the war of a marked lack of consent to British colonial rule in the Northern Territories of the Gold Coast.

During the war, the main structures of the colonial administration and the colonial economy of the Gold Coast, as well as the dynamics of African societies, appeared to change little. There was continuity, in particular, in the ways in which local Africans took the opportunity to shape the evolving, though unequal, colonial relationship and turn it as far as they could to their advantage. Of course, patterns of domination varied across the empire, "penetrating deep in some societies" but "involving a comparatively superficial contact with others."[64] In the case of the Gold Coast, there continued to be a relatively weak colonial administration. The few British administrative officers floated, as it were, on the surface of the territory, communicating for the most part with only a small number of their African subjects, such as chiefs, clerks, and certain members of the Western-educated elite. They remained largely ignorant of the lives of the rest.

A major aim of this study is to consider the variety of constraints under which all participants in the colonial relationship in the Gold Coast colony operated in this period so dominated by the world war. The viability of the colony depended on a healthy balance

62. J. Allman and J. Parker, *Tongnaab: The History of a West African God,* (Bloomington, Indiana, 2005), p. 73.
63. R. Rathbone, "World War I and Africa," p. l.
64. A. Loomba, *Colonialism/PostColonialism,* 2nd ed. (London, 2005), p. 9.

of trade—but the international export trade in cocoa could no longer be relied upon during the war. This inescapable fact redefined the options open to Africans, as well as to the British, in a constantly changing wartime context. As in the other three, all nonsettler colonies of British West Africa (Nigeria, Sierra Leone, and the Gambia), the First World War sharply exposed just how minimal was colonial government in the Gold Coast—and how it was increasingly incapable of meeting African aspirations. This new, postwar, African evaluation of colonial rule, in the light of wartime experience, leads us to a reconsideration of Richard Rathbone's view that "continuity and discontinuity were finely balanced" in such African colonies as the Gold Coast in the war period.[65]

This period is not merely the chronological halfway point in the colonial history of the Gold Coast; it is a decisive moment. The First World War represents a pivotal discontinuity in the history of the Gold Coast. In their study of the British colony, Kenya, in this period, Lonsdale and Berman argued that "the legitimacy of the colonial state was hitched to the oxcart of African accumulation."[66] The First World War appears to mark the moment when the oxcart began to become unhitched in the Gold Coast. The sources do not reveal a definitive picture. But in the long term, the additional impact of the interwar depression and another world war increased frustration, undermined legitimacy, and led to the mass demand in the late 1940s, not merely for reform, but for an independent African government.

This study falls into sections marking three periods: before the war, the years of war, and the immediate aftermath. The aim will be to assess the impact of the First World War on the Gold Coast colony, together with the significance of Clifford's colonial administration. We will look first at the prewar economy and finances, along with an evaluation of the character and potential of British colonial government at that time. Secondly, covering the war period, three chapters consider the impact of the disruption of shipping and trade on the economy and finances of the territory and its people; while a further three chapters examine the impact on British policy and programs, the unevenness of British administration, and the significance of wartime conditions for evolving colonial relationships. The final chapter looks at the immediate postwar period and draws conclusions regarding the importance of the war in the history of the Gold Coast and the nature of British colonial rule in this part of equatorial Africa.

65. *Ibid.*, p. 5.
66. J. Lonsdale and B. Berman, "Coping with the Contradictions," p. 497.

List of Abbreviations

ADC	Assistant District Commissioner
AETC	African and Eastern Trading Corporation
AGC	Ashanti Goldfields Corporation
ARPS	Aborigines Rights Protection Society
BBWA	Bank of British West Africa
BCGA	British Cotton Growing Association
CC	Chief Commissioner
CFAO	Compagnie Francaise de L'Afrique Occidentale
CO	Colonial Office, London
CPP	Convention Peoples' Party
DC	District Commissioner (District Officer)
ERDC	Empire Resources Development Committee
FO	Foreign Office
GCR	Gold Coast Regiment
JAH	Journal of African History
LegCo	Legislative Council
MOH	Medical Officer of Health
NCBWA	National Congress of British West Africa
NT	Northern Territories
PMO	Principal Medical Officer
PC	Provincial Commissioner
PRAAD	Public Records and Archive Department of Ghana
PRO	Public Records Office, now the National Archive (UK)
PWD	Public Works Department
SCOA	Societe Commerciale de L'Ouest Africaine
SPG	Society for the Propagation of the Gospel
SSO	Senior Sanitary Officer
UAC	United Africa Company
TAMS	Tropical Africa Medical and Sanitary Advisory Committee
WACB	West African Currency Board
WAFF	West Africa Frontier Force
WAMS	West Africa Medical Service
WO	War Office

Ghana During the First World War

Section I
Prewar

Chapter 1

The Gold Coast's Prewar Economy: Production for Export

At the heart of the economic relationship in the Gold Coast colony in this period between British rulers and African ruled lay production for the export trade—largely in cocoa and gold. The colony's existence and continuing viability depended on the export trade, and that meant above all the production and export of cocoa.[1] Far from being passive colonial subjects, Africans remained in control of this agricultural production throughout the colonial period in British West Africa, and they seized trading opportunities to market cash crops. They were, as this study will show, active participants in a flourishing capitalist economy. African farmers, traders, and brokers, along with European shipping and merchant companies, all gained—though unequally—from contributing to the extraordinary prewar boom in cocoa exports in the Gold Coast. This trading boom was stimulated both by the Western demand for chocolate and by the fast-growing African demand for European and American imports. It was, above all, cash from selling cocoa that gave many Africans of the Gold Coast the means to buy imported manufactured goods and Western food. Rewards from the export-import trade may be said to account, to a significant degree, for the prewar acquiescence in British colonial rule in the Gold Coast.[2]

Africans in the Gold Coast, however, were responding here not so much to colonial rule as to global economic conditions concerning supply, demand, and prices. British colonial officials in the colony facilitated, while at times attempting to modify, production and trading relationships. For the most part, however, they were spectators, with a different perspective from that of their African subjects. Anxiety regarding the soundness of the Gold Coast's economic and financial base led them to a number of interventionist initiatives—both to protect the cocoa crop and to promote diversification—but these had little or no effect. Meanwhile they continued to underestimate African sensitivities regarding land and its use. For their part, African farmers, brokers, traders, and laborers made choices and decisions that suited their own perceived interests. They largely defied the colonial government's attempts to modify their farming or marketing techniques or to get them to grow alternative crops. In overseas trade, they remained the prime movers in the prewar production and export of cocoa.

African farmers, though colonial subjects, had always controlled agriculture in the Gold Coast colony, including the production of cocoa, the major cash crop. An African from the Gold Coast, Tetteh Quarshie, a Ga, was traditionally credited with being the

1 See Appendix II, "Principal Exports from the Gold Coast 1905–1914," page 281.

2. Thus it is not necessary to argue that in the Gold Coast it was "anti-German propaganda," once the war had started, that "led to relative acquiescence to colonial rule": K. Akurang-Parry, *Africa and the First World War*, p. 56.

first (in 1879) to bring cacao to the mainland of West Africa from the island of Fernando Po—where William Pratt, a half-West Indian, half-African from Sierra Leone, had planted cacao seedlings from the West Indies. It seems that both the Basel mission and the Wesleyan mission had experimented with cocoa in the Gold Coast earlier than this, but regardless of who was the first, farming entrepreneur or missionary, planting increased rapidly in the late nineteenth century in the forest regions, spreading out from Eastern Province. The Gold Coast first officially exported cocoa (121 lbs) in 1885. Cocoa exports then increased at a phenomenal rate. In less than thirty years, by 1911, the quantity exported had risen to 88.9 million lbs, and the Gold Coast colony had overtaken Ecuador to become the largest producer of cocoa in the world. Just before the First World War, in 1913, the colony produced 20% of the total world production of cocoa.[3]

In the context of this prewar cocoa boom, there was little incentive for the colonial government to intervene in the economy of the colony. (Only in the context of the disruption of the war would it become clear to British officials that they had little power to intervene, even when they wanted to, in either cash crop production or any part of the export trade.) Just before the First World War, the new governor, Sir Hugh Clifford, patronizing but appreciative, acknowledged the critical role played by African farmers in the Gold Coast: "The remarkable achievement" of the cocoa boom was an achievement of "a purely native industry."[4] Large European trading companies such as Swanzy, Millers, or the African Association either bought direct from African farmers or employed African brokers as middlemen. Exports were then shipped to the markets of Europe (and some to the United States) by these big companies or by smaller European or African traders, most often in the boats of one of the two large European shipping companies, the British Elder Dempster Company or the German Woermann Line.

British officers in Whitehall or Accra did not believe government should intervene directly in trade. Nongovernment capitalist relations define much of the colonial relationship in this prewar period. Here was evidence, from a British perspective, that the imperial policy of laissez-faire worked. Trade was seen by British officials as normally the business of private commercial companies: "Our great European merchant firms control amongst them our imports and exports making their profit on both." The government "had no wish to disturb the happy condition they at present control."[5]

A minimal colonial administration provided little more than a basic framework to facilitate this trade. It intervened, indirectly, in imposing customs duties on imports as the main source of taxation and hence of government revenue. In this way the government benefited from the colony's economic success. It took pleasure in, and derived income from, the rapid spread of the main cash crop, cocoa, and it contributed by providing law and order and by constructing some of the necessary transport infrastructure. The arrival of a new, energetic governor, Sir Hugh Clifford, in December 1912, led to a period of greater government activity before August 1914 with, for example, a drive to extend the railway into the cocoa districts north of Accra. Improving transport was seen by Clifford as not only benefiting all involved in the trade, Europeans and Africans, but also ultimately as benefiting the whole colony by generating wealth that could be used to improve health and education.

---

3. Clifford, to the Legislative Council, *LegCo* 28/11/14, re. 1915 Estimates, *Gazette* 158, 14/10/14, CO99/85.

4. Clifford, *LegCo* 3/10/13, re. 1914 Estimates, *Gazette* 87, 4/12/14, CO99/85.

5. Acting Gold Coast colonial secretary Robertson, *LegCo* 26/3/13, *The Gold Coast Government Gazette* (henceforth referred to as "*Gazette*") 24/5/13, CO99/39.

Thus, just before the war, prospects were bright for the Gold Coast. Clifford found the financial position of the colony in 1913 "thoroughly sound and satisfactory."[6] The value of the total seaborne trade exceeded that of 1912 by 25%. Record exports of gold and timber helped to account for this rapid increase, but the biggest contribution was made by cocoa. Annual exports of cocoa were rising ever more rapidly from just over £1.5 million in value in 1912 to nearly £2.5 million in 1913, when they exceeded the value of gold exports.[7] As the new governor was well aware, "the prosperity of the Colony and Ashanti mainly depends upon the flourishing condition of the cocoa industry."[8]

But there were concerns. British officers on the coast, afraid that the cocoa crop was vulnerable, believed that priority should be given to protecting the colony's main cash crop from serious damage, if not disaster, as a result of disease or predators. The paradox here was that the more successful the cocoa industry became in the Gold Coast, the greater the colonial government's anxiety. But African farmers resisted active official intervention. As the agricultural department reports for this prewar period show, when the colonial government began to attempt a shift from its role of enthusiastic spectator of agricultural production to that of trainer or even manager, it enjoyed notably little success. African farmers and traders, far from being passive recipients of colonial initiatives, reacted with indifference or opposition to what they saw as ill-judged government advice.

British officials had little success in persuading African farmers to take the action they believed necessary to protect the cacao trees from serious blight or pest damage. The dramatic increase in cocoa production was due to the spread of farms planted over a wider area, as in Ashanti, rather than to an increase in yields per acre. British officers feared a large scale epidemic breaking out as a result of shifting cultivation and abandoned, unweeded farms with diseased pods left on the trees. The pattern of close planting of up to 500 to 800 trees per acre (in contrast with 300 per acre in Trinidad) could produce a very good return in the short term, but British officials feared that disease or blight would spread quickly if they took hold.[9]

African farmers did not share these fears and therefore often did not cooperate with the colonial officials. Agricultural department staff recognized the farmers' reasoning: that many abandoned cocoa farms, effectively left fallow, subsequently recovered and the land could be reused (even if this produced a smaller crop). It was only later recognized by British officials that weeds performed a useful function in helping to keep moisture in the ground. But the British agricultural officers were increasingly alarmed at the growing number of diseases and pests threatening the single most valuable cash crop in the colony. For example, thread fungus, as well as weevils, mold, white ants, and rats caused damage to the cocoa crop in Eastern Province in 1910. By 1911, bark louse and root fungi had become widespread, especially in southern Ashanti. Voracious insects, three species of capsids known locally as "cocoa bugs,"[10] had been identified in 1910, and by 1912 were causing damage to about 25% of the crop. And in 1913, a new fungoid disease, stem

6. *Ibid.*

7. See, e.g., Clifford, re. 1914 Estimates, *LegCo* 3/10/13, *Gazette* 87, 14/10/13; Clifford, re. 1915 Estimates, *LegCo* 1915, *Gazette* 158, 4/12,/14.

8. Clifford, confid. to Secretary of State Lewis Harcourt (see Principal Officials, Appendix I), 2/ 4/9/14, CO96/548/39121.

9. *Agricultural Department Reports* for 1911, *Gazette* 22/11/12, CO99/86, and for 1913, *Gazette* 14/11/14, CO99/147. And C. Gunnarsson, *The Gold Coast Cocoa Industry 1900–1939. Production, Prices, and Structural Change* (Sweden, 1978), p. 50.

10. Sahlbergella singularis, sahlbergella distantiella, and helopeltis bergrothi.

canker, otherwise known as "black pod," was observed attacking "neglected unkempt farms."[11]

Danquah's study of a formidable range of insect, vertebrate, fungoid, and pathogenic viral attacks and diseases, to which cocoa—not an indigenous plant—had become subject in the Gold Coast in the period before the First World War, shows that British officers' alarm at this time was justified. Trees tended to become more vulnerable as they got older. Additional alarm was raised by reports of very damaging outbreaks of witch broom fungus or pod rot among cacao trees elsewhere, such as in Ceylon (1906), Java (1908), Surinam (1905–12), and Trinidad (from 1911).[12] Not surprisingly, the British administrators on the West African coast saw the threat from a different perspective from that of local farmers. They feared the Gold Coast cocoa crop might not be sustainable.

However, British officials could be quite unrealistic about their powers, in contrast with African agency. They did not always recognize that the colonial government lacked the means to insist on what they believed to be essential measures. Coercion was not an option given the shortage of officers and finance and the scale of planting. Although cocoa bylaws officially gave chiefs legal powers to insist on "proper husbandry," they were acknowledged to be "practically a dead letter," even though agricultural officers naively called on them to be "rigidly enforced."[13] They were largely unenforceable. Most chiefs could not insist on unpopular, labor-intensive, and therefore expensive, farming methods. Indirect rule relied on chiefs' cooperation, but much British government advice was seen by the African farmers as simply not practicable—or necessary.

The result was that colonial government advice concerning cocoa production—even apparently good advice—tended to be rejected or ignored by African farmers. For example, British staff on tour (there were only nine traveling instructors for the whole colony in 1913) advised against such habits as "careless hacking with cutlasses" when pruning or harvesting. This was later supported by research in the 1920s of the assistant Gold Coast government mycologist, H. A. Dade, in conjunction with research in London at the Imperial Bureau of Mycology and in studies of plant pests at the Royal Botanic Gardens at Kew. This research suggested that one of the ways that fungoid spores were transmitted was through machete wounds on the trees. The British colonial administration desired efficient agricultural practices but lacked the means, as well as sufficient knowledge, to achieve them. Cocoa farmers were suspicious of visits from government officials, fearing interference and controls. Nor were they much interested in advice from government model farms, of which there were 300 by 1911.[14]

Clifford was also concerned about the shortage of trained agricultural officers, both British and African, but he came up against racist attitudes among officials in London and Accra against appointing Africans to posts of responsibility. Clifford did not share the prejudice of those Colonial Office officials who doubted "natives" could be fully trained as agricultural instructors.[15] British agricultural officers were not prepared at this time to

11. *Agricultural Department Quarterly Report: 31/3/13; Gazette* 24/4/13, CO99/58.

12. See F. Danquah, *Cocoa Diseases and Politics in Ghana 1909–1966,* (New York, 1995).

13. *Agricultural Department Reports: 1912, Gazette* 13/12/12, CO99/106; *1913, Gazette* 14/11/14, CO99/147.

14. *Agricultural Department Quarterly Reports:* 31/3/12, *Gazette* 25/5/12, CO99/21; 13/3/13, *Gazette* 19/7/13, CO99/58; 30/6/13, *Gazette* 1/11/13, CO99/93; 30/9/13, *Gazette* 6/12/13, CO99/103. And see R. J. Southall, "Cadbury of the Gold Coast 1907–1938: The Dilemma of the Model Firm in a Colonial Economy," unpublished PhD thesis, (Birmingham, 1975), p. 52.

15. Green (See Principal Officials, p. 277) CO Minute 14/10/12, CO96/521/32401.

accept Africans on an equal footing as curators or assistants. (Each of the experimental agricultural stations in operation by 1913—Aburi, Tarkwa, Kumasi, Kyebi, and Pleko-Blongo—was supervised by a European curator.) The director, Tudhope, the only fully qualified agriculturalist in the agriculture department, let it be known that if a "negro" were made assistant agricultural director, the white staff would resign—a remark which provoked the Liberal Secretary of State for the Colonies Lord Harcourt to comment dryly "that the late Mr. W. Wilberforce would be disappointed with the slow progress of Negrophilism."[16]

Meanwhile, encouraged by the new governor, the colony's agricultural department set up a small-scale experimental training scheme just before the war. Six farmers were chosen by chiefs for a special course at Aburi, the botanical garden just inland from Accra, so that they could give instructions when they returned home. These African instructors were given lists of tips such as not planting cocoa too closely, applying tar on tree wounds, and using kerosene emulsion to kill cocoa mosquitoes.[17] The scheme was judged by officials as a success and was continued later during the war years. Encouraging "natives" to help themselves also included persuading farmers in the Aburi-Nsawam district in 1913 to form an association to improve methods of farming. But such initiatives, however well intentioned, were successful on only a very small scale.

African producers also proved immune to officials' pleas to prepare the cocoa more carefully for the market. There were many complaints from the agricultural officers in the period before the war that African farmers did not ferment the beans adequately—either because they could not be bothered or because they did not understand the process.[18] These British officials were constrained by having no means by which they could insist on improved quality, even though they were convinced that more careful fermentation would have the effect of raising the price of Accra cocoa—whether the world price in the futures market or the price that the European companies on the coast were prepared to pay.

The African farmers' perspective on producing cocoa for the market was different. They explained that there was no point in preparing the cocoa beans more carefully, because buyers for the trading companies did not normally differentiate between beans which had been fermented and dried and those which had not.[19] Only the chocolate manufacturers, notably Cadbury, had the reputation of consistently encouraging better farming and fermenting practices by buying better quality beans and paying higher prices for them. Cadbury, from the time of its first shipments from the Gold Coast in 1908, was seen by the government as the model firm practicing "responsible capitalism."[20] Cadbury also enjoyed African approval, as seen in the local press and in the lifelong friendship established in 1909 between W. Cadbury and Konor Mate Kole of Eastern Krobo, one of

16. Harcourt, CO Minute 16/6/14, CO96/541/8030.

17. *Duties of Local Instructors* 1/10/13, Tudhope, director, agricultural department ADM11/1/500, PRAAD.

18. E.g., *Agricultural Department Report* 31/12/13, *Gazette* 21/3/14, CO99/26.

19. Clifford to Harcourt, dispatch: *Tour of the Eastern Province 10–26 February 1913*, CO96/528/9916.

20. *Agricultural Department Report 1913, Gazette* 14/11/14, CO99/147. And see R. J. Southall, "Cadbury on the Gold Coast 1907–1938," p. 89, and N. Edwards, *Cadbury on the Gold Coast. A Brief Survey of the Commercial and Social Activities of Cadbury Brothers Ltd. 1900–1954,* (Bournville, 1954), pp. 5–6.

the two nominated African unofficials in the Legislative Council at this time.[21] For the most part, Africans continued to market agricultural products as they had done before.

African intermediaries, too, played a critical role in the cocoa trade, a role that was not welcomed by British officials, who believed the local marketing system was a destabilizing factor. Officials' reports at this time reveal British officers' ignorance and prejudice concerning trading practices and the role of African "middlemen," a derogatory word in official records, although European trading companies also acted as middlemen between African producers and European manufacturers.[22] European companies bought cocoa from African brokers who, responding to demand, tended to buy wholesale at a low price without differentiating between different quality cocoa. A Gold Coast government report of 1912 was dismissive of "hordes of youths," mainly from the coast towns, who, acting as buyers, were said to "scatter over the cocoa districts" at the start of the season "with no more qualification than simple writing and arithmetic."[23] This is an example of an African initiative which was not well understood and was therefore distrusted by British officials.

In fact, the cocoa brokerage system played an essential and positive role in providing credit, quite separately from the official bank.[24] This system often involved payments to farmers in advance of harvesting the crop. A network of largely African brokers worked on behalf of big company operators in the ports, down to the smallest inland buyers. This arrangement suited Gold Coast farmers, many of whom were short of ready cash or heavily in debt.[25] Nor did British colonial officials at this time recognize that, among the chain of intermediaries, many farmers themselves acted as traders. It was twenty-five years later, in 1938, that the Nowell Commission estimated that one in every ten farmers was also a trader.[26] Clifford's advice in February 1913 shows that he initially shared these generally negative views of middlemen: selling produce on trees to "speculators … must be discouraged."[27]

However, it was typical of Clifford that he followed up on the issue, sought more information, and was prepared to change his mind. Two months later, he had the sense to call merchants to a meeting in Accra to discuss how the quality of cocoa put on sale could be improved. He concluded that the issue was more complex than he had initially supposed

21. *Ibid.*

22. For prejudice against trade among British officials, see C. Erlich, "Building and Caretaking. Economic Policy in British Tropical Africa 1890–1960," *The Economic History Review* XXVI, 4, 1973, pp. 650–651. And compare with Nigeria: A. I. Nwabughuogu, "From Wealthy Entrepreneurs to Petty Traders: The Decline of African Middlemen in Eastern Nigeria 1900–1950," *JAH*, 23, 1982, p. 366.

23. *Report of Eastern Province 1912, Gazette* 11/10/13, CO99/84.

24. See R Fry, *Bankers in West Africa. The Story of the Bank of British West Africa Ltd.*, (London, 1976), pp. 105–106.

25. See P. Hill, *The Gold Coast Farmer. A Preliminary Survey* (London, 1956), pp. 48–83; R. Southall, "Cadbury on the Gold Coast 1907–1938," pp. 28–31, 99–120; and J. G. Deutsch, "Educating the Middlemen: A Political and Economic History of Statutory Cocoa Marketing in Nigeria 1936–1947," unpublished PhD thesis, (London, 1990). For the risks for a West African broker, see O. Awolowo, *Awo. The Autobiography of Chief Awolowo*, (London, 1960), Chapter 8, "My Business Adventures," pp. 92–103.

26. R. Beckman, *Organizing the Farmers. Cocoa Politics and National Development in Ghana* (Uppsala, 1978), pp. 46–47. And A. Boakye-Boaten, "Indigenous Retail Trade and Markets in Asante During the Colonial Era 1902–1945," *Bulletin of the Ghana Geographical Association*, 17, 1975, pp. 31–32.

27. Clifford to Harcourt, dispatch: *Tour of the Eastern Province 10–26 February 1913*, CO96/528/9916.

and "was not capable of an easy solution."[28] He now appreciated the constraints of the commission system and the impossibility of producing a uniform grade of cocoa when the industry was in the hands of such a large number of small peasant proprietors. Government intervention, he decided, would cause more harm than good. The reality, however, was that the colonial administration did not have the means to intervene effectively even if it had wanted to.

The anxiety of British officials in the Gold Coast before the First World War concerning the growing dependence of the colony on one cash crop, cocoa, has been widely ignored in the literature. British officers worried about the damaging long-term effects on the colony of a lack of diversification of agriculture, with so many African farmers concentrating on cocoa and abandoning other cash crops such as palm oil and palm kernels. The role of Clifford and his administration has been omitted and Governor Guggisberg mistakenly given the credit for initiating British concern—though only later, in the 1920s.[29] But before the war, as early as 1913, Tudhope (director of agriculture in the Gold Coast colony since 1909) warned: "It is never safe to depend entirely on one crop."[30]

Far from promoting monoculture, senior British officials realized at this time that it would make the colony's "open" economy even more vulnerable to fluctuations in demand and price on the world markets, as well as to the effects of natural disasters that might ravage the crop. Fell (provincial commissioner in West Ashanti since 1905) expressed a common anxiety among British officials in 1914: "In many parts of the colony all the eggs, so to speak, have been put into the one basket in the shape of cocoa."[31] In the event of any widespread disruption of the cocoa trade, these British officers feared that the stability of the colony would be threatened, to the detriment of both African producers and British traders. Concern about the lack of diversification of cash crops, as well as concern about the neglect of farming sufficient local food, was echoed in the African press, as in editorials in the *Gold Coast Leader*, for example, nine months after the outbreak of the war.[32]

However, African farmers remained the key players in agricultural production in the colony. They took the initiative and chose what to grow. They switched to the crop that gave the best immediate return for their investment of time and money. By contrast, palm oil production, for example, required periods of particularly intensive work.[33] Far from diversifying in this prewar period, many African farmers were cutting down palms to make way for cocoa trees, even though this was condemned as "a mischievous practice" by British agricultural officers.[34] Although there remained an international demand for palm oil—for products such as industrial lubricant, soap, and margarine—the rapid

---

28. Clifford to Bonar Law 1/8/16: copy of letter, Gold Coast 541 in *Gold Coast/Cocoa, Miscellaneous Reports 1910–1926*, The Royal Botanic Gardens, Kew, 10.32, pp. 85–91.

29. E.g., R. H. Green & S. H. Hymer, "Cocoa in the Gold Coast: A Study in the Relationship between African Farmers and Agricultural Experts," *Journal of Economic History*, 26, 1966, pp. 299–319; and A. A. Boahen, *Ghana: Evolution and Change*, p. 117.

30. *Agricultural Department Report 31/3/13 Gazette* 19/7/13, CO99/58.

31. Fell, PC W. Ashanti, to Clifford, 24/2/14, Clifford to Harcourt, dispatch: *Trek through Ashanti, January to March 1914, 12/3/14*, CO96/528/746.

32. E.g., *Editorial Notes, Gold Coast Leader*, 31/07/15. For improvement in harvesting local foodstuff in 1916, see editor's notes, *Gold Coast Leader*, 10/6/16.

33. Inez Sutton, "Labor in Commercial Agriculture in Ghana in the Late Nineteenth and Early Twentieth Centuries," JAH, 24, 1983, p. 466.

34. *Agricultural Department Report 1910, Gazette* 3/2/12, CO99/8.

expansion of cocoa farms in the Colony and Ashanti in the years just before the Great War was matched by an equally rapid contraction of palm oil production. The quantity and value of palm exports from the Gold Coast fell heavily.[35] A fertile belt of palm trees remained just inland, running between eight and twenty-five miles from the sea along most of the breadth of the Colony, especially in Central Province, but much was left unattended. The neglect was always worse in periods of drought, as in the 1912–1913 season when palms had to be buried in bunches in pits and covered with leaves until there was water to extract the oil. This practice confirmed the reputation of the product as a hard oil that contained much dirt.[36] In short, cocoa was much easier to cultivate.

Many African farmers therefore preferred growing cocoa, despite the continuing overseas demand for other crops such as palm products and rubber. It was estimated in 1912 that only 30% of the palm crop was being gathered, despite a wide market for the kernel as well as for oil from the fruit husk, or pericarp.[37] The rise in the market for palm kernels, as opposed to palm oil, was largely due to demand from Germany, where they were crushed and used to make cattle cake. Producing kernels required less labor in Africa than working on the pericarp, which had to be processed on the coast, as otherwise the oil turned rancid on the journey to Europe. Although the value of palm kernel exports rose to a record in 1912, it fell in 1913, affected not only by low rainfall that year but also by African farmers' continuing neglect of palm products in favor of cocoa.

The main reason why British officials could not dissuade an increasing number of African farmers from switching to cocoa or extending their cocoa farms was simply that cocoa was the most profitable crop. It was sometimes suggested by British officials that the widespread neglect of palm products was due to high transport costs. Yet transport costs per ton mile were similar for cocoa.[38] Price was the crucial difference. In 1914, before the outbreak of war, £47 was the price for a ton of cocoa compared with £19.5 per ton for palm oil and £14.8 per ton for palm kernels.[39] With no means to adjust prices or to force compliance, the local British government could only try to persuade farmers that retaining some diversification, some "judicious mixture" of produce was, in their view, more prudent.[40] From the colonial point of view, what mattered more than any single product, such as cocoa, was the Gold Coast's continuing capacity to pay for itself. But given the mixture of confidence and ignorance in much of the colonial officers' advice, it is hardly surprising that African farmers took little notice of warnings about dependence on one crop. Their perspective was bound to be different. With relatively little information about either the whole territory or the international context, the concern of African producers was for the most part with the immediate needs of their individual cocoa farms, whereas the colonial government was preoccupied with the economic foundation and future financial viability of the colony.

Nor was the powerlessness of the colonial government to dictate prices well understood by most of the local population. The chiefs of Peki, for example, when they met Governor

35. See Appendix II.

36. *Agricultural Department Quarterly Report 31/12/12, Gazette* 21/3/14, CO99/26.

37. G. Hunt, unofficial memo, *LegCo* 4/11/12, CO96/526/34941.

38. *Agricultural Department Report* 1913, *Gazette*, 14/11/14, CO99/147. And see B. Ingham, *Tropical Exports and Economic Development. New Perspectives on Producer Response in Three Low Income Countries*, (London, 1981), pp. 22–23.

39. I. Sutton, "Labor in Commercial Agriculture in Ghana," p. 467.

40. *Agricultural Department Report, 30/6/13, Gazette* 1/11/13, CO99/93; and see Western-educated reaction in e.g., *editorial notes, Gold Coast Leader, 3/6/16.*

Clifford during his trek of the Trans Volta districts in September 1913, urged him to intervene to increase the prices paid by merchants for "native" produce. They also wanted him to lower prices for imported goods such as corrugated iron roofing—which, as one of the chiefs explained, was not only more durable, even if much hotter than thatch, but also "increased their dignity."[41]

Meanwhile, further prewar government efforts to halt the decline of other cash crops, such as rubber, met with little success because there was too little demand for low grade rubber and too low a price compared with cocoa.[42] Most of the rubber was collected from wild vines in the forest region, though the agricultural department did report some success with handing out para rubber seedlings. But Clifford doubted whether rubber could ever be produced sufficiently cheaply in the Gold Coast, even on plantations, given that 2s a pound from the Bonsu Estates was still twice as much as it cost to produce rubber on plantations in Ceylon or Malaya, two of his previous postings.[43] Plantation rubber from South and Southeast Asia now dominated the world market, accounting for 60% of the world's supply. With the world price for African varieties of rubber collapsing just before the First World War and many farmers in the Gold Coast switching to cocoa, it was hardly surprising that the colony's rubber exports fell drastically in 1913 to the lowest level since 1908.[44]

Other attempts by the colonial government at encouraging substantial diversification by introducing new cash crops, such as copra and cotton, also failed in this period. Seed coconuts from Ceylon were handed out by officials in the hope that they would flourish along the littoral of the southeast in the Keta and Ada districts, but little systematic cultivation was undertaken because African farmers were not initially attracted by the very slow return on the time and money invested.[45] The British Cotton Growing Association (BCGA) briefly regarded cotton as a promising prospect in the Northern Territories, where there were already scattered local African small-scale cotton growing and weaving in the prewar period. However, the BCGA concentrated its main efforts in Africa at this time in Uganda and Northern Nigeria, although the Northern Territories of the Gold Coast did initially seem promising.[46] There continued to be "a thriving trade" in local garments in the Northern Territories made from "native" cotton. Little European cotton cloth was obtainable in the north except through Kumasi market.[47] But in addition to un-

---

41. Clifford to Harcourt, dispatch: *Trek of the Trans Volta District September 1913, 7/10/13*, CO96/528/746.

42. E.g., *Report of Central Province 1911, Gazette* 10/8/12, CO99/55; and *Report of Eastern Province 1912, Gazette* 11/10/13, CO99/84.

43. Clifford to Harcourt, dispatch: *Tour of the Eastern Provinces 10–26 February 1913*, 3/3/13, CO96/528/9916.

44. See R. Austin, *African Economic History. Internal Development and External Dependency* (London, 1987), p. 140; J. Forbes Munro, "Monopolists and Speculators: British Investment in West African Rubber 1905–1914," *JAH*, 22, 2, 1981, p. 263; and *Table of Exports 1905–1914,* Appendix II.

45. Governor Thorburn's Address on the 1912 Estimates, *LegCo* 6/11/11, *Gazette* 6/1/12, CO99/29; and *Agricultural Report 1913, Gazette* 14/11/14, CO99/147.

46. *Report on Ashanti 1911,* 23/4/12, Thorburn to Harcourt 30/5/12, CO96/517/18726. The BCGA had been formed in 1902 with Manchester backing to promote cotton growing in the Empire because of problems obtaining American supplies during the 1861–1865 civil war and during the 1890s boll weevil infestation. See D. C. Dorward, "British West Africa and Liberia" in A. Roberts (ed.), *The Cambridge History of Africa, Volume 7, 1905–1940,* (London, 1986), p. 407.

47. Armitage, Chief Commissioner NT, informal diary, 10/11/13, ADM 56/1/177, PRAAD.

reliable rainfall and a sparse population, transport in the north was inadequate and expensive. The reluctant conclusion of the agricultural department in 1913 was that there was little likelihood of cotton being profitably grown in the Gold Coast as a cash crop for the international market. The claim that cotton "took hold" in the Northern Territories before 1914 is thus not borne out by the records.[48] The price offered was too low, with too much labor involved to be worth it. Another attempt by British colonial officials to diversify agricultural production in the Gold Coast colony had failed.

At the same time, Clifford's relative neglect of the north, which was to increase the gulf between the Northern Territories and the rest of the colony, was evident before the war. In 1913, the new governor concluded that without a viable cash crop, the Northern Territories were not a priority when compared with "the necessity ... of providing an efficient means of transport in the more accessible districts of the Colony and Ashanti which have already attained to a certain degree of development and prosperity."[49] Northerners continued as migrant laborers or subsistence farmers or participants in local trade, in such products as yam, cattle, and goats. Unusually for Clifford, economic considerations outweighed paternalism in formulating British policy in the north—with serious repercussions, as will be seen, for the Northern Territories.

The small Gold Coast agricultural department, undaunted, continued to energetically investigate a whole range of vegetable products (including in the north) in an attempt to identify new cash crops for the future benefit of the colony. Clifford and his officials judged the investigation to be in the mutual interests of the metropolitan country and the local African population. Experiments with growing soya, hemp, ginger, cinnamon, maize, rice, tobacco, and groundnuts were carefully monitored in this prewar period. There were successful demonstrations of growing sisal in the Northern Territories, where peppers were also distributed, and good results with rice were reported in Tamale.[50] In Kumasi there was success with arrowroot and cassava, while samples of these products, and many more, such as castor oil seed, shea butter (from fruit of the wild shea tree, sold to Africans as food and used in Europe in the manufacture of soap and skin creams) and shea kernels (a food preservative), guinea grain, coffee, black pepper, and chillies were sent off to be assessed by the Imperial Institute in London or to the Royal Botanic Gardens at Kew.[51] But only timber and kola nuts were able to hold their own, in a modest way, in the face of the ever-expanding cocoa trade.

Nowhere was African independent enterprise more evident under colonial rule in this period than in the kola trade.[52] Kola was in a class of its own as a forest product that was exported by sea (to Nigeria) as well as being carried across inland frontiers, but for which there was no market in Europe or America. Demand for kola as a mild stimulant, particularly in Muslim or partially "Islamized" areas of the interior of West Africa, was sustained throughout the period. A record quantity was shipped in 1912, in addition to what was traded overland.[53] The government could not obtain the overall figure, let alone

48. L. H. Gann & P. Duignan, *The Rulers of British Africa 1870–1914,* (London, 1978), p. 314.

49. Clifford to Harcourt, 27/1/13, CO96/527/5493.

50. *Agricultural Department Reports: 1910, Gazette* 3/2/12, CO99/8; *1912, Gazette* 13/12/13, CO99/106; *for quarter ending 31/3/13, Gazette* 19/7/13, CO99/58.

51. *Ibid.*

52. See E. Abaka, *"Kola Is God's Gift": Agricultural Production, Export Initiatives and the Kola Industry of Asante and the Gold Coast, c.1820–1950,* (Athens, Oxford, Accra, 2005).

53. Clifford, Address on the 1914 Estimates, *LegCo* 3/10/13, *Gazette* 14/10/14, CO99/87.

supervise the trade, which was, as Archer, the comptroller of customs in the Gold Coast, complained, "completely in the hands of illiterate and very suspicious Hausas."[54] It seems that these African traders succeeded in keeping their livelihood free from colonial government interference.

What is therefore striking about the evolving trading relationships in the Gold Coast colony already, in the years just before the Great War, is the independent initiative of African producers in contrast with the limited knowledge and the limited powers of the colonial government. In persisting with a preference for producing cocoa, African farmers and traders seized what economic opportunities were available and responded to the international demand for their products. They largely disregarded local British officers' advice, itself often a confused mixture of unrealistic admonition with doses of common sense. Thus African farmers also ignored British concerns about the dangers of a lack of diversification. With very limited resources, the agricultural officials of the local British administration searched methodically, but in vain, for new cash crops. They tried to persuade the local farmers, but their suggestions tended to be ignored. Nonetheless, their persistent efforts should be acknowledged.

However, there were related issues that roused African farmers into outright opposition to British imperial policy—above all, concerning rights to land and land use. Colonial rule depended on African cooperation and African enterprise in cash crop production. Yet British colonial authorities were perennially insensitive to what was always a very sensitive subject: ownership and control of land. One issue at this time involved monopoly rights over land use. Just before the war, in 1913, the British imperial government in London encouraged British companies to apply for monopoly rights to set up depericarping machinery to extract palm oil. Lever Brothers, which at that time had obtained the official palm oil processing monopoly in the Gold Coast, was widely suspected of having done a private deal with the British government.

African spokesmen found themselves supported—though to no avail—by British commercial interests on the West African coast, against the imperial government in London. Secretary of State for the Colonies Lord Harcourt received strong protests from the London, Liverpool, and Manchester chambers of commerce.[55] The British and African unofficial members of the Gold Coast legislative council also fiercely opposed the bill. W. H. Grey, the senior British unofficial and spokesman for the British traders, argued the case strongly that "it is an undoubted fact that competition is good for trade and monopoly is bad for trade and the country generally."[56]

But Harcourt, and his London officials, claimed that without modern machinery to extract the oil more efficiently, the palm oil industry would die, and that setting up such machinery would be financially feasible only if a company were guaranteed exclusive rights to process the oil. Only then could West African farmers compete with plantations in South and Southeast Asia.[57] Thomas Hutton Mills, the African barrister and unofficial member of the legislative council, supported by the other unofficial African member, Konor Mate Kole, and by the ARPS (the Aborigines' Rights Protection Society based in Cape Coast), argued vigorously for the urgent need to protect African ownership of land.

---

54. P. L. H. Archer, comptroller of customs, *Trade Report 1912, Gazette* 3/5/13, CO99/34.

55. Ellis (see Principal Officials, p. 277), CO Minute 7/11/12, CO96/524/35197. For a description of this "storm of protest" see D. Kimble, *A Political History of Ghana*, pp. 46–48.

56. W. H. Grey, *LegCo* 26/3/13, *Gazette* 24/5/13, CO99/39.

57. Harcourt to E. D. Morel (editor, *The African Mail*), 17/10/12, CO96/526/32876.

They had no doubt that a monopoly, in this case of processing machinery, would interfere with the rights of "native" landowners to deal with the products of their land as they wished.[58]

The colonial relationship of rulers and ruled was further complicated by Governor Clifford finding himself in the awkward position of agreeing with the opposition rather than with his superiors in London. Much to the irritation of officials in Whitehall, he persisted in questioning Colonial Office policy. Clifford and his officials on the coast believed that monopolies were undesirable. Such legislation ran counter to the principle that the Governor adhered to: that all land belonged to the local inhabitants, with the colonial government acting as trustee.[59] Politically Clifford proved to be right, in that the issue stirred up a lot of bad feeling. Lever Brothers soon abandoned its unsuccessful oil mills in West Africa (in Sierra Leone and Nigeria as well as the Gold Coast) and set up plantations in the Congo. What had been confirmed, meanwhile, was a colonial governor's inability to counter a strategic policy decision made in London.

Strong African opposition to British policy was aroused—again, just before the war, but in this case successfully—against the colonial government's plan to protect forests. On this matter, Clifford and his officers were on the other side, opposing the local population. Any such government intervention was once more seen by Africans as a threat to their rights over land. This was hardly surprising, considering previous British insensitivity in the handling of the 1890s Land and Forest Bills.[60] Sale of timber was rising fast, reaching a record level in 1913.[61] But British officers were concerned that forests were "gradually degenerating and disappearing."[62] As in the Axim area in the southwest of the Colony, the problem was indiscriminate felling of timber for short-term gain, despite the knowledge that mahogany took 150 to 200 years to mature. There was also a general retreat of the forest as farmers encroached to plant cocoa or, in northern Ashanti, groundnuts. The four members of the Gold Coast forestry department might spend two-thirds of their time traveling, but they could not stop the deforestation.[63] Nor did the Gold Coast government have the means to conserve the colony's forests in the face of widespread local opposition.

Agbodeka's suggestion that the government on the coast was simply trying to preserve agricultural forest products for British use during this period is not convincing.[64] Rather, officers such as Thomas Chipp (director of forestry, trained and first employed at the Royal Botanic Gardens at Kew in southwest London) urged government designation of forest reserves in the belief that deforestation would damage the environment, adversely affecting the local population as well as the export trade in timber. For example, forest shade was used to protect food crops as well as cocoa trees.[65] Here again, the British officers

---

58. Hutton Mills, *LegCo* 26/3/13, *Gazette* 24/5/13, CO99/39.

59. Sir George Fiddes (see Principal Officials, p. 277), CO Minute 19/8/13, Clifford to Harcourt 24/3/13, CO96/529/13459.

60. See D. Kimble, *A Political History*, pp. 330–357.

61. *Trade Report* 1913, *Gazette* 25/4/14, CO99/35.

62. H. M. Thompson, *Forestry Report 1908*, quoted by Acting Governor Bryan to Harcourt 21/10/12, CO96/522/35648.

63. *Forestry Reports: 4th quarter 1912, Gazette* 22/3/12, CO99/22; *1912 Report, Gazette* 27/9/13, CO99/80; *3rd quarter 1913, Gazette* 22/11/13, CO99/10. Also G. D. Hazzledine, article in *The African Mail*, enclosure in Acting Governor Bryan to Harcourt 16/7/12, CO96/525/22384.

64. F. Agbodeka, *Ghana in the Twentieth Century*, p. 20.

65. See reports sent to the Royal Botanic Gardens, Kew, by Thomas Chipp, director of forestry, *Miscell. Reports West Africa, Including Liberia 1865–1916*, MS. Kew, pp. 146, 184–186, 191.

took a long-term perspective; but in the face of fierce and sustained African opposition to any interference in land use, or misuse, the government could not deliver.[66] Nothing had been done to preserve the colony's forests by the time war broke out in August 1914.

Also concerning land rights, Africans successfully opposed any government interference in the sale of land concessions. There was considerable concern among British officials in the Gold Coast and in London at the extent of land alienated by chiefs to companies, reported by the close of 1912 as a total of 1,800 square miles.[67] Although the Colonial Office concluded that it could not forbid concessions, Harcourt, the Liberal secretary of state, feared that uncontrolled speculation could lead to future generations being "in the position of labourers on the lands which their ancestors owned or occupied under the communal system."[68] This reflected the well-known concern of the British imperial government to avoid the creation of an impoverished and landless, and therefore perhaps lawless, African population. Harcourt's paternalism can be seen in his belief that it was the moral duty of colonial government to protect "natives" from untrammeled economic forces. In practice, though, rather than British rulers imposing regulations and controlling a passive subject population, Africans were largely successful in standing up for what they believed to be inalienable rights to their land—and to its disposal.

Another major problem affecting the export trade that the government felt itself unable to address in the prewar period was a perceived shortage of labor in the colony. The mining companies, almost exclusively involved in exporting gold, claimed that they suffered acutely from labor shortage.[69] They certainly did not suffer in silence. Gold was the second most valuable export of the colony after cocoa, even if it accounted for only 2% of world production.[70] The Chamber of Mines was dominated by the four largest companies: Ashanti Goldfields Corporation Ltd., Prestea Block A Ltd., Abosso Gold Mining Corporation Ltd., and Tarquah Mining and Exploration Company Ltd. These companies looked to both the local government and the Colonial Office for aid in obtaining labor, having received particular government assistance with recruitment in the Northern Territories in the period 1907 to 1910.[71] The daily average "native" labor force in the Gold Coast gold mines in 1914 was 17,400. The gold mine companies wanted special legislation with regard to the "recruitment, engagement and control of natives working in the mines," as well as lower railway rates.[72] Was the Colonial Office not aware, they complained, of

66. For discussion of opposition to the Forest Bill of 1911 and the subsequent government attempts at compromise, see D. Kimble, *A Political History,* pp. 363–367. Also J. A. Belfield's *Report,* CO Minute 18/6/12, CO96/525/18878; and *Forestry Report 4th quarter 1913, Gazette* 18/4/14, CO99/32.

67. Official estimates of the extent of concessions in 1913 varied wildly: from 1,084 square miles (Belfield) to 14,829 square miles (the West African Lands Committee), see C. Ilegbune, "Concessions Scramble and Land Alienation in British Central Ghana 1885–1915," *African Studies Review,* 19, 1976, p. 23. Estimates of total areas in square miles: the Colony: 24,200; Ashanti: 20,000; NT: 35,800. *Colonial Office List* 1912–20, CO941/171/241.

68. Harcourt, CO memo, West African Lands Committee 20/12/12, CO96/523/575.

69. For the long history of labor problems in the mines in the Gold Coast, see J. Silver, "The Failure of European Mining Companies in the Nineteenth Century Gold Coast," *JAH,* 22, 4, 1981, pp. 511–529.

70. Gold Coast colony 1913: export value of gold: £1,648,769; of cocoa: £2,489,218, *Trade Report 1913, Gazette* 25/4/14, CO99/35.

71. For requirement on northern chiefs to provide labor for mines, roads, carriers, etc., see D. Kimble, *A Political History,* pp. 41–42; and R. Thomas, "Forced Labor in British West Africa: The Case of the Northern Territories of the Gold Coast 1906–1927," *JAH,* XIV, 1, 1973, pp. 79–89.

72. Deputation of West African Chamber of Mines to Governor 10/1/12, CO Minute 22/4/12, CO96/516/12361. And see *Trade Report* 1919, CO98/32.

"the huge amount of British capital at stake"? [73] However, there was in fact no hope of the South African-style legislation the mines companies demanded, not merely because London officials disapproved of such legislation but because it had been shown that it was not possible to pass unpopular laws in the Gold Coast, such as the Forest Bill, in the face of widespread opposition.

The real problem lay in the companies' failure to offer sufficient pay. While African producers responded to prices, African laborers responded to wage levels. Miners' wages remained largely static in the period before the Great War: for example, the 1s 3d per shift for unskilled workers such as shovelers and surface laborers. In contrast with the mines, cocoa farmers could offer sharecropping, as well as a higher wage. Average annual labor rates in the 1910s have been estimated as £25 for a miner and £40 for a cocoa laborer.[74] But despite their cries for help, the mining companies were doing well. They were getting around the labor shortage in the Gold Coast colony by importing cheap labor from elsewhere, such as Sierra Leone, Nigeria, Togo, and Liberia.[75] They also recruited from the Northern Territories of the Gold Coast itself, this being a region that offered few alternative employment opportunities. Mines export figures for 1912 were a record for the Gold Coast, and the rise in production continued, up 12% in 1913.[76]

Again British officials did not agree among themselves. It was London officials rather than local British officials who stood up to the mining interests. The Gold Coast government under Clifford, as under his predecessor Thorburn, was sympathetic to the labor problems of the mines companies. In contrast, Colonial Office officials were distinctly unsympathetic. The companies had relied on northern chiefs to supply much of the labor needed to operate the mines, since this labor came largely from areas without cash crops, such as the Northern Territories. The effects of poor working and living conditions were made worse by chiefs often producing men who were in poor health rather than sending able-bodied recruits. Conditions in the mines were "so exacting and unpleasant" that it was no wonder that the African miners left at "the first opportunity."[77] In 1913 Clifford sent to London a very favorable description of a number of mining villages where there had clearly been recent improvements. But Colonial Office officials noted how uncharacteristically uncritical was his glowing report with reference to such aspects as the water supply and electrical lighting. There was no mention of conditions underground and the rates of such diseases as TB and phthisis. Clifford appeared "to be holding a brief for the mines," having, it was said by London officials, been shown only what the companies wanted him to see.[78]

---

73. Letter to *Financial News* re. *4th Annual Report of the West African Chamber of Mines,* Enclosure 12/1/12, CO96/526/1204.

74. I. Sutton, "Labor in Commercial Agriculture in Ghana," p. 81.

75. *Report on the Mining Industry 1912, Gazette* 19/8/13, CO99/67; and see N. Van Hear, "Northern Labor and the Development of Capitalist Agriculture in Ghana," unpublished PhD thesis, (University of Birmingham, 1982), p. 34.

76. *Reports on the Mining Industry: 1912, Gazette* 19/8/13, CO99/67; *1913, Gazette* 14/11/14, CO99/147.

77. J. A. Belfield's *Report* in Acting Governor Bryan to Harcourt 28/8/12, CO96/525/27267.

78. Fiddian (See Principal Officials, p. 277) and Ellis, CO Minute 8/5/13, Clifford to Harcourt, CO96/530/17773. The continuation of poor conditions was later confirmed by Professor Simpson's 1924 *Report* investigating the high death rate among mines laborers, which led to the Mines Health Areas Ordinance of 1925. D. Kimble, A *Political History*, p. 43; and J. Crisp, *The Story of An African Working Class. Ghanaian Miners' Struggle 1870–1980,* (London, 1984), p. 49.

The Colonial Office would not agree to bringing in cheap labor from outside West Africa, such as Indian coolies, as the companies requested. The explanation given was that such indentured labor, used elsewhere in the Empire for agricultural work, was not suitable for mining. This was certainly judged to have been the case in the Rand.[79] Besides, London officials did not believe the labor problem in the Gold Coast to be so acute as to need outside assistance.[80] The gold mining companies were left to tackle their labor recruitment problems themselves.

There were, however, no immediate grounds for concern, with the colony's export trade booming and African farmers producing at an ever-increasing rate for export to a range of European and American destinations. The dramatic rise in exports in 1913, at 25% over 1912, was mainly accounted for by cocoa, with the addition of other exports such as gold, timber, and kola.[81] Although there was a considerable dependence on foreign markets in the prewar period, Britain took by far the greatest share, 68%, of the total value of the colony's exports of nearly £5.5m in 1913. But a significant proportion of exports were sold elsewhere. In terms of value, Germany, taking 17%, was second to Britain. Cocoa provided an increasing proportion of exports to Germany and France, with Germany the chief customer for palm kernels and France the chief customer for palm oil. The major commodity shipped direct to the United States was timber. Most timber (largely mahogany), including that shipped to Germany and Britain, found its way eventually to the American market. Before the First World War, the proportion of trade exported to Germany was much higher in the British West African colonies of Nigeria and Sierra Leone than in the Gold Coast as a result of the demand for palm products, especially palm kernels. In 1913 more than half the total value of all produce exported from Nigeria, and just under half the total value of exports from Sierra Leone, went to Germany.[82]

In spite of some concerns regarding cocoa, there was no reason to suppose this pattern of flourishing free trade should not persist just as successfully during the rest of Clifford's term of office as governor of the Gold Coast. As he declared in 1913, "the trade of this colony has never before attained to such proportions as those which exist today. The progress of recent years has not only been steady but rapid."[83] The colonial government's role, Clifford believed, was to provide a skeletal administration and a basic transport and communications infrastructure to make the international export trade possible. Meanwhile, African farmers in the Colony and Ashanti regions of the Gold Coast made their own commercial decisions as they continued to expand production, especially of the highly successful cash crop, cocoa.

African farmers chose what to produce for export, in the light of demand—the prices offered by the trading companies. In the Gold Coast, a majority favored cocoa over palm products or rubber. African producers were not, on the whole, interested in experimenting

79. P. Richardson, "The Recruiting of Chinese Labor for the South African Gold Mines 1903–1908," *JAH*, XVIII, 1, 1977, pp. 85–108.

80. Flood (See Principal Officials p. 277), CO Minute 26/7/12, Sir John Moffat to Harcourt, 24/7/12, CO96/526/23441.

81. *Trade Report* 1913, *Gazette* 25/4/14, CO99/35.

82. *Trade Reports: 1912, Gazette* 3/5/13, C099/34; *1913, Gazette* 25/4/14, C099/35. Also see A. Osuntokun, *Nigeria in the First World War*, p. 23, and F. Cole, "Sierra Leone and World War I," p. 259.

83. Clifford re. 1914 Estimates, *LegCo* 3/10/13, *Gazette* 14/10/13, C099/87.

with alternative crops. The African farmers' priority was to retain independent control of their land and land use. It was clear that over these issues they could, as they had in the past, mount a widespread and formidable opposition to the British colonial rulers—even if they did on occasion wish the government would intervene on their behalf with the traders to obtain a better price for their crops. But British officials did not intervene; they were powerless to insist either on diversification of crops or on what they believed to be essential standards of production.

Cocoa was, as has been shown, not the only commodity in the export trade. To take another case, the export of timber also raises the question of who was in control of the Gold Coast's economy in this period. The foreign market for timber, an example of the pressing demand for raw materials in the world economy and the readiness of Africans in the Gold Coast to meet it, won out against the paternalistic concerns of colonial officials about good husbandry and conserving forests into the future.

The British colonial administration in the Gold Coast was limited in its effectiveness. On the one hand, Clifford and his government deplored monopolistic practices, but found themselves unable to persuade Colonial Office officials in Whitehall to their point of view. They lacked the powers to resist decisions made in London, even when European traders as well as the African unofficials and the African press joined Clifford in noisy opposition to monopoly. On the other hand, they could not detach their African subjects from an increasing dependence on one fragile cash crop, cocoa. The considerable prewar efforts of the small agricultural department to diversify agricultural production in the Gold Coast were largely unsuccessful (and have been neglected in the existing literature).

British colonial officials in the Gold Coast thus had little influence on the colony's export trade before the First World War. The local government's position remained that of a slightly uneasy spectator of the activities of African farmers and traders and European companies. It did not control production or marketing. The gold mining companies acted independently, and African farmers and traders took little notice of British officials' advice concerning agriculture. Also, British officials failed to effectively address the problem of how to obtain the African labor required by both European commercial companies and the coast government, even before the outbreak of war. The local British government tried to protect the African population from decisions made by the metropolitan government in London (such as the granting of a monopoly in palm oil processing to a British trading company) and from what the local British government believed might jeopardize long-term economic stability, such as the effects of poor husbandry and of monoculture.

This did not insure it against criticism from African spokesmen in the legislative council and in the African press. In 1913, an editorial in the main local newspaper, the *Gold Coast Leader*, spoke for the African population: "We should like to see more of the profits of trade going into the pockets of the natives." Was it not possible to develop big "native" trading corporations in the colony as trade expanded, since only much larger African organizations could counter-balance the ever larger European expatriate companies?[84] Here is evidence not only of contemporary voices in the local African press already raising major issues concerning the colony's inequitable economic structures, but also of a widespread prewar confidence that the export trade was set to continue to expand.

---

84. *Editorial, Gold Coast Leader*, 19/7/13.

While the colonial administration on the coast had little room for maneuver, and constraints already visible did not augur well for what might happen in conditions of war, for the time being the Gold Coast colony was prospering. This was thanks to global economic conditions rather than to the policies of its British administration. Meanwhile, numerous Africans were both responsible for and benefiting from the colony's evolving economic relations with the rest of the world. These favorable economic conditions were providing the Gold Coast government with sufficient funds for the new governor, Hugh Clifford, to harbor ambitious development and welfare plans for the colony in this prewar period.

Chapter 2

Clifford's Prewar Plans: Financing Development and Welfare

The Gold Coast colony was still embryonic when Clifford arrived, but the new governor had ambitious plans for the territory. These went beyond merely giving the colonial state firmer foundations. He wanted to be in a position to finance what British contemporaries termed "development" and "welfare." Thus he wanted to encourage trade to the utmost, in order to fund from its proceeds not only an improved infrastructure but also a program of social services that would benefit both Europeans and Africans. During the prewar trade boom he was fortunate to have much of the funding he needed, though he faced opposition at times (more from British officials in London than from his African subjects) as well as the pressing need for a stable currency. But he achieved a number of successes before the First World War. These—especially in the areas of transport, public works, health, and education—promised well for the future of his governorship.

Soon after his arrival in December 1912, Governor Clifford summarized his aim: to adopt policies that promoted "the moral and intellectual advance of the population."[1] For Clifford, the purpose of construction plans in the Gold Coast colony, especially an up-to-date transport and communications infrastructure, was primarily to create the conditions in which the colony's export and import trade could flourish. Trade was critical, because the greater the amount of trade, the more government revenue from customs duties could be used to finance welfare projects. Clifford argued that money should be spent on applying modern science and technology to benefit the African public, such as constructing an improved water supply in Accra and other coastal towns and providing Western medicine and Western education across the colony.[2] Although several construction schemes had been launched by previous governors, such as Sir John Rodger, Clifford gave them new urgency and scope.[3]

The transport facilities of the Gold Coast colony were described by Clifford as more backward than in any dependency known to him in his more than twenty-nine years of public service in Southeast Asia and the Caribbean. He was determined to improve railways, roads, and harbors, and also to develop a telegraph and telephone network. The framework of the Gold Coast colony was still being formed at this time with, for example, no final decision yet made concerning a new site for the capital; where to construct a deepwater harbor; routes for certain main roads such as a main north-south arterial road linking Tamale with Kumasi; and railways to connect the cocoa regions north of Accra and Central and Eastern Province with ports along the coast. Meanwhile, in 1913, a substantial surveying team had yet to complete the task of mapping the Northern Territories.[4]

---

1. Clifford to Harcourt, 1/10/13, CO96/537/1/136.
2. See, for example, Clifford to Harcourt re. program of road construction of Sir John Rodger, Governor Gold Coast (1904–1910), 11/3/13, CO96/528/2/10706.
3. Clifford to Harcourt, 11/3/13, CO 96/528/1. For Rodger, see p. 277.
4. Clifford to Harcourt, 8/7/13, CO96/532/6.

The colonial relationship firmly linked the African population to global capitalism. The international export and import trade was flourishing, with many Africans buying goods from abroad that materially improved their standard of living. As a result, government revenue and commercial profits were both rising fast. But revenue in the colony came very largely from a single source: indirect taxes on imports. These, by their nature, provided only limited funds, and they were vulnerable to fluctuations in trade. But there was no other major source of taxation apart from railway rates. The imperial government in Britain expected colonies to pay for themselves and not be a charge on the metropolis. It seemed that welfare projects could be financed by economic growth in British colonies over time, but Clifford wanted the colonial government to play a more immediate and active role. He did more than merely inform officials in Whitehall of his aspirations for the Gold Coast. In order to win them around, he spent much time and energy in lengthy argument and correspondence with London. In the absence of private investment in the Gold Coast, as in the other West African colonies, he advocated financing development and welfare not only with revenue from customs but also with loans raised on the London money market. By 1914 the governor had, despite a struggle over finances, succeeded in turning the tide of colonial policy and obtaining permission from London to use more funds across the board: for more African medical and teaching staff and more government schools, though not for "Africanisation."

Indeed, the main criticism of Governor Clifford at this time came not from the African population of the colony but from prejudiced British officials (both in the colony and the Colonial Office). For example, they opposed Clifford's plans (based on his positive experience of employing "native" staff in former postings, such as in the Malay States) for the "Africanisation" of both the medical and legal professions.[5] Meanwhile, there was African approval of the new governor's successful drive to increase funding in the colony—despite initial concern about the British attempt to extend colonial powers by, for example, standardizing the currency. In particular, the subsequent rapid completion of new public buildings by the early war period was appreciated by the African newspaper, the *Gold Coast Leader,* as "a credit to the energy of the new administration."[6]

By the time of the outbreak of war, the administration of the Gold Coast under Sir Hugh Clifford had also become committed to a major transport scheme of rapid railway construction. Concerning transport, roads remained very much in second place in Clifford's plans. Like Lugard, Clifford believed that the means to achieve economic improvement and growth could be encapsulated in a single word, "transport," or more specifically, "railways." A railway line from Sekondi to Kumasi already existed, built between 1898 and 1903 to service the mines in Tarkwa and Obuasi and, by carrying troops if necessary, to control Ashanti. What was now needed, British officials strongly believed, was for the colonial government to extend the Accra-Akuepem railway, begun in 1909, into the rapidly expanding cocoa districts to the north of Accra. The ultimate aim was to link Accra to Kumasi, capital of the Ashanti, either directly or by joining the Sekondi line. This plan partly reflected the growing importance of Accra as the commercial and the administrative capital of the colony (from 1878), whereas Cape Coast had declined from the 1870s.[7]

---

5. See, for example, Clifford re. 1914 Estimates, *LegCo* 3/10/13, *Gazette* 14/10/13, CO99/87.
6. *Gold Coast Leader*, 2/1/15.
7. *Consulting Engineer's Report 19/2/12*, CO96/524/6703.

For three years before Clifford's arrival, the Gold Coast government had been trying to get permission from London for a fifteen-mile railway extension to Koforidua. But they had been unable to obtain Colonial Office agreement, despite the fact that this was the center of a rich farming area—primarily of cocoa, but also of palm oil, rubber, kola, and gum copal (a base for making varnish and lacquer) where "valuable tropical produce lies rotting on the ground for want of means of transport."[8] The Colonial Office response had been typically cautious and parsimonious. Permission was finally given in 1912 to extend the railway for a mere two miles, to Mangoase, but no further, given that the colony had to provide the funds. "One cannot at the present moment safely allow an addition of £1.5 million to the Gold Coast debt."[9] (The public debt stood at nearly £2.5m at this time, whereas government revenue and expenditure stood at just over £1m each.)[10] Meanwhile the existing railway system, in particular the Sekondi-Kumasi line, had been allowed to run down and urgently required proper maintenance.[11]

Clifford believed that further railway construction in the Gold Coast would be justified by the economic benefits to all involved in the international trade, both Europeans and Africans. He told his superiors in London not only that "railway construction is the one most important and most immediate need of the Gold Coast" but also that the colony could afford it.[12] In 1913 he called for further loan funds—but market conditions were reported as not being sufficiently favorable. It was not possible to borrow at 3% or even 4%, considered a high rate at the time. The governor's solution was to pay for the cost of railway extensions out of the colony's extensive surplus balances.[13]

Clifford's concentration on railways was hardly surprising given the context. This was the great age of railway construction across the world. All over the Empire, in Canada, Australia, and India, for example, and also in regions of informal empire such as Latin America, railways were integrating local economies into the world economy, exporting raw materials and importing manufactured goods. Across Britain's tropical empire in this period, including the African colonies, development was seen by colonial governments as dependent on railways opening up sources of trade and, through rail rates, providing public funds.[14]

Indeed, this "railway imperialism" included more than economic arguments: railways were viewed by the British colonial administrators as more than just a means of transport. Clifford himself argued that improved transport led to more efficient administration with easier access not only for maintaining law and order, but also to enable the spread of education and, he believed, "the civilizing influence of Europeans."[15] He might have added that it also provided the means to police a territory. In contrast, African comment concentrated on practical trading needs such as the frequent demand for a coastline railway or a coastline road to link Accra with Central Province.[16]

---

8. *Ibid.*

9. Ellis, CO Minute 1/2/12, CO96/524/5413.

10. *Blue Book* 1912, CO100/62.

11. *Railway Report 1911, Gazette* 24/8/12, CO99/61. Also Clifford to Harcourt, 7/10/12, CO96/521/31607.

12. Clifford to Harcourt, 11/3/13, CO96/528/10706.

13. Clifford to Harcourt, 26/5/13, CO96/531/20352.

14. The closest parallel is perhaps with the Uganda railway, built at the same time as the Sekondi-Kumasi line and similarly designed for a range of administrative, economic, and potentially military purposes.

15. *Ibid.*

16. E.g., *The Gold Coast Nation*, 26/11/14 and 10/6/15.

It took the exceptional determination and drive of the new governor to persuade the Colonial Office that railways were a major priority on which money should be spent immediately. Within six months of arriving at his post, Clifford had, remarkably, turned around Colonial Office opinion to his views: instead of accumulating large balances, "every available shilling" was to be invested to accelerate development and "consolidate the prosperity of the people."[17] London officials now agreed: "This is no time to starve the Gold Coast railway which after all more than pays its way and is developing traffic rapidly."[18] It was estimated that the total expenditure for the colony, of approximately £1.08m, would in 1914 exceed the total revenue by around £500,000—but this was no longer seen as a cause for alarm. The difference was to be met by dipping into the surplus balances of, perhaps, £lm by the end of 1913. In the longer term it was believed that trade would be stimulated, and therefore revenue, including railway rates, would rise.

Sir Hugh Clifford's forceful personality and administrative experience played a major part in winning metropolitan backing for, in this case, a forward policy on railways—illustrating that a powerful governor had the potential, in the short term at least, to make a personal impact on a relatively small tropical colony. His lengthy and impassioned pleas won support in the Colonial Office. Though his plans were "ambitious," they were not, it was now agreed, beyond the resources of the colony.[19] Clifford's energy, determination, and paternalism were evident in his ambitious plans for completing a wide range of improvements—including the provision of electric lighting in the main towns. Railways would help provide the funds.

Clifford's railway schemes were certainly ambitious. The secretary of state's approval of the extension to Koforidua, announced in March 1913, was to be only a first step. The governor intended the line to reach Kumasi, variously estimated at between 152 and 175 miles, depending on the route chosen. He argued that once the Accra line north was linked at some point to the Sekondi-Kumasi line, it would be possible to shift the capital of the colony. The Kwahu plateau was the site he suggested as being in a central position, equidistant between Accra and Kumasi, with the advantage of a better climate, at 1,500 to 2,300 feet above sea level.[20] Colonial Office officials agreed that a new capital was likely if all these railway extensions were sanctioned, although the choice might well, they thought, be Kumasi. A change of site would allow the governor to move out of Christiansborg Castle on the edge of Accra. This was once a slave fort, vividly described by Clifford as not only damp, ill-ventilated, and plagued by mosquitoes and yellow fever, but also "depressing to the spirits," with the deafening roar of the surf and the smell of the sewage and refuse tipped onto the shore.[21]

A wide range of the African population responded positively in this prewar period to the colonial government's plans. Officials noted the popular demand for railway construction, as seen in petitions received. For example, in a letter to the governor of July 1913, chiefs in the Koforidua district declared they would even waive their rights to land needed for construction, as they were "conscious of the benefits" of the proximity of a railway. This provoked approving paternalistic comments in London: "The people

17. Clifford, re. 1914 *Estimates*, *LegCo* 3/8/13, *Gazette* 14/10/13, C099/87.

18. Flood, CO Minute, Clifford to Harcourt, 13/8/13, C096/534/575.

19. Sir John Anderson (see Principal Officials, p. 277), CO Minute 26/5/13, C096/531/20352.

20. Clifford, *LegCo* 1/3/13, *Gazette* 5/4/13, CO99/26; and Clifford to Harcourt, 11/2/13, CO96/528/10706.

21. Clifford to Harcourt, 7/4/1913, C096/529/216.

are just as keen to have a railway as Sir Hugh Clifford is to build one," and " ... another instance of the progressive character of the Gold Coast native."[22]

The African demand for improved transport—far from any grandiose aim of British officials—reflected immediate economic need. It was Clifford who had declared himself "much struck" by the sight in Mangoase in January 1913 of "a continual string of heavily laden bearers carrying sacks of cocoa on their heads" en route from Koforidua.[23] At this time the cost of such human porterage per ton mile was about thirty times more expensive than rail transport. With a heavy sixty lbs as the average load, it took about thirty-six carriers to move a ton of goods.[24] There were other examples of the African demand for improved rail transport. Commissioner of Western Province Maxwell reported that in "palavers" with chiefs while on trek in 1913, he had received frequent requests for more steam engines—known locally as *okataka*, or "iron that walks on iron"—and for more railway extensions to transport cash crops to the ports.[25]

Constructing roads, on the other hand, was not given the same priority as constructing railways by the British administration of the Gold Coast at this time. For Clifford, government transport policy should be unambiguous: "Efficient transport facilities mean the construction not of roads but of railways." Railways rather than roads were a good source of revenue for the government, "a direct engine for taxation."[26] And railways were "a far cheaper venture" than metalling roads to make them suitable for motor traffic.[27] The Colonial Office also argued that Britain was behind both France and Germany in railway development in West Africa, especially in the case of the Gold Coast and Sierra Leone.[28] They were inclined to agree that in the absence of draft animals and indigenous wheeled forms of transport, money should not be spent on more trunk roads, as "railways are much more economical."[29] It was even argued in London that "road and railway construction must be regarded as to some extent mutually exclusive owing to the extreme scarcity of labour in the Gold Coast."[30]

Given what followed, it is important to understand the colonial government's thinking here. The priority the government gave to railways was partly justified by the fact that it was both difficult and expensive to construct roads that could withstand very heavy motor vehicles. Many reports before the war describe road surfaces as very badly damaged. Just inland from the coast in Eastern Province, for example, the Accra-Dodowa road was said to have become little more than "a pit."[31] The main reason for this was the excessive weight of most trucks, such as the German and Austrian trucks used by the Swanzy trading company, which weighed five tons when fully laden. "A few monstrous motor lorries ...

22. Flood, Green, CO Minute re. enclosure, letter from Chiefs in the Koforidua area, July 1913; Clifford to Harcourt, 9/11/13, C096/538/413301.

23. Clifford to Harcourt, 28/1/13, CO96/527/5676.

24. See J. Hogendorm, "Economic Initiative and African Cash Farming: Pre Colonial Origins and Early Colonial Development" in L. H. Gann & P. Duignan (eds.), *Colonialism in Africa, iv: The Economics of Colonialism,* (Cambridge, 1975), p. 296.

25. John Maxwell, PC, Western Province, *Report on Western Province 1913, Gazette* 29/8/14, C099/103.

26. Clifford, *LegCo* 3/8/13, *Gazette* 14/10/13, CO99/87.

27. Clifford to Harcourt, 10/3/13, C096/528/150.

28. Sir John Anderson, CO Minute 27/2/13, C0554/676959.

29. Ellis, CO Minute, Clifford to Harcourt, 4/6/12, C096/525/77256.

30. Green, CO Minute, Clifford to Harcourt, 10/3/13, C096/528/150.

31. Flood, CO Minute, Clifford to Harcourt, 4/12/12, C096/523/40501.

churned up the roads into quagmires or reduced them to powder."[32] Many vehicles were fitted with solid, and therefore very heavy, rubber tires, and some steam traction engines with trailers even had steel wheels. In 1913 Clifford complained of a truck journey on poor roads in the Winneba district of Central Province as "the noisiest, most comfortless and least smooth running vehicle upon which it has ever been my misfortune to travel."[33] The Gold Coast government passed a series of Orders in Council in 1913 to ban motor vehicles over two tons in weight without pneumatic tires. But the problem remained that most roads were simply trampled earth tracks. Tons of cocoa were still rolled by laborers along such tracks down to the ports on the coast. The ravages of the tsetse fly meant that in the coastal and forest regions of the southern two thirds of the colony, animal transport could not normally be used, and there was still little in the way of any mechanized transport.

As early as 1913, both African and European merchants wanted the government to construct roads suitable for the new light motor vehicles that were beginning to be imported as feeders to the railways. Clifford was not in favor. Metalling roads (the Kumasi-Ejura road cost £1,000 to £2,000 a mile) was judged too expensive to be an economic option.[34] His dismissal of roads in the colony as merely "makeshifts which cannot adequately supply the place of railways" led the senior unofficial, Grey, to inform the governor, less than a year before the war, that "there is an impression in the public mind that your Excellency is against roads altogether."[35] The governor was still insisting in 1913—in a debate which pre-dated the war—that "for many years, it may be for many generations to come" only the railway could relieve the colony's "crippling transport difficulties."[36]

His African subjects disagreed, and took action. The construction of a network of roads suitable for the new light motor traffic was a particular African initiative.[37] The sources reveal that this extraordinarily rapid commercial revolution in motor transport was begun by Africans just before the First World War. It is usually dated as beginning in the 1920s: for example, Michael Crowder wrote that "commercial road transport was not to become feasible in West Africa until the *late* twenties."[38] Yet long before this, motor traffic was increasing as a result of farmers and local traders improving old roads and constructing new ones.[39] An increasing number of light Ford cars and light American trucks were imported from Britain during 1913 by European companies such as Swanzy and Millers. Vehicle imports into the colony rose by 68% in 1913.[40] Over half of these were sold to Africans in Central Province in the districts of Sekondi, Winneba, Cape Coast, and Saltpond—all cocoa-growing districts without a railway.

The transport department reported "great changes" in the motor service that year, 1913. Hired light motor trucks with high road clearance now provided a "great saving in time and expense," such as an estimated saving of £3 a journey on the Kumasi-Ejura road.

32. Clifford, "Recent Developments in the Gold Coast," *Journal of the African Society,* XVIII, LXXII, July 1919, p. 249.

33. Clifford to Harcourt, dispatch: *Trek of the TransVolta Districts, September 1913, 7/10/13,* C096/528/746.

34. Clifford to Harcourt, 10/3/13, CO96/528/150.

35. *Report of the Select Committee, LegCo* 11/10/13, *Gazette* 3/1/14, C099/1.

36. Clifford to Harcourt, dispatch: *Visit to Togo, 30/10/13, C096/536/36154*; and see Clifford to Harcourt, 10/3/13, CO96/528/150.

37. See the African initiatives taken during the war in Chapter 7.

38. *West Africa under Colonial Rule,* p. 278. My italics.

39. *Trade Report 1913, Gazette* 25/4/14, C099/35.

40. *Blue Book 1913,* CO100/63.

One particular journey recorded by the transport department in 1913 could now be completed in eight hours, though it had previously taken carriers nine days.[41] Figures given for light motor vehicles in the Gold Coast before the war, as only fourteen touring cars and two trucks, are clearly an underestimate.[42] The total number of motor cars and trucks imported into the colony in 1913 alone, 135 (including two for the government), was then far exceeded in 1914, when 318 were imported (including six for government use). There were clearly sufficient numbers of motor vehicles on the roads by April 1914 to merit a ban on general motor vehicles traveling over ten mph and motorcycles and cars from traveling at more than twenty-five mph.[43] Before the war, the few government cars included a Wolseley that could by now cover the sixty-one miles between Kumasi and Ejura in just over three hours.

These developments prompted several officials in the Colonial Office to express serious concern about the local colonial government's relative neglect of road construction in the Gold Coast. Sir George Fiddes argued that "railways are not a solution, for the more railways we build, the more roads we want as feeders."[44] In June 1913, Secretary of State Lord Harcourt agreed to the setting up of the West African Transport Committee to review transport policy for the whole of the British West African coast, to which vehicle manufacturers and merchants such as Swanzy (who were in the process of sending twenty-three light Ford trucks to the Gold Coast at the time) could give evidence. As Flood observed, the mercantile community in the Gold Coast was bound to press for government provision of metalled roads, as it would save them money, given that the average cost of road construction in 1913 was £781 a mile.[45] But no new policy or instructions had been sent to the colony by this London committee before the outbreak of war just over a year later.

In short, what Clifford achieved before the war was London's agreement with the necessity for, and immediate financing of, a major government drive to construct more railways. He had not yet taken on board the dramatic changes in road transport underway as early as 1913. In contrast, African producers and traders responded more quickly to these innovations. They were already, before the war, taking initiatives to improve and extend roads for use by the light motor vehicles that were now being imported and were available in increasing numbers for sale or hire. Africans were responding, according to their own needs, as active players in the now globally linked economy of the colony.

Considerable government expenditure was also committed just before the war to improving the harbors of Accra and Sekondi in order to facilitate overseas trade to the benefit, the governor believed, of all in the colony. Extending the breakwaters at both ports was intended to allow lighters to come in alongside the jetties so that passengers and cargo could be landed on the beach without having to use surf boats. Unfortunately, it became clear during construction that one effect of the breakwater at Accra was a rapid accumulation of sand, countering the effort to obtain a minimum depth of five feet alongside the jetty at low tide. Sand pumping plants were installed, but as the British unofficial, Grey, commented dryly in the legislative council, "it looks as if money is being

41. *Transport Department Report 1913, Gazette* 24/10/14, CO99/134.

42. *The Times*, 1 Jan 1924, in M. Crowder, *West Africa Under Colonial Rule*, (London 1968), p. 312.

43. Order in Council, *Gazette* 4/4/1914, CO99/30.

44. Fiddes, CO Minute, Clifford to Harcourt 10/3/13, CO96/528/150.

45. Flood, *ibid.*

thrown into the sea."[46] Anxiety was also expressed by officials in London as to whether the works could be sustained at "any reasonable cost."[47] However, if work was stopped, the harbor at Accra would rapidly silt up, and the trade of the port, with its increasingly important role given the extension of the railway, would be ruined. As Ellis commented, they were caught in "a sand trap."[48]

Clifford's attitude to the Accra harbor fiasco was characteristically robust, but he was not initially aware of the extent of the constraints. He believed that further heavy expenditure had to be incurred because good port facilities were a vital necessity for the colony: "It is not open to us to accept defeat."[49] But a further ominous sign had been reported early in 1913. Fuel supply needed for the sand pumps had been "erratic and expensive." Pumping operations had even had to stop briefly because of shortage of fuel during the coal strike in England.[50] At least good progress was being made with Sekondi harbor, where Clifford also ordered further major construction, including a second jetty, in 1913. Investigations were underway too concerning the construction of a deepwater harbor in the Colony suitable for oceangoing steamers. The choice was likely to be Sekondi, given the harbor conditions there and the needs of the Western Province trade, including exports of timber and minerals.[51]

In contrast to port facilities, the government construction of waterworks at Accra and Sekondi just before the First World War provided tangible benefits of "modernization" to the African population of the colony. Work had seemed to proceed just as frustratingly slowly as the harbor construction, and for some of the same reasons, such as the shortage of skilled and unskilled labor, which was partly due to the government failure to pay sufficient wages. Costs were also a concern, with estimates having constantly to be revised upwards since work had begun in 1910. However, the provision of a temporary pipe-borne water supply to Accra from January 1913, at the height of the dry season, was a cause for much self-congratulation among British officials, a "notable achievement."[52] By March 1914, with further work on two large storage reservoirs, the Accra waterworks were able to produce 200,000 gallons a day. This government project was, as Clifford realized, unique in the Gold Coast colony in bringing benefit to all classes of the population. "It has done more, I think, to add to the prestige of the government and the confidence felt in it by the bulk of the native inhabitants in and about Accra than anything that has happened for many years."[53] And by 1914, much more such "modernization" was planned by Clifford's administration for the immediate future, including a third Accra reservoir; the completion of the Sekondi waterworks; waterborne sewerage and drainage systems for Accra and Sekondi; and pipe-borne water supplies for the other main towns of the Colony and Ashanti, such as Cape Coast and Kumasi.

British and African views tended to diverge over issues relating to the development of the territory's towns. Clifford was initially preoccupied with the shortage of housing for colonial officials. He inherited from his predecessors, particularly Governor Sir John Rodger, projects to build government officers' houses in Accra and military officers'

46. Grey, *LegCo* 6/11/11, *Gazette* 1/1/12, C099/1.
47. Fiddes, CO Memo 7/10/12, C096/524/31534.
48. *Ibid.*
49. Clifford re. 1914 Estimates, *LegCo* 3/10/13, *Gazette* 14/10/13, C099/87.
50. Annual Report of Resident Engineer, Accra Harbor Works 1912, Clifford to Harcourt, 1/3/13, CO96/528/131.
51. Green, CO Memo 13/5/13, C096/539/16423.
52. Clifford re. 1914 Estimates, *LegCo* 3/10/13, *Gazette* 14/10/13, C099/87.
53. Clifford to Harcourt, 30/3/14, C096/543/210.

quarters in Kumasi. He also had plans for further buildings, once these were completed. But responsibility for the construction of government buildings lay with the notoriously inefficient public works department, whose officials blamed very slow progress and rising costs on the shortage and expense of labor and on problems obtaining bricks, timber, and lime from England. Colonial Office officials, however, accused the PWD of "lethargy" in preferring to import materials rather than following the example of the mines companies by organizing supplies of local timber and bricks.[54] Just before Clifford's arrival in 1912, an exasperated official in the Colonial Office commented that "the Gold Coast must be a wilderness of unfinished and roofless bungalows."[55]

In contrast, the main African concern was with a recent British segregation order that disregarded the needs of local African residents of the colony's towns. This was the imperial requirement that European housing be segregated, for health reasons, from a quarter of a mile to a mile away from "native quarters." Segregation of European and African housing on health grounds had been accepted as official policy in British West Africa just before Clifford's tenure of office. The policy was the result of Robert Koch's identification of mosquito-borne malaria and the identification of *stegomyia* yellow fever mosquitoes in mining villages following the 1910 yellow fever epidemic. It was largely based on contemporary scientific research that suggested African children were the main carriers of malarial parasites. But whoever or whatever might be carriers, the policy failed to take into sufficient account the distance that mosquitoes can fly.[56] Segregation was expensive and provoked complaint from both African and British unofficials in the Gold Coast. The British merchants' representative, Grey, appealed for "common sense," pointing out that the segregation orders were in nobody's interest, with European firms having spent large sums on existing housing. He accused the sanitary officers of being quite unrealistic. They only appeared to consider satisfactory "a site in the middle of the Sahara desert."[57]

Before the war, the African unofficial, Thomas Hutton Mills, argued forcefully that it was the government's duty to improve conditions in existing towns for the protection of all, rather than simply remove Europeans and neglect Africans.[58] Clifford privately agreed. This was another issue on which the British imperial rulers of the colony did not speak with one voice. The governor spent much time and effort early in 1913 trying to persuade the Colonial Office officials in London to reconsider the segregation proposals, which he believed both impracticable and impossible to justify. Not only would Europeans be forced to travel "excessively" from their separate dwelling to their mixed place of work, but the "natives," as principal taxpayers, were to have their money spent on protecting Europeans instead of on the development of the colony. "So selfish a policy could not bear examination," wrote Clifford, and he also sharply criticized the enthusiastic supporters of the scheme in the Gold Coast, the sanitary branch of the medical department, as "an autocracy uncontrollable by the governor."[59]

But there were London officials, especially Fiddian (spokesman for Tropical Africa Medical Work), who could be relied upon to back the policies of the medical and sanitary

54. Ellis, CO Minute, Acting Governor Bryan to Harcourt, 1/4/12, C096/516/9968.
55. Flood, CO Minute re. 1913 Estimates, 31/10/12, C096/522/36321.
56. See R. Dumett, "The Campaign Against Malaria," p. 171; and K. D. Patterson, *Health in Colonial Ghana*, pp. 39–40.
57. Grey, *Report of Select Committee, LegCo*, 11/10/13, *Gazette* 3/1/14, CO99/1.
58. Hutton Mills, *LegCo* 1/1/13, *Gazette* 5/4/13, C099/26.
59. Clifford to Harcourt, 8/3/13, CO96/528/10704.

officers on the coast against the judgment of the governor. Fiddian dismissed Clifford's scruples, and referred sarcastically to a governor writing twenty-one typed pages of first principles (on public health and housing) within a mere three months of his arrival in the colony. In Fiddian's confidently haughty view, "The money the colonial government gets out of the West African native in customs, railway fares, and stamps is for the privilege and benefits the British domain has given him."[60] At Fiddian's suggestion the matter was referred to the Tropical Africa Medical Sanitation Advisory Committee (TAMS) in London, which had been set up by the Colonial Office in 1909 under Assistant Secretary of the Colonies Lord Crewe, who was known to be in favor of segregation. The insulting regulations for British West Africa remained in place.

The other major public buildings under construction just before the war reveal both the local colonial government's priorities and the problems that arose from failing to train Africans. To improve the work of the administration, there were to be new government offices in Accra to house the secretariat, customs, and treasury, as well as an enlarged chamber for the legislative council. Further plans for Accra included a general post office headquarters, a new police barracks, and a European hospital—with a "native" hospital to follow—and a new government house, which was also likely to be in Accra. Colonial Office officials constantly bemoaned the fact that the PWD was "hopelessly behind," and urged that more efforts be made to train "natives." This failure to train Africans across the board was to cause particular problems once staffing was reduced in the war. However, the governor was praised by London officials for his "herculean effort" to get the department abreast of its work.[61] For Clifford, the PWD remained "the weakest spoke in the wheel of this administration."[62] The African barrister and prominent spokesman, J. Casely Hayford, agreed, describing the department in 1913 as "the acme of ineffectiveness."[63]

In some respects, the colonial administration of the Gold Coast at this time—and hence its competence—remained very primitive. There were therefore plans, too, for rapid improvements to communications, with considerable concern being expressed in the Colonial Office at, for example, the condition of the post and telegraph service. "This matter is most urgent in the Gold Coast, where the telegraph system has broken down almost, through lack of repair and supervision."[64] "The wires are rotten, the poles are falling in all directions and the staff are below the mark in numbers and efficiency."[65] Complaints from the mercantile community helped to spur officials to act. Grey related that a telegram sent by the governor from Akuse to Accra, a five-hour cycle journey, had taken three days. His main recommendation was for improved training and pay for the African clerks.[66] The Colonial Office acknowledged that extra expenditure, as on transport, was essential. "We have tried cheese-paring for some time in the Post Office and I think it is time we had a try at the effect of generous expense."[67] By 1913 Clifford had obtained Colonial Office permission for a new GPO in Accra, a 40% increase in staff, and improved pay. Successful experiments with wireless telegraphy had been achieved, and also in 1913,

60. Fiddian, CO Minute, Clifford to Harcourt, 8/3/13, CO96/528/107704.

61. CO Minute, Clifford to Harcourt, 17/4/13, C096/530/242.

62. Clifford to Harcourt, 20/8/13, C096/534/599.

63. J. Casely Hayford, *The Truth about the West African Land Question,* (London, 1913), p. 111.

64. Ellis, CO Minute, Thorburn to Harcourt, 1/10/12, C096/525/30829.

65. Green, CO Minute, Acting Governor Bryan to Harcourt, 29/8/12, CO96/520/29189. See also CO Memo 2/1/13, C096/522/39701.

66. Grey, *LegCo* 6/6/12, *Gazette* 17/8/12, CO99/59.

67. Ellis, CO Minute, Acting Governor Bryan to Harcourt, 29/8/12, C096/520/29181.

badly needed telegraph extensions and repairs were completed, as over the one hundred-mile distance in the Northern Territories between Tamale and Gambaga. There were as yet only four telephone exchanges, all in Accra, but there were plans to extend the telephone service as soon as possible to Sekondi, Tarkwa, and Dodowa.[68]

The African population of the colony was, of course, affected by these programs of development and welfare. They paid for them: not directly, but by indirect taxation. Direct taxation had been strongly resisted in the Gold Coast.[69] It was clear from the effects of the public outcry over the land and forest bills in the 1890s that the government had no power to withstand a popular campaign and widespread opposition over taxes. In August 1898, Joseph Chamberlain, on receiving a deputation from the Gold Coast over the Land Bill, had tried to argue the case for direct taxation as a means to develop the country. He had been given a short answer: any form of hut or poll tax was unacceptable and would be impossible to collect.[70]

Indirect taxation, on the other hand—in the form of import duties—was easy to impose and to administer. Africans were buying a wide range of imported goods in this prewar period, despite the fact that customs duties raised the price of imports, typically by 10%, even before the huge wartime increases. They were able to buy rifles, gunpowder, and spirits (rum was now replacing gin as the favorite liquor), for example, as well as kerosene for lighting and a whole range of foods such as beef and pork, bread, flour, rice, sugar, and salt. Out of £1,230,850 total revenue (1912), customs dues at £735,470 formed by far the largest item—railway rates (£329,399) was the only other major source.[71] Quantities of all categories of imports, especially cotton, metal goods, and provisions, were rising in the prewar period as a result of increased purchasing power among the local population from the sale of agricultural exports, especially cocoa.

For many residents of the Colony and Ashanti, this prewar period was one of increasing prosperity. Fuller, chief commissioner of Ashanti, noted the growing demand, and the speed with which agencies of European firms were opening stores along the Kumasi-Ejura road: "More wants are being developed day by day among the people."[72] Markets were also spreading alongside the railway lines selling imported goods such as cotton cloth, clothes, and tinned provisions. Evidence that the standard of living was rising in the more prosperous cocoa districts could be seen in the sales of corrugated iron roofing and construction of "better houses" and "more sanitary" yards and compounds, as well as in the consumption of imported provisions and the purchase of luxuries.[73] Not surprisingly, the value of commercial imports rose sharply in 1912 and again in 1913, with reports of a growing demand from Africans for a mixed range of products including, for example, furniture, rice, flour, soap, kerosene, oils, greases, perfumes, cigarettes, cheap cigars, pipe tobaccos, and European tweeds and flannels.[74]

---

68. *Post and Telegraph Report 1912, Gazette* 13/12/12, C099/106; Clifford to Harcourt, 23/7/13, C096/533/523; Clifford re. 1914 Estimates, *LegCo* 3/10/13, *Gazette* 14/10/13, C099/87.

69. For earlier popular resistance to government attempts to impose direct taxation, 1850–1862, see D. Kimble, *A Political History*, pp. 169–191.

70. *Report of the Proceedings of the Deputation, Representing the Kings and Chiefs of the Gold Coast, to Chamberlain, 5 May 1898*, enclosure in Thorburn to Harcourt, 8/1/12, C096/515/3000.

71. See *Blue Book 1912*, CO100/62.

72. Fuller, *Ashanti Report 1911*, 23/4/12, C096/517/18726.

73. *Report of Eastern Province 1912, Gazette* 11/10/13, C099/85; and *Railway Report 1911, Gazette* 24/8/12, CO99/61.

74. *Trade Reports:* 1912, *Gazette* 3/5/13, CO99/34; 1913, *Gazette* 25/4/14, C099/35.

In view of forthcoming wartime dislocation, it is worth noting here that many of these imports purchased by Africans in British West Africa came from Germany. This was to cause considerable difficulty when all ties were broken at the outbreak of war. By 1913 Germany was second to Britain in terms of value of imports to the colony: indeed, British firms had steadily lost ground in the provision of a wide range of popular commercial imports such as earthenware, metal goods, building materials, beer, lemonade, beads, and vehicles.[75] Agricultural implements such as machetes, hoes, and cutlasses were mostly of German origin, including those imported from Holland. German imports such as iron implements, cement, candles, coarse cotton cloth, wearing apparel, furniture, cigars, and perfumery were cheap, and popular with the local African population. An effective printing process meant that the color designs on the German cotton cloth were more stable and better able to cope with the African sun and damp than were English dyes. Cotton cloth was often sold white or off-white, to be printed or dyed locally, though Dutch wax block prints, based on local designs of Indonesian batik prints, were also popular.[76] Most drugs and chemicals, including many medicines, were from Germany. German traders also imported a high proportion of furniture sold in the colony and were responsible for almost all imports of enamel bowls, cheap cutlery, and cheap sewing machines. The traveler Mary Gaunt had noted in the Gold Coast colony in 1910 that "enamelled iron basins are as common now on the coast as they are in London town."[77] And German companies were strong competitors too, in terms of astute trading practices. These included packaging their goods more attractively, being much quicker than British firms to imitate successful lines, and giving generous credit terms. And German traders had a reputation for quicker delivery than their British rivals.[78]

Meanwhile, however, government welfare projects were subject to limitations. The governor had little room for maneuver, and his goal of extending "civilisation" met a number of obstacles, not all of them financial. There were British officials both in London and in the territory who did not support his plans to expand the provision of medical treatment and open up such professions to Africans, while his program for extensive educational reform, including more government schools, needed London's agreement for more staff and for funds to be made available. But Clifford managed to overcome several of these constraints—while his efforts raised African expectations of what the colonial government would soon provide.

Just before the war, as noted already, officials in both the colony and in London sought to block Clifford's reforms of the medical service. The two, related, issues were the provision of medical services for Africans and the training of Africans as doctors. The official priority of the fifty-three British doctors of the West African Medical Service in the Gold Coast in 1913 was to care for the health of the handful of Europeans. This was at a time when the population consisted of a total of 2,291 Europeans, of whom 510 were officials and 1,781 non-officials—among a total population of about two million Africans.[79] Doctors were responsible for monitoring outbreaks of infectious diseases such as smallpox, sleeping sickness, blackwater fever, and yellow fever. The commission of inquiry on yellow fever

---

75. A. Osuntokun, *Nigeria and the First World War*, p. 24; and Trade Report 1912, *Gazette*, 3/5/13, CO99/34.

76. *Ibid.*

77. M. Gaunt, *Alone in West Africa*, (London, 1912), p. 97.

78. *Trade Report 1912, Gazette* 3/5/13, CO99/34; and see A. Osuntokun, *Nigeria in the First World War*, p. 24.

79. *Medical and Sanitary Report 1912*, Clifford to Harcourt, 12/8/13, CO96/534/573.

in West Africa had been set up in 1912 following a serious outbreak in 1910 when nine Europeans—and an unknown number of "natives"—died. However, the prejudice of the British medical officers in the Gold Coast Medical Service precluded adequate training not only for African doctors but also for African auxiliaries such as vaccinators (pleaded for by the senior British unofficial, Grey), who could have eased staff shortages. Entrusting "native" dispensers with the treatment of sleeping sickness was deemed, by the prejudiced and exclusively white West African Medical Service, to be "out of the question."[80]

Opinion in the Colonial Office was divided. Although Ellis declared himself personally in favor of appointing African doctors, the main London spokesman on health issues, Fiddian, shared the jaundiced views of the colony's medical officers, as can be seen in such absurd comments as "medical details of officers' illnesses might afford much interesting gossip for native tea parties."[81] He claimed that it would take "generations" for Africans "to be on a par in morals, or manners even, with the black and coloured doctors of the West Indies."[82] Yet Fiddian could also consider it "rather scandalous" that the building of the "native" hospital in Accra, sanctioned in 1909, had had to be postponed yet again, as it had been agreed that work should only begin once the European hospital (long delayed through PWD inefficiency) was completed.[83] It was not uncommon in this period to find British officials simultaneously expressing racial prejudice and paternalism.

The exclusion of African doctors since 1902 from the West African Medical Service remained a major African grievance. The issue of health care for the African population was constantly raised by the unofficials in the legislative council in this period. Clifford's predecessor, Governor Thorburn, had simply repeated a common reason put forward for not employing African doctors: European officials objected to being treated by a "native."[84] One African doctor, Dr. Reindorf, made persistent and well-publicized, though ultimately fruitless, efforts to enter the Medical Service between 1910 and 1913.[85] Yet this was at a time when there were still a few African medical officers—appointed before 1902—practicing in the main public medical service in southern Nigeria and in Sierra Leone.

For Clifford (though not for many other officials both on the coast and in London) the concentration on the health of Europeans (largely a result of the fears of the "white man's grave") could not be justified. Highly contrasting opinions were held at this time concerning the danger to Europeans of the climate of the West African colonies. A British official in London described them as "the most pestilential holes on earth."[86] On the other hand, *The African Mail* insisted that many parts of the region were "as healthy as Brighton."[87] Clifford, with his iron constitution and his habit of cycling in shirt sleeves on his tours of the Colony and Ashanti, was more sympathetic to the latter view. As a biographer

80. *Medical Officer Wade's Report* in Acting Governor Bryan to Harcourt, 1/4/12, CO96/516/9893. And see Grey, *LegCo* 6/11/11, *Gazette* 6/1/12, CO99/1.

81. Fiddian, CO Minute, 23/7/12, CO96/519/23062.

82. Fiddian, CO Minute, Acting Governor Bryan to Harcourt, 20/5/12, CO96/517/15441.

83. Fiddian, CO Memo re. 1913 Estimates. 31/10/12, CO96/522/36234.

84. Thorburn, *LegCo* 6/11/11, *Gazette* 6/1/12, CO99/1; and see D. Kimble, *A Political History*, p. 106.

85. He was finally in 1919 appointed as a medical officer to a new subsidiary, "Native Medical Service."

86. Flood, CO Minute, re. the War Office query on health conditions in West Africa, CO554/3/10304.

87. *The African Mail*, 30/5/13, enclosed in *Statistics re: Non-Officials printed for Parliament April 1913*, CO554/3/3615.

observed, "His physical stamina became legendary in all the areas of the Empire in which he served."[88] Clifford certainly felt that it was his duty to challenge the "legend" that West Africa was "a hot bed of disease"; although he acknowledged that yellow fever was a danger, he considered the temperature in the colony compared favorably with Ceylon and Malaya (as it did, uniquely, on the Accra plain), and that the incidence of other diseases such as malaria and cholera was similar, if not rather less.[89] However, Colonial Office officials noted that death and invalidity rates were higher among officers in the British West African colonies than elsewhere in the Empire.[90]

The governor was quite determined that "the benefits of European medical science" should be made readily accessible to Africans in the immediate future.[91] Clifford was not a man to accept a policy without subjecting it to rational scrutiny, and he was also convinced that he was morally right. He was "much struck by the small extent to which the native population is at present benefited by the expenditure incurred on account of curative medicine" when compared to Britain's Far Eastern colonies.[92] Although he was told there were too few Europeans to supervise a dispensary scheme such as he had seen in Ceylon, Clifford argued that skilled medical assistance should be provided in not just the principal European centers, but also in areas outside, such as Kwahu.[93] However, British policy continued to be one of concentrating medical resources and expertise in a few centers rather than the French system of training numbers of subsidiary African health workers. There was to be no equivalent in the British West African colonies to the field posts and auxiliary African medical staff of French West Africa. Yet Clifford's attitude does not support Dumett's argument that in the Gold Coast in this period, the colonial government "wanted to restrict its responsibilities for ministering to the needs of the entire African population."[94]

Clifford switched his arguments to the question of cost: "Africanisation," opening up the profession to Africans and thereby replacing Europeans with "efficient native practitioners," would, he said, provide "a cheaper machinery." European personnel were expensive, with seventeen months' pay for twelve months of work, together with the cost of passages home and back when on leave. The Gold Coast was spending £36,000 per annum on its medical budget but giving treatment to only 3% of the population, compared with 20% spent in Ceylon. "The medical treatment of the bulk of the native population is a duty which the government cannot for ever continue to shirk."[95] From his liberal paternalist viewpoint, training "the native" was, for Clifford, a major rationale for colonialism. It was "no small

---

88. H. Gailey, *Clifford*, p. 9.

89. Clifford to Harcourt, 14/10/13, CO96/537/37984. For contemporary views that contrast with Clifford's, see Alan Burns (posted to Nigeria in 1912, the same year Clifford arrived in the Gold Coast) in C. Allen, *Tales from the Dark Continent. Images of British Colonial Africa in the 20th Century*, (London, 1979), p. 23; and S. Leith-Ross, *Stepping Stones. Memoirs of Colonial Nigeria 1907–1960*, (London, 1983).

90. Flood, CO Minute, Clifford to Harcourt, re. *Medical and Sanitary Report 1911*, 6/2/13, CO96/52/6603. For death/invaliding rates, see, e.g., L. Gann & P. Duignan, *The Rulers of British Africa*, p. 230. In 1902 the death rate for a European official in West Africa during the first year's residence had been 1 in 7. R. Dumett, "The Campaign against Malaria," p. 156.

91. Clifford re. 1914 Estimates, *LegCo* 3/10/13, *Gazette* 14/10/13, CO99/87.

92. Clifford to Harcourt, 3/3/13, CO96/528/133.

93. See. e.g., K. D. Patterson, *Health in Colonial Ghana*, p. 16.

94. R. Dumett, "Disease and Mortality Among Gold Miners of Ghana," p. 1.

95. Clifford to Harcourt, 27/5/13, CO96/531/20353; also Fiddian, CO Minute 15/7/13, CO96/532/483.

part of the business of our administrative system in the Crown colonies to develop the capacities of the native population, and gradually train and educate natives for the performance of work which owes its inception to our initiative."[96]

Support for Clifford's campaign came from different quarters during 1913. There were questions in the House of Commons asking for information about the numbers of European and "native" doctors in West Africa.[97] British commercial representatives were also critical: "It is time the inhabitants of the Colony obtained more value for money than is expended on the Medical Department."[98] Clifford finally received the welcome reassurance from the Colonial Office that the senior sanitary officer was officially only an "advisor" to government and "can in the last resort be overruled."[99] Equally important, the Liberal Secretary of State Lord Harcourt now expressed his own concern about the lack of "native" medical officers in the Gold Coast. He declared privately that he was "increasingly impressed by the necessity of doing something in this matter, though I realise the difficulties."[100] Therefore, toward the end of 1913 there were grounds for the African unofficial Hutton Mills's optimism that Clifford was winning the battle and that there would at last be financial provision for "native" medical staff in the Gold Coast in the near future.[101]

As with the provision of medical services, the spread of Western education was an aspect of colonialism strongly welcomed by the local African population. African demand for more government schools was to spur Clifford and his officials to seek London's approval for their provision. In Ashanti, for example, a "growing interest in education," especially among illiterate parents, led to many applications for government schools. Chiefs were anxious for their sons to be educated so that they could compete with literate coast people and "no longer remain at the mercy of alien clerks."[102] After his trek through the Trans Volta districts in September 1913, Clifford noted that he had found "a pretty general desire in many parts of the country to see a government school established."[103] He was concerned at how few government schools were provided, deploring the fact that there were none at all in the southwest between Dunkwa and Half Assini. In the whole of Western Province, "very little has been done to improve the social, intellectual and moral condition of the people."[104]

Thus little education had yet been provided by the government, as distinct from the missions. Of the five secondary and 378 primary (or "elementary") schools in the whole colony by 1913, only eleven (primary) were government schools.[105] A major African

96. Clifford Memo, re. *Principal Medical Officers' Conference, November 1912,* 14/4/13, CO554/233.

97. *Hansard,* 29/1/13, CO554/3/233.

98. Grey, *Select Committee, LegCo* 11/10/13, *Gazette* 3/1/14, CO99/1.

99. Harcourt to Clifford, 8/7/13, CO Memo 11/6/13, CO554/19781.

100. Harcourt to Butler, 29/3/13, re. articles by E. Morel in *The African Mail,* 28/3/13, CO554/11081.

101. Hutton Mills, *Select Committee, LegCo* 11/10/13, *Gazette* 3/1/14, CO99/1.

102. *Report on Ashanti 1911,* 30/5/12, CO96/517/18726 and *Report on Ashanti 1914,* quoted in K. Busia, *The Position of Chief in the Modern Political System of Ashanti,* (London, 1951), p. 132.

103. Clifford to Harcourt, dispatch: *Trek through the Trans Volta Districts, September 1913,* 7/10/13, CO96/528/746.

104. Clifford to Harcourt, dispatch: *Trek from Dunkwa to Axim, November–December 1913,* 8/2/13, CO96/528/746.

105. Of the 534 secondary school students and 25,510 pupils in primary schools, the government had taken on responsibility for educating only 2,239, at elementary level. *Blue Book 1913,* CO 100/63.

concern was the lack of a government secondary school. The African unofficials, Hutton Mills and Konor Mate Kole, supported by the British unofficial, Grey, urged the government to provide a secondary school like King's College, Lagos. The government response before Clifford's arrival in the colony had been that the time was "not yet ripe."[106] The issue of government secondary education was then raised in October 1913 in front of the new governor, and Clifford promised to give the proposal due consideration. The government ran one teacher-training college in Accra; this was the only institution of further or higher education provided by the government, other than the Accra Technical and Industrial School, where twenty-five students learned woodwork and metalwork. Otherwise, higher education could only be obtained outside the colony: in Lagos, Freetown, Britain, or the United States.

There was also considerable African concern at the failure to attract Africans into teaching in the immediate prewar period. Many pupil teachers or assistant teachers were untrained, unable to write grammatically, and showed very little grasp of arithmetic. According to Hutton Mills, the standards of teaching were generally low and the whole system of education required "reconstruction."[107] The problem was a financial one that the government had the power to remedy. What was at issue were both the teachers' starting salary and promotion prospects. Those who passed sixth or seventh grade standard in primary school and became clerks were immediately better off than teachers, who were still unable to catch up with third class clerks' wages after seven years of teaching. Many missions could not afford even the low government rates and had difficulty obtaining and retaining teachers on £25 a year. Robertson, as acting governor when Clifford was on leave, recommended in June 1914 that government teachers' salaries be raised.[108] This won support in the Colonial Office, where it was acknowledged that even after this additional expense, "the Gold Coast will still be spending little on education."[109]

Recruiting European staff, both as teachers and as inspectors, was also a problem before the war, again because the pay was not sufficiently attractive. Inspection was important because the government needed to keep some check on the standard of those schools deemed fit to receive a grant. Clifford shared the concern of the Gold Coast education department at the idea of leaving school inspections to DCs, for lack of inspectors, rather than using the services of trained professionals.[110] The London official, Flood, agreed that education in the Gold Coast was in "far too backward a state" already, and that more qualified inspectors were badly needed.[111] But no action had been taken to increase the number of inspectors (from only five for the whole colony) before war broke out in 1914.

However, just before the war, there had been a positive response among Colonial Office officials to Clifford's persuasive case concerning the urgent need for more educational

---

106. Hutton Mills, and Acting Governor Bryan, *LegCo* 28/10/12, *Gazette* 28/12/12, CO99/100.

107. Hutton Mills, *LegCo* 28/10/12, *Gazette* 28/12/12, CO99/100.

108. Clerks were paid £36 p/a as probationers, rising to £42–£72 p/a over seven years. The starting salary for teachers, after two years of training on no pay, was £42 p/a. Acting Governor Robertson to Harcourt, 8/6/14, CO96/545/445. And see H. McWilliam, *Development of Education in Ghana*, (London, 1959), pp. 46–47.

109. Green, CO Memo re. Education Department Establishment and Salaries, 22/6/14, CO96/553/22876.

110. Clifford to Harcourt, 15/11/13, CO96/527/3966; also Meetings of the Board of Education 8/5/11, *Gazette* 9/3/12, CO99/15; and 19/2/12, *Gazette* 24/5/13, CO99/39. And Ellis, CO Memo re. Inspection of Schools 17/10/12, CO96/525/32897.

111. Flood, CO Minute, Clifford to Harcourt, 15/11/13, CO96/527/3966.

provision in the colony. Out of a total budget of just over £l million in 1913, only around £25,000 was spent on education (of which £9,000 were grants to mission schools). Yet, in contrast, £57,000 was spent on the medical department and £37,000 on sanitation. It was acknowledged in London that "the insignificance of the amounts spent on education and native health in the Gold Coast is certain to invite criticism."[112] For these London officials, Western education was not (as it was for Clifford) a moral imperative, but rather a response to administrative needs and African demand to aid economic development. They nevertheless accepted that more government money had to be spent on education in the Gold Coast. There were plans for more government elementary schools and technical training, and, for the first time, some government secondary and higher education. There would also be more African, as well as more British, teachers and more funds. And it was recognized that more school places and training were needed for girls. Relatively few girls went to school, though there were as yet few employment opportunities for educated women.[113]

As was the case with the import trade—regarding, as we have seen, the German origin of very many manufactured goods imported into the Gold Coast—so Germans (and Swiss Germans) played a huge role in education in the Colony at this time, notably the Basel and Bremen missionaries. It was certainly cheaper and less trouble for the Gold Coast government, as elsewhere in British Africa, to continue to depend on missions to provide most Western education, and especially to rely on the Basel mission, which was mostly concentrated in Eastern Province but also ran some schools in Ashanti. Just before the war, the Basel (Swiss-German) mission was responsible for the largest number of government-assisted schools, and this contributed to the disparity in educational provision. By 1912, around two-thirds of all schools in the colony, ninety-two, were sited in Eastern Province (the most prolific area for cocoa production). Elsewhere, there were forty-five in Central Province; seventeen in Western Province; seven in Ashanti; and only two, both government schools, in the Northern Territories.[114] Compared to the sixty-four Basel schools, the Wesleyans (mostly in West and Central Provinces) ran a larger number, though few of comparable quality.[115] The German Bremen mission ran twenty-three elementary schools.[116]

The Basel mission played a particularly important role in the Gold Coast colony in this prewar period. They were nicknamed "the scrubbing mission" by other Protestant groups on the coast—because of their emphasis on vocational and technical training—but many cocoa farmers in states such as Kwahu and Akyem Abuakwa in Eastern Province were literate due to the work of Basel missionary teachers.[117] Some of these African "scholars" contributed to modernizing African society, while others challenged traditional African authorities through *asafos* (commoner organizations or companies).[118] Both the

112. Green, CO Minute in Clifford to Harcourt, 17/4/14, CO96/545/2070; and *Blue Book 1913,* CO100/63.

113. In 1912, for example, 4,503 girls compared with 18,971 boys, *Blue Book 1912,* CO100/62.

114. At Tamale and Gambaga, the latter established only in 1912. Just 142 out of the 367 mission schools merited government grants-in-aid.

115. Only 31 of 135 qualified for government assistance. Other missions were relatively small, including the Catholic mission (33 schools).

116. *Blue Book 1913,* CO100/63.

117. R. Parsons, *The Churches and Ghana Society,* (Leiden, 1963), p. 119.

118. See J. Simensen, "Commoners, Chiefs and Colonial Government," e.g., pp. 46–50 and 187–189.

Basel mission and the small German Bremen mission were highly commended by British officials for efficient management. The Basel mission was singled out for special government praise for its strong emphasis on manual work. Its agricultural and carpentry instruction were said to be "far in advance" of other schools.[119] The Basel mission, in addition, performed a unique service through its book depot in Accra. It acted as the main supplier to the government as well as to other mission schools, the Foreign Bible society, and the local reading public. It was also notable for educating more girls proportionally than either the government or the other main mission, the Wesleyans, and it made a major contribution, too, to teacher training, having set up two teacher-training institutes, at Akropong and Abetifi.

In the year and a half of Clifford's governorship before the outbreak of war, African expectations concerning educational reforms, to be made possible by much greater government spending, were firmly raised. Clifford announced that he planned on his next tour to devote much closer study to the whole question of education in the colony.[120] No changes were planned in the overall pattern of provision, however. Western education would continue to be very largely independently run, by missions rather than by government, and provided above all by German or Swiss German missionaries—an awkward factor once war had been declared.

A problem in the financing of welfare programs, and a further sign of teething troubles in the infancy of the Gold Coast colony, was the absence of an acceptable, universal, and stable currency—a key element for the development of sound trading conditions. Innumerable African transactions proved exceptionally difficult to regulate. A wide mixture of coins had long been in use on the West African coast, including British gold and silver, from three pence pieces up to double florins (4s), crowns (5s), and sovereigns (20s). British silver coins, especially the 1s piece, were apparently the most popular. But there were also French "napoleons," Spanish and South American "doubloons," and US "eagles." Such coins were still in use at this time, although an ordinance of 1880 had officially demonetized foreign silver dollars.[121] The lowest denominations consisted of the British bronze coinage: 1d, a halfpenny, and a farthing. French five-franc pieces were the foreign coins in greatest demand in Ashanti and the Northern Territories, where African traders coming across the frontiers, mainly with cattle, sought money to pay their French taxes. French cattle traders were unable to use British silver in French colonies, though they did ask for gold.[122]

There might be widespread agreement that some form of uniform currency was needed, but there was certainly no agreement between British and Africans on the form it should take. Two particular problems had arisen as a result of African insecurity concerning trading conditions: hoarding, and a lack of coins of sufficiently low denominations. The local African population needed coins of a wide range of value. But much of the gold

---

119. See S. Prempeh, "The Bremen and Basle Missions and Their Successors in the Gold Coast," unpublished PhD thesis, (Aberdeen, 1977); *Education Department Reports* 1911, *Gazette 7/9/12* CO99/65, and 1912, *Gazette* 11/10/13, CO99/85; *Report on Eastern Province* 1913, *Gazette* 26/9/14, CO99/122.

120. Clifford, *LegCo* 3/10/13, *Gazette* 3/1/14, CO99/1.

121. There were similar reports elsewhere in British West Africa, e.g., foreign dollars taken across the frontier from Porto Novo in Dahomey, to Lagos, and into Northern Nigeria via Hausa caravans. D. Kimble, *A Political History*, p. 37. And see *The African Mail*, 21/8/14.

122. Acting Governor Bryan: *Evidence to the West Africa Currency Committee*, 15/12/11, in Thorburn to Harcourt, 14/2/12, C0554/8/6783. R. Fry, *Bankers in West Africa*, p. 73.

and silver coin in circulation soon disappeared, hoarded and either made into jewelry on account of its intrinsic value or buried in the earth for security. These were the means of saving and protecting coin; few of the African population used banks. Also, lower coin denominations were still not low enough for many African market transactions. The result was that old African forms of currency, such as measures of gold dust or "ackie" (valued at 4s 6d) from Ashanti, continued to be used inland in the more remote districts. Although an ordinance of 1889 had officially demonetized gold dust, it continued to be used as a currency—to the advantage of the local authorities that controlled its use, as it was difficult to weigh precisely.[123] Small cowrie shells were also still used, usually valued as twelve and a half strings (forty cowries in a string) exchanged at 3d, or as one "head" of cowries (fifty strings or 2,000 cowries) rated at 1s. Bartering, little practiced on the coast or in the vicinity of larger towns up-country, was quite common in the Northern Territories, where Muslim caravan traders came south over the border to exchange cattle, sheep, local cloth, and leather for kola and salt.[124]

In order to help spread the money economy, prevent hoarding, and provide lower-denomination coins, a subsidiary British West African nickel-bronze currency had been introduced by the government in June 1912. This included coins to the value of 1d, a halfpenny, and one tenth of a penny. The aim of this policy was, in the words of a British Treasury official, to prevent English silver coin from "being absorbed at such an enormous pace by a semi-civilized community."[125] Officials in the colony were pleased to report that the coins had been "readily taken up" in the main trading centers. But there was some confusion that might give rise to inflation: the tenth was often thought of as one-eighth and the farthing as one halfpenny. The inflated value seems to have included the intrinsic value of the metal.[126] Even so, by June 1914 the use of these new coins led to optimism (which was to prove premature) in the Gold Coast Treasury that cowries were gradually becoming extinct as a form of currency.[127]

Another recommendation of the 1912 West Africa Currency Commission in London was also accepted: that there should be a distinctive British West Africa silver currency, convertible at a fixed rate of exchange into sterling. These silver coins (2s, 1s, 6d, and 3d) were proclaimed as legal tender in the Gold Coast in June 1913. They could be exchanged for up to £10 in value at the Bank of West Africa in London or Liverpool. Clifford hoped that releasing more money into circulation would stimulate the economy, especially as the majority of the agricultural population "had not yet learned the art of financial investment."[128] It is difficult to judge whether this was as inflationary a policy as it sounds: much currency put into circulation still disappeared, either hoarded or used as ornaments. The Gold Coast government tried to encourage the local population to

123. D. Kimble, *A Political History*, p. 37. And see J. Simensen, "Commoners, Chiefs and Colonial Government British Policy and Local Politics in Akim Abuakwa, Ghana, under Colonial Rule," unpublished PhD thesis, (University of Trondheim, 1975), p. 55; and K. Arhin, "Monetization and the Asante State," in J. Guyer (ed.), *Money Matters. Instability, Values and Social Payments in the Modern History of West African Communities*, (London, 1995), pp. 97–110.

124. Acting Governor Bryan, Evidence to the West Africa Currency Committee, 15/12/11, in Thorburn to Harcourt, 14/2/12, CO554/8/6783.

125. S. Armitage Smith, Treasury representative on the Emmott Committee on West African currency, 1912, in R. Fry, *Bankers in West Africa*, p. 70.

126. Acting Governor Bryan, *LegCo* 28/10/12, *Gazette* 28/12/12, C099/100.

127. Gold Coast Treasury to Royal Mint, 23/6/14, C096/545/488.

128. Clifford re. 1914 Estimates, *LegCo* 3/10/13, *Gazette* 14/10/13, C099/87.

save, but in a different way. Clifford hoped that the extension of banking facilities would help spread the money economy further, and that as wealth increased and education spread, more money would stay in general circulation. The Bank of West Africa, founded in 1894, had five branches by 1914: Accra, Sekondi, Cape Coast, Axim, and Kumasi, with a further five agencies in the Colony at Winneba, Saltpond, Tarkwa, Obuasi, and Dodowa.[129] But the problem remained that the local African population were not confident that the colonial government would provide enough coin, especially at the time of the cocoa harvest. The result was that they defied the government by continuing their own strategies of hoarding, avoiding banks, and making good in their own way the lack of small denomination coins crucial for markets and up-country trading.

African concerns about the money supply continued up to the outbreak of war. They were reinforced by the row that developed between British officials in London, in the Colonial Office, and the Treasury, early in 1914, over the repatriation of silver coin and the provision of new coin to West Africa.[130] Hostility between the Treasury and the Colonial Office was well established by 1914, with Treasury mistrust of Colonial Office financial commitments. Sir George Fiddes complained at the late delivery of coins from the Royal Mint, and explained to work colleagues that "the natives" would not accept very worn coin.[131] In the Gold Coast, silver coins were always in great demand and often in short supply in October at the start of the cocoa season, when much of the crop was bought in advance. The problem was made worse by the Treasury's perennial concern that over-issue of currency in a colony could destabilize the currency at home if it were suddenly converted and flooded back into Britain.[132] The Mint refused for some time to reimburse the West Africa Currency Board for the coin it had been forced to send out to the Gold Coast to bridge the gap during the period of the cocoa harvest in 1913–1914. No amicable agreement had been reached with the Treasury before war intervened, bringing new problems concerning supply of coinage.

London officials were much more sanguine than officials in the colony about the possibility of solving the coinage problems by introducing a West African paper currency. There was as yet little paper money in circulation except for a few Bank of England notes. Early in 1914, the West Africa Currency Board proposed paper denominations of £1 upwards. Gold Coast Treasurer Reece was not in favor, arguing, in his crude description, that "the native wants glitter in bulk."[133] His fellow officials on the coast, including the governor, also believed that any attempt by London to force acceptance of paper money at this time would be inadvisable and premature. However, pressure to introduce paper notes was to become much greater in the difficult circumstances of war. Here as elsewhere, British colonial administrators and Africans active in the money economy had different preoccupations, attitudes, and preferences, and the colonial state was as yet unable to establish the currency it wanted.

Overall, however, this prewar period appeared to be the beginning of a highly productive era. Trade, and therefore also government revenue, was rapidly increasing, and a new

129. *Blue Book 1914*, CO100/64.

130. See S. Constantine, *The Making of British Colonial Development Policy*, p. 12; and B. Ingham & C. Simmons, *Development Studies and Colonial Policy*, p. 247.

131. CO to Treasury, 28/2/14, C0554/20/7652.

132. See J. Guyer, "The Currency Interface and Its Dynamics," in J. Guyer (ed.), *Money Matters*, p. 11.

133. Reece, memo, West Africa Currency Board, 3/4/14, C0554/19/12610.

phase of greater government spending, urged by Clifford's administration, was now agreed upon by the Colonial Office. Clifford was confident that he had turned the tide of British policy in the Gold Coast in the 1913–1914 period—with new government commitments to spending in tune with African demand for further modernizing projects in the colony. The colonial government's attitude to trade remained laissez-faire; this was hardly surprising, as trade was flourishing, and laissez-faire did not preclude the colonial government's actions to improve the colony's infrastructure—the trading context—while not itself trading. There seemed no reason to be concerned in this prewar period over the increasing dependence of the Gold Coast population on a whole range of German imports, or on teething troubles concerning African reluctance to accept the new paper currency. Officials concentrated their attention on import duties, which formed the backbone of government revenue, and with efforts to achieve a standardized and stable currency. All appeared to be set for increases in government resources to be used for welfare and development in the Gold Coast colony. There was no hint yet of the disruption to come with the outbreak of a world war in August 1914.

On the other hand, there was a negative consequence of the African focus on the export trade. There were frequent complaints from the Gold Coast's agricultural department in this period that local food was expensive and in short supply because there was insufficient food production in successful cocoa districts.[134] Farmers' neglect of food production for "more profitable employments" was partly responsible for the increasing cost and even shortages of local food, as in Ada, Keta, and the Volta River districts.[135] In July 1912, the chief of Teimang tribunal bemoaned abandoned food farms: "The zeal for readily obtained money in the cocoa future" made farmers "forget themselves."[136] According to Director of Agriculture Tudhope, towards the end of 1912 food prices in some areas of Eastern Province were nearly 200% over three years before. In Central Province in 1913, little had been grown in the way of a second crop of maize because of cash crops, even though dependence on the first maize crop was dangerous, as stores were often destroyed by weevils.[137] Cash crop farming was diverting efforts from domestic to export production.[138] And farmers either could not switch back into major food production, or not switch quickly enough, to alleviate shortages and take advantage of sudden demand. Meanwhile, it is likely that part of the problem in some rural areas was a diversion of food supplies to the markets of the growing urban areas on the coast. The Gold Coast government did not have the means to force farmers to grow what they considered to be adequate amounts of food alongside cash crops.

Thus, before the war, there were already problems for African wage earners, with the cost of living, and especially the cost of food, high and rising. Criticisms of the British administration could bring concessions. For example, clerks in the printing department

134. E.g., *Ashanti Report 1912,* Clifford to Harcourt, 26/8/13, C096/535/635; and *Agricultural Department Quarterly Reports 31/3/13, Gazette* 19/7/13, C099/93; *30/6/13, Gazette* 1/11/13, C099/93.

135. *Trade Reports: 1912, Gazette* 3/5/13, C099/34; *1913, Gazette* 25/4/14, C099/35.

136. Chief of Teimang tribunal to Francis Crowther, Secretary of State for Native Affairs, 19/7/12, ADM 11/1/412. PRAAD.

137. Tudhope, *Agricultural Quarterly Department Report 3/12/12, Gazette* 1/3/13, C099/15; *Report of the Eastern Province 1912, Gazette* 11/10/13, C099/84 and Clifford to Harcourt, dispatch: *Tour of the Eastern Province 10–26 February, 13/3/13,* C096/528/9916 ; and for Central Province: *Agricultural Quarterly Department Report for quarter ending 31/12/13, Gazette* 21/3/14, C099/26.

138. See Barbara Ingham's critique of Hla Myint's vent-for surplus theory in B. Ingham, *Tropical Exports and Economic Development,* p. 90.

in Accra successfully appealed for an increase in wages in January 1912, arguing that high rents and the increasing price of foodstuffs meant that it was impossible to live on their existing salaries.[139] In July 1913, clerks in the commissioner's office also petitioned for more pay and better promotion prospects. The response from the Colonial Office in London was sympathetic: "We shall certainly have to agree to some improvement in pay, owing to the increase in the cost of living in the Gold Coast."[140] Sensitive economic and financial issues already impinged on the overall prewar relationship between British and Africans at this time—the focus of the next chapter.

139. *Clerks' Memorial,* 9/1/12, in Acting Governor Bryan to Harcourt, 18/7/12, C096/519/24560.
140. Green, CO Minute, Clifford to Harcourt, 30/7/13, C096/533/546.

Chapter 3

The Limits of Colonial Rule: Prewar British Administration

Though colonial rule in the Gold Coast was secure, a striking feature in this prewar period is how little government there was. The administration lacked sufficient numbers at all levels, from the British district commissioner to African employees. There was also a serious lack of funds and capacity to achieve British goals and meet African aspirations. The British, of course, controlled the political agenda. In the central administration, no significant political role was given to Africans, though two of the four nominated unofficial representatives on the legislative council were African. The British colonial authorities largely ignored the Western-educated Africans—and their views in the African press, such as calls for a democratic alternative to British Crown Colony government. The governor tended, instead, to concentrate on indirect rule through the chiefs.[1] Senior clerk remained the highest administrative post open to "natives," and little training or Africanization was undertaken.

And yet the British struggled if they ever appeared to disregard African interests. They remained highly dependent on chiefs. This "indirect" rule allowed them to engage with established, "traditional," authorities—and it was cheap. Even so, this relationship was problematic: it needed managing and was always subject to change. British government was especially minimal in the North, and remarkably light, too, in Ashanti, where by now violent opposition to British rule had given way to acquiescence. Indeed, active opposition to colonial rule was not a feature of the Gold Coast at this time. But the potential of the British remained slight. They lacked above all, perhaps, knowledge of the complexities of African society, even of basic facts about the territory. Clifford went on tours of his domain in 1913 and 1914, just before the war, like a peripatetic medieval European king—and with the similar dual purpose of reinforcing the British claim to authority and finding out what was going on. He did learn much (and records of his tours inform us, too). Even so, the British government was to enter the war period with very little competence for coping with troubled times.

There was widespread demand from both British and Africans for more, as well as more effective, government in the colony at this time—though there was not necessarily agreement as to what that might be. One example of difference arose from the British failure to reform a system of municipal administration that was largely responsible for the poor condition of the colony's towns. The elected African members were always in a minority, so that the councils were, in fact, run, or rather not run, by a few overworked British officials from a number of different departments such as the PWD, the medical and sanitary department, and the department of native affairs. These officials were

1. The division between the "Western-educated" elite and the "traditional" elite of chiefs and elders could be blurred by family connections or individuals straddling both categories.

constantly needed by their own department and were frequently changing places with each other as each in turn went on leave. The result, as the British unofficial, Grey, had put it in 1911, was "a farce"—a description that was echoed by the African newspaper, *The Gold Coast Nation*, two years later.[2] Yet British officials in London and on the coast maintained that such town councils were essential "to teach the natives the rudiments of self government."[3] As has been pointed out, this paternalistic view reflected British experience of nineteenth-century British towns such as Bradford or Manchester, rather than an African experience of twentieth-century towns in West Africa.[4]

Both British and African unofficials in the legislative council subjected the whole concept of town councils in the Gold Coast to a barrage of devastating criticism in the prewar period. According to Grey, "native" members of the councils were simply ignored: "The town councils are really nominated by the government and I think that it is reasonable to ask the government to be responsible for them."[5] It was quite clear to the incoming governor that the local population had no confidence in what Hutton Mills called "an absolutely useless institution."[6] It was one of Clifford's strengths that he listened to such arguments with an open mind. He had come to the conclusion by July 1913 that in such towns as Accra, Sekondi, and Cape Coast, the colony's town council system needed "some very radical alterations."[7] But the war then postponed much-needed reforms.

From the moment of his arrival on the coast in December 1912, the new governor was also highly critical of officers who tried to impose measures without attempting to obtain local African support. The sanitary officers were a case in point. Clifford was convinced that provision of adequate sanitation was "a moral obligation" for the colonial government as well as "a practical necessity."[8] The sanitary officers of the Gold Coast worked in the sanitary branch of the Gold Coast medical department, which had been set up in 1910 under Dr. T. E. Rice, the SSO (Senior Sanitary officer). They had drawn up an extensive program of preventative action to control the spread of infectious diseases, but they had failed to win over the population. According to Clifford, these sanitary officers saw their main role as "punitive" rather than "educative."[9] As a result, the sanitary inspector had come to be regarded by the African population of the Gold Coast in this prewar period as "a malignant type of police officer."[10]

Government intervention here, even if well-intentioned, was seen by the local African population as interference. For example, fines had been imposed for not covering water receptacles, but inhabitants of Accra claimed that these were unfair, as the government had failed to prevent mosquitoes from breeding in pools and bushes around the city.[11] Many of the numerous sanitary bylaws could not be enforced. Regulations had been

---

2. Grey, *LegCo* 6/11/11, *Gazette* 6/1/12, CO99/1; and *The Gold Coast Nation*, 4/9/13.

3. Thorburn, *LegCo* 6/11/11, *Gazette* 6/1/12, CO99/1.

4. A. Casely-Hayford & R. Rathbone "Politics, Families, and Freemasons in the Colonial Gold Coast" in J. F. A. Ajayi & J. D. Y. Peel (eds.), *People and Empires in History. Essays in Memory of Michael Crowder,* (London, 1992).

5. Grey, *LegCo* 26/3/13, *Gazette* 24/5/13, CO99/39.

6. Hutton Mills, *LegCo* 6/11/11, *Gazette* 6/1/12, CO99/1.

7. Clifford to Harcourt, 21/7/13, CO96/5333/512.

8. Clifford to Harcourt, 6/2/13, CO96/527/6603. And see R. Dumett, "The Campaign Against Malaria and the Expansion of Scientific and Sanitary Services in British West Africa, 1898–1910," *African Historical Studies*, 1, 2, 1968, pp. 153–197.

9. *Ibid.*

10. Thorburn to Harcourt, 1/7/12, re. *Medical and Sanitary Report 1911,* CO96/518/20235.

11. Hutton Mills, *LegCo* 26/3/13, *Gazette* 24/5/13, CO99/39.

drawn up concerning the siting and maintenance of rubbish heaps, latrines, wells, water holes, animal pens, and buildings; and the reporting and containing of infectious diseases. Fines were high, ranging from 10s to 20s for noncompliance, and chiefs and headmen were threatened with further draconian punishment if they failed to report immediately any case of smallpox or anthrax. This officially incurred a £25 fine, with or without three months' hard labor.[12] However, British administrators tended to overestimate their power to enforce unpopular measures, either by their own efforts or through the chiefs. Many of the regulations remained a dead letter. Only under the 1927 Native Administration Ordinance were native tribunals given the powers to obtain fines, and therefore also the incentive to prosecute.[13] According to the Reverend Lochman of the Basel mission station at Nsaba in 1912, chiefs did not worry much about sanitation. They offered gin to get people to clear roads or dig a new latrine. "The best or the only sanitary police are the vultures or the carrion kites."[14]

Officials in the metropole supported the Gold Coast sanitary officials rather than the governor. It was galling for Clifford that entrenched opinion blocked his path, such as that of Rice, backed by Fiddian, the London official with responsibility for tropical medical affairs. The limits of a governor's authority in some matters of detail were apparent when Clifford found that Rice could apparently veto his plans in this period (for example, his efforts to get the segregation housing order revoked) by appealing directly to the tropical Africa medical and sanitary advisory committee (TAMS) in London. [15]

There remained an urgent need to improve the sanitary conditions in the coastal towns and in the expanding settlements in cocoa districts. Swedru in Central Province was one such town that aroused concern.[16] This had been "an insignificant bush village" two or three years previously, but it had become a rapidly growing town of about 2,000 inhabitants by the time of the governor's visit in 1913.[17] Similarly, villages at the back of Winneba that had been collections of huts four years before had, like Konyaku, become new towns, but without any sanitary arrangements. The fouling of the streets and the beach were common in coastal towns such as Cape Coast, where four-fifths of the rooms were judged "unfit for human habitation."[18] In contrast, Clifford, on his prewar tours of the Colony and Ashanti, was very impressed by the sanitary condition of inland villages, which reflected "the West African's love of cleanliness and order in the vicinity of his house."[19] It was a common belief among British colonial officials of this period that "traditional" rural Africa was superior to Westernized urban Africa.

---

12. *Sanitary Bye-Laws, The Native Jurisdiction Ordinance No 5, 1883, Gazette* 24/2/12, CO99/11.

13. R. Gocking, "British Justice and the Native Tribunals of the Southern Gold Coast Colony," *JAH*, 34, 1993, p. 101.

14. The Rev. Lochman, Basel Mission, 17/10/12, *Report for West African Lands Committee*, CO96/523/571.

15. Clifford to Harcourt, re. *Medical and Sanitary Report 1911*, 6/2/13, CO96/527/6603.

16. See M. Owusu's study of Swedru, *Uses and Abuses of Political Power. A Case Study of Continuity and Change in the Politics of Ghana*, (Chicago, 1970).

17. Clifford to Harcourt, dispatch: *Trek Accra to Dunkwa, October–December 1913*, 8/11/13, CO96/528/746.

18. *Report of the Medical and Sanitary Department 1911*, Thorburn to Harcourt, 1/7/12, CO96/518/20235.

19. Clifford to Harcourt, dispatch: *Trek: Dunkwa to Axim, November–December 1913*, 8/12/13, CO96/528/746.

Accra was a particular concern. In 1913, the African unofficial, Hutton Mills, described its "very unsatisfactory sanitary state" as "astonishing" given that it had been capital of the Colony for forty years.[20] The Colonial Office was aware that other West African capitals, such as Conakry in French Guinea and Lome in German Togoland, were better laid out and maintained, with electric street lighting installed from 1912.[21] In the Gold Coast, only in Sekondi, as a result of the construction of railway workshops, was provision of electric light imminent in 1914. On the other hand, the Accra improvement committee (set up in 1908 as a result of an outbreak of bubonic plague) "had overseen good work" with the demolition of slums and building of new drains in areas of Accra such as Jamestown and Usshertown.[22]

An assumption among British colonial officials at the time, in London as well as on the West African coast, was that the central political administration of the British West African territories had to be run exclusively by British officers. Yet from the time of his arrival on the coast in December 1912, Clifford held the view that a major obstacle to the efficient administration of the whole colony was the shortage of (British) personnel. Reform and development, he believed, required more British staff as well as more funds. In 1913, out of the 740 British officials in the colony, only 573 were (on average) in post at any one time. The majority of the rest were on leave; a few were unfit. [23] Most departments had long complained of being short-staffed. And London officials had long recognized that a major cause was the difficulty of obtaining men from Britain on the existing salaries.[24]

Clifford decided in the first instance to concentrate on the fact that the political administration was threadbare—even before the war took its toll. One major deficiency was that there were too few DCs. Although it was recognized that it was not desirable to give new ADCs control of districts, the dearth of officers, as in Eastern Province, meant that ADCs were in charge of Akuepem, Keta, and the Volta River districts in 1912. Meanwhile, three DCs had to take turns acting as commissioner of Eastern Province during the year.[25] Administrative officers were being asked to fill appointments in the law department and the secretariat, even though the staff of each province was "somewhat seriously undermanned."[26] There were instances of medical officers being used as ADCs, as in Ada in 1913, depleting what small medical provision existed. More ADCs were needed to allow DCs to travel, as in Elmina, Saltpond, Apam, Sekondi, and Half Assini. Individual officers, as Clifford described it, tended to be "moved from post to post with so bewildering a frequency that they had been precluded from acquiring a deep and intimate knowledge of any one district or of any of its chiefs or peoples."[27] Yet this was in

20. Hutton Mills, *LegCo* 26/3/13, *Gazette* 24/5/13, CO99/39. For similar descriptions of Freetown at this time, see Dr. Clearkin's report of 1914 in L. Gann & P. Duignan, *The Rulers of British Africa*, p. 302; and F. Cole, "Sierra Leone and World War I," pp. 144–145.

21. *Report of Consul General Wallis, Dakar*, to Edward Grey, FO, 22/4/12, FO to CO, 23/5/12, CO554/14988.

22. Clifford, *LegCo*, 3/10/13, *Gazette* 3/1/14, CO99/1; and *Report of Accra Improvement Committee, Gazette* 19/4/13, CO99/29.

23. There were thirty invalidings as well as six deaths among the Gold Coast officials in 1913, *Medical and Sanitary Report 1915*, 20/5/16, CO96/567/372.

24. Ellis, CO Minute, Acting Governor Bryan to Harcourt, 6/5/12, CO96/517/13896.

25. *Report of Eastern Province 1912, Gazette* 11/10/13, CO99/87.

26. Clifford re. 1914 Estimates, *LegCo* 3/10/13, *Gazette* 14/10/13, CO99/87.

27. Clifford to Harcourt, 25/6/13, CO96/532/409; and Clifford, *LegCo* 3/10/13, *Gazette* 14/10/13, CO99/87.

a colony, unlike Clifford's experience of Malaya, where transport was difficult and frequent traveling round the district often impossible. Officers were not "on tour" (in post) in the colony for more than twelve months at a time, and seldom served consecutive postings in the same district. As Clifford made clear, in these circumstances, efficient British supervision of the local African administration of chiefs and elders (under "indirect" rule) was "an impossibility."[28]

On his extensive tours of the Colony and Ashanti in 1913, the governor received many requests from local people to have a DC posted in their area. Here again are instances of a local demand for more colonial government rather than less. Clifford interpreted this as "one of the most striking testimonies to the character of British administration"—although he did admit that there might be factors such as prestige and "some purely economic advantages" to explain the enthusiasm. Yet he still believed it also reflected "a genuine feeling of confidence in British administrative officers."[29] However, in remote areas in Western Province, for example at Wenchi, the inhabitants were clearly reluctant to see the arrival of government officers and viewed the posting of a DC there with considerable suspicion.[30]

In 1913–1914, the Colonial Office was persuaded by the new governor of the need for a modest increase in the numbers of Gold Coast expatriate political staff. There was agreement in the first instance for a few extra posts in the Colony, with three additional DCs and one ADC, raising the number of political officers there from thirty-four to thirty-eight. As a result of these additions, by August 1913 the political administration of the whole colony consisted of seventy-four officers: ten PCs, four traveling commissioners, twenty-five DCs, and thirty-five ADCs. Clifford was also successful in arguing the case for an increase in the staff of the secretariat. As he pointed out, there were in fact fewer officers in the secretariat than had been recommended in 1903, although the work had, of course, greatly increased. There was the additional disadvantage that the Gold Coast colonial secretary was obliged to act as governor for five out of every seventeen months, and then was himself absent from the colony on leave for an additional five months, so that he was only able to work at his post for seven months out of every seventeen.[31] This inevitably affected those below him in the secretariat, who had to shift posts accordingly. As Clifford complained, this "hand to mouth" system of running the colony was no longer sufficient. The Colonial Office concurred. Although there was some concern that "Sir Hugh Clifford is recommending large increases in every direction," the predominant view at the Colonial Office in June 1913 was favorable: "The time has gone by for cutting down staff in West Africa."[32]

Clifford was not only concerned about quantity, given the number of staff available, but also about quality—the training and knowledge of British officers. The colonial administration lacked information and understanding, so Clifford set out to encourage British officials to learn much more about the people they ruled. And he aimed to make each department and the staff of each province self-sufficient so that they could cope with their own relief postings. He was determined to ensure that individual officers served several tours in succession in the same post. Encouraging officers to acquire "native"

28. Clifford to Harcourt, dispatch: *Tour of the Eastern Province 10–26 February 1913*, CO96/528/9916.

29. Clifford to Harcourt, dispatch: *Trek through Ashanti, January–March 1914*, CO96/528/746.

30. Clifford re. 1914 Estimates, *LegCo* 3/10/13, Gazette 14/10/13, CO99/87.

31. Clifford to Harcourt: 23/6/13 CO96/532/401; 26/6/13, CO96/532/411; 22/8/13, CO96/534/606.

32. Flood, CO Minute, 26/6/13, CO96/532/411; also Green, CO Minute, 26/6/13. CO96/532/412.

languages was part of the drive to improve the quality and efficiency of the administration of indirect rule. As a result of Clifford's determination, in 1913 the Secretary of State approved a permanent pensionable income of £25 a year to any officer who attained proficiency in any language other than Hausa.[33] It was the new governor's aim that knowledge of "native" languages should be "the general rule," not, as with an officer like Rattray, the "startling exception."[34] It was also announced that anthropology courses in native law, customs, origins, and religion were available free for officers at the Imperial Institute while they were on vacation.[35] Clifford's successor, Guggisberg, was given credit by Kimble for "a new approach" in 1922 in encouraging officers to study local history and customs, but clearly much in this field, as in so many others, was initiated by Clifford. His support for officers pursuing such interests continued in the war period, as can be seen in his backing for Claridge's *A History of the Gold Coast and Ashanti* in 1915.[36]

Meanwhile, the Gold Coast administration had problems attracting sufficient African labor. The PWD, ever behind schedule, and aware of the call for more efficiency, always found excuses for delays, including the difficulty of finding workers.[37] It was true that labor could be hard to obtain or expensive because the need for carriers persisted. However, more often than not, the government's labor scarcity, like that of the mining companies, arose as a result of how much, or rather how little, it was prepared to pay. British officials, especially Colonial Office officials, considered wages unduly high in the Gold Coast when compared to the eastern colonies of the Empire, even though it was recognized that the general cost of living was also high.[38]

African perception of the labor problem was different. The labor rate was seen as too low. Skilled workmen such as carpenters, masons, smiths, and mechanics were paid on average only between 1s 6d to 4s 2d a day. The government rate for laborers and carriers, including hammock men, was normally 1s a day plus 3d subsistence money for food. Contract laborers or carriers working in permanent "gangs" could usually earn fractionally more: 25s a month and 3d a day subsistence. The critical factor was that these figures did not change in the years just before the Great War—regardless of rising government revenue and the fluctuating demand for labor according to the cocoa season. There was always acute difficulty in the Gold Coast in obtaining labor at the time of the cocoa harvest, when carriers and laborers on farms could command high wages. African cocoa farmers in the Colony and Ashanti were the most successful at attracting labor, including migrant labor from the north, in this period.[39]

It would seem that the colonial government in this instance had the means but not the will to ease their labor shortage. The cause was simple: both African producers and

---

33. *CO Circular No 25,* 25/6/13, *Gazette* 12/7/13, CO99/55.

34. Clifford to Harcourt, 12/3/13, CO96/528/153. Rattray's major work on Ashanti was published just after the war period: R. S. Rattray, *Ashanti,* (London, 1923).

35. *CO Circular* 23/5/13, *Gazette* 21/6/13, CO99/45.

36. D. Kimble, A *Political History,* p. 486; Sir H. Clifford, *Introduction* to W.W. Claridge, *A History of the Gold Coast and Ashanti,* (London, 1915).

37. PWD Enclosure, 23/4/12, in Acting Governor Bryan to Harcourt 3/5/12, CO96/517/15538.

38. Flood, CO Minute on *Blue Book 1911,* 29/7/12, CO96/519/23629. See also D. Moore & F. G. Guggisberg, *We Two in West Africa,* (London, 1909), p. 59, re. cooks receiving "absurdly high wages" of £4 a month. Domestic servants of British officials on the coast were paid on average £1.10 to £2 a month, with cooks on £1 to £5 a month.

39. See R. Southall, "Cadbury on the Gold Coast" p. 22; and N. Van Hear, "Northern Labor," pp. 34–35.

European trading companies paid more. British officers knew this. There were many instances when African employees made their dissatisfaction clear, as for example when police recruits complained they could get a higher wage outside the force or when "a restlessness among the warders for a better salary" was noted in the colony's annual prison report. Even after long government service, many carriers of the transport department voted with their feet for higher rates elsewhere, moving into such jobs as transporting cocoa for African farmers.[40] The railway maintenance engineer at Sekondi explained his difficulty in obtaining labor during 1912: it was simply that trading and timber logging companies paid higher wages. The unofficials in the legislative council argued the same case. As Hutton Mills pointed out, the government needed to pay more if they wanted to get better recruits into the police.[41] And Grey, speaking for the wider British merchant interest (in terms which were typical of his day) explained to the local colonial officials why "intelligent young men" were not joining the Post and Telegraph department: staff were insufficiently paid by the government, whereas mercantile firms found "a well paid native of experience practically as good for supervision and office work as a European."[42]

Some parts of the Gold Coast were more undergoverned than others. Marked regional disparities continued and were, in some cases, accentuated in this prewar period. For example, despite the official integration of the Northern Territories into this colonial administrative structure, the officers of the dependency felt isolated and considered the region to be "much neglected" by the coast.[43] One of the reasons for this neglect was that the Northern Territories were seen merely as an Ashanti hinterland "tacked on to the Gold Coast," having been acquired not for their economic value but because it was considered strategically undesirable that they should fall to either the French or the Germans at the time of the partition of Africa.[44] Yet they comprised a substantial proportion of the colony: about 40 percent of the land mass and perhaps a fifth of the population. The ignorance of the civil administration in Accra was partly due here to the lack of interchange of officers. The majority of officers in the north remained military personnel, even though a civil administration had been instituted there in 1907.[45] Army sappers, obtained through the War Office, were still engaged at this time, just before the war, in the first topographical survey of Ashanti and the Northern Territories, and were not expected to complete their work until 1915.[46] Armitage, the chief commissioner of the Northern Territories, had been heartened by Governor Thorburn's interest in the north on his tour in February 1912, but Thorburn had been forced to retire as a result of ill health and was never able to write up his recommendations for the Colonial Office.[47]

---

40. *Police Report 1911, Gazette* 13/7/12, CO99/49; *Prisons Report 1912, Gazette* 31/9/12, CO99/70; *Transport Department Report 1911, Gazette* 10/8/12, CO99/58.

41. *Railway Department Report 1912, Gazette*, 28/5/13, CO99/100; and Hutton Mills, *LegCo* 28/10/12, *Gazette* 28/10/12, CO99/100.

42. Grey, *LegCo* 6/1/12, *Gazette* 6/1/12, CO99/1.

43. Armitage to Ellis, 12/9/12, CO96/525/32491.

44. Lord Selborne, *Report on the Northern Territories 1898–9,* in R. Bening, "Colonial Development Policy in Northern Ghana 1898–1950," *Bulletin of the Ghana Geographical Association,* 17, 1975, pp. 65–66. See, e.g., M. Staniland, *The Lions of Dagbon: Political Change in Northern Ghana,* (Cambridge, 1975), p. 39.

45. Armitage, 29/10/12, Enclosure in Acting Governor Bryan to Harcourt, 4/12/12, CO96/523/40502; also, Flood, CO Minute, Clifford to Harcourt, 27/1/13, CO96/527/3138.

46. CO to War Office, 1/1/12, CO96/516/9895; also, Acting Governor Bryan to Harcourt, 1/5/12, CO96/516/15433.

47. Armitage to Ellis, 12/9/12, CO96/525/32491.

The incoming governor, Clifford, did not include a visit to the Northern Territories on his extensive prewar treks across the Colony and Ashanti, and never expressed any interest in the region. In fact it was the one area he never visited, except for the fringes, when accompanying the German Governor of Togo, the Duke of Mecklenburg, on a visit to Ashanti in January 1914. On that one occasion he passed through Yeji on his way to Krachi and the border of Togo. (Clifford bade farewell to his visitor on January 31, 1914, expressing the hope—just six months before the start of the First World War—that "one of the results of this visit may be increased friendship and mutual understanding between ourselves and our German neighbours in this part of West Africa."[48]) It was the middle of the dry season, and Clifford's few recorded impressions were negative. He described what he saw as like Northern Ashanti, a "desolation" of scrub, stubble, dust, and intense heat. He also commented on the apparent sparseness of the population and the "very unsatisfactory" system of transport, with only a few poor roads. And that was it. He never went back, both because the war intervened and because it seems that he did not believe the Northern Territories were a priority.

Minimal government and minimal expenditure in the Northern Territories were justified, according to Clifford, because the inhabitants were only just settling down to the benefits of Pax Britannica. In his view, British rule had rescued the population from "the tyranny of the slave raiders" and now provided "the blessings of security and peace."[49] British control had only officially been asserted right across the protectorate when opposition in the Tong Hills in the far northeast was suppressed as recently as 1911: the inhabitants were now finally said to be "acquiescing" to British rule "in a thoroughly satisfactory manner."[50] But there were still scattered incidents in the region just before the war, which should have warned the Gold Coast government that the African perspective here was very different and that they should not take law and order in this northern region for granted. For example, the Chief of Mamprussi settled a fight between villages in April 1913 in which two were killed and compounds were burned.[51]

Overall transport costs remained too high for a successful contribution by the Northern Territories to the international trade. Thorburn had argued for expenditure in the Northern Territories to make cash crops viable there. Samples of shea butter sent to London had been valued at £28 5s a ton, but the head load cost per ton from Tamale to Kumasi was £30, before adding the rail freight charge from Kumasi to Sekondi. The cost per ton by canoe on the Volta, from Tamale to Ada, was £23 10s, five times the rate of the journey from Ada to Liverpool. At Colonial Secretary Harcourt's intervention, an experiment was inaugurated in 1913 with a government river transport service between Yeji and Tamale using wooden canoes and steel pontoon boats from England.[52] But Clifford believed the priority had to be opening up "the more accessible and richer districts of the Colony and Ashanti." He regarded any similar projects in the north as "premature." Most Colonial Office officials in 1913 agreed with him: "Our present policy for the Northern Territories

48. Clifford to Harcourt, dispatch: *Trek through Ashanti, January–March 1914*, CO96/528/746.

49. *Report on the Northern Territories 1912,* Clifford to Harcourt 14/7/13, CO96/532/479. See also Sir H. Clifford, "United Nigeria," *Journal of the Africa Society,* 21, 1921–1922, p. 4, in P. Hetherington, *British Paternalism and Africa 1920–1940,* (London, 1978), p. 50.

50. Thorburn to Harcourt, 23/2/12, CO96/517/19407.

51. P. C. Navarro to Acting CC, NT, Tamale, 7/5/13, *Native Affairs & Riots*, ADM56/1/165, PRAAD.

52. *Report,* Tudhope, Director of Agriculture, 28/5/12, Enclosure in Acting Governor Bryan to Harcourt, 12/7/12, CO96/519/23634. See also Thorburn to Harcourt, 10/8/12, CO96/526/25356; 7/5/12, CO96/517/17841; and 6/6/12, CO96/517/19406.

should be to keep the district in order and to leave the natives as much as possible to themselves."[53] Apart from being a revealing contemporary comment on the limited extent of colonial ambition, this observation failed to acknowledge financial imperatives. Without cash crops, there were no means by which the region could pay its way. Government expenditure on the Northern Territories in 1913 came to a total of around £79,000, whereas revenue added up to under £3,000.[54]

The British colonial administration had shot itself in the foot regarding any hope of collecting revenue from the Northern Territories: the only exports of any value were cattle driven through the northern protectorate to Ashanti, but caravan tolls had been abolished in 1908. The aim of the British administration was to encourage cattle herders, both from French territory across the northern border and from within the Northern Territories, to bring their cattle south to Kumasi. However, African traders apparently believed that payment of tolls was a guarantee of government protection; therefore, many now assumed it was no longer a safe route and diverted east through Togo. The result was that it took twenty years for the revenue from the Northern Territories to recover. From just over £18,000 in 1906–7, it fell dramatically to only £3,500 in 1907–8, and only recovered to £19,000 in 1926–7.[55]

Clifford saw the Northern Territories as separate and backward. "Until the Colony and Ashanti have been thoroughly opened up and developed, the Northern Territories must be content to await their turn."[56] This was very similar to the attitude in other hinterland areas of British West Africa that were also seen useful only as labor reserves, for example, Sokoto and Bornu in Nigeria and Koinadogu district in Sierra Leone. The north's contribution to the southern economy was, in fact, important. The Colony and Ashanti were dependent on northern labor to provide, for example, carriers, seasonal farm workers, miners, police, and soldiers. By August 1914 the Gold Coast Regiment was almost entirely manned by men from the Northern Territories or from the French territories further north.[57]

Though minimal government was the norm throughout the colony in this period, the Northern Territories were exceptional in Clifford's eyes. Contrary to his usual advocacy of expansion and development, Clifford sought to restrict government and expenditure in this region even more than officials in London. In June 1914, Clifford even called for a reduction of staff in the Northern Territories. He recalled how Harcourt had shown a "somewhat special interest" in the Northern Territories, referring to them as "the Cinderella of the Gold Coast," just before he, Clifford, took up his appointment as governor in December 1912.[58] But he continued to argue that there were far more urgent calls on the

53. Reminiscent of Governor Hodgson's attitude in 1899: against "a single penny more than absolutely necessary" being spent on the Northern Territories. Green, CO Minute, Clifford to Harcourt, 27/1/13, CO96/527/5493. Harcourt, CO Minute, Clifford to Harcourt, 27/1/13, CO96/527/5493. *Report,* Migeod, transport officer, 23/7/13, Enclosure in Clifford to Harcourt, 1/8/13, CO96/534/ 28689.

54. Clifford, LegCo 3/10/13 in G. E. Metcalfe, *Great Britain and Ghana. Documents of Ghana History,* (London 1964), pp. 544–546. And see *Report on the Northern Territories 1919,* in K. Dickson, *A Historical Geography of Ghana,* (London, 1969), p. 175; and Section I, chapter 1 re. the failure of the BCGA cotton growing experiment.

55. M. Staniland, *The Lions of Dagbon,* pp. 44–45.

56. *Report on the Northern Territories 1912,* Clifford to Harcourt, 14/7/13, CO96/532/479.

57. Concerning the extent to which the growth of the cocoa industry in Ashanti was due to labor from the north, see *Report on the Northern Territories 1913,* in P. Ladouceur, *Chiefs and Politicians: The Politics of Regionalism in Northern Ghana,* (London, 1979), p. 48; and R. Bening, "Colonial Development Policy in Northern Ghana," p. 76.

58. Clifford to Harcourt, 9/4/14, CO96/543/15158.

colony's money in the more profitable southern regions. In his view, fewer administrative officers were needed in the north in light of what he described, with no firsthand knowledge, as the "sheep-like docility" of the population. There were very few British officials there. An average of thirty-one Europeans (of whom twenty-eight were officials) were resident among the local population, which was believed then to be around 362,000 (now considered a substantial underestimate) in an area of 31,000 square miles.[59]

Clifford's judgments concerning the manning of the north were to prove embarrassing three years later, during the war. Although there were only nineteen political officers in the region and only two-thirds of these were on duty at any one time, Clifford had pronounced this number to be "in excess of requirements," and the nine medical officers, who "did little beyond keeping these British officers healthy," to be "a deplorable waste both of money and men." Far from being "Cinderella," the Northern Territories were, according to Clifford's dismissive flourish, "*l'enfant gâté*" of the Gold Coast.[60] However, Clifford's judgment that there were more than enough British administrators in the Northern Territories was questioned by Colonial Office officials at the time, and he was criticized for "unnecessary acerbity" towards the chief commissioner of the Northern Territories, Armitage, whom Ellis in the Colonial Office ambiguously described as "a very straightforward, honourable and exceedingly pompous man of no great brain power."[61] The reverse side of Clifford's positive drive and his energetic, liberal, paternalistic disposition was his capacity for a fierce inflexibility of mind, from which old Coasters such as Bryan (the Gold Coast colonial secretary when Clifford arrived in 1912) and Armitage, and the whole of the Northern Territories, were to suffer.

In contrast, the other dependency, Ashanti, received nothing from the new governor except praise and appreciation. Economic prospects were "bright and promising" as a result of the rapid expansion of the cash crop farming of cocoa. Ashanti, unlike the Northern Territories, was solvent, and the people were said to express "an increasing and sincere loyalty towards the Crown and Government" that was "very gratifying."[62] On a tour in April 1913, Clifford was impressed not only by "a very spirited" war dance on the Kumasi cricket ground to celebrate his arrival, but also by the "great frankness and intelligence" displayed by the Kumasi chiefs in his discussions with them the following day.[63] Kumasi itself he described as "the finest and best built town in this part of West Africa."[64] On his trek across Ashanti between January and March 1914, he found it to be "exceedingly pleasant and favourable."[65]

Although it was less than fourteen years since the Ashanti "revolt" of 1900, there appeared to Clifford to be no suspicion or distrust between Ashantis and European officers. British officials on the coast believed that this harmony was only threatened by the possibility that certain educated "natives" of the Colony might intrude into the courts of

---

59. *Report on the Northern Territories 1912 (Census 1911)*, Clifford to Harcourt, 14/7/13, CO96/532/479.

60. "The spoilt child," Clifford to Harcourt, 9/4/14, CO96/543/15158.

61. Flood, CO Minute, Clifford to Harcourt, 9/4/14, CO96/543/15158. Ellis, CO Minute, Clifford to Harcourt, 9/4/14, CO96/543/15158.

62. Clifford to Harcourt, re. *Report on Ashanti 1912*, 26/8/13, CO96/535/635.

63. Clifford to Harcourt, dispatch: *Tour of the Western Province of Ashanti and the Central Province, April–May 1913*, CO96/528/9916.

64. Clifford re. 1914 Estimates, *LegCo* 3/10/13, *Gazette* 3/1/14, CO99/1.

65. Clifford to Harcourt, dispatch: *Trek through Ashanti January–March 1914*, 12/3/14, CO96/528/746.

law in the Ashanti region. In terms that were typical of contemporary Europeans, Clifford described how the Ashanti had won the respect of the British officer as "a first class fighting man" whose spirit had been "tamed but not broken."[66] He was, however, of the opinion, given "the superior physical and mental energy" of the Ashantis, and the fact that their military organization still existed and their national pride was still intact, that the *Asantahene* (king), Prempeh, should not be allowed to return from exile in the Seychelles. The Colonial Office agreed with Clifford that although there were no signs of opposition, it would nevertheless "be dangerous to give a rallying point to this proud and warlike confederation."[67] As with the Colony, Clifford obtained approval just before the war for an increase in the number of British administrative staff: in Ashanti three to four officers, to add to the existing seventeen, were promised for August 1914. This was to govern a population of about 300,000 in an area of about 20,000 square miles, mostly living in thickly forested areas where travel was slow and difficult.[68]

Clifford did not plan any changes to the role played by Africans in the central administration of the colony. Far from there being any policy of Africanization, African officials—as elsewhere in British Africa—were to remain restricted to the status of clerks. The only small change initiated was in pay. Modest reform was initiated in 1913 in the separate salary structure of the Native and Clerical Subordinate Service with small rises in initial and maximum pay. Clerks formed the largest single African employed group in the colony. The highest salary went up by £10, to £210, and the lowest by £2, to £42. But the probationary salary of the first year of employment remained the same (since, astonishingly, 1896) at £36 p.a.[69] Colonial Office approval was easily obtained in 1913: "Government clerks in West Africa are usually fairly hard worked and are not overpaid."[70] A special bonus was also agreed for the clerks in the governor's office, who Clifford realized were under "severe and almost constant strain," as their work had almost doubled due to the extent and exceptional length of his official correspondence. Clifford often spent five hours before nine a.m. on such work so that he could spend the rest of the day on administrative duties. Officials in the Colonial Office in London privately expressed sympathy with the governor's clerks in the Gold Coast with the mischievous suggestion that perhaps the bonus should be extended to "all who had to read and attempt to digest Sir Hugh Clifford's despatches...."[71]

The two African unofficials in the Legislative Council provided the only source of African opinion formally sought at this time in colonial political decision making in Accra. Clifford instituted minor reforms just before the war to improve communication with all four unofficials there, of whom the two nominated Africans were Konor Mate Kole of Eastern Krobo and Thomas Hutton Mills, the Accra barrister. As in the other colonies of British West Africa, the legislative council was a purely consultative body. This pattern of membership had remained unchanged since 1895, despite African petitions for much wider representation, including elections.[72] Meanwhile, the British unofficials had not been happy with the way that orders had tended to be passed as a matter of course in

66. *Ibid.*
67. Clifford to Harcourt, 12/3/14, CO96/542/12788.
68. Clifford to Harcourt, 23/3/13, CO96/542/186, and 23/6/13, CO96/532/401.
69. *1921 Census Table of Occupations,* D. Kimble, A *Political History,* p. 45.
70. Flood, CO Minute, Clifford to Harcourt, 30/7/13, CO96/523/546.
71. CO Minute, Clifford to Harcourt, 5/9/13, CO96/536/677.
72. E.g., *Chiefs' Petition to King in Council, LegCo* 18/11/12, CO96/522/36322. See also D. Kimble, *A Political History,* pp. 13–15.

such a way as "to turn council meetings into a farce."[73] Governor Clifford therefore set up a select committee to study the annual supply bill in detail, with heads of department present to explain the estimates. The aim was to give both British and African unofficials a much better understanding of how policies had been formed, with greater opportunity to comment on the provisions of the bill.[74]

Beyond this, however, there was little attempt at this time on the part of the British administration to forge links with Western-educated Africans—a small but prominent and vocal element in local society. British officials often expressed strong irritation with the ARPS (the Aborigines Rights Protection Society, which at this time largely represented wealthy coastal Western-educated Africans in Central Province) and its criticism of government.[75] The Colonial Office tended on this issue to be much less critical.[76] Yet Flood wrote irritably in 1913 that ARPS members "needed to be told exactly what their place was in the scheme of things."[77] But what was it? These Western-educated Africans had not been found a place in the British colonial "scheme of things" in the Gold Coast. Clifford's attitude was ambivalent. His recognition of the need for more Western education and Africanization was appreciated.[78] But he did not welcome the comments of the Accra and Cape Coast journalists who criticized the paternalistic and autocratic features of "Crown Colony" government. As the London official, Flood, observed: "Sir Hugh Clifford does not love the native press in West Africa."[79] The Colonial Office view was in this instance more tolerant. The *Gold Coast Leader*, the main colony weekly newspaper (with a circulation of 57,200 compared to the *Government Gazette* circulation of 65,350) was said to be harmless and certainly not nearly as violent in its expression as an ordinary provincial opposition paper in Britain.[80] Clifford, however, defended the principle of a free press when it was challenged from outside the colony, as can be seen in his prewar response to the Duke of Mecklenburg's complaint about articles in the *Gold Coast Leader* attacking German policies in Togo.[81]

In this period, Clifford also argued the case for Africanization of the legal profession—as he had for the medical profession. He believed African lawyers (excluded from native tribunals under the 1883 Native Jurisdiction Ordinance) should be allowed to practice in the public service of the Colony. This would help the administration where political officers had to serve in the legal department because of staff shortages, even though they did not have sufficient technical knowledge. Clifford's solution was to make three crown counsel appointments: one senior European crown counsel and two junior "native" barristers. He set out the case to the secretary of state in terms of a general policy. "Little by little, I am convinced, it should be the policy of this government to replace Europeans by native officers ... one of the primary objects of our presence here should be, I submit, gradually to accustom and adapt selected natives of the colony to positions in the public service of

73. Hunt, Grey, *LegCo* 27/3/12, *Gazette* 31/8/12, CO99/87.
74. Clifford re. 1914 Estimates, *LegCo* 3/10/13, *Gazette* 14/10/13, CO99/87.
75. E.g., Thorburn to Harcourt, 12/6/12, CO96/518/20234.
76. Green, Harcourt, CO Minute, Thorburn to Harcourt, 12/6/12, CO96/518/20234.
77. Flood, memo re. Clifford's Tour of Western Province, 8/12/13, CO96/538/44638.
78. E.g., by Hutton Mills, *LegCo* 1/5/14, *Gazette* 13/6/14, CO99/55.
79. Flood, CO Memo, 18/11/13, CO96/538/854.
80. Green, CO Memo, 18/11/13, CO96/538/854; *Blue Book 1912,* CO100/62. And see D. Kimble, *A Political History,* p. 555.
81. Clifford to Sir John Anderson, 17/6/13, CO96/531/23243.

increased trust and responsibility."[82] Again, seemingly to impress Whitehall, he emphasized that these were not "sentimental theories." They took into account "practical and economic considerations." The terms were not intended to be seen as generous. It was simply that "natives" were cheaper to employ. The government "did not necessarily have to" provide lodgings for "native" officers, many of whom were expected to be able to live at home on low salaries.[83] There is no record in the administration files that any investigation was undertaken to check how this policy might be received by the local population.

Clifford's pressure produced a cautious, though generally favorable, Colonial Office response at this time. It was agreed that there had been "native" judges in the Gold Coast in the past, so there might as well be an experiment now with "native" crown counsel. Two European officers and only one "native" were to be appointed in the first instance. E. C. Quist was the first such appointment, as African Crown counsel in 1914, with a second "native" to be appointed subsequently if the experiment was successful.[84] Once again, Clifford's experience in Ceylon contributed to his relatively liberal judgment. He certainly hoped for a rapid expansion of the scheme. As he told the Gold Coast legislative council in October 1913, in Ceylon all barristers, including the solicitor general, were "natives."[85]

As far as the government of the Gold Coast was concerned, indigenous chiefs provided convenient, ready-made, and effective intermediaries with African society. Clifford believed that the "tribal system," evolved by the inhabitants of the colony, was crucial as "the natural machinery for the administration of the people."[86] There was, in his view, no alternative. However, the potential instability of "native" society was a constant source of concern, given the need to use the chiefs as "direct instruments" of the colonial administration.[87] Profound social and economic changes were taking place in African society, induced partly by the spread of cash crops and commercialization of land use. These changes, over a period of time, were themselves a threat to order and stability, as they undermined the authority of many of the chiefs and elders whom the British needed to use in their ad hoc form of "indirect rule."[88] Increasing agricultural wealth led to a loosening of the hold of chiefs over their people, so that they had difficulty finding Africans to enroll as government carriers or, for example, take on the upkeep of roads as required under the Roads Ordinance.

But nowhere was the colonial government directly threatened. None of the "disturbances" reported by the Secretary for Native Affairs before the war—such as occasional "riots" reported in Central Province and Western Province in 1912—was described as of a "political"

82. Clifford to Harcourt, 25/6/13, CO96/532/410.

83. *Ibid.*

84. Flood, Ellis, CO Minute, Clifford to Harcourt, 25/6/13, CO96/532/410. See D. Kimble, *A Political History*, p. 101.

85. Clifford re. 1914 Estimates, *LegCo* 3/10/13, *Gazette* 14/10/13, CO99/87.

86. Clifford, *LegCo* 11/10/13, *Gazette* 3/1/14, CO99/1. For a discussion of this informal indirect rule policy, see D. Kimble, *A Political History*, pp. 455–505.

87. Clifford, *LegCo* 3/10/13, *Gazette* 14/10/13, CO99/87. For increased government control over chiefs in the Chiefs' Ordinance 1904, including the Governor's final decision re. election and destoolment, see R. Stone, "Colonial Administration and Rural Politics in South Central Ghana 1919–1951," unpublished PhD thesis, (University of Birmingham, 1975), p. 75.

88. The administrative system of the Gold Coast was at this time neither wholly direct nor wholly indirect. See, e.g., Lord Hailey, *An African Survey*, (London, 1938), p. 471.

character (by which was meant, directed against the colonial government).[89] Yet they obviously were political in a broader sense. "Riot" was a loose term denoting a serious breach of the peace, usually with some participants seriously injured or killed. Colonial officials were reassured by comments such as the following, added to the official record of a land boundary fight between Jappa and Sum in Western Province in 1912 (in which three were killed): "The attitude of these people towards the government is quite peaceful."[90]

The British colonial administration's political agenda went little further than to keep the peace and to see that judicial processes were duly followed in the local maintenance of order and law. But these were not easy tasks. There were numerous disputes, of several kinds: for example, between different ethnic groups; between head chiefs and subordinate chiefs; and between "traditional authorities" of chiefs and elders and the "young men" of independent wealth earned mostly from cash crop farming, some of whom were organized into rival companies of *asafos*. Disputes over succession to the stool, and funeral customs (as at Debisu in January 1912), were a common cause of fights, as were land boundaries, the extent of a chief's jurisdiction, and chiefs' demands for labor or fees.[91] Judicial cases—and some chiefs—could go back over a very long period. The continuing Saltpond–Kormatin dispute (over the extent of the jurisdiction of the chief of Anomabu) dated from 1844 in the Maclean era.[92] The Muslim Hausa chief Musa of Cape Coast, where the growing numbers of Wangaras disputed both his jurisdiction over their community and the fines imposed, reminded a British court in 1914 that he had been in post since 1860.[93] Clifford expressed his concern about "endless litigation" between Africans, for example over land, which he observed was "almost as ruinous" as the petty tribal warfare it had replaced.[94] Plaintiffs who were unhappy about a tribunal judgment could appeal to the British commissioner's court. But such transfers could be a problem, as illiterate chiefs commonly did not keep tribunal records.[95] African lawyers were judged to be the main beneficiaries when land cases came in front of British courts. As Flood in the Colonial Office commented wryly in January 1914, lawyers grew rich while the chiefs grew poor.[96]

Chiefs were clearly seen by both the British and the African unofficials as needing government support. Grey's suggestion was that chiefs should collect a land or poll tax instead of attempting to impose forced labor.[97] But Governor Thorburn had, not surprisingly, been skeptical as to whether anyone would be willing to pay such a tax.[98] The African unofficials, Konor Mate Kole and Hutton Mills, both emphasized that chiefs' dependence on court fees and fines made them very unpopular. They argued strongly that chiefs'

89. Acting Governor Bryan to Harcourt, 10 September 1912, CO96/521/30698; *Report of the Department of Native Affairs 1912, Gazette* 9/8/13, CO99/65.

90. Riot at Jappa, 12/2/12, ADM 11/1/378, PRAAD.

91. Report on Riot at Debisu, 21/5/12, ADM 11/1/402, PRAAD. And see, e.g., R. Stone, "Colonial Administration and Rural Politics," pp. 21, 56–81.

92. Saltpond–Kormanti file: 1844, 1880s, 1890s, 1900s, riots of 1907, 1908, 1910. ADM11/1/726, PRAAD.

93. Letter, 24/11/14, ADM 11/1/501 PRAAD. (Chief Musa died in 1927.)

94. Clifford to Harcourt, dispatch: *Trek from Accra to Dunkwa October–December 1913*, 6/11/13, CO96/528/746.

95. DC G. Freeman, Saltpond, 31/8/16. ADM11/1/635 PRAAD.

96. Flood, CO Minute, 13/1/14, CO96/541/3997. And see J. Simensen, "Commoners, Chiefs, and Colonial Government," pp. 61, 88, 165.

97. Grey, *LegCo* 6/11/11, *Gazette* 6/1/12, CO99/1.

98. Thorburn, *LegCo* 6/11/11, *Gazette* 6/1/12, 0099/1.

income was insufficient for the whole range of duties concerning law and order and provision of labor that the government now expected them to perform, at a time when personal service by their subjects on farms and building houses was no longer widely available. Like Grey, the African unofficials believed that the government needed to pay chiefs a regular stipend or agree on some form of tax as extra income.[99] However, there were no means to enforce such a tax, and British officials did not believe that the Gold Coast government could afford to pay all chiefs a salary out of current revenue. Such a scheme harked back to the Tax Ordinance of 1852 under which government stipends were given to chiefs. The issue was discussed again in 1879–1880 under Governor Ussher but was only considered possible if direct taxation was imposed. This was rejected because of the risk of renewed trouble. The population of the Gold Coast colony had firmly rejected direct taxes in the 1850s.[100] Protests against the proposal to introduce a poll tax on one occasion involved "several thousand armed men, from all the coastal villages between Accra and the Volta."[101]

Strengthening the chiefs' judicial authority appeared to the colonial administration to be a solution to the litigation problem. Just before the war, officials expressed general satisfaction with the 1910 amendments to the 1883 Native Jurisdiction Ordinance. The authority of "native" tribunals had been underpinned by making them compulsory courts of first instance for issues not covered by British law: "There is little doubt that the Ordinance has greatly enhanced the prestige of the Chiefs."[102] But there was a problem not apparently appreciated by British officials at the time. Without inspection or proper regulation of such tribunals, it was possible for the "traditional" African elite of chiefs and elders to exploit their position with extortionate court fees and fines.[103] Such practices undermined the position of chiefs in the long term, with commoners tending to avoid the tribunals, using DC courts in preference. As Arhin pointed out, the British initiative was typical of the tendency of the colonial administration to "put traditional authority into considerable jeopardy even as it sought to buttress it."[104]

Clifford valued hierarchy as a means to sustain social stability. He became convinced in 1913, on his first tour of the Gold Coast, that priority should be given to strengthening the powers of head chiefs. Mate Kole, the unofficial, and head chief of Manya Krobo, not surprisingly agreed. He strongly criticized a shortcoming in the terms of the Native Jurisdiction Ordinance: its failure to distinguish different ranks of chiefs and its treating them all as equal. This, he declared, had been interpreted as "a declaration of freedom and enfranchisement" to sub-chiefs, as well as encouraging "the growing tendency among men of means encroaching on the dignities of chiefs by making unto themselves swords,

99. K. M. Kole, Hutton Mills, *LegCo* 6/11/11, Gazette 6/1/12, CO99/1; K. M. Kole, *Select Committee, LegCo* 11/10/13, *Gazette* 3/1/14, CO99/1. For chiefs' economic dependence on tribunal fees and fines, see, e.g., R. Stone, "Colonial Administration and Rural Politics," p. 34.

100. D. Kimble, *A Political History,* pp. 172–191.

101. *Ibid.*, p. 176. The idea of direct taxation was to re-emerge later in a different form with stool treasuries and local taxes in the 1930s. See R. Stone, "Colonial Administration and Rural Politics," pp. 68, 117.

102. *Report of Eastern Province 1912, Gazette* 11/10/13, CO99/85. For the increasing interweaving of the British and African judicial systems, see R. Gocking, "British Justice and the Native Tribunals," pp. 93–113.

103. See J. Simensen, "Rural Mass Action in the Context of Anti-Colonial Protest: The Asafo Movement of Akim Abuakwa," *Canadian Journal of African Studies,* 8, 1, 1974, pp. 29–32.

104. K. Arhin, "The Pressure of Cash and the Political Consequences in Asante in the Colonial Period," *JAH,* 3, 1976, p. 468. And see F. Agbodeka, *Ghana in the Twentieth Century,* p. 73.

drums, and sticks and otherwise posing as chief."[105] He pointed out that in the days before head chiefs of the Colony had voluntarily placed themselves under the King of England, they had had their own soldiers and executions to enforce obedience. They now had the right to expect the forces of the colony to support them, as in the head chiefs' tribunal.[106] Clifford made a commitment in 1913 to draw up proposals for further amendments to the Native Jurisdiction Ordinance on his next tour.

The colonial government clearly needed, and took some steps, to be better informed about local affairs in all their complexity. For example, the West African Land Committee, set up by the Colonial Office in London, was at this time attempting to disentangle the nature of customary land tenure from a mass of contradictory submissions from both British officials and chiefs. It was important for the British administrators to find out whether private ownership in some form now existed alongside communal ownership, since there were many instances of friction, as when chiefs attempted to collect a third of all cocoa grown on stool land as legitimate rent.[107] But British officials did not perceive many of the subtleties, such as the distinction between ownership and occupation. Often, what really counted was control of fruit-bearing farms.[108] Harper, commissioner of Eastern Province, suggested at this time that government eliminate one source of friction by undertaking a systematic demarcation of all tribal boundaries. But this too seriously underestimated the problem, especially given that boundaries tended to be defined by village allegiance rather than, as in Britain, by land demarcation.[109]

One of the few ways a governor could become better informed and more closely in touch with his colonial subjects was through personally touring his territory. After his arrival in the Gold Coast colony in December 1912, Clifford traveled extensively in 1913 and the early months of 1914 in order to familiarize himself with as much of the colony as possible. He completed four major treks across the length and breadth of the Colony and Ashanti, covering 3,430 miles: 2,710 by land and 720 miles by sea, in just over a year.[110] It was a remarkable feat of physical energy and determination, especially as he was already in his thirtieth year of tropical service when he became governor of the Gold Coast at the age of forty-six.[111] By early November 1913 he was able to claim he had met every principal chief in the Eastern and Central Provinces of the Colony. "I hope that my recent journeys will help to bring the native chiefs into rather closer touch with the central government."[112] By March 1914, when he returned from Ashanti, the final trek of his first tour, he was able to claim that he had seen more of the Colony and Ashanti than any other European alive or dead.[113]

Certain features surprised and impressed Clifford from the beginning of his travels across the territory, such as what he rather patronizingly described on his tour of Eastern

105. K. M. Kole, *Select Committee, LegCo* 11/10/13, *Gazette* 3/1/14, CO99/1.

106. *Ibid.*

107. E.g., Furley, PC, *Report of Central Province 1912, Gazette* 27/9/13, CO99/80.

108. See P. Hill, *The Gold Coast Farmer,* and A. Robertson, *The Dynamics of Productive Relationships,* p. 77.

109. Harper, PC, *Report of Eastern Province 1912, Gazette* 11/10/13, CO99/85; and see R. Stone, "Colonial Administration and Rural Politics," p. 35.

110. Clifford to Harcourt, dispatch: *Trek through Ashanti January–March 1914*, 12/3/14, CO96/528/746.

111. Clifford was seventeen when he began service as a cadet in the Malay States.

112. Clifford to Harcourt, dispatch: *Trek from Accra to Dunkwa October–December 1913*, 6/11/13, CO96/528/746.

113. Clifford, speech on return from Tour of Ashanti, *Gazette* 12/3/14, CO99/23.

Province as "the curiously democratic native constitution" by which a chief who abused his power was likely to be "destooled" (dethroned), "nowadays by no means an uncommon practice."[114] Clifford's surprise concerning "democratic practices" suggests he was inadequately briefed by his officials. There is no indication that British officers fully grasped the systems of local African checks against authoritarian practices of chiefs.

In fact, Clifford had come to the conclusion that the government might have to intervene to protect some head chiefs from destoolment. No fewer than four paramount chiefs of the Eastern Province were removed by their people during 1913. There were only seven destoolments between 1904 and 1908, but twenty-three between 1909 and 1913.[115] Systems of "native" government were said to be breaking down in towns and villages where many of the inhabitants were newcomers, owing no allegiance to the local chief.[116] British officials, including the new governor, were distanced from such disputes and somewhat puzzled by them. They did not understand the full importance of popular councils or commoner *asafo* organizations in Akan states that challenged what were seen as irregular practices of the stool hierarchies.[117] Nor was there apparently any recognition of the effect of the British policy (largely from 1895) of recognizing paramount stools in order to create a conveniently hierarchical system of indirect rule.[118]

The main concern of British officers had been to identify the chiefs and elders responsible for running local African affairs. But Clifford failed to reconcile two beliefs: on the one hand, that democratic institutions "cannot be safely tampered with" and, on the other, that the government should support chiefs whose unpopularity was "due to the fact that they are more enlightened and progressive than their subjects."[119] Here was one of the main contradictions inherent in the practice of indirect rule. As Rathbone has commented, the British colonial government was never to achieve a satisfactory balance between intervention and allowing a degree of autonomy.[120]

However, Clifford was optimistic that the government would be able to create greater social stability by reinforcing the authority of chiefs and bringing them into closer cooperation with the government. He attempted to support chiefs by increasing their judicial powers, in order to harness their authority to help with administration. Early in his governorship, Clifford commented on the "extraordinary difficulties" in setting up effective administration using chiefs and the tribal system when the only check was the DC. The whole machinery was "lamentably deficient."[121] He intended to improve communication by arranging a series of regular *durbars* where chiefs of each province could bring matters of interest to their native communities, to be "freely debated" personally with the governor and top officials. He also hoped that as a result of his re-

---

114. Clifford to Harcourt, dispatch: *Tour of the Eastern Province 10–26 February 1913*, 3/3/13, CO96/528/746.

115. D. Kimble, *A Political History*, p. 490.

116. See, e.g., J. Simensen, "Commoners, Chiefs, and Colonial Government," p. 29.

117. For selective bibliography re. extensive literature on *asafos*: see E. Wrangham, "The Gold Coast and the First World War," p. 75.

118. See D. Henige, "Akan Stool Succession Under Colonial Rule—Continuity or Change?" *JAH*, XVI, 2, 1975.

119. Clifford re. F. Crowther, *Report on the Department of Native Affairs 1913*, 24/3/14, CO96/543/13456.

120. R. Rathbone, *Murder and Politics in Colonial Ghana*, (New Haven, 1993), pp. 60–61.

121. Clifford to Harcourt, dispatch: *Tour of the Eastern Province 10–26 February 1913*, CO96/528/9916.

organization of the administration it would be possible for officers to be in closer touch with the chiefs and peoples of their districts. It was, he declared, his "earnest wish to see the authority of the chiefs supported by all government officers; and the chiefs and their principal advisors taken into the confidence of the government, and habitually consulted when any matter affecting them and their people is under consideration." This was a well-meaning, relatively liberal, consultative vision, but it did not encompass democratic reform of Crown Colony government. Enfranchisement was considered as only a far distant goal.[122]

That the British government of the Gold Coast was as yet minimal in its impact on the local inhabitants struck Clifford most forcibly on his visit to the remoter parts of Western Province in 1913. A vignette of this time tells us much about colonial rule here. In the heavily forested Sefwi-Bekwai area, he was interested to note that the people were unable to believe a governor was actually visiting—and that they were clearly nervous. Clifford did not comment on how the size of the governor's entourage (264 people) must alone have created a formidable impression. The party consisted of seven Europeans, three "native" clerks, 130 carriers and one carriers' headman, a military escort of thirty-three, twelve governor's house boys and cooks, seven personal servants of other Europeans, four PC hammock boys, twenty-two DC hammock boys and carriers, five women and children, and forty other hammock boys. Camp and office equipment, general stores, and mineral water were carried in loads averaging sixty-nine lbs over 620 miles of "rough terrain." Even Clifford, who walked most of the way, wrote of "the great physical exertion of the journey." But the formalities were maintained. Before entering Enchi, the governor, a broadly built man well over six feet tall, retired into a bush hut to change into white dress uniform—an action that was likely to have made his African hosts even more nervous.[123]

Around Wioso there were no Europeans, no mission, no school, only a strong local fetish and, to Clifford's amazement, slavery being practiced quite openly. Although there were still at this time domestic slaves, or "pawns," attached to many households in such towns as Accra and Cape Coast, they could at least appeal to European officers for their freedom. Slavery had officially been abolished under the 1874 Ordinance. Pawning (people working off a debt in lieu of payment) had supposedly been abolished in 1880.[124] But here in the Western Province of the Gold Coast, as late as 1913, slavery existed on quite a different scale, with slaves, instead of Hausas or Wangaras, being used to carry rubber or cocoa to Kumasi or Cape Coast. Clifford had to inform the local *omanhene* (chief) that slave "palavers" (a form of public bargaining or market) were illegal.

Officials acknowledged that the western frontier of the colony had been "quite neglected"; the deputy conservator of forests, Palfreman, warned that some "natives" in the region who had never seen a white man were "very intractable"—and that slavery and human sacrifice were likely to die out only gradually, with the opening up of the country.[125] The widespread planting of cocoa would, it was believed, slowly lead to development and better communication. A new district was about to be created in the western frontier

122. Clifford re. 1914 Estimates, *LegCo* 11/10/13, *Gazette* 3/1/14, CO99/1.

123. Clifford to Harcourt, dispatch: *Trek from Dunkwa to Axim November–December 1913*, 8/12/13, CO96/528/746. See front cover portrait for a glimpse of this formal colonial attire.

124. D. Kimble, *A Political History*, p. 11.

125. Flood, Green, Co Minute, Clifford to Harcourt, 8/12/13, CO96/528/746. Also, Flood, CO memo re. Clifford's tour of the Central Province, 8/11/13, CO96/538/41332.

area, with a DC and school at Wioso, despite the opposition of the local omanhene, which was attributed to the fear that guns would be confiscated and fetish practices suppressed.[126]

The reality was that there were still whole areas of the colony in 1913 that were little affected by British rule. Crowther, the commissioner for native affairs in the colony, expressed surprise that there was "almost entire immunity from riot and disorder," given that this was a country "where large tracts are so little in touch with civilisation."[127] Crowther failed to note that the disorder that did occur at this time mostly took place in coastal towns where there was closer contact with the colonial administration, rather than in remote inland areas. The governor naively expressed the hope that the Fanti armed companies of the principal coastal towns, the *asafo,* were now being replaced by the kind of "local football teams" that met him with displays of bands and banners when he entered Mankessim towards the end of 1913.[128]

Yet the new governor was undaunted by the lightness of the colonial impact thus far. More expenditure was now committed for construction and more staff, and plans laid to improve the administration and provide more services. There was no reason to doubt that all would be paid for out of the growing wealth of the colony's trade, which was producing a steady increase in government revenue and the colony's surplus balances. Meanwhile, Clifford had, as Green in the Colonial Office wrote appreciatively, inspired his officers with some of his own energy.[129]

What he had done so far was apparently also appreciated by the unofficial legislative council representatives of both the European community and Western-educated Africans. Grey assured him in May 1914 that the sixteen months of his governorship had had a greater effect than anything he, Grey, had yet seen in his eight years in the colony, and that the "natives" had a feeling for him such as they never entertained for any governor since he, Grey, had been in West Africa. More significantly, the African unofficials were effusive in urging him on. Clifford won their support for his reforming agenda at this time: his interest in "native" affairs, his recognition of the value of education, and his determined efforts to promote Africanization, including "native" appointments of lawyers and "native" medical practitioners.[130] Clifford also received praise from the African press.[131] He seems to have gained from comparison with the unpopular contemporary governors of Sierra Leone and Nigeria at this time, Merewether and Lugard, as well as from comparison with his predecessor in the Gold Coast, Thorburn, referred to by *The Gold Coast Nation* as "the silent governor," who had been forced to retire prematurely as a result of poor health.[132]

No one could describe Clifford as "silent." He was persistent, determined, energetic, even driven, outspoken when he felt it necessary, and not afraid either to make decisions or to rescind them if he was subsequently persuaded they were impractical or morally

126. Clifford to Harcourt, 25/3/14, CO96/543/193.

127. Crowther, *Report on the Department of Native Affairs 1913,* Clifford to Harcourt, 24/3/14, CO96/543/13456.

128. Clifford to Harcourt, dispatch: *Trek from Accra to Dunkwa October–December 1913*, 8/11/13, CO96/528/746.

129. Green, CO Minute, Clifford to Harcourt, 27/8/13, CO96/535/641.

130. Grey, K. M. Kole, and Hutton Mills, *LegCo* 1/5/14, *Gazette* 13/6/14, CO99/55.

131. For typical comment, see *The Gold Coast Nation*, 17/4/13 and *The African Telegraph and Gold Coast Mirror,* 14/11/14.

132. *The Gold Coast Nation*, 15/08/12, NP 12/9 PRAAD.

wrong. In some instances, at least, he had won battles with fellow British officials, locally and in London, such as with the Gold Coast sanitary officers. He had, in a short time, made some contribution to improving the relationship between rulers and ruled in the Gold Coast, and local expectations were high as to what might be achieved while he was governor.

The overall picture at this time remains, however, somewhat mixed. On the one hand, thanks largely to favorable global conditions, along with African as well as European enterprise, the prewar economy of the Gold Coast prospered.[133] This made British colonial rule the more acceptable, and by now it was indeed well established and facing no overt challenge. On the other hand, it still amounted to little more than a holding operation. Both political and administrative competence lagged far behind what the new governor wanted. Clifford's discovery, noted above, that slavery persisted in the territory decades after it had officially been abolished, was a sobering experience and spoke of a wider reality. As he concluded: "Perhaps it is as well to recognise ... that, except in the matter of the suppression of overt acts of lawlessness, and in the improvement of the material prosperity of the people, and the practical development of the Colony's economic resources, British rule in many parts of the Gold Coast has so far done little more than effect a change in the surface of things."[134] In his overall assessment of what colonial rule amounted to, Clifford was free of delusion. He acknowledged that the legislative council had promulgated an enormous volume of laws over the previous twenty years—without taking into account the inadequacy of the machinery to carry them out. He concluded wistfully in 1913 that, except in the towns where there were government institutions, "the administration of the colony is to a great extent theoretical, rather than practical, and exists on paper rather than in fact."[135]

Clifford and his officials were involved in a country of which they still knew and understood little, and where there were inevitably difficulties in their relations with both Africans and private European trading companies. Clifford left for England for his delayed leave in May 1914. He intended to discuss his plans for the Gold Coast directly with the secretary of state and Colonial Office officials in London before returning to continue his work of modernizing the colony.[136] But within three months of his departure, Britain was to be at war with Germany. There was no doubting the personal competence and ambition of the new governor, but it was not at all clear how successfully British colonial rule in the Gold Coast might cope with the damaging repercussions of the imminent global conflict.

---

133 See Appendix III, "Gold Coast Imports and Exports 1910–1919," page 283.

134. Clifford to Harcourt, dispatch: *Trek from Dunkwa to Axim, November–December 1913*, 8/12/13, CO96/528/746.

135. Clifford to Harcourt, dispatch: *Tour of the Eastern Province 10–26 February 1913*, 3/3/13, CO96/528/9916.

136. Clifford, *Speech on Return from Ashanti, Gazette* 12/3/14, CO99/23. (He was also concerned that Lady Clifford would have the chance to recuperate from her severe tropical illness.)

Section II

War

Chapter 4

The Gold Coast's Lifeline: The Impact of the War on Shipping and Trade

The Great War had global consequences that threatened to undermine the relationship between the British colonial rulers and their West African subjects in the Gold Coast. The main factor was the disruption to the international trade on which the colony's economy and finances depended. On the day that the declaration of war was announced, August 5, 1914, a British imperial proclamation was issued in the colony banning all trade, business, and shipping with the German Empire.[1] Yet Germany was until then second only to Britain as exporter, importer, and shipper to and from the colony. Trade was subjected thereafter to further wartime regulations, along with severe fluctuations in demand and price.

A major problem for the duration of the war, seriously affecting trade in both exports and imports, was the shortage of shipping. The losers from this shipping shortage were the main African producers, traders, and shippers, as well as smaller European trading companies—and government revenue. After the initial shock of the declaration of war, British officials hoped that the seaborne mercantile trade would soon begin to recover.[2] But it did not. The number of ships and total tonnage available to carry the colony's trade were to decline to alarmingly low levels in 1917. By 1918, the viability of the whole colony was threatened.

From the start of the war, the British colonial government intervened in the economy to an unprecedented extent. However, its attitude remained reluctant and its actions limited. Though primarily established to facilitate the exploitation of the Gold Coast's economic potential, the government had not hitherto felt it appropriate to intervene in economic relations in general, or shipping in particular. The evidence suggests that its essential approach was not consciously ideological but simply pragmatic—laissez-faire by default—reflecting what worked, who could be depended upon, and what was cheapest. This made possible a largely welcome competition, before the war, between companies exporting and shipping goods from the Gold Coast. In the challenging new context of global war, however, there was a strong economic tendency towards monopolization: in the now dangerously exposed world of intercontinental shipping, only the fittest would survive. Little could be done to prevent one British shipping line, Elder Dempster, from establishing itself as increasingly monopolistic and dominant (though paying a big price in losses at sea). While such developments confirm the relatively limited significance of official British personnel in the Gold Coast at this time, they need to be understood primarily as illustrating the context—the near severance of the colony's lifeline—for all the internal developments in the Gold Coast during the war years, to be explored in subsequent chapters of this study.

---

1. *Government Proclamation* 5/8/14, *Gazette* 5/8/14, C099/28/71. Governor Clifford was on leave in Britain when war broke out.
2. Acting Governor Robertson, *Confidential Dispatch printed for Parliament* 19/8/14, CO96/547.

Emergency action in 1914 reflected the extent of the colony's dependence on food and fuel imports before the war. At its outbreak, Governor Clifford was away on leave in Britain, so it fell to the acting governor, Robertson, eager to avoid local shortages, to approve unprecedented government intervention to try to control supplies of food and fuel. The alarm was raised when the British shipper Elder Dempster (now the main shipping line to the coast), acting swiftly and apparently independently, suspended all ordinary sailings to West Africa. It then announced a punitive 50% increase in passenger and freight rates.[3] As a result, the Gold Coast government briefly took over major stores, including all food stores in Accra; bought 1,000 gallons of gasoline; and gave instructions to buy up rice throughout the colony. According to the subsequent complaints of a number of merchants in the Gold Coast, some trading stores up-country were briefly taken over by overenthusiastic DCs. General supplies were judged as sufficient for just four months.[4] Robertson expressed particular concern at the consequences of a total cut in imports of rice and coal, though Ellis in the Colonial Office was more sanguine, saying that locally grown food and wood could act perfectly well as substitutes.[5] The issue of import substitution was to re-emerge later in the war in response to shortages and high prices. The problem was that not only the white population but also, by this time, "a large part of the Europeanized natives" in British West Africa depended heavily on imported food, such as the 7,500 tons of rice then imported annually into the Gold Coast.[6]

The colonial government had no remedy, of course, for the lack of ships. However, the immediate disruption and confusion of the start of the war seemed to pass relatively quickly. Alarms were raised initially by rumors, such as sightings of "steamers in the sky" and warships off Ada.[7] But by the time Clifford returned to the colony in September (via Togo, with Lome now in British hands), ships were once more arriving offshore, and trade was apparently operating as usual. Indeed, Clifford was optimistic at this stage that he could restore "normal" conditions to the Gold Coast.[8] However, the governor was to find that even his will and energy could not summon the "normal" quantity of personnel, supplies, and funds—or ships.

The shortage of shipping was not only one of the most serious problems hampering the colony's trade for the whole of the war, but also one of the first to make itself felt. The average of only twenty-five ships (average tonnage: 56,429 tons) on the coast of the colony between August and November 1914 contrasted unfavorably with the forty-two (average tonnage: 97,051 tons) in the same period the year before, in 1913.[9] The initial shortage reflected the loss of German shippers, with some German and Austrian ships

---

3. *Elder Dempster Notices: 11 & 16 August 1914,* C0554/23. And see P. N. Davies, *The Trade Makers. Elder Dempster in West Africa. 1852–1972,* (London, 1973), p. 185; and A. Olukoju, "Elder Dempster and the Shipping Trade of Nigeria During the First World War," *JAH,* 33, 1992, pp. 255, 271.

4. Telegram, Acting Governor Robertson to Harcourt, 12/8/14, C096/547. Compare with emergency measures taken elsewhere in British West Africa, e.g., food rationing in the Gambia: see P. Hatton, "The Gambia, the Colonial Office, and the Opening Months of the First World War," *JAH,* VII, 1, 1966.

5. Ellis, CO Minute. Telegram, Acting Governor Robertson to Harcourt, 12/8/14, C096/547.

6. Manchester Chamber of Commerce to CO, 25/8/14, C0554/19. See also Liverpool Chamber of Commerce, *Report of Proceedings of Trade Conference at the Colonial Office,* 19/8/14, C0554/21.

7. Flood, CO Minute, Acting Governor Robertson, *Confidential Dispatch printed for Parliament* 12/8/14, C096/547 and Acting Governor Robertson, *Confidential Dispatch printed for Parliament,* 19/8/14, CO554/21.

8. Clifford, confid. to Harcourt, 8/9/14, C096/547.

9. Telegram, Clifford to Harcourt, 18/12/14, C096/550.

seized as prizes of war, as well as a number of ships requisitioned by the Admiralty for war use. Although there was some recovery after the first few months of the war, the number and tonnage of steam ships entering ports in the colony during 1915 were down by nearly 50% when compared with just before the war.[10]

From late 1916, shortage of shipping space became even more acute for the Gold Coast than elsewhere in West Africa. This was the result of new imperial wartime regulations under the Board of Trade, with preference—over the Gold Coast's cocoa—increasingly given to freightloads of palm products and groundnuts from other regions. In terms of exports, Clifford had a relatively weak hand to play. Apart from food protein, edible nuts from neighboring colonies could also provide oil as a lubricant and glycerine used in the manufacture of munitions. These new measures were brought in to limit shipments to Britain of what were now labelled "non-essential imports," such as cocoa. With an increasing number of steamers sunk by enemy action in the last four months of 1915, Nigeria was now allocated more shipping space than the Gold Coast. In addition, by 1917 many homeward bound ships from Nigeria either bypassed the Gold Coast altogether or offered only a small proportion of space in a ship's hold for cocoa. Elder Dempster agents reported that some ships from Nigeria were ignoring requests for cocoa shipments from the Gold Coast and filling up on the return journey with palm oil and palm kernels from Sierra Leone and groundnuts from the Gambia.[11]

The major cause of the sharply reduced provision of ships to the Gold Coast in 1917 was the high number sunk by the enemy that year. In February 1917, the Germans resumed unrestricted submarine attacks on Allied shipping in a campaign centered in the North Atlantic. Of the twenty-nine ships Elder Dempster lost from enemy action during the whole of the war, twenty-one were sunk in 1917.[12] The West Africa "run" was only fully integrated into the British convoy system and awarded some protection in 1918. That the seaborne trade to and from Europe survived at all was, as the inhabitants of the Gold Coast were frequently reminded by their government, due to the protection of the British navy.[13] As the shipping shortage worsened during the last two years of the war, the Gold Coast government was unable to find any ways of obtaining relief for the colony. The contrast with the prewar period was stark: by 1918 the number of steamships anchoring off Gold Coast ports had fallen by 60% compared with before the war: in 1913, 692 steam vessels had anchored off Gold Coast ports; in 1918 the figure fell to just 210. The addition by 1918 of forty-six sailing vessels (twenty-two from the United States) only slightly eased the situation.[14]

The shipping shortage exacerbated the other two major problems affecting the colony's exports during the war: fluctuating demand and fluctuating prices. Demand for cocoa

10. *Trade Report 1915, Supplementary 1, Gazette* 1/5/16, CO99/30.

11. *Trade Report 1916*, 9/7/17, C096/580/430; *Trade Report 1917, Gazette* 21/5/18, C099/33/1; and Slater, Colonial Secretary, memo on the Gold Coast Cocoa Trade in Clifford, confid. to Long, 23/8/17, C096/581.

12. The main steamers trading on the West African coast sunk by enemy action were: one in 1914; four in 1915 (including the *SS Falaba*); none in 1916; twenty-one in 1917 (including the *SS Abosso, SS Apapa*, and *SS Gold Coast*) and one in 1918 (*SS Baratu*). P. N. Davies, *The Trade Makers, Appendices: Table 16*, pp. 408–409.

13. Acting Governor Slater, *LegCo* 25/10/15, *Gazette* 25/11/15, C099/29/101; also Clifford, *LegCo* 23/10/16, *Gazette* 23/10/16, C099/31/17.

14. Total tonnage 1913: 1,515,197 tons; 1918: 488,366 tons. Tonnage of sailing vessels 1918: 50,819 tons. *Trade Reports: 1914*, C098/24; *1916*, C098/26; *1917*, C098/28; *1918*, C098/30.

initially fell, then appeared to steady uncertainly in 1915, rose suddenly in 1916, and then fell drastically in 1917 and 1918, only to rise dramatically and then crash with the sudden boom and slump that followed the end of the war. The development of a particular wartime demand for other agricultural products such as rubber and palm oil could not compensate the Gold Coast financially for these periods of sudden collapse in the dominant cocoa industry, which were all the more dramatic in contrast with the uninterrupted boom of the prewar period. There was some compensation, however, in the sustained export of minerals: gold, for example, while manganese came to be mined in the Colony for the first time.

Only the British shipping company with an effective wartime monopoly, Elder Dempster, and a few large expatriate trading companies were to gain from wartime conditions. Elder Dempster had been in a dominant position even before the war, when it owned almost all the ninety-two British ships on the West Africa run. There had been fifty-one German ships, thirteen of which were captured. Holt's of Liverpool had at first only three, then four, ships for the West African coast, but two of these were lost in the German U-boat campaign of 1917–18. Lever Brothers opened their own line in 1916, but three of their six ships were also sunk.[15] Elder Dempster's main competitors on the West Africa run were eliminated at the outbreak of war when the cartel, the West African Shipping Conference, collapsed once the other members, the German Woermann line and the Hamburg Bremen Shipping Company, were no longer able to operate. Competitive edge initially, then conditions of war—rather than deliberate government policy—saw Elder Dempster hold and increase its dominance during the war years.

Although successful pressure was brought to bear on Elder Dempster to reduce its initial unilateral rise in rates from 50% to 25%, there remained widespread anger among British and African traders at the way the company took advantage of its position. It was clear that new wartime insurance costs were being passed on to the trading companies by the Elder Dempster shipping line in extra freight charges.[16] As one British shipper complained to *The Daily News*, Elder Dempster's action was "tantamount to a request from the steamship company to pay their own merchants."[17] The high freight and passenger rates that the shippers charged were subsequently passed on by the merchants to the African producers in the form of lower prices paid for agricultural products such as cocoa. This had the effect of reducing Africans' purchasing power at a time when import prices were rising—a cause of considerable frustration. Wartime shortages of imports also contributed to lowering government income from indirect taxation on which the revenue depended.[18] Meanwhile, rates were raised again, partly reflecting the increased insurance premiums as a result of the shippers' risk of being struck by German torpedoes.[19]

The British colonial government disliked monopolistic practices, but there was little it could do except adjust to a new situation: the colony's international trade, and therefore also government revenue, became heavily dependent during the war on the one major

---

15. The 92 British ships = 274,000 tonnage; and the 51 German ships = 133,000 tonnage. See P. N. Davies, *The Trade Makers*, pp. 194–195; and C. Leubuscher, *The West African Shipping Trade 1909–1959*, (Leyden, 1963), p. 31.

16. CO Memo, Trade Conference, 19/8/14, C0554/21.

17. *The Manchester Guardian*, 14/8/14 in BCGA to CO, 14/8/14, C0554/23.

18. For the similar situation in Nigeria, see A. Olukoju, "Elder Dempster and the Shipping Trade of Nigeria," p. 266.

19. *Government Circular* 3/10/16, *Gazette* 18/11/16, CO99/30/82; also, Acting Governor Slater, secret to Harcourt, 28/12/16, C096/547.

British shipping company, Elder Dempster. The company's cooperation was normally necessary if extra ships were required.[20] The Colonial Office relayed Admiralty advice that merchants were free to charter their own ships. More freight could also be obtained by chartering extra ships through Elder Dempster. But the shortage of shipping made chartering very difficult as well as expensive. Before the war, although a deferred rebate system had tied merchants to shipping with the conference lines, it had also to some extent protected smaller companies by guaranteeing them shipping space. This was no longer the case during the war. In addition, Elder Dempster tended to act as if it still held rights of "primage," the prewar practice of penalizing attempts made to ship outside the "ring."[21] For example, in 1916 a number of British timber merchants at Axim reported that they were being refused all shipping facilities by Elder Dempster because they had also chartered their own schooners to ship mahogany logs to America. It was clear that although Elder Dempster did not have enough ships itself, it was determined to make it impossible for exporters—British or African—to obtain tonnage elsewhere.[22] The expense of chartering ships and the new free-for-all of the war period (with no guaranteed shipping space for small companies) led to small European traders and many African traders being squeezed out.[23]

Early in the war, the governor suspected that the "practical monopoly" which the Elder Dempster shipping company then enjoyed in British West Africa had led to its "serving its own interests rather than being stirred into making great exertions" to meet the needs of the colonies. Apart from its fleet of steamships, Elder Dempster dominated harbor services, including tugs, lighters, and surf boats, and controlled a network of interests in Liverpool as well as interests in timber and mining in West Africa. It also enjoyed a particularly close relationship with the Bank of West Africa, which regarded the shipping line and the largest trading companies as the most reliable of its creditors.[24] Official British government control of the West Africa shipping run was only imposed later in the war. Early in 1916 the Shipping Control Committee was set up by the British government in London under the chairmanship of Lord Curzon. Control of all shipping was finally placed under the Ministry of Shipping only in May 1917.[25]

It was easiest for the largest of the European trading firms to cope with wartime conditions. The major merchant companies, on which much of the prosperity of the Gold Coast colony depended at this time, were the four main buyers of cocoa responsible for buying half the cocoa crop in 1914: Swanzy, Millers, the Africa Association (together referred to as "the combine"), and (until it was taken over in December 1917) the Basel mission trading company, or "factory." During the war (apart from the Basel Mission) they were to become even more dominant as a result of smaller competitors—many of which were relatively small African traders—being squeezed out by new restrictions,

20. P. N. Davies, *The Trade Makers,* p. 188.

21. Green, CO Minute, Telegram, Clifford to Long, 14/12/14, C096/550. Telegram, Clifford to Long, 14/12/16, C096/573.

22. Ellis, Read, CO Minute, Acting Governor Slater to Long, 18/12/16, C096/574/937.

23. See C. Leubuscher, *The West African Shipping Trade,* pp. 17–32.

24. The special relationship dated from when the Bank had originated as "little more than a department of Elder Dempster & Co." when founded in 1894 by Sir Alfred Jones, Elder Dempster's first chairman; see R. Fry, *Bankers in West Africa,* p. 24.

25. Contrast with South Africa, where "the South African government controlled Union Castle and Union Castle controlled the Conference," R. Berridge, *The Politics of the South Africa Run. European Shipping and Pretoria,* (London, 1987), p. 219; P. N. Davies, *The Trade Makers,* pp. 108–124, 161, 181–187; and C. Leubuscher, *The West African Shipping Trade,* pp. 19–32.

expenses, and risks. The larger firms also found it less difficult to cope with irregular sailings, a feature of the war years caused partly by shipping and manpower shortages and partly by severe congestion at those ports such as London and Liverpool that remained open to commercial shipping.

British imperial edicts and German U-boats largely shaped the pattern of trade with Britain and the rest of Europe during the war. Nor was the local government responsible for (even if it was much relieved by) the greatly increased trade between the Gold Coast and the United States, which proved so vital to the colony at this time. Within the constraints of wartime prohibitions and shortages, British officials for the most part accepted the view that external political forces and the market would dictate demand and supply and therefore also price levels. Laissez-faire was not—since it could not be—abandoned either as a policy preference or as normal practice.

In most respects, British officials in the Gold Coast colony were powerless to defend their own or their subjects' interests—despite the government officially acquiring new powers during the war. From January 1916, British Imperial Orders in Council for merchant shipping required that government licenses be obtained for permission to ship cargo to foreign ports in British vessels.[26] This meant that the allocation of licenses, introduced because of the extreme shortage of shipping space, was officially left to the governor's discretion.[27] But unofficially—and therefore not formally recorded (or referred to)—Elder Dempster continued to have the main say in shipping space allocation in the Gold Coast colony. The British Gold Coast officials took the line of least resistance, believing that they had no option but to allow the exceptionally free hand enjoyed by Elder Dempster during the war. This arose because of the practical impossibility of the small number of colonial officials setting up and running a new licensing scheme or being involved in the detail of allocating shipping space in the context of wartime staff shortages. The government's ultimate priority was to ensure that trade and government revenue were sustained during the war. This meant that the main shipping line, and the main traders it favored, had to be encouraged rather than hampered. As elsewhere in British West Africa, they continued to dominate the trade.[28]

The wartime licensing system thus favored the large established expatriate trading companies rather than small African (or European) firms. Licenses were granted to regular shippers and shipping space initially allocated according to the proportion of space used by each firm before the war. One problem that arose from this system was that the smaller, often African, shippers were badly affected by the lack of any records of prewar shipments on the German Woermann Line.[29] The larger trading firms also obtained priority because they were seen by Elder Dempster as financially more reliable, with their greater reserves of capital and their control of major warehouse storage space. Moreover, the big European trading companies shipped in bulk, with the effect that their goods were easier to handle than were lots of smaller assignments from the African and smaller British trading firms. But it was also in the interest of the Elder Dempster shipping company to favor a merchant "combine" of the larger expatriate companies in the Gold Coast, as was the case in Nigeria,

26. New Orders in Council 1/1/16, C099/30/5.

27. Telegram, Clifford to Long, 9/10/18, C096/593.

28. See A. Olukoju, "Elder Dempster and the Shipping Trade of Nigeria," p. 264; and F. Cole, "Sierra Leone and World War I," pp. 315–320.

29. A. Olukoju, "Elder Dempster and the Shipping Trade of Nigeria," p. 261.

to reduce the threat of other companies seeking to charter their own ships and challenging its effective shipping monopoly.[30]

Meanwhile, the colonial government was, not surprisingly, blamed for failing to protect the interests of the smaller African and European shippers. There were frequent complaints throughout the war that the combine prospered at their expense and was monopolizing the available tonnage.[31] In 1917, the colonial government denied the accusation and defended Elder Dempster, arguing that it could not be expected to keep regular space for "small spasmodic shippers"—a category which would have been largely African.[32] The colonial administration of the Gold Coast colony was now seen by the local population to be clearly favoring the larger European shippers and traders.

The Gold Coast government did, however, make one bold—and much resented—venture to intervene in allocation of shipping space. Clifford decided in late 1917 to grant licenses to a few leading African chiefs involved in the export of cocoa. But this government initiative, far from being widely welcomed, provoked a sustained outburst of fury from both African and European shippers. The whole incident reflected the increasing tension of the ever-worsening constraints on trade. Clifford believed that a handful of key head chiefs in the main cocoa growing districts needed the extra fillip of government support. But the main British chambers of commerce in Liverpool, Manchester, and London, as well as the Association of West African Merchants, protested in the strongest possible terms.[33] Expatriate shippers headed by Elder Dempster, all obviously used to having their own way without serious government interference, bombarded the Colonial Office with complaints.[34]

Clifford was responding to an African initiative here—but one that was not representative of African interests generally. He had been convinced by Nana Ofori Atta, the astute *okyenhene* (king) of Akyem Abuakwa in Eastern Province, that chiefs and their farming communities should be allowed to ship cocoa direct to Britain, even if they had never shipped before.[35] There was no possibility of new special licenses being granted by the Board of Trade, which instead advised the governor to make room for new shippers by reducing existing shippers' allocations. Clifford was well aware that such a move would be extremely unpopular and that the trade and revenue of the colony depended on the cooperation of the larger merchant companies. So he asked permission

---

30. A. Osuntokun, *Nigeria in the First World War,* p. 38.

31. E.g., complaint of Theo Vasner & Co. to CO, 2/5/16, and Bonar Law's reply, CO96/57; Manchester Chamber of Commerce to CO, 16/5/18 and Long's reply, C096/594.

32. See E. J. P. Brown's question and the acting colonial secretary's reply, *LegCo* 25/10/17, *Gazette* 26/11/17, C099/32/76.

33. This association of large British firms operating in West Africa had been founded in 1916 officially to assist the government war effort. See, e.g., J. G. Deutsch, "Educating the Middlemen," p. 73.

34. Memo, Joint Deputation Chambers of Commerce London, Liverpool and Manchester and Association of West Africa Merchants to CO, June 1918, in Clifford, confid. to Long, 3/10/18, C096/593. Also Liverpool Chamber of Commerce to CO, 13/6/18, CO96/594; and London Chamber of Commerce to CO, 21/6/18, CO96/590.C096/594.

35. Telegram, Clifford to Long, 13/11/17, C096/582. Also Clifford, confid. to Long, 10/12/17, C096/583. Nana Ofori Atta, enstooled in 1911, was an unofficial member of *LegCo* from 1916. Both he and his state, Akyem Abuakwa, a major center of cocoa production in Eastern Province, were regarded by the colonial government, including Clifford, and by very many Africans in the Gold Coast, as "synonymous with modernization and progress." R. Rathbone, *Murder and Politics,* p. 11.

instead to transfer to a number of chiefs the export licenses of the Anglo-Belgian company and the Basel trading company that had been declared enemy property in December 1917.[36]

For Clifford, government intervention was eminently sensible in the context of extreme depression in the cocoa industry during the 1917–1918 cocoa season. "The sole object of the scheme is to afford small relief to farmers," he wrote.[37] It was perhaps also a useful way of diverting anger aroused by the new cocoa export duty.[38] Licenses were to go to paramount chiefs in Eastern Province on the grounds that farmers there produced more than 50% of the total amount of cocoa from the entire country. Clifford was scathing about the outcry of the merchants "who naturally dislike any scheme whereby even a few farmers are partially enabled to dispense with their services as middlemen."[39] He contrasted the plight of the African farmers, paid the lowest ever prices for cocoa since February 1917, with the "unprecedentedly large profits" enjoyed by the much bigger expatriate buyers and shippers. Clifford was in no doubt that Swanzy, Millers, and the African Association—the "combine" with monopolistic practices that he deplored—were especially annoyed, as they had imagined that they would secure all, if not most, of the Basel trading company's licenses, once these were confiscated as enemy property.[40]

Clifford's relatively limited yet very controversial intervention into the Gold Coast's international export trade proved more laudable in intention than in execution. The main European firms calculated that their strongest argument against the government's action was to focus on the neglect of African interests rather than their own. The governor was accused of favoring certain chiefs at the expense of African as well as European firms and at the expense of the majority of African producers.[41] A complaint of the Accra Chamber of Commerce, representing both African and European traders, claimed to be concerned with abuses of the system. For example, one of the beneficiaries of the scheme was the *Ga Mantse* of Accra, who had immediately sold his license to "speculators" rather than recognizing local African shippers and traders who felt they should have received the export licenses in the first place.[42] Within the state of Akyem Abuakwa, there was opposition to Ofori Atta's shipping scheme, since it was feared that his raising a loan from the Colonial Bank, partly to charter a steamer, was nothing less than illegally mortgaging his stool.[43] Although a few hundred tons of cocoa from Eastern Province and Ashanti were now directly shipped by chiefs through this government initiative, it did not solve the shipping problem, even for the favored chiefs and cocoa farmers. Possession of an export license unfortunately did not guarantee that the holder could ship. It was "notorious" that more licenses for goods were issued than the ever-diminishing supply of shipping space could accommodate.[44]

---

36. Telegram, Clifford to Long, 13/11/17, C096/593/597.
37. Telegram, Clifford to Long, 19/8/18, C096/590.
38. R. Southall, "Cadbury on the Gold Coast," p. 153.
39. Telegram, Clifford to Long, 19/8/18, CO96/590.
40. Clifford, confid. to Long, 3/10/18, C096/593.
41. Memo, Joint Deputation Chambers of Commerce London, Liverpool and Manchester and Association of West Africa Merchants to CO, June 1918, Clifford, confid. to Long, 3/10/18, CO96/593.
42. Africa Trade Section, Liverpool Chamber of Commerce to CO, 27/12/18, C096/594/726.
43. This accusation contributed to the attempt to destool Ofori Atta in Kyebi in November 1918. See J. Simensen, "Commoners, Chiefs and Colonial Government," pp. 141–146.
44. Harper, Acting Colonial Secretary, replying to E. J. P. Brown, *LegCo* 29/10/18, *Gazette* 9/11/18, C099/33/81.

The relationship between African shippers and traders and British colonial officials thus deteriorated rapidly in the war as a result of the cumulative impact of prevailing conditions and government policy. Africans—other than a handful of chiefs in Eastern Province—found themselves ignored by the government and excluded from an adequate license and shipping space allocation. The African unofficial E. J. P. Brown argued the case for "legitimate native shippers" across the colony but especially for those in his own region in the ports of Central Province, such as Cape Coast. *The Gold Coast Nation,* also representing interests in Central Province, claimed that Eastern Province and Ashanti had been favored concerning shipping space during the war.[45] In September 1918, Clifford reluctantly sent on to London a letter addressed to the secretary of state from what he referred to as "a body which styles itself the Association of Native Shippers and Planters."[46] They complained vigorously that special licenses to ship cocoa had been granted by the Board of Trade in 1917 and 1918 to old and newly established European firms and to certain chiefs, but none had been allocated to African shippers, even though they had raised the matter with the governor as early as May 1917. Such a policy, they argued cogently, "aims at shutting out from the open market legitimate Native Merchants and others and introduces and perpetuates a sort of economic servitude inconsistent with Imperial ideals."[47] Their angry stand was supported in the local African press: "Native" shippers had suffered "disabilities" before the war but wartime conditions had certainly "aggravated" the situation.[48] Colonial rule was being subjected to a new, more critical, review.

The reaction of local British officials to the plight of these African traders was not particularly sympathetic. The acting comptroller of customs in the Gold Coast, Mitchell, acknowledged that thirty to forty small "native" shippers had "no doubt been hard hit," but he added that many others had been too, as a result of the current shipping difficulties.[49] It is true that the petitioners were not aware of some of the constraints. The Gold Coast government was not in a position to dictate to either the Board of Trade or to the other two Ministries in London—Food and Shipping—which by 1918 also had a say in how much cocoa could be shipped into Britain. The situation had also been made worse by the heavy losses from the German U-boat campaign. Clifford's dismissive comment concerning "native shippers and planters" was clearly affected by their criticism of his colonial administration as well as their bypassing the governor with a direct appeal to London, which Clifford clearly resented.

There was a lack of consistency here in Clifford's response to African needs. In contrast with his support for a number of leading chiefs in their role as major cocoa producers, Clifford failed to support established African shippers and traders in the colony's export trade. He did not recommend any special consideration being given, their position being "unfortunately far from uncommon at the present time."[50] The smaller surf ports of the

45. E. J. P. Brown, *LegCo* 29/10/18, *Gazette* 9/11/18, 0099/33/81. *The Gold Coast Nation,* 8–15/6/19.

46. An instance of a standard British criticism that such African organizations were not genuinely representative. Compare with the Nigerian Combine's dismissal of African shippers in Lagos, in A. Olukoju, "Elder Dempster and the Shipping Trade in Nigeria," pp. 261–262; or Clifford's well-known attack on the NCBWA (National Congress of British West Africa) in 1920, quoted in M. Crowder, *West Africa Under Colonial Rule,* p. 428.

47. *Petition of Association of Native Shippers and Planters,* Clifford, confid. to Long, 25/10/18, C096/593.

48. Editorial, *Gold Coast Leader,* 18/8/17; and 28/9/18.

49. Mitchell, Comptroller of Customs, Enclosure 2, Clifford, confid. to Long, 25/10/18, CO96/593. And see P. N. Davies, *The Trade Makers,* pp. 197–204, 408–9.

50. Clifford, confid. to Long, 25/10/18, CO96/593.

Colony, together with their African traders and nearby farms, also lost out in the war. Accra was the main port for cocoa shipments, and Sekondi had beaten first Winneba and then Ada to achieve second place for itself just before the war. During the war, the gap widened between Accra and Sekondi (the premier ports) and the other ports along the coast. Some, like Denu and Prampram, had largely ceased to function by the end of the war because the declining number of steamers tended to call only at the major ports. The experiment of allocating licenses by port during the war failed to reverse the trend, partly because small ports were also affected by the decline in non-cocoa products such as rubber and gum copal.[51]

Elder Dempster took the opportunity of the wartime reduction in competition to strengthen its position further. P. N. Davies, writing an official history, argued the Elder Dempster case. Considering the extra costs of the war and the depreciating value of money, he judged the shipping line's returns in real terms as "quite moderate," its profits "not extortionate," and its freight charges "never excessive."[52] But as A. G. Hopkins noted, "the author identifies a bit too closely with the company and its interests."[53] Elder Dempster's role in keeping the West African trade going during the war, before all shipping came under British government control, was certainly crucial for the colony. Yet it is also notable that the shipping line made substantial profits overall, rising throughout the war years, even during the worst of the trade depression in the Gold Coast in 1918. From its comfortable monopolistic perch, Elder Dempster dug in its claws in preparation for the revival of competition once peace returned.[54]

The war caused the partial severing of the Gold Coast's economic lifeline, its link through shipping with the rest of the world. Prewar shipping patterns were broken by reductions in demand as well as by German U-boats and further distorted by both the trend toward monopoly and the licensing of shipping space for a reduced number of Gold Coast exporters. The British colonial authority was largely a spectator here. It was incapable of major influence: nervous, anyway, of intervening, for fear of disrupting such trade as could take place (and revenue as could accrue) in the increasingly difficult wartime conditions, yet at times capable of mistaken individual interventions.

Trading conditions for African shippers deteriorated markedly during the war. The wartime issuing of licenses and allotment of shipping space were unofficially left to the major European shipping and trading firms to negotiate between themselves. Governor Clifford's one small intervention to aid African chiefs and cocoa farmers in the Gold Coast was much resented by both the small European and the small African exporters and shippers. African shippers did not receive a fair proportion of licenses and expressed their anger to colonial officials in both Accra and London. As a result of trading restrictions with Britain, many African shippers went out of business. Some were bought up by larger European companies, while others turned to the growing trade with the United States. The wartime conditions of international trade revealed competing African and European

51. Official closing down of ports: Denu (1916); Adjua, Shama, Prampram (1919); Dixcove, Atuabo, Apam, Elmina (1921). *Trade Reports: 1913, Gazette* 25/4/14, CO99/35; and *1918*, CO98/30. And see also K. Dickson, "Evolution of Seaports in Ghana: 1800–1928," *Annals of the Association of American Geographers*, 55, 1965, pp. 98–111

52. P. N. Davies, *The Trade Makers*, p. 198.

53. A. G. Hopkins, "Review of P. N. Davies, The Trade Makers," *JAH*, XV, 3, 1974.

54. Appendices, Elder Dempster & Co. Ltd., *Table of Results 1911–1925*. And P. N. Davies, *The Trade Makers*, p. 457.

interests—each seeking to maximize what economic opportunities were still available and to minimize damage to their trade. The Gold Coast colonial government's interventions to mitigate the effects of disruptive global conditions from 1914 were piecemeal and occasional. They were unprecedented too, and received unprecedented criticism from Africans involved in the colonial economy, as we shall see in the next chapter.

Chapter 5

Wartime Disruption of the Gold Coast Economy: British Responses

The Gold Coast suffered greatly in wartime conditions, not only from the shipping shortage but also from acute and unpredictable fluctuations in the international demand for the goods it exported—especially for cocoa, the major cash crop. The substantial deterioration in trading conditions at the outbreak of war, and for most of the long war years, prompted reaction from all parties: from Africans who were in any way involved in the Gold Coast's economy as well as from government and the major expatriate enterprises, the trading companies and the mines.

British and African interests were both at stake here in conditions that no one could control—including, most visibly, the colonial officials who were supposed to be in charge. It was not just fluctuating trade conditions that they could not govern, but also the perceptions and responses of their own subjects, whether capitalist expatriates, or African farmers, or laborers (or immigrants). What the Gold Coast economy could contribute to the British war effort was again not within their own competence to determine or manage—as we will see most clearly from their repeated attempts to sustain the cocoa crop and diversify the products of African farming. Not only did the powers of the colonial government prove limited in minimizing the war's disruption of the Gold Coast economy; Africans who before the war might have regarded the British administration as competent and confident, associating it with a period of economic boom and the prospect of further benefit, now reacted increasingly skeptically to policies during the war that proved too often inadequate or irrelevant.

During the First World War in the Gold Coast, there was no greater economic concern to British or Africans involved in export production than the changing fortunes of cocoa. War conditions caused dramatic fluctuations in demand and huge variations in prices paid to producers. As a result, African cocoa farmers could not be sure of such income as they had come to rely on for their purchase of imported goods, and the British administration could not be sure of its revenue. The responses of both parties revealed the seriousness of the impact of the war on the Gold Coast economy and exposed the apprehensions of a colonial administration out of its depth in these new and unforeseen circumstances.

At the beginning of the war, the fall in demand for cocoa was immediately reflected in the prices. A revival in late 1915 accelerated into a cocoa boom in 1916. But this proved to be short-lived. There followed a plunge into depression in 1917 and 1918, aggravated by the restrictions placed first on cocoa imports into Britain and then, in the second half of 1918, by the restrictions on imports into, first, France and then the United States.[1]

Demand for cocoa plummeted almost at once. Despite the requirement of a guarantee of destination, there were suspicions towards the end of 1914 that a large proportion of

1. See Appendices II and III.

the cocoa sold in Europe was reaching Germany and the German army. The result was a British Order in Council of January 1915 prohibiting the export of cocoa to all countries in Europe except France, Russia, Belgium, and two neutral states, Spain and Portugal. Germany had taken not only 17% of the Gold Coast cocoa crop in 1913, but also a substantial proportion of the cocoa exported in British ships to Hamburg (the center of the world cocoa trade before the war). Some of this was then distributed to countries such as Holland and Denmark.[2] Estimates suggested that Germany imported more than half the total Gold Coast cocoa crop, partly for its own use and partly for re-export. By 1914, Germany had become one of the world's largest consumers of cocoa, second only to the United States, taking an estimated one-fifth of the world supply.[3] The trading company Swanzy reported that at the news of the trade ban in January 1915 to all but allied or neutral states in Europe, all buying briefly stopped in Liverpool, and the price of Accra cocoa suddenly dropped from £40 a ton to only £10 a ton.[4]

Another problem concerned the supply of sugar required for the manufacture of chocolate and of cocoa as a drink. It was estimated that just under 40% of the world production of sugar came from sugar beet from countries directly affected by the war: Germany, Austria, Russia, France, and Belgium. It was obvious that not only would there be a shortage of sugar, despite British government efforts to obtain new supplies of cane sugar from the West Indies, South America, Java, and Mauritius, but also that a portion of the 1914 cocoa crop would have to be stored for a period.[5] Nor would British troops on the Western Front sustain demand. While German troops were rumored to be drinking cocoa—*The Daily Chronicle* proclaimed: "British cocoa for Germany! How we are feeding the enemy!"[6]—the War Office could not be persuaded to introduce cocoa into British army rations. It was said that the British "Tommy" simply wanted his tea, nor were French or Russian troops interested.[7]

There were to be further restrictions. By 1916, a shortage of shipping produced its own damaging effect. The 1915–1916 revival of the cocoa trade did not last, and neither the local British government nor the Colonial Office could do anything to help as the cocoa market suddenly plunged downwards in December 1916, mid-season, largely because of the shortage of ships. African producers suddenly found that buying had practically stopped, and trading firms such as Cadbury now faced the problem that their local storage was full.[8] About three-quarters of the crop had been picked, but only half had been sold.[9] This sudden downturn in the cocoa trade in 1916 was also partly due to a sudden drop in British demand. Large stocks of cocoa had accumulated in Britain by this time as a result of manufacturers' shortage of labor and machinery for processing.

By 1917, the prospects were bleak for Gold Coast cocoa. There were now restrictions on the quantity of cocoa allowed into Britain—with priority given to products judged

---

2. See R. Southall, "Cadbury on the Gold Coast," p. 139.

3. CO memo, Telegram, Clifford to Harcourt, 22/9/14, CO554/21; *Report of Restriction of Enemy Supplies Committee,* 19/12/14, Telegram, Clifford to Harcourt, 11/12/14, CO96/555. R. Southall, "Cadbury on the Gold Coast," p. 139.

4. Telegram, Clifford to Harcourt, 11/12/14, CO96/555.

5. See P. Davies, *The Trade Makers,* p. 188.

6. CO memo, press extracts, November/December 1914, 12/12/14, CO96/552.

7. *Restriction of Enemy Supplies Committee,* 19/12/14, Telegram, Clifford to Harcourt, 11/12/14, CO96/555.

8. Telegram, Acting Governor Slater to Bonar Law, 14/12/16, CO96/573; Manager of the Bank of West Africa to Sir George Fiddes, CO, 22/12/16, CO96/573.

9. Telegram, Acting Governor Slater to Harcourt, 28/12/16, CO96/574.

to be more essential to the war effort, such as edible nuts—and the large stocks of cocoa in London and Liverpool were estimated as a year's supply. By the end of August 1917, the new annual quota for the Gold Coast of 22,000 tons of cocoa (half that of the previous year) had already been shipped. Production was now down to the level of 1912, and only 25% of the crop was placed on the market.[10] Cadbury complained that because they had not been able to ship enough, much of their good quality stock had had to be destroyed. They were therefore threatening to cease operations and to leave the coast altogether.[11] More bad news came from the Ministry of Shipping: the freight charge on cocoa exported from West Africa to Britain was to be increased from £3 6s 6d a ton to £7, which would "tend to depress still further the prices offered to the native producers."[12]

That the cocoa trade of the Gold Coast colony survived the final two years of the war was mainly a result of the phenomenal growth in sales to the United States and, to a lesser extent, to France. The explanation for there not having been even greater dislocation and distress in 1917, when the 22,000-ton quota to Britain was full, was that between January 1 and July 31, a further 25,000 tons was exported, of which rather more than two-thirds was shipped to the United States and rather less than one-third to France.[13] The United States and France between them thus received about half of the total amount exported. It was companies like Cadbury, which did not use these new outlets, that suffered most. Cadbury, however, on the strength of its good relations with the British government, was able to win unique concessions from the Board of Trade for itself and its new partner, Fry. Its 1918–19 license allocation was brought forward to allow shipment of more cocoa in storage from January 1, 1918, and it obtained a new license to ship an additional 500 tons to Britain in April 1918.[14]

These new markets, above all the American market, saved Gold Coast cocoa exports in 1917 and 1918. Governor Clifford saw this growth in demand from the United States as "the most notable feature" of the colony's trade of 1917.[15] A direct trade across the Atlantic, avoiding European waters, developed strongly at this time: the total amount of cocoa shipped across the Atlantic in 1917 was three times higher than the previous year. The United States now took more cocoa from the Gold Coast colony than did Britain. Cocoa exports to the US rose rapidly from under 10,000 tons in 1916, to reach a height of nearly 70,000 tons in the postwar boom of 1919.[16]

But there was to be a nasty turn to this story of trade recovery. As a result of acute shortage of shipping, the French government imposed a ban on cocoa imports, which caused a sudden fall in the trade with the Gold Coast in 1918. Only 2,539 tons of cocoa were exported to France in 1918, as opposed to 9,988 tons in 1917.[17] Even more serious

10. Clifford, confid. to Long, 12/12/17, CO96/583.

11. Slater, memo in Clifford, confid. to Long, 23/8/17, CO96/581.

12. Harding (deputy, Niger Department Section) CO Minute, Slater, memo in Clifford, confid. to Long, 23/8/17, CO96/581.

13. 17,593 tons of cocoa were exported to the United States and 7,991 tons exported to France. Slater, *Memo on the Cocoa Trade*, in Clifford, confid. to Long, 23/8/17, CO96/581.

14. R. Southall, "Cadbury on the Gold Coast," pp. 157–165.

15. Clifford, 1918 Estimates, *LegCo* 25/10/17, *Gazette* 26/11/17, CO99/32/76; also *Trade Report 1917*, 30/4/18, *Supplementary 1*, *Gazette* 21/5/18, CO99/33.

16. For the substantial increase in cocoa consumption in the United States between 1914 and 1918, see Table 5, *Consumption and Prices of Raw Cocoa during the First World War*, in R. Southall, "Cadbury on the Gold Coast," p. 140; and *Blue Book 1920*, CO100/70.

17. *Blue Book 1920*, CO100/70.

were restrictions in the American trade in 1918. In July that year, the United States government decided to revoke all licenses for importation of cocoa into the United States, except a limited proportion from South and Central America and the West Indies.[18] This was partly due to the sharp decline in the quality of the cocoa shipped to the United States. Careful fermentation, a labor intensive practice, tended to be neglected during difficult periods for the trade. The American ban in 1918 finally raised the prospect of ruin for the cocoa trade of the Gold Coast. It was now unclear how the colony's cocoa trade—and therefore also its general finances—could survive. It was certainly fortunate for the Gold Coast colony that the First World War ended when it did.

Prices paid to African producers reflected the unprecedented fluctuation in demand for cocoa during the war, though the dominant trend was of price depression, which was to bring about, as we shall see, both suffering and grievance. Before the war, African cocoa farmers benefited from a price of 20 shillings per sixty lb load (the standard unit of measurement). In September 1914, however, little cocoa was being offered for sale, partly as a result of a very dry season, but mostly because the price had fallen to less than half the price of 1913, to 10 shillings per sixty lb "load." (The futures price had fallen as low as 7s 6d at the outbreak of the war).[19]

It was at this point, in September 1914, that Clifford publicized his proposal to save the industry from "permanent damage" by the government fixing a minimum price for cocoa—of 12s 6d per load. [20] Clifford was able to report in early December 1914, however, that after late rains, the cocoa crop was beginning to come in satisfactorily at prices of 12s to 14s per load—much higher than expected.[21] But far worse was to follow: at the end of that same month, the cocoa price plunged dramatically to only 3s to 9s a load, causing, as Clifford acknowledged, "hardship and discontent."[22] Following the 1915–16 revival of the cocoa trade, the shipping shortage was next blamed for a renewed fall in the prices paid to farmers, from 18s to only 10s a load of sixty lbs. This was in fact the better price given at the railway centers: extremely low prices were now offered elsewhere, such as a mere 2s 6d in Kwahu.[23]

Average prices for cocoa fell so low in outlying areas in 1917 that they did not cover the cost of carriers for the African farmers. Even in coastal towns the fall in prices was dramatic. In Cape Coast, a sixty-lb load of cocoa had been worth 18s in 1913. By 1917 its value was down to 8s. It was estimated by the officials on the coast that an average price of about 10s a load was needed to cover the costs to the farmer of picking, fermenting, and transporting in order to allow him "some moderate profit." But the current price of cocoa in Kwahu was now said to be merely "the price of a cake of soap."[24] As Slater

18. Telegram, Long to Clifford, 13/8/18, in telegram, Clifford to Long, 7/8/18, CO96/591; also Clifford, confid. to Long, 13/7/18, CO96/591.

19. *Blue Book 1914,* CO100/64.

20. Telegram, Clifford to Harcourt, 5/9/14, CO96/547; Clifford, confid. to Harcourt, 24/9/14, CO96/548; *Agricultural Department Report for quarter ending 30 September1914, Gazette* 12/12/14, CO99/29/161; Clifford, confid. to Harcourt, 24/9/14, CO96/548.

21. Clifford to Harcourt, 2/12/14, CO96/550/911.

22. Telegram, Clifford to Harcourt, 11/12/14, CO96/555.

23. Acting Governor Slater, secret to Bonar Law, 28/12/16, CO96/547.

24. *Report of the Central Province 1917,* 13/6/18, CO96/590/331. Also Harper, Furley, reports in Slater's memo re. the cocoa industry, in Clifford, confid. to Long, 23/8/17, CO96/581.

commented in August 1917: "In all probability, local prices will remain dead, or at least uncertain and capricious, during the next cocoa season."[25]

British officials were at a loss to reduce, let alone reverse, the negative effects of the war on the colony's major export trade. Twice they considered trying to fix prices—but they did not actually attempt this. They also contemplated buying up the whole cocoa crop—but decided they could not afford to. Either measure would have protected African producers. In the event, the one major measure they did adopt was to impose an unpopular export tax on cocoa—which appears to have been passed on by the trading companies to African producers in the form of further reductions in prices paid to them. This did nothing to relieve African grievances and only fueled discontent and protest.

It was the immediate downturn in demand and prices in late 1914 which first prompted Clifford to suggest a policy of minimum price fixing. But the Colonial Office viewed expensive government interventionist schemes with considerable caution.[26] The Board of Trade was asked to find out whether lower prices would lead major manufacturers in Britain to substitute British-grown cocoa for that from South America, the West Indies, and Ceylon. But Gold Coast cocoa was already the cheapest on the world market.[27] Also there would continue to be a demand for a proportion of the finer grades and special flavor cocoas such as those from Guayaquil, Bahia, and Venezuela, as well as for "Accra" cocoa. It was not well understood by British officials that manufacturers needed to blend different grades, mixing both fine criollo cocoas from the Americas with the heavier grade forastero amelonado beans (such as "Accra cocoa"), which remained the basis for making chocolate.[28] Therefore manufacturers would never buy only Accra cocoa, however cheaply it was sold. The decision of the Secretary of State for the Colonies in London, that there should be no dramatic government intervention in the Gold Coast economy at this time, was also influenced by a short-lived trade recovery early in the war.[29] There was, briefly, general satisfaction all around. The Secretary of State Harcourt's response reflected enthusiasm and relief: "The Gold Coast is wonderful!"[30] The idea of government intervention was, for the moment, put aside.

Two years later, an unprecedented export tax on cocoa was imposed to protect government revenue. The financial position of the Gold Coast colony had become "very critical."[31] For the first time in the war, London officials expressed fears for the future revenue of the colony and raised the question as to whether all development schemes should not be cut forthwith.[32] The heavy dependence on a single cash crop and a single source of taxation placed the Gold Coast colony in an especially vulnerable position, as many of the colonial officials had predicted before the outbreak of war. The result was

---

25. Slater, memo re. cocoa industry, in Clifford, confid. to Long, 23/8/17, CO96/581.

26. CO Memo, *Trade Conference*, 19/8/14, CO96/548. Fiddes, CO Minute, Telegram, Clifford to Harcourt, 5/9/14, CO96/547; Ellis, Green, CO Minute, Telegram, Clifford to Harcourt, 22/9/14, CO96/548.

27. CO to the Board of Trade, 6/10/14, Telegram, Clifford to Harcourt, 22/9/14, CO96/548; and *Trade Report 1913*, *Gazette* 25/4/14, CO99/29/35.

28. Board of Trade to CO, 13/10/14, CO96/522. Also R. Southall, "Cadbury on the Gold Coast," pp. 10–11; and K. Dickson, *A Historical Geography*, p. 171.

29. Harcourt, draft letter, telegram, Clifford to Harcourt, 11/12/14, CO96/555.

30. Clifford to Harcourt, 2/12/14, CO96/550/911; Harcourt, CO Minute, telegram, Clifford to Harcourt, 2/12/14, CO96/550.

31. Clifford to Bonar Law, 15/12/16, CO96/576.

32. Flood, CO Minute, 23/12/16, Clifford to Harcourt, 13/11/16, CO96/572/840.

that, from October 1, 1916, cocoa exporters were required to pay a tax of £2 10s a ton. Before the war, the Gold Coast government had imposed customs dues on only imported goods, but with imports now in short supply, the government urgently needed to raise more revenue from other sources. There was a precedent in British West Africa: Governor Lugard had imposed export duties in Nigeria in August 1916, including £2 6s 8d per ton on cocoa. In the Gold Coast, neither the Colonial Office nor the local government agreed to the request of the four main cocoa buying firms, Swanzy, Millers, the Africa Association, and the Basel Trading Company, that cocoa stocks bought before October 1 and awaiting shipment should be exempt from the new duty. London officials were unmoved by the merchants' pleas concerning the cocoa trade: "They make enough money on it usually."[33]

British officials did not explore whether such an export tax on merchants would further depress the prices paid to African farmers. In the local African press, the farmers were reported as even more at the mercy of the merchants' rings, now that there was no longer competition with German traders: "On whom will such taxation fall but the poor native producer?"[34] The African unofficials' attempt to limit the damage by making the cocoa export duty a strictly temporary measure during the immediate revenue crisis was defeated in the legislative council.[35]

In 1917, Clifford again raised the possibility of government intervention to fix a minimum price for cocoa. His reservation was the obvious difficulty of fixing a price that would be equitable, given the variety of transport costs. There was also the danger that intervention—if the price was set too low—might deter farmers from bringing as large a proportion of the crop as possible to market. The governor, aware of these constraints, including evidence from the prewar agriculture reports, also feared that if the crop was not properly harvested, long-term damage could be done to the industry with the spread of disease.[36]

There is no evidence for what Agbodeka claimed was as an "unsavoury alliance" between the government and merchants to keep prices as low as possible.[37] It was rather in the interest of both traders and colonial administrators to ensure that the general population of the colony had money in hand to buy imports. The alternative suggestion of the Liverpool chamber of commerce—that the government purchase the whole of the season's cocoa—was seen by British colonial officials as quite impractical on grounds of cost. Clifford estimated, at the end of that year, 1917, that to buy the whole crop, the government would need something like £1,350,000: that is, the mean of the total annual government revenue.[38]

But by August 1918, the prospects for cocoa were so poor that Grey, the leading British unofficial and spokesman for the trading firms, presented another scheme of government intervention to save the colony and to finance the next cocoa crop. His idea was that the combine firms should also participate, so they and the government together would buy 25,000 tons each at an agreed price.[39] However, no serious consideration of this latest emergency plan to save Gold Coast cocoa exports had taken place before, with peace suddenly imminent, restrictions were eased in October 1918.[40]

---

33. Flood, CO Minute, Association of West African Merchants to Bonar Law, 14/9/16, CO96/576.
34. *The Gold Coast Nation*, 21/9/16.
35. *LegCo* 25/9/16, *Gazette* 4/11/16, CO99/31/78.
36. Clifford, confid. to Long. 23/8/17 CO96/581; and 3/10/18, CO96/593.
37. F. Agbodeka, *Ghana in the Twentieth Century*, p. 31.
38. Clifford, confid. to Long, 12/12/17, CO96/583.
39. Clifford, confid. to Long, 1/11/18, CO96/593.
40. CO Minute, telegram, Clifford to Long, 19/10/18, CO96/593.

As trade conditions fluctuated, so did the opinions of British officials concerning the effect of wartime trading conditions on African cocoa producers. In 1916, Clifford appeared sanguine regarding the impact of the export tax. He made clear to the secretary of state his belief (or wishful thinking) that "up to the present time the natives of the Gold Coast and Ashanti have suffered no hardship and comparatively little inconvenience" as a result of the war. They could therefore, in his view, "properly be required to contribute substantial sums" to funds which were ultimately needed to develop the resources of the colony.[41]

This position, however, ignored the evidence. Some African farmers had already staged a protest of some significance: early in the war, they tried to raise the very low prices for cocoa by withholding from the market a substantial proportion of the cocoa crop. Clifford noted that, from the first months of the war, cocoa farmers had begun to "hold up" the crop if a satisfactory price was not offered. Cocoa hold-ups are usually associated with the 1930s and the effects of the Depression, but they began earlier. They were first reported in the Gold Coast in 1908, with a further important hold-up in 1910. More followed the outbreak of the Great War. There were also hold-ups elsewhere in British West Africa at this time, as among groundnut producers in Nigeria in 1915.[42] There were also other, less dramatic, responses to falling prices. Even if they could not force up the price, many Gold Coast farmers were able to compensate for the low fluctuating prices by harvesting more thoroughly and marketing a greater quantity—though only as long as there was an adequate supply of shipping to allow them to export the cash crop.

Clifford and Slater (the Gold Coast colonial secretary) often repeated the claim that the African population of the colony was not suffering unduly from the effects of the war—until the acute trade depression in the Gold Coast in 1917 and 1918. The colonial officials on the coast were relatively isolated from much of the African population. Their main concern was to persuade London to agree to further tax raises to maintain both the revenue and Clifford's development plans. Slater reported on the "gratifying unanimity" of officials and merchants that the cocoa export duty was having no effect on the trade. It was, he said in December 1916, "generally agreed" that the grower was "unconscious of its incidence."[43]

London officials in the Colonial Office, however, were not convinced that African producers were "unconscious" of low prices. The Gold Coast government's claim, that the purchasing power of "the natives" was as yet unaffected by the war, was judged to be "odd" given the sudden drop in payment for cocoa in December 1916 from an average of 18s to 10s a load.[44] Local African comment was less ambiguous: according to the leader in *The Gold Coast Nation* in December 1916, "Ruin stares the producers in the face. People ask where is this going to end?"[45] How such prices affected the different forms of hired

41. Clifford, re. 1917 Estimates, to Bonar Law, 13/11/16, CO96/572/840.

42. Clifford to Harcourt, 1/8/16, CO96/568/541; also *Report of Central Province 1914,* 29/3/15, *Gazette* 6/9/15, CO99/29/8. And see J. Miles, "Rural Protest in the Gold Coast: The Cocoa Hold-ups 1908–1938," in C. Dewey & A. Hopkins (eds.), *The Imperial Impact: Studies in the Economic History of Africa and India,* (London, 1978), p. 154; F. Agbodeka, *Ghana in the Twentieth Century,* p. 95; and A. Osuntokun, *Nigeria in the First World War,* pp. 38–39.

43. Acting Governor Slater, secret to Bonar Law, 28/12/16, CO96/547.

44. Flood, CO Minute, telegram, Acting Governor Slater to Bonar Law, 28/12/16, CO96/574.

45. *The Gold Coast Nation,* 21/12/16.

labor employed by African cocoa farmers was apparently not observed, and certainly not recorded, by local British officials.[46]

Finally, only during the depression following the 1917–1918 cocoa season could there be no question that the cocoa farmers of the Gold Coast were in fact suffering and felt bitter about the new export tax. The relationship between the colonial administration and African farmers came under pressure. The governor took the precaution of reducing the cocoa export duty temporarily, in November 1917, on the grounds that there was a perceived threat to social stability.[47] The cocoa price fell during 1917 to an average of only 4s to 5s a sixty-lb load, and it was popularly believed that buyers were using the tax as a lever to depress prices. Cocoa farmers were reported, not surprisingly, as "aggrieved" that the government was taxing the industry at a time of new restrictions on importing cocoa to Britain and a difficult season of very heavy rains. In a confidential memo to Secretary of State Walter Long in August 1917, Governor Clifford now at last admitted that the economic hardship as a result of the war was "a bitter experience" for the African producers—though he did not as yet admit that the export duty on cocoa was a contributory factor.[48]

It was clear by now that the cocoa farmers of the Gold Coast were not receiving an adequate share of the profits accumulated by expatriate trading companies in the later war years—even though it was always in the interest of the European import-export companies to set a price for imports that was not so low as to destroy Africans' purchasing power. African resentment about the low prices was directed against the European trading companies. *Omanhene* Nana Ofori Atta and chiefs of Akyem Abuakwa had raised this issue on the occasion of Sir Hugh and Lady Clifford's visit to Kyebi in September 1916. They had told the governor that in the absence of definite government measures, it was "beyond doubt that some of the merchants have been taking undue advantage of the ignorance and illiteracy of the native farmers even though African producers in the Gold Coast were riding the storm with remarkable resilience and enterprise."[49] The cocoa growers' resilience had been noted by Clifford before the war when he praised their "calm philosophy" and their ability to remain "undaunted" even when "handicapped by natural difficulties." During the long war period, the African farmers of the colony were to need all "the qualities of courage, energy and patience" that Clifford had cited in 1913.[50]

In another respect, the war brought change to the exporting of cocoa in the form of new African entrepreneurship. A large number of new "native" brokers, or "free sellers," had come into the cocoa market as a result of the considerable reduction in the number of agents used by the main mercantile firms. It was possible for these new African traders to charter schooners to the United States, or pay relatively high freight charges to ship

46. For discussion of this lack of contemporary evidence re. African labor, see N. Van Hear, "Northern Labor," pp. 5–24; and A. Robertson, *The Dynamics of Productive Relationships*, pp. 66–73.

47. Telegram, Clifford to Long, 2/11/17, CO96/582. The Cocoa Export Duty Amended Ordinance reduced the rate from one-quarter to one-fifth of a penny per pound (from 1s 3d to 1s a load), 1/12/17, *Gazette* 22/11/17, CO99/32/74. It was then raised to 2s 6d a load in July 1919. By 1919–1920 it accounted for approximately one quarter of government revenue, and became a particularly important source of revenue once trade spirits were banned after the war, in September 1919. See P. Hill, *Gold Coast Farmer*, pp. 112–113; and D. Killingray, "Repercussions of World War I," pp. 44–45.

48. Clifford, confid. to Long, 23/8/17, CO96/581.

49. Address, *Omanhene and Chiefs of Akyem Abuakwa*, 22/9/16, enclosure in Clifford to Bonar Law, 22/9/16. CO96/571/683. Ofori Atta was shortly to join the legislative council; for portrait, see front cover.

50. Clifford, *LegCo* 3/10/13, *Gazette* 14/10/13, C099/87.

cocoa on them, without the license that was needed for exporting to Britain—though chartering became more difficult once the US entered the war, with many ships now needed to transport American troops across the Atlantic.[51] These new independent African buyers had little knowledge of the product, and they certainly had few storage facilities. Beans were kept in outhouses in "native" compounds, or on open verandas, or even left for months in the open air on the beach at Accra. The cocoa was then stowed "carelessly" by these "speculators" and often reached the United States in an unmarketable condition given that stored cacao easily develops mold as a result of fungal or insect damage.[52] Here was an example of African entrepreneurship that was misguided. British officials were justified, in this case, in their concern for preserving the quality of the product.

For the African cocoa farmers throughout the war period, the hardship lay in the decline in the local price. Despite all the constraints on shipping to Europe in 1917, as a result of the new markets more cocoa was exported that year than ever before, and still more awaited shipment. But the price paid to farmers in the colony had fallen to 8s a load, then to 6s 6d and even to 5s a load of sixty lbs, or about £10 a ton. Yet there was little "price-sensitivity" here: cocoa farmers could not quickly switch to other commodities. Cocoa was not a product to be taken up and then abandoned at will. It took seven years to grow a cocoa bush to maturity. But prices did determine the extent to which farmers harvested and marketed their crops, as the early hold-ups clearly demonstrate.

Another long-term worry for colonial officials, which continued from before the war, was the increasing incidence of disease and pests affecting cacao trees, especially where farms were left untended and pods left unharvested on the trees. There was particular anxiety about the effects of abandoned farms in the periods of depression during the First World War. Wartime conditions—with low prices, and crops not being harvested and marketed—appeared to threaten an epidemic that would permanently damage Gold Coast cocoa and jeopardize its future as a viable and valuable cash crop. However, British officials and African cocoa farmers made different assessments of this problem. In the event, the limits of British competence were to be starkly exposed.[53]

Much of the growth in production of cocoa came from large areas such as Ashanti that had been planted long before the war and had now reached fruit-bearing maturity. One major problem was that farms had often been extended way beyond farmers' ability to husband the trees. As Polly Hill observed, many so-called "absentee" or "negligent" farmers were in fact spending much time traveling in their effort to supervise scattered holdings.[54] Rumors that the cocoa crop would not be purchased at all, as well as collapses in price and the effects of a drought in 1914, all contributed to farms being abandoned on an unusual scale in Eastern and Central Province of the Gold Coast that year. Another problem for farmers was that labor was "exceptionally scarce" as a result of the war with, for example, up to 2,000 carriers sent to the Togo campaign.[55]

---

51. R. Southall, "Cadbury on the Gold Coast," p. 152.

52. *Trade Report 1918*, *Gazette* 5/5/18, CO99/33/34; Director of Agriculture Tudhope to Professor Dunstan, the Imperial Institute, 8/3/18, CO96/595; and Tudhope's *Interim Report on Agriculture*, 23/10/18, CO98/31.

53. E.g., *Agricultural Department Report 30 September 1915*, *Gazette* 11/12/15, CO99/29/105; Clifford, re. 1917 Estimates, *LegCo* 23/10/16, *Gazette* 23/10/16, CO99/31/16; and Acting Governor Slater, *LegCo* 23/10/16, *Gazette* 11/11/1, CO99/31/79.

54. P. Hill, *Studies in Rural Capitalism in West Africa*, (London, 1970), p. 27.

55. *Agricultural Department Reports: 31 December 1914*, *Gazette* 13/3/15, CO99/28/14; and *30 June 1915*, *Gazette* 11/9/15, CO99/29/71. See also D. Killingray, "Repercussions of World War I," p. 47.

Insect damage, other predator damage, and fungoid diseases increased on cocoa farms during the war period.[56] Already by mid-1915, in a period of heavy rains, there were reports (from Ashanti, for example) of "neglected" farms, with unpicked fruit half eaten by squirrels and rats and decaying on and under cocoa trees. In some villages west of Kumasi, farmers were paying "fetish doctors" to drive away the increasing number of insect pests from cocoa farms.[57] There was great concern again in 1917 that the rapid spread of white thread fungus, which was reducing the crop in Central Province and parts of Ashanti such as the Kintampo area, might endanger the whole industry. The rains, which were exceptionally heavy leading up to the 1917–1918 cocoa season, encouraged the spread of another fungoid disease, black pod. Meanwhile, blight caused by insects—capsid bugs such as *sankonuabe* (sahlbergella) and "cocoa mosquito" (helopeltis bergrothi)—was a major problem in, for example, Juaben.[58] The message of neglect was the same everywhere in 1917: "From every cocoa district come reports of gardens standing deep in weeds, of disease spreading unchecked, and of pods rotting unplucked from the trees."[59]

In the early war period, British "expert" opinion was characteristically divided about whether or not there was a serious threat to Gold Coast cocoa. Officials on the coast and staff at the Royal Botanic Gardens at Kew expressed much more concern than did Colonial Office officials in Whitehall. In September 1914, Clifford wrote to London of his immediate wartime fears that if farmers did not receive an adequate price for their cocoa, pods would be left un-harvested and disease would cause permanent damage.[60] Ellis in the Colonial Office was much more sanguine. In his view, cocoa trees would not be injured if one year's crop was left to rot.[61] But "expert" opinion in London disagreed with this. During the war, a steady stream of letters to the Colonial Office from Sir David Prain, the director of the Royal Botanic Gardens at Kew, referred to the unfortunate fate of the coffee industry in Ceylon and urged that action be taken to protect the Gold Coast cocoa industry from "eventual extinction."[62] In the Gold Coast, Director of Agriculture Tudhope strongly supported this view, calling for more staff and even for coercive measures to force farmers to pick the crop, clear away the pods, and generally care for their cocoa farms. Slater too declared himself impressed with the need to act against "negligent farmers," with chiefs, as before the war, still failing to enforce the unpopular cocoa by-laws.[63] British officials believed they faced two equally unwelcome options: to try to use force directly, or to undermine chiefs by putting pressure on them to implement unpopular measures.

Given the evidence and advice at the time and since concerning disease, blight, and pests, it hardly seems fair for Southall to dismiss the attitude of the Gold Coast agricultural department as one of "morbid fear." The spread of disease subsequently—for example,

---

56. See F. Danquah, "The Capsid, Black Pod, And Swollen Shoot Cacao Diseases," p. 71; and Section 1, Chapter 1 re. capsids, black pod, beneficial effect of weeds, etc.

57. *Agricultural Department Report 30 September 1915, Gazette* 11/12/15, CO99/29/105.

58. Harding, PC, *Report on the Central Province 1917,* 13/6/18, CO96/590/331. *Sankonuabe* (Twi) means "go back and pick palm nuts." Tudhope, *Inquiry into the Gold Coast Cocoa Industry,* 9/3/19, CO98/31. And F. Danquah, "*The Capsid, Black Pod and Swollen Shoot Cacao Diseases,*" p. 73.

59. Philbrick, PC, *Report on Eastern Province 1917,* 9/3/18, CO96/591/389.

60. Clifford, confid. to Harcourt, 24/9/14, CO96/548.

61. Ellis, CO Minute, telegram, Clifford to Harcourt, 5/9/14, CO96/548.

62. Sir David Prain, director, Royal Botanic Gardens, Kew, quoted in Acting Governor Slater to Harcourt, 10/9/15, CO96/560/742. See also Sir David Prain to Colonial Office, e.g., 20/9/16, 3/2/17, 8/1/18, in *Miscellaneous Reports 1910–1926, Gold Coast Cocoa,* 10.32. Kew.

63. Director of Agriculture Tudhope, 3/7/15, Enclosure 1, Acting Governor Slater to Harcourt, 10/9/15, CO96/560/742.

the viral disease of swollen shoot—showed that agricultural officers had grounds for their fears.[64] There were good reasons for believing that the Gold Coast's cocoa industry was vulnerable. However, one key constraint remained the same as before the war: the government had no power to enforce any particular farming methods on the African producers. Slater accepted that "no close European supervision is really practicable" given that there were perhaps 240,000 acres under cocoa. Yet he believed that "peaceful persuasion" was insufficient and suggested DCs be given legal powers to impose fines when on tour. This view was echoed two years later in 1917 by Harding, commissioner of Central Province, who felt that fines should be imposed for the neglect of farms just as they were for neglecting upkeep of roads.[65] But this was unrealistic given the local supervision, let alone cooperation, that would have been required to adopt it. Where were the personnel? The whole of the colonial administrative and political service, always short-staffed, was now badly depleted as a result of the war. The new European staff promised just before the war never materialized, and the agricultural department had no locally trained Africans to replace them.

African producers could not be coerced. As Fiddian in the Colonial Office pointed out, "natives" of the Gold Coast could not be compelled to earn money for themselves and the British traders.[66] Tudhope reported in frustration that African cocoa farmers "laugh at my officers" when they offered advice about not allowing pods to get overripe on the trees and about selling only well-fermented cocoa.[67] The African farmers' response suggests that, given the conditions of the market, including the low prices and high cost of labor, they found the British officials' advice quite impractical, even derisory. Production costs—in this case, labor costs—had to be kept as low as possible. This had long been the strength of "Accra cocoa" in the world market: that compared to plantation cocoa from the Americas, costs could be kept low to tide producers over difficult times.

Far from being able to dictate production methods, the very small agricultural department in the Gold Coast was not even able to collect sufficient data on cocoa for a detailed picture of the whole industry. Green and Hymer accuse the agricultural department of failing to note "acreage, investment yields, age distribution of trees, size of farms and institutional patterns."[68] But such a task was quite beyond the numbers of officials available. Criticism of the lack of systematic investigation may be appropriate for a later period, but, as Green and Hymer themselves note, the staff in 1915 consisted of only one administrator, seven European and ten African garden staff, one inspector, thirteen African field instructors, and two technically trained agricultural research officers.[69] It is hardly surprising that the Director of the Royal Botanic Gardens at Kew should urge the government that more expenditure, including more staff, was a worthwhile investment.[70]

---

64. R. Southall, "Cadbury on the Gold Coast," p. 21. See, e.g., "Report on Cacao Pod Disease of the International Institute of Tropical Africa," *The Guardian,* 5/5/98; and "Focus Curse of the Witches' Broom, Report on The Threat to the World's Chocolate Supplies," *The Sunday Telegraph* 10/5/98.

65. Acting Governor Slater to Harcourt, 10/9/15, CO96/560/742; also *Report of the Central Province 1917,* 13/6/18, CO96/590/331.

66. Fiddian, CO Minute, Sir David Prain, Kew, to CO, 3/2/17, CO96/585.

67. *Agricultural Department Report for Quarter Ending 30 September 1916, Gazette* 25/11/16, CO99/31/83.

68. R. Green & S. Hymer, "Cocoa in the Gold Coast," pp. 301–306.

69. *Ibid.*

70. Sir David Prain to CO, 9/11/15, *Miscellaneous Reports 1910–1926, Gold Coast Cocoa,* 10.32, Kew, pp. 75–78.

Colonial Office officials were more realistic. Responding to the persistent demands from Kew, Ellis commented that Sir David Prain failed to understand the contrast between cocoa farming in British West Africa and European cocoa plantations of the West Indies. "Native" farmers in West Africa, Ellis claimed, were well aware of the diseases but "would not endure the remedies." Ellis wrote of Prain, "he doesn't sufficiently recognize the limited extent of our authority over the greater part of the Gold Coast. Any attempt to enforce rigid regulations involving the destruction of infected plantations would have to be made very gradually, otherwise it would provoke serious disturbances" (as of course it did much later, in the 1940s).[71] Comments in the local African press confirmed this view. According to *The Gold Coast Nation*, for example, any such legislation would inhibit cultivation and "kill the goose that lays the golden eggs."[72]

Left to themselves, the Gold Coast farmers did, in the event, harvest and market much of their cocoa. Tudhope, after touring the Colony and Ashanti in the middle of the depression of the 1916–1917 cocoa season, declared the news as "distinctly reassuring": that the whole of the crop (perhaps 100,000 tons) was, after all, being gathered—despite or perhaps because of low prices per load. Yet possibly half of this was withheld from the market and stored in farmers' own houses—to await higher prices—and much was likely, according to the merchants, to be unsaleable. But Tudhope and his officials were nevertheless greatly relieved that the "vitality" of the trees was no longer "menaced," and that next season's crop was no longer "seriously prejudiced."[73]

The agricultural department in the Gold Coast did what it could to improve cocoa production throughout the war period. Agricultural training schemes were introduced to compensate for the lack of British staff and the fact that British agricultural officials had "so little control of the industry."[74] Two West Indian instructors were added to the permanent staff in 1915, but the department would employ African "natives" only as "learners." Six such "learners" were taken on in 1915 (raised to twenty-six by 1918) to act, when trained, as local advisors—a cheap way of spreading agricultural knowledge in the cocoa districts.[75] There was also a continuation of the 1913 experiment at Aburi of appointing local cocoa instructors selected by chiefs.[76] By 1918, there were sixteen in Eastern Province and twelve in Ashanti, though in some cases a wry comment on the instructor is included, such as that he went home to live on his salary "scrupulously refraining from labor, even the proper cultivation of his own farm."[77] Despite staff shortages, six more small agricultural substations were established during the war, including two in the cocoa districts of Western Province, as well as a small agricultural school at Assuantsi in Central Province.[78] But much other work had to be cut back during the war years. There was less itinerant instruction, no government-organized agricultural shows, and few pamphlets, for lack of paper.

---

71. Ellis, CO Minute, Sir David Prain, Kew to CO, 9/11/15, CO96/563; also acting Director of Agriculture, 21/12/15 Enclosure 1, Clifford to Bonar Law, 1/8/16, CO96/568/541; and Ellis, CO Minute, Acting Governor Slater to Long, 17/1/17, CO96/577/45.
72. Editorial, *The Gold Coast Nation*, 6/7/16.
73. Tudhope, Director of Agriculture, Acting Governor Slater, secret to Long, 28/12/16, CO96/547.
74. Tudhope, Enclosure 2, 11/11/17, Clifford, confid. to Long, 12/12/17, CO96/583.
75. Acting Governor Slater to Bonar Law, 11/8/15, CO96/559/654; and 10/9/15, CO96/560/742.
76. *Agricultural Report 1914*, 26/3/15, *Gazette* 30/7/15, CO99/560/742.
77. *Agricultural Report 1918*, 30/4/19, CO98/30.
78. Clifford re. 1919 Estimates, *LegCo* 28/10/18, *Gazette* 9/11/18, CO99/33/82.

More serious was the effect of wartime retrenchment on the agricultural department's research. The first government mycologist, R. H. Bunting, appointed in 1914, had to postpone his investigations into black pod.[79] The department's attempt to interest farmers in preparing cocoa butter and chocolate was not a success. Preparation was difficult, and there was, ironically, no local market for chocolate.[80] Tudhope's inquiry as to whether mills could not be erected on the coast to extract the fat for shipment led the Colonial Office to ask Lever Brothers about the possibility of using their palm kernel crushing factory at Lagos. But it was decided that the presses could not be used for so slithery a substance as cacao.[81]

Nor could the government enforce the careful fermentation of beans that the scientists in London at both Kew and the Imperial Institute frequently urged to improve the quality and durability of Accra cocoa.[82] Even if there had been enough staff to act as government inspectors at the ports of shipment, merchants could still have refused to buy at the higher price that would alone have made the preparation worthwhile for the farmers. As the London official, Flood, acknowledged in 1915, "Owing to the war and the huge freight charges, the price paid to the native is probably so low that it doesn't pay to take any trouble over the crop."[83]

The disincentive, as before the war, was that the farmers were not offered a sufficiently raised price for well-fermented cocoa to compensate for the extra time and labor that effective fermentation required: only 1s to 2s more per load in 1914 and down to between 6d and 9d more per load in 1915.[84] As before the war, there were appeals to the government to intervene to ensure a better price, as for example by the *Omanhene* of Nsawam at the durbar there in December 1915.[85] Although "dry" cocoa survived storage more successfully (fermented for up to a week and then spread out to dry), it was easier for the merchants to buy cocoa of one consistent grade from the middlemen. This did not then require separate shipment, which would have posed a problem, given the very reduced allocation of freight space during the war. Clifford did not rule out the idea of some system of inspection and controls to help ensure consistency of quality once "normal times" returned.[86] But the London official, Flood, hesitated "before adding one more to the wise laws which are ineffective in West Africa for lack of machinery."[87] Flood was clearly not alone in the Colonial Office in his dismissal of Kew as getting "pretty excited over this," and in his support for the laissez-faire view that any controls would be an "unwarranted interference into private rights of trading."[88]

Encouraging cooperative farming appeared to be the most promising form of government intervention to aid cocoa production in the war period by, for example, enabling farmers

---

79. F. Danquah, "The Capsid, Black Pod, and Swollen Shoot Cacao Diseases," pp. 58–9.

80. *Agricultural Report 1918,* 30/4/19, CO98/30.

81. Tudhope to Professor Dunstan, Director of the Imperial Institute, 8/3/18; and Harding, CO Minute, CO96/596.

82. See, e.g., Arthur Hill, assistant director, Royal Botanical Gardens, Kew to CO, 10/9/15 in *Reports on Gold Coast Cocoa,* 10.32. Kew, pp. 23–26.

83. Flood, CO Minute in Assistant Director, Kew, 10/9/15, CO96/563.

84. *Agricultural Department Report for Quarter Ending 31 December 1914, Gazette* 13/3/15, CO99/28/14; also *Report of Committee of Inquiry into the Cocoa industry, Sessional Paper,* 30/10/19, CO98/31; and R. Southall, "Cadbury on the Gold Coast," pp. 63–64.

85. *The African Mail,* 28/4/16.

86. Clifford to Bonar Law, 1/8/16, CO96/568/541; and Clifford to Walter Long, 20/10/18, CO96/593/597.

87. Flood, CO Minute, Sir David Prain, Director, Kew, to CO, 10/9/15, CO96/560/742.

88. Flood, CO Minute, Clifford to Bonar Law, 1/8/16, CO96/568/541.

to get advance funding. There had been a small-scale response to the agriculture department's initiatives before the war, with one instance being the formation of a cocoa producers' association in the Birrim district in 1911 (which included both Kyebi districts, Akyem Abuakwa and Kwahu) and the Larteh planters' union, which negotiated with Cadbury in 1909.[89] Beckman's claim that the first government support for such cooperatives was in the late 1920s ignores these earlier ventures.[90] The conditions produced by the war now appeared to favor such organizations. By the end of 1914, sixty-three farmers in the Aburi-Nsawam district, under the guidance of the agricultural department, had formed an association of cocoa growers, which led to a marked improvement in the condition of farms in the Koforidua and Akuapem hills. In the following year, membership rose to ninety and better fermentation methods were noted in the area. But attempts to set up a similar association in Kwahu were not successful, as farmers were said to be interested only in a better price for their cocoa. But this too was obviously the aim of the Aburi-Nsawam farmers. However, their initial enthusiasm waned as they found that the careful farming and preparation of beans urged by the agricultural department did not impress the brokers, who mostly continued to buy in bulk at a uniform price, regardless of quality.[91]

But Clifford hoped to encourage such cooperative ventures in order to help correct what he saw as the discrepancy, accentuated by wartime conditions, between the profits for African producers and those for European traders. In September 1916, 200 members of the Aburi-Nsawam Association attended a meeting in the hope of grading their cocoa and shipping it direct to the United Kingdom.[92] However, nothing was achieved until the governor, in his controversial intervention into the cocoa export trade (as we have seen) granted a limited number of export licenses to chiefs in 1918. Farmers of the association were then finally able to ship direct a consignment of 700 bags of cocoa, with the somewhat reluctant assent of the local *Omanhene*. The lack of enthusiasm seems partly due to the association being dominated by immigrant farmers outside the traditional structure of society.[93] Tudhope welcomed the association's success, hoping for many "properly constituted unions of farmers" in the future, guided by members of the agricultural department.[94] Although the governor recognized that there had been no tradition of such cooperative farming in the region, he too hoped associations would spread and help to raise the quality of cocoa as well as the price, perhaps by taking on credit functions and by cutting out the need for middlemen altogether.[95]

Pledging—in which middlemen or retailers made purchases in order to resell—became much more common in the case of farms (as opposed to pledging crops only) in this period.[96] African farmers were, it seems, rather more receptive to cooperative ventures at this time because the war had damaged the brokerage system. The usual money-lending

---

89. See N. Edwards, *Cadbury on the Gold Coast,* p. 6. Compare with the Agege Planters' Union, 1907, in Nigeria, in J. G. Deutsch, "Educating the Middlemen," p. 36.

90. B. Beckman, *Organizing the Farmers,* p. 91.

91. *Report of Eastern Province 1914,* 6/9/15, *Supplementary Gazette* 10/6/15, CO99/29/8; *Agricultural Department Reports: 31 December 1914, Gazette* 5/6/915, CO99/28/42; *30 June 1915, Gazette* 11/9/15, CO99/29/71; *30 June 1916, Gazette* 16/9/16, CO99/31/66.

92. *Agricultural Department Report 30 September 1916, Gazette* 25/11/16, CO99/31/83.

93. See J. Simensen, "Commoners, Chiefs and Colonial Government," p. 152.

94. *Agricultural Department Report 1918,* CO98/30.

95. Clifford, 1917 Estimates, *LegCo* 23/10/16, *Gazette* 23/10/16, CO99/31/76.

96. See Tudhope's *Interim and Final Reports, Sessional Papers on the Gold Coast Cocoa Industry 1918–1919,* CO98/27, CO98/31; also Polly Hill's discussion and reference to the Mampong/Akuapem area in P. Hill, *The Gold Coast Farmer,* p. 61.

networks were not working adequately during the latter part of the war and subsequent slump. One sign of this was the petition of Eastern Province chiefs in 1918 calling on the government to set up an agricultural bank. Long-term indebtedness and mortgaging (with advances paid at times of high prices) were to spread rapidly during times of depression, as in the Colony in the last year of the war.[97] And "chronic debt" led to neglect of husbandry.[98] The wealthier cocoa farmers with extensive farms were not the only ones affected. Small farmers and those in marginal areas also suffered. For example, in the Goaso district of Ahafo most cocoa farmers were heavily in debt in the early 1920s, often with crops mortgaged three to four years in advance. The postwar slump following the immediate postwar boom exacerbated, even if it did not initiate, such indebtedness.[99]

The postwar association of farmers in Akuapem did not fit neatly into the pattern of government-approved African farming cooperatives that Clifford had advocated, since their focus was not on quality but on collective bargaining for higher prices. In December 1921, Akuapem farmers started an association of their own to counter the extreme fluctuations in the cocoa price that they had suffered both during and after the war. At the beginning of the season, cocoa was selling at 15s a load in Koforidua but fell to 10s. The farmers then joined together to forbid sales at less than 15s. This cocoa hold-up was so successful that it became for a period virtually impossible to buy cocoa at all in Akuapem. The farmers experienced the satisfaction of forcing acceptance of their price through their own independent cooperative action. As a result of this successful campaign, other hold-ups followed, as in Densu near Mangoase.[100]

The war had revealed just how vulnerable was the industry on which the finances of the colony depended. Clifford, frustrated at how little the administration could achieve in wartime, hoped that a careful review of all these problems would reveal solutions that could be applied once peace had been restored. In 1917, a government inquiry was set up to assess the impact of the war on the cocoa industry of the Gold Coast. The director of agriculture, Tudhope, who had been on the coast since 1907, was given the task in 1917 of conducting a major investigation. Tudhope collected the observations of different interests involved in the trade. He traveled extensively through most of the cocoa-growing districts in the Colony and Ashanti, armed with lengthy questionnaires for members of the mercantile firms as well as African brokers and farmers. By March 1919 he had traveled 2,000 miles, largely on foot and bicycle, and about 220 miles by rail and motorcar. Notwithstanding his being a senior figure in the British government of the Gold Coast, he was well received by local people and "hospitably entertained" on his travels. But he had to acknowledge that farmers were often suspicious and reluctant to give him information, such as the size of farms, for fear that detailed information could lead to the imposition of government taxes or penalties concerning pests or diseases.[101]

Tudhope expressed sympathy with "the unfortunate farmer" in 1918 and was clearly aware of "the extraordinary feeling of pessimism" in the last few months before the Armistice, made worse by the ravages of the influenza epidemic in September, and the

---

97. G. Austin, "The Emergence of Capitalist Relations in South Asante Cocoa Farming, c. 1916–33," *JAH*, 2, 28, 1987, p. 270.

98. J. Miles, "Rural Protest in the Gold Coast," p. 162.

99. P. Konings, *The State and Rural Class Formation in Ghana: A Comparative Analysis*, (London, 1986), p. 62.

100. *Report of Eastern Province 1921*, CO98/38. And see D. Kimble, *A Political History*, pp. 50–51.

101. *Sessional Papers: Final Report on the Gold Coast Cocoa Industry 1919*, CO98/31.

acute shortage of coin. In his full report in March 1919, he concluded that exporters and cocoa buyers did not want any form of government interference in the trade, but that cocoa farmers did want some protection.[102] Tudhope believed that government intervention—to improve methods of production and standardize selling procedures—was needed and would eventually be welcomed by producers. His proposed regulations included fixed buying centers, licensed buyers, and standard measures. But he also proposed fines to discourage what he believed to be "careless" farming that damaged the prospects of all farmers by overextending farms and abandoning farms that were suffering from disease.[103] But such measures were unenforceable. In short, Tudhope's proposed remedies of 1918–1919, like the draft bill drawn up on Clifford's instructions in October 1916, were too draconian in theory and impossible to police in practice. The 1916 bill would have given the government powers to declare a cocoa area infected and have it brought under the control of the agricultural department, while fining "careless" farmers the huge sum of £50.[104]

Tudhope and his department have come under attack, mostly unfairly, in some of the existing literature on the Gold Coast in this period. He might have been unrealistic in his belief that the government had the means to enforce such regulations, but what he wrote is hardly a "sustained campaign" against the cocoa industry of the colony, as Geoffrey Kay argued.[105] Kay suggested that Tudhope's "attack" was part of "a crusade against the industry" conducted by the department of agriculture.[106] This is a distortion. Tudhope was consistent in his concern for what he judged to be a very unstable situation, and in his efforts to save Gold Coast cocoa from "disaster." He believed that only a strong remedy in terms of government action could save the colony's cocoa production.[107] "Sustained campaign" more accurately describes attacks such as these made on him and his department.[108] Tudhope was criticized at the time in the local African press for wanting more controls over cocoa production and for blaming "native" middlemen, yet there was also widespread agreement with his view that farmers needed to prepare their cocoa more carefully and with his acknowledgment of what farmers had achieved in very difficult times.[109] It is interesting that there is no evidence that the local African population perceived agricultural officers as hostile. On the contrary, agricultural officers were praised in the African press for their efforts and their advice and "genuine concern" for people's benefit over the years.[110] Later, too, at the time of the subsequent 1937–8 cocoa hold-up, it was said to be the political officers rather than the agricultural officers who were distrusted by the local African population.[111]

Kay also accused the Gold Coast agricultural department of being "technically inadequate" and of having no better scientific measure for dealing with diseases affecting cocoa than

102. *Sessional Papers: The Gold Coast Cocoa Industry 1918–1919,* 0098/31.

103. Tudhope, *Interim Inquiry 1918, Final Report 19191 Sessional Papers: The Gold Coast Cocoa Industry 1918–1919,* CO98/27 and CO98/31.

104. Enclosure 6, Clifford, Minute, 6/1/16, also Enclosure 7, *Bill for Better Control of Diseases of the Cocoa Plant* 1916, in *Sessional Papers on the Gold Coast Cocoa Industry,* CO98/27.

105. G. B. Kay, *The Political Economy*, p. 12.

106. *Ibid.*, p. 14.

107. *Ibid.*, p. 238.

108. E.g., R. Green & S. Hymer, "Cocoa in the Gold Coast," pp. 299–319.

109. *Gold Coast Leader*, 22/2/18, NP 12/9, PRAAD.

110. *The Gold Coast Nation*, 3/11/17.

111. R. Stone, "Colonial Administration and Rural Politics," p. 134.

the African farmers.[112] Although this was largely true, it omits any reference to the department's continuing efforts to obtain what expert knowledge it could. There were barely any trained agriculturalists on the coast. Officers were always begging for more staff (though, as we have seen, they argued against the appointment of Africans). Because of the increasing pest and fungoid attacks on cocoa, the agriculture department had appointed the first government entomologist in 1910 and the first mycologist in 1914.[113] Officers were constantly collecting data and sending samples to Kew, and they also continued to obtain what scientific advice they could from the Imperial Institute, even during the war. In addition, they experimented both on the model farms and at the botanical gardens at Aburi in the Gold Coast.

Green's and Hymer's accusation that the department was "neither inclined towards, nor capable of, scientific investigation of the best way to grow cocoa" is thus only partly accurate, and certainly misleading.[114] Farmers were advised that more careful farming practices produced heavier yields which were much less prone to disease. This, in turn, hardly merits Agbodeka's judgment that agricultural department officials were aware of the threat to cocoa in this period but "did nothing about it."[115] They took great care to communicate the results of their investigations even though they had no means to enforce what they believed to be good practice. It was, as we have seen, African producers who ultimately determined production and the quality of produce.

The arguments of the paramount chiefs of the main cocoa districts, to whom the bill was circulated for comment in 1916, were unanswerable then and were still unanswerable in 1919. For example, Konyer Mate Kole of Manya Krobo argued that such legislation would discourage cocoa farming and create great distrust between farmers and government, represented in this instance by the enforcing agents—the agricultural officers and DCs. African newspaper comment agreed. They asked why farmers should be "treated as criminals."[116] Rumor spread that the government was planning ways of taking away the cocoa farms from African farmers in order to claim for itself ownership of production. Among Ofori Atta's criticisms was the comment that almost every cocoa plantation in the colony would qualify as "an infected area," given that almost all were subject to some disease or pest. As the *Omanhene* of Akuapem observed: "High prices alone will make the native put in more elbow grease."[117]

Clifford therefore finally decided such a law would be impossible to implement, given the scale of the problem and the shortage of staff. Kay argues that the bill was put aside by Clifford for the purely political reason that such legislation would stir up too much resentment against the government.[118] But this assumes that the colonial government had the power to enforce such measures. Clifford was of course concerned to maintain stability, but he also recognized that the colonial government on the coast simply did not have the necessary degree of control to make such a law operable. But perhaps the dramatic fluctuations and uncertainties that had affected the cocoa industry so severely during and

112. G. B. Kay, *The Political Economy*, p. 13.

113. See F. D. Anquah, "The Capsid, Black Pod and Swollen Shoot Cacao Diseases," pp. 58–64.

114. R. Green & S. Hymer, "Cocoa in the Gold Coast," pp. 307–309.

115. F. Agbodeka, *Ghana in the Twentieth Century*, p. 119.

116. Editorial, *Gold Coast Leader*, 1–15/7/16.

117. Enclosure 9, Konor Mate Kole, 16/3/16; Enclosure 12, Omanhene Eastern Akyem, Nana Ofori Atta, 2/10/16; Enclosure 12, Omanhene Akuapem, 28/9/16, *Sessional Papers on the Gold Coast Cocoa Industry*, CO98/27.

118. G. B. Kay, *The Political Economy*, p. 15.

immediately after the war would now encourage the local African population to diversify by producing a greater proportion of other vegetable products for export, thereby reducing the colony's dependence on the one major crop.

Kay claimed that it was only after the war that the Gold Coast government turned to a policy of export diversification in order to gain more control over agricultural production "by stealth," once attempts to introduce effective regulation over cocoa had failed.[119] But there was nothing either new or secret about British officers' concern to discourage monoculture, as their prewar efforts and discussions demonstrate. The colonial government continued during the war with its efforts to persuade farmers of the danger of relying, in an uncertain world, on selling one export: "The agricultural department constantly advise the farmers not to stake all upon the success or failure of a single product."[120] A similar effort to encourage diversification occurred in other British African colonies at this time, as in Sierra Leone, where farmers were urged to produce rubber, coconuts, and cocoa to reduce their dependence on palm products.[121] But only the Gold Coast colony was so dependent on a single cash crop.

Ironically, the Gold Coast agricultural department has also been strongly criticized by Green and Hymer for persisting in spending time and money on "non-cocoa and in most cases non-economic" crops. They concluded, however, that the search for diversification "would have been justified had it succeeded in finding major new cash crops, but it did not."[122] The colonial officers can hardly be blamed for lack of hindsight. They continued to take a long-term view. Their aim, in the interest of both the international trade and the local African population, was to ensure that agriculture in the Gold Coast remained viable. The search for economic crops, with the help of the Royal Botanic Gardens at Kew and the Imperial Institute in Kensington, cannot be lightly dismissed as being "confused with decorative horticulture" or as mere dabbling with "exotic plants."[123]

In the early war years, British officials' efforts in the Gold Coast were largely concentrated on trying to save a range of agricultural exports, apart from cocoa, from disappearing altogether. But it was more the vicissitudes of the cocoa industry than the efforts of the government that were responsible in the later war period for the brief revival of other cash crops in the Gold Coast, such as palm products, rubber, and copra. Depression in the palm industry grew worse at the beginning of the war, with farmers complaining bitterly in 1914 at the drop in prices. Plantations received even less attention than in previous years.[124] The decline appeared so general that Tudhope feared that the palm oil industry would soon "die a natural death" in the Gold Coast, with exports the lowest ever by 1915, down to one-sixth of what they had been in 1910.[125] He hoped that European factories that could extract a higher grade oil with a high percentage of glycerine, useful in the making of munitions, would halt the decline. But European palm oil companies were hard hit by shortages of staff and machinery.[126]

119. *Ibid.*

120. Acting Colonial Secretary, *LegCo* 17/5/17, *Gazette* 24/11/17, C099/32/75.

121. F. Cole, "Sierra Leone and World War I," pp. 279–280.

122. R. Green & S. Hymer, "Cocoa in the Gold Coast," pp. 306–7.

123. *Ibid.*

124. See, e.g., *Report of Eastern Province, 1914, Supplementary Gazette* 10/6/15, C099/29/8; and *Report of Western Province 1914, Supplementary Gazette* 6/9/15, C099/29/8.

125. *Trade Report 1915, Gazette* 1/5/16, C099/30/1.

126. *Agricultural Department Report 1914, Supplementary Gazette* 30/7/15, C099/29/6; and *Report of Central Province 1915. Supplementary Gazette*, 26/6/16, C099/30/2.

African producers and British officials in the Gold Coast shared an interest in the palm kernel trade during the war. Though cocoa commanded a better price, the greater initial problem was the loss of the German market for palm kernels. The colonial government made reassuring noises but had no practical remedy. In October 1915 the governor and the special committee set up in London to review the West African trade in edible and oil-producing nuts and seeds insisted that every effort was being made to find alternative outlets.[127] In May 1916, this London committee recommended an export duty on palm kernels shipped for crushing outside the British Empire. Their aim was to expand the market for palm kernels in Britain by encouraging the development of a British palm kernel-crushing industry that would be able to compete with Germany after the war.[128] But Clifford, backed by his executive council, argued strongly against such a tax. He claimed (in contrast with his apparent current indifference concerning the effect of the export duty on cocoa) that the £2 levied on palm kernels would be passed on to the producer in lower local prices. As he pointed out in late 1916, the price of palm kernels in Liverpool, at just over £22 a ton, had not changed since the outbreak of the war, but the price on the coast was already between £3 and £6 lower.

There was a British West African precedent: Lugard had imposed export duties in Nigeria on palm oil, palm kernels, and cocoa.[129] With exports declining in palm products and less than half the prewar annual quantity exported in 1915, Clifford feared "the final extinction" of the palm kernel industry in the Gold Coast.[130] Despite the governor's best efforts to have the bill dropped over the next couple of years and the unprecedented unanimous vote against the bill by both British and African unofficials in 1918, the export duty on palm kernels at £2 a ton was finally made law in October 1919—after Clifford had left the colony.

In the interest of both the African export economy and the colonial government's finances, Clifford had at least succeeded in delaying imposition of the new tax until after the war. The duty on palm kernels was subsequently withdrawn in 1922 because, just as Clifford had predicted, it was having a damaging effect on the trade.[131] Here was another example of a complex colonial relationship. Africans and local British officials joined forces (even though unsuccessfully) against officials in London. This was reminiscent of the struggle before the war over the granting of a monopoly of palm oil processing to Lever Brothers. In both instances Clifford felt he had been proven right.

However, in 1916 African producers had responded to the increasing demand for palm products in France and the United States. The revival in the palm trade was partly due to the uncertain prospects for cocoa by the end of that year, but also there were fewer government restrictions on the palm trade than on cocoa and timber. The ministry of munitions in Britain now allowed regular shipments of palm oil to Marseilles, and special permission was also granted to export palm kernels to the United States, since the main European market at Hamburg had been eliminated. When there was cargo room, the

---

127. Steel Maitland (Parliamentary Under-Secretary of State for the Colonies) was chair of this committee, and both Lugard and Clifford were members. Clifford, *LegCo* 25/10/15, *Gazette* 25/11/15, C099/29/101. And see W. Hancock, *Survey of British Commonwealth Affairs, II*, pp. 113–115.

128. See D. Kimble, *A Political History*, p. 52.

129. Clifford to Bonar Law, 8/11/16, C096/572/823; and A. Osuntokun, *Nigeria in the First World War*, p. 37.

130. Clifford, quoted in Acting Governor Slater to Bonar Law, 5/12/16, C096/573/913. The main palm kernel-producing areas were Krobo in Eastern Province, the Winneba and Saltpond districts in Central Province, and the Adjua-Dixcove area of Western Province.

131. D. Kimble, A *Political History*, pp. 53–55.

kernels were shipped on America-bound steamers carrying mahogany logs from Axim and Half Assini.[132] It was unfortunately not possible, because of detrimental storage effects, to ship kernels in the same hold as cocoa. In Western Province, the revival of interest in the trade in palm kernels was also due to the prohibition of timber exports to Britain.[133]

African producers then had to make new entrepreneurial decisions in response to a sudden downward spiral in exports of palm products in 1917, largely brought about by the acute shortage of shipping. Unable to trade enough overseas, many African farmers now looked to the home market. To the alarm of British officials on the coast, the prospects of the future recovery of the palm industry were now threatened by the increasing number of palm trees cut down to make palm wine for sale in the colony (at a time when imported liquor, now largely whisky and gin rather than rum, was very expensive). Felling the trees for palm wine, rather than tapping them, produced a better quality wine and a higher return in the short term. Palm trees were worth 1s to 2s, but the seller could obtain 10s for wine from a cut tree.[134] The local African population of the Gold Coast (as also in Sierra Leone at this time) often chose this alternative use for their palm trees. There was a different perspective here. British colonial administrators in West Africa were anxious about the long-term future of the export trade, whereas African producers were, of necessity, more concerned with making good their immediate financial losses. The generally low price for palm also encouraged some farmers to fell trees and switch to cocoa.[135] Bylaws were introduced in 1918 in an attempt to discourage this practice, with fines of £1 for each rubber or palm tree cut down—but there were no means of enforcing such regulations.[136] In September 1917, London officials suggested a conference on oil palm cultivation in West Africa with representatives from the Imperial Institute and Kew, but it had to be postponed, as the Gold Coast and Nigeria were too short-staffed during the war to spare the officers to attend.[137] So there were no practical steps that the British colonial governments could take and not even a chance to discuss the matter, while the war lasted.

That the British government did not control agricultural production in the West African colonies, and that its role was essentially little more than an observer and adviser, was not well understood in Britain at this time. This was illustrated in the House of Commons in October 1917 when a bland question was asked: whether, in the light of the increase in imports of cheap margarine from Holland, "steps were being taken to acquire the oil palm forests of West Africa."[138] The British colonial government on the Gold Coast had been in no position to "acquire" African land and challenge forest rights before 1914, and was in an even weaker position in the middle of the war, with resources of men and money severely reduced. As Clifford was well aware, "abysmal ignorance with regard to

---

132. Telegram, Acting Governor Slater to Bonar Law, 14/8/16, C096/569. Also, Axim merchants to CO, 28/8/16, C096/569/615.

133. Furley, PC, *Report of the Eastern Province 1916, Supplementary Gazette*, 9/11/17, C099/32/4; and *Report of Western Province 1916, Gazette* 29/10/17, C099/32/3.

134. *Report of Eastern Province 1917*, 9/7/18, CO96/591/389; and *Agricultural Department Report 1918*, CO98/30.

135. *The Gold Coast Nation*, 10–17 March 1917. See also Atterbury, P. C., *Report on Central Province*, 6/4/22, in Guggisberg to Churchill, 14/8/22 in *West Tropical Africa: Oil Palm 1916–1928, Miscellaneous Reports*, 10.2. Kew, pp. 131–147; and Ellis, CO Minute, Clifford to Bonar Law, 22/8/17, CO96/581/591. And compare with Sierra Leone, see F. Cole, "Sierra Leone and World War I," p. 309.

136. *Bye-Laws* 4/7/18, ADM 11/1/713, PRAAD.

137. Clifford to Long, 25/1/18, C096/587/57.

138. Sir J. D. Rees, *Hansard*, 18/10/17, *Gazette* 16/2/18, C099/33/8.

tropical dependencies" was "very general" in Britain.[139] But there was also a lack of data on the coast. Government information concerning production and exchange of the non-cocoa rural economy, as well as details of cocoa sharecropping and brokerage, were strictly limited.[140]

African producers then had to adapt once again to dramatically changing trading conditions. The year 1918—which saw the worst slump in cocoa exports in West Africa, and was therefore an especially serious period in the Gold Coast—saw a sudden unexpected revival in the palm trade. Britain was able to process more palm kernels, since crushing centers had now been developed during the war in London, Liverpool, and Hull. The war had also "rendered a great service to West Africa" since "millions of Europeans" who had previously "only thought of eating butter" were now, because of high butter prices, "learning to eat margarine."[141] Palm oil exports from the Gold Coast, given priority shipping space, rose dramatically in value to over three times the figure for 1917. From May 1917, vegetable oils could only be bought and sold in the UK under license, and maximum prices were fixed.[142] Even more oil might have been exported, but fruit on previously abandoned farms did not produce a very good yield, and there was an acute shortage of barrels or puncheons needed as containers for shipping. An increase in local sales, too, with the purchase of palm oil for food and soap-making, helped reduce the surplus—there being no similar storage problem on the coast, as the oil was often kept in gasoline tins.[143]

Exports of rubber followed a similar pattern to palm products in the war period. Initial depression was followed by a revival as cocoa prices fell and wartime demand rose. On the outbreak of war, the agricultural department continued its prewar policy of giving out para rubber seedlings, but "the energies of the people" were said to be "chiefly centred on cocoa."[144] Much wild or "vine" rubber, as in Ashanti, was destroyed with the extension of cocoa farms.[145] Low prices were still the problem, with an increasing quantity of cheaper, finer rubber being produced on plantations in the Far East: in Java, Malaya, and Ceylon. It was now "doubtful if the indigenous rubber will ever again command a price which will pay the native his tapping and transport expenses."[146] In the Gold Coast, rubber exports fell 50% in quantity and 75% in value in 1914. The few plantations that existed suffered wartime shortages of materials and personnel: for example, in 1915 the Avrebo Rubber company near Axim was having to use palm wine as a coagulating agent for latex because of a lack of acetic acid, and the Prestea rubber plantation, the largest in the colony, was short-staffed, with both European managers called up by the French army.[147]

African producers responded astutely to the dramatic revival in demand for rubber in 1916. The amount of rubber exported from Ashanti in 1916 was over twice that of the

139. *Clifford,* "Recent Developments in the Gold Coast," pp. 243–244.

140. See discussion in B. Ingham & C. Simmons, *Development Studies and Colonial Policy*, pp. 230–240.

141. *The African Times and Orient Review*, October 1918.

142. See A. Osuntokun, *Nigeria in the First World War*, pp. 47–48.

143. *Agricultural Report 1918,* C098/30.

144. *Agricultural Department Report for quarter ending 30/6/15, Gazette* 11/9/15, C099/29/71.

145. *Ibid.*

146. *Forestry Department Report 1914, Supplementary Gazette* 13/5/15, C099/28/2; also *Agricultural Department Report 1914,* 26/3/15, *Supplementary Gazette* 30/7/15, C099/29/6.

147. *Agricultural Department Report for quarter ending* 30/6/15, Gazette 11/9/15, C099/29/71; and *Report of Western Province 1915, Supplementary Gazette* 3/7/16, C099/31/3.

year before, even though it was a particularly bad year for locust damage to para rubber trees.[148] In the Sefwi district of Western Province, whole villages were involved in collecting vine rubber from the forest, while "native" rubber plantations expanded in the Axim area.[149] The war in this instance stimulated production, with good prices continuing in 1917. Companies such as West Africa Rubber Plantations in the Birrim district of Eastern Province reported output up by 100%. Officials were pleased to note examples of the mixed farming they advocated, as in Central Province, where the Scottish Cooperative Wholesale Society was planting rubber trees as permanent shade for cocoa.[150]

But rubber did not escape the widespread depression in the international trade as a result of the lack of shipping in what later proved to be the final year of the war. In 1918, rubber exports suddenly fell by nearly half in value and over half in quantity due to a prohibition on rubber being imported into the United Kingdom because of the acute shortage of shipping space. Increased exports to the United States were not enough to compensate for this loss of the UK market, and exports of rubber from the Gold Coast never rose to such heights again.[151] Prices and quantities fluctuated bewilderingly in the early postwar period, to the point of the product being almost eliminated in 1922, though it rose again in 1923 to around half the prewar level.

During the war, the Gold Coast agricultural department also continued its efforts to encourage diversification by growing copra as an additional export crop. There had been some progress in establishing coconut trees in the Ada and Keta districts in the southeast littoral by 1914, but further west along the coast, in the Ningo area towards Accra, there was less interest. African farmers concentrated on stock, especially pigs, left to roam in the mudholes on the edge of the lagoon and the marshes. "The people seem quite contented with their lot and seem somewhat sceptical of added riches in the shape of copra." Slater, however, was "strongly impressed" with the possibilities of coconut cultivation, as a "valuable second string to cocoa."[152] Unfortunately, the port of Keta had been badly affected by the outbreak of war, because German merchants from Hamburg had previously dominated shipping near the border with Togo. The result was that copra now fetched only a low price.[153]

However, Governor Clifford was appreciative of African enterprise and remained optimistic about the future of copra in the colony as "a very valuable native industry."[154] He was impressed by the great increase in coconut palms that he saw in Keta in September 1916.[155] Clifford believed that the establishment of large-scale production, second in importance only to cocoa, was a real possibility in the long term, given that the littoral was admirably suited to growing coconut trees. The African press praised the British colonial government's efforts to retain a variety of cash crops in the colony with, for example, officers giving out seed nuts and a £2 bonus for every 150 coconut palms successfully es-

148. *Report on Ashanti 1916*, 15/8/17, C096/581/510.

149. *Report of Western Province 1916*, *Supplementary Gazette* 29/10/17, C099/32/3. From 647,982 lbs 1915 to 2,215,973 lbs in 1916.

150. *Report of Central Province 1917*, CO98/28.

151. *Agricultural Report 1918*, C098/30.

152. Acting Governor Slater to Bonar Law, 6/8/15, C096/559/638.

153. *Agricultural Department Report* 1915, *Gazette* 13/5/15, C099/28/14.

154. Clifford to Bonar Law, 5/10/16, No. 722 in *Gold Coast Cocoa, Miscellaneous Reports 1910–1926*, 10.32. Kew, p. 131.

155. Clifford to Bonar Law, 4/9/16, C096/569/643.

tablished in any one year.[156] Although much coconut palm seed distributed in Eastern and Central Provinces failed for lack of care (with a proportion consumed by bush pigs, sheep, and goats) the copra industry in Keta and Ada districts continued to grow in 1917.[157] It was difficult to calculate the amount exported because much was taken to Lome for shipment as a result of the continuing shortage of steamers at Keta.[158]

But copra in turn shared in the general depression of trade in the Gold Coast in 1918, with a major drop of around 86% in value and quantity. France, usually the main customer, took virtually none that year for lack of shipping.[159] For Tudhope, the fall in demand from farmers for rubber and coconut seedlings dismally reflected the "apathetic interest" of "these dull times."[160] British officials tended to blame the African farmers rather than the wartime constraints on trade. Furley, now secretary of native affairs, had to remind frustrated officers that compulsory methods and penalties were not a practical option as there was "no means at hand to enforce legislation ... along the whole coast line."[161] But despite wartime setbacks, copra was established in the Gold Coast colony in this period, and twenty years later it was still making progress in the coastal area.[162]

The fortunes of timber exports from Western Province followed a different path. An earlier prewar collapse of the British market was followed eventually by a period of revival during the last phase of the war due to the expansion of the American market. The boom of 1913 had been followed by a sudden slump in 1914, just before the outbreak of war. A drought meant that the Ankobra river fell too low to float logs down to the coast. Prices also fell because of substantial stocks in the UK after the abnormally heavy shipments of the year before. The war then largely closed down the German market and the wider cabinetmaking trade in Europe, with the result that timber suddenly became "practically unsaleable."[163] Much was left lying in the bush, with the African buyers and cutters in the Axim and Half Assini area especially hard hit. Sekondi was also badly affected because German firms had dominated the lumber trade there in the prewar period. By 1915 the timber industry had "fallen to pieces"; with exports down by around 63% in quantity and value, the depression in the area worsened.[164] However there was some revival of demand for timber within the colony later in the war because of the shortage of fuel. There was no shortage of African initiative: before the war there had been only one small sawmill north of Sekondi, but by 1917 a "native" processing industry had developed in the Koforidua and Tafo areas of Eastern Province.[165]

---

156. See, e.g., *Editorial Notes, Gold Coast Leader*, 28/6716; and *Agricultural Department Notice*, 23/9/16, C099/31/68.

157. *Agricultural Report for quarter ending 3O/9/16, Gazette 25/11/16, C099/31/83; Report of Central Province 1917, 13/6/18. C096/540/331; and Report of Eastern Province 1917*, 9/7/18, C096/591/389.

158. *Agricultural Department Report 1918*, CO98/30.

159. *Trade Report 1918, Supplementary Gazette*, 15/5/19, C099/34.

160. *Agricultural Department Report 1918*, C098/30.

161. J. T. Furley, secretary of Native Affairs to acting colonial secretary, 19/6/18, ADM 11/1/583, PRAAD.

162. Copra production: 656 tons in 1913; 2,000 tons p.a. in 1936–1937. Lord Hailey, *An African Survey*, p. 915.

163. *Report of Western Province 1914*, 6/12/15, *Supplementary Gazette*, 8/4/15, C099/29/8; *Forestry Department Reports for fourth quarter of 1914, Gazette* 27/3/15, C099/28/17; and *Department Report, Supplementary Gazette* 13/5/15, C099/28/2.

164. *Report of Western Province 1915, Supplementary Gazette* 3/7/16, C099/31/3.

165. C. Tsey, "Gold Coast Railways. The Making of a Colonial Economy 1879–1929," unpublished PhD thesis, (Glasgow, 1986), p. 300.

It was the American trade rather than any British government initiative that "stemmed the tide of ruin."[166] In 1916 only fifty logs were exported to the UK from Western Province; a doubling of timber exports in 1918 was only made possible by the number of schooners available to carry logs across the Atlantic. The value of mahogany had now increased, as it was in demand for making airplane propellers, particularly with the depletion of supplies of walnut. As a result, Professor Groom of the Imperial Institute predicted a great international demand for mahogany once peace was declared.[167] But increasingly propellers were made of metal, and by 1923 timber exports from the colony were well down on their prewar value.

However, the experience of war was instructive: it was recognized in London in the immediate postwar period that the Gold Coast and Nigeria were the nearest parts of the Empire possessing large tropical forests, and that they might well be an important resource in any future conflict. Systematic investigations were therefore planned into mahogany, gums, resins, bark oils, and dyes.[168] European demand for African mahogany *(khaya ivorensis)* did finally begin to increase in the mid-1920s, and supply improved with the opening up of sources in the Eastern and Central Provinces following the completion of the Accra-Kumasi line in 1923 and the Huni Valley-Kade line in 1927.[169]

The shipping shortage meant that even supplies of kola, normally the most reliable of the vegetable exports, fluctuated during the war. The problem was that, despite the advantage of being sold very largely within the African continent (mostly in Nigeria), much kola was sent by sea. In 1914, over half the kola produced in the colony was grown in Ashanti, and most was exported by Hausas through ports in Western Province.[170] The upturn in the cocoa trade and the shortage of ships, together with the effect of an import duty in Nigeria, reduced kola exports in 1916 to their low point of the war.[171] Once more, however, African farmers adapted. Kola production rose again during the following two years as cocoa declined. Detailed information on the overland trade is lacking, but in 1917 Cardinall noted a flourishing trade, men walking north through Navrongo with head loads of kola.[172] Kola exports reached a record level in 1918 when a regular steamer service was once more maintained along the coast. By that year, the agricultural department was experimenting with kola cultivation.[173] From 1914, kola overtook timber in the Gold Coast as the second most profitable vegetable export after cocoa. But the gap between cocoa and kola remained huge. By the end of the immediate war period, in 1923, cocoa exports were worth £6m, whereas the total value of kola exports only came to just over £300,000.

---

166. *Report of Western Province 1916, Gazette* 29/10/17, C099/32/3.

167. Professor Groom, Imperial Institute, to the Crown Agents, 7/10/18, C096/594; and *Trade Report 1918, Supplementary Gazette,* 15/5/19, C099/34/1.

168. Memo, "Colonial Research Needed into Forests, West Africa 1921, West African Tropical Forests 1905–1921," *Miscellaneous Reports,* 10.2., Kew.

169. See K. Dickson, *A Historical Geography,* p. 178.

170. *Agricultural Report 1914, Supplementary Gazette* 30/7/15, C099/29/6.

171. *Report on the Blue Book 1916*, 25/8/17, C096/581/582; *also Report on Western Province 1915, Supplementary Gazette* 3/7/17, CO99/31/3.

172. A. W. Cardinall, *The Natives of the Northern Territories of the Gold Coast,* (London, 1920), p. 96.

173. *Agricultural Department Report 1918*, C098/30 and acting Governor Slater to Milner, 8/10/19, *in Gold Coast 817. Gold Coast Agricultural Department 1903–1907, Miscellaneous Reports,* 10.32, Kew, p. 60.

It was not immediately clear what would happen in the war period to another possible cash crop, cotton, already in decline before the outbreak of the war.[174] As we have seen, it had been hoped that cotton would prove a crop suitable for the north of the colony, but the British Cotton Growing Association (BCGA) was already considering withdrawing from the Gold Coast colony in 1914.[175] The experience of the Association since establishing a station in the Northern Territories in 1910 had been that the poor soil could barely produce sufficient food for the local population, let alone sustain a flourishing cotton export industry. Clifford and Slater remained convinced that there were no prospects that cotton would ever be a profitable industry in the Gold Coast.[176] Perhaps only large-scale coercion could have produced cotton exports in such conditions, as practiced in the north of the neighboring French colony of the Ivory Coast in this same period.[177] But such a policy was out of the question in the British territory. The British colonial administration of the Gold Coast did not consider using force—even if manpower had been available.

However, there was concern among British officials about the political effects of abandoning cotton cultivation at this time. Armitage, the chief commissioner of the Northern Territories, saw it as a breach of faith. In the Colonial Office, Flood was nervous over the possibility of social unrest in the north: "We have induced these people to plant cotton and our government in the Northern Territories is so paternal in character that any sudden stoppage could perhaps have serious results in shaking the natives' faith in the 'white man'."[178] Clifford was more positive. The government would continue to help "natives" who grew cotton by keeping open the ginnery at Labo Labo (in a central position on the banks of the Volta) and by continuing to purchase cotton once the Association left the coast.[179] The local cotton industry continued as before but only on a very small scale, in both the Northern Territories and around Keta in Eastern Province.

Given staff shortages, longer tours, and economies, it is surprising that the British officials in the Gold Coast continued so assiduously during the war to seek other possible crops that might one day reduce the colony's dependence on cocoa. In the Northern Territories, sisal and hemp plots and groundnuts were encouraged. Coffee was planted in Eastern Province and groundnuts in the Axim area of Western Province. But British officers were scornful of the suggestion from London that the Northern Territories might be made into a wheat-producing area. There was little prospect of growing cereal, as in the temperate zones. One of the many hazards seen in the north in 1917 was a swarm of locusts, reportedly sixteen miles long.[180] There had been some success with maize, but exports were restricted as a result of the shipping shortage.[181] Another crop suggested because of acute wartime shortages was sugar.[182] As a result of experiments on agricultural

174. CO Minute, Clifford to Harcourt, 28/9/14, C096/548/733.

175. Armitage, quoted in *Director of Agriculture's Report on the British Cotton Growing Association in the Gold Coast Colony*, 10/6/15, C096/558/480.

176. Enclosures, Armitage, Tudhope, re. BCGA in Acting Governor Slater to Bonar Law, 28/8/15, C096/559/710.

177. T. Bassett, "The Development of Cotton in Northern Ivory Coast 1910–1965," *JAH*, 29, 1988, pp. 272–273.

178. Flood, CO Minute, Acting Governor Slater to Bonar Law, 28/8/15, CO96/559/710.

179. Clifford to Bonar Law, 23/8/15, C096/564; CO to BCGA 3/9/15, Acting Governor Slater to Bonar Law, 28/8/15, CO96/559/710; Clifford to Bonar Law, 20/10/15, C096/594.

180. Acting Governor Slater to Long, 14/3/17, CO96/578/174; Enclosure 5, Moutroy-Read, 19/3/17, Clifford, confid. to Long, 6/6/17, C096/580.

181. *Report of Central Province 1917*, 13/6718, C096/590/331.

182. *"Our Food Supply,"* editorial, *The Gold Coast Nation*, 17–24/12/14.

stations with locally grown sugar cane, Tudhope believed that sugar could flourish and urged government action for the often cited reason: "The Gold Coast is too much dependent on one industry, cocoa."[183] But, as the Colonial Office was aware, there was no evidence that growing sugar for export was feasible given the climate, soil, and labor costs of the Gold Coast colony.[184] And no such innovation could ever be achieved unless the colony's African farmers were convinced of its practical value to them.

Colonial officials also supported experiments with varieties of local food crops to improve the local diet, such as cassava in the Northern Territories and onions along the lagoon near Keta, where conditions were said to be similar to Antigua.[185] Rice proved profitable, especially since imported rice had become scarce and expensive. Agricultural officers distributed seedlings in the hope of a future possible cash crop, but it was grown ever more widely for local consumption rather than for export, as in Western Province, where it was especially in demand in the mining villages.[186]

The gold of the "Gold Coast" was the colony's second most valuable export after cocoa in this period, but the British colonial government intervened less to support the export of minerals during the war. The main effect of the war for the mining companies was to slow or stop prospecting and development, thereby inhibiting rises in production and profits. But despite constant difficulties in obtaining supplies and labor, the larger mining companies mostly managed to sustain production levels. Overall, there was only a small reduction in gold output in the war period.[187] And manganese (used in the production of steel) was now an additional mineral exported from the Gold Coast. The mines suffered inconvenience and rising production costs as a result of the war, but with the price fixed by the gold standard, mining companies could not pass on increased costs in higher prices.

The official British government attitude towards the mining companies remained largely laissez-faire. Although the companies continued to seek government aid to ease their labor shortage, especially at times of exceptional demand as on cocoa farms in 1916 and in the immediate postwar boom, they were expected to cope on their own with the inconveniences of the war—not only shortages of labor but also the high price of coal and patent fuel. And Clifford's administration largely kept to the sidelines when local mines personnel clashed with London officials of the Colonial Office. For example, in August 1914 there were strong complaints from mine managers that the Admiralty in Britain had commandeered a steamer chartered by the mines that had been unloading coal at Sekondi. London officials in the Colonial Office were unsympathetic: "If the Admiralty want coal or colliers they must have them whether all the mines in the Gold Coast shut down or not."[188]

However, Ellis did acknowledge that with the annual gross value of gold production at £1.5m, "gold is very useful just now."[189] Companies such as Ashanti Goldfields began

---

183. Tudhope, Director of Agriculture, to CO, 14/2/18, C096/596.

184. Ellis, CO Minute, Tudhope to CO, 14/2/18, CO96/596.

185. *Agricultural Department Reports: 30/6/15, Gazette* 11/9/15, C099/29/71; *Department Report 1914*, 26/3/15, *Supplementary Gazette* 30/7/15, C099/29/6; *30/9/16, Gazette* 25/11/16, C099/31/83.

186. Clifford to Long, 10/12/17, C096/583/767.

187. T. E. Anin, *Gold in Ghana,* (London, 1990), p. 15. And see Chairman of Ashanti Goldfields Corporation, Lord Bessborough, summing up re. the impact of the war at the 21st Ordinary General Meeting, Holborn, 17/12/18, AGC. MS. 24,661.5.p. 34.

188. Flood, CO Minute, telegram, Acting Governor Robertson to Harcourt, 13/8/14, CO96/547.

189. Ellis, CO Minute, telegram, Acting Governor Robertson to Harcourt, 22/8/14, CO96/547. Also *Report on the Mining Industry 1914, Supplementary Gazette* 8/9/15, CO99/29/9.

preparations for reverting, where they could, to large-scale gathering of wood fuel and the use of steam power. But fuel remained in short supply. Anthracite was now scarce, often of poor quality, and very expensive.[190] By August 1916, even the main AGC Obuasi mine was "in a precarious state" because of lack of fuel.[191] Two major companies, Prestea and the Abbontiakoon Mines, complained in 1916 that Elder Dempster (which had had a near monopoly as shippers of coal, silver, and cement since the turn of the century) had failed to adhere to contracts for supplies of coal, and were filling their boats with "more remunerative cargo."[192] But London officials felt that the Elder Dempster fleet, with many ships requisitioned and other ships lost to torpedo attack, was not in a position to carry the full amount of coal needed—and not only by mines—along the West African coast.[193]

Clifford had been accused before the war of being too close to the mining companies. Now, he tended to ignore their difficulties and remained reluctant to intervene. "The war has not adversely affected the output of the mines and labour conditions," he wrote in April 1915.[194] But the mines suffered from the British government ban on the export from Britain of a whole range of products such as lubricating oils and zinc needed for gold precipitation or oil for gas-fired engines. Companies such as Ashanti Goldfields struggled to overcome the difficulties of shortages and the rising costs of steel machinery and parts such as joists, plates, bars, wheels, and rails. Anxiously awaited stocks in 1915 included fuses and explosives, as well as grinding plates and steel balls.[195] Meanwhile, the lack of shipping and government wartime regulations and restrictions affected transport of bullion as well as incoming supplies. Orders came from the Bank of England as the submarine danger intensified to ensure that no more than first £100,000, then £50,000, worth of raw gold be shipped on any one steamer.[196]

African concern, in contrast, focused on labor practices and deteriorating working conditions in the mines. Essential parts became scarce, and such supplies as were available were of poor quality. The British government allowed shell discard steel to be used, but it was hard and brittle. Hacksaw blades, hammers, and drills often broke after only one day's use. "Hammer boys" at Obuasi were discontented with the poor tools they were given, as they were only paid if their job was completed. Cast steel naves did not last as long as the spares formerly obtained from Krupp. Safety was also affected: poor quality iron caused cages to crack. Valves and even nuts and bolts were scarce, and spares such as ball valves and wire nails could no longer be obtained from Hamburg, their usual source.[197] In the Gold Coast, experiments were made with scrap iron balls and firebricks made from local clay, but they were not very successful and cost more. Palm oil lamps

190. Admiralty to CO, 31/8/14, CO96/551. See AGC correspondence: Watkins (manager AGC, Obuasi) to Mann (secretary, London Office), 5/12/15, AGC. MS. 14,171.38.

191. Mann to Samson (acting manager, Obuasi), 8/8/16, AGC MS 14,170.32; and to Watkins, 12/3/18, 14,170.43. See also *Report of Western Province 1916, Supplementary Gazette* 29/10/17, CO99/32/3; and West African Chamber of Mines to Governor, 28/11/16 in Clifford to Long, 8/1/17, CO96/586.

192. P. Davies, *The Trade Makers*, p. 150.

193. Flood, CO Minute, West African Chamber of Mines to CO, 14/3/16, CO96/576.

194. Telegram, Clifford to Harcourt, 26/4/15, CO96/557.

195. E.g., Watkins to Mann, 17/2/15, AGC MS 14,170.33; Mann to Samson, 26/3/15, 14,170.29; Samson to Mann, 24/4/15, 14,170.37.

196. Crown Agents to CO, 24/8/14, CO96/551; Bank of England to CO, 3/8/16, CO96/57; Bank of England to CO, 7/9/16, CO96/576.

197. Samson to Mann, 24/8/17, AGC MS 14,171.42. Also Watkins to Mann, 13/4/16, 14,171.42; Samson to Mann, 21/6/16, 14,171.39; Watkins to Mann, 19/9/16, 14,170.40; Mann to Watkins, 31/10/16, 14,170.32.

were of little use. Nor was the available palm oil much good as lubricating oil: it corroded bearings because it was dirty and had a high acid content.[198] Some alternative sources were found in the United States, but American supplies could be expensive. The West Africa Chamber of Mines was informed by the Colonial Office that little could be done to ensure the importation of urgently needed dynamite from either the United States or South Africa.[199] The mining companies were on their own.

Shortage of skilled and unskilled labor remained a problem for both the colonial administration and the commercial companies throughout the war period. There were the usual complaints from the mine companies about the lack of skilled labor available, and requests for permission to import more foreign labor. In December 1914, Clifford saw no objection to increasing the numbers of skilled Chinese to above the total of the twenty-six who had apparently been working satisfactorily in the Colony for over three years.[200] But the issue was raised in 1914, both in the House of Commons and in the local press, warning of the threat to "native" interests of an unlimited supply of Chinese labor in the mines. Colonial Office officials were also hostile. Harcourt advised against the introduction of such "coolie" labor on the grounds that experience elsewhere in the Empire showed that it tended to provoke local opposition. The possibility of large-scale importation of indentured labor into the Gold Coast colony had been raised in the 1890s and early 1900s but rejected. In an initial experiment in 1896, fifteen Chinese miners had been brought from Kuala Lumpur.[201] A bill to restrict such labor in the Gold Coast colony was duly drawn up in 1915.[202] Meanwhile, European staff were called up for military service. As a result, Clifford was sympathetic to requests from the West African Chamber of Mines and Ashanti Goldfields in 1916 that their employees be released from military duty. With the agreement of the War Office, mines were placed on the list of reserved occupations.[203]

However, the main reason for the persistent shortage of skilled labor was the failure to introduce training schemes for Africans before the war, an omission which was felt keenly by expatriate companies as well as by the coast government in this period. For example, in 1915 management at the AGC Obuasi mine was belatedly instructed by the head office to train "natives" as mechanics.[204] Meanwhile, a number of the skilled African labor force in the Gold Coast were recruited to work abroad during the war. Some were sent with the East African expeditionary force as mechanics and drivers. Also Lever Brothers, after persistent efforts, and against the wishes of the Gold Coast government, finally obtained permission from the Ministry of Food in 1918 to send some skilled artisans

---

198. Watkins to Mann, 13/4/16, AGC MS 14,171.39; Watkins to Mann, 17/4/17, 14,171.41; Mann to Watkins, 9/11/14, 14,171.36; and Watkins to Mann, 20/2/17, 4/4/17, 14,171.41; 13/12/17, 14,171.42; 20/2/18, 14,171.38.

199. Mann to Samson, 6/8/14, 14/8/14 and to Watkins, 26/8/14, 4/9/14, also Watkins to London Office, 28/10/14, 31/10/14. AGC. MS 14,170.28; and Watkins to Mann, 17/12/15. AGC. MS. 14,171.38.

200. Clifford, confid. to Harcourt, 31/12/14, C096/550.

201. Clifford, confid. to Harcourt, 31/12/14, CO96/550; *Gold Coast Leader* 25/7/14; Acting Governor Robertson, confid. to Harcourt, 2/8/14, CO96/522; Clifford to Harcourt, 16/3/15, CO96/556. A. Phillips, *The Enigma of Colonialism*, p. 38. Local opposition elsewhere, see P. Richardson, "The Recruiting of Chinese Indentured Labor," pp. 85–108; and P. Richardson, *Chinese Mine Labor in the Transvaal*, (London, 1982). Law, 24/11/15, C096/561.

202. Harcourt to Clifford, 16/4/15, C096/556; also Clifford, confid. to Bonar Law, 24/11/15, CO96/561.

203. Clifford to Harcourt to Clifford, 16/4/15, C096/556; also Clifford, confid. to Bonar Law, 20/1/16, CO96/565/48; Ashanti Goldfields to CO, 3/2/16, CO96/578.

204. Samson to Mann, 16/4/15, AGC. MS 14,71.29.

and coopers to the Belgian Congo to help one of its associated companies with machinery and containers for palm oil and palm kernels.[205] Governor Clifford was known to be against such exporting of Gold Coast labor. However, Ellis in the Colonial Office commented laconically: "In these times of war when we have to look anywhere for our bread and butter, or rather margarine, we can't be as 'pernickety' about black labourers as in peace time."[206]

Apart from these issues regarding skilled labor, the shortage of unskilled labor in the Gold Coast also persisted during the war period, with competition between mines, government, and farmers. Government call-up of carriers in August 1914 caused immediate disruption in the mines, with reports from the main AGC Obuasi mine of "a stampede of boys into the bush" when recruiters were believed to be near. The camp became "more or less deserted" before European staff could reassure workers that no more carriers were needed.[207] The African miners' reaction tells us much about the supposed "voluntary" nature of government carrier recruitment during the war. Spokesmen for the mines complained to the government about the "2,000 carriers" sent to East Africa in 1916, arguing that Indians in East Africa should have been used instead.[208] But military recruitment took priority and led to the formal suspension in April 1917 of any government aid with labor recruitment to the mining companies, even though there had been government assistance in 1916 for both gold and manganese mines.[209] The mines companies were also competing, as usual, with demands for labor on cocoa farms. This was a particular problem in the wartime boom period in cocoa production during the 1915–1916 cocoa season.[210] However, as cocoa prices slumped in the Gold Coast to their lowest levels ever in 1917 and 1918, the shortage of labor in the Gold Coast eased—but not for long. Labor again became extremely scarce in late 1918 and 1919 as a result of the ravages of the 1918 influenza epidemic followed by the demands of the postwar boom.[211]

It was in the First World War period that African workers began to combine in organized protests in the Gold Coast. Low rates of pay were the major reason for labor problems in the mines. Miners on strike at Obuasi in 1917 and 1919 complained that most rates had changed very little between 1913 and 1918 despite the high rise in the cost of living during the war.[212] Pay had increased only marginally for the lowest paid miners, such as a rise of 3d for surface workers.[213] Continuing "disturbances," culminating in the Tarkwa strike in

---

205. Ministry of Food to Long, 14/5/18, C096/595.

206. Ellis, CO Minute, Ministry of Food to Long, 14/5/18, CO96/595.

207. Samson to Mann, 11/8/14, AGC. MS 14,171.36; Mann to Samson, 26/8/14, 14,171.28.

208. West African Chamber of Mines to Bonar Law, 1/8/16, C096/576. Gold Coast war service: 11,487 (WAFF: 9890; Carrier Corps for E. Africa: 400; Motor Transport: 1,197). From "Report on the Combatant Manpower of the Native Races of British West Africa 1923," in D. Killingray, *Repercussions of World War I in the Gold Coast*, p. 46.

209. Letters Fanti Consolidated Mines Ltd and Abontiakoon Mine, Tarquah, to Armitage, CC, NT, 1916–17, ADM/56/1/84, PRAAD. And see Section 1, Chapter 1.

210. See, e.g., *Agricultural Department Reports: for quarter ending 31/12/15, Gazette* 18/3/16, C099/30/23; *for quarter ending 30/6/16, Gazette* 16/9/16, C099/31/66; *and Agricultural Department Report 1918,* CO98/30.

211. R. Thomas, "Forced Labor in British West Africa," pp. 89–92. Also, *Consulting Engineers' Report,* 30/9/17, AGC. MS 24,661.5; West African Chamber of Mines to CO, 1/8/16 and CO Minute, CO96/576; Clifford, *LegCo* 28/10/18, *Gazette* 9/11/18, CO99/33/82; and R. Southall, "Cadbury on the Gold Coast," pp. 124–125.

212. See D. Killingray in M. Page (ed.), *Africa and the First World War,* p. 165.

213. *Report on the Mines 1913, Gazette* 14/11/14, CO99/28/147; *Report on the Mines 1918,* CO98/30.

1920, led to agreements to pay a further 3d to the lowest paid.[214] But labor rates in the mines continued to be well below average agricultural wages. The average wage per day at the end of the war period was 5s for a miner and 15s for a cocoa carrier.[215] Furthermore, African miners lost jobs when peripheral mines were shut down. In 1918, some mining companies in severe difficulties, such as the Abosso gold mining company, threatened permanent closure and were referred to a committee of the Treasury set up to investigate relief to low grade gold mines.[216]

The mines were able to continue recruitment, despite low wages and poor conditions, because of the very low rates paid generally in the Gold Coast for unskilled labor from the north of the territory. The Colony and Ashanti were heavily dependent on migrant labor, which accounted for nearly half the mines labor force of 19,000 in 1917.[217] Unskilled labor in Ashanti in 1917 was mainly supplied by northerners, whose pay at the rate of 1s a day plus 3d for subsistence had remained unchanged since 1911. Such low rates explain why laborers needed for work on the roads were said "to come and go at their own convenience."[218] Army pay, also at 1s to 1s 3d per day, was below pay to miners and police.[219] But all these rates were above the standard labor rate in the Northern Territories, where carriers and other laborers were still only paid 6d a day in 1917. This is lower than the figure of 9d a day given by Kimble as the lowest wage for general laborers in government employment in the Gold Coast at this time.[220] Not surprisingly, such northern laborers were said to be "increasingly difficult to obtain."[221] This was one major reason for the number of northerners recruited into the GCR of the WAFF (The Gold Coast Regiment of the West Africa Frontier Force), the constabulary, the police—and the mines.

The mines companies' preferred solution for solving their labor problem was, as before the war, to import cheap labor from the Northern Territories—or from other colonies nearby—rather than to try to attract local labor by improving wages and conditions. Before the war about a third of mining labor had been of foreign origin.[222] The immediate labor problem for some mines was eased in 1916 by the lifting of the ban on recruitment from Togo. Thanks partly to the efforts of the governor, a large contingent from Lome as well as 400 northerners from Tamale were brought in to work the manganese deposits in the Abbontiakoon mines in 1916. Thousands of Togolese were also working on farms in Eastern Province by 1917.[223] However, the acute shortage of labor in early 1919 after the influenza epidemic led the Nigerian government to refuse the Gold Coast gold mines permission for recruitment, for lack of workers for the Nigerian tin mines. Also Colonial

214. J. Crisp, *The Story of an African Working Class*, pp. 44–46.

215. See *Gold Coast Handbook 1923.*

216. Abosso Gold Mining Company to CO, 28/10/16, 21/10/18, CO96/596.

217. J. Crisp, *The Story of an African Working Class*, p. 42.

218. *Report on Ashanti 1917,* Clifford to Long, 13/6/18. C096/590/329.

219. See D. Killingray, "Repercussions of World War I," p. 49.

220. D. Kimble, *A Political History*, p. 45.

221. *Report on the Northern Territories 1917,* Clifford to Long 1/7/18, C096/591/377.

222. See R. Szereszewski, *Structural Change in the Economy of Ghana 1891–1911,* (London, 1965), p. 56; and N. van Hear, "Northern Labor," p. 34.

223. Ford, manager Abbontiakoon Mine, to colonial secretary Gold Coast, 2/9/16, Clifford to Bonar Law, 2/10/16, C096/571/709. *Trade Reports* at Kpeve, cited in I. Sutton, "Labor in Commercial Agriculture in Ghana," p. 478.

Office officials advised against recruiting in Sierra Leone after the heavy losses among the large number of carriers sent from Sierra Leone to East Africa.[224]

The main fall in the output and value of gold came immediately after the end of the war. Materials were still in short supply and expensive, and labor very hard to obtain, especially during the sudden postwar cocoa boom of 1919 and 1920. The gold mining industry was always badly affected by the attraction of higher labor rates in the cocoa trade. Now there was also a new demand for labor on postwar government projects such as railway building. Some idea of how serious a problem this had become can be seen from the decreasing number of African miners employed in the 1914–1919 period. In 1914 the daily average total "native labour force" of the Gold Coast mines companies had been 17,400 workers. This fell to 10,759 in 1918, and to only 8,939 in 1919. By this time gold accounted for a very much smaller proportion of the total exports of the colony than before the war: cocoa had risen to 76% and gold fallen to just 13% of the total.[225]

However, mining output increased overall during the war in that a new mineral, manganese, an essential alloy used for hardening steel, began to be exported from the colony for the first time. By 1923 it had overtaken kola as the third most valuable export after cocoa and gold. Kitson, the colony's very able and energetic director of geological surveys, had in May 1914 discovered large deposits of manganese near Tarkwa, about thirty-three miles from Sekondi. (It was also Kitson who, during the First World War, suggested a dam across the Volta to generate electricity for mines and railways and who found industrial diamonds in the Birrim district in 1919.)[226] Analysis by the Imperial Institute in London proved that the Tarkwa manganese was of high grade (50–55% purity). However, the development of manganese was not immediate: in July 1915 the Colonial Office was told by the Ministry of Munitions that Britain already had sufficient manganese for steel manufacture, including an ample supply from India. Nor was the British Government immediately interested in the "fair quantities" of good quality bauxite, used to produce aluminum, that Kitson had found on the Kwahu plateau in Eastern Province. However, by the summer of 1918, manganese had become an important new export from the Gold Coast. The Colonial Office had begun to show interest in the manganese and considered a government takeover of the Darwen Mostyn company that had successfully begun mining operations. The deposits were not only conveniently close to the railway, but also more extensive and of a higher grade ore than had been previously supposed.[227] By April 1918 new rail track was being completed to link into the main line, and output had reached 6,000 tons a month, with a large quantity of 15,000 tons of ore awaiting shipment.

Wartime demands in Britain were by now urgent for whatever manganese could be shipped. No one could know that the war would be over before the end of the year—and manganese was therefore given priority shipping space. The constraint was, again, the shortage of shipping tonnage. The only other manganese deposits worked on any scale in the British Empire were

---

224. Ellis, Harding, CO Minute, Clifford, confid. to Milner, 26/3/19, C096/598.

225. *Trade Report 1919,* CO98/32.

226. Enclosure, *Report by Kitson, Director of Geological Survey of the Gold Coast,* 27/7/15, Acting Governor Slater, confid. to Bonar Law, 4/9/15, CO96/560; also *Report of Geographical Survey 1914* in Acting Governor Slater, confid. to Bonar Law, 8/9/15, CO96/560; and Ministry of Munitions to CO, 28/7/15, CO96/563. See *Geological Survey Report* in Clifford to Long, 10/4/17, CO96/579; and P. Greenhalgh, *West African Diamonds 1919–1983; An Economic History,* (London, 1985), p. 3.

227. Darwen Mostyn & Co. to CO, 8/3/16, CO96/576; Wassaw Exploratory Syndicate to CO, 2/10/16, CO96/571.

in India, and the Gold Coast had the advantage in quality and freight charges. By this time, 1918, the Ministry of Munitions revealed that British stocks of manganese ore and ferro-manganese were less than 50% of the amount considered necessary (with consignments from India lower than expected), and that there would have been "trouble" but for the West Africa supply.[228] In 1916, around 4,000 tons of manganese were exported from the Gold Coast. By 1918, this had risen to over 33,000 tons. Despite startling fluctuations in the postwar boom and slump, manganese exports had risen to over four times their 1918 level by 1923.

There were not the same labor recruitment problems in these open cast manganese mines. The less demanding and less dangerous conditions of work, as later in the diamond mines, attracted labor away from the gold mines.[229] This confirms (as London officials had warned before the war) that, as well as rates of pay, conditions of work needed to be improved in the gold mines for the companies to obtain the numbers of African miners they required. By the mid-1930s, the Gold Coast had become the third largest manganese producing country in the world, after the Soviet Union and India.[230] The war period had not only increased the contribution of a new mineral, manganese, to the exports of the colony but also brought the prospect that others, bauxite and industrial diamonds, would follow suit.

The wartime labor shortage in the mines softened the Gold Coast government's attitude to greatly increased immigration into the colony. Though they were officially committed to preventing immigration, unofficially they welcomed its contribution to easing the labor problem in the colony. Nor was such immigration a new phenomenon. Before the war, immigrants entered from German territory into the Gambaga district in the northeast province of the Northern Territories in 1911 and 1913 to avoid forced labor and to find seasonal agricultural work. Others from French territory crossed into the northwest province of the Northern Territories in 1911 and 1913 to avoid heavy taxes, and into the southwest of the Colony in May 1914 to avoid forced labor.[231] Before the war, British officials, both on the coast and in London, had been sympathetic to immigrants seeking to enter British territory to escape taxes, forced labor, or military service—although it had not been thought advisable, in view of maintaining good relations with neighboring European governments, to encourage such immigration in any way. This remained official policy during the war. But it had already been noted by the Colonial Office before the outbreak of war that immigrants were a useful source of labor for the Gold Coast colony.[232]

Immigration into the Gold Coast grew in the war years, provoked by French conscription. This immigration was on a scale that was impossible to police, even though DCs were instructed to cooperate with French authorities across the frontier, as in Enchi in February 1916.[233] Some Africans also escaped across frontiers to avoid recruitment on the British

---

228. Telegram, Clifford to Long, 8/7/18, CO96/591; Ministry of Munitions to CO, 25/7/18, CO96/595.

229. T. E. Anin, *Gold in Ghana,* p. 16.

230. By 1930 production had reached 420,000 tons. See R. Dumett, "Africa's Strategic Mineral During the Second World War," *JAH,* 26, 4, 1985, p. 400.

231. *Report on the Northern Territories 1911,* Thorburn to Harcourt, 29/7/12, C096/519/322; *Report on Eastern Province 1912, Gazette* 11/10/13, C099/25/85; *Intelligence Reports,* Clifford, secret to Harcourt, 18/6/13, C096/531; 2679/13 CO96/536; 22/5/14, C096/544. Also Clifford, dispatch to Harcourt, *Trek through Ashanti January to March 1914,* 12/3/14, C096/746. And A. Asiwaju, "Migrations as Revolt: The Example of the Ivory Coast and the Upper Volta before 1945," *JAH,* XVII, 4, 1976, pp. 577–594.

232. Flood, CO Minute, Clifford, dispatch to Harcourt, *Tour of Ashanti 1914,* 12/3/14, CO96/746.

233. Flood, CO Minute, *Intelligence Report,* Clifford, secret to Bonar Law, 12/2/16, C096/565.

side (in Navrongo-Zuarungu district in the northeast province and in Lawra in the northwest province of the Northern Territories), but the exodus from British Africa was small in comparison with the influx. It was also small in comparison with the scale of emigration from carrier recruitment in Sierra Leone in 1915 and 1917.[234]

The scale and severity of conscription in British territories was in marked contrast with the much greater scale and severity of the French policies. The French experience persuaded the British recruiter Colonel Haywood that conscription (introduced in Britain itself in 1916) was inadvisable in the Gold Coast, as it could threaten the stability of the colony. There were reports of a serious and widespread revolt being suppressed with "the utmost severity" in the northwest of the French-held Ivory Coast in March 1916 as a result of forced recruitment.[235] By June 1916 smuggling was said to have practically stopped across French frontiers because of the danger for the smugglers of being caught up in the French conscription drive. Those from the Gold Coast who needed to cross the border now applied to local DCs for certificates of nationality. Towards the end of the year, the French closed roads connecting with Western Province to try to prevent locals from escaping across the frontier into British territory.[236] Officially, the British government in Accra acceded to the request of the Governor General of French West Africa to pass ordinances under which any person crossing into Ashanti or the Northern Territories was liable to arrest and deportation.[237] But there were neither the means nor the incentive to enforce such laws.

With immigration from neighboring French colonies rising sharply in 1917, it was clearly impossible for DCs and members of the west frontier preventative service to patrol the whole border with the Ivory Coast. It was very difficult, often impossible, to identify immigrants. For example, in heavily forested areas new arrivals easily mingled with the locals and were often of the same ethnic group. Arrivals from across the Ivory Coast frontier who owed allegiance to the paramounts of Sefwi Aowin and Beyin were said to have been given a warm welcome when they arrived in the Gold Coast.[238] The DC in the Aowin district of Western Province estimated that there were as many as 12,000 to 15,000 refugees in the south and about 300 in the north of his district in early 1917. Some were old men fleeing fines and imprisonment for supposedly concealing sons from conscription.[239] Asiwaju's figures only refer to the Assinie cercle where, according to the French, over 12,000 crossed the frontier into the Gold Coast in 1916–17. But Kodiale Kassy, the paramount of Assinie, estimated 18,000 fled from that cercle alone.[240] The official total of 18,900 refugees from the Ivory Coast by June 1917 therefore appears to be a considerable underestimate. [241] Refugees from French areas listed a whole range of complaints against French authorities, from forced conscription to forced labor without pay; arbitrary arrest

---

234. R. Thomas, "Military Recruitment," pp. 77–79; D. Killingray, "Repercussions of World War I," p. 53; F. Cole, "Sierra Leone and World War I," pp. 64–68, 114; D. Killingray & J. Matthews, "Beasts of Burden," p. 12.

235. *Intelligence Report,* Clifford, secret to Bonar Law, 19/5/16, C096/566.

236. *Intelligence Report,* 30/6/16, Clifford, secret to Bonar Law, 15/8/16, C096/569; and *Intelligence Report,* Acting Governor Slater, secret to Bonar Law, 29/11/16, C096/573.

237. *Ashanti Ordinance 9 1915,* 29/12/15, Clifford to Bonar Law, 10/1/16, C096/565/23; also *Northern Territories Ordinance 6 1915,* Clifford to Bonar Law, 10/1/16, C096/565/22.

238. Clifford, confid. to Long, 3/5/17, CO96/576.

239. Report, Maxwell, PC Western Province, 9/2/17, Acting Governor Slater, confid. to Long, 15/2/17, CO96/578.

240. A. Asiwaju, "Migrations as Revolt," p. 590.

241. Clifford, confid. to Long, 26/6/17, CO96/580.

and imprisonment without trial; "heavy and humiliating labour for chiefs"; and a range of high direct taxes such as the poll tax, the tax on logs, and requisitioning. [242]

Slater appreciated that any large-scale forcible repatriation at this time could incite "grave local disturbances" and also damage Colonel Haywood's "voluntary" recruitment drive in the Gold Coast between January and April 1917. Meanwhile, such immigrants provided a very useful source of labor in the Gold Coast. So there was more than one reason for the government's reluctance to make much effort to send immigrants back—despite, to Governor Clifford's irritation, the increasingly imperious tone of the lieutenant governor of the Ivory Coast. The French colonial administration of Upper Volta (formerly French Soudan, now Burkina Faso) was also said to give "regular indignant attention" to the flight of subjects across the frontier to the Gold Coast.[243]

As the French realized, chiefs on the British side of the frontier were benefiting from the influx of young men.[244] The colonial government also benefited. Labor employed by the PWD on roads in the Colony in February 1917 was largely from French colonies.[245] Maxwell, commissioner of Western Province, wanted more inhabitants for the west of the Colony, a region that had never been densely populated, as the mines had taken most of the young men. He sought permission to settle immigrants in new villages along the line of pioneer roads, with land to farm, thus providing labor for roads as well as increasing local food production.[246] No official sanction could be given, but that did not prevent arrivals from providing a welcome injection of unofficial labor. Hundreds more refugees entered the colony early in the following year, 1918. Relatively few were repatriated, despite Clifford finally being instructed by London in April 1918 to frame a deportation ordinance for the whole colony.[247] As Crowder knowingly pointed out, the only sure way the British could have discouraged this immigration effectively was by a recruitment policy to match that of the French.[248]

Colonial Office officials agreed with Clifford that the British were not bound by treaty to send immigrants back, but they were uneasy about the problem of not appearing to cooperate with their wartime ally. There was also awareness that major decisions soon needed to be made with the French concerning the long-term future of the German colonies, Togo and Cameroon.[249] Ellis acknowledged the desperate need of the French, by 1917, for more men, but the result of the conscription drives was that "several Gold Coast officers have told me the natives hate the French more than they do the Germans."[250]

---

242. Acting Governor Slater, confid. to Long, 16/4/17, C096/579, For strong qualification of the "voluntary" nature of recruitment, with chiefs expected to provide manpower, see R. Thomas, "Military Recruitment in the Gold Coast," pp. 57–59, and J. L. Atterbury, *Interview with Emigrants,* 22/2/17, Enclosure 3, Clifford, confid. to Long, 3/5/17, CO96/576.

243. J. Gregory, "Review of J. Marchal, Chronique d'un Cercle de l'AOF Recueil d'Archives du Poste de Ouahiougya (Haute Volta) 1908–1941 (Paris, 1980)," *JAH,* 24, 3, p. 422. Also D. Cordell & J. Gregory, "Labor Reservoirs and Population: French Colonial Strategies in Koudougou, Upper Volta 1914–1939," *JAH,* 23,1982.

244. French Ambassador to FO, 21/4/17, FO to CO, 25/4/17, C096/584.

245. Acting Governor Slater to Long, 7/2/17, C096/578/103.

246. Report, Maxwell, PC Western Province, 9/2/17, Acting Governor Slater, confid. to Long, 15/2/17, C096/578.

247. Clifford, confid. to Long, 19/8/18, C096/592.

248. M. Crowder, *West Africa Under Colonial Rule*, p. 261.

249. See B. Digne, *Imperialism's New Clothes. The Repartition of Tropical Africa 1914–1919,* (New York, 1990).

250. Ellis, CO Minute, Clifford, confid. to Long, 29/6/17, CO96/580.

With the French Western Front in Europe coming under renewed German pressure, French recruitment intensified in 1917 and early 1918. In the Cercle du Mossi (Upper Volta), French demands were listed as 10,000 men; groundnuts, pepper, rice, and corn from each village; and donkeys to convey food for the troops.[251] This was the context for the British Foreign Office letter to the French ambassador in 1917 that included the smug statement that any forcible expulsion of immigrants from the Gold Coast would be "contrary to the spirit in which the colony is administered."[252] Despite the ambassador's reply that an amnesty for migrants from the Ivory Coast had been announced several months before, the British solution was to do nothing (except enjoy the benefits of the extra labor).[253] A formal British assurance was given in the finest tradition of civil service obfuscation: the Gold Coast government would always assist the French, but at present nothing could be done to add to the efforts already being made.[254]

Overall, the Gold Coast government played a very limited role in ensuring that the colony's export trade survived wartime upheavals—especially concerning the loss of ships and markets. But from the perspective of African producers, the colonial government in some respects played too active a role, exacerbating difficult conditions by imposing extra tax burdens and threatening to interfere in agricultural production. The British impositions of high taxes (including, for the first time, export taxes) and intervention in the form of trading regulations and shipping licenses were certainly unprecedented. Such actions fed African disillusionment and grievance—but so did the government's inability to normalize trading conditions. Overall, Africans tended not to welcome the few achievements of which the British colonial government proved capable.

Meanwhile, the British colonial administrators' attempts to steer Africans away from monoculture were neutralized by the farmers' own estimates as to what was in their best interests. The British were revealed as lacking the means to enforce what they believed to be best practice. Despite the major wartime fluctuations in demand and price—and official promptings—cocoa remained by far the predominant vegetable cash crop. For the British, the war offered an opportunity to persuade Gold Coast farmers to diversify, and encouraged by the governor, officials continued the search for new export crops. Boahen's statement that during the colonial period each African colony "was made to produce a single cash crop or two, and no attempts were made to diversify the agricultural economy," is not borne out by evidence for the Gold Coast at this time.[255] Nor is his contrasting comment that, in the Gold Coast, it was Guggisberg in the 1920s who was "the first to realize the dangers of a mono-crop economy and to attempt to do something about it."[256] Green and Hymer also misleadingly give the credit to Guggisberg rather than Clifford.[257]

Conditions brought about by the First World War, above all the lack of ships to transport produce, affected all the main vegetable exports: palm oil, palm kernels, rubber, timber, kola, and copra, as well as cocoa. But in the event, and despite the British colonial officials'

---

251. Intelligence report, 31/3/18, Clifford, secret to Long, 28/6/18, C096/590.
252. FO to the French ambassador, 9/8/17, C096/580.
253. French ambassador to FO, 18/10/17; FO to CO, 23/10/17, C096/584.
254. Read, CO Minute, Clifford, secret to Long, 28/6/18, CO96/590.
255. A. Boahen, *African Perspectives on Colonialism*,(Baltimore, 1987), p. 101.
256. A. Boahen, *Ghana: Evolution and Change*, p. 112.
257. R. Green & S. Hymer, "Cocoa in the Gold Coast," p. 312.

best efforts to avoid the creation of a monoculture, the war only briefly slowed the forward march of cocoa, the most resilient of the vegetable products in terms of supply and demand. By 1920, cocoa exports had risen to 83%, the highest proportion to date of the total exports of the colony. All other crops formed a minuscule proportion of total vegetable exports. Even so, the unnerving experience of the Great War (and subsequently of the Depression), with sharp fluctuations in demand and price for cocoa exports and the exposure of how vulnerable the undiversified economy could be, was to encourage a much bolder and more interventionist government policy, such as marketing boards, in the next major conflict in the early 1940s.

It is clear that although some effects of the war were similar in each of the four British West African territories, there were also effects that were unique to the Gold Coast. All the British West African colonies, for example, suffered in the war period from reduction in shipping, the loss of markets, the high price of imports, manpower diverted to serve war needs, the reduction of public works, and the spread of major epidemics. But whereas Nigeria and Sierra Leone (both with a greater dependence on the German market than the Gold Coast) and the Gambia (dependent on the French market and groundnut processing in northern France) were initially badly hit by wartime dislocation, the trading conditions for these three colonies improved once Britain organized its own processing and once edible nuts were given priority during the war on account of their glycerine as well as their protein content. The other British African colonies (Nigeria, Sierra Leone, and the Gambia) were able to benefit more from the implementation of the convoy system for the West African trade in the final year of the war. In addition, the port at Freetown remained the busiest in West Africa as the main naval and coaling station on the coast, both strategically important with regard to the Atlantic and able to function as a halfway stage between Britain and Simonstown on the Cape.[258]

The Gold Coast suffered more as the war dragged on because of its dependence on cocoa, a nonessential crop in terms of war needs. The severe trade depression in the colony in 1917 greatly worsened in 1918 as a result of the highest ever levels of tax, the restrictions on food exports to the UK, and finally, above all, as a result of the new 1918 restrictions on cocoa exports to France and the United States. For the first time, in 1918, the viability of the Gold Coast economy was seriously threatened. The coincidence of this crisis with the influenza epidemic caused—if only for a while—real concern among British officials for the stability of the colony. The Armistice, followed by a rapid trade revival, came just in time for the Gold Coast.

For now, though, laissez-faire remained largely intact as the general approach of the British authorities to the economic life of the Gold Coast in this period. For example, there was no colonial government interference with labor rates in the mines. Indeed, the large expatriate mining companies were expected to fend for themselves, and, like the main expatriate commercial trading companies, they rode the storm. In the mines' case, this was not just despite government inaction (over recruitment), but because of it—notably, inaction towards the significant numbers of immigrants entering the colony and helping to ease the labor shortage. For once, and in a period of highly porous colonial borders, government inability to act proved something of a blessing. There was limited scope, too, for government-inspired import substitution, even though by 1918 there were still serious shortages of virtually all mechanical spare parts such as valves, as well as candles, cement,

258. F. Cole, "Sierra Leone and World War I," pp. 12, 217–8.

and lime. The limestone deposits (found in 1915 by Kitson, the director of geological survey) could not yet be worked commercially.[259] In view of shortages, there had been calls in the African press during the war for domestic manufacture of a range of products, including soap, sugar, and rum. It was African initiative that was responsible for the little import substitution that took place: brick-making, for example, and wood products.[260] Imported soap was said to be beyond the price that could be afforded by local consumers, so that "native-made" soap from palm oil (as in Sierra Leone at this time) to some extent took its place.[261]

The war period therefore confirmed that the African population of the Gold Coast were not passive subjects but active players, in a wide range of roles, in this challenging economic context. Meanwhile, as we have seen, cocoa hold-ups and mining strikes also gave direct expression to African dissatisfaction—expressed in the legislative council as well as in the newspaper columns of *The Gold Coast Nation* and the *Gold Coast Leader*. In a number of respects, the war period presented British colonial rule in an unfavorable light—which government commitment to development and welfare projects, the focus of the next chapter, would struggle to modify.

259. Mann to Watkins, 23/4/18. AGC MS 14,170.35; Watkins to Mann, 26/2/18, and 29/5/18, 14,171.43; Mann to Samson, 30/7/18, 14,170.36. And see K. Dickson, *A Historical Geography*, p. 199.

260. E.g., editorial notes, *Gold Coast Leader*, 22/9/14; editorial, *The Gold Coast Nation*, 17–24/12/14.

261. *Report on the Blue Book 1919*, CO98/32 and see F. Cole, "Sierra Leone and World War I," pp. 305–306.

Chapter 6

Public Revenue, Private Income and the Currency: Wartime Financial Management

It was, of course, not only the export trade of the Gold Coast that was disrupted by the war but also the flow of imports: food and manufactured goods. This had serious effects on both public revenue and the private finances of innumerable African consumers. A related, fundamental aspect of colonial economic management at this time was the government's attempt to establish a uniform and universal currency. This in turn prompted African responses and initiatives. The context from 1914 was one of shortages of imported goods and greatly increased prices which, by 1917 and 1918, had reached unprecedented levels due to the extreme shortage of shipping, reduced consumer manufacture in Europe, and government trading restrictions.

The situation for the local African population was aggravated by the colonial government imposing ever higher taxation during the war years. Customs duties provided the main source of revenue for the government. But imports became scarce and expensive. The revenue fell. The critical priority for Clifford and his officials was to ensure, despite this, that normal administration could continue unimpeded. Although construction projects were largely abandoned halfway through the war, the high taxation—and inflation—remained. By raising customs duties and railway rates, the government contributed further to the sharp rise in the cost of living in the Gold Coast colony in the war period. It was essential that Africans enjoyed sufficient income (from selling exports) to be able to buy imports, on which not only government revenue but also Governor Clifford's prewar development and welfare plans largely depended. A stable currency was also a priority here. But in this wartime context of reduced proceeds from exports and high prices of imports, the colonial government had no alternative but to constantly raise taxes, thereby reducing Africans' purchasing power.

From the start of the war, the African population of the Gold Coast faced shortages of imports and high prices. The immediate problem was that new sources of supply had to be found to replace Germany, which had been second to Britain as importer into the colony in 1913. Although Germany had provided a minor proportion of the whole, the figures do not reveal the difficulties for the local population caused by the sudden loss of the major source of particular categories of imports, such as agricultural tools: axes, machetes, hoes, and knives.[1] Supplies of metal goods and quantities of certain cotton goods, "largely the product of enemy countries," fell 33% in quantity in Western Province

1. Germany: 11% of the value of imports; UK 70% rising to 79% in 1915. *Trade Report 1918, Supplementary Gazette* 15/5/19, CO99/34. The value of metal goods imported in to the colony fell from £120,985 in 1914 to £87,946 in 1915, *Trade Report 1915, Supplementary Gazette* 1/5/16, CO99/30.

in the last quarter of 1914.[2] With imports generally in short supply, government revenue initially fell but then rose again in December 1914 with "a rush" of (high-priced) goods to make up for what had not been shipped in the previous three months.[3] The value of commercial imports was sustained in 1915, but again the figures are deceptive: the value remained high because prices rose. Average wholesale prices of imports were 11% to 25% higher than in 1914—and quantities fell. Supplies of cotton goods, for example, were down in 1915, mostly due to shipping and manufacturing difficulties in England.[4] Imports were also reduced because of restrictions on exporting a whole range of foods from Britain such as flour, butter, condensed milk, cheese, eggs, sugar, and jam, and because of restrictions on goods from Europe to prevent "surreptitious trading with the enemy."[5]

The initial problem in the Gold Coast was shortage of supply rather than demand. In this context, while quick to criticize importers for overcharging, the *Gold Coast Leader* also called on Africans to be less dependent on foreign goods. They should, for example, adapt their diet. Given that the price of imported rice had doubled in the first year of the war, they should grow their own or switch to locally produced *kenke*; do without tea and coffee; and eat fresh fish rather than tinned salmon, herrings, and sardines.[6] Meanwhile, there was clearly popular resentment in the colony at the very steep rise in prices from the moment war was declared. A previous editorial in the *Gold Coast Leader* expressed a popular view blaming the large expatriate companies for hiking up prices in August 1914: "The combined firms are allowing no grass to grow under their feet."[7] As long as export prices, and especially the cocoa price, held up sufficiently and enough could be shipped, African producers still had cash in hand to buy imported goods. It was noted in 1916 that the local consumer "does not refrain from purchasing even at greatly enhanced prices when the commodities he needs are available."[8] This, of course, applied only as long as African purchasing power was sustained. It fluctuated in the early war period and then fell in the trade depression of 1917 and 1918.

Any threat to imports also threatened Clifford's entire development and welfare program for the Gold Coast. Clifford was determined that major public works would be continued despite the war. He was not a man to give up his plans without a struggle, and he clearly found the intrusion of the war frustrating. He expressed as much in a personal letter to Sir John Anderson at the Colonial Office in late 1914: "Here things are settling down into their appointed groove, but it is rather a dreary job, as you may imagine, trying to run the machinery at less than half the power and making the best of a side track."[9] Deficit budgeting had been agreed on in 1913 as a result of Clifford's successful plea before the war for a bold financial strategy of using surplus funds to pay for development. The governor planned to cover the deficit in the 1915 estimates by using up practically all these surplus balances.[10] But this policy was risky in wartime, with resources now strictly

2. *Report of Western Province 1914, Supplementary 8, Gazette* 6/9/15, CO99/29.

3. Clifford, *LegCo* 26/11/14, re. *Estimates for 1915, Gazette* 4/12/14, CO99/29/158.

4. *Trade Report 1915, Supplementary Gazette* 1/5/16, CO99/30.

5. Harcourt to West African Chamber of Mines, 20/8/14, re. meeting on West African Trade, 19/8/14, CO96/553/13; Clifford to Harcourt, 28/1/15, CO96/555/87; also Customs Notice, *Gazette* 27/2/15, CO99/28/10. Exception was made for Scandinavia, Holland, Switzerland, and Italy.

6. *Gold Coast Leader*, editorial, 31/7/15. *Kenke* is corn: soaked, fermented, boiled, and mashed.

7. Editorial, *Gold Coast Leader*, 22/8/14.

8. *Trade Report 1915, Supplementary Gazette* 1/5/16, CO99/30.

9. Clifford to Sir John Anderson, CO, 19/11/14, Enclosure in Clifford to Harcourt, 2/12/14, CO96/550/911.

10. Clifford to Harcourt, 2/12/14, CO96/550/991.

limited and shipping in ever shorter supply. A further loan was unlikely to be forthcoming in the near future even if the war ended quickly. Colonial Office officials urged caution. Clifford was now told that funds could not be drawn below the safety margin of £150,000 of assets over liabilities, and there should therefore be further economies and additional taxation, as in contemporary Nigeria under Governor Lugard.[11]

The African population of the Gold Coast thus faced much higher taxation during the war.[12] The revised customs tariffs of 1915 were justified by Clifford to the African population as a means to save further cuts in government works. But the raising of the general *ad valorem* rate from 10% to 12.5%, which further raised the price of imports to African consumers, was criticized in the African press as "bewildering in its bureaucratic autocracy."[13] Additional duties were now also attached to specific items such as tobacco, sugar, salt, spirits, beer, and wines, which doubled the duty on most of these products. For the first time, specific duties were imposed on matches, cigarettes, soap, candles, coffee, tea, and cordage. Their inclusion clearly indicates the high level of African demand for these products by this time—as well as emphasizing the wide extent of African grievance.[14] The plan to abolish duties on imported foodstuffs, which had been under consideration for some time before the war, was now, not surprisingly, put aside.[15]

Of course, British administrators and African subjects each saw the new taxation in a very different light. The governor was confident that the new indirect taxation, together with the recovery of trade, would relieve the anxiety felt in the Colonial Office about the financial position of the Gold Coast in 1915 and into 1916.[16] The governor at this stage was sanguine: "Additional taxation, in the direction of increased customs duties, can be imposed without inflicting hardship upon the people of the colony and its dependencies, and without having any appreciable or permanent ill-effect upon local commerce."[17] Clifford had no proof for this claim in May 1915. It is what he wanted to believe, and certainly what he wished London to believe.

The African press painted a completely different picture. In the same month, May 1915, the African population of the Gold Coast was said to be finding it hard to make ends meet, with prices up on average 40% to 50%, yet pay unchanged; as a result of paying more for food and clothes since the outbreak of war, "the majority of us are always in debt."[18] Readers were advised to go "back to the land" to cultivate their own foodstuffs as a substitute for imported food.[19] The war had clearly brought hardship to the growing population of the coastal towns and revealed the extent of their reliance on imports.

---

11. Flood, Ellis, CO Minute in Clifford to Harcourt, 2/12/14, CO96/550/991. See the sinking net excess of assets over liabilities: 1913, £1,006,988; 1914, £463,118; 1915, £292,822. *Blue Books 1913*, CO100/63, *1914*, CO100/64, *1915*, CO100/65.

12. Telegram, Clifford to Harcourt, 18/1/15, CO96/555.

13. Editorial, *The Gold Coast Independent*, 4/11/15.

14. *Blue Book 1915*, CO100/65; Clifford, confid. to Harcourt, 20/1/15, CO96/555; Harcourt to London, Liverpool and Manchester Chambers of Commerce, 30/11/15, CO96/561/898. These rates were to apply uniformly across the colony to Lome. The trans Volta customs area, with lower duties to stimulate trade with Togo, was abolished in 1914 following Togo's capture by British and French forces. N. A. Cox-George, *Studies in Finance and Development*, pp. 47–49.

15. Clifford, confid. to Harcourt, 20/1/15, CO96/555.

16. Clifford to Harcourt, 20/3/15, CO96/556/247.

17. Clifford to Bonar Law, 1/5/15, CO96/577/377.

18. Editorials, *Gold Coast Leader*, 1/5/15, 22/5/15.

19. See, e.g., editorials, *Gold Coast Leader*, 31/7/15, 3/6/16 and *The Gold Coast Nation*, 7–14/1/15; and 26/8/15.

Whether this dependence had arisen as a byproduct of overconcentration on cash crop farming, or as a result of consumer choice, is less clear.[20] The complaints in the local newspapers reveal African consumers' dependency on international manufactured goods (as well as the enhanced material standard of living that colonial rule had promoted in the years before the war). The exhortation to go "back to the land" suggests that patterns of African production had become somewhat distorted even before the war.

Higher taxes continued to be imposed in the Gold Coast during the early war period to maintain construction work, and above all to maintain government revenue. The finances of the colony deteriorated in April 1915 with unexpectedly heavy capital expenditure on the railway leading to a temporary suspension of general public works. As a result, Clifford argued that railway rates should be raised. They had been lowered in July 1912 to stimulate trade, but a rise, as a temporary war measure, "would lead to the mines contributing their share."[21] The 15% added to the railway rates from May 1915 was thus effectively a war tax. Officials in the Colonial Office still believed there could be no local objections, as "the Gold Coast is lightly taxed and prosperous."[22] But coastal officials did not report to London the references in the African press to the hardship caused by the new taxation.[23]

Clifford, one year into the war, was keen to resume railway construction. What was needed was finance for such development. The aim was to raise revenue from a range of higher taxes, such as increased spirit licenses, judicial fees, and telegraph and telephone charges. British officials justified these new rates by the need to finance new stretches of railway track, which would in turn stimulate trade and increase government revenue. This had indeed been shown in March 1915 with the opening of the Mangoase-Koforidua section of rail north of Accra, described by Slater as "an instantaneous success" carrying "thousands of barrels and bags of cocoa."[24] Clifford finally won permission in November 1915 for work to be resumed on the northern extension of the Accra railway, for which a deficit budget was again prepared in the estimates for 1916, with the difference to be met out of the steadily diminishing surplus balances.[25] It appeared that the Gold Coast colony had weathered the storm, with the 1915–1916 cocoa season largely responsible for a "gratifying increase" in the value of exports, bringing the prospect of increased purchases of imports and thus of increased tax revenue.[26]

Clifford still did not accept, in mid–1916, that his long-term plans for the colony would need to be shelved for the duration of the war. He remained committed to financing construction, if necessary from additional taxation. But higher customs dues raised prices of imported goods even further—to the detriment of the African population. By May 1916 customs revenue had still not risen enough to reassure the governor that development works in the Colony and Ashanti were secure. The result was that, for the first time, plans were drawn up for an export tax on cocoa. The Colonial Office was once again assured

20. See, e.g., R. H. Green & S. Hymer, "Cocoa in the Gold Coast"; and J. Hogendorn's modified version of Hla Myint's "vent for surplus theory" in P. Duignan & L. H. Gann (eds.), *Colonialism in Africa Vol. IV*, pp. 289–291.

21. Clifford to Harcourt, 26/4/15, CO96/557.

22. Green, CO Minute, telegram, Clifford to Harcourt, 26/4/15, CO96/557.

23. See, e.g., editorial notes, *Gold Coast Leader*, 29/5/15.

24. Acting Governor Slater, confid. to Bonar Law, 30/9/15, CO96/560.

25. Estimated surplus balances: 31/12/15: £248,000; 31/12/16: £192,186, Acting Governor Slater to Bonar Law, 5/11/15, CO96/561/894.

26. Slater, *LegCo* 25/10/15, *Gazette* 25/11/15, CO99/29/101.

by the governor (ignoring African complaints) that the prosperity of the colony had "so far been little if at all affected by the war."[27] The London official, Flood, however, now doubted whether railway schemes should be allowed to continue during the war, at a time when it would be more prudent to build up the colony's surplus balances: "This is no time for public works on a large scale."[28]

Clifford could not continue indefinitely to ignore the rise in the cost of living in the Gold Coast colony. He initially acknowledged its effect on the expatriate community rather than the African community. In late 1916, six months after seeking to reassure the Colonial Office that the prosperity of the colony was almost untouched, the governor was prepared, confidentially, to argue a case for a revised salary scheme for European officers on the grounds of "a greatly enhanced cost of living occasioned by the war." He estimated, for example, that by November 1916 his own household's expenditure was 56% higher than it had been for the rather larger governor's household of 1913.[29] A number of senior coast officials produced data to back up their claim for a war bonus at this time. Crowther, Secretary for Native Affairs, estimated that by mid-1916 the overall cost of living for officers during the war had risen by 30%. Local foodstuffs had not gone up quite as much, but many items obtained from the coast as well as from overseas, including fowl, eggs, fish, imported meat, milk, and mineral water, had risen by 50% to 100%. The Gold Coast treasurer's list of "absolute necessities" was headed by whisky, which was selling at 57s a case in July 1916, up from the prewar price of 42s. All such rises, he noted, contributed to "financial strain" which was "a direct result" of the war.[30] But the governor had not yet publicly drawn the conclusion that innumerable Africans—whose pattern of purchases was clearly not identical to that of Europeans—were also victims of some of the same high prices as European officers.[31] C. B. Nettey (the *Asafoatso* of the Gbese quarter in Accra) suggested tactfully to Crowther, secretary of native affairs, that Clifford could not be "properly informed": "I am quite sure that his Excellency the Governor does not know to what extent the people of Accra are suffering."[32]

The war caused major fluctuations in supply, but there were good periods as well as bad. Commercial imports, which had declined 4% in value in 1915, rose dramatically, by 56%, in the boom year of 1916.[33] Much of this rise in the value of imports, as for example the 84% rise in the value of imported provisions, was due to much higher prices. But there was also a general increase in the quantity imported in 1916, with the exception of cotton goods, soap, and gin.[34] More earthenware was imported to compensate for the loss of German enamelware, and exceptionally high figures for some items such as perfumery and beads are explained by alternative suppliers in Europe and the United States only at that point replacing the prewar German and Austrian sources.[35] In particular,

27. Clifford, confid. to Bonar Law, 8/5/16, CO96/566.
28. Flood, CO Minute, Clifford, confid. to Bonar Law, 8/5/16, CO96/566.
29. Clifford, confid. to Bonar Law, 8/11/16, CO96/572.
30. Other steep price rises included potatoes (from 9s a case just before the war to 23s 6d); kerosene (from 11s a case to 15s or 20s); sugar (from 2s 9d a 7 lb tin to 5s); eggs per box (from 8s up to 13s 6d); and milk per bottle (from 10d to 1s 3d). Enclosures, Crowther, Commissioner for Native Affairs, and Reece, Treasurer, in Clifford, confid. to Bonar Law, 8/11/16, CO96/572.
31. Long to Clifford, 20/2/17, CO96/572; Clifford, confid. to Bonar Law, 8/11/16, CO96/572.
32. C. B. Nettey to Crowther, Secretary of Native Affairs, 5/10/16, ADM 11/1/620, PRAAD.
33. *Summary of Trade Report 1916*, Acting Governor Slater to Long, 9/7/17, CO96/580/430.
34. E.g., the 53% increase in the value of sugar imported was calculated as 20% due to the increase in quantity.
35. *Trade Report 1916, Gazette* 1/5/17, CO99/32.

the import trade with America, already on the rise before the war, "took a sudden leap forward" in 1916.[36] It was mainly due to this new source of supply that the standard of living for both Africans and Europeans in the colony did not deteriorate further. The United States' contribution to the value of imports into the colony doubled between 1913 and 1916, and had thus more than taken the place, in terms of value, held by Germany before the war. The chief imports from the United States continued to be beef, pork, flour, vehicles, petroleum, and rum. As a result of shortages from the loss of the German market, the United States was also now an important supplier of metal goods, building materials, cement, and sugar.[37]

Even when the colonial government revenue was buoyant and the books balanced, in 1916, Clifford still sought increases in taxation: not to keep the government afloat, but to finance his development and welfare plans. High prices combined with the higher duties contributed to a "bumper year" for customs revenue, up over 36% overall.[38] As a result of new taxation (including the export duty on cocoa imposed for the first time from October 1916, as well as higher railway rates) the books balanced for the first time since 1912.[39] The governor therefore decided when drawing up the estimates for 1917 that the colony still had the wealth and resources to bear further taxation on top of the £500,000 which had been collected as additional taxation since 1915. The surplus balances had fallen sharply between 1913 and 1915 but had risen satisfactorily during 1916 as a result of the trade recovery, the new taxes, and cuts in government expenditure. Although there was no hope of floating the additional substantial loan for railway and public works construction that would have been launched but for the war, financial prospects seemed good during the initial trade boom of 1916. It was estimated, optimistically, that in 1917 the revenue would exceed £2 million for the first time in the history of the colony.[40]

African opinion continued to be ignored. As late as November 1916, Clifford was still claiming, when making a case to London for further taxation to finance development, that "the natives of the Gold Coast and Ashanti have suffered no hardship and comparatively little inconvenience through the Empire being at war."[41] The *Gold Coast Leader* was arguing, meanwhile, that taxes should fall, not on the African population, but rather on the European trading companies concerned only "for their economic dividend."[42] Then economic prospects suddenly deteriorated drastically, so that Clifford's ambitious expenditure proposals, put forward "with all the force at his command," were now dismissed by Sir George Fiddes, permanent under-secretary of state for the Colonies, as "really absurd."[43] The bottom fell out of the cocoa market in December 1916 with a lack of tonnage to ship exports and a fall in demand from the manufacturers. "Anything going

---

36. Clifford, *LegCo* 25/10/17, *Gazette* 26/11/17, CO99/32/76.

37. *Trade Report 1916, Gazette* 1/5/17, CO99/32. As a result of these increases in American imports the proportion of imports from the United Kingdom fell from a high point of 79% in 1915 to 75% in 1916.

38. *Trade Report 1916, Gazette* 1/5/17, CO99/32. Rises in quantity included wearing apparel up 71%, provisions up 111%, and metal goods up 197%.

39. Revenue: £1,835,989; Expenditure: £1,465,946. *Blue Book 1916,* CO100/66.

40. See fluctuating surplus balances: 1913: £1,006388; January 1916: £292,822; December 1916: £662,864. Clifford to Bonar Law, 13/11/16, CO96/572/840. Also Clifford, *LegCo* 25/10/17, *Gazette* 26/11/17. CO99/32/76.

41. Clifford to Bonar Law, 13/11/16, CO96/572/840.

42. Editorial, *Gold Coast Leader,* 31/8/16.

43. Fiddes, CO Minute, Clifford to Bonar Law, 13/11/16, CO96/572/840.

wrong with trade will hit the whole revenue … the purchasing price will fall and with it the volume of imports and customs revenue," he continued. Expenditure on construction in the colony, so long defended by Clifford, had to stop: "All our steel is needed for killing Germans in France and Flanders and not for building railways in the Gold Coast." Instead of such "luxuries," the colony should build up accumulated reserves for after the war, when money would still be hard to get but materials would probably be cheaper. Fiddes even suggested that taxation could be reduced to its pre-1915 level. "However much Sir Hugh Clifford may press … he must be made to understand the war comes first."[44] The message to the Gold Coast government in January 1917 from Walter Long (now secretary of state in place of Bonar Law) was unequivocal: there were to be no more large-scale development works in the colony while the war lasted.[45]

The whole Empire was expected to play its part at this critical stage in Britain's war against the Central Powers. Money raised from local taxation in overseas possessions was now to be used, not for local development, but for subsidizing the imperial war effort. A telegram from the Colonial Office later the same month, January 1917, ordered the Gold Coast government to invest £500,000 of the colony's surplus balances (now estimated at £680,000) in the Imperial War Loan. No reference to Fiddes's suggestion of lowering taxes after the forced halt to development was included.[46] Slater's concern that the colony's funds would not now be "readily accessible" even at the end of the war was dismissed by Colonial Office officials. He was informed that few colonies had liquid balances as large as the Gold Coast, yet all were doing what they could to contribute to the war effort, such as Malta buying Exchequer bonds.[47] What was not mentioned here was the reason why the liquid balances of the Gold Coast colony were exceptionally high. A major proportion had recently been extracted from the African population in tax (such as the new export tax on cocoa as well as higher import duties and railway rates) and less had been spent on development than planned, because of wartime cutbacks. A justification offered by the Colonial Office for this money being spent by the British imperial government was that it would help to ensure that colonial subjects would continue to benefit from remaining subjects of the British, as opposed to the German, Empire.

In 1917, taxes were set to rise further. The colony's surplus balances were being taken away for use by the metropolitan country at a time when the local population was suffering from an acute lack of shipping, exceptionally high freight rates, and very low prices for cocoa. It was clear that with the revival of the German submarine campaign, all imports from Britain would be reduced to a minimum and little could be made up from other sources.[48] The prospect of a severe shortage of revenue and the sudden collapse in the cocoa market necessitated a complete revision of the estimates for 1917 and yet higher taxation.[49] Clifford sought to reassure the legislative council that the causes of all the problems were "temporary and artificial." The end of the war "would have an electric

---

44. *Ibid.*

45. Long to Acting Governor Slater, 12/1/17, CO96/572/840.

46. Fiddes, CO Minute, telegram, Long to Acting Governor Slater, 20/1/17, CO96/577.

47. Telegram, Acting Governor Slater to Long, 24/1/17, CO96/577; Ellis, CO Minute, telegram, Acting Governor Slater to Long, 24/1/17, CO96/577.

48. Reece, treasurer, memo. Enclosure 1, Acting Governor Slater to Long, 7/12/17, CO96/578/103.

49. Estimates for 1917, 24/1/17: total revenue over expenditure as £100,000. Estimates for 1917 (only nine days later) as £34,000. Revenue for the year now estimated as £1.5m rather than £2m. Acting Governor Slater to Long, 7/12/17, CO96/578/103.

effect … upon local prosperity and upon public revenues." But meanwhile, a deficit of over £100,000 was anticipated by the end of the year.[50] A wide range of additional taxes were therefore imposed. Telegraph and postal rates were again increased, including a rise of 1s on parcels; duties on spirits and vehicle licenses also rose in 1917, as did hospital fees. European trading firms were using parcel post because cargo boats were slower, and wartime freight charges were higher, than the mail boat; cargo freight rates had risen at least 40% since the outbreak of the war.[51]

There could be no debate now, in 1917, as to whether to proceed with development and welfare projects in the territory. The dramatic fall in customs revenue took place as feared in 1917, with the total value of imports down by more than £2.5m to around half the level of 1916: "a bad set-back."[52] Shortage of supply was now the critical factor, with quantities of most imports reduced by half or more, and prices therefore considerably raised. Some of the decreases in quantity were in soap, gin, and food imports such as bread, biscuits, beef, and pork. Only liquid fuel and petroleum, almost all from the United States, increased both in quantity and value. The proportion of the colony's imports provided by the United States rose from 15% to 22%, but this was partly accounted for by more goods being shipped direct to avoid German U-boats, rather than via British ports. Despite the American contribution, the overall reduction in the quantity of imports meant that the sum raised by import duties fell by 38% in 1917. The decrease in quantity was greatest for *ad valorem* goods, down 47% compared with the boom of 1916. As noted by Archer, the comptroller of customs, the loss of revenue would have been far greater but for the higher prices of commodities.[53]

At last, in the depression of 1917, came an important, though belated, public recognition by Clifford of the impact of wartime economic conditions on his African subjects. He finally publicly acknowledged that a large number of the local population now depended on a whole range of imported goods such as cotton cloth, soap, kerosene, matches, cutlasses, building materials, furniture, and enamel bowls. He even recognized in a speech to the legislative council that deprivation of such articles, and the "standard of comfort" to which "natives of the Gold Coast" had become accustomed, caused "very genuine privation."[54] Yet British officials remained uncertain about the extent to which the purchasing power of the local population had been reduced as a result of the war. Archer, comptroller of customs, argued that even in 1917 the demand for imported goods was still as great as ever despite the "crushing prices"; he blamed the decline in import revenue on the difficulty of procuring goods from overseas rather than any shortage of money in the colony.[55] It was clearly difficult for British officials on the coast to make an assessment of the financial resources of the African population, especially given the tendency to hoard coin rather than bank it. It remained very difficult to judge how much money was in circulation.

There was no consistent British view from the provinces. On the one hand, the commissioner of Eastern Province, Philbrick, suggested that the purchasing power of "the

---

50. With £500,000 invested in the War Loan, only £200,000 surplus remained to draw on, and half of that would have gone by the end of 1917. Clifford, *LegCo* re. 1918 Estimates 25/10/17, *Gazette* 26/11/17, CO99/32/76.

51. Clifford to Long, 22/5/17, CO96/579/329. See also *Blue Book 1917*, CO100/67.

52. Comptroller of Customs Archer, *Trade Report 1917*, *Supplementary Gazette* 21/5/18, CO99/33.

53. *Ibid.*

54. Clifford, *LegCo* 25/10/17, *Gazette* 26/11/17, CO99/32/76.

55. Comptroller of Customs Archer, *Trade Report 1917*, *Supplementary Gazette* 21/5/18, CO99/33.

natives" could not be tested in 1917, as imports were in such short supply.[56] On the other hand, Harding, commissioner of Central Province, claimed that the cost of living for Europeans and "the educated native community" had risen startlingly. He estimated that by that year, 1917, every article imported into the colony cost approximately 70% more than before the war. Many small inland stores had closed, and those still open were "sadly reduced in stock," with prices often beyond locals' ability to pay.[57] Overall, however, as in many other respects, British officials were ignorant about life in African society. The reduction in British staff during the war only made this worse.

With economic prospects no better for 1918, it was the African unofficial members of the legislative council who led the way in arguing that the Gold Coast government should reduce taxation. The attack was concentrated on the export duty on cocoa. Nana Ofori Atta, head chief of an important cocoa-producing kingdom in Eastern Province and by this time the leading African unofficial in the Gold Coast colony, argued that retention of the tax could not be justified, given that it had been agreed that it would be reduced or removed altogether if there was a collapse in the cocoa market. Buyers were telling producers that they would have paid more for the cocoa but for the government duty.[58] Moreover, as two of the other African unofficials in the now enlarged legislative council (Casely Hayford and E. J. P. Brown) pointed out, the government had previously justified new taxes by the need for capital expenditure on railway extensions and public works—but all such projects had now been indefinitely postponed. However, both the British officials and British unofficials agreed with the governor that such taxation was simply part of the war burden that had to be borne by the present generation, African as well as British.[59] By this time the financial position of the colony was such that the tax on cocoa was necessary to cover basic government expenditure. Of the total of £805,000 from customs duties, £170,000 was provided from the duty on cocoa.[60]

The British government in the Gold Coast had always had to tread warily with regard to taxation. To placate African critics, the export duty on cocoa was lowered from one-quarter to one-fifth of a penny per lb. The government planned to cover the expected revenue shortfall from the new surplus balances that were now accumulating as a result of high wartime taxation and expenditure cuts. But with the outlook concerning both shipping and restrictions on exports extremely bleak, Colonial Office officials judged that the colony's surplus balances needed to be conserved, not depleted, and taxes in the colony increased rather than decreased. The colony was now said to be paying the penalty for "too hasty commitment" to large development works.[61] This might have been true, but it was hardly fair, in that London had firmly backed Clifford's construction projects, both before the war and during the early war period.

There was a limit to what Africans could be expected to pay. One suggestion discussed in the Colonial Office at this time as a solution to the financial problems of the Gold Coast colony was to devolve all local expenditure, as on sanitation and the water supply,

---

56. Philbrick, P. C., *Report of Eastern Province 1917,* 9/7/18, CO96/591/389.

57. Harding, P.C., *Report of Central Province 1917,* 13/6/18, CO96/590/331.

58. N. O. Atta, *Okyenhene* of Akyem Abuakwa, to Governor, 17/10/17 in Clifford to Long, 10/12/17, CO96/583/767.

59. Clifford to Long, 10/12/17, CO96/583/767.

60. Calder, CO Minute, Clifford to Long, 10/12/17, CO96/583/767.

61. Calder (principal clerk, West Africa Section) CO Minute, Clifford to Long, 10/12/17, CO96/583/767. Net excess of assets over liabilities: £862,709 in 1917; £791,897 by the end of 1918. *Blue Books: 1917,* CO100/67; *1918,* CO100/68.

to local authorities to be paid out of rates.[62] As the experience of municipal authorities in the large coastal towns of Gold Coast had not been a happy one, it was proposed that chiefs and headmen of each "political district" act as a sort of county council, with the DC as president.[63] The idea that such controversial administrative structures could be set up in the colony in the middle of the war and receive the necessary active cooperation of the local population was remarkably naive. British coast officials were not alone in being guilty of a lack of realism.

The imposition of direct taxation was also discussed. Colonial Office officials claimed that customs duties were too narrow a basis for taxation in a colony the size of the Gold Coast. The London official, Calder (principal clerk in the West Africa section of the Colonial Office), proposed a form of direct tax such as the 5s hut tax in Sierra Leone. He argued that all inhabitants of the colony had benefited from roads and railways as well as from the end of slavery and tribal wars, and yet there were still Africans who did not buy European goods and so did not contribute to the cost of European administration. Others, he believed, could pay far more. The size of nongovernment contributions to the British war effort (£8000 per year for 1915–1917, and eleven airplanes at £1,500 each) proved, in his view, that there was money on hand.[64] It was just as well for the British officials that their African subjects who had given this money did not realize their tax potential would be judged from the size of their war contributions. Nor is there here any recognition of the extent to which chiefs put pressure on their people to raise "voluntary" contributions for the war.

Clifford's own powerful arguments against any form of direct taxation in the Gold Coast were well known to the Colonial Office. Given the long history of opposition to direct taxes in the colony, the governor had good reason to believe they would indeed give rise to "acute discontent" and cause "widespread disturbances," especially in a period of commercial depression during the war.[65] Also, such taxation would be very difficult and expensive to collect. Clifford suggested as an alternative the possibility of raising the export duty on cocoa after the war.[66] Clifford's comment here for London officials was for private consumption only. It was certainly not the understanding of the African unofficials that the export duty was anything other than an emergency wartime measure. At the same time, it was clear that direct taxation would not be acceptable to the African population and could endanger order in the colony. Common sense prevailed. The conclusion in London was that direct taxation "must wait for a more convenient season and a new governor."[67]

Not all officials in the Colonial Office at this time were indifferent to local conditions. Ellis argued against direct taxation, believing it would be possible neither to obtain local African cooperation nor to set up the necessary machinery with a depleted staff. He feared a revolt, as with the Egba rising in Nigeria in June 1918 in reaction to Lugard's imposition of direct taxes during the war.[68] Yet drastic measures were required to keep up the revenue if the surplus balances were not to be drawn upon again: dipping into the surplus balances,

---

62. These local rates and mining royalties were the only two forms of direct taxation in the Gold Coast. See N. A. Cox-George, *Studies in Finance and Development,* pp. 51–52.
63. Calder CO Minute, Clifford to Long, 10/12/17, CO96/583/767.
64. *Ibid.*, £80,000 was raised by local subscriptions in the Gold Coast during the war.
65. Telegram, Clifford to Long, 29/3/18, CO96/589.
66. Clifford, confid. to Long, 28/5/18, CO96/590.
67. Ellis, CO Minute, telegram, Clifford to Long, 29/3/18, CO96/589.
68. See A. Osuntokun, *Nigeria in the First World War,* pp. 126–130.

or advances on the war loan, would deprive the colony of resources in the postwar period.[69] Lugard had set a precedent for a massive increase in customs duties when he imposed a surtax of 25% on most imports into Nigeria as early as November 1914.[70] Ellis now suggested, as an alternative to direct taxation in the Gold Coast, a further huge rise in *ad valorem* duties (provisions exempted) from 12.5% to 25%.[71] The *ad valorem* rate, 10% at the start of the war, was raised to 12.5% in 1915. Governor Clifford now sought a balanced increase, calculating that a further rise was unavoidable but wanting to limit it to what would be acceptable to the local population. He obtained London's agreement that the rise should be to 20% rather than the 25% proposed by Ellis (except for provisions, which were to stay at 12.5%, with an extra duty on spirits of 1s a gallon).[72] Even so, that month Clifford expressed his anxiety to Secretary of State Walter Long: "I fear that 1918 is going to be a pretty black time for the colony."[73]

Now that considerable economic hardship was widely expected, the governor felt a powerful rallying cry was needed. Clifford had already warned the general public that "testing times" lay ahead with his belated acknowledgement that the inhabitants "have begun to experience, with some acuteness, the adverse effects of the war."[74] He felt it necessary to justify sacrifices made by the African population of the Gold Coast, announcing in *The Government Gazette* in the strongest terms that things might have been much worse. The physical safety of the civilian population of the colony would, he declared, have been threatened but for the protection of the Royal Navy. Using dramatic and emotional imagery, he declared that without such protection there would have been bombing from aircraft or warships, and Zeppelin raids such as those in London and the south coast of England, with the streets of Accra "strewn with the mutilated bodies of men, women, and children." The people of the Gold Coast should "cheerfully accept their share of sacrifice as proud members of the Empire" alongside "the Mother Country" and "the great self-governing Dominions."[75] The emphasis was on the contrast between the desirability of the British, as opposed to the German, Empire.

1918 was indeed to prove the most "testing time" for the colony. It was far from certain whether the population would "cheerfully" accept sacrifices. In February 1918 Clifford forwarded to London petitions for a war bonus for both administrative services, the European and the Native Subordinate and Clerical staff, each of which had cited the effect of "enhanced prices" for imported goods.[76] Each community was suffering from these wartime privations, if unequally. The PMO (principal medical officer), Dr. Rice, claimed at this time that it was "generally admitted" that the value of the currency had halved.[77] One European senior surveyor complained that the purchasing power of his salary in

---

69. Clifford to Long, 29/3/18, CO96/589. Also Slater, Colonial Secretary, *Memo of Executive Officers of the Gold Coast*, Enclosure 2, Clifford to Long, 25/2/18, CO96/588/106.

70. A. Osuntokun, *Nigeria in the First World War*, p. 29.

71. Ellis, CO Minute, Clifford to Long, 10/12/17. Also telegram, Long to Clifford, 31/1/18, CO96/583/767.

72. Long to Clifford, 16/5/18, telegram, Clifford to Long, 29/3/18, CO96/589.

73. Clifford to Long, 25/1/18, CO96/587/55.

74. Clifford, *LegCo*, 25/10/17, *Gazette* 26/11/17, CO99/32/76.

75. *Ibid.*

76. Clifford to Long, 25/2/18, CO96/588/106.

77. *European Officers' Petition*, Enclosure 1; and *Report*, Dr. Rice, PMO, Enclosure 2, Clifford to Long, 25/2/18, CO96/588/106. A similar claim, that the value of the sovereign had halved since the start of the war, was made in Sierra Leone at this time. F. Cole, "Sierra Leone and World War I," p. 344.

1918 was less than when he had arrived in the colony in 1912.[78] African staff produced figures both from leading trading firms and the market clerk of Accra. Boots, blankets, and sugar were said to have risen 200% in price since August 1914. Matches were reputed to have risen 300%, and a whole range of food rose 100%, such as flour, rice, salt, potatoes, fowl, eggs, and bread.[79] And African clerks too, in the *Further Petition of Native and Clerical Subordinate Staff,* cited the ever-increasing costs of not only all imports but also of local food and rents.[80] It is unfortunate that British officers failed over the war period to keep figures of market produce that could be used to gauge the cost of living in the colony. More precisely, one problem was the tendency of traders in local markets to sell by a bewildering variety of containers, such as "bag," "tin," "spoon," "cup," and "bowl," rather than using any standard measures.[81]

Yet it was clear that the cost of living was high and rising as the war continued into its fifth year, with no end in sight. Shipping available for the West African trade had been further reduced by the destruction of ships in the 1917 German U-boat campaign. Also, much of the British merchant fleet was by now being used for military purposes with, for example, 60% of the American armies for France and their supplies being transported across the Atlantic in British ships.[82] Meanwhile, the increased cost of local produce was attributed not only to farmers cultivating cash crops at the expense of food crops but to food producers raising their prices. Demand for local foodstuffs rose because of the shortages and high prices of imported provisions. There was also greater pressure on food supplies in towns like Accra, where large numbers had arrived in the war looking for work, such as an influx of immigrants from Togo. And food supplies were also affected by an unusually dry year in 1918, after exceptionally heavy rainfall in 1916 and 1917.[83]

It was a mark of how dire the situation had become in the Gold Coast by the summer of 1918 that the Gold Coast government decided it had to intervene to try to fix a maximum price for certain imported foods. British officials believed that new paternalistic and protectionist measures were called for. The local African press had noted with approval the fixed prices for main articles of food, including rice, imposed in 1916 by the government in Sierra Leone as a result of serious food shortages.[84] New food export restrictions in Britain and subsequently in the United States led to a crisis in the Gold Coast in 1918.[85] The items of food and drink that were now listed as subject to a fixed maximum price were flour, sugar, butter, lard, rice, salt, tea, and unsweetened milk. Schedules were set out for the different ports with some slight variation in price. The maximum price set for flour was 5s more in Keta than in Accra, but sugar was nearly 5s cheaper. Different weights were given (each with a maximum price) to make local marketing easier. For

78. *European Officers' Petition re: War Bonus,* Enclosure 1, and Postmaster General, Accra, Enclosure 3, in Clifford to Long, 18/9/18, CO96/592/546.

79. *Petition of Native Clerical and Subordinate Services,* Enclosure 4, Clifford to Long, 25/2/18, C096/588/106.

80. *Further Petition of Native Clerical and Subordinate Staff,* Enclosure 4, Clifford to Long, 18/9/18, CO96/592/546.

81. *Blue Book 1918,* CO100/68. For discussion concerning the impossibility of drawing up an accurate cost of living index because of the lack of data re. domestic goods and services, see B. Ingham & C. Simmons (eds.), *Development Studies And Colonial Policy,* p. 240.

82. Clifford, *LegCo* 28/10/18, *Gazette* 9/11/18, CO99/33/82.

83. Acting Treasurer Lewis, memo in Clifford to Long, 25/2/18, CO96/588/106.

84. E.g., *The Gold Coast Nation* 3/8/16; and see F. Cole, "Sierra Leone and World War I," p. 219.

85. *Blue Book 1918,* CO100/68; and Clifford to Long, 19/8/18, CO96/592/478.

example, maximum prices for flour were listed per barrel, per 7 lb tin, and per 4 lb tin; rice was weighed by the 50 or 25 lb bag; and butter by the 2 lb or 1 lb tin.[86]

But this government intervention seems to have had little effect. Not surprisingly, European and African officials claiming the need for a further war bonus did not report any leveling off in prices.[87] Rather than the government taking over control of stocks, as had happened briefly on the outbreak of war, there were simply government appeals to the public for restraint—an indication that officials were in fact unable to control prices. In September 1918, supplies of flour were in danger of completely running out, and so "the greatest economy" and avoidance of waste was called for. With sugar supplies also running very low, the population was asked to "place themselves on rations" and informed that the allowance of sugar in England at this time was only 2 lb per person per week.[88] Butter and cheese had become prohibited exports from the United States in 1918, and licenses to export all other American foodstuffs were much reduced.[89] All imported provisions were thus in extremely short supply in the colony just before the end of the war. The colonial government, neither in control of prices nor able to institute effective rationing, would have found itself in a very difficult position if the war had not ended in November 1918.

The colony's trade and revenue were wholly dependent on a stable currency. Nothing better illustrates the colonial relationship in the Gold Coast throughout the war period than the differing attitudes and responses to the currency problem. Africans complained of the shortage of coin, especially of small denominations, but the government continued to give priority to obtaining a uniform currency that would not be hoarded for its intrinsic value. There had been a problem obtaining enough coin from the Royal Mint before the war, so it was hardly surprising that wartime conditions brought further shortages. Indeed, Clifford warned London that not only might the normal trade of the colony founder if the government failed to overcome currency problems, but there might also be serious public disorder. Above all he was very concerned that paper money should not be forced on an unwilling populace. As we shall see, however, Africans reacted in unforeseen ways to the British government's currency interventions.

Unprecedented fluctuations in the demand for cocoa during the war brought unprecedented fluctuations in demand for coinage, which the British authorities did not handle very adeptly. The immediate contraction of trade at the beginning of the war led to a fall in demand for coin. The West Africa Currency Board (WACB) therefore found itself with a large amount of surplus, which it was required to send back to London to be converted into English silver. It was expensive to ship back because of the new freight rates, but £530,000 of silver coin was repatriated between August and November 1914. However, prices then quickly recovered, with the result that in December 1914—at the height of the cocoa season—the Board had to produce £100,000 of new silver currency for West Africa.[90] Coinage required seasonally for the cocoa crop of the Gold Coast constituted the most important—and most difficult—issue the WACB had to address.

86. E.g., *Orders by Food Controller in Extraordinary Gazettes:* 15/6/18, 15/8/18, CO99/33; 20/8/18, CO99/33/87; 2/12/18, CO99/33/99; 14/11/18, CO99/33/87; 2/12/18, CO99/33/94; 10/12/18, CO99/33/99.

87. Enclosures 3 and 4 in Clifford to Long, 18/9/18, CO96/592/546.

88. *Public Warning Notices* 11/9/18, *Gazette* 14/9/18, CO99/33/58.

89. *Regulation, War Trade Board, Washington, Extraordinary Gazette* 14/12/18, CO99/33/100.

90. See R. Fry, *Bankers in West Africa*, pp. 77–78.

The first major wartime shortage of coin occurred early in the 1915–1916 cocoa season. London officials refused to admit there was a crisis, but Clifford believed they failed to appreciate that crucial African and British interests were at stake. He considered the situation "most serious" because buying cocoa might well have to be suspended at the height of the season, with dire effects on African farmers' purchasing power and hence on the revenue.[91] Because of the shortage of silver coin in Britain, the WACB had in early October 1915 again given instructions to their agents on the coast, the Bank of West Africa, to repatriate a certain amount of silver. But they were then "with startling suddenness" faced at the beginning of the new cocoa season (1915–1916) with a complete change in the scale of demand for coin in the Gold Coast.[92] All the colonies of British West Africa were affected by shortage of silver coin, made worse by a large crop of groundnuts coming onto the market in Nigeria at the same time as the usual major demand from the cocoa industry in the Gold Coast. The Bank of West Africa announced that £2m worth of coin had been used to buy the Gold Coast cocoa crop but a further £2m was needed immediately, and it only held £259,000. A further £155,000 of new silver coin had been promised from London, with the mines requiring £25,000 a month.[93]

The governor saw himself as defending the interests of the African farmers and traders against the insensitivity of the Colonial Office. Clifford now decided, against London's advice—and despite the extent of the immediate financial crisis—not to issue paper money to cover the coin deficiency. He sent an urgent telegram to London in December 1915 to emphasize the extreme seriousness of the situation: half the season's cocoa crop was still unsold simply for lack of coinage. Clifford feared that a sudden attempt to force the population to accept notes in lieu of coin would not only mean that much cocoa would not be put on the market, but would also "fatally prejudice" attempts in the future to persuade "natives" to use paper money.[94] Any attempt to impose a note issue, without people being able to see that paper money was backed by cash and could be redeemed when wanted, would fail and be "highly damaging to the prestige of the government."[95] Clifford believed that if paper currency was introduced without the guarantee of a date fixed for possible conversion, there would be not only real hardship in the colony but "acute discontent."[96]

It is clear that the governor considered the challenges to the colony as both economic (the fate of the export trade) and political (the continued cooperation of the African population). He believed it was essential that an adequate amount of coin be sent to the colony immediately. As Clifford noted, only the combine firms gained from inadequate government provision of currency. They had coin with which to buy because they alone imported general merchandise. As a result they could now set a low price without competition from either smaller traders or produce buyers like Cadbury.[97] Clifford denied what some London officials maintained—that the shortage of coin was the fault of the local population and could be remedied if all the silver hoarded on the coast were realized.

---

91. Telegram, Clifford to Bonar Law, 28/11/15, CO9/561.

92. Memo, West African Currency Board Memo in Clifford, secret to Bonar Law, 4/12/15, CO554/30. See, e.g., F. Cole, "Sierra Leone and World War I," p. 69; and R. Fry, *Bankers in West Africa,* p. 78.

93. Telegram, Clifford to Bonar Law, 28/11/15, CO96/561; also *West African Currency Board Report for year ending 30/6/15,* CO554/26.

94. Telegram, Clifford to Bonar Law, 4/12/15, CO96/561.

95. *Ibid.*

96. Clifford, secret to Bonar Law, 4/12/15, CO96/561.

97. Telegram, Clifford to Bonar Law, 4/12/15, CO96/561.

In defense of the African public, and in line with his views on trusteeship, the governor argued that it was the colonial government's responsibility to put money into circulation on a scale to meet public need.

Clifford pointed out to London officials that one reason for there being more hoarding and less money in circulation than usual was that, since the outbreak of war, "natives" had been exhorted by the government to economize. With imports scarce and expensive, some of the local population had planted more food and so needed to buy less. Also confidence had been damaged because of the "abnormally low price" paid for cocoa for most of the 1914–1915 season. The crop had been sold for only £800,000 compared to £2m in 1913, "so sudden and so serious a fall in the collective income of the richest sections of the agricultural community" must have caused "considerable uneasiness and apprehension."[98] Clifford's insistence that it was not his African subjects but "those entrusted with supplying cash for use in the West African colonies" who were "primarily responsible" for the present shortage was clearly a direct criticism of the WACB, the Royal Mint, and the Treasury. However, if there was not enough silver coin available to send, then the only "practical possibility," Clifford had to accept, reluctantly, was to issue notes in the near future that were convertible locally and not simply in London.[99]

The governor had good reasons for his conviction that the state of the currency was causing anxiety and instability in the colony. The shortage of silver and sudden drop in cocoa prices in early December 1915 caused panic among African farmers and brokers. Word had spread that Great Britain and her allies were losing in the struggle with Germany and that all money in England had been exhausted. One of the British unofficials, Parker, warned Clifford that such fears might lead to a run on the bank.[100] As usual, rumors spread rapidly—a result of the colonial government's failure to institute effective channels of communication.

The governor's reaction to these rumors reflects how important was the issue of currency for the stability of the colonial economy and the colonial relationship. On December 6, 1915, Clifford summoned a meeting of chiefs and "leading members" of the "native" community to the courthouse in Accra, where he gave a speech that was translated sentence by sentence into Ga. Copies in Ga and Twi were subsequently distributed through the cocoa districts. The governor sought to reassure the population by telling them that the German fleet was trapped in its home ports by an effective naval blockade. The Allies had suffered an initial disadvantage in not being well prepared for war, but now men and armaments were available on a vast scale. The reason that British West Africa was short of coin was simply that the skilled mechanics and machines at the Royal Mint were involved in making munitions. Clifford urged patience. There would be a shortage of coin for some time to come, but it was merely a temporary inconvenience. The governor added a homely, paternalistic touch that he clearly thought would evoke a response in his African audience: Germany had been reduced to "collecting its cooking pots and turning them into munitions."[101] Clearly officials in the British colonial government felt the need of their own propaganda to win the confidence of their African subjects.

The initial response of Colonial Office officials to Clifford's serious concern about the currency was remarkably cavalier. The Bank of West Africa's view was dismissed as "unduly

98. Clifford, secret to Bonar Law, 4/12/15, CO96/561.
99. *Ibid.*
100. *Ibid.*
101. *Ibid.*

alarmist."[102] Coastal officials were accused of getting their figures wrong; the situation of shortage of coin in the colony was described as merely "unpleasant"; "natives" had to be induced to lodge silver coin in the Bank.[103] Such comment and suggestions displayed ignorance and lack of imagination. It was also typical of the tendency of London officials to ignore the judgment of their "man on the spot"—when it was convenient to do so. Clifford was told that the Treasury would, if necessary, lend the WACB "a parcel of notes" in preference to gold.[104] The governor had to realize that there was no alternative to notes, as there was no chance of new coinage before March. Sir George Fiddes (assistant under-secretary of State for the Colonies in the Colonial Office) was not amused by Clifford's lack of cooperation over the issue of paper currency, commenting in a headmasterly tone, "He really must do as he is told and make the best of it."[105]

Hoarding persisted, and London officials were forced to recognize that there was no simple remedy regarding the currency that the government of the Gold Coast could adopt. The majority of the local African population had no experience of, nor any confidence in, either banking or paper money, and viewed them from a different cultural, as well as economic, perspective. This was much better understood in Accra than in London. The governor feared that an appeal to the local population to deposit their silver in the bank could create suspicion, even panic.[106] The popular prejudice against placing savings in a bank was said to be partly due to the delay in getting money out, but also partly due to concern that bank clerks might divulge to customers' relatives how much money had been deposited.[107] Nor had the majority of the African population any experience of paper currency, which was in any case in higher denominations than many day-to-day transactions required. Privately it was accepted in the Colonial Office that it was "at least possible that the whole of the (Currency) Board's stocks as well as those of the Bank may be exhausted at a very early date."[108] Some firms stopped buying cocoa on the coast for lack of coin, and were reported to be considering collecting imperial silver and shipping it out to West Africa themselves. But the acute shortage of coin made necessary the use of some form of paper money as a result of the war. It was therefore decided in 1915, and Clifford had to accept, that British Treasury currency notes should be sent to the colony and assurances be given, as to Cadbury, that shipment of coin in comparatively small quantities would be resumed by the end of January 1916.[109]

The immediate crisis of shortage of silver coin was thus solved at the close of 1915 even if, as Clifford had frequently warned, paper currency was not universally accepted in the colony.[110] Treasury notes circulated in Eastern Province, where an abnormal demand for specie had arisen because of the increased value of imports.[111] However, the bulk of the £75,000 worth imported into Sekondi in Western Province in December 1915 was not put in circulation because of doubts as to whether "the natives," except in the large towns,

102. Fiddes, CO Memo, 15/11/15, CO554/28.

103. *Ibid.*

104. *Ibid.*

105. Fiddes, CO Minute, Bank of West Africa to Fiddes, CO, 6/12/15 in Clifford to Bonar Law, 4/12/15, CO96/561.

106. Telegram, Clifford to Bonar Law, 4/12/15, CO96/561.

107. *The Gold Coast Nation,* 11/1/17. And see P. Bauer, *West African Trade,* (London, 1954), p. 8

108. Fiddes, CO Minute, telegram, Clifford to Bonar Law, 28/11/15, CO96/561.

109. Fiddes, CO Minute, Cadbury to Bonar Law, 29/12/15, CO96/564.

110. Crowther, *Report on Native Affairs 1915,* 4/5/16, Enclosure in Clifford, confid. to Bonar Law, 26/5/16, CO96/567.

111. *Report on Eastern Province 1915, Supplementary 4, Gazette* 14/7/16, CO99/31.

would receive them without "unmerited suspicion."[112] Many farmers preferred continuing the usual practice of selling their cocoa on credit and receiving IOUs over accepting paper money.[113] In fact, only a limited number of the total of £225,000 worth of Treasury notes imported into the colony in 1915 were circulated because "the native is very conservative and does not take readily to innovations of this nature."[114] The manager of the main Ashanti Goldfields mine at Obuasi decided to pay miners only 15% of their wages in paper money to start with, in December 1915, for fear of "considerable trouble."[115]

In the context of the war, even though there appeared to be no alternative to circulating some form of paper currency, Clifford seemed to be right: it was not popular. For example, the West African Rubber Plantations company informed the Colonial Office in April 1916 that the shortage of silver coin in the Gold Coast was causing serious labor difficulties, as "the natives were very bitter against, and dubious of, paper currency."[116] Steps were taken in June 1916 to repatriate the British Treasury notes because the Royal Mint had finally succeeded in producing and shipping a supply of coinage, and the immediate panic had subsided.[117] But during 1916 the WACB initiated a cautious attempt to test the waters with the circulation of a small number of West African currency notes. It was announced in September 1916 that the Board planned to issue some 20s and 10s notes in the Gold Coast and Sierra Leone, as already in Nigeria, "to test their suitability." They were to be issued against silver kept locally and would be accepted for all dues payable to the government.[118]

As the war continued, it became clear that Clifford had been overanxious about whether the African population of the colony would accept paper money, but his caution and reassurances helped to alert London and to reconcile local opinion. First reports indicated that the higher denominations of notes were being used but that there was little acceptance of small denominations. By the last quarter of 1916, notes (mostly 20s and 10s, of which some 46,000 were in circulation) were in use in the absence of sufficient coin, but the smallest denomination, of a few 2s notes, had not been widely accepted.[119] The introduction of 2s notes reflected the acute shortage of small change. To encourage their use, it was announced that small notes would be accepted in payment of all government dues, such as railway, customs, and post office rates.[120] It remained difficult for the government to calculate the impact. The local manager of the Bank of West Africa in Ashanti reported in 1916 that it was impossible to judge whether new notes were circulating, because disappointingly few locals used the bank.[121] A year later, in 1917, there were few notes circulating in Ashanti, with the result that the population there was still not used to paper money.[122]

African conditions played a part here. Although in the event the £1 and 10s notes had been—according to officials—"willingly accepted" by African traders and shopkeepers

112. *Report on Western Province 1915, Supplementary 3, Gazette* 3/7/16, CO99/31.

113. Acting Treasurer Lewis, Enclosure 1, Memo, 24/8/18, CO554/37/493.

114. *Trade Report 1915, Supplementary Gazette* 1/5/16, CO99/30.

115. Watkins to Mann, 17/12/15, AGC MS.14, 171.38.

116. West Africa Rubber Plantations Company to Bonar Law, 7/8/16, CO554/32.

117. R. Fry, *Bankers in West Africa,* p. 79.

118. *West African Currency Board Report for year ending 30/6/16,* CO554/30; also *Notice, West African Currency Board, Gazette* 9/9/16, CO99/31/64.

119. Clifford, *LegCo* 2/11/17, *Gazette* 10/12/17. CO99/583/767.

120. *West African Currency Board Notice, Gazette* 19/12/16, CO99/32/5.

121. *Report on Ashanti 1916*, Clifford to Long, 15/8/17, CO96/581/510.

122. *Report on Ashanti 1916,* Clifford to Long, 15/8/17, CO96/581/510; *Report on Ashanti 1917,* in Clifford to Long, 13/6/18, CO96/590/329.

(ever astute commercial practitioners), the reason paper notes had not "won their way into the ordinary native market places" was as much a result of practical inconvenience as lack of confidence. Clifford was perceptive, compared with his contemporaries, in appreciating the disadvantage that "the average native, when wearing his ordinary cloth, is an even more pocketless creature than the well dressed European lady of 1910."[123] It was easier and safer for "natives" to knot silver coins into a corner of their clothes than to store paper notes. Paper rapidly deteriorated in the damp tropical climate, and there were other dangers, such as fire or white ants. It was therefore, as Clifford pointed out, "only natural, that the ordinary native should be very reluctant to keep his money in a form in which it is liable to be eaten or reduced to a handful of dust in the course of a few days, or even hours."[124]

The currency situation deteriorated further in 1918, with notes as well as coin in ever shorter supply. Clifford admitted that the Gold Coast Treasury was "in great need of ready money" when he asked for permission to use £70,000 of the Basel Mission factory money in July 1918.[125] Part of the problem was the "huge sums" owed to the Gold Coast by the War Office to cover the expense of sending the Gold Coast Regiment to East Africa, which the Colonial Office was pressing the War Office to repay.[126] Clifford was still not in favor of making the West African currency notes legal tender in August 1918, though urged to do so by the local Chambers of Commerce.[127] However, the circulation of the notes had steadily increased since their introduction in the latter half of 1916, making it possible for the Currency Board to reduce the coin backing to 75% of their value in October 1917 and to 50% in 1918.[128]

Even so, by the beginning of the cocoa season in late October 1918, the shortage of silver coin threatened to become so serious that the governor was forced to change his policy. A bill to make the West African currency notes legal tender was passed, although Clifford remained reluctant and confessed that he viewed the situation of forcing paper money on the African population of the colony "with considerable uneasiness and anxiety."[129] He planned to issue a circular to chiefs in cocoa districts to assure them, with "the formally pledged word of the government," of the value of the currency notes as a medium of exchange. Clifford, well-intentioned though patronizing, hoped that such an explanation to "the more intelligent classes of natives" and (through the political officers) to the local people of their districts would reduce to a minimum the "embarrassment" to the government of substituting paper for silver currency. The governor wanted to avoid any panic that might lead to more hoarding and concealment of silver "on an unprecedented scale."[130]

Considerable care was taken in both the preparation and the production of the West African currency notes to promote their use by the local population. In early November it was announced that the West African currency paper notes (red for 20s, green for 10s, and blue for 2s) were to become legal tender, backed by coin in London, even though

---

123. Clifford to Long, 27/10/18, CO554/37/604.

124. *Ibid.*

125. Telegram, Clifford to Long, 4/7/18, CO96/591.

126. Calder, CO Minute, telegram, Clifford to Long, 4/7/18, CO96/591.

127. Chambers of Commerce (Accra and Eastern Province) to colonial secretary, Accra, 18/7/18, enclosure in Clifford to Long, 24/8/18, CO554/37/493.

128. West African Currency Board to Long, 14/1/18, CO554/38/52.

129. Clifford to Long, 27/10/18, CO554/37/604. "Legal tender": currency prescribed by law in which payment may be offered to meet a financial obligation.

130. *Ibid.*

they could not immediately be turned into money on the coast. They were to be used in stores and markets and for paying wages.[131] As in the French territories, an exact reproduction of the relevant silver coin was printed on the notes to help reassure illiterates: the £1 note had a picture of a 10 florin piece, the 10s note a 10s coin, and the 2s a florin. Also printed on the back of all notes was an endorsement of the values of the notes in Hausa (Hausa words, in Arabic writing). The inclusion of Hausa was partly for trading purposes and partly to ease payment to troops and police.[132]

The trading boom immediately after the war—welcome at the time as an economic fillip—led, however, to a new currency crisis. By mid-November 1918, just after the Armistice, currency notes were circulating in the colony with only a minimal coin reserve: notes to the value of £109,045 with a coin reserve of only £39,045. The Currency Board was in favor of further reducing the coin reserve to only 25% of the value of the paper currency to allow the banks to release more silver coin into circulation.[133] The government was able to reassure the Colonial Bank in Accra that, with the end of hostilities, £30,000 in notes and £70,000 of silver had just been shipped from England.[134] Before this there had been no guarantee of safe arrival. For example, £10,800 of silver coin was lost at sea in the early months of 1918 as a result of enemy action.[135]

The sudden postwar revival of trade and shipping, and high import prices, had led to a demand for currency on an exceptional scale. By mid-December 1918, the situation deteriorated sharply again, with yet more coinage urgently needed. The governor once more warned the Colonial Office of "serious trouble" if enough silver coin were not immediately received. There was not enough silver to exchange for the notes that were now being presented in great numbers at the banks. Africans were testing the colonial government's credibility. Clifford warned that the need for more silver was "most urgent," including £60,000 required before December 31 simply for miners' wages and pensions for members of the Gold Coast Regiment after the completion of war service.[136] The West African Chamber of Mines had informed the government that miners, largely from the north of the colony, would not accept paper money, and that notes were unacceptable to miners from other territories.[137]

A particular problem the government had not been able to solve during the war was the lack of sufficiently low denominations of currency. It would seem that this had an inflationary effect, though it is impossible to be certain of the overall picture. There were not only different denominations of British coins being used but also, as before the war, a range of other coinage and traditional forms of currency such as cowries or "shell money," especially in the more marginal areas. Clifford called for low-denomination notes of 1s, 6d, and 3d. The Currency Board responded by putting a West Africa currency note of 1s

131. Clifford to Long, 4/11/18, CO96/593/642.

132. Bank of British West Africa, 8/7/18, Enclosure 4, Clifford to Long, 24/8/18, CO554/37/493. West African Currency Board to Long, 22/4/18, CO554/38/52.

133. West African Currency Board memo, 12/11/18, CO554/38.

134. Telegram, Colonial Bank, Accra, to CO, 9/11/18, CO96/593; telegram, Long to Clifford, 11/11/18, CO96/593. The Colonial Bank had been set up in the Colony in 1917 and was by now (despite few reserves) a small scale rival and irritant to the Bank of West Africa.

135. *Report of the West African Currency Board*, 25/1/19, CO554/42.

136. Telegrams, Clifford to Long, 11/12/18, 13/12/18, 21/12/18, CO554/37.

137. West African Chamber of Mines to Acting Colonial Secretary, Accra, 30/7/18. Enclosure 3 in Clifford to Long, 24/8/18, CO554/37/493.

into circulation in January 1919, even though they knew the 2s note had not been popular.[138] Clifford's government had also been unable to wholly compensate for the shortage of silver coin by increasing the subsidiary British West African nickel-bronze currency introduced into the colony in 1912. According to the District Manager of the Bank of British West Africa, these coins, both the one penny (1d) and halfpenny values, were well liked over the whole of the Gold Coast, although he believed the one-tenth coin was only in demand in the Northern Territories.[139] But reports from officers in the field to the Treasury in Accra in 1915 reveal that one-tenths were also "in very common use" in markets in eastern districts of Eastern Province, where they were seen piled up for use as change by sellers of spices, herbs, and sweetmeats. However, they were not normally used as exchange in the main cocoa districts, which were wealthier and where the price of food was comparatively high.[140]

Africans responded to the colonial government's currency adaptations with initiatives of their own. They made use of the nickel-bronze coinage in ways that the British colonial administrators had not foreseen. The holes in the center of the nickel-bronze coins, intended for stringing purposes, were put to a variety of uses. The metal, increasingly rare because of wartime shortages, appears to have been more valuable, like silver, as jewelry. Nickel coins were also commonly used as counters for gambling—and even as washers for buildings, being much cheaper and easier to obtain than the real thing. Crowther reported seeing one-tenth coins serving as washers for galvanized iron roofing in Eastern Province.[141] This coinage became steadily more scarce during the war, until shipments from the UK finally stopped altogether in 1917 because of the cost of production, and because nickel and copper were needed for military purposes.[142]

The local African population also compensated in a whole variety of other ways for the general shortage of coins during the war, and especially the shortage of low-denomination coins. Barter was still common in the Northern Territories, even though more money had come into the protectorate in recent years as a result of migrant northern laborers seeking employment in the south and bringing money back with them. But also, more importantly, the supply of nickel coinage had never been enough to banish cowries from the markets.[143] The verdict of the Gold Coast Treasury in June 1914 just before the war that cowries were becoming extinct had proved premature.[144] It was not a case of the population in the Northern Territories or in eastern districts of Eastern Province, such as Ada and Keta, or in parts of Ashanti "reverting" to the use of cowries during the war

138. Telegram, Clifford to Long, 11/12/18, CO554/37. And *Report West African Currency Board for year ending 30/6/15,* CO554/42.

139. *Report, District Manager Bank of British West Africa,* 26/6/15, CO554/24/157. As before the war, the tenth was often taken as an eighth. See Section I, chapter 2.

140. Acting Commissioner of Eastern Province Crowther, to Treasury, Accra, 26/6/15, in Acting Governor Slater to Harcourt, 2/1/15, CO554/24/888.

141. Replies to Treasury questionnaire, in Acting Governor Slater to Harcourt, 2/1/15, CO554/24/888.

142. Ellis, CO Minute, West African Currency Board to Long, 7/5/17, CO554/34.

143. Armitage, *Report on the Northern Territories 1917,* 3/6/18 in Clifford to Long, 1/7/17, CO96/591/337. A similar shortage of low denomination coins contributed to the retention of the manilla in Southeastern Nigeria; see B. Naanen, "Economy Within an Economy: The Manilla Currency, Exchange Rate Instability and Social Conditions in Southeastern Nigeria 1900–1948," *JAH,* 34, 1993, pp. 425–446.

144. Gold Coast Treasury to Royal Mint, reply to questionnaire, 23/6/14, CO96/545/488.

or of the cowrie "reappearing" in 1919, as some of the secondary literature suggests.[145] In these areas, cowries, lower in value than any coin, had never stopped being used as a medium of exchange, even if they were rare elsewhere. The provincial commissioner at Sekondi declared in 1915 that he had only once ever seen cowries used in Western Province.[146] But they had remained a major form of currency in the Northern Territories, where they were still used in preference to silver, particularly in the payment of head money for wives. "Every family has their store of cowries and the small amount of one-tenths received only represents a small fraction of the value of stored or buried cowries."[147]

More "shell money" was put into circulation in periods when European currencies were unstable or in short supply, as during the First World War. Redundant shell was used for house decoration or crushed for lime content, but cowries, even if increasingly scarce, continued to be used as currency in the mid-1920s.[148] Indeed, they were still reputedly in use in the late 20th century on the northwest frontier of Ghana and Burkina Faso.[149] "Shell money" was a currency that could cross frontiers; it was light, durable, stable, and difficult to counterfeit. In such ways, African ingenuity and resourcefulness compensated to some degree for the inadequacies of colonial provision.

Although cowries had an advantage over official national currencies in cross-border transactions, it was coins, such as the one-tenth piece (about 8 cowries), that appeared to be seeping away across northern frontiers. There were suspicions in the northeastern province of the Northern Territories that the chiefs in French Moshi country, who were well supplied with cowries, were deliberately trying to buy up what they could of British West African nickel coinage in cross-frontier payments for cattle. It is likely that this was mainly required for exchange to pay tax to the French authorities.[150] With no direct tax in the Gold Coast, there was no comparable need for coin on the British side of the frontier.

In the case of currency, the war period proved a valuable learning experience for British officials, who were previously unfamiliar with the complexities of African economic custom and practice. Crowther, as acting commissioner of Eastern Province, realized that farthings and half farthings would be more useful to local people in the markets, and fit more easily into the local pattern or coinage, than tenths.[151] But it was not thought

---

145. E.g., N. Van Hear, "Northern Labor," p. 98.

146. Provincial Commissioner, Sekondi, reply to Treasury questionnaire, 31/7/15 in Acting Governor Slater to Bonar Law, 2/11/15, CO554/24/888.

147. Acting Chief Commissioner, Northern Territories quoted by Acting Treasurer Davies, *Treasury Report,* 19/10/15 in Acting Governor Slater to Bonar Law, 2/11/15, CO554/24/888. See also Acting Treasurer Davies, *Treasury Report,* 19/10/15 in Acting Governor Slater to Bonar Law, 2/11/15, CO554/24/888.

148. K. Arhin, *West African Traders,* p. 74.

149. See J. Hogendorn & M. Johnson, *The Shell Money of the Slave Trade,* (London, 1986), pp. 150–155.

150. Commissioners, North Western Province and North Eastern Province of the Northern Territories, quoted by Davies, *Treasury Report,* 19/10/15, Acting Governor Slater to Bonar Law, 2/11/15, CO554/24/888. About half the value cited for exchange with cowries before the war (see Section I, Chapter 2). West African Currency Committee, 15/12/11, in Thorburn to Harcourt, 14/2/12, CO554/8/678.

151. For the common units used in markets and native tribunals, see E. Wrangham, "The Gold Coast and the First World War," p. 152. Acting Commissioner of Eastern Province Crowther, 23/8/15, in Acting Governor Slater to Bonar Law, 2/11/15, CO554/24/888. For smaller values, see Ramseyer and Kuhne (1875) and Rattray (1923) in Kwame Arhin, "Monetization and the Asante State," in J. Guyer (ed.), *Money Matters,* p. 100.

practicable in the Colonial Office to change low coinage denominations during the war. The immediate problem was the lack of coin of any kind. Yet it was subsequently recognized that useful investigative work had been undertaken by officers in the coast in the war period, and that the information would be referred to the Currency Board to be acted upon after the war.[152]

The war exposed to its subjects the shortcomings of the colonial government—in this instance, its inability to provide a sufficient steady supply of currency. It is not clear whether the effects of the shortage of coin would have been mitigated earlier if notes had been circulated as legal tender before the end of 1918. Governor Clifford had tried hard to steer the colony through a sequence of currency crises to avoid paper currency being forced on the colony before he felt its people were ready for it. One advantage of the postponement was that it allowed time for the population to get used to paper money gradually, before it became the crucial means of exchange.

Disruption of the flow of imports into the Gold Coast during the First World War put both public and private finances under great pressure. The deterioration in the standard of living of Africans was due to the colonial government's financial policies as well as to the economic impact of world war. Ironically, Clifford's prewar policy of using the colony's surplus balances to finance development and his determination to complete his construction plans led, during the war, to higher levels of taxation than might otherwise have been imposed. In the legislative council just before the armistice (in late October 1918), Clifford defended his record.[153] He argued that only the increased taxation, especially the export duty on cocoa, together with the trade recovery of 1915 and the 1916 boom, had enabled government finances to survive the "acute economic depression" of 1917 and 1918, the last two years of the war.[154] He did not mention here another factor that had led to high taxation for Africans: the sums siphoned off to the imperial exchequer as the colony's contribution to the Empire's war. A significant way in which the Gold Coast government was financed over the war period was that reserves were run down to below their 1913 level.[155]

Clifford had been left in no doubt, in his dealings with London, of the main concerns of the Colonial Office. It was not how Clifford could maintain his ambitious spending plans or protect his African subjects from the inconveniences of war. It was how the Gold Coast could help sustain the home country. Meanwhile, the local administration was capable only of policy initiatives which added to, rather than reduced, African privations. Suffering shortages, high prices, and a collapse in their purchasing power, Africans responded both by criticizing the government and by taking measures of their own. However, they were not driven to active opposition to the government that (in Clifford's view, at least) the imposition on them of direct taxation would have provoked. At the same time, Clifford's judgment (for public consumption) that "the war has not materially interfered with the actual capacity of this colony either as a producer or as a consumer" did not focus on the crucial international constraints within which the colonial economy

---

152. Fiddes, CO Minute, Acting Governor Slater to Bonar Law, 2/11/15, CO554/24/888.

153. It is worth observing perhaps that Clifford cannot be blamed for having failed to predict the length—or indeed the sudden termination shortly afterwards—of the war.

154. Clifford, *LegCo* 28/10/18, *Gazette* 9/11/18, CO99/33/82.

155. See N. A. Cox-George, *Studies in Finance and Development,* p. 57.

operated.[156] The war had revealed, to many of the local African population as well as to British officials, the extreme vulnerability of the "open" economy of the colony: "open" to unprecedented fluctuations in world prices and variations in demand and supply.[157] It was not clear at the time whether the wartime disruption to trade was just a temporary blip, but it was clear that continued acquiescence by Africans in British colonial rule would depend on improved trading conditions.

As Jeffrey Herbst has commented, "there is no better evidence of the problematic nature of colonial control of West Africa ... than the uncertainty of the British authorities about their ability to impose a new currency on the territories they nominally controlled."[158] The situation in the Gold Coast during the First World War supports this general judgment. Here Clifford and his officials were indeed anxious, rather than merely uncertain, regarding the consequences of coin shortage and the introduction of paper money. They remained ignorant in some respects of how Africans were coping—but they knew more about local conditions than did the more sanguine Colonial Office. Once again, within the global trading constraints, and in response to currency concerns, it was Africans who largely determined what the colonial government could—and could not—do in the Gold Coast. While the governor sought to steer London officials and the colony's population to his point of view, Africans made what they judged to be the most effective use of such coin and notes and traditional currencies as were available in the difficult circumstances of wartime shortages and disrupted trade.

Meanwhile, as we shall see in the next chapter, the problematical state of public (and private) finances severely restricted the Gold Coast government's spending in the war years—and this in turn complicated its relationship with Africans of the territory.

---

156. Clifford, *LegCo* 28/10/18, *Gazette* 9/11/18, CO99/33/82.

157. D. Seers, "The Stages of Development of a Primary Producer in the Middle of the Twentieth Century," *Economic Bulletin of Ghana*, 7, 1963.

158. Jeffrey Herbst, *States and Power in Africa, Comparative Lessons in Authority and Control*, (Princeton, 2,000), p. 206.

Chapter 7

Wartime Development and Welfare: British Projects and African Enterprise

The agenda of British colonial governments in Africa at this time included, as noted before, both development and welfare projects. For the embryonic territory of the Gold Coast, the priority for developing infrastructure was transport: railways and roads. British colonial rule—especially under Clifford—was also committed to welfare: the concept of "trusteeship" incorporated attempts to safeguard and enhance the quality of life of the African as well as the European population. The priorities here were to extend health provision and increase opportunities for Western education. African assessment of colonial rule may be said to have depended as much on "development" as on "welfare" (in addition, of course, to changes in their material standard of living), since development in the form of improved transport infrastructure, in particular, benefited all Africans involved in overseas trade.

However, as a result of the war, few of Clifford's development and welfare plans were achieved, and many were put on indefinite hold. As early as October 1914, Clifford recognized privately that the war would mean that many of his plans for the development of the Gold Coast colony would have to be curtailed or postponed: "All expenditure has had to be cut down ruthlessly and most of my cherished schemes are knocked on the head for a long time to come."[1] For such a determined and energetic governor, the constraints were bound to be frustrating. "It is very disappointing, of course, and substitutes the nauseous task of retrenchment for the much more congenial task of rapid development."[2] What was unforeseen at this time was that the war, far from being "likely to last for many weary and anxious months," would last as long as four years.[3] It became increasingly difficult to overcome the doubts of London officials about continuing major public works in a British colony while the Empire was at war.

African prewar expectations were thus dashed as the extent of wartime cutbacks became clear. There was no sign of the promised modernity through development—and, as we shall see later in this chapter, Africans became frustrated by the perennial inadequacy of both medical and educational services in the war years. For a while, little changed. For example, Clifford's first priority after news of the outbreak of war was to continue development of the northern extension of the Accra railway. He succeeded in maintaining work on this railway construction until it was finally stopped, on London's orders, late in 1916. At this point, he still considered railways as the crucial government priority, with roads merely as feeders to the rail heads. As we shall see, it was African agency that produced the remarkable road revolution in the colony which, begun before the war, now

1. Clifford to Fell, 5/10/14. T. E. Fell, *Letters from the Gold Coast 1987–1915*, MSS. British Empire, s. 316 (l) Rhodes House.
2. *Ibid.*
3. *Ibid.*

gathered pace throughout the war years.[4] Africans took other initiatives too, such as in pursuit of educational provision, but this accompanied a wider critique that any improvements arising from colonial rule were being outweighed by its costs.

Clifford fought doggedly to ensure that railway construction proceeded as planned. Just before the war, all had seemed well in place, with the Gold Coast considered to be "well off generally" in July 1914, once a loan had finally been raised for development works.[5] Clifford had obtained permission for a long-term rail strategy to link up the Accra-Koforidua line through the Kwahu plateau to Kumasi, at the estimated cost of £1,200,000. The Colonial Office was enthusiastic about this further investment in the infrastructure, recognizing that the railways were directly responsible for between a third and a quarter of the colony's revenue.[6] The extension to Koforidua was then completed in October 1914, after the outbreak of war. The first eight miles of the line to the north of Koforidua towards Tafo were constructed by the end of the year. Despite the shortage of trucks, goods began to be transported by British and African traders. As Clifford argued, it had been "abundantly proved" that every section of line completed brought in a "handsome return."[7]

But by 1915, Colonial Office officials were beginning to apply the brakes, with a "stop-go" policy for the railway works applied that year—apparently the result of a vacillating Colonial Office being pressured by a powerful governor. Clifford received instructions from Secretary of State Lord Harcourt in January 1915 that "all, or nearly all" development work had to be stopped.[8] The sum allotted for the railway would have to be halved, even though Ellis acknowledged, "It is hard on Sir H. Clifford who has set his heart on seeing a decent railway programme put through in his colony but it is, I fear, inevitable."[9] Clifford continued with more limited construction but still argued strongly as follows: "It can be asserted with absolute confidence that there is no more directly remunerative service upon which the funds of this colony can be expended than the construction of the northern line through the cocoa producing districts."[10] Then, in April, orders were suddenly given for work to be stopped altogether for six months because of high capital expenditure, such as expensive rolling stock, as a result of the war.[11] The issue was largely expense rather than, as has been suggested, shortage of materials and labor.[12]

---

4. For an earlier version of this study of road transport in the colony, see E. Wrangham, "An African Road Revolution: the Gold Coast in the Period of the Great War," *Journal of Imperial and Commonwealth History*, 32, 1, January 2004, pp. 1–18.

5. Ellis, CO Minute, Acting Governor Robertson to Harcourt, 6/7/14, CO96/546/531.

6. Acting Governor Slater, *LegCo* 25/10/15, *Gazette*, 25/11/15, C099/29/101; and Flood, CO Minute, Acting Governor Robertson to Harcourt, 6/7/14, CO96/546/531.

7. Clifford to Harcourt, 2/12/14, C096/550/911.

8. Telegram, Harcourt to Clifford, 27/1/15, CO96/550/911.

9. Ellis, CO Minute, telegram, Clifford to Harcourt, 27/1/15, CO96/550/911.

10. Clifford to Harcourt, 20/3/15, C096/556/247.

11. The governor blamed Cruickshank, the general manager of the railways, for failing to keep account of the extent of liabilities. And see Flood, Green, Ellis, Fiddes, Sir John Anderson, CO Minute, Clifford to Bonar Law, 1/5/15, C096/577/377.

12. See G. Chada, "Labor Protest, Group Consciousness and Trade Unionism in West Africa. The Radical Railway Workers of Colonial Ghana 1900–1950," unpublished PhD thesis, (University of Toronto, 1981), p. 21. Also Bonar Law to Acting Governor Slater, 16/6/15, CO96/577/377. Acting Governor Slater to Bonar Law, 4/9/15, C096/560/733; and Acting Governor Slater to Bonar Law, 29 July 1915, C096/559/610.

Yet in October 1915, there was a sufficient trade recovery for the governor to be allowed to proceed with yet more railway construction. Clifford received permission from London to extend the railway north through rich cocoa districts at least to Tafo, nearly fourteen miles from Koforidua, at an estimated cost of £3000 a mile. This was seen as a potentially very profitable investment, with likely government revenue of about £20,000 a year. What directly affected the African population, although it was accepted without comment by British officials, was that the estimated cost of £81,500 would have to be met by further raising indirect taxes.[13] Yet this was a time when the cost of living for Africans in the colonial economy had already risen very sharply. Development during the war came at a high cost. For the African population, prices were already unusually high, and substantial wartime taxation raised the price of imports even higher.

British perspectives were by now very different. At the Colonial Office, Sir George Fiddes argued that continued construction would "assist after the war in the recuperation of the Empire."[14] For Clifford and his officials in the Gold Coast colony, the priority remained extending railways into the most profitable cocoa districts. This explains why, despite wartime expenses and shortages, work was in "full swing" on the Koforidua-Tafo section of the line as late as July 1916, and permission was granted even then for work to proceed with the link between Koforidua and Kumasi, a distance of 146 miles.[15] Clifford was anxious that work should also proceed from Kumasi towards Kwahu. The cocoa districts to the east and southeast of Kumasi "very urgently" needed transport facilities.[16] He also planned surveys to investigate the possibility of a railway route near the coast in Central Province.[17]

Clifford's sense of urgency regarding the link between the Accra and Sekondi-Kumasi lines was partly prompted by the need to relieve pressure on the port of Accra. Landing goods was easier at Sekondi harbor than at Accra, which was in "a precarious condition" and was losing revenue through congestion and the lack of facilities. The situation threatened to get worse as the harbor became increasingly silted up.[18] The general congestion in Accra was visibly worsening: " … the queue outside Accra station every morning has not a dissimilar appearance to the Strand in the neighbourhood of a popular music hall."[19]

However, construction costs were mounting to what became, in late 1916, a level that was unacceptable to London. Already in 1915 the war was making it increasingly difficult and expensive to obtain necessary imported supplies. In September, Fiddes warned that the Treasury would not support buying American rails, out of concern for increasing British indebtedness to the United States.[20] A month later the Crown Agents confirmed that there could be no guarantee that rails would be delivered from Britain, where rail makers were occupied making steel for shells. Obtaining rails from Canada "would at all

13. Acting Governor Slater, *LegCo* 25/10/15, *Gazette* 25/11/15, C099/29/101; and Acting Governor Slater, secret to Bonar Law, 30/9/15, C096/560.

14. Ellis, Fiddes, CO Minute, Clifford to Bonar Law, 18/6/16, C096/570/667.

15. Flood, CO Minute, Crown Agents to Bonar Law, 15/11/15, CO96/562; Ellis, CO Minute, Clifford to Bonar Law, 18/6/16, C096/570/667; Flood, CO Minute, and Clifford, confid. to Bonar Law, 27/7/16, C096/568.

16. Clifford to Bonar Law, 13/11/16, C096/572/840.

17. Clifford, *LegCo* 23/10/16, *Gazette* 23/10/16, C099/31/76.

18. Clifford, confid. to Bonar Law, 27/7/16, C096/568.

19. Clifford to Bonar Law, 18/9/16, C096/570/667.

20. Sir George Fiddes, CO Minute, Acting Governor Slater to Bonar Law, 30/9/15, CO96/560.

events keep the matter within the Empire."[21] Investigations were undertaken to see whether there was any timber in West Africa that was resistant to "white ants and such drawbacks" and could therefore be used for sleepers. Eventually some stock including rails was located in storage in Nigeria. But costs continued to rise sharply. By late 1916 the construction cost per mile had risen to over £9,000, three times higher than the previous year.[22] Rolling stock and coal were still very expensive and in short supply, even though savings had been made with wood used as fuel to power the trains.[23]

From the middle of 1916, the opinions of London officials and Clifford's government began to seriously diverge. Several Colonial Office officials were expressing ever graver doubts as to whether the Gold Coast should continue with ambitious development schemes during a war. Other railway schemes in British West Africa had been halted in 1915, such as the extension of the Sierra Leone railway and the construction of the eastern Nigeria railway north of the Enugu and Udi coalfields.[24] By September 1916 there were questions in London as to whether money should not rather be lent to the Imperial Government until the end of the war. By the end of November 1916, with the need for military recruits, London officials such as Ellis and Flood were convinced that work on the Gold Coast railways would finally have to stop.[25] They argued that the labor of between 6,000 and 8,000 men on railway construction in the Gold Coast colony could not be justified when soldiers were needed for the East Africa campaign and for service on the inland water transport system in Mesopotamia. It was also noted that the governor had claimed that there was already a shortage of labor in the colony, with insufficient men to meet the needs of the gold and manganese mines. In December 1916, cocoa prices finally collapsed and the economic prospects for the Gold Coast colony for 1917 became dire. Clifford's construction plans were now condemned in London as "absurdly ambitious."[26] Yet, despite the war, he had, remarkably, succeeded in keeping them going for two and a half years; only by the close of 1916 did the war finally put a stop to his schemes for the construction of new railway lines.

Clifford's priorities remained different from those of officials in London. He tried hard—with somewhat desperate arguments—to save the development plans for the Gold Coast that were so dear to him, and also to retain the colony's labor force for much-needed works in the colony. For example, he suggested that the "natives" of the Colony and Ashanti were not well fitted by temperament for military service abroad, being mostly "landed proprietors" who were not keen to leave agriculture.[27] This assessment, however, was hardly consistent with Clifford's prewar description of the Ashanti as "a first class fighting man."[28] Taking manpower from a colony that was so sparsely populated could, he claimed, threaten its stability. He argued that increased taxation had been justified to the population of the Gold Coast as the only way development could continue during

21. Crown Agents to Bonar Law, 15/11/15, C096/562. For the work of the Crown Agents, see R. Kesner, "Builders of Empire: The Role of the Crown Agents in Imperial Development 1880–1914," *Journal of Imperial and Commonwealth History*, 5, 3, 1977.

22. Reports, Waller, manager of Gold Coast Railways, 1/9/16, Enclosure 1, Clifford to Bonar Law, 18/6/16, CO96/570/667; Also Enclosure 1, Clifford to Bonar Law, 18/9/16, C096/570/667.

23. Flood, CO Minute, Clifford to Bonar Law, 10/8/16, C096/568/574.

24. D. C. Dorward, in A. Roberts (ed.), *The Cambridge History of Africa*, p. 426. And see Section III, Chapter 7.

25. Ellis, CO Minute, Crown Agents to CO, 27/11/16, C096/574.

26. Flood, CO Minute, Clifford to Bonar Law, 13/11/16, C096/572/840.

27. Clifford, confid. to Bonar Law, 13/12/16, CO96/576.

28. See Section 1, Chapter 3. Also Clifford to Harcourt, dispatch: *Trek Through Ashanti 1914*, 12/3/14, CO96/528/746.

the war. If this spending were stopped, the population would feel cheated, and it would be hard for the government to resist remitting taxes. Abandoning construction would thus have "deplorable local effects" while adding very little to the manpower for East Africa, Egypt, or Mesopotamia.[29] But London officials had no intention of allowing remission of taxes, and African and European voices that drew attention to African hardship remained unheard.

Unprecedentedly high taxation was now inflicted on the Gold Coast population regardless of whether development projects were being undertaken or not. The higher rail rates led to reduced passenger traffic from the time of the first wartime tax rises in 1915. Normal goods traffic was also reduced because some mines had closed and there were fewer imports. By 1918, there was something of a one-sided haul of railway goods in the colony. Empty, or nearly empty, rail trucks now dominated the journeys inland as a result of the shortage of manufactured imports, although more local food was now transported by rail in the space available.[30]

The effects of the war bit deep. Short of money, materials, and men, the railway infrastructure of the colony steadily deteriorated during the war. This affected both African producers and European trading companies. Clifford recognized that after the war reconstruction would need to take priority over new extensions.[31] By 1916, the permanent way of the Sekondi-Kumasi line was in "a deplorable state," with both rails and sleepers "seriously deteriorating." The war stopped the annual renewal of ten miles of the worst part of the track.[32] Damaged steel sleepers had to be replaced by wooden ones, and there were frequent derailments, with twenty-ton vans sliding off badly worn rails. On the worst section of track, about forty-five miles of the Sekondi-Kumasi line, there were nine derailments in the last two months of 1916, and an average number of two per week in January 1917. There was little the government could do to reduce the danger of accidents other than lowering speeds.[33] Occasionally badly needed stock reached, or nearly reached, the colony. Two locomotives were finally shipped in 1918 after long being on order for the Accra railway. Unfortunately, one of them came to grief in the Accra roadstead. The heavy surf and the poor condition of the harbor with the lack of adequate landing facilities led to the boiler and various parts being lost overboard.[34]

British transport priorities reflected wartime needs. There was an increase in firewood traffic for the mines. Mining companies were, like the railways, using wood because of the shortage and high price of coal. An extra hazard of burning wood for the railways was due to the fact that the locomotives had been designed for coal. As a result, in 1918 the governor was given permission to pass legislation to absolve the railway from compensation claims for damage to customers' goods from sparks.[35] As we have seen, the

---

29. Clifford, confid. to Bonar Law, 13/12/16, C096/576.

30. C. Tsey, "Gold Coast Railways," p. 312.

31. Clifford, *LegCo* 28/10/18, *Gazette*, 9/11/18, CO99/33/82.

32. *Railways Report 1916*, Clifford to Long, 25/7/17, C096/580.

33. Clifford to Long, 10/12/17, C096/583/767. Acting Colonial Secretary, *LegCo* 17/5/17, *Gazette* 2/6/17, C099/32/42. The overall figure was 96 derailments in 1917, and 103 in 1918 (cf. 65 derailments in 1911). Derailments at stations were largely due to worn-out switches. *Railways Report 1918*, C098/32. See also *Railways Report 1911*, *Gazette* 24/8/12, C099/26/61.

34. *Railways Report 1918*, CO98/32.

35. Clifford to Long, 10/12/17, C096/583/767. Foodstuffs transported by rail: 12,000 tons 1916; 28,000 tons 1918; see C. Tsey, "Gold Coast Railways," p. 312; also *Railways Report 1917*, C098/30 Clifford to Long, 25/9/18, C096/592/555.

British imperial government was particularly concerned about obtaining manganese, an essential ingredient in steel production. Trucks of manganese ore, exported since September 1916, caused a heavy weight on the southern section of the Sekondi-Kumasi line. In June 1918, the Ministry of Munitions in London emphasized the need to strengthen the main line, as safe delivery of manganese was by now "a matter of national importance."[36]

The wartime search for fuel thus put new pressure on the colony's railway network, to the detriment of other users, whether government officials, farmers, or traders. An increasing proportion of mining capital was spent to complete tram lines and acquire boilers that could be used to burn wood, even though steam-fired engines were less efficient. Locomotives, put to heavy use to obtain firewood for fuel, could not be replaced, and were now competing with cocoa "specials" for space on the railway lines. This problem was made worse in 1916 by additional "specials" conveying soldiers to Sekondi en route to East Africa. Meanwhile, the shortages of bearings led to a large number of ore trucks remaining idle.[37]

By the end of the war, the railways were also suffering from staffing problems. The problem was partly the result of too few Africans having been trained before the war. The African unofficial Casely Hayford was told as late as May 1917 that every endeavor was now being made to belatedly train "natives" for "responsible duties" in the railway department.[38] Apart from military secondments, shortages arose because British staff assigned to the Gold Coast were required to administer the railway in Togo. In October 1918, the Crown Agents also reported problems in recruiting artisans such as fitters and platelayers from Britain, as wages were not as attractive as in England.[39]

Moreover, the beginnings of African worker organization and unionization in the colony grew out of railwaymen's grievances relating to pay and conditions of service during, and immediately after, the war.[40] There were strikes of skilled railway workmen at Sekondi in July 1918. An unpopular change in the schedule of working hours in June 1918 had brought to a head a number of complaints. These concerned the lack of sick pay, the failure of management to provide tools at a time when prices were rising sharply, and, for artisans, the lack of pensionable status in contrast with the provision for clerks.[41] Railway workers also complained about the increased cost of food, clothing, and rents since the outbreak of the war. The prices of carpenters' tools had risen sharply, with small saws up from 5s to 7s 6d and squares up from 3s 6d to 5s. In June 1918, mechanics

36. The Colonial Office therefore contacted Lugard in order to obtain materials from stocks at Kaduna junction in Nigeria: Ministry of Munitions to Long, 3/6/18, C096/595.

37. Watkins to Mann, 17/12/15, AGC MS.14,171.38; Samson to Mann, 13 July 1916, 14,171.40. Watkins to Mann, 30/7/15, 28/8/15, AGC MS 14,171,37; 25/10/15, 17/12/15, 14,171.38; 2/10/16,14,171.40; 25/1/17, 14,171 41.

38. Casely Hayford, *LegCo* 17/5/17, *Gazette* 2/6/17, C099/32/42.

39. Crown Agents to Long, 14/10/18, C096/594.

40. E.g., The Railway Workers' Association, Sekondi 1923. See R. Jeffries, *Class, Power and Ideology in Ghana, The Railwaymen of Sekondi,* (London, 1978), pp. 28–35: compare with the 1920 Artisans and Laborers' Union. For miners' organized activity see J. Crisp, *The Story of an African Working Class,* pp. 43–46. And for the range of strikes across the continent in this period, see A. Boahen, *African Perspectives,* p. 72.

41. See G. Chada, "The Radical Railway Workers," pp. 168–208; and C. Tsey, "Gold Coast Railways," pp. 217–221.

reported that most prices in local markets had risen by 50% to 60% during the war.[42] They had clearly experienced a substantial fall in real wages.

Turning from railways to roads, we encounter one of the most significant occurrences of the war period in the Gold Coast. There was such change here that we may speak of an African road revolution. What is so striking is that this radical change was generated by local Africans responding to changing wartime conditions. Whereas the British administration "on high" failed—after 1916—to provide improved railway services, Africans "below," already participating as key players in the economy, succeeded in providing themselves and the territory with a greatly enhanced road network.

In retrospect, we can see that this "road revolution" was already underway just before the First World War. Though road transport was still at this time far more expensive than rail, numbers of motorized vehicles (especially light American Ford cars and trucks with high road clearance) were increasing rapidly and costs were falling.[43] And the fact that roads did not require the same injection of government-raised capital was to be a great advantage in time of war. It should be noted that at this time there were three broad categories of roads in the Gold Coast: main "government" roads, built and maintained by the PWD; "pioneer" or "district" roads built by chiefs and local people under DCs and maintained by chiefs under the Roads Ordinance; and "native" roads built by Africans, mostly chiefs or cocoa growers, independently of government.[44]

Official British policy, as before the war, was to concentrate on roads that acted as feeders to existing railways, such as the road constructed in 1915 through the thickly cultivated Koforidua and Akuse region. DCs were urged to encourage improvements in chiefs' roads, with the advice of the PWD, so that they could carry light vehicles, but there was to be no new government work on roads if it could be avoided. In November 1915, Slater expressed the hope that money might be saved if Africans built more of their own roads.[45] It was obvious in Western Province, for example, that large sums would have to be spent on town roads "at some future date."[46]

The Gold Coast government's favoring of railways, as well as retrenchment, meant that the transport needs of coastal towns were neglected in this period. The local Chamber of Commerce in Sekondi drew attention in 1915 to the urgent need for adequate roads, including linking roads with neighboring villages like Chama and Amoaful. Also a lack of planning had led to buildings being constructed on the edge of Sekondi, where there were no roads at all. The trading lobby noted the irony: Sekondi, the largest port in the

42. For example, a small bag of rice from 3s 9d to 15s a bag; kerosene oil from 3s 6d a tin to 10s 6d; khaki trousers from 4s 6d a pair to 10s 6d; cassava: 6 "big ones" for 3d to 3 "small ones" for 6d; matches from 3d per packet to 1s a packet; and house rent from between 5s and 8s up to 18s to 20s a month: Acting Governor Slater to Long, 19/7/17 re. *Report of Committee on Conditions of Service of Native Mechanics of the Railway Department Sessional Papers on Gold Coast Government Railway Workers' Pay 1919,* CO98/31.

43. See R. Southall, "Cadbury on the Gold Coast," p. 172.

44. For an analysis of road-building in the Gold Coast during British colonial rule in a longer and wider perspective, see K. O. Akurang-Parry, "Colonial Forced Labor Policies for Road Building in Southern Ghana and International Anti-Forced Labor Pressures 1900–1940" in *African Economic History*, 28, 2000, pp. 1–25.

45. Acting Governor Slater to Bonar Law, 5/11/15, C096/561/894. See Section I, Chapter 2.

46. *Report on Western Province 1914,* 8/4/15, *Supplementary 8, Gazette* 6/9/15, C099/29.

colony and the terminus of the main railway line, still had no roads with satisfactory surfaces, apart from the graveled sections between government offices. The population still had to depend on head-transport, which meant that food was expensive. Rents in Sekondi were also high, with the result that the cost of living, aggravated by wartime conditions, worsened a labor shortage that was said to be the worst in the Colony.[47] The Colonial Office response, that this was "no time for town development," ignored the possibility of upgrading existing tracks for use by the growing number of light trucks and cars belonging to African farmers and traders, as well as to expatriate companies and government officials.[48]

British officials' attitude towards road transport did begin to change during the war—but more as a result of its growing usefulness for the administration rather than its usefulness for trading purposes. By the early war period, there were enough roads of a sufficient standard to allow most officers to cycle, or even motor, through their districts. The condition of many roads in Eastern and Central Province was gradually improving as a result of the 1913 prohibition against trucks without pneumatic tires, even though "motor roads" were often little more than "a track which a Dodge truck or tough Ford car could negotiate in the dry season without falling to pieces."[49] Clifford appreciated the improvements when he went on a tour of Keta district in September 1916. Motorized travel was now quite common. Gone were the days, only seven years earlier, in 1909, when a new English employee of Cadbury on arrival in the colony had been given merely a bicycle and a tent.[50] Clifford motored across the frontier from Lome and made his way from the southeastern corner of the Gold Coast back to Accra. The *Fia*, or head chief, of Awuna accompanied the governor part of the way in his own Ford car. Clifford obviously enjoyed driving his new Studebaker, proudly recording that he had covered the fifty-six miles between Akuse and Christiansborg in two hours fifteen minutes. He had even managed to go above his average twenty-five mph on one good stretch, where he had exceeded thirty-three mph. (He does not mention that twenty-five mph was in fact the speed limit for the colony.) He was impressed at the extent to which such roads had improved over the last three years, and gave credit to the increased efficiency of the PWD—responsible for the main roads—as well as to the effect of the ban on heavy trucks.[51]

Given that all departments were "understaffed and overworked," the small fleet of government motor vehicles (ten cars and eleven trucks) proved a real boon in saving time and energy during the war.[52] This was clear from the bad feeling that had arisen between coast officials as to who should have use of the few official cars available. In January 1917, the senior judge, King Farlow, expressed considerable irritation that other senior officials not only had official cars but even used them in Accra to drive to the Club.[53] Acting

47. Sekondi Chamber of Commerce, enclosure, Manchester Chamber of Commerce to Bonar Law, 13/5/15 and Ellis, CO Minute, Sekondi Chamber of Commerce to PC, Western Province, 7/4/15, CO96/562.

48. Flood, CO Minute, Acting Governor Slater to Bonar Law, 21/6/15, C096/558/515. And Flood, Ellis, CO Minute, Manchester Chamber of Commerce to Bonar Law, 13/5/15, C096/562. See also *Report of Select Committee, LegCo re. Supply Bill 1916,* Acting Governor Slater to Bonar Law, 5/11/15, C096/561/894.

49. C. Wrigley, in A. Roberts (ed.), *The Cambridge History of Africa,* p. 84. And see: *Report on Eastern Province* 1914, 10/6/15 and *Report on Central Province* 1914, 29/3/15, *Supplementary 8, Gazette,* 6/9/15, CO99/29.

50. N. Edwards, *Cadbury on the Gold Coast,* p. 7.

51. Clifford to Bonar Law, 4/9/16, C096/569/643.

52. *Report on Blue Book 1916,* Clifford to Long, 25/8/17, CO96/581/528.

53. Acting Governor Slater to Long, 19/1/17, C096/577/51.

Governor Slater was wholly unsympathetic, noting smugly that he and the governor were happy to use bicycles or walk, and had together recently walked nearly seventy miles. But the London official, Ellis, judged "the bush shirt, shorts and bicycle method of progression" which Slater, Commissioner of Eastern Province Harper, and Clifford himself, favored, as not necessarily appropriate for the dignity required of senior officers. It had "caused great offence" to the chief of Peki, for example, when the governor had arrived in informal fashion (as he occasionally liked to do) on one of his prewar tours.[54]

Toward the end of 1917, with government expenditure cut to the bone, Clifford had to justify retention of the by now thirteen government cars to a skeptical Colonial Office. One reason he gave was that the opening up of the railway had brought the tsetse fly to Accra, depriving horses of their relative immunity. He also argued that the only practicable means of covering the distance between the governor's residence at Christiansborg and government offices was now by car. Cars were also necessary for the very busy colonial secretary, and for the efficiency of the medical department, PWD, and the police. The commissioners of the provinces of the Colony made heavy use of their cars which had, for example, allowed Harding, commissioner of Central Province, to cover 800 miles in only a few weeks. There was now a station car at Cape Coast for the use of a number of officers, and more were needed elsewhere, as at Saltpond where the "segregation area" was up a hill some distance away from the town. Chief Commissioner Fuller of Ashanti used his own car and drew a motor allowance, though Clifford felt that it was unreasonable to expect officers to provide their own cars, especially considering the increased cost of living as a result of the war.[55]

Clifford's lengthy and successful defense of government cars makes it clear how useful they had become to the colonial government's administration during the war, now that there were fewer officers in the colony but many more roads made accessible to motor traffic. He still argued that railways were the priority to address the economic needs of the colony, but, as he commented in November 1917, "in the Gold Coast the advent of the motor car has done a great deal during the past five years to solve the transport problem which has so long shackled administrative work in this part of West Africa." The governor, however, was irritated by the Colonial Office instruction that no government car should ever be used for private purposes. How could officers be asked to draw the line? According to Clifford, a car was sometimes necessary for "dinner, Club, Church, calls." In the absence of "hackney carriages" (taxis)—readily available, he implied to London officials—and rickshaws, a car was "much more of a necessity" and "less of a luxury" in West Africa than elsewhere.[56] But the response of officials in the Colonial Office was wholly predictable, given the shortage of gasoline. The use of cars "for pleasure purposes," as in England for the duration of the war, was strictly prohibited for officials.[57]

To add to the colonial government's shortage of labor, the war also came at a time when the transport department of the Gold Coast colony was still heavily dependent on carriers. Both improved roads and the new light motor vehicles, with their high road clearance, were badly needed on the outbreak of war—when all the department's permanent gangs of carriers left with the troops for Togo. When the Togo campaign ended in September 1914, 500 of the total of between 1,600 and 2,000 (about half were permanent

54. Acting Governor Slater to Long, and Ellis, CO Minute, 25/1/17, C096/577/78.
55. Clifford to Long, 16/11/17, CO96/583/729.
56. *Ibid.*
57. Long to Clifford, 16/11/17, CO96/583/729.

carriers of the Transport Department) set off for Cameroon. More carriers were enlisted in 1915, bringing the total for the Cameroon campaign from the Gold Coast to 3,300. Many of the carriers who came back from the Cameroons at the end of the campaign in May 1916 had been two and a half years on duty with no respite, and many were ill. Half the British carriers of the Cameroon campaign were invalided. Guinea worm and gonorrhea were especially common, and those infected needed a long convalescence. Unlike soldiers, carriers did not receive a pension or disability allowance.[58]

Not surprisingly, there was no great enthusiasm for enlisting for East Africa. Only about 400 carriers from the Gold Coast left for the East Africa campaign in 1916, whereas the total number of carriers recruited from Sierra Leone was over 13,000.[59] In the Gold Coast, the establishment of permanent gangs of carriers of about 220 men became possible again only in 1918, when there were few military or construction requirements and an unprecedented trade depression, but it was estimated that 75% of these men succumbed to the influenza epidemic. Although only two died, many required a long convalescence. With carriers in such short supply and locally hired carriers in Kumasi "unsatisfactory," it would have been convenient for the transport department to have been able to rely simply on motor vehicles, especially with its additional wartime responsibility of the embarkation and disembarkation for large numbers of troops at Sekondi port: in 1917, 2,000 troops used the port and 1,000 men passed through on transfer.[60]

During the war, the transport department had great difficulty keeping its department vehicles running or its staff working normally. The new trucks (two Albion trucks had arrived in 1914) were insufficient as a substitute for carriers, and the condition of the roads caused frequent breakdowns. Unmetalled roads were often impassable in the rainy season, especially during the exceptionally heavy rains of 1917. On the Kumasi-Ejura road, the metalled-granite section was hard on tires, while the unmetalled section was hard on springs. Once the cocoa season began, casks were rolled along the road, and their metal fastenings often fell off, with disastrous results. Tires were said to be "rendered quite unrepairable in consequence." By 1915 the tires had worn out on the two Albion trucks and there was no possibility of getting replacements. One Ford truck obtained from Togo was no substitute. The department had to hire trucks when they were needed. In early 1917, a large supply of tires suddenly arrived, but they were not good quality and did not last. The transport department could not obtain a skilled European mechanic because of the war, and so had to use an untrained employee of Millers (Swanzy Transport). By 1918 it had three Ford trucks, but spares were so short that two of them were cannibalized to keep the third going, and gasoline was so scarce that it was often mixed in equal quantities with kerosene.[61]

With severe expenditure cuts in both 1917 and 1918, what little government money could be spared for roads had to be spent on urgent repairs. The abnormally heavy rains of 1916 and 1917, together with increased road traffic, caused severe damage to road surfaces and bridges all over the colony. Some roads, such as the Dodowa-Somnanaya road near the coast, were in a state of "serious deterioration." Wartime shortages also

58. *Transport Department Reports 1914,* CO98/24; *1915,* CO98/25; *1916,* CO98/26.; and see D. Killingray & J. Matthews, "Beasts of Burden," pp. 14–18.

59. See D. Killingray, "Repercussions of World War I," p. 47 and F. Cole, "Sierra Leone and World War I," p. 108.

60. See *Transport Department Reports 1917,* CO98/27; 1918, CO98/28.

61. *Transport Department Reports 1914,* C098/24; 1915, CO98/25; 1917, CO98/27; 1918, CO98/28.

prevented replacing wood and swish with cement culverts.[62] New roads were badly needed, as we have seen, not only for the new townships developing on the edge of coastal towns like Sekondi, but also for the rapidly growing towns on the railway such as Koforidua and Tafo.[63]

Yet at no point in this period did the British colonial administration prioritize road construction. Although the Gold Coast government now at last saw money spent on roads as a good investment, Colonial Office officials saw it as an extravagance in the war. They were, however, reassured that the "natives" employed in mending roads were largely immigrants who had fled across the frontier from French colonies and were not eligible for recruitment.[64] But roads were an easy target for London's cuts. The Colonial Office in January 1918 ordered expenditure on roads reduced to no more than was "urgently necessary."[65] Yet the appalling condition of the colony's roads was graphically described in the *Gold Coast Leader* that same month: "If you arrive at Accra on a rainy day, you will be much disappointed with the capital of the Gold Coast. Besides a few yards of macadamized road you will walk or drive to your lodging in mud almost all the way."[66]

Thus the war postponed urgently needed government work to improve the road network. The PWD built sixty-seven miles of roads in 1914 but only just over twelve miles in 1915.[67] There were still extraordinary gaps, such as the lack of any road along the coast connecting Accra to Winneba. The normal way to travel the thirty-five-mile distance was still to go along the beach—unchanged since conditions described by the English lady traveler, Mary Gaunt, in 1910.[68] Surveys for the construction of an Accra-Axim coast road began only in 1916. It was still not possible to drive from Sekondi to Accra in 1918, although there had been many calls in the African press for government action to improve communication between the coastal towns.[69] In an appeal for government roads in the *Gold Coast Leader*, attention was drawn to Britain's own experience of colonization: "People point to and admire Roman roads in Britain."[70] But Clifford's construction plans would have strained the budget of the Gold Coast colony in peacetime, let alone with the British Empire at war. The reality was that cutbacks continued. Most of the district roads planned for Ashanti, for example, were deferred until after the war. Without a railway, the development of the Northern Territories depended on motorized roads to the south and the coast, but there was a marked disparity between the regions in government funding for roads: in the 1918 estimates, the Colony was to receive £40,000, Ashanti £7000, and the Northern Territories £550.[71]

But African enterprise succeeded where colonial government failed. In the Gold Coast, the main network of "motorised" roads, built just before and then during the war, was

62. Report in *The Gold Coast Independent,* 15/6/18.

63. Slater, *Memo on Gold Coast Estimates, LegCo,* Clifford to Long, 10/12/17, CO96/583/767. Also *Report on the Northern Territories 1917,* Clifford to Long, 1/1/18, CO96/591/377.

64. Acting Governor Slater to Long, 7/12/17, C096/578/103.

65. Long to Clifford, 30/1/18, C096/583/767.

66. Article, *Gold Coast Leader,* 26/1/18.

67. Clifford to Bonar Law, 1/10/16, CO96/571.

68. M. Gaunt, *Alone in West Africa,* (London, 1912), *passim.*

69. See, e.g., editorials, *Gold Coast Leader,* 22/5/15 and 3/8/18.

70. Editorial, *Gold Coast Leader,* 24/2/17.

71. Slater, *Memo on Gold Coast Estimates, LegCo,* Clifford to Long, 10/12/17, C096/583/767; also *Report on Western Province 1916, Gazette* 29/10/17, C099/32/3; and Slater, *Memo on Gold Coast Estimates, LegCo,* Clifford to Long, 10/12/17, CO96/583/767.

constructed by Africans. The war period saw many local initiatives by African chiefs and people, including cocoa farmers who were quick to see the trading opportunities in constructing all-weather roads, as well as making existing roads fit for motor traffic. This was achieved despite the many natural obstacles, including tropical forest and rivers, such as the Volta River north of Kumasi. The technical developments in motor transport—dating from before the Great War—provided the great incentive for Africans to improve roads. The new lightweight vehicle transport was quicker and usually cheaper than using carriers, who were "daily becoming more difficult to obtain."[72] It was the first mechanized form of transport that was sufficiently flexible to suit the indigenous trade as well as the international export trade.[73] The revolution in road transport was also to be of huge cultural significance, with distances appearing to shrink as a result of the new mobility.

During the war, an increasing number of "motorised" roads, constructed locally by Africans, were being surfaced relatively cheaply with enough laterite gravel to be able to support light vehicles. One such road in one of the largest cocoa-producing areas in Ashanti was a ten-mile branch road that linked Afiduasi village with the main Ejura road. By May 1915, cocoa could be transported by truck on this road rather than being rolled in a barrel. This saved the high costs of labor—a saving of 35s a ton—at a time in the war when labor was often unobtainable. Four months later, in September 1915, the acting governor, Slater, described how exhilarated he had felt when driving on a seventeen-mile stretch of a "native" road near Koforidua that was suitable for "light if somewhat adventurous motor traffic."[74] Although Slater loyally supported Governor Clifford's view that railways were still the best solution to the colony's transport problems, he now argued that work on roads suitable for light motors was practical, especially if constructed by local enterprise "with but slight assistance from local government." Examples included a fifty-mile stretch between Togo and the Volta, and about eighty miles of roads in Eastern Province—built at virtually no cost to the government. One of these was the good road up the Kwahu scarp, supervised by the DC but undertaken entirely by Kwahu chiefs. By 1916, almost all the major roads in Eastern Province and Central Province could be used by light motor trucks, including Koforidua to Mpraeso (completed 1915); the Krobo plantations road, Nsawam to Asamankese; and Accra to Kpong via Dodowa and Akuse. The Nsawam to Cape Coast and Sekondi road was finished in 1920.[75]

By 1916 also, many chiefs' roads had been made passable for light motor traffic, including twenty-five miles of engineered motor roads in Eastern Province constructed for African customers by Italian and Greek contractors. Clifford was full of admiration for one such road, about ten miles long and built with only local African investment, to link the new houses along the ridge between Aburi and Akropong with the Adawso-Mangoase road built by the PWD. This new road had been built not for commercial purposes but to enable cocoa farmers, whose cocoa gardens were down on the plain, to return by car to spend weekends with their families living on the ridge. Clifford declared

72. *Report on Central Province 1917,* Clifford to Long, 13/6/18, C096/590/331.

73. See P. H. Drummond-Thompson, "The Impact of Motorised Road Transport on the Organization of Internal Trade in Nigeria: 1919–1945," unpublished MA thesis, (SOAS, London University, 1983), p. 40.

74. *Report of PWD 1914,* Acting Governor Slater to Bonar Law, 25/9/15, C096/560/782.

75. Acting Governor Slater to Bonar Law, 25/9/15, CO96/560/782; also *Report on Eastern Province 1915, Supplementary 4, Gazette* 14/7/16, CO99/31. And see K. Dickson, "The Development of Road Transport in Southern Ghana and Ashanti Since About 1850," *Transactions of the Historical Society of Ghana*, 5, 1, 1961, p. 40.

that he knew no other "native" population anywhere in the tropics that would be prepared and able to do this: that is, be able to put up that kind of money (the Italian contractor was paid £800 per mile) and, through "natural self reliance," take action themselves without even trying to obtain financial aid from the government.[76] The governor also became aware of the development of local road transport as a result of other African initiatives. An increasing number of motor vehicles were owned by Africans, some of whom ran half a dozen cars and fleets of trucks.[77] By September 1916, half the fifty cars and trucks in Nsawam were owned by Africans. Truck parks had become new distributive centers, sometimes attracting their own local markets.[78] By now, advertisements for American four-cylinder "touring cars," at around £350, were beginning to appear regularly in the *Gold Coast Leader*.[79]

It was due to local African efforts that the state of Akyem Abuakwa in Eastern Province was made accessible to motor traffic in 1916. Some African initiatives took the form of seeking government funds for their projects. Nana Ofori Atta, on the occasion of the Governor and Lady Clifford's visit to Akyem Abuakwa in late September 1916, asked for government help to complete the Kyebi road joining "hitherto untapped towns" in the west of the district. The people of the region were said to have an "ardent desire" to improve roads, but lacked equipment: "the present meagre supply of tools has not helped the people very much."[80] However, the government too suffered from the constraint that metal goods (largely supplied by Germany before the war) were scarce and expensive. Clifford approved this local enthusiasm for making roads to facilitate trade, but still felt that the priority should be railway construction. Government contribution to roads in this area came only later, in the 1920s, after the end of the war. [81]

The purpose of much of this road building was to sustain the cocoa-producing cash crop economy; therefore it varied in its intensity across the country. Most of the new roads were built in the Colony, especially to link the cocoa-producing areas to the coast. There was also substantial African road construction in Ashanti during the war period, but less in the Northern Territories. The extension of the road system and the use of light trucks in Ashanti enabled cocoa to be brought to the railhead at Kumasi from districts where the pods would often previously have been left to rot on the trees for lack of transport. Many Ashanti chiefs were said to be constructing "excellent roads" between villages in the bush in 1917.[82] Not only cocoa producers were affected. One unforeseen outcome was the threat of overfishing Lake Bosumtwi. Motor transport now allowed fish to reach Kumasi market much more quickly, so that fresh fish as well as dried fish were in great demand. In 1918, the chief commissioner obtained legal reinforcement of the local African regulations (backed by religious sanctions) against overfishing: no fish hooks or fishing boats were allowed on the lake, only reed nets and logs.[83] Fuller described "wild excitement" among the local population at the first journey by motorcar to the southwest

---

76. Clifford to Bonar Law, 22/9/16, C096/571/683.
77. *The Gold Coast Nation*, 23/9/16.
78. Crowther, *Report on Native Affairs 1916*, Acting Governor Slater, confid, to Long, 25/1/17, C096/577.
79. See, e.g., *Gold Coast Leader*, 17/2/17, and 2/6/17.
80. N. O. Atta, in Crowther, *Report on Native Affairs 1916*, Acting Governor Slater, confid. to Walter Long, 25/1/17, CO96/577.
81. See R. Addo-Fening, "Akyem Abuakwa c.1874–1943," pp. 370–375.
82. *Report on Ashanti 1917*, Clifford to Long, 13/6/18, C096/590/329.
83. *Ashanti Ordinance Amendment*, Clifford to Long, 11/10/18, C096/593/566.

province of Ashanti in March 1918 with a cavalcade of fourteen cars on a trip to Lake Bosumtwi from Kumasi on the August bank holiday.[84] Compared to the central and southern forest regions, it was relatively easy to construct roads in the savannah of the Northern Territories, although local resentment concerning forced labor on the roads—organized by chiefs—contributed, as we shall see, to wartime disturbances in the region.[85] Motor traffic was slow to penetrate the north. In 1918, only British officers with cars "in perfect running order" were advised to risk the "lonely roads" beyond Ejura, where accidents could go unreported and it could be difficult to repair a car so far from base.[86]

Road building by the local African population in this period has been taken as an indication of local wealth and ingenuity, but it can equally be seen as a reflection of frustration and impatience. Self-help was the only alternative now that the colonial government had moved, despite higher taxes, into a wartime phase of much reduced development. In 1916, the *Gold Coast Leader* urged its readers to take action themselves: "The cry of the hour is for roads, more roads!"[87] In May 1917, Nana Ofori Atta called for government recognition of the extra work undertaken by chiefs in improving and maintaining roads and suggested an increase in the quarterly allowance for such work. But the official response was vague: each case would be dealt with on its merits.[88] One illustration of the keen interest in motor transport in the Gold Coast colony was the "ready response" to the appeal for drivers (as distinct from carriers) for service in the East African campaign. The great majority of those enlisting from British West Africa (largely untrained or only partly trained) were from the Gold Coast. By May 1918, 575 of these had been sent overseas and another 200 were waiting to be transported from Accra. A total of 993 trainee drivers were recruited into the mechanized transport section of the Gold Coast regiment over the war period.[89]

The remarkable increase in the road network in the colony during the war years was, then, largely an African initiative. Three quarters of motor roads built since August 1914—450 miles out of 600—had been, as Clifford acknowledged just after the war, "voluntarily constructed by the natives themselves."[90] The local African population has not been given sufficient credit in the literature for this achievement, which contrasts with the sharp relative decline in government provision in this period as a result of cuts in expenditure for both PWD and "pioneer" roads. The shortage of funds had led to many "pioneer" roads, as between Axim and Half Assini in the southwest, being wholly abandoned and overgrown with weeds and bush.[91] The lack of funds and staff made it difficult even to complete the necessary surveys. At the end of the war, as trade quickly revived and the whole colony "galvanized into life," there was an urgent need to make good the neglect of government roads during the war. By the close of 1918, in the extraordinary surge of activity after the Armistice, roads in the cocoa districts of Eastern Province were described as "thronged" with planters, traders, carriers, bicycles, motorcycles, lorries, and cars.[92]

---

84. Fuller, diary, 24/3/18 and 5/8/18, ADM 12/5/160, PRAAD.
85. E. Wrangham, "The Gold Coast and the First World War," pp. 216–217.
86. *Report of the Transport Department* 1918, CO98/30.
87. Editorial, *Gold Coast Leader*, 29/4/16.
88. N. O. Atta, Slater, *LegCo* 17/5/17, *Gazette* 24/11/17, C099/32/75.
89. Clifford, *Brief Summary of Assistance in Men; Money and Material furnished by the Gold Coast Colony to the Imperial Government.* Enclosure in *Empire at War,* 17/6/18 (prospectus of book to be undertaken by Royal Colonial Institute and Oxford University Press), C096/590/345. And see D. Killingray & J. Matthews, "Beasts of Burden," Table II, p. 10.
90. Clifford, "Recent Developments in the Gold Coast," 17/6/19, p. 249.
91. *Reports on Western Province 1918, Ashanti 1918, Eastern Province 1918,* C098/30.
92. *Ibid.*

The provision of motorized roads between the regions was uneven before 1914; during the war this unevenness increased. For example, Eastern and Central Provinces, the main cocoa regions, were relatively well provided for. Motor cycles and cars—new motor vehicles on the new road network—were said to be "the usual forms of transport" for European officials by the end of the war. Bicycles had become common, whereas being transported in a hammock was now rare. But there were still no main motor roads in Western Province, and none in prospect except plans for the coast road to Accra.[93] Elsewhere motor transport was growing rapidly as a result of local African initiative: Fuller, in Ashanti, noted somewhat patronizingly that several sections of good motor roads had been "built by the natives themselves without any supervision."[94]

That Clifford's administration failed to make a substantial contribution to road building was due partly to his policy of concentrating on railways and partly to the interruption of the war. Before the war, the governor had taken the line, according to Flood's somewhat exaggerated description, that "roads were no use and railways were the only thing."[95] Though cheap light Ford cars and trucks were already being imported in small quantities in 1913, the governor was still arguing, right up to the end of 1916 when railway construction was stopped on account of the war, that it was railway rather than road construction that would solve the colony's transport problems and lay the basis for the future prosperity of the Colony and Ashanti. He acknowledged the growing network of roads suitable for light motor traffic and largely constructed by local people as "a most striking and encouraging development,"[96] but he still insisted that roads were relatively unimportant. However, by the end of the war, Clifford's perspective had at last changed. The war had prevented his railway schemes from being realized, and yet, despite this great setback, transport in the Gold Coast had improved out of all recognition since his arrival in the colony in December 1912. There was not the same need for trams or light railways now that there were large supplies of light motor trucks. These were relatively cheap and easy to maintain and could be used on roads that local people had constructed. There had been, he said, "an extraordinary development of our rural road system," which had made a crucial difference in the cocoa districts when the quantity of cocoa exports had risen dramatically.[97]

This revolution in road transport has often been dated erroneously in the literature as occurring only after the end of the First World War.[98] But we have now seen how it had begun before the war and gathered pace during the war years. In his last major address to the legislative council of the Gold Coast, in October 1918, Clifford was unstinting in his praise for the African achievement concerning road construction. "The native population, to whose enterprise the phenomenal growth of the cocoa industry is now due, has once again demonstrated its alacrity to avail itself of such material advantages as circumstances may place within its reach."[99] It was a strange situation for Clifford.

---

93. *Report on Central Province 1918, Report on Eastern Province 1918, Report on Western Province 1918.* C098/30.

94. Fuller, diary, 6/8/19, ADM 12/5/160, PRAAD.

95. Flood, CO Minute. Clifford to Bonar Law, 13/11/16, C096/572/840.

96. Clifford, *LegCo* 23/10/16, *Gazette* 23/10/16, C099/31/76. Also see Section I, Chapter 2; and Clifford, confid. to Harcourt, 30/9/13, C096/536.

97. Clifford, *LegCo* 28/10/18, *Gazette* 9/11/18, CO99/32/82.

98. See, for example, A. McPhee, *The Economic Revolution in British West Africa,* (London, 1926), p. 42; A. Boahen, *Ghana: Evolution and Change,* p. 99; and R. Southall, "Cadbury on the Gold Coast," p. 26.

99. Clifford, *LegCo* 28/10/18, *Gazette* 9/11/18, C099/32/82.

There had been, despite the war, "a veritable revolution" in transport in the Gold Coast during his term of office, but it had not taken the form he expected or advocated. It had been, not a government-led railway revolution, but an African-led road revolution. Moreover, here was an example of how colonial rule (unintentionally) could provide opportunities for African enterprise and achievement that were to have a major impact on the development of the territory.

Concerning other forms of construction, the governor comes across in official and unofficial records as concerned for the living conditions of everyone in the Gold Coast—including his own. Though inevitably focused on the ever-present issue of funding, sources offer a wide-ranging glimpse of what conditions were like. Lack of money and materials from the start of the war immediately affected both work in hand and plans for building projects—a number of which were specifically for the colonial government administration. The first casualty was a new Government House in Accra, even though Clifford later described Christiansborg as "barely habitable."[100] Work on the "palatial" GPO, the European hospital, and government offices, well underway by August 1914, was not finished until September 1915 because of wartime budget cuts and the scarcity (and expense) of supplies such as iron, steel, and cement. The European hospital, begun in 1912, was only usable in 1916 when money was at last found for a water supply. In Accra, work on the new police headquarters was suspended for much of 1915 and then completed in the boom year of 1916. As Slater commented, it was as well such government building projects, including the "magnificence" of the first legislative council chamber, had been begun before the war.[101] Despite their almost exclusively colonial purpose, these new public buildings were seen as prestigious and even received approval in the local African press as "a credit to the new administration."[102]

Work on government housing such as segregated bungalows for officers and quarters for the GCR regiment in Kumasi and officers' quarters in Cape Coast slowed down or stopped during the war. Clifford's determination that housing be improved for government officers arose out of his conviction that living and working conditions were crucial for the morale and efficiency of those in the colonial service. He had been horrified at the "deplorable conditions" in the Gold Coast, more similar to "temporary camp" in Malaya twenty-five years earlier than to "the permanent establishment of a Crown Colony of the first rank."[103] Lack of staff curtailed much PWD work. No more foremen were available once the war began, which London officials hoped might "compel them to utilize natives more."[104] But the usual major block to Africanization applied: once a department was short-staffed, it was almost impossible to find the time during the war for training to make up for the lack of training programs set up before the war. African unofficials were nevertheless understandably highly critical of the failure to employ Africans to fill vacancies in the PWD during the war.[105] Many PWD staff were seconded for military service or

100. Clifford to Harcourt, 21/7/14, CO96/553; Clifford, *LegCo* 28/10/18, *Gazette* 9/11/18, CO99/33/82.

101. Acting Governor Slater to Bonar Law ,9/9/15, CO96/560/741; and 5/11/15, CO96/561/894.

102. Editorial, *Gold Coast Leader*, 2/1/15. And see the photographs proudly displayed in Lady Clifford, *Our Days on the Gold Coast*, (London, 1919).

103. Clifford, *LegCo* 28/10/18, *Gazette* 9/11/18, CO99/33/82.

104. Ellis, CO Minute, Clifford to Harcourt, 9/4/15, CO96/577/303.

105. Hutton Mills, *LegCo* 19/8/18, *Gazette* 2/11/18, CO99/33/77.

employed purely on war work such as building temporary housing and hospital extensions in Accra and Kumasi for troops returning from East Africa or preparing topographical surveys, war maps, sketches, and photographs of the colony and Togo for military intelligence.[106] In 1916 the governor deplored the shortage of skilled labor in the PWD, including clerks: "It is practically impossible to obtain a qualified man."[107]

In addition, major building projects directly affecting the African population were delayed as a result of the war, such as the construction of a new "native" hospital, a rest house for chiefs visiting Accra, an asylum, and a prison. Also postponed were buildings planned for expanding towns such as Nsawam and Koforidua (intended as the future headquarters of Eastern Province in place of Accra) and a new hospital at Keta.[108] Clifford was concerned, too, at the condition of certain African residential areas in the coastal towns, where little was being spent because of the need to make savings during the war. Despite staff shortages, in the boom year of 1916 there was a major effort to improve the deteriorating housing situation in Accra. Under Clifford, the PWD constructed two model compound houses and provided materials for local people to construct their own houses. The Colonial Office was impressed with news that over 260 families had benefited: "an excellent development."[109] The PWD was also involved, in this year of "extraordinary building activity" in Accra, in evacuating some of the most congested areas of African habitation and organizing housing to the west of the Korle lagoon.[110]

There were economic and health incentives to rid Accra of the worst of its slums. The trade of the port of Accra was seriously affected not only by a shortage of labor but also by periodic epidemics.[111] The aim was to relieve "deplorably overcrowded" sections such as the Sempe area, where a large number of immigrant laborers lived, largely Kru and Fante, including boatmen, beach and warehouse workers, town council laborers, and fishermen. But by 1917, expenditure was "subject to relentless retrenchment." With materials scarce, even badly needed repairs could not be undertaken. Work was also urgently needed in the new townships of Sekondi (including housing for government clerks), in old towns such as Cape Coast and Kumasi, and in new towns such as Tafo and Koforidua.[112] Wartime shortages also delayed the installation of electric lighting in Sekondi (using a generator from the railway workshops) until May 1, 1917, and postponed work to provide electric lighting elsewhere in the colony.[113]

The war did, however, bring a few side benefits. The lack of government housing for expatriates was no longer "acute," simply because war had reduced the number of officials on the coast.[114] Also the Gold Coast PWD (as in Nigeria) had been forced to use more local materials such as timber and limestone. In Eastern Province in 1917, for example,

---

106. *PWD Report 1914*, CO98/30; Clifford to Bonar Law, 25/10/16, CO96/571/777. By the end of 1915, nineteen had been seconded for military service.

107. Clifford, confid. to Bonar Law, 24/7/16, CO96/568.

108. Clifford to Harcourt, 2/11/14, CO96/549/82; Clifford, *LegCo* 28/11/14, *Gazette* 4/12/14, and *LegCo* 23/10/16, *Gazette* 23/10/16, CO99/31/76; Clifford to Bonar Law, 13/11/16. CO96/572/840.

109. Fiddian, CO Minute, Clifford to Bonar Law, 6/9/16, CO96/569/648.

110. *PWD Report 1916*, CO98/26.

111. Colonial Secretary Slater, Clifford to Bonar Law, 20/9/16, CO96/571/688.

112. *Report on Central Province 1917*, 13/6/18, CO96/590/331; *Report on Eastern Province 1917*. 9/7/18, CO96/591/331.

113. Clifford to Long, 10/12/17, CO96/583/767; and *Gold Coast Leader*, 19/5/17.

114. Acting Governor Slater to Bonar Law, 9/9/15, CO96/560/741.

500 tons of limestone were excavated at Labadi, the eastern end of Accra, and used for plastering.[115] Clifford also had the satisfaction of obtaining permission from London to relax the 1913 segregation regulations (a radius of 440 yards required between European and "native" houses) because of "the present critical state of the country's finances." European officers were thus allowed to live in permanent quarters in the new police barracks in Accra.[116] In 1918 the governor could not resist pointing out the contrast between prewar restrictions and the advantage of the greater flexibility induced by the war: "The tyranny of expert medical opinion exercised by the professional advisers of the Colonial Office in those days was more autocratic and certainly more exacting than it has since become."[117]

It had become clear that such projects as the harbor works in Accra and Sekondi would also be targets for wartime cuts. But these would jeopardize the Gold Coast's lifeline: Clifford was aware that not only his development plans but also the crucial international trade itself depended on the two main harbors functioning adequately. But by the close of 1914, the loan funds for the harbor schemes were almost exhausted, and the prewar plan of floating a loan in 1915 had to be shelved. Work on the breakwater and jetties at Sekondi continued on a reduced scale in 1915, but was then suspended in 1916 for the duration of the war.[118] Accra harbor posed a different problem. The demands on the port's facilities continued to grow. A record shipment of 11,700 bags of cocoa was loaded on the *SS Eboe* at Accra on November 15, 1915. Capital expenditure, as on slipways and warehouses, had been cut, but the running cost of dredging, already high, was rising rapidly.[119]

Conditions of war, with no regular supply of fuel for the pumps, made it much harder to judge whether it was possible to stop Accra harbor from silting up with sand. When the shortage of coal in August and September 1914 interrupted regular pumping, the quantity of sand accumulating in the harbor became "immediately visible."[120] The small sand pumps removed a quarter of a million tons of sand during 1915, but a new, more powerful pumping plant was needed to ensure that an adequate depth of water remained in the harbor. Pipes were laid waiting for this pump to remove the sand to the Korle Gono lagoon. The breakwater, near completion by the end of 1915, was intended to allow larger boats to use the sheltered jetties rather than having cargo carried in small craft through the surf.[121] But as the London official Flood commented dryly, in February 1916 the coast appeared to be following the breakwater out to sea "with some vigour."[122]

Expenses mounted, with the local colonial government not daring to stop pouring money into the pumping operation for fear of the sand choking the harbor completely.[123] Conditions then seriously deteriorated when the wartime coal shortage stopped all three

---

115. *Report on Eastern Province 1917,* 9/7/18, CO96/591/399. A. Osuntokun, *Nigeria in the First World* War, p. 52.

116. Clifford, confid. to Bonar Law, 1/5/15. CO96/557.

117. Clifford, *LegCo* 28/10/18, *Gazette* 9/11/18, CO99/33/82.

118. Acting Governor Slater to Bonar Law, 5/11/15, CO96/561/894; *Coode Matthews Engineers' Report,* 18 January 1916, Crown Agents to Bonar Law, 21/1/16, CO96/574.

119. *Accra Harbor Works Report 1915,* Clifford to Bonar Law, 21/2/16, CO96/565/128.

120. Clifford, *LegCo* 28/11/14, *Gazette* 4/12/14, CO99/29/158.

121. Acting Governor Slater, memo re. expenditure, Accra Harbor Works, 14/9/15, CO96/560/750; and Slater to Bonar Law, 5/11/15, CO96/561/894.

122. Flood, CO Minute, *Accra Harbor Works Report 1915,* Clifford to Bonar Law, 21/2/16, CO96/565/128.

123. Acting Governor Slater to Bonar Law, 14/12/16, CO96/573/926.

sand pumps for six weeks in April 1916.[124] By the time continuous pumping began again in October, the silting-up process had gained so much ground that there was little hope that the accumulation of sand could ever be removed. Also in April, the breakwater, only just completed, was badly damaged by unusually heavy surf that undid six months of sand clearance.

Trading facilities were by now so congested that merchants called on the government for a wholly new scheme for Accra harbor, but new heavy expenditure was out of the question during the war. Meanwhile the engineers still claimed that regular pumping would clear the sand and reduce maintenance costs. But with coal increasingly hard to find, a conclusive trial was impossible.[125] The Crown Agents made every effort to increase supplies from Britain, while the Gold Coast government in 1917 obtained some coal from Durban in South Africa, but the problem was that 500 tons of expensive patent fuel were needed every month to keep the pumping plant going night and day.[126] By 1917, Slater admitted that locally "all the unofficials and many of the officials have long been convinced that the present harbour scheme is a failure."[127] Nor had officials in London ever been enthusiastic. Ellis echoed his warning from before the war: "The harbour is a trap for sand and gold."[128] As Clifford acknowledged gloomily in November 1917, even with no further interruptions to pumping, it would take four years to get the harbor back to its 1912 condition.[129]

A crisis point was reached in 1918 when it finally became clear that the extension of the breakwater had led to an accumulation of sand in Accra harbor that the pumps would not now be able to counter. Despite the £40,000 spent on pumping sand in 1917, it was impossible for boats to land people at the jetty because it was by now "high and dry" in sand.[130] Clifford went to see the situation for himself. On September 28, 1918, a motorcar was driven out across the beach at low tide to a point within a few yards of the seaward end of the breakwater, "illustrating in a forcible manner the failure of pumps to cope with the siltage."[131] The pump at the end of the jetty was landlocked and could only be kept in action manually. It was now clear that all that the pumping had ever been able to achieve was to delay, to some degree, the settling down of a natural equilibrium between sand and sea. Clifford concluded that all pumping operations should cease forthwith. He believed that sometime in the future this would allow the construction of a deepwater harbor with a pier running out to sea, where ships would be able to lie alongside an island breakwater. But such an expensive project would have to await a time when a loan could be raised at a reasonable rate. The only expense agreed to was repairing the breakwater to forestall even greater expenditure at a later date.[132]

The deterioration of shipping conditions at Accra during the war contributed to the postwar decision to construct a deepwater harbor in Sekondi. Because the beach had

---

124. *Intelligence Report,* Clifford, confid. to Bonar Law, 18/8/16, CO96/926.

125. Costs rose from £12,000 in 1916 to over £35,500 in 1917, Clifford to Long, 19/5/17, CO96/579/325.

126. *Blue Book 1916,* CO100/66; *Blue Book 1917,* CO100/67.

127. Colonial Secretary Slater, 14/3/17, Enclosure 1, Clifford to Long, 19/5/1, CO96/579/325.

128. Ellis, CO Minute, *Accra Harbor Works Report 1916,* Acting Governor Slater to Long, 17/4/17, CO96/579/240. Ellis, CO Minute, *Hobbs, Resident Engineer's Report,* 15/5/17, Enclosure 8, Clifford to Long, 19/5/17, CO96/579/325; also Ellis, CO Minute, Crown Agents to Long, 16/2/17, CO96/584.

129. Clifford to Long, 20/11/17, CO96/583/750.

130. Clifford to Long, re. *Accra Harbor Report 1917,* 16/2/18, CO/588/99.

131. Telegram, Clifford to Long, 7/10/18, CO96/593.

132. Clifford to Long, 30/10/18, CO96/593/607. Clifford to Long, and Flood, Colonial Office Minute, 28/12/18, CO96/594/730.

flattened out in Accra, boatmen there had to carry cargo through the water for a considerable distance, so that heavy packages were often damaged. Few boats could reach smooth water, and even surf boats had to go some distance through breaking waves before they were properly afloat. The result was that at certain states of the tide, boats had to be loaded in the surf itself.[133] Goods were not only doused with a fine salt spray, but water could often be seen pouring from a sling of cocoa when it was being lowered into a ship's hold.[134] Without the distraction of the war and the shortages of fuel, building materials, and loan funds, the Accra harbor scheme would not have been left to run for so long as "a costly and expensive failure."[135]

Clifford also regretted that the war interrupted plans for other construction projects to modernize the colony. Extending water supplies and drainage facilities to the main towns of the Gold Coast was high on the agenda. He did see brought to completion major works initiated by his predecessor, Governor John Rodger, such as the Accra waterworks, which provided pipe-borne water from January 1914, and the Sekondi water scheme, which was finally completed in July 1917.[136] But many other water projects planned by Clifford, such as provision of pipe-borne water to Cape Coast and Kumasi (for which preliminary investigations had already taken place) were put aside as of "academic interest" only, because of the war. Water schemes for other towns were to be long delayed: for example, until 1928 for Cape Coast and until 1934 for Kumasi.[137]

Some London officials now questioned whether such "expensive water works" were needed at all. Ellis asserted that locals were usually immune to substances in the water and could therefore depend on wells and rainwater, whereas Europeans could simply distill water for drinking. However, Fiddian, the main Colonial Office spokesman on public health in West Africa, reminded his colleagues that typhoid fever had been introduced into the region by Europeans and that "natives" were anything but immune to such complaints as guinea worm. Also, provision of piped water encouraged the destruction of local wells that bred mosquitoes. Mosquitoes were reported to breed in anything, from crab holes and the remains of wrecks on the coast to the enormous snail shells in Ashanti villages or the thousands of empty "fizzy water" bottles thrown away near railway stations. Ashanti Goldfields employed their own "mosquito brigades" to pick up "promiscuous tins and bottles."[138]

Drainage schemes were also an early casualty of the war, despite the danger to public health. Fuller bemoaned the lack of adequate sanitation in Kumasi, where there were no modern means of transporting night soil, and there was now no money for constructing drains to carry away either surface water or sewage.[139] And the war also made it more

133. Main superintendent, *West African Lighterage and Transport Company Report,* Clifford to Long, 28/12/18, CO96/594/730.

134. District supervisor customs, Accra, 1/5/19, Enclosure, Acting Governor Slater to Milner, 1/5/19, CO96/599/356.

135. Clifford, *LegCo* 28/10/18, *Gazette* 9/11/18, CO99/33/82.

136. *Report on Eastern Province 1914,* 10/6/15, *Supplementary 8, Gazette* 6/9/15, CO99/29.

137. Clifford, *LegCo* 28/11/14, *Gazette* 4/12/14, CO99/29/158; also Acting Governor Slater to Bonar Law, 14/9/15, CO96/560/749. And see E. Wrangham, "The Gold Coast & The First World War," p. 177.

138. Ellis, Fiddian, CO Minute. Acting Governor Slater to Bonar Law, 14/9/15, CO96/560/749. *Medical and Sanitary Report 1915,* CO98/25. For a description of the snail trade, e.g., in the Ahafo district, see A. W. Cardinall, quoted in F. Wolfson, *Pageant in Ghana,* (Oxford, 1958), pp. 217–224; *MOH Inspector Report,* Obuasi, 27/11/14, AGC. Ms. 14,171.37, p. 164.

139. Fuller, diary, 3/9/17, ADM 12/5/160, PRAAD; and *PWD Report 1918,* CO98/30.

difficult to maintain the purity of the Accra water supply. By April 1915, there was anxiety about the impurities in the water and the comparative failure of the filtration plant.[140] It took the Crown Agents some time to find an inspector, as all their chemists were "now making gas or high explosive."[141] By 1918 a better standard of purity of water had at last been achieved, with successful lime treatment of algae pollution and distillation of water using charcoal rather than anthracite coal. Also the cleaning of one of the two reservoirs, built before funds ran out, had led to the discovery of unexpected occupants: a large number of fish and five crocodiles.[142] After the war, Guggisberg made a strong case that water supplies and drainage schemes be given a high priority. "A good loan" was required at the earliest possible date to compensate for "the five valuable years lost in the development of this country."[143]

Telegraph reconstruction plans also suffered from wartime cuts, but one good effect of the war was that the urgent need for more trained staff during the war sped up Africanization in this field. Despite Clifford being "most anxious" to improve the "far from satisfactory" communications in the Gold Coast, it was a struggle merely to maintain services, given the shortage of trained supervisors. [144] The postmaster general and six other members of the department joined the signals on the expeditionary force to Togo and were then posted to Togo with nine African members of the department.[145] Other staff, too, were seconded and could not be replaced because of, for example, a general demand for telegraph engineers for military purposes. Trained African staff were badly needed, with the result that a small sum was belatedly set aside in 1917 to help with more systematic training of "native" technical staff.[146] There was no problem finding recruits at a time when fewer commercial jobs were available as a result of cutbacks. By the end of that year, sixty-six Africans qualified as telegraphers at the Accra and Cape Coast telegraph schools, and the experiment of employing female telegraph clerks was producing "very promising results."[147]

Although the post and telegraph department was described as "seriously handicapped" for lack of money and trained supervisors, the hard work of telegraph reconstruction continued during the war on a reduced scale.[148] About 1,400 miles of telegraph line were constructed, while the number of post offices and agencies rose.[149] Again the expectation was for much more, once the war finally ended. J. E. Symonds of the Royal Engineers (senior inspector of telegraphs) described the usual routine work of mapping routes, supervising clearing of sites, and setting up poles, with work occasionally interrupted by wires coming down in heavy rains or tornadoes. But during the war, in 1918, he came

---

140. Telegram, Harcourt to Clifford, 29/4/15, CO96/557.

141. Flood, CO Minute, Crown Agents to Bonar Law, 20/7/15, CO96/562.

142. *Intelligence Report, Accra Waterworks* and Flood, CO Minute, 23/12/15, CO96/561; Clifford, *LegCo* 28/10/18, *Gazette* 9/11/18, CO99/33/82.

143. Guggisberg, *LegCo* 9/10/19, *Gazette* 13/10/19, CO99/34/86; Guggisberg, *LegCo* re. 1920 Estimates 26/11/19, *Gazette* 8/12/19, CO99/34/100.

144. Clifford to Harcourt, 20/3/15, CO96/5567247.

145. *Post and Telegraph Department Report 1914, Supplementary 7, Gazette* 28/8/15, CO99/29.

146. Clifford to Long, 10/12/17, CO96/583/767.

147. *Post and Telegraph Department Report 1917,* CO98/28.

148. There were sixteen European staff vacancies in 1916. Examples of work were the Accra-Lome line, and the Sekondi-Kumasi line, where wiring was completed to Tarkwa by the end of 1915. *Post and Telegraph Department Report 1915,* CO96/25.

149. There had been sixty-nine post offices or agencies in 1913. By 1917 the number had reached 102. Clifford, *LegCo* 9/11/18, *Gazette* 28/10/18, CO99/33/82.

across new hazards. While working in the Cape Coast district, Symonds noticed small coils of copper wire cut down from the telegraph poles. An elderly man was found in the vicinity collecting the copper to give to goldsmiths to make bracelets.[150] Similar instances of missing wiring ("wilful damage") were reported elsewhere in the Colony in September and November 1918.[151] The economic hardship of that year seems to have encouraged such private enterprise.

Clifford's plans to modernize the communications system in the colony had to be postponed as a result of the war. The post and telegraph department remained badly underfunded throughout the war, though the volume of work rose, especially in the boom year of 1916, with increased provision of telegraph, telephone, and wireless communication.[152] Only small sums were spent on telephones during the war, with new switchboards coming into operation, as in Tarkwa and Sekondi, and the first long distance telephone trunk line between Accra and Koforidua completed in 1918.[153]

To retain the acquiescence of its African subjects, there had to be some tangible benefits to colonial rule. Alongside the higher standard of living before 1914 arising from international trade—now damaged by the war—Governor Clifford had promised improved provision of welfare services, especially health and education. He had stated that he saw it as part of his duty as a colonial governor, and of Britain's duty as the imperial power, to extend the benefits of Western science and philosophy to the "native" population.[154] He had every reason to believe that the necessary funds would be met both by taxes on the profitable overseas trade and by using the colony's surplus balances. African hopes were raised. But what priority could be given to the colony's welfare services during a world war? To the governor's great disappointment, the war severely restricted the implementation of his liberal plans for health and education. It would be left to his successor, Guggisberg, to carry forward and augment Clifford's program after the war.

At the time of the outbreak of the war, Clifford was still fighting his own battle against entrenched British colonial medical opinion on the coast. Since arriving in the colony in December 1912, he had argued strongly for more money and more staff for medical services, including trained African doctors and dispensers. This was to ensure that, rather than money being spent almost exclusively on the very small number of Europeans, the health of the local African population would at last receive more attention. Some commentators have argued otherwise. Concerning public health, the government of the Gold Coast has been criticized for having "neither the resources, nor the will, for anything more than piecemeal works projects and clean-up campaigns."[155] But Clifford had the will. The question was—especially given the war—would he have the resources? Meanwhile, the state of public health in the Gold Coast colony was now no longer of such

---

150. J. E. Symonds, Royal Engineers, Senior Inspector Telegraph, the Gold Coast, 14/9/18 in *Diary 1909–1922,* Book 4. Mss. Afr. r.165, Rhodes House.

151. *Post and Telegraph Department Report 1918,* CO98/30.

152. From a high point of over £14,000 in 1914, the Post and Telegraph extraordinary budget plunged to a record low of only just over £2,500 in 1918. *Blue Books 1914,* CO100/64; *1918,* CO100/68.

153. *Report on Western Province 1915, Supplementary 3, Gazette* 3/7/16, CO99/31; *Post and Telegraph Department Report 1918,* CO98/30.

154. See, for example, the start of Chapter 2.

155. R. Dumett, "Disease and Mortality Among Gold Miners of Ghana," p. 3.

interest to some officials in London: "In these days of wholesale slaughter, a little yellow fever more or less is hardly noticeable."[156]

Despite wartime preoccupations, Clifford continued his struggle for "native" medical practitioners to be accepted into the West African Medical Service in the Gold Coast. He wanted not just more doctors, but more African doctors. It had finally been agreed just before the war that African doctors should be employed in a separate "Native Medical Service" rather than the European-run "West African Medical Service."[157] This concession produced a second-rate scheme. The compromise still rankled with the governor, who declared in January 1915 that he had "never pretended to be satisfied with it." For Clifford, the principle at stake was even more obvious and striking at a time of war, when the "natives" were expressing their "utmost loyalty" to the British government and assumed they "could count upon fair play" in the British Empire and "upon equal opportunities with Europeans."[158]

Clifford weakened his case with exaggeration here. It is doubtful whether any African in the Gold Coast colony at this time was sufficiently optimistic to believe "equal opportunities" were offered. Clifford himself considered lower grades of pay and less favorable leave as justified for African doctors, on the grounds of their being able to live more cheaply and more healthily in West Africa than Europeans. But the governor wanted to emphasize the unacceptability of a color bar "such as no government of any Crown Colony in the Empire, with which I am acquainted, has attempted to establish." And the really galling aspect was that all this was "for the purpose of keeping the West Africa Medical Service as an all-white institution." He also believed the policy to be impolitic. It was not advisable at this time of war to perpetuate a justified grievance among the educated "native" community.[159]

Clifford had consistently argued a powerful case for African doctors being accepted into the public West Africa Medical Service, but he was powerless to deliver, even in the circumstances of the severe shortage of European medical officers during the war. In the Colonial Office, Fiddian judged it impossible to compare the "developing civilisation" of Ceylon (as Clifford and Slater did ad nauseam from their previous experience) with the bulk of the population of the Gold Coast, who were, in Fiddian's extremely prejudiced view, "simply savages," with "practically no community of ideas with Europeans." In February 1915, he included the old arguments: "The average European officer wants a European doctor," and "putting black men in West Africa in authority over white men" was "unthinkable"—views that were very similar to those expressed by Chamberlain and his officials in 1902.[160] Fiddian failed to mention here that there had been African doctors in the West African Medical Service in the Gold Coast up to 1902. In 1915, there were still four African doctors in the public service in Nigeria and three in Sierra Leone, though no new posts for African doctors in the public medical service were being created in these colonies at this time, and vacated posts were being left unfilled.[161] However, Fiddian did

156. Fiddian, CO Minute. Telegram, Acting Governor Robertson to Harcourt, 18/8/14, CO96/547. For the similar attitude regarding Sierra Leone, see F. Cole, "Sierra Leone and World War I," pp. 147–152.

157. Clifford to Harcourt, 25/7/14, Harcourt to Acting Governor Robertson, re. TAMS Committee decision, 8/8/14, CO554/23.

158. Clifford, confid. to Harcourt, 21/1/15, CO96/555.

159. Clifford, confid. to Harcourt, 21/1/15, CO96/555.

160. Fiddian CO Minute, 18/2/15, Clifford, confid. to Harcourt, 21/1/15, CO96/555; Fiddian, CO Minute, Clifford to Harcourt, 25/7/14, CO554/23. And see D. Kimble, *A Political History*, p. 98.

161. *Gold Coast Leader*, 27/3/15. And see R. Dumett, "The Campaign Against Malaria," p. 194.

refer to the possibility in "the distant future" of a medical school in West Africa. One day, the rank and file of the medical service on the coast might be "natives," with a few Europeans simply acting in a supervisory capacity.[162] In the meantime, arrangements were made to advertise six African posts in the auxiliary medical service. Duties would normally be "entirely concerned with the indigenous population and more especially with the poorer classes," and would usually be in stations away from large towns.[163]

As a result of secondments as well as shortage of funds, wartime cuts began to bite deep into what little medical provision there was in the colony. By 1916, eleven medical stations were closed (six in the Colony, one in Ashanti, and four in the Northern Territories), and provision was officially made for only forty-six European medical officers in the Gold Coast (down from fifty-five in 1913) and for only two of the six posts (to save money) agreed for African medical officers in the Native Medical Service.[164] Only the number of vaccinators was to be allowed to increase, from one to four. Slater noted the absurdity of the situation. It was "almost incredible" that there was only one vaccinator in a "progressive" colony such as the Gold Coast, especially when a regulation existed by which all children were supposed to be vaccinated within three months of their birth. In fact, vaccination usually only took place when there was an outbreak of smallpox. There was a financial incentive for increasing the vaccination program: serious financial losses occurred when ports had to be quarantined, and there was particular concern to protect the two most important ports of Accra and Sekondi, on which the colony largely depended. In this instance economic need acted as a driving force for obtaining agreement that there should be a program of training "native" staff as vaccinators.[165] However, the officers of the Gold Coast medical department—who appear to have preferred seeing services cut to accepting any "native" into their ranks—spent time in 1915 arguing vigorously against including any West Indian doctors into the depleted West African Medical Service. Such views were not unique to officers in the Gold Coast. A similar mixture of financial constraint and racial prejudice was to be found elsewhere, for example, in the British West African colony of Sierra Leone.[166]

Only "an insignificant fraction" of the population of the colony (consisting largely of Europeans, Africans in government employment, and a few educated Africans) were actually treated by government medical officers. As Clifford confided, "It is as well to recognize that the bulk of the natives derive direct benefit from the Medical Department only in the cases of epidemic disease."[167] Clifford's case stood: that a major reason why the medical service in the colony was so limited in its scope was to satisfy prejudice, at the expense of popular health needs. Meanwhile, as a result of staff shortages, London accepted that annual reports could be shortened and simplified. Medical records continued to be kept, although the forms recording, for example, the minutiae of sanitary returns were set aside during the war. These give an insight into the extraordinary detail of

162. Fiddian, CO Minute, endorsed by Harcourt, 18/2/15, Clifford, confid. to Harcourt, 21/1/15, CO96/555.

163. Clifford, confid. to Harcourt, 12/4/15, CO96/557.

164. Tweedy, Acting PMO, memo, Clifford, confid. to Bonar Law, 24/12/15, CO96/561; Acting Governor Slater to Bonar Law, re 1916 Estimates, 5/11/15, Draft approval of Estimates, Bonar Law to Acting Governor Slater, 11/1/16, CO96/56/894.

165. Acting Governor Slater, *LegCo* 25/10/15, re. 1916 Estimates, *Gazette* 25/11/15, CO99/29/101.

166. Tweedy, acting PMO, memo, Clifford, confid. to Bonar Law, 24/12/15, CO96/561; and F. Cole, "Sierra Leone and World War I," p. 146.

167. Re. *Medical and Sanitary Report 1914,* Clifford, confid. to Bonar Law, 8/9/15, CO96/564.

imperial supervision—with records normally kept of, for example, the average number of cartloads of refuse per day, or pails of excreta, and how they were dealt with in every main town of the colony.[168] As Clifford observed, the statistics in the medical and sanitary department reports did not bear much relation to plans for the general health of the whole community.[169]

Of course, Clifford was not indifferent to expatriate needs, especially those that affected the administration of the colony. One health-related issue which inspired him to write extraordinarily lengthy dispatches to London in 1916 was whether British officers' children should be allowed to live with their parents in West Africa. Clifford was keen that they should. But British government officers' children were not allowed into West Africa, as a result of Lord Crewe's ruling in 1910, even though they were allowed elsewhere in the tropics, such as in India and Ceylon. Perhaps the fact that Clifford saw so little of his own children added edge to his writings on this subject.[170] His initiatives were part of a campaign to counter what he believed to be a false impression of the dangers of the West African climate, and West Africa's image as the "white man's grave." The governor also wanted to raise the morale of British government officers by making living conditions more familiar and less expensive. He considered that far too many single men were inclined to "picnic" when on tours of duty in West Africa instead of making comfortable homes for themselves, which would have been far better for their general health and well being. In addition, those who had children had the crippling expense of maintaining two households, one in Africa and one at home. Kuklick has given credit for improved practice solely to Guggisberg, omitting Clifford's earlier role in arguing the case for British officers to be allowed to establish normal family life in the colony.[171]

Colonial Office officials, comfortably settled in London or the Home counties, were indifferent. Sir George Fiddes saw some potential in such an experiment: "It would probably claim a few little victims but will be a powerful stimulus for the amelioration of conditions on the coast."[172] Meanwhile, it was suggested by Ellis in London that the reason Basel and Bremen missionaries' children showed no ill effects was that German mothers were better at looking after their children. The wives of British officials were "drawn from a class which is in the habit of handing over the care of children largely to servants."[173] Despite Clifford's efforts, however, in 1918 the London TAMS (Tropical Africa Medical Sanitary Advisory) Committee finally decided on health grounds against changing the regulations to allow officers to bring children to West Africa.[174]

African concerns were more immediate and wide-ranging. They focused on the diminishing medical services provided by the colonial government for the African public. On this issue Africans again wanted more, and more effective, colonial rule—not less. During his visit to Akyem Abuakwa in September 1916, Clifford heard of the local

---

168. Clifford to Bonar Law, 23/11/15, Fiddian, Colonial Office Minute, CO96/561/707.

169. For a discussion of the government's failure to collect accurate medical/mortality data, see R. Dumett, "Disease and Mortality among Gold Miners of Ghana," pp. 8–13.

170. See H. Gailey, *Clifford*, pp. 81–82.

171. Clifford to Bonar Law, 13/3/16, CO96/566/172. See H. Kuklick, *The Imperial Bureaucrat. The Colonial Administrative Service in the Gold Coast 1920–1939*, (Stanford, 1979), pp. 123–124.

172. Sir George Fiddes: Sir Frederick Lugard, memo, CO Minute, Bonar Law to Clifford, 16/8/16, CO96/567.

173. Ellis, CO Minute, Clifford to Long, 25/1/18, CO96/587/55.

174. TAMS memo, August 1918, Clifford to Long, 25/1/18, CO96/587/55.

population's "grief" at the removal of the dispensary from Kyebi to Kwahu.[175] Although officially a "temporary measure," there appeared to be no prospect of services returning to "normal" during the war. It was also quite common for medical officers who remained in post to have to act as DCs, which took them away from their medical duties.[176] By May 1916, with eighteen medical officers from the Gold Coast now in the Cameroons, the total number of medical officers in the colony was reduced to thirty-eight, of whom twelve or thirteen would normally be on leave at any one time. There were therefore regularly only twenty-five government doctors for a European population of up to 631 government officials and 1,306 non-officials, and for an African population of around two million. Whole districts in the Northern Territories were described as "shut down as far as medical work is concerned," with sanitary inspection "at a standstill."[177]

Medical provision was thus pitifully small during the war, yet Colonial Office officials, unlike Governor Clifford, showed little concern. They judged provision only in terms of servicing the European community and therefore deduced that the medical service had been overstaffed before the war.[178] But Clifford continued to argue that "active assistance" should be extended much more widely to the "native" population. He calculated in 1916 that only about 3% of the African population were receiving any medical treatment at all from the West African Medical Service. Although the principal medical officer, Dr. Rice, defended the service—with his calculation that 48,153 Africans had received some treatment from European doctors in 1916—Clifford's claim remained true, that "the vast majority of the taxpayers" were not receiving the "benefits of modern medical science." The governor deplored this as "a serious reproach" to the administration of the colony. He looked forward to the time when, instead of government hospitals and dispensaries only being sited where political officers were posted, there would be a complete system of rural hospitals and dispensaries as in Ceylon.[179] As we have seen, Clifford was a lone voice in this key area of government health provision. His was a much more generous view than that expressed by London officials in the Colonial Office. For example, Flood asked scathingly if "natives" "exhibit any wild longing" for European medical treatment. Clifford's proposal for enough white doctors to service the whole community was dismissed as "an unjustifiable extravagance."[180]

There were as many requests from Africans for government medical services as there were for schools. One example, illustrating the concern of head chiefs in Eastern Province to obtain government dispensaries in their divisions, had been reported to the Colonial Office in July 1916, three months before Flood wrote the comments above.[181] In contrast with the attitude of the Colonial Office, Professor Simpson, chairman of TAMS, agreed with Clifford that more trained personnel were needed and that the "native" population should benefit more from medical science. Simpson's recommendation was that the question should be "vigorously taken up when the war was over."[182]

---

175. N. O. Atta, Okyenhene of Akyem Abuakwa, address to Governor 22/9/16, Clifford to Bonar Law, 22/9/16, CO96/571/683.

176. Clifford to Bonar Law, 23/11/16, CO96/572/816. cf. Chapter 3 and Chapter 9.

177. *Medical and Sanitary Report 1915,* Clifford to Bonar Law, 20/5/16, CO96/567/372.

178. Fiddian, CO Minute, Clifford, confid. to Bonar Law, 8/8/16, CO96/568.

179. Clifford to Bonar Law re. *Medical and Sanitary Report 1914,*11/10/16, CO96/571/740. Rice, Memo, 17/12/18, Clifford, confid. to Milner, 5/3/19, CO96/598.

180. Flood, CO Minute, Clifford to Bonar Law, 11/10/16, CO96/571/740.

181. *Report on Eastern Province 1915, Supplementary 4, Gazette* 14/7/16, CO99/31.

182. Extract, minute of Meeting TAMS, 5/12/16, *Medical and Sanitary Report 1914,* Clifford to Bonar Law, 11/10/16, CO96/571/740. For Simpson's own investigations in 1924 and the influential

In the meantime, the sanitary condition of the main coast towns, and especially Accra, deteriorated as a result of the shortage of funds during the war period. Sewage continued to be dumped in the sea or into trenches inland, while rubbish was often used to fill up holes and swamps.[183] The School of Tropical Medicine in Liverpool received information from a local paper, the *Eastern Star and Akwapim Chronicle,* in 1916, about the threat of diarrhea and dysentery in Accra as a result of the lack of sewers and inadequate rubbish removal. African residents explained that European officials were not always aware of the conditions. They did not experience the stench of latrines "in these days of segregation areas."[184] Perceptions differed: officials in the Colonial Office regarded such complaints as unreasonable. There was an admission that the drains in Accra might be only in what was euphemistically described as "an intermediate state," but a full sewerage system would have to await the end of the war.[185] In contrast, sanitary improvements were achieved, exceptionally, at Kyebi in the African state of Akyem Abuakwa in Eastern Province, where Nana Ofori Atta installed new drains and latrines as well as lighting in the town between 6 pm to 5 am, at his own expense—another illustration of African initiative in the context of wartime cuts.[186]

The main concerns of government officials were disease and epidemics rather than "nuisance"—preoccupied as they were with the economic and financial health of the whole territory. Officers were satisfied that the general health of the residents of Accra had much improved as a result of the new water supply. With the government's prewar provision of piped water, there were fewer recorded cases of, for example, worm and blackwater fever. But Clifford expressed his grave concern at the "menace" to public health when he inspected "deplorably insanitary conditions" in Accra in August 1916.[187] Rats remained a problem at stations along the railway line and in the main towns: the average number of rats caught each month in Accra in 1916 was 642.[188] There were cases of bubonic plague in March 1917 in the densely populated areas of Accra and in Tema village just outside Accra. It was difficult for officers to ascertain the extent of epidemics because local people were usually able to conceal the sickness unless someone died. Although there was a demand for sanitation to be provided by government, local priority during an epidemic might be to avoid the unwelcome attention of sanitary officers and thereby the economically damaging effect of Accra being declared an infected area and placed in quarantine.[189]

It is not surprising that medical provision could not keep up with local needs in wartime, and that the health of the population was therefore at risk. Conditions were especially

---

1925 Report on the Sanitary Condition of the Mines and Mining Villages of the Gold Coast and Ashanti, see, e.g., R. Dumett, "Disease and Mortality Among Gold Coast Miners," pp. 11–13.

183. *Medical and Sanitary Department Report 1915,* CO98/25.

184. *The Eastern Star and Akwapim Chronicle,* 3/11/15, enclosure in *Liverpool School of Tropical Medicine to Bonar Law,* 21/2/16, CO96/576. See similar complaints in other local papers e.g., editorial notes, *Gold Coast Leader,* 16/9/16.

185. Fiddian, CO Minute, Liverpool School of Tropical Medicine to Bonar Law, 21/2/16, CO96/576.

186. N. O. Atta, Okyenhene of Akyem Abuakwa, 22/ 9/16, address to Governor, Clifford to Bonar Law, 22/9/16, CO96/571/683.

187. Reported cases of worm declined dramatically from 123 in Accra in 1913 to only four in 1918. *Medical and Sanitary Report 1918,* CO98/30; also Clifford to Bonar Law, 10/8/16, CO96/568/569.

188. Assistant Colonial Secretary Welman, memo, *Report on the Blue Book 1916,* printed for Parliament; Clifford to Long, 25/8/17, CO96/581/528.

189. Telegram, Acting Governor Slater to Long, 6/3/17, CO96/578; Acting Governor Slater to Long, 16/3/17, CO96/578/183; telegram, Acting Governor Slater to Long, 23/3/17, CO96/578; Acting Governor Slater to Long, 23 March 1917, CO96/578/194; Acting Governor Slater to Long, 18/4/17, CO96/579/245.

difficult in those towns with a rapidly growing population. It seems that disruption of the export trade in cash crops, and especially cocoa, accelerated urbanization at this time. It was estimated that the population of Cape Coast increased by 8,000 between 1914 and 1915 to a total of nearly 19,300, comparable with the total population of Accra at the start of the war. Sekondi increased by about 3,000 in the same period, to just over 12,250. A major expansion in the size of Accra also took place in 1915–1916, from around 19,000 to 25,000. The main towns varied in overall area and density of population. Cape Coast covered an area of 2.5 square miles in this period, with Sekondi 3 square miles, Accra 4.5 square miles, and Kumasi 9 square miles. Unfortunately this urban expansion coincided with war and reduced public spending. New towns in the cocoa districts just inland in the Colony, apart from the exception made for Koforidua, could no longer be carefully supervised by government officers such as building inspectors. As Clifford acknowledged: "Naturally the time of a great war is not the time for the active realization of any town planning schemes."[190]

The climate and particular weather conditions during the war years made matters worse. Unfortunately, exceptional rainfall in 1916 and 1917 coincided with what even the Colonial Office now accepted as a severe lack of medical staff as a result of the war, to the detriment of the local population.[191] The total annual rainfall in Accra in 1916 (over forty-one inches) was nearly double that of 1915. The level of rainfall increased at almost all stations in 1917, doubling at Ejura in Northern Ashanti from thirty inches to seventy-nine inches. Fuller, the chief commissioner of Ashanti, complained in September 1917 that the rain was constant—raining every day, far in excess of what was usual.[192] In Tamale in the Northern Territories, the rains were the highest on record, over nine inches above the level of 1916, causing flooding of the Volta river and infecting water supplies. Rainfall only returned to normal throughout the colony in 1918. This heavy rainfall led to "an abnormal amount of sickness among the native population."[193]

The *Gold Coast Leader* reported during the abnormal rainfall of 1917 that "a perpetual gloom seems to overhang the atmosphere." There was at this time a marked increase in malaria, dysentery, influenza, whooping cough, chronic rheumatism, bronchial pneumonia, and TB. Records of Accra show how closely the malarial curve followed the curve of rainfall in 1917.[194] The main killers in 1916 appear to have been pneumonia and TB (together with bronchitis in the mines), though many cases were never seen by European

190. *Medical and Sanitary Report 1915,* Clifford to Bonar Law, 20/5/16, CO96/567/372; also *Medical and Sanitary Report 1914,* Clifford to Bonar Law, 11/10/16, CO96/571/740; *Medical and Sanitary Report 1916,* Clifford to Long, 15/5/17, CO96/579/313. For the limited accuracy of official figures re. towns, see R. Dumett, "Disease and Mortality Among Gold Coast Miners," p. 5.

191. Flood, CO Minute, Acting Governor Slater to Long, 3/3/17, CO96/578/156. Maxwell, *Report on Western Province 1917,* 1/7/18, Clifford to Long, 2/8/18, CO96/591/445; *Report on Ashanti 1917,* Clifford to Long, 13/6/18, CO96/590/329; *Report on the Northern Territories 1917,* Clifford to Long, 9/7/18, CO96/591/377; *Medical and Sanitary Report 1917,* Clifford to Long, 9/7/18, CO96/591/393.

192. Fuller, diary, 24/9/17, ADM 12/5/160, PRAAD.

193. *Medical & Sanitation Report 1917*, 9/7/18, CO96/591/393.

194. Report, *Gold Coast Leader,* 1/9/17. See also *Medical and Sanitary Report 1916,* Clifford to Long, 15/5/17, CO96/579/313; *Report on Ashanti 1916,* 15/8/17, CO96/581/510; also Assistant Colonial Secretary Welman, memo, *Report on the Blue Book 1916* printed for Parliament, Clifford to Long, 25/8/17, CO96/581/528; *Medical and Sanitary Report 1917,* Clifford to Long, 9/7/18, CO96/591/393; Clifford, *LegCo* 25/10/17, *Gazette,* 26/11/17, CO99/32/76.

medical officers or were simply reported to them as "coughs."[195] Certainly Maxwell, the chief commissioner of Western Province, believed that TB accounted for 50% of deaths in 1917 in his region, where the coastal towns of Sekondi-Dixcove district were said to be the most unsanitary areas as a result of "the promiscuous keeping of pigs."[196] "Starvation" was added to the official list of causes of death in 1917, without comment, with twenty instances in Kumasi and two in Accra. These records do not give explicit information about the very poor, or whether individual officers believed that prewar conditions of poverty were exacerbated by hardship as a result, specifically, of wartime conditions.[197] The increased incidence of disease also affected European officials and unofficials, although the higher rates of invalidism were probably also due to longer tours and there being fewer personnel to cope with the work in the war.[198]

Even so, and despite the war, some long-term health projects were completed that directly benefited the local population. A "native" hospital was opened in Kumasi (said to be "much appreciated" by the local population), another "native" hospital in Saltpond, and a dispensary in Koforidua—all in 1915.[199] The large new "native" hospital in Accra, however, planned as early as 1909, still awaited the release of more funds: Korle Bu hospital in Accra was finally opened only in 1924 by Guggisberg.[200] In June 1917, Clifford outlined a plan for after the war of setting up a number of small dispensaries scattered over the colony, which would increase the provision of outpatient treatment available for the local African population.[201] In the light of this, Clifford also planned a lying-in hospital in Accra that would act as a school of midwifery under European management. The aim was to try to reduce the number of infant deaths, thought to be partly the result of untrained midwives. A lying-in hospital and midwifery school—Lady Clifford's great interest—were finally achieved a decade later. African infant mortality was very difficult to assess because many chiefs and people were reluctant to register children's births, but it was thought to be "extremely high."[202]

In the short term, wartime cuts in funding bit deep in a number of ways. Expenditure on the medical department sank in the war from £63,500 in 1915 to only just over £36,000 in 1918.[203] Medical research such as investigations into sleeping sickness and yellow fever had to be abandoned. The free distribution of quinine as a prophylactic to school children, initiated by Clifford before the war, was discontinued in 1918 as a belated war economy.[204] A committee of inquiry into the increasing incidence of TB and phthisis (silicosis caused by the inhalation of silicon dioxide) in the main mining settlements such as Tarkwa also

---

195. *Medical and Sanitary Report 1916,* Clifford to Long, 15/5/17, CO96/579/313. And see R. Dumett, "Disease and Mortality Among Gold Miners of Ghana," pp. 13–15.

196. Maxwell, *Report on Western Province 1917,* 1/7/18, Clifford to Long, 2/8/18, CO96/591/445.

197. *Births and Deaths Registration Report 1917,* Clifford to Long, 16/5/18, CO96/590/267. And see J. Iliffe, *The African Poor: A History,* (Cambridge, 1988).

198. *Medical and Sanitary Report 1916,* Clifford to Long, 15/5/17, CO96/579/313.

199. *Report on Ashanti 1916,* Clifford to Long, 9/7/18, CO96/591/393.

200. *Medical and Sanitary Report 1915,* Clifford to Bonar Law, 20/5/16, CO96/567/372. Another instance of there being insufficient acknowledgement of Guggisberg's predecessor's efforts and plans.

201. Clifford to Long, 11/6/17, CO96/580/376.

202. *Sanitary Report, Accra 1916*, Clifford to Long, 11/9/17. CO96/582/570; *Medical and Sanitary Report 1917*, Clifford to Long, 9/7/18, CO96/591/393.

203. *Blue Book 1915*, CO100/65; *Blue Book 1918*, CO100/68.

204. Clifford re. 1918 Estimates, to Long, 10/12/17, CO96/583/767.

had to be postponed because of the war.[205] One British medical officer suggested chillingly that little could be done about such disease in what was seen as the long years ahead of colonial rule: "We must simply let it kill off the most susceptible, and immunise the others in the course of generations."[206] Nonetheless, some efforts were made to encourage preventative action, such as circulating leaflets in mining areas, urging people to keep their housing well ventilated—and not to spit.[207] But it is not clear whether there were enough literates to pass on such messages.

Reductions in the government medical service, as in the other British West African colonies, were most severely felt during epidemics. In many stations in the Gold Coast, only dispensers remained when medical officers had been withdrawn, such as at Keta, Ada, and Elmina in 1917.[208] But people did not always bother to attend government "native" hospitals when medical officers were not in attendance.[209] There were scattered outbreaks of infectious diseases throughout the war period, as before, but with even fewer medical staff at hand. The outbreaks of plague in Accra and then in Axim in 1917 were relatively confined and short-lived, as were the outbreaks of smallpox and anthrax in the Northern Territories between 1916 and 1918.[210] But along with the generally high rate of disease noted in 1916 and 1917, they weakened some Africans' resistance to the devastating influenza pandemic of 1918.

The international phenomenon of the influenza pandemic was on a wholly different scale. Such epidemics, affecting European and African alike, did not of course recognize racial distinctions. But it was certainly made worse in the Gold Coast, as in other colonies, by the lack of medical knowledge and trained personnel. The influenza epidemic reached the coast on August 31, 1918, via a ship from Freetown, and then spread all over the country. The scale of the outbreak meant that few were able to be treated. Many of the fifty non-official Europeans who died in the Gold Coast, twenty-five from complications arising from influenza, were not within reach of medical aid when they became ill.[211] The violent effects of the epidemic, the worst since 1891, are described in Koforidua in mid-September: the town was "silent and empty," with businesses closed, the market "more or less deserted," and funeral processions "a common sight." After five weeks it had virtually gone, but left survivors weak and debilitated and requiring a long convalescence.[212] At Obuasi mine, survivors were reported at the end of December as still having "lost all energy and go."[213]

Given the sudden spread and virulence of the disease and the minimal level of British administration and communications in this West African territory, it is not surprising that it was difficult for the government to give any useful advice or remedy. A high proportion of the population of the whole colony was affected in what has been described as "the worst single demographic disaster" in the area's history.[214] Overcrowding in the

205. *Report of PMO on Mines Phthisis and TB 1916,* SSO Report, 14/11/17, PMO Report 10//1/18, Clifford to Long, 18/9/18, CO96/592/544. See R. Dumett, "Disease and Mortality Among Gold Miners in Ghana," pp. 15–16.

206. Dr Bruce, Abosso, Enclosure 1, in Clifford to Long, 18/9/18, CO96/592/544.

207. Dr Watson, Appendix A, 25/5/17 in Clifford to Long, 18/9/19, C096/592/544.

208. *Medical and Sanitary Report 1917,* Clifford to Long, 9/7/18, CO96/591/393.

209. Report on the Northern Territories in 1917, letter, Clifford to Long, 1/1/18, CO96/591/377.

210. *Return of Diseases and Deaths, Sanitation Report 1918,* Clifford to Milner, 1/3/19, CO96/591/393.

211. Dr. A. Ingram, *Influenza Report,* 6/2/19, Clifford to Milner, 1/3/19, C096/591/393.

212. *Koforidua Influenza Report,* 19/9/18, Clifford to Milner, 1/3/19, CO96/591/393.

213. Watkins to Mann, 29/12/18, AGC Ms. 141,171, 44.

214. K. D. Patterson, *Health in Colonial Ghana,* p. 64.

main coastal towns such as Accra, Cape Coast, and Sekondi, where sanitation had worsened during the period of the war, probably also contributed to the spread of the infection. In Axim, about 80% of the population caught the influenza, and perhaps 40% in Sekondi. Young children and young adults between 20 and 30 were especially vulnerable, falling victim to secondary infections such as dysentery, bronchitis, pneumonia, or meningitis. Able-bodied laborers could die the same day that they first appeared sick. Fuller estimated that about 2% of the population died in Ashanti, with approximately 9,000 deaths. The Northern Territories were particularly hard hit, with some 80% of the population in both the northeastern and northwestern provinces of the Northern Territories affected and an overall death rate of perhaps 7%. The mortality rate in Accra was high, possibly 5%. Throughout the colony at least 4% of the population died.

Official figures are likely to be underestimates. The contemporary official estimate of just over 60,000 deaths in all was based on the 1911 census total of 1.5m, as opposed to the more likely total population figure of over 2m.[215] Precise figures were impossible to obtain. For example, sick miners were carried or "railed away" to villages, and many deaths, especially of children, were never recorded. Even so, we may conclude that the mortality rate was higher in coastal and northern areas than in the forest regions, where the population was better protected against cold winds. In the north, people were badly affected by the harmattan—the dry land wind blowing from the north into this region, mainly between December and February. The harmattan was particularly strong and cold in 1918, coinciding with a long drought. Cultural factors also played a part here: those who were especially affected were those who normally wore no clothes or few clothes and were unaware of how important it was to wrap up and prevent the development of secondary pulmonary infections.[216] And clothing played a part elsewhere, too, as Claridge described when on duty in Togo: Africans along the coast were vulnerable when they sat down dressed only in damp cotton cloth after getting overheated or being soaked by rain.[217]

In the crisis of this flu epidemic, the British colonial administration was tested and was seen by its African subjects to fail. Not surprisingly, perhaps, the ravages of the influenza epidemic, coinciding with the worst months of the war for the colony's shipping and trade, caused expressions of anger against the Gold Coast government. Some people gave vent to "very natural resentment at this visitation."[218] In particular, the government was held responsible for the shortage of European and African doctors as well as for inadequate public health measures. But criticism of Clifford's clearly well-intentioned

---

215. K. D. Patterson, "The Influenza Epidemic of 1918–19 in the Gold Coast," *JAH,* 24,1983, pp. 485–502; D. Ohadike, "The Influenza Epidemic of 1918–19 and the Spread of Cassava Cultivation in the Lower Niger: A Study in Historical Linkages," *JAH*, XXII, 1981, pp. 379–91; Fuller, diary, 15–17/1/18, and 10/4/19, ADM 12/5/160, PRAAD; *Gold Coast Leader*, 19/10/18, NP/12/9, PRAAD; F. Cole, "Sierra Leone and World War I," pp. 213–245. And for comparison elsewhere on the continent, H. Phillips, *"Black October: "The Impact of the Spanish Influenza Epidemic of 1918 on South Africa,"* (Pretoria, 1990); C. Perrings, "Good Lawyers But Poor Workers": Recruited Angolan Labor in the Copper Mines of Katanga 1917–1921," *JAH,* XVIII, 2,1977; C. Van Onselen, "Worker Consciousness in Black Mines: Southern Rhodesia 1900–1920," *JAH,* XIV, 2,1973.

216. *Koforidua Influenza Report,* 19/9/18, Clifford to Milner, 1/3/19, CO96/591/393. See K. D. Patterson, "Influenza Epidemic of 1918–19 in the Gold Coast," pp. 495–50; Samson to Mann, 21/10/1918, AGC. Ms. 14,171.44.

217. Claridge, Senior Medical Officer Togo, Enclosure 3, *Report on Togo 1917,* 16/7/18, CO96/591/407.

218. Dr A. Ingram, *Influenza Report,* 6/2/19, Clifford to Long, 1/3/19, CO96/591/393.

regime was muted compared with, for example, "the abusive press campaign" against the government in Sierra Leone.[219] As elsewhere on the West African coast, the epidemic led to food shortages.[220] With schools and offices shut and religious services and festivals postponed, "a general depression" was said to have settled on the population. If it was not the British who were at fault, or solely at fault, there had to be alternative culprits. Some Africans blamed "bad fetish." In Ashanti when priests in Wam and Berekum tried to revive the Afunsoa fetish custom, there was a widespread belief that the epidemic was due to the malignant influence of witches.[221] But the government also remained an obvious target. It was fortunate for the British officials that the Armistice and rapid revival of trade, as well as a drop in the incidence of the disease, came to their rescue in the last weeks of 1918.

The severity of the influenza outbreak raised critical questions about the adequacy of the whole medical and sanitary provision in the Gold Coast colony, as well as in the other British West African colonies, and in Britain itself.[222] In October 1918, the *Gold Coast Leader* raised the questions: "Where are the doctors? Where are the pathologists? Where are the men of science?"[223] The government was blamed for failing to encourage the necessary training and specialization. Also that month, African unofficials grilled the government in the legislative council. E. J. P. Brown, who had become one of the African unofficials in the Gold Coast, asked why African doctors and nurses had not been employed to make up for the reduced number of Europeans. The answer given—that there had been insufficient European staff to undertake training of Africans—was considered unsatisfactory. Why had not more staff been appointed and more money and systematic training been given before the war? The government was hardly generous in its response: it was hoped that after the war the number of African nurses could be increased "to no less than six."[224] The PMO could only agree with Casely Hayford, also recently appointed as an unofficial in the Gold Coast, that the number of medical officers was barely sufficient for routine work and was "undoubtedly inadequate" for a major epidemic, as was the number of hospitals. Even if there was no known cure for the influenza, medical advice could have been given on how to avoid, or how to deal with, secondary infections. The truth was that there were whole areas of the country with little or no medical aid at all.[225]

Nana Ofori Atta, the leading African unofficial in the legislative council, questioned why African doctors were not used to assist British medical officers, on a temporary basis if necessary. It was clearly too much for one doctor to be given responsibility for five districts, as in Koforidua. The PMO's defense in that case was that attempts were being made to get hold of another European medical officer, and that there had been no

219. See, e.g., report, *Gold Coast Leader,* 19/10/18. And see F. Cole, "Sierra Leone and World War I," pp. 239–240.

220. Cf. Nigeria, see D. Ohadike, "The Influenza Pandemic of 1918–19," p. 383.

221. *Report on Ashanti 1918,* CO98/30. For similar beliefs elsewhere on the continent at this time, see D. Killingray, "War & Society in Africa 1914–20," paper given to the African History seminar, SOAS, London University, November 1989, p. 12.

222. See, e.g., Sierra Leone, in F. Cole, "Sierra Leone and World War I," p. 240.

223. *Gold Coast Leader*, 19/10/18, NP 12/9, PRAAD.

224. Acting Colonial Secretary Harper, *LegCo* 29/10/18, *Gazette* 9/11/18, CO99/33/81.

225. Casely Hayford, *LegCo* 29/10/18, *Gazette* 9/11/18, CO99/33/82; Rice, PMO, *LegCo* 29/10/18. *Gazette* 9/11/18, CO99/33/82. And see D. K. Patterson, "The Influenza Epidemic of 1918–19 in the Gold Coast," p. 493. See *Gold Coast Leader,* 28/8/15, and R. Addo-Fening, "Akyem Abuakwa c.1874–1943," pp. 279–281.

applications from "suitable candidates" for the two posts for "native" doctors.[226] But this answer failed to acknowledge that there had been insufficient European doctors appointed to the colony before the war, which contributed to the shortage of medical personnel, and also that "suitable" "native" candidates would have required training, of which there was very little before the war. It is likely that the shortage of African candidates was also partly due to the relatively poor remuneration offered, as well as to the requirement that "native" medical officers should work in outstations, where there was little chance of supplementing their salary with private practice.

The colony's medical service had been weighed in the balance and found wanting. This was not only in the exceptional circumstances of the influenza pandemic. Clifford's plans for African doctors, nurses, dispensers, vaccinators, and sanitary inspectors had been frustrated not only for lack of funding (made worse by the war) but also as a result of prewar opposition from other British officials. Clifford had challenged the conventional wisdom and practice of the West African Medical Service and its supporters in the Colonial Office in London. As Clifford acknowledged, he had not won the whole fight, but after "a somewhat strenuous campaign," he had (as he said with some satisfaction in October 1918) achieved certain "modifications."[227] Clifford's struggles before and during the war played a major role in ensuring that the medical and sanitary officers' restrictive influence over government policy in the Gold Coast, and over Colonial Office policy in London, was never the same again. But African confidence in the governor's ability to deliver, in this case vitally needed modern Western medical treatment, was damaged in the war period.

Along with medical services, Western education was given high priority in Clifford's administration—being at the heart of the "civilising mission," as he perceived it. This was a crucial part of what Clifford, and his successor Guggisberg, promised would be achieved for the local African population of the colony. Governor Clifford may have been "a pragmatic colonial administrator," but he was not merely concerned with the administrative and economic needs of clerks and artisans, as Gailey, his official biographer, seems to suggest.[228] Clifford argued that Britain had a trusteeship role and a moral responsibility for Africans' welfare and progress beyond the core colonial agenda of keeping order and promoting trade at minimum expense. But the Great War intervened. Concerning education, reforms such as the planned increases in numbers of teachers and inspectors and higher salaries never materialized, and reforms had to be postponed. And the war was to have one particular impact in the Gold Coast: rather than expanding educational opportunities in this period, the government of the Gold Coast was to become preoccupied with taking over, even if temporarily, the Bremen and Basel mission schools, on account of their German personnel. This was perhaps the single major way, apart from trade, in which the war being fought against Germany came directly to the colony. Ironically, as a result the government was to spend more money on education in the Gold Coast than ever before, but with barely any increase in overall provision.

The local African demand for Western secular education, articulated most loudly in Eastern and Central Province, was as pressing during the war years as before. An increasing number of requests for government schools was received from Twi-speaking areas, even

---

226. N. O. Atta, *LegCo* 29/10/18, *Gazette* 9/11/18, C099/33/81.
227. Clifford, *LegCo* 28/10/18, *Gazette* 9/11/18, CO99/33/82.
228. H. Gailey, *Clifford*, p. 87.

though there were many Basel schools in this region. Since the outbreak of war, these Swiss-German schools had come to be known locally as "German" schools. In 1916 Nana Ofori Atta persuaded the governor of the need for a government school at Kyebi, capital of the African state of Akyem Abuakwa, requesting "a purely English education" as distinct from the existing local Basel school. The government made a financial contribution: a PWD officer supervised the building, and the okyenhene provided the land and the labor.[229] In the early war period, London still advocated more government schools "for so important a service as education on which too little has been expended."[230] Crowther, the commissioner for native affairs, judged such government schools to be "more efficient and less disturbing to native society than missions."[231]

Even so, several London officials were less happy with the provision of secular government schools. Ellis revealed uncompromising prejudice as well as ignorance when he declared that he did not believe in nondenominational schools where no religious teaching was given. "The heathen savages of West Africa" needed the "missionary spirit."[232] A teacher from Europe "will not go out for the love of John Stuart Mill ... to undertake the education of little nigger boys." What was needed in the teaching profession, he claimed, was "not half as much intellectual as moral qualifications."[233] The aim, according to this view, was to continue to leave education as far as possible to the missionary societies (irrespective of their country of origin and irrespective of the war), with a government right of overall supervision. Mission schools were not only cheaper but also agencies of "civilisation," and produced a well-ordered and appreciative population. Lessons on "The Rights and Duties of a British Subject" were added to the school curriculum in 1916, although there was the irony, noted by Flood, that "no one seems to know what duties are and it is always bad to make people think about rights."[234] Fiddian's sarcastic comment was that he was sure "some exquisitely unsuitable English text book" would be chosen.[235]

Yet the missionaries of the society that ran the most schools in the colony were to be deported in the fourth year of the war. This was despite unanimity between British officials in London and Accra on this subject, as well as the widespread demand from Africans in the Gold Coast, that provision of Western education be substantially increased—through either secular or religious schools. The relatively small number of German Bremen missionaries in the colony was finally deported in July 1916. This was followed by the banning of the Swiss Basel mission in December 1917. Given that the war was a very difficult period of retrenchment and shortage of staff, what led the Gold Coast government to take such drastic action? There was certainly no intention or desire at the start of the war on the part of either the governor or the Colonial Office to disturb the status quo. Indeed,

229. Clifford to Bonar Law, 11/7/16, CO96/567/485.

230. Green, CO Minute, Acting Governor Slater, confid. to Harcourt, 19/5/15, CO96/558; Harcourt to Acting Governor Slater, 12/7/15, CO96/558.

231. Crowther, *Report on Native Affairs 1915,* 4/5/16, Clifford, confid. to Bonar Law, 25/5/16, CO96/567. And compare with Lugard's similar view, in J. Mangan, *The Games Ethic and Imperialism. Aspects of the Diffusion of an Ideal,* (London, 1986), pp. 101–121.

232. Ellis, CO Minute, *memo, Anti Slavery and Aboriginal Protection Society re: Education in West Africa* 3/4/14, CO554/23. Compare with the similar views of Secretary of State Lord Kimberley in 1880, in D. Kimble, *A Political History,* p. 72.

233. *Ibid.*

234. Flood, memo, *Draft Education Bill, 1916.*

235. Fiddian, CO Minute, Clifford to Bonar Law, 20/12/16, CO96/574/947.

the arrangements made to deport 162 Germans in November 1914 specifically excluded the twenty "or so" who were missionaries.[236]

Before 1914, the Basel mission had an impressive record. Its major contribution to education in the Gold Coast—providing a good education at no cost to the government—was viewed very favorably by British officials in London and on the West African coast.[237] The secretary of the Africa section of the mission had written from Basel at the beginning of the war, as a precaution, to appeal to the British government to protect its missionary work and to treat the mission like the International Red Cross. He wished to make clear that the Basel missionaries were wholly loyal to the local government. Although the mission was partly German, the origin and headquarters of the mission were in Switzerland, and the Basel mission factory, the trading society which donated sums to the mission, was run by a Swiss firm. The Colonial Office reassured the Basel mission at this time, in August 1914, that its work was highly valued and that its property would be protected .[238]

But as the war continued with no end in sight, local Africans began to receive contradictory messages from the British administration in the Gold Coast concerning Germans, whether missionaries or not. On the outbreak of war, a proclamation was issued to chiefs in the colony warning them that anyone molesting or insulting Germans who had lived among them for years "as friends and guests" would be severely punished.[239] There were no reports of anti-German feeling at this stage. German traders, with their easy credit terms for African traders, were popular along the West African coast.[240] Nevertheless, it soon became difficult for the population of the Gold Coast to know how to regard Germans, with government pamphlets accusing Germany of atrocities in Belgium and misrule in Togo.[241] There was also disagreement in the African press during the war as to whether Germans should be allowed to stay in the Gold Coast. But there was also acceptance of the governor's decision to treat the missionaries as "honourable enemies."[242] Among the few negative comments of 1914 listed in an intelligence report were claims that some Basel missionaries were responsible for pro-German propaganda, with portraits of the Kaiser displayed in certain Basel schools.[243]

Although the Basel trading society was Swiss-run, Clifford was concerned that all but two or three of its personnel were German, and rumors abounded among British and African residents alike of covert hostile practices by German residents. For example, there were rumors in January 1915 that an employee of the Basel mission factory had fired a signal rocket from the beach at Ada when it was believed that a German cruiser, the *Karlsruhe,* was in the vicinity. (It was not known at the time that the *Karlsruhe* had been destroyed off the West Indies on November 4, 1914). There were also warnings in the press about a possible German attack, such as the advice given in *The African Telegraph*

236. Clifford, confid. to Harcourt, 19/11/14, CO554/18. See also S. Prempeh's study, "The Bremen and Basle Missions and Their Successors in the Gold Coast," unpublished PhD thesis, (University of Aberdeen, 1977).

237. See Section I, Chapter 2.

238. Letter, Rev. W. Oettli, secretary of the Africa Section, Basel Mission Society, Basel, to Harcourt, 14/8/14, CO96/553/13.

239. Green, CO Minute, Oettli to Harcourt, 14/8/14, CO96/553/13.

240. See, e.g., A. Osuntokun, *Nigeria in the First World War,* p. 72.

241. Editorial, *Gold Coast Leader,* 28/11/14.

242. *Gold Coast Leader,* e.g., 20/2/15, 2/12/16, 12/5/17.

243. Ellis, CO Minute, Oettli to Harcourt, 14/8/14, CO96/553/13.

and Gold Coast Mirror in January 1915: "Should hostile aircraft be seen, take shelter in the nearest house, preferably in the basement ... do not stand about in crowds and do not touch unexploded bombs." Alarm had been heightened by the news just received of the bombing of the east coast of England, including Scarborough.[244] The same paper, *The African Telegraph and Gold Coast Mirror*, published "War Pictures Weekly," in anti-German "Boys Own Style" articles during 1914 and 1915.[245]

There were important economic and administrative issues at stake for the British government of the colony. Clifford did not want either the mission or the Basel trading society disturbed, jeopardizing the good order and economic well-being of the colony. Yet there was a lobby of British traders, including Grey, the senior British unofficial in the legislative council and main agent of the trading society Swanzy, who from commercial interest as well as enhanced patriotic sentiment urged the governor to ban all "enemy subjects" from the colony's trade. But Clifford did not want to see one of the main purchasing agencies driven out of the cocoa market by false accusations, which would then give a virtual trading monopoly to a few British firms. The Basel factory managed to continue supporting the Basel mission without most of its German personnel, once all Germans were excluded from trading in November 1914.

Thus six months after the start of the war, it still suited the British colonial administration in the Gold Coast to retain the Swiss-German Basel mission and its trading factory and the small number of German Bremen mission schools. The work undertaken by the Basel mission, especially in Eastern Province and Ashanti, and the contribution it made to local African education, were still substantial. Apart from mission settlements and farms, there were day and boarding schools and two training colleges, all "admirably conducted." London officials also agreed with Clifford's concern at the expense that would be incurred if the government had to maintain all the colony's schools itself, and also acknowledged the advantage of retaining trading competition for the trading "combine" (Swanzy, Millers, and the Africa Association).[246] The governor had been disconcerted, however, to discover that twenty-two of the twenty-eight Basel missionaries in the Gold Coast were in fact German. Yet the German missionaries of the Bremen and Basel missions and their families, fifty-nine in total, were allowed to remain in January 1915—with the restriction that they could not leave their residence or travel outside a five-mile radius without permission of the DC.[247]

It was a question of what was possible as well as what was desirable. Clifford and his key officials did not consider that there was any option but to keep these two missions in the Gold Coast at this time. For the government to take over all the sixty-four Basel and fifteen Bremen schools was "not within the range of practical politics now or in the near future." These schools together made up nearly half the total number of the 143 mission-assisted schools in the entire colony. Clifford also considered the work of the Basel mission as "vastly superior in quality to any other missionary society." Even if a majority of the German missionaries were found to hold hostile political views, their power to do any harm was "very greatly restricted"; nonetheless he was slightly alarmed that they were the

244. Clifford, secret to Harcourt, 10/1/15, CO96/555/75. And P. Hatton, "The Gambia, the Colonial Office, and the Opening Months of the First World War," *JAH*, VII, 1,1966, p. 128. See also see, e.g., *Gold Coast Leader*, 6/2/15.

245. *The African Telegraph and Gold Coast Mirror*, e.g., 14/1/15.

246. Flood, CO Minute, Acting Governor Slater, confid. to Harcourt, 19/5/15, CO96/558.

247. Clifford, secret to Harcourt, 10/1/15, CO96/555/75.

only white men in the Gold Coast who could converse freely with Africans in the vernacular languages, which neither the Wesleyans nor the Roman Catholic missionaries were able to do.[248] Fuller, the chief commissioner of Ashanti, agreed that taking over such a large number of schools would involve an unacceptably large outlay for the colonial government, and that education in the Gold Coast would suffer without these "fine peace-loving and teaching set of men." They were also praised by Mayall, the acting director of education, for their high standards and "excellent management."[249]

Yet concerns persisted: for example, that in Eastern Province the Bremen mission at Peki had alerted Germans across the Togo border at the time of the outbreak of the war. Crowther was confident that local people in Peki and Awuna remained wholly loyal to the British and "strongly anti-German"—though he claimed that the German-speaking Swiss, as well as Germans, continued to obtain German newspapers, "war news dictated in Berlin," and distribute them to "native" catechists and pastors.[250] Some officers' reports to the governor simply reflected prejudice. Hinson, ADC in Winneba, criticized the Basel mission for "its unwholesome combination of trade, export and shipping, with worship of God."[251] He was uneasy at seeing circular letters for the Basel missionaries linking Germans in West Africa with Basel mission stations in India and China, especially as some of the missionaries were known not only to have relatives in the German army but also to have had military training themselves. The acting PC for Western Province, Bartlett, noted that "the Basels" always had the best map of any district—confirmation that they were "simply an instance of the world wide ramifications of the German spy system."[252]

From the middle of 1915, Colonial Office officials in London were also faced with a steady barrage of unsubstantiated accusations against the Basel mission. These were sent by personnel from other departments of state: the Foreign Office, the War Office, and the Home Office. For example, the Foreign Office forwarded the increasingly virulent dispatches of Grant Duff, the British minister in Berne, for whom the Basel mission was "a nest of German theologians" and "merely an insidious association for the diffusion of the gospel according to William II."[253] Colonial Office officials countered that there was no evidence of the mission doing any harm in the Gold Coast.[254] The War Office passed on the views of the chief censors in Accra and Britain that all Germans in the colony should be interned or deported. They claimed that it was impossible to check all lines of communication, and several German pastors and missionaries were said to be "naturally anti-British in their sympathies."[255] The Colonial Office was able to reply that all German

248. Clifford, quoted by Acting Governor Slater, confid. to Harcourt, 19/5/15, CO96/558.

249. Chief Commissioner Ashanti Fuller, 26/1/15, Enclosure 2, and Acting Director of Education Mayall, 26/12/14, Enclosure 1, Acting Governor Slater, confid. to Harcourt, 19/5/15, CO96/558.

250. Acting PC Eastern Province Crowther, 11/1/15, Enclosure 4, Acting Governor Slater confid. to Harcourt, 19/5/15, CO96/558.

251. ADC Winneba Hinson, 6/2/15, Sub-enclosure 3, and Acting PC Western Province Bartlett, 3/12/15, Enclosure 6, Acting Governor Slater, confid. to Harcourt, 19/5/15, CO96/558.

252. *Ibid.*

253. Grant Duff, Berne, to Under Secretary of State Lord Grey, FO, 11/8/15, enclosure, Grey, FO, to Bonar Law, 19/8/15; Grant Duff to Grey, FO, 17/9/15, enclosure, Grey, FO, to Bonar Law, 30/9/15; Grant Duff to Grey, FO, 8/12/15; enclosure, Grey, FO, to Bonar Law, 20/12/15, CO96/562.

254. Green, CO Minute, Grey, FO, to Bonar Law, 30/9/15, CO96/562.

255. Chief Censor, WO; and Chief Censor, Accra, 30/8/15, Enclosures in Grey, FO, to Bonar Law, 23/9/15; also WO Minute, 18/9/15 and Chief Censor, Accra, 30/8/15, copies enclosed in WO to Bonar Law, 17/9/15, CO96/563.

missionaries were very carefully watched in the Gold Coast.[256] The Home Office also wanted control of the Basel trading society on the grounds that its profits went to German missionary work, which consisted "largely of political propaganda." Colonial Office officials realized that commercial competitors such as Swanzy and Millers were behind this accusation, partly out of resentment that this commercial rival (whom they hoped to "squeeze out" of the trade) was not subject to British war taxation.[257] To satisfy the Home Office, an element of United Kingdom control over the Basel factory was introduced in the form of a British-based company, Werner's, whose members agreed to act as sole agents.[258] The Basel missionaries and the Basel trading society were therefore allowed at this stage to remain in West Africa.

But pressure to exclude all Germans from all British colonies mounted sharply in 1916, especially in London. The longer and more bitter the general conflict, the more likely that the presence of "enemy subjects" living and working freely in the Gold Coast would become unacceptable to the government in Britain, regardless of their value to the colony and regardless of any evidence there might be of their political neutrality. Orders finally came from London in March 1916 that the German Bremen mission be closed and its missionaries deported. Action was delayed because Clifford was away on tour, but the Bremen missionaries were duly told in mid-June 1916 that they had to leave the Gold Coast forthwith, although they had previously been assured that they would only be deported if they were "disloyal." They were now instructed that "imperial reasons" made it imperative that they leave. They were given just two days to pack. The issue of compensation was put aside for the time being, as was the question of whether the mission would be allowed to return after the war.[259] The education department in the Gold Coast, already very short-staffed, was now saddled with running the Bremen Lutheran schools on a "modest and economical scale." Clifford, however, hoped to persuade the United Free Church of Scotland, which already had a mission at Calabar, to take over the educational as well as the religious work of the mission, with some government aid. He declared at this time that if the management and direction of religious affairs were left to "native" pastors and catechists too long, it would lead to "speedy degeneration."[260]

There was mounting pressure on the Colonial Office from other departments of state in London during 1916 to deport all the Basel missionaries from the Gold Coast. In July 1916, the Foreign Office "advised" the Colonial Office that the Gold Coast should sever its relations with the Basel Society, irrespective of the mission's record in the colony.[261] The supporting papers sent to the Colonial Office consisted mainly of the usual hysterical dispatches from Grant Duff, for whom the Basel Mission was now "a Pan German Association disguised" and "an organ, even in time of peace, for the spread of Kultur

256. Flood, CO Minute, WO to Bonar Law, 17/9/15, CO96/563.

257. Flood, Ellis, Fiddes, CO Minute, Home Office to Bonar Law, 20/11/15, CO96/563.

258. Fiddes, CO Minute, Home Office to Harcourt, 3/12/15, CO96/563.

259. Bonar Law to Clifford, 13/3/16, in telegram, Clifford to Bonar Law, 8/6/16, CO96/567; telegram, Clifford to Bonar Law, 17/7/16, CO96/567; memo, Colonial Secretary Slater to Clifford, 26/6/16; Enclosure 5 in Clifford to Bonar Law, 17/7/16, CO96/568/503. Also see E. Grau, "The Evangelical Presbyterian Church (Ghana and Togo) 1914–1916. A Study in European Mission Relations Affecting the Beginning of an Indigenous Church," unpublished PhD thesis, (Hartford, 1964), p. 43. Also Director of Education Oman, 31/8/16, Enclosure 1, and Townsend, CO Minute, 16/10/16, Enclosure 5, Clifford, confid. to Bonar Law, 20/10/16, CO96/571.

260. Clifford to Bonar Law, 17/7/16, CO96/568/503; and Clifford, confid. to Bonar Law, 20/10/16, CO96/571.

261. Grey, FO, to Bonar Law, 31/7/16, CO96/574.

combined with money making. Its religion is merely a cloak."[262] Also enclosed were dispatches from Hertslet and Beale, the British consul general and vice consul in Zurich, agreeing that the missionary society was in reality a German political organization.[263] It was clear to Colonial Office officials that the Foreign Office had finally decided that the Basel mission and its factory were one and the same, and that both were German at heart.[264]

There was no single agreed British view, even in 1916. The preferred solution of Clifford's administration was still to allow the Swiss Basel mission, purged of its German elements, to continue in the Gold Coast in cooperation with the United Free Church, thus saving the local government from having to take on all the organization and expense itself.[265] Yet increasingly London officials were coming around to the view that there was no option but for the Basel mission to go, and if so, the sooner the better for all parties.[266] Ellis wanted more precise information concerning Basel loyalties: for example, did they teach in German or English? Did they teach religion or politics? Did they pray for the King or the Kaiser?[267]

Much now depended on the governor. The Colonial Office had been happy to leave Clifford the final word on the subject, despite the increasing number of denunciations of the mission from many quarters, mostly far from the colony. In October 1916 the Secretary of State for the Colonies, Bonar Law, officially accepted that the Basel mission would be excluded from British Africa, as the Foreign Office formally urged. But concerning the Gold Coast, this would not be before satisfactory arrangements had been made to take over the mission's extensive work.[268] The governor was left with some responsibility, in this case for the timing of the missionaries' departure. Although the tone of much of the British press was by now dramatically anti-German—for example, the call of the *Daily Mail* for the withdrawal from overseas of "the black flag of a nation of spies and criminals"—the situation was allowed to drift on into 1917 with German missionaries still in post.[269] A year after Lord Grey's official letter from the Foreign Office to the Colonial Office about deporting the Basel missionaries and closing the mission and its trading society, no action had yet been taken against the Basel mission in the Gold Coast. As late as August 1917, Clifford expressed his disapproval of the French and British governments' decision to deport all German missionaries from occupied Togo.[270] But the Gold Coast administration found itself in an increasingly anomalous position, with Germans allowed to remain there but not elsewhere on the continent.

In December 1917, however, Clifford completely changed his mind on the subject. It was the devastating effects of the German U-boat campaign and the deaths of key British

262. Grant Duff, Berne, to Grey, FO, 10/7/16 and 13/7/16; also British Consulate General Zurich Hertslet, to Grey, FO, 11/7/16; and Vice Consul Zurich Beale, to Grey, FO, 10/7/16, enclosures, Grey, FO, to Bonar Law, 31/7/16, CO96/574.

263. *Ibid.*

264. Flood, CO Minute, Grey, FO, to Bonar Law, 21/9/16, CO96/576.

265. Tennyson (legal advisor to the CO), CO Minute. Grey, FO, to Bonar Law, 3/8/16, CO96/575.

266. Flood, CO Minute, Grey, FO, to Bonar Law, 27/9/16, CO96/575.

267. Ellis, CO Minute, Grey, FO, to Bonar Law, 3/8/16, CO96/575.

268. Bonar Law to Grey, FO, 2/10/16 in Grey, FO, to Bonar Law, 27/9/16, CO96/574; Grey, FO, to Bonar Law, 22/9/16, CO96/574.

269. *The Daily Mail* 9/9/16, quoted in W. R. Louis, *Great Britain and Germany's Lost Colonies 1914–1919,* (London, 1967), p. 76.

270. Clifford, confid. to Long, 1/8/17, CO96/581; Clifford, confid. to Long, 27/7/17, CO96/580.

officials and a number of Gold Coast citizens that altered the general climate of opinion in the colony among both British and African residents, and in particular changed the governor's views. The first of the two major losses in 1917 was in April when the *SS Abosso* was sunk. Reece, the treasurer, and his wife, and Inspector General of Police and Prisons Collins were among a large number of officials, unofficials, and residents of the colony who were drowned. In December a second major disaster struck when the *SS Apapa* was torpedoed, again with heavy losses among residents of the Gold Coast, both British and African, including Attorney General Townsend, Comptroller of Customs Harragin, and Senior Assistant Colonial Secretary Farrar.[271] The grief was shared by British and Africans. According to an editorial in the *Gold Coast Leader*: "The common suffering has tended to draw the government and the governed together."[272]

An incident immediately following news of the deaths of those aboard the *SS Apapa* seems to have been the final straw concerning Clifford's attitude to the Basel missionaries. Four members of the mission were said to have noisily celebrated the sinking of the *SS Apapa* in a room opening on to the high street in Accra, not far from the Accra Club. Similar shouting and singing were subsequently reported to have taken place in August when the *SS Karina* sank. However, it is interesting to note that none of the three principal witnesses could speak German, and two were agents of rival firms.[273] Whether or not the accusations were justified, they were enough to convince key players in the Gold Coast such as the governor, members of the executive and legislative councils, and African journalists, that all Germans and German sympathizers would have to leave the colony. Occasional incidents, speeches, pamphlets, and newspaper articles that had appeared on the coast in the past—purporting to show that some of the missionaries sympathized with the German cause—all contributed to the emotional effect at this time of mourning. Accusations included failure to express loyalty to the Crown, as when loyal statements were said to have been deleted from the Akropong Basel school's jubilee pamphlet in September 1917.[274] The governor was now finally convinced that the Basel mission was "an enemy institution."[275] The strain of the long tours, the overwork, and the deaths of his only son and then his beloved brother in France in 1916 were all to militate against Clifford making a dispassionate judgment.

British officials now viewed the government takeover of the Basel schools and the sale of the Basel factory or trading company with relative equanimity. The governor now believed that the education department could run the educational work of the mission, even if not as efficiently or extensively as it had been run by the Basel missionaries. Religious work could, after all, be continued by "native" pastors. As to commerce, Clifford suggested that the trading firm's assets, estimated at nearly £lm, should not be sold as one lot, because then only the Combine would be able to afford them, and this sale would thereby strengthen their monopoly. If they were sold in a number of smaller lots, English buyers and "well to do natives" would not be excluded.[276] The Colonial Office readily concurred with the governor's change of heart. Sir Herbert Read, assistant under-secretary for the Colonies, agreed that the missionaries' loyalty was suspect: it was dangerous to

271. Telegram, Clifford to Long, 6/12/17 and draft, Long to Grey, FO, 8/12/17, CO96/583.

272. Editorial, *Gold Coast Leader* 5/1/18.

273. See S. Prempeh, "The Bremen and Basle Mission," p. 105.

274. See M. Gannon, "The Basle Mission Trading Company and British Colonial Policy in the Gold Coast 1918–1928," *JAH,* 24, 1983, p. 505.

275. Clifford, confid. to Long, 14/12/17, CO96/583.

276. *Ibid.*

leave them in a "lightly administered" colony when civil staff were depleted and the bulk of the military staff were in East Africa.[277] There was little hard evidence to justify the expulsion of the Basel mission. All material printed by the mission headquarters in Basel was pacifist. The Basel mission magazine of December 1916 deplored the war as likely to "curtail European influence, shake the authority of the White Races, and weaken Christianity in its struggle with other religions."[278] By this time in Britain, pacifism was widely viewed as pro-German.

There had been growing British concern from mid-1917 that German interests seemed to be taking the opportunity to stir up the African population in the colony against their British rulers. The Basel mission press published reports of popular discontent with the government of the Gold Coast. Such reports announced that the shortage of money and lack of transport for cocoa in the Gold Coast were giving rise to a growing cry of "Africa for the Africans," echoed by Marcus Garvey's later call in the 1930s.[279] But there was support in the African press for the governor's decision to expel German missionaries. It seems that one effect of the economic slump was to encourage local anti-German feeling.[280]

Anti-German sentiment was so strong among British officials during the last twelve months of the war that there were no qualms concerning the deportation of the Basel missionaries. The missionaries were interned in December 1917 in Accra where, as German prisoners of war, they were placed under military guard. Two pairs of field glasses, one diary, and one map were the sum total of "suspect articles" confiscated before the majority of the missionaries were deported that month, and the remainder early in the new year of 1918.[281] To the Gold Coast government's relief, the United Free Church of Scotland did finally agree to take over the Basel Mission work and buildings, provided that the Gold Coast education department ran the schools and paid the teachers. The schools would revert to their grant-aided status once the Scottish mission felt able to take over the educational work, which took place in April 1920.[282]

The Basel society had presented a strong defense of its assets as the property of Swiss nationals and therefore of neutrals, and of its wider neutrality. They claimed that there had never been, and could not be, any proof of their missionaries' disloyalty to the colonial government. Accusations such as "celebrating" the sinking of ships were dismissed by the mission as "absurd." The government had failed to record the missionaries' many acts of loyalty and sympathy, such as letters of commiseration and attendance at funeral services for those drowned. The loud celebrations were defended as simply a birthday toast. [283] But the carefully argued protest of the Basel mission was ignored, while the governor, with all the enthusiasm of a recent convert, now wholly condemned the mission, its publications, and its past practices. That the mission in the Gold Coast had relayed news of the Ashanti war to the German government in Togo in 1900 and then congratulated the

---

277. Sir Herbert Read, CO Minute, Clifford, confid. to Long, 14/12/17, CO96/583.

278. *Basle Mission Magazine,* 12/16, enclosure, Grey, FO, to Long, 2/1/17, CO96/584.

279. *Report of 102nd Meeting of Basle Mission,* quoted by British Minister Horace Rumbold, Berne, enclosure, Grey, FO to Long. 2/8/17, CO96/584.

280. *The Gold Coast Nation,* 6/4/18.

281. Clifford, confid. to Long, 11/1/18, CO96/587. And see N. Smith, *The Presbyterian Church of Ghana 1835–1960,* (Accra, 1966), p. 150.

282. United Free Church of Scotland to Long, 2/1/18; Clifford, confid. to Long, 9/4/18, CO96/589; and *Education Report 1920,* CO98/34.

283. W. Preiswerk-Imhoff, Basle Mission Secretary, to Long, 30/7/18, CO96/595. H. Debrunner, *A History of Christianity in Ghana,* (Accra, 1967), p. 287.

Kaiser on his birthday in 1902 were now all cited by Clifford as proof of long-festering "disloyalty."[284] He urged that the Basel mission "never again be suffered to resume operations in the Gold Coast."[285] (In fact, the first few Basel missionaries did return in 1925–26). Clifford had no hesitation concerning the sale of the trading society and recommended the expropriation of the Basel mission property for use by the Scottish Mission.[286]

Consequently, the Gold Coast government was faced with major expenditure on education at a time during the war when funds were extremely short. The finances as well as the responsibilities of the education department were transformed. In 1914, the total annual government expenditure on education had been just under £25,000. But in 1918, the additional cost of taking over the Bremen and Basel schools alone added £15,000 to department costs. Clerical work previously undertaken by twenty-five missionaries was now the responsibility of clerks in the education department.[287] In Ellis's view, the substantial addition to educational expenditure made all the more necessary the proposed increases in taxation.[288] At the time of the outbreak of the war, there were sixty-eight foreign missionaries present (out of a total of 152 missionaries in all) most of whom, forty-six, were German. By 1918 there were only four foreign missionaries left.[289] Ironically, the colonial government rejected foreign missionaries' services at a time of an acute shortage of both teachers and administrators. There was one period in 1917 when, as a result of secondments and leave, Oman, the Director of Education, found himself the only member of the educational administrative staff in the colony.[290]

The deportation of the German and German-Swiss missionaries from the Gold Coast in 1916–1917 was merely one of the disruptive effects of the First World War, on just one of Britain's African colonies, but the way the decision was finally reached reflects more widely on the way in which colonial power was then exercised. The governor remained officially under the King in Council (and under the Cabinet via the secretary of state for the colonies), and unofficially, on a day-to-day basis, under instruction from Colonial Office officials in Whitehall. The Colonial Office was not only obliged to defer to decisions of the Cabinet and Parliament, but was also subject to pressure from other departments of state, such as the Foreign Office, the War Office, and the Home Office. And yet it is interesting that after prolonged delays, it was only when Governor Clifford himself finally pressed for the Basel mission to be closed down in the Gold Coast that action was taken. It does appear that, perhaps especially during the war, a governor of Clifford's caliber and drive could be given considerable latitude in some aspects of running a colony. This confirms Rathbone's picture of this period as one of "maximal local, pro-consular initiative with minimal metropolitan interference."[291]

It is also apparent that the anti-German hysteria of World War I was not confined to Britain. In the Gold Coast, the Basel and Bremen missionaries were its victims, while the administration, and above all the local African people (with the diversion of government

284. Clifford, confid. to Long, 18/6/18, CO96/590.

285. Clifford, confid. to Long, 12/9/18, CO96/592. See, e.g., C. K. Graham, *The History of Education in Ghana from the Earliest Times to the Declaration of Independence,* (London, 1971), p. 151.

286. Clifford, confid. to Long, 12/9/18, CO96/592.

287. Oman, Director of Education, Estimates, Clifford to Long, 18/4/18, CO96/589/217. Also *Blue Books: 1914,* CO100/64; *1918,* CO100/68.

288. Ellis, CO Minute, telegram, Clifford to Long, 17/4/18, CO96/589.

289. Clifford, confid. to Long, 2/10/18, CO96/593.

290. Director of Education Oman, *Education Report 1912,* CO98/28.

291. R. Rathbone, "World War I and Africa," pp. 1–2.

resources), paid the price. Apart from the immediate disruption to education and the delay in increasing educational provision, there was literally a high price to pay in 1928 when the Imperial government required the colony to bear the cost of the £305,000 compensation to the Basel trading society.[292] There is an element of contradiction here: British officials wanted Africans to be educated (and many officers believed it should be a religious education), yet a major proportion of the missionary agents of that education were expelled from the colony on the contrived grounds that they were fomenting anti-British feeling among Africans. This perhaps in turn suggests less British confidence in the colonial British-African relationship than was officially acknowledged.

Africans took steps to fill some of the gaps left by the foreign missionaries. African catechists took on religious and administrative responsibilities—with all established missions affected to some degree. African leadership was also seen in African Christian revivalist movements that arose in the war period, notably that of Prophet Harris in the area of Western Province that was suffering from the depression in the timber industry in 1914. As a result of "Krooman" Harris's preaching, thousands were said to have "forsaken heathenism, destroyed their fetishes and built little churches."[293] His follower, John Swatson, left "a trail" of "Christ churches" in the Tano region in 1915–1916, most of which were soon absorbed into the Anglican Diocese of Accra.[294] Similarly, Samson Oppong established his African church in Ashanti just after the war, in the depression induced by the influenza epidemic and the postwar slump. The major missions, Wesleyan (or Methodist), Anglican, and Catholic, were all reported to have gained adherents in this period as a result of African initiatives.[295]

The economic insecurities of the war period, together with the impact of the influenza pandemic, appear to have led to much wider expressions of African religious belief in this period. The earliest "Tigari" and "Kundi" shrines in northwest Ashanti that M. J. Field could trace seem to have dated from the First World War.[296] In 1916 Ofori Atta raised concerns about the revival of the "Kune" fetish (similar to the suppressed "Aberewa" fetish), which originated in Ashanti and, he claimed, "deceived and robbed" his people.[297] A month later, C. B. Nettey, *Asafoatse* of the Gbese quarter in Accra, partly blamed the increasing cost of living in Accra on an increase in fetishism among women traders.[298] In Sierra Leone, Islam was also reported to have gained adherents in this period as a result of the physical and psychological stress induced by wartime conditions—which may also have been the case in the Gold Coast.[299] McCaskie has pointed out that anti-witchcraft cults, such as the "Hwe me so" cult that spread from Appolonia in the southwest to villages around Lake Bosomtwe in the period of the postwar slump, tended to flourish in conditions of apprehension and uncertainty.[300]

---

292. See M. Gannon, "The Basle Mission Trading Company," pp. 512–515.

293. J. H. Oldham (ed.), *The International Review of Missions*, VI, 21/1/17, p. 44.

294. G. M. Haliburton, "The Anglican Church in Ghana and the Harris Movement in 1914," *Bulletin of the Society for African Church History*, 1, 1963–4, p. 102. Also, P. Jenkins, "The Anglican Church in Ghana, 1905–24," *Transactions of the Historical Society of Ghana*, XV, (i), 1974.

295. G. M. Haliburton, *The Prophet Harris*, (London, 1971), p. 147.

296. M. J. Field, *Search for Security: An Ethno-Psychiatric Study of Rural Ghana*, (London, 1960), p. 90.

297. Ofori Atta to Furley, PC Eastern Province, 22/9/16, in ADM 11/1/637, PRAAD.

298. C. B. Nettey to Secretary for Native Affairs, 5/10/16, in J. Parker, *Making the Town. Ga State and Society in Early Colonial Accra*, (Oxford, 2000), p. 178

299. M. J. Field, *Search for Security*, p. 90; and F. Cole, "Sierra Leone and World War I," p. 160.

300. T. McCaskie, "Anti-Witchcraft Cults in Asante: An Essay in the Social History of an African People," *History in Africa*, 8, 1981, pp. 137–142.

Clifford identified a continuing "genuine hunger for education" on the part of the local population. But with the expense of running the Bremen and Basel schools at a time of wartime economies, there were no funds to undertake additional education projects. A handful of new government schools had been opened earlier in the war, as at Enchi, the first government school in Western Province; at Kyebi and Obo in Eastern Province; at Juaso in Ashanti; and at Wa in the Northern Territories. By the end of the war, there were forty-nine more schools and 6,200 more pupils enrolled than when the governor had arrived on the coast in 1912. But Clifford was frustrated at the relative lack of progress. The overall sum spent on education was still, he said, "pitifully small" and the department understaffed because of the war.[301] By 1918 there was no money for new schools, and African press comment on the government's educational record was pretty damning. For example, this statement in the *Gold Coast Leader* in February 1918: "Our government has not bothered much about our education so far."[302] Nonetheless, Clifford believed that there had been no alternative to the government taking on the expense of running the extra seventy-nine Basel and Bremen missions schools. The result was that by 1918 the education department of the Gold Coast had become responsible for 60% of schools in the colony, in sharp contrast with only 8% in 1914.[303]

Clifford also regretted the wartime disruption to the little technical education offered in the colony. The African demand for technical training (as for the mines and for motor mechanics) was on the increase. He believed that expanding government technical training was essential as soon as the war was over.[304] The premises of the Accra Technical College had frequently been taken over by the government during the war. The college was closed for six months in 1915 to house prisoners of war, then used to house the Basel missionaries prior to their deportation between December 1917 and March 1918. The governor regretted that there were more applications for the Accra Technical School in 1916 than there were places, especially with the large number of motor vehicles now being imported from the United States and the urgent need for mechanics.[305] This was at the time when the Basel Mission training shops at Christiansborg were forced to close.

At the same time, there continued to be too few Africans seeking teaching qualifications, apparently due to poor pay. The governor accepted that teachers would have to be paid more, and teacher-training facilities had to be greatly improved, with colleges needed in Central and Western Provinces as well as Kumasi. Untrained monitors were often used in government and mission schools in this period when few trained teachers were available.[306] During the war, the normal program of the sole government teacher training institute in Accra had been disrupted and students housed in police barracks when the building was commandeered, like Accra Technical College, to house prisoners of war. The only two private teacher-training colleges, the Basel seminaries at Akropong and Abetifi, had also been "much disorganised" due to staffing problems, even before the Basel missionaries were deported. All the main missionary societies, notably the Basel and Bremen missions and the Presbyterian Church of Scotland and Methodist missions, suffered from greatly reduced numbers of missionaries sent out during the war, estimated as only about half

301. Clifford, re. Estimates 1919, *LegCo* 28/10/18, *Gazette* 9/11/18, CO99/33/82.

302. "*Africanus*," *Gold Coast Leader*, 2/2/18.

303. Clifford, *LegCo* 28/10/18, *Gazette* 9/11/18, CO99/33/82.

304. Clifford, *LegCo* 28/10/18, *Gazette* 9/11/18, CO99/33/82.

305. Accra Technical School, 1914: 56 students; 1915: 73 students. Clifford, *LegCo* 23/10/16, *Gazette* 23/10/16, CO99/31/76.

306. See N. Smith, *The Presbyterian Church of Ghana*, p. 169.

the prewar number. For example, in 1915 the White Fathers' School at Navrongo was closed for the duration of the war because of shortages of staff and funds.[307]

Meanwhile, Africans in the Gold Coast renewed their demands for government provision of secondary education. The war affected the decision as to whether the government (as distinct from the missions) would provide new secondary schools. Clifford, backed by the colony's board of education, continued to believe that universal compulsory primary education should be the government's priority. However, as before the war, the African unofficials continued to argue the urgency and necessity of establishing a government secondary school similar to those in Sierra Leone and Lagos. The majority of pupils in the Gold Coast were said by Hutton Mills to have "a smattering knowledge of various elementary subjects" in what he decried as merely a "loathsome partial education."[308] Mate Kole, the Konor of Manya Krobo, recalled Governor Rodger, more than a decade before, promising a high school for sons of chiefs. Higher education was also needed, he argued, if Africans were to take on important posts in public service, let alone for the governed to understand matters of public interest as the colonial government wished.[309] And there were arguments in the African press to try to convince the government of the need for better educational provision: "incompetent semi-educated clerks" were "not making for good communication between chiefs and government."[310] Newspaper articles called for provision of a British West African university—an issue to be taken up later by the National Congress of British West Africa ((NCBWA) in its postwar conference calling for educational as well as political reform.[311]

Key local British officials (in this instance, including the governor) were opposed to government secondary schools at this time, partly because of the impact of the war: the colony was not yet "ripe" for government provision of secondary education. There was only one secondary assisted school, the SPG school at Cape Coast. Secondary-level education was also provided independently at Mfantsipim (the Wesleyan school at Cape Coast), at Accra grammar school, and at the Basel seminaries for training teachers and pastors at Abetifi and Akropong.[312] But Clifford believed that given the state of the colony's finances as a result of the war, the government should concentrate in the immediate future on primary education—even though he recognized that a secondary institution comparable to the Royal College in Trinidad was needed at some time in the future.[313]

Before the outbreak of war, the British aspired to promote "development" and "welfare" in the Gold Coast. At one level, these twin objectives represented Governor Clifford's mission to bring the benefits of "civilisation" to West Africa. At another, they served sensible and practical goals: to develop the infrastructure of the territory—such as railways, roads, and harbors—in order more easily to exploit its economic potential; and to demonstrate to Africans, through the provision of medical and educational services, that British colonial administration could be beneficial for them.

307. S. Prempeh, "The Bremen and Basle Missions," p. xxii.
308. Board of Education, *Report on Secondary Education 1915*, Hutton Mills, 31/8/15, CO98/27.
309. Mate Kole, Konor of Eastern Krobo, 7/10/15, in *Sessional Papers, Education,2,1915*, CO98/27.
310. *The Gold Coast Nation*, 25/5/16.
311. E.g., *Gold Coast Leader*, 16/11/18.
312. Acting Governor Slater, *LegCo* 25/10/15, *Gazette* 25/10/15, CO99/29/101.
313. For example, editorials, *Gold Coast Leader*, 4/3/16 and 1/9/17; and editorial, *The Gold Coast Independent*, 13/7/18; and see Clifford, *LegCo* 28/10/18, *Gazette* 9/11/18, CO99/33/82.

Clifford appears to have been as frustrated as those he governed by how wartime conditions made it impossible to achieve all his targets. The African population found that it was not only rail and road construction that were affected by wartime conditions: building schemes throughout the colony were halted for the duration of the war and the immediate postwar period. In 1914, Clifford had only just succeeded in obtaining London's assent for the rapid completion of a wide range of substantial construction work, ranging from hospitals to harbors and waterworks. When war intervened, shortages of money, materials, and manpower made a serious impact. Developments that would have helped to raise the standard of living for the African population, as well as for expatriates, were postponed. But for the interruption of the Great War, Clifford would have seen through to completion a very substantial program of public works and improved communications. This was recognized at the time by officials in London, where Flood noted in 1915: "Sir H. Clifford's energetic measures were beginning to bear fruit, and it is a pity that the war has stopped the progress which had been maintained."[314]

As for welfare, Clifford's interest in improving and expanding Western education in the Gold Coast had won him African support. His frustration at the way the war delayed progress and distorted educational provision made him determined to ensure that educational reforms would be put into effect as soon as possible once the war was over. He did not appear to concede that he had himself contributed to the delay during the war with the deportation of a large number of (missionary) teachers. After the frustration of wartime postponements and the unexpected and extensive diversion of government effort and funds into taking over the Bremen and Basel schools in the Gold Coast, plans remained in hand after the war for substantial improvements to educational provision in the colony. Indeed, Clifford's overall contribution to the expansion of the colonial government's role in education in the Gold Coast—as in other policy areas—has been underrated. It was he who initiated discussion and committed the colonial government to new levels of funding and a much wider provision of Western education, as with Western medical care. Immediately after the war, Clifford set up a special education committee in the colony with an open agenda to make recommendations for improvements in the educational system. And this committee was unprecedented in having five African unofficials as members, as well as representatives of the main missions.

Africans welcomed development and welfare—advocating, to this extent, more colonialism rather than less. We have seen how disappointment and frustration led to verbal criticism and, at times, active protest, as in the railway strikes. Their other response was development and welfare "from below": initiatives in education, for example, and above all in the road revolution. This was some compensation for shortcomings of the British administration—but those failings meant that an assessment of the costs and benefits of colonial rule was looking rather different by 1918. The war had seen higher taxes—yet there were also cuts in development and welfare provision. Any previous balance between the demands of colonial rule, on the one hand, and what it provided, on the other, was being upset. The governor might be proud of the new Council Chamber in Accra, for example, and the GPO building.[315] But many plans affecting other towns of the Colony and Ashanti, as well as Accra, had to be shelved—and these included matters of immediate concern to the African population of the colony: provision of hospitals, housing, water supply, drainage, and lighting.

314. Flood, CO Minute re. *PWD Report 1914,* Acting Governor Slater to Bonar Law, 25/9/15, CO96/560/782.

315. Clifford, *LegCo* 28/10/18, *Gazette* 9/11/18, CO99/33/82.

From an African perspective, the war period brought (as we have seen above) economic disruption and a deterioration in their standard of living; we now see how it brought disappointment with development and welfare projects indefinitely postponed. Perhaps the story of the unavailing sand pumps in Accra harbor is an allegory of the colonial period at this time: the failure of the Europeans' attempt to order Africa as they wanted. While the African response did not amount to active opposition to colonial rule, the fruits of war—or rather the lack of them—were contributing to a closer and more critical monitoring of a British colonial rule that was, as yet at least, unable to fulfil its promises. As the following chapter demonstrates, in one region of the Gold Coast in particular, manifestations of discontent amounted to more than mere criticism.

Chapter 8

Wartime British Rule: Unevenness and Division

There were already marked differences between the various regions of the Gold Coast territory before 1914; the war was to exaggerate these and confirm a pattern for the future. The differences arose partly from their respective economic activities. The cultivation of cash crops, especially cocoa, in the Colony and Ashanti, in addition to the large gold mines in the southwest of the Colony, contrasted with patterns of migrant labor from the north. In particular, differences between Ashanti and the Northern Territories were reinforced by uneven administration through chiefs. A robust system in Ashanti contrasted with a weak British model of indirect rule in the north. This pattern was confirmed by Clifford's own self-fulfilling assessment: that Ashanti was of central importance and value, while the Northern Territories contributed very little and remained a liability. The war period was thus to see the Colony and one of its dependencies, Ashanti, drawn yet closer together, largely through participation in the cocoa trade—but it also saw a widening of the gap between these two regions and the north.

To understand the contrasts in the nature of the colonial administration in these three regions at this time—the original Colony, Ashanti, and the Northern Territories—we must look at African as well as British perceptions. While generally in the Gold Coast the hand of British government was slight, significant regional variations reflected both geographical position and historical background. Among the Ashanti, there was by 1914 apparent acquiescence to British rule (to the relief of formerly anxious British officials), primarily on account of the benefits of international trade—as well as concern for the eventual return of the Asantahene from exile. The Ashanti revolt of 1900 was relatively recent, but the governor and his officials were to be pleasantly surprised by the "loyalty" of the Ashanti during the war and by their sustained and productive farming of cash crops, especially cocoa.[1] By contrast, for the Northern Territories colonial rule by 1914 had brought little if any economic benefit, but rather taxation and forced labor. When opportunities arose during the war, in the north there were sporadic attempts to resist British rule. This region remained relatively poor, unproductive, and neglected. For Clifford it was an area of little interest, with no immediate economic prospects. He focused on it only reluctantly as a result of the periodic breakdown of British control. Otherwise the war provided the governor with the excuse and the opportunity for continuing to ignore the Northern Territories.

At the beginning of the war, Clifford and his officials believed there was a "very definite risk" that a reduction in the normal quota of troops stationed in Ashanti could tempt any who were disaffected to act against the government.[2] Care was taken to ensure that an

1. In 1900, a number of Ashanti had besieged the British fort at Kumasi. The revolt failed and led to Ashanti's formal annexation by the British.
2. Clifford to Harcourt, 24/9/14, C096/548/60.

adequate military presence was retained in Ashanti, and the army's request for recruits from this region was refused on the grounds that a "levy of Ashantis would be a very nasty proposition."[3] But, in the event, reports continued to be reassuring: towards the end of 1914 Chief Commissioner Fuller described "a spirit of the most eager loyalty towards the administration" and "implicit trust" in the ultimate victory of the British government.[4] A major reason for this support was clearly the substantial economic benefits of cash crop farming of cocoa, which affected a wide sector of the local population.

Yet there continued to be unease in the Colonial Office during 1915 concerning the attitude of the Ashanti—or rather the lack of European military staff in the region. The situation in Kumasi was judged to be "most serious," with only three British officers for 360 soldiers, while the people had retained their military organization, and many held arms. Despite "the evidences of good will," it was feared that the Ashanti might possibly be "worked on by rumours or by German agents."[5] This concern deepened as a result of a riot at Goaso in the Ahafo region of Northern Ashanti in March 1915, even though this was not sparked by hostility to the government. The disturbance (one of several since August 1914 in the Central Province in the Colony) was attributed to "the unrest and excitement" caused by the outbreak of the war and the invasion of Togoland.[6] Such fighting was mostly between local military companies or *asafos;* the incident at Goaso, for example, was the result of a local dispute that involved the chiefs and people of Mim against the *Omahene* of Kukuom. Cardinall, the ADC, was praised for effective intervention in what was considered by British officers to be "quite a wild place and full of fetish."[7] There was no evidence of anti-British feeling in any of these riots, though they did draw attention to the large supply of guns available. Importing guns had practically ceased, but blacksmiths were able to manufacture copies, and local people demanded retention of guns for hunting and to protect crops.[8]

In contrast with such concerns, Ashanti remained generally peaceful and prosperous. As Fuller, chief commissioner of Ashanti, noted in 1914, small retail businesses had spread along the main roads radiating from Kumasi, and shops were now established in villages "that were scarcely known a few years ago."[9] Towards the end of 1915, farming and trading in Ashanti were flourishing despite the war. It seems that many chiefs wanted to be seen to be firmly associated with the British war effort. Contributions to the War Fund were "characterized by lavish generosity." One Ashanti chief gave the whole of the year's cocoa crop of his division; another donated £1,000.[10] Whether their subjects were as keen on these war contributions is not recorded, but there was no major outcry. By the end of 1915 there was little government anxiety concerning Ashanti, even though the region had been "practically denuded" of British-led troops.[11] By 1916 few troops at all were left quartered in Kumasi. It had been the headquarters of the GCR before the war, but was now little more than a recruiting depot.

---

3. Flood, CO Minute, telegram, Robertson to Harcourt, 17/8/14, C096/547.
4. Reported by Clifford, *LegCo* 28/11/14, *Gazette* 4/12/14, C099/29/158; Fuller, *Report on Ashanti 1914,* Acting Governor Slater to Bonar Law, 30/8/15, C096/559/717.
5. Green, CO Minute, telegram, Clifford to Harcourt, 16/4/15, C096/547.
6. Clifford, secret to Harcourt, 24/9/14, Clifford, confid. to Bonar Law, 1/5/15, C096/557.
7. Flood, CO Minute, Clifford, confid. to Harcourt, 1/1/15, CO96/557. And see J. Dunn & A. Robertson, *Dependence and Opportunity. Political Change in Ahafo,* (London, 1973).
8. Ellis, CO Minute, Clifford, confid. to Harcourt, 1/1/15, C096/557.
9. Fuller, *Report on Ashanti 1914, Blue Book 1914,* C098/24.
10. Acting Governor Slater, *LegCo* 30/10/15, *Gazette* 5/11/15, C096/561/894.
11. *Ashanti Blue Book 1915,* Clifford to Bonar Law, 27/7/16, C096/568/529.

That the dependency was under control with such a depleted number of officers was due, according to Fuller, to "the exemplary conduct of the Ashantis and their steadfast loyalty throughout the trying years of the hostilities."[12] The African population of Ashanti was thought to be about 300,000 but was probably more.[13] There were only 277 Europeans in Ashanti in 1916, made up of forty-one officials and 236 "others" (for example, merchants, bankers, miners, and eight missionaries). Of these, approximately 105 were in Kumasi (with a population of about 24,000). By 1917, the average total number of Europeans resident in Ashanti was only 180.[14] As a result of the reassuring calm, as well as the serious shortage of troops needed for the East Africa campaign, the GCR was finally opened up to Ashantis from early 1916.[15] Had there been in Ashanti a determined wish to throw off British rule, these conditions during the First World War provided every opportunity. No such action was taken.

A high proportion of army recruits, as well as a majority of unskilled workmen in Kumasi at this time, were from the Northern Territories. Unskilled labor rates were still commonly only 6d a day in the North (at a time when average earnings for "the poor" were given as 9d a day in Sierra Leone), but were twice that or more (1s to 2s) a day in Kumasi, as on cocoa farms in Ashanti or the Colony. Given these rates of pay, it was not surprising that "natives" were leaving the Northern Territories "in yearly increasing numbers."[16] Over half the population of Kumasi in 1916 (12,000 out of just under 24,000) were described as "northerners," with the rest (apart from Ashanti) including 4,000 coastal people and 2,000 "other."[17] The official "Ashanti" recruits to the army were largely men from the Northern Territories or from further north, from French territory. Ashanti chiefs paid between £5 and £35 (usually about £20–£25, according to Fuller) to get men to enlist so that they could demonstrate their "loyalty" to the government without having to try and find reluctant Ashanti recruits. Paying northerners to go instead was a neat way out of an impasse. It was reported that twenty to thirty northerners were enlisting each week in Kumasi in March 1917.[18] They were reacting to economic opportunities available to them in the context of the colony at war.

Meanwhile, the Ashanti, formerly so hostile to British rule, were cooperative—and this allowed the administration to function with very few civilian personnel. Armitage, CC of the Northern Territories, had been present in Ashanti immediately after the 1900 conquest. He believed that although there had been "grave errors" in the treatment of the Ashanti in the past, its people had come to realize that British administration was now bringing prosperity. King Prempeh's seizure and deportation at that time had been "grossest treachery." Armitage sympathized with the Queen Mother, Ya Kia, who, when Governor

---

12. Sir Francis Fuller, *A Vanished Dynasty—Ashanti,* (London, 1921), p. 228.

13. The 1911 census total for the Ashanti population of 287,814 seems to have been a considerable underestimate, as perhaps was the 1921 census of over 400,000. Clifford, *LegCo* 23/10/16, *Gazette* 23/10/16, C099/31/76. *Report on Ashanti 1916,* Clifford to Long, 15/8/17, C096/581/510. *Report on Ashanti 1917,* Clifford to Long, 13/6/18, C096/590/329.

14. *Ibid.*

15. See D. Killingray, "Repercussions of World War I," p. 51.

16. Armitage, CC, NT, to Colonial Secretary, Accra, 16/4/15, ADM 56/1/84, PRAAD.

17. *Report on Ashanti 1917,* Clifford to Long, 13/6/18, CO96/590/329; also *Report on the Northern Territories 1915,* CO98/25; I. Sutton, "Labor in Commercial Agriculture in Ghana," p. 479; and F. Cole, "Sierra Leone and World War I," p. 279.

18. Fuller, diary 21/1/18, ADM 12/5/160, PRAAD; Clifford, secret to Long, 31/5/18, CO96/590; and see R. Thomas, "Military Recruitment," pp. 60, 74–81; and D. Killingray, "Repercussions of World War I," pp. 50–51.

Hodgson visited the deposed Prempeh at Elmina in 1901, was said to have removed the clay pipe from her mouth just long enough to mutter, "All white men are liars."[19] But since these events, "a sullen and suspicious race," in Fuller's words, had been transformed into "a contented and prosperous people."[20] The anniversary of "Coomassie Day" in July 1919, commemorating the lifting of the siege of the Kumasi fort with thirty-three old soldiers, passed uneventfully.[21]

The critical factors in changing Ashanti attitudes were growing wealth and a rising material standard of living. Imported goods were bought largely with profits from the cocoa trade. The new positive attitude was illustrated in a statement issued by the Council of Kumasi chiefs in 1918: "The government is administering our country. It has done well. Kumasi is prosperous. If the government wants more land to make Kumasi bigger, we will give it."[22] This confidence survived the hardship of the final two years of the war when Ashanti suffered the same deepening commercial depression as the Colony and the same cuts in public services. By 1918, government expenditure in Ashanti had slumped to only £47,204, compared with £188,123 in 1914.[23] Kumasi chiefs were then said to have "expressed great glee" at the news of the Armistice and to be looking forward to a new boom in the cocoa trade.[24] The peace celebrations in August 1919, held in Kumasi as in Accra, reflected this Ashanti enthusiasm, involving a total of between 15,000 and 20,000 people and the largest gathering of chiefs Fuller had ever seen (under about one hundred huge umbrellas). Entertainments included gun salutes, fireworks, sixteen school children's bands, and also, ironically, a massed war dance.[25]

Yet British rulers still believed in the necessity of maintaining a visible presence in Ashanti, despite the general calm. Neither Slater nor the Colonial Office thought it wise to reduce the number of administrative posts in Ashanti in 1917. A recommendation that five officers be released on military service in January 1917 would have involved closing down newly opened stations at Wenchi, Goaso, and Ejura. Slater believed this was not safe, because control was needed "over the wilder people who never saw a white man."[26] There was agreement in the Colonial Office that closure of stations might lead to rumors of the white man leaving, as had already occurred in the Northern Territories, with the danger of a renewal of intertribal wars. Experienced officers were also needed in 1917 to help raise recruits for carriers and the WAFF.[27] Such caution seemed vindicated when there were occasional violent incidents, as with the border dispute in Bekwai in mid-1917 when heavy drinking led to several "natives" being wounded in a fight between two villages.[28] Shortage of staff in 1917 led to the closing down of the new DC station at Goaso, an area as unknown to the governor as the Northern Territories. Closure did not, as it

19. Armitage, Enclosure 3, Clifford to Long, 19/2/18, C096/588/104.

20. Fuller, *A Vanished Dynasty,* foreword.

21. Fuller, diary, 15/7/19, ADM 12/5/160, PRAAD.

22. Acting Chief Commissioner of Ashanti Philbrick, Enclosure 1, Clifford to Long, 20/3/18, CO/588/104. And see W. Tordoff, *Ashanti Under the Prempehs 1888–1935,* (London, 1965), p. 177.

23. Clifford to Long, 10/12/17, C096/583/767; also *Report on Ashanti 1918,* C098/30.

24. Fuller, diary 21/11/18, ADM 12/5/160, PRAAD.

25. Fuller, diary, 23/8/19, ADM12/5/160, PRAAD.

26. Acting Governor Slater, confid. to Long, 19/1/17, C096/568.

27. Flood, CO Minute, Acting Governor Slater, confid. to Long, 19/1/17, CO96/568.

28. PC Ashanti Philbrick, *Report on Riot at Dominase, Bekwai;* Acting Governor Slater, confid. to Long, 2/8/17, C096/586.

turned out, prompt any local disturbance, though it did postpone hygiene improvements until government activity was finally resumed there as late as 1926.[29]

Continuing concern—albeit ungrounded—about possible political instability during the war was the main reason for not yet conceding to the Ashanti request for the return of their king, the Asantahene, from exile. The Ashanti petition of February 1918 was carefully couched in flattering terms such as "the great benefit that has accrued by reason of the British occupation and pacification." An important section of Ashanti society clearly believed that their "loyalty" and cooperation over the previous sixteen years, and especially during the war, would now be rewarded.[30] The following month Fuller judged that "things in general seem wonderfully quiet in Ashanti." Apart from a few stool disputes, as usual, the only contest appeared to be the Sekondi–Kumasi cricket match then underway.[31] British officials were divided as to whether Prempeh should ever return. But the governor was wholly against allowing him back to the Gold Coast, and all were opposed to a return during the war, when the cocoa market was disrupted and some young men were "restless and discontented," though precisely who and why are not revealed.[32] According to Fuller, once peace returned, the Ashantis should be rewarded "for their excellent attitude since the outbreak of the war."[33] It was not clear whether this would include Prempeh's return. The matter was taken up by the new governor, Guggisberg, when peace was restored. In the event, the end of Prempeh's long exile in 1924 clearly owed something to the proofs of Ashanti stability and "loyalty" during the difficult years of the war.

Although British perception of Ashanti was changing in this period, it was still only a protectorate without full Crown colony status. The African unofficial, E. J. P. Brown, argued in November 1918 that "the remarkable practical loyalty" shown by the Ashanti during the war had earned them the privilege of the system of trial by jury. But officials on the coast were wary of clever, articulate, and opinionated Africans, and they were not keen to give an opportunity for "native" barristers to extend their practices from the Colony into Ashanti, including increasing litigation and contested cases. Harper's reply was uncompromising: Ashanti was not "at present adapted or ripe" for such change.[34] Barristers and solicitors were specifically excluded from courts in Ashanti and the Northern Territories until 1933. Only from 1934 would the legislative council pass laws for Ashanti and the Northern Territories as well as for the Colony.[35]

A study of this period confirms that, despite often unfavorable wartime conditions—with disrupted trade and fluctuating prices and demand—the Ashanti were now active and accommodating trading partners. They had accommodated to a trading relationship that was now bringing them substantial economic benefit while allowing many of their institutions and customs to remain intact. The political grievance was not British rule, as such, but the continuing exile of Prempeh, the Asantahene. But there were grounds

29. See J. Dunn & A. Robertson, *Dependence and Opportunity*, pp. 115–118, 164.

30. *Petition for the Return of King Prempeh*, 16/2/18, enclosure, Clifford, confid. to Long, 12/6/18, C096/590.

31. Fuller, diary, 29/3/18, ADM 12/5/160, PRAAD.

32. Clifford to Long, 19/2/18, C096/588/104; Acting Chief Commissioner Ashanti Philbrick, 5/2/18, Enclosure, Clifford to Long, 19/2/18, CO96/588/104.

33. Chief Commissioner Ashanti Fuller, 1/6/18, Enclosure 5, and see Sir Herbert Read, CO Minute, Clifford to Long, 19/2/18, CO96/588/104.

34. E. J. P. Brown, Harper, *LegCo* 29/10/18, *Gazette* 9/11/18, C099/33/81.

35. D. Kimble, *A Political History*, pp. 325, 536.

for hope that the British government would reconsider this issue after the end of the war. And the British acknowledged that the area was steadily growing in economic importance—with an increasing volume of trade and excellent roads suitable for motor traffic being built by local people. By the end of the war period, the Ashanti were no longer simply referred to as "a martial people." Their loyalty was no longer questioned. In October 1918, Clifford summarized the change: in the process of a remarkable expansion of cocoa farming, the Ashanti had succeeded in turning their "swords and spears into hoes and machetes."[36]

In the early war period, the colonial administration was more worried about the stability of the other protectorate, the Northern Territories. The last incidents of armed opposition to British rule in the north had been as recent as 1911, in the Tong hills in the northeast province of the region. Officials questioned how securely the Northern Territories were attached to the rest of the Gold Coast colony. The allegiance of the Moslem population was a particular concern. When Turkey joined the war, some *mallams* attempted to stir up neighboring French territory, though "not a single fanatical Mohammedan ventured to preach sedition in the Protectorate."[37] Initially, the area remained peaceful.

However, the extent to which a visible British presence needed to be maintained in the Northern Territories was never given sufficiently careful consideration by the Gold Coast government. Clifford's administration had drawn up plans just before the war to reduce the number of British officers in the north and to withdraw some of the medical officers (many of whom performed DC as well as medical duties) to Ashanti, despite Chief Commissioner Armitage's opposition.[38] Clifford believed Ashanti and the Colony were ripe for development, but the Northern Territories would have to wait their turn. The war did speed up proposed cuts in staffing of the Northern Territories. By 1915 there were no longer any medical officers to take charge of the "native" hospitals in the north at Yeji, Wa, Bawku, or Zuarungu ("Zoueragu").[39] In October 1914, Clifford expressed some concern that reduction of personnel for war duties and "the slackening of administrative control" in the Northern Territories "might be misunderstood by the natives."[40] Nevertheless, the governor assured London—without, as Colonial Office officials commented wryly, any firsthand experience of the area himself—that the duties of such officers in the Northern Territories were "peculiarly light."[41] Clifford's ignorance of the north, and the fact that he never visited the region, were to contribute to the problems of the British administration there both during and after the war.

The question was: how few officers could the British get away with in their minimal rule of the Northern Territories? Despite Clifford's assurances, with only eleven political officers (four officers were on leave and six seconded for war service), the administration

36. Clifford, *LegCo* 28/10/18, *Gazette* 9/11/18, C099/33/82.

37. Armitage, Chief Commissioner of the NT, *Report on the Northern Territories 1914,* Acting Governor Slater to Bonar Law, 30/8/15, C096/559/715.

38. Acting Governor Robertson to Harcourt, 27/7/14, C096/547/671.

39. *Report on the Northern Territories 1915,* C098/25.

40. Clifford to Harcourt, 13/10/14, C096/549/766; Flood, Ellis, CO Minute, *Annual Confidential Report on Officers for 1914,* Clifford, confid. to Harcourt, 4/4/15, C096/557.

41. *Ibid.*

of the Northern Territories had become seriously understaffed by October 1915.[42] District stations at Zuarungu and Bawku in the northeast were closed. At the time, Slater reported this as a decision made at Armitage's suggestion and with the governor's approval.[43] There was thought to be adequate security with a company of the WAFF in the protectorate as well as detachments of the Northern Territories constabulary, described as "a queer force—as much soldiers as police."[44] Out of a total WAFF establishment of 370, 140 had contributed to the military invasion of Togo, and a force of twenty-five stayed on in Yendi.[45]

Partly as a result of understaffing and to the governor's anger and embarrassment, the British administration of the Northern Territories fell apart dramatically in 1916. In the first main incident, in April, a fight broke out over a local land dispute among members of one of the northern peoples, the Fra Fras, in Bongo. Constables were fired on, and one was killed. This trouble culminated in July with the shooting by the Northern Territories constabulary of a total reported at the time of eighty-four people. Meanwhile in Bawku, an unidentified number of people and a further two constables were killed in a separate incident in June. There had been complaints from chiefs in this area that people had been refusing to obey orders since the GCR company at Zuarungu and Navrongo left for the Togo campaign at the start of the war.[46] The British station at Bawku had been closed in February 1916, but four months later, a handful of constables attempted to insist on Fra Fras building bridges in the area.[47] By the end of the year, 1916, it was clear that the number of deaths—in Bongo at least—had been greatly exaggerated. It was thought by then to be between fifteen and nineteen—although it was acknowledged to be very difficult to identify accurate figures.[48] Both Clifford and Armitage realized that the diminished British presence, with the closure of administrative stations and apparent withdrawal of the British, had led to the troubles, but they did not agree (as we shall see shortly) as to who was responsible.

A further flare-up in the Northern Territories occurred in 1917. Some warning of the volatility of the situation had been given in February 1917 by the acting chief commissioner, Moutray Reade, when he described the Northern Territories protectorate as "like an active volcano liable to eruptions."[49] A month later, in March, many villages in the Bole district were said to be in revolt as a result of a "fetish man's" preaching. Slater, as acting governor, took no chances. A company of constabulary and a company of the GCR were immediately sent up from Kumasi. It was estimated that as many as 1,200 locals were "disaffected." However, with constabulary converging on the Bole and Daboya country from Kumasi, Tamale, and Wa, order was restored by the end of the month. One cause of the unrest

---

42. Clifford to Bonar Law, 11/10/15, C096/560/831.

43. Armitage to Colonial Secretary, 9/3/15, Acting Governor Slater, confid. to Bonar Law, 28/7/15, C096/559.

44. Flood, CO Minute, Clifford to Bonar Law, 5/8/16, C096/568/557.

45. Acting Governor Slater, confid to Bonar Law, 1/7/15, C096/559.

46. See R. Thomas, "The 1916 Bongo 'Riots' and Their Background: Aspects of Colonial Administration and African Response in Eastern Upper Ghana," *JAH*, 24, 1983, pp. 57–75; and R. Thomas, "Military Recruitment in the Gold Coast," pp. 57–83.

47. Slater, secret to Bonar Law, Intelligence Report, 29/11/16, CO96/573.

48. Acting Governor Slater, confid to Bonar Law, 28/11/16, C096/573; also Armitage, *Report* 11/12/16, enclosure, Acting Governor Slater, confid. to Long, 3/1/17, C096/577.

49. Moutray Reade, quoted in Acting Governor Slater, confid. to Long, 7/2/17, C096/578; see R. Thomas, "Military Recruitment," pp. 57–83; and D. Killingray, "The Colonial Army in the Gold Coast," pp. 284–288.

was said to be the belief that the power of the white man was waning. There were rumors that "the constabulary had to go to help the British" in East Africa because "they were being beaten by the Germans, and the time was therefore ripe for the people to win back control of their country."[50]

Slater now acknowledged that this incident was partly antigovernment and that the immediate cause of the unrest was the 1917 British military recruitment drive.[51] This was a thinly populated area where chiefs had already had considerable trouble before the war fulfilling government demands for relatively poorly paid labor. At a time when the recruitment drive had already exacerbated tensions, the DC, Sheriff (known to be a heavy drinker), took sides in a local dispute between rival chiefs and, to the satisfaction of the chief of Bole, rashly arrested and humiliated Yabum, the Paramount of Gonja. The Senyon government rest house was subsequently burned down, and local people declared "the white man's power is finished in the Northern Territories."[52] Once troops reached the area, Moutray Reade sought to reassure the population that the government did not intend to force people to enlist, nor were rumors true that men recently recruited for labor in the manganese mines were going to be sent away as soldiers.[53]

The Northern Territories proved to be so explosive because in this region, in contrast with the Colony and Ashanti, the balance of advantage in the colonial relationship remained solidly weighted against local African interests. Poor communications as well as poor soil and a difficult climate meant that the Northern Territories had not been able to participate in the fruits of the cash crop export trade as had the Colony and Ashanti. Tensions in the society were exacerbated by British colonial wartime intervention and recruitment for the army, the police, and the mines, and for carriers. This placed heavy demands on northern chiefs to supply labor when, even before the war, chiefs in the north were not widely respected by their subjects. Many had been imposed by the British or had had their powers increased by the British and were simply regarded as government agents. The British dependence on "indirect" rule, and especially on recruitment through unpopular chiefs, was provocative, especially at a time when the British presence, on whose support northern chiefs depended, was reduced. This was interpreted by the local African population as British weakness or even as permanent British withdrawal. There seems to have been little acceptance of colonial authority (or that of its agents, the chiefs) in a region where, in contrast with Ashanti, labor demands rather than economic benefits characterized the administration in the eyes of the local population—both before and during the war.

Armitage claimed that it was not the British administration but certain disaffected groups in the local African society that were to blame. The fighting in Bongo in April 1916 was not, he believed, merely directed against the colonial government. It was the result of "young men" attacking chiefs in a dispute over land. Behind the "young men" were certain "evilly disposed old men" who stirred up trouble with accusations that the

---

50. Telegram, Acting Governor Slater to Long, 18/3/17, C096/578; telegram, Acting Governor Slater to Long, 22/3/17, C096/578; Acting Governor Slater, confid. to Long, 22/3/17, C096/578.

51. Telegram, Acting Governor Slater, confid. to Long, 29/3/17, C096/578.

52. Acting Governor Slater, confid. to Long, 6/4/17, C096/579.

53. Moutray Reade, 19/3/17, enclosure, telegram, Acting Governor Slater to Long, 14/3/17 and Moutray Reade, Enclosure 2, 30/3/17, Acting Governor Slater, confid. to Long, 13/4/17, C096/576. And see R. Thomas, "Military Recruitment," pp. 72–74.

chiefs were simply working for the government.[54] According to the chief of Zuarungu, these old men had never been reconciled to the British occupation. They were said to retain "a fanatical hatred of chiefs" and to "put every obstacle in the way of their young men getting in touch with civilization."[55] This description fits with Rattray's researches in the 1930s concerning the problems of trying to operate a system of indirect rule in the north of the Gold Coast. Tensions were exacerbated as a result of the peculiar nature of chieftaincy in much of the region, with the dual system of relatively new incoming chiefs, now supported by the British, alongside the original priest kings, or *tendaana*.[56]

But there is no doubt that the British colonial administration was indeed responsible for much of the resentment and tension in African society; in this case, in the north of the colony. Chiefs had from the outset of British colonial rule taken on an unpopular role by being obliged to provide carriers and workers for government buildings and roads. Such labor, obtained by "requesting" chiefs, was not recognized by colonial officials as "forced."[57] But African perception was different, as Clifford to some extent perceived: "It is sad to see that "work for the white man" is apparently the main impression of the meaning of British Rule on the minds of the natives of the Northern Territories."[58] It was in the interest of northern chiefs to acquiesce to the British administration's manpower demands. Dependent on the British presence, they considered it worth their while to make large contributions (out of local taxes they charged) to the British Imperial War Fund. These came to nearly £2,000 in 1915, despite widespread poverty in the region made worse by the effects of the war. The loss of labor was apparently preferable to any imposition of direct tax, as required over the border in French territory, though there were complaints by village chiefs at the loss of young male agricultural workers. Armitage struggled to convince a gathering of 500 at Bongo on November 21, 1916, that everyone in the whole colony benefited from the government's development program: for example, "Roads are to a country what veins are to our bodies."[59]

In fact, for many, migrating in search of work was a necessity, as for those "northerners" who were in fact from French territories coming south or east across the borders into the Gold Coast to take advantage of higher wage rates in order to pay their taxes.[60] However, Roger Thomas estimated that the percentage of "foreign" northern recruits into the Gold Coast regiments of the West African Frontier Force fell from about 59% in 1914 to only about 5% in 1918, as a result of Blaise Diagne's recruitment drive in French West Africa that year.[61] This put more pressure on finding recruits within the Gold Coast. The Gold

---

54. *Armitage Report* 11/12/16, Enclosure 1, Acting Governor Slater, confid. to Long, 3/1/17, C096/577. See also R. Thomas, "The 1916 Bongo Riots," p. 71.

55. Chief of Zuarungu, quoted by Breckenridge, PC, NE Province, *Inquiry into Disturbances.* 20/11/16, Enclosure A, Acting Governor Slater, confid. to Long, 3/1/17, CO96/577; also *Report on the Northern Territories 1918,* C098/90.

56. D. Kimble, *A Political History,* pp. 487–490.

57. See, e.g., R. Bening, "Colonial Development Policy in Northern Ghana," p. 72; and R. Thomas, "Forced Labor in British West Africa," p. 98. For work demands and low rates of pay, see also M. Staniland, *The Lions of Dagbon,* pp. 45–46.

58. Clifford, Minute, 22/5/17, *Report on the Proceedings of the Chief Commissioner's Court, Northern Territories,* 2/4/17, Clifford, confid. to Long, 6/6/17, CO96/580.

59. *Armitage Report* 11/12/16, Enclosure 1, Acting Governor Slater, confid. to Long, 3/1/17, C096/577.

60. Armitage, CC, NT, informal diary, 29/10/17, ADM 56/1/117, PRAAD.

61. Clifford, *LegCo* 2/11/17, quoted in Clifford to Long, 10/12/17, CO96/583/767. See F. Bourret, *Ghana, The Road to Independence,* p. 85; and R. Thomas, "Military Recruitment," pp. 58–61.

Coast government's "call" for carriers, as with the 4,000 men reported collected from farms in the Tamale district in 1914, made the problem of insufficient food being grown in the region even worse. Large numbers of carriers were not uncommon: for example, 960 were employed in Salaga in 1914 transporting PWD loads. Many were recruited, or rather were impressed, by northern chiefs. And not all who left returned.[62]

In the British recruitment campaign in the Northern Territories between April and July 1917, the numbers recruited "dwarfed" the campaigns in the Colony and Ashanti combined.[63] But it was not a good time of year to get people to enlist. In the Bole region, there were wholesale desertions on the road as a result of the recruiting drive coinciding with harvesting food crops, as well as with unusually heavy rains and flooding. The usual period of the year for migrant workers to spend in the south was between the end of October and April or May, to coincide with work on southern farms in the cocoa season. They could then return north in time for harvesting local crops. British recruiting officers were overoptimistic in expecting that more than a handful of half-clad men, many forcibly enlisted by chiefs and in poor health, would march the 300 miles to Kumasi in such conditions. Some were in poor physical shape. A training center was established at Tamale with huts for 450 men. The aim was for recruits to get used to the diet and the uniform before marching through Ashanti, thus avoiding the ridicule that greeted northerners, who were mocked for being in "a state of semi-nudity."[64] Recruiting was more successful, however, in early 1918, with over 1,500 enlisting, "despite the curses of the old men."[65]

Economic instability in the staple cattle trade contributed to the impoverishment of the northern region and local tension at this time, during the war. By 1918 there was a big reduction in the number of livestock driven south, a result not only of low rainfall and an outbreak of rinderpest in 1917, but also of "disturbances" in neighboring French territory, where many roads had become unsafe due to wartime compulsory conscription and high taxation.[66] The rinderpest epidemic of 1917 reinforced government determination to set up a proper veterinary service in the north after the war. Occasional visits by British officers in the war period simply aroused local suspicion that the government was planning to impose taxes, with the result that cattle were often hidden from the veterinary inspector.[67]

It is not clear whether the war also contributed to impoverishment by reducing the volume of internal trade passing north and south through the protectorate. No accurate figures were kept. Apart from the cattle trade, sheep and goats as well as hides and dried fish from the Niger were brought south, while kola was transported north from Ashanti. An element of barter remained within this northern trade. Salt evaporated from lagoons in the southeast of the Colony was still carried north up the Volta by Ada boatmen in canoes and exchanged for such products of the Northern Territories as yams, fowl, shea butter, local cloth, and horns of bush cow and antelope. There were some stations on the

---

62. Armitage, *Report on the Blue Book 1914,* CO98/24; *Provincial Commissioner's Report* 6/3/15, ADM 56/1/84, PRAAD; also Armitage, *Report on the Northern Territories 1914,* Clifford to Long, 1/7/18, CO96/591/377. And see N. Van Hear, "Northern Labor," p. 100.

63. Clifford, *LegCo* 28/10/18, *Gazette* 9/11/18, CO99/33/82.

64. *Report on the Northern Territories 1917,* Clifford to Long, 1/7/18, CO96/591/377; see R. Thomas, "Forced Labor in British West Africa," pp. 100–102.

65. See, e.g., D. Killingray and J. Matthews, "Beasts of Burden," p. 9.

66. Acting Governor Slater to Bonar Law, 30/8/15, CO96/559/715; also Acting Governor Slater to Bonar Law, 5/11/15, C096/561/894. Also, ADC Palfreman, Enclosure 1, 24/5/17; Clifford, secret to Long, 25/6/16, CO96/580.

67. *Report on the Northern Territories 1916,* CO98/26.

main trade routes where statistics were kept, but there had been no compulsory registration since tolls had been abolished in 1908, and many caravans, especially those with livestock, passed through at night unrecorded.[68] A whole range of imports from the coast were sold across northern borders by the time of the outbreak of the war, such as cotton and woolen materials, metal and enamel goods, tobacco, tinned provisions, and beads. But many imported goods that cattle traders wanted to buy in Kumasi were said to be becoming unobtainable or prohibitively expensive during the war.[69]

Nevertheless there is no evidence for the sweeping comment that "the colonial system destroyed African domestic trade."[70] Some local manufacture was stimulated as a result of the shortages and high prices of imports during the war. For example, higher prices were paid for northern "native" cloth in Kumasi in 1918, with 305 "loads" being carried south to Ashanti that year, as opposed to only three loads in 1917. There was a similar increase in demand for local cloth elsewhere in West Africa during the war, such as in the Ivory Coast.[71] Also the value of Ada salt shot up during and immediately after the war because of the scarcity and high cost of imported salt as a result of shipping shortages and raised import duties.[72]

But such trade did not improve the condition of the general population of the northern region, acknowledged by Chief Commissioner Armitage in 1917 as being "miserably poor." Those who found work in Ashanti and the Colony would return "with little if anything beyond a suit of white clothes, a cap, and possibly an umbrella" (reminiscent of the district officer's clerk in Joyce Cary's novel, *Mister Johnson*) as well as the "meagre savings" some brought home after work in the south.[73] Armitage blithely predicted a gradual improvement in the Northern Territories as "natives" came to realize the benefits of peace brought them by British occupation.[74] However, the incidents of lawlessness in 1916 and 1917 seemed to show that many northerners were unconvinced of the benefits of British colonial administration. Benefit was judged by economic prosperity rather than by the degree of law and order.

A major source of tension contributing to such disturbances was British interference with chieftaincy. This arose from the British dilemma—not uncommon in equatorial Africa—of not having found, and thus having to try to manufacture, an effective hierarchy of chiefs. The administration had been seeking to "consolidate" various tribal groups in the Bongo area with subchiefs and headmen placed under a paramount chief. There had been previous British attempts to strengthen the powers of paramount chiefs in the Northern Territories, as in Wa in the period of British administration before 1907. But much remained as it had been in this earlier period of colonial rule: the use of chiefs to

---

68. Armitage, enclosure, *Report on the Northern Territories 1917*, Clifford to Long, 1/7/18, CO96/591/377.

69. *Report on the Blue Book 1914*, CO98/24.

70. S. Amin, "Underdevelopment and Dependence in Black Africa. Origins and Contemporary Forms," *The Journal of Modern African Studies*, 10, 4, 1972, p. 523.

71. *Report on the Northern Territories 1918*, CO98/30. And see T. Bassett, "The Development of Cotton in Northern Ivory Coast," p. 275.

72. I. Sutton, "The Volta River Salt Trade: The Survival of an Indigenous Industry," *JAH*, 22, 1981, pp. 48–51.

73. Armitage, enclosure, *Report on the Northern Territories 1917*, Clifford to Long, 1/7/18, CO96/591/377. Joyce Cary, *Mister Johnson*, (London, 1939); and P. Ladouceur, *Chiefs and Politicians*, p. 49.

74. Armitage, enclosure, Clifford to Long, 1/7/18, CO96/591/377.

provide forced labor, British officers' ignorance of local constitutional practices, and the locals' lack of respect for chiefs.[75] The attempt to create a tighter hierarchical political structure of indirect rule was under even greater strain once British officers were seen to be withdrawing during the war.

One effect of the war was to reveal the vulnerability of many northern chiefs. They were seen as part of the colonial administration in the Northern Territories, which used them in a form of rule that in many ways was more direct than indirect.[76] Fra Fra chiefs made clear that their authority depended on a British presence. Without "their commissioner," their power was undermined, as when closure of the station at Bawku had given rise to rumors that the white man was about to abandon the country. Similar rumors arose when government stations were withdrawn elsewhere, as in Borgu in northern Nigeria.[77] According to the chief of Nangodi, in the north of the Gold Coast colony, as soon as news came that the white man had gone—which became a common saying once the station at Zuarungu was closed—"out came the bows and arrows." The chief of Kologu was immediately threatened by the Tallensi: "The white men had made me chief and now that the white men had gone they would kill me and have no chief."[78] Similar submissions illustrated local antagonism directed against chiefs who demanded forced labor under direction from their British masters. The chiefs of Bole and Sambolugu were accused by their people of having "made them work for the white man."[79] They now refused to work on the roads. When Armitage toured the area in November, he made a point of giving ostentatious support to "deserving chiefs" by giving them presents for their "loyalty," such as silver medallions, to display their acceptance of British overrule.[80]

The incidents in the Northern Territories also revealed further tensions among British officials in the north of the Gold Coast territory. British officers squabbled while the region threatened to spiral out of their control, with Africans fighting each other. Wartime conditions exposed the unstable nature of the administration. With so few officials, personalities mattered. The breakdown of law and order could be blamed on individual officers rather than on the weak administrative structure and the shortage of British personnel. Clifford, appalled at the mismanagement of the Bongo and Bawku incidents in 1916 and the number of deaths, wrote a massive dispatch in September. He sought to absolve himself, and in the strongest terms blamed the breakdown of law and order not on understaffing but on three named northern officers: Armitage, Chief Commissioner; Wheeler, acting PC for the North Eastern Province; and Castellain, the DC at Navrongo (then known as "Navarro"). Clifford blamed Armitage for allowing the stations to close—though in August 1914 Armitage had urged that stations be kept open in the Northern Territories to maintain order. Closures had then been forced on the northern administration

75. E. Wrangham, "The British Occupation and Early Administration of the Northern Territories of the Gold Coast 1897–1907," unpublished MA thesis, (SOAS, London, 1973), pp. 33–42.

76. Armitage to acting colonial secretary, 10/7/16, Enclosure 8, Clifford confid. to Bonar Law, 18/9/16, CO96/570. And see P. Ladouceur, *Chiefs and Politicians*, pp. 42–44.

77. M. Crowder, "The First World War and Its Consequences" in A. Boahen (ed.), *General History of Africa VII, Africa Under Colonial Domination 1880–1935*, (London/New York, 1985), p. 291.

78. *Report on Native Affairs & Riots*, 16/11/16, ADM56/1/165, PRAAD; Chiefs of Languid, Kologu, Bongo, and Head Chief of Navarro Sambolugu, *Statements of Chiefs*, 16/11/16, PC of NE Province Breckenridge, *Inquiry into Disturbances*, 20/11/16, Enclosure A; also Armitage Report, 11/12/16, Enclosure 1, Acting Governor Slater, confid. to Long, 3/1/17, CO96/577.

79. *Ibid.*

80. *Ibid.*

by cuts in staffing.[81] This lesson was learned, but only later. As Fuller, chief commissioner of Ashanti, wrote in 1919: "Opening up and shutting down stations leads to a lot of dislocation and confusion."[82]

Again in 1917, concerning Bole, Clifford blamed individual northern officers rather than addressing demands or the underlying weakness of the administrative structure increasingly exposed by the war. Sheriff, disgraced, was sent home an invalid after contracting blackwater fever. Moutray Reade was criticized by the governor for poor supervision, for irregularities in judicial procedure, and for allowing the withdrawal of a large detachment of constabulary that had been ordered to Kumasi on its way to joining the East African expeditionary force. Moutray Reade now typified for Clifford the officer who still seemed to regard the region as under military occupation and the population as requiring "pacification"—though on closer acquaintance he absolved Armitage from having such an attitude. Civil administration was relatively recent, only officially replacing the military in 1907.[83] The Gold Coast colony remained only nominally a unitary state.[84] Whereas southerners in the Colony already sat on the legislative council, Ashanti representation was granted as late as 1946, and the first nominated northerners took their seats only in 1950. Clifford, moreover, had no firsthand knowledge of the region.

The governor's reaction reveals how inadequate was his and the coast government's understanding of conditions in the Northern Territories. Clifford claimed that the problem of closing stations could have been overcome if officers had trekked (traveled around their districts) more frequently—an accusation that could in fact be levied against himself concerning the north. British rule here, as elsewhere, relied on a British presence, and this often meant, with the shortage of officers, depending on a peripatetic administration. But the struggle for political officers of combining office work and trekking had been made much more difficult as a result of wartime staff reductions. It had become impossible for an officer in the field to perform all the duties expected of him. One result tended to be selective reporting.[85] In addition, the awkward truth was that a government circular had been issued to the whole service in May 1915 announcing that traveling locally should be undertaken only where "urgently necessary." Clifford's defense in September 1916, that he was "appalled" that Armitage had interpreted this to mean there should be as little travel as possible in the Northern Territories, was unconvincing.[86]

Failures in the British command structure had led to the violent British reprisals against Africans in the northeast province of the Northern Territories. Clifford accused Wheeler and Castellain (with some justification, once fighting had begun) of delays followed by "highly inappropriate punitive measures," including the mid-1916 burning of compounds and the seizure of cattle that members of the constabulary had divided among themselves. (Castellain was typical of administrators in the north in having a military background—in his case, in the South African War and constabulary.) The governor was outraged and mortified by Castellain's casual comment after fifty-nine people had been reported killed

81. Clifford, confid. to Bonar Law, 18/9/16, CO96/570.
82. Fuller, diary 8/8/19, ADM12/5/160, PRAAD.
83. Clifford, confid. to Long, 6/6/17, C096/580.
84. R. Rathbone, "World War I and Africa," p. 1.
85. See H. Kuklick, *The Imperial Bureaucrat,* p. 6.
86. Clifford, Minute, 18/9/16, Enclosure 2, confid. to Bonar Law, 18/9/16, CO96/570. It was estimated in 1922 that the average area and number of subjects per administrative officer was 1,953 sq ml and 34,204 people in the NT, as opposed to 1,006 sq ml and 17,425 people in Ashanti, and 593 sq ml and 27,253 people in the Colony. See M. Staniland, *The Lions of Dagbon,* pp. 46–47.

in one day in July: "A few more expeditions like this and I think the natives will realize that the white man still lives."[87] Slater admitted that Castellain had only been following the "usual and authorized form of punishment" in ordering destruction of compounds. But he condemned the whole action, including the burning of houses and crops, as "excessive"—adding, with reference to recent events in the European war, that the "ill-advised delegation of dangerous duties" to the constabulary had led to actions that compared with "the worst of the atrocities in Belgium."[88]

Armitage explained that as chief commissioner he had tried to counter the rumors that all the English were leaving the country, reminding northern chiefs that they should be grateful to be spared the misery of war while "sitting peacefully in their villages protected by the power of the British Empire." According to Armitage, Castellain had done his best to patrol the district frequently and took action only when in danger. Some constables had been killed with poisoned arrows, and his patrol had been surrounded by "hundreds of armed men" concealed in the millet. "Coast experts" (among which Armitage clearly included the governor) failed to appreciate the need for some sort of display of armed force in a region that had only supposedly been "pacified" in 1911. "Unless drastic methods had been adopted, the whole countryside would have been ablaze."[89] "Drastic methods" included sending in constables with two maxim guns as well as destroying compounds and driving away cattle and sheep, and Armitage also cited instances of two other local conflicts in 1914 and 1915 (in the Lobi district in the northwest and in the Navrongo district in the northeast) where swift action by the constabulary had apparently prevented further trouble.[90]

In bitter terms, Clifford nonetheless blamed Chief Commissioner Armitage for not keeping himself sufficiently informed and for lack of overall control.[91] The strain of the war was by now seen to be seriously affecting the governor's judgment. Clifford's indictment of the old coaster, Armitage, was written in extraordinarily unrestrained language that reflected long hours, long tours, and considerable frustration—as well as his great personal grief at the recent loss of his son. In addition, there was in September his "agony of apprehension and anxiety" for his wife's safety on her sixth sea journey through the danger zone. He admitted to Fiddes that he was preparing the 1917 estimates on only three hours sleep a night.[92] Clifford was a man who drove himself unmercifully. He was to spend from seventy-two to ninety hours a week on paperwork during his next posting in Nigeria after the war—excluding the time he still spent writing novels. A year later he had to retire early, at sixty-three, when a combination of depression and a stroke led to permanent residence in a nursing home. As his faithful subordinate, Slater, wrote, the strain was beginning to tell as early as 1915, even on Clifford's "iron constitution."[93] In his official 1916 dispatch, Clifford publicly described Armitage as "dangerously unfit" to administer the Territories, being "so complacent, so childishly vain, so gullible, so credulous and so inefficient," his judgment "warped" and his vision "distorted." In addition, he argued that

87. *Ibid.*

88. Acting Governor Slater confid. to Bonar Law, 28/11/16. CO96/573.

89. Armitage to Colonial Secretary, 4/11/16, Reply to Governor's Minute of 15/9/16, Enclosure 1 A, Acting Governor Slater, confid. to Bonar Law, 28/11/16, C096/573.

90. *Ibid.*

91. Clifford, Minute, enclosure 2,15/9/16, and Castellain as quoted by Clifford, confid. to Bonar Law, 18/9/16, CO96/570. And R. Thomas, "The 1916 Bongo Riots," pp. 61, 69.

92. Clifford to Sir George Fiddes, CO, 15/9/15, CO96/570.

93. Slater to Sir George Fiddes, CO, 18/9/15, CO96/570.

Wheeler should be put on half pay and arraigned before the executive council and Castellain relieved of his post and indicted, even though Clifford was hesitant to withdraw too many European officers from the administrative staff of the Northern Territories at the same time.[94]

It seems that London officials in the Colonial Office were more concerned with the governor's sanity and stability than with the number of Africans killed in the Northern Territories. It was considered in London to be unacceptable for a governor to prejudge officers as guilty before the Secretary of State had heard their case. As Sir George Fiddes noted: Clifford's "stream of insulting invective" was "grossly unfair" on the accused, and from any other governor the whole "lamentable performance" would have raised "grave doubts as to his mental balance."[95] The Colonial Office concluded that the officers in the Gold Coast should all remain in post, provided that Clifford and Armitage could resolve their differences sufficiently to work together. The governor was censured for the violence of his language and his threat to resign despite the regulation that, during the war, officers of the Crown could not resign without permission.[96]

Clifford's reaction to the wartime incidents in the Northern Territories is also indicative of some aspects of his style of governorship: a personal rule that was autocratic towards many British officials, especially towards inflexible "old coasters," but generally protective towards the African population. Colonial Office officials, though appreciative of his considerable abilities, criticized Clifford's "overweening vanity" and "intolerance of opposition." However, in terms of personalities, Armitage was also judged to be vain, as well as "gloomy and touchy," having long been annoyed that the governor had failed to visit the Northern Territories and "belittles their importance."[97] Armitage was rightly suspicious that the governor wanted to replace him, an old "coaster," with his own man, Fell, who had biked extensively with Clifford up and down Ashanti. The governor's only venture into the north had been to Yeji, where he had "mortified" the chief of Prang by appearing on his own, on a bicycle, without any retinue except for the local DC. For Clifford, Fell was a kindred spirit, "a man's man" and someone who "loves trek work"—someone, indeed, who agreed that the Northern Territories was "essentially a bush and shorts job, and not a white uniform dress coat job."[98] For such British officers, one of the pleasures of colonial service appears to have been its similarity to scout camp.

The troubles in the Northern Territories revealed the strain and low morale of officers in the depleted and isolated British service there resulting from both the war and Clifford's governorship. As Armitage reflected: "The depression caused by this terrible war weighs heavily on all of us here, where news is so scanty and fragmentary."[99] The hapless Wheeler—demoted to half pay and aggrieved that the governor had put the worst possible interpretation on the charges against him—died of yellow fever at Gambaga. It seems that his previous lethargy, including recklessly granting his "native" constables a free hand and failing to keep Armitage fully informed, had been partly caused by ill health. The

94. Clifford, confid to Bonar Law, 18/9/16, C096/570.

95. Sir George Fiddes, CO Minute, Clifford, confid. to Bonar Law, 18/9/16, C096/570. And see H. Gailey, *Clifford,* pp. 104, 134, 180–184.

96. Steel Maitland, CO Minute, Acting Governor Slater to Bonar Law, 28/11/16, CO96/573. Ellis, CO Minute, Clifford, confid. to Bonar Law, 18/9/16, CO96/570.

97. Ellis, CO Minute, Clifford, confid. to Bonar Law, 18/9/16, CO96/570.

98. Clifford to Fiddes, 15/9/16, Clifford, confid. to Bonar Law, 18/9/16, CO96/570.

99. Armitage to Ellis, 5/5/16, Clifford, confid. to Bonar Law, 18/9/16, CO96/570.

governor's furious censure and plans to humiliate him publicly appear to have been the last straw and, according to Armitage, induced "severe mental strain."[100] For Armitage, the pressure of work and acute anxiety induced by Clifford's charges against him were seriously affecting his own health, and he too feared a nervous breakdown.[101] His explanation of his own inaction included the poor communications in the north. Not only were there very few officers, but the main telegraph line between Tamale and Gambaga had been damaged by lightning at the critical moment. Armitage's defense was all the more telling by being relatively restrained. He had served six different governors in the Gold Coast since 1894, and yet, as he commented wryly, he was now branded "as a sort of engaging lunatic" by a "great—if ruthless—man" who had not "the faintest idea of the conditions obtaining in the "protectorate." Armitage believed, with some justification, that his main crime had been "to question Sir Hugh Clifford's infallibility." This referred to discussions in 1914 when he had challenged the governor's policy of fostering the growing wealth of the Colony and Ashanti and spending as little money as possible on the north, as it had no commercial prospects.[102]

The Colonial Office officials in Whitehall absolved no one involved (officers named in dispatches, the governor, members of the secretariat, and of the executive council) from a share of responsibility for the events in the Northern Territories protectorate. But they too had contributed: by supporting Clifford's concentration on the Colony and Ashanti and by ignoring prewar requests for increases in staff and expenditure in the north. The Colonial Office also, with some justice, saw Clifford as prejudiced against the Northern Territories, in contrast to his predecessor, Thorburn, and as failing to appreciate the importance of the north as a supplier of labor for the Colony and Ashanti.[103] London officials did acknowledge that administration of so large an area (approximately 31,000 square miles) with so small a staff and poor transport "must inevitably be rough and ready."[104] With very few roads suitable for motor traffic, travel was very slow. Most government stations were two to three days distance from each other, and the journey from Kumasi to Tamale took two weeks, including the time taken to cross the Volta at Yeji. In contrast, it took only two days from Accra to reach Kumasi.[105] It was therefore now suggested that DCs should do a couple of tours in the Colony before being sent to remote places in the north.[106] London also noted Armitage's criticism of the attempt to obtain "native" recruits in an area that was only just recovering from Samory's invasion of 1896 and 1897, twenty years before, when large numbers of men had been killed and women and children sold into slavery.[107] In neighboring French territory in the Lorha district to the northwest, there was frequent fighting over recruiting and taxation and reports that many Lobis had been killed.[108] British officials were only too happy to criticize the French, but the incidents in the Northern Territories in 1916 and 1917 were salutary reminders that all was also not well on the British side of the frontier.

100. Wheeler to Armitage, 10/10/16, ADM 56/1/213, PRAAD; telegram, Acting Governor Slater to Bonar Law, 5/11/16, C096/572. Also Armitage to Colonial Secretary, 4/11/16, Enclosure 1 A, Acting Governor Slater, confid. to Bonar Law, 28/11/16, CO96/573.

101. Telegram, Armitage to Bonar Law, 4/11/16, C096/572.

102. Armitage to Colonial Secretary, 4/11/16, Enclosure 1 A, Acting Governor Slater, confid. to Bonar Law, 28/11/16, CO96/573.

103. Armitage to Ellis, 5/5/16, Clifford to Bonar Law, 18/9/16, CO96/570.

104. Steel Maitland, CO Minute, Acting Governor Slater to Bonar Law, 28/11/16, CO96/573.

105. *Ibid.*

106. Ellis, CO Minute, Clifford, confid. to Long, 6/6/17, CO96/580.

107. Armitage, Enclosure 12, Clifford, confid. to Long, 6/6/17, CO96/580.

108. ADC Palfreman, Enclosure 1, 24/5/17, Clifford, secret to Long, 25/6/17, C096/580.

Despite the troubles of 1916 and 1917, the Northern Territories continued to be neglected, due to Clifford's lack of interest and the continuing demands of the war. But for the war, Clifford would have perhaps toured the north and obtained a different perspective on the protectorate. It is possible that this would have led to measures to integrate the north more successfully with the rest of the colony. Colonial Office officials urged Clifford to undertake his delayed tour of the Northern Territories in the dry season of late 1917 and early 1918.[109] But Clifford produced a number of reasons as to why he believed it was not practicable: the arrival of the governor's "rather large caravan" needing food and carriers would be unjustifiably expensive in wartime and would hinder recruitment, and he should not be absent from his administrative headquarters for such a long period when the next cocoa season was likely to be "a somewhat trying time" for the rural population of the Colony and Ashanti.[110] Despite this rationale, one gets the impression that Clifford did not want to go.

As before the outbreak of the war, the governor saw the colonial government's relationship with the north as wholly different from its relationship with the Colony and Ashanti. He did not believe there was any good reason for spending time touring a region with no prospect of economic development. As Ellis in the Colonial Office noted, "the Northern Territories are stagnant, and will continue to stagnate until communications are improved so as to render some export possible."[111] During the remainder of the war, Clifford continued to argue that a tour of the Northern Territories was "essentially a peace-time job."[112] He was concerned that the journey would take at least four months, and he did not believe he should leave his post for so long—especially when the colony might be attacked by a submarine off the coast. This claim did not seem so far-fetched at the time. There was a report of a submarine attack on Monrovia and on an Elder Dempster boat, the *SS Burutu*, off the Liberian coast in April 1918. Men and guns were sent that month to reassure the inhabitants of Sekondi, where a submarine attack was expected.[113] Rumor spread fast in the war period. Under pressure from senior officials at the Colonial Office, Clifford at last announced to the legislative council in October 1918 that his tour of the Northern Territories was imminent. But news of the end of the war intervened.[114] By this time, too, he was aware that his period as governor was coming to an end. He was clearly happy to leave a tour of the Northern Territories to his successor.

The poverty and relative neglect of the Northern Territories before and during the war meant that its population was particularly vulnerable to natural disasters. A series of epidemics rendered northern farmers "prostrated" and "lacking in all energy."[115] There were outbreaks of smallpox, anthrax, and measles early in 1918. At least 425 children died of measles in Bolgatanga in May 1918. The influenza epidemic practically put a stop to trade during the last quarter of the year, especially when the French authorities placed

---

109. Ellis, CO Minute; Clifford, confid. to Long, 6/6/17, CO96/580.

110. Clifford, confid. to Long, 14/10/17, C096/582.

111. Ellis, CO Minute, *Report on the Northern Territories 1916,* Clifford to Long, 21/12/17, C096/583/801.

112. Private letter, Clifford to Sir Herbert Read, CO, 5/3/18, CO96/591; Fuller, diary, 12/4/18, ADM 12/5/160, PRAAD; *Gold Coast Leader,* 27/7/18; F. Cole, "Sierra Leone and World War I," p. 123.

113. *Ibid.*

114. Sir Herbert Read, CO Minute, Clifford to Sir Herbert Read, CO, 5/3/18, CO96/591. Also Clifford, *LegCo* 28/10/18, *Gazette* 911/18, CO99/33/82.

115. *Report on the Northern Territories 1918, CO98/30. K. D. Patterson, Health in Colonial Ghana,* pp. 68, 99–105. And N. Van Hear, "Northern Labor," p. 12.

a *cordon sanitaire* around posts and stations forbidding people to pass. The effects of previous epidemics as well as malnutrition appear to have made the northern population particularly vulnerable to the influenza pandemic. The effect of all this and the drought—with eleven inches less rainfall in Tamale, Wa, and Gambaga in 1918 compared with the heavy rains of the year before—seriously disrupted the harvest. The decimation of herds from rinderpest had also reduced the amount of animal protein available.[116] An additional problem, "very troublesome" in 1918, were lions in the northwest province, where they took a heavy toll of cattle during the year. Herdsmen complained bitterly of the wartime lack of gunpowder needed to protect their cattle (with only a very small amount manufactured locally). There were similar complaints in 1918 in Koinadugu, in the northwest of the Sierra Leone protectorate, concerning the ravages of wild animals and the lack of gunpowder.[117] Local trade only began to revive in the mid-1920s after the severe impact of this sequence of epidemics and shortages.

The combination of Clifford's governorship and wartime cuts and the better transport and cash crop farming of the south led to an increasing disparity between the northern protectorate and the rest of the Gold Coast in the war period. The African unofficial E. J. P. Brown expressed a common southern view in 1918 when he asked why the Colony had to be financially responsible for the Northern Territories and why they could not, like Togo, pay their own way.[118] Many such criticisms of the northern region were expressed in the local press by Western-educated Africans: for example, the complaint in *The Gold Coast Independent* that colonial rule there "merely absorbs our revenue and yields nothing in return."[119] But in his final major speech to the legislative council in October 1918, Clifford belatedly defended the Northern Territories from the charge that they were simply a burden on the rest of the colony. He now emphasized the contribution they made to the colony in terms of labor, including 90% of the recruits to the army.[120] The war had at least made the British coast government more appreciative of the contribution of the Northern Territories as a source of manpower. However, there continued to be unresolved problems. Many soldiers were no longer needed by the colonial government after the end of the war. According to Armitage, such recruits had enjoyed "a healthy camp life" with more money than they knew what to do with before suddenly being discharged in December 1918. This led to some incidents when chiefs' authority was challenged, with chiefs themselves subjected to insults as mere "bush men." However, little is recorded of ex-servicemen in the Gold Coast immediately after the Great War, in contrast with evidence of their impact elsewhere in West Africa, as in Guinea.[121]

The episodes in the Northern Territories during the First World War, in 1916 and 1917, reflected how thinly the colonial administration was spread in the Gold Coast colony. That the wartime labor demands and withdrawal of officers had placed British control of the area in jeopardy revealed the fragility of the British colonial administration. During

116. *Ibid.*

117. *Report on the Northern Territories 1918,* CO98/30. And F. Cole, "Sierra Leone and World War I," p. 354.

118. E. J. P. Brown, *LegCo* 29/10/18, *Gazette* 9/11/18, CO99/33/81.

119. Editorial, *The Gold Coast Independent,* 13//7/18.

120. Clifford, *LegCo* 28/10/18, *Gazette* 9/11/18, CO99/33/82.

121. *Report on the Northern Territories 1918,* CO98/30. And see A. Summers and R. Johnson, "World War I and Social Change in Guinea," *JAH,* XIX, 1, 1978, pp. 25–38; and see J. Lunn, "Kande Kamara Speaks," in M. Page, *Africa and the First World War,* pp. 28–53.

the war, British officials became increasingly jittery. The irony was that Ashanti, where violence was expected, remained calm—whereas the Northern Territories, apparently calm, erupted into violence. The fundamental difference lay in the unequal development and treatment of the two dependencies: Ashanti prospered as part of the southern cash crop economy, while the north remained neglected except for its use as a source of labor, with northern chiefs treated primarily as government recruiting agents.

The Gold Coast was never seen by its colonial rulers as a single undifferentiated entity, and during the war British officials continued to favor whichever administrative methods were cheapest and most practical. The result was that a different relationship between British officials and African subjects continued to evolve in each of the three distinct regions: of the Colony, Ashanti, and the Northern Territories. In terms of investment and economic development, the north was left increasingly far behind in this period, and here too the British administration was especially ignorant, provocative, and occasionally, brutal. There were limits to Clifford's sense of imperial obligation and trusteeship, especially during the strains of war. The interwar period was to see the role of the Northern Territories confirmed, in the eyes of the colonial administration, as little more than a labor reserve for the south.[122]

We have just noted that colonial administration was spread thinly, especially during the war, and seen how a stretched service struggled to administer the north—and struggled, too, to respond coherently to the unintended consequences of underadministration there. The strains on the service were not limited to one region, however, or to one stratum of officials. As the next chapter shows, strains and tensions characterized much of the business of the British government of the Gold Coast during the First World War and in turn contributed to the way in which relationships between British rulers and African ruled were to evolve in the colony.

122. N. Van Hear, "Northern Labor," pp. 117–118.

Chapter 9

The Colonial Relationship: Stresses and Strains

The war exposed how limited was the British colonial presence in the Gold Coast. The colony was short-staffed even before 1914; during the war the British were engaged in little more than a holding operation. Though colonial rule was to prove secure, British officers became seriously anxious, concerned that the local African government of chiefs and elders was becoming increasingly unstable. In Ashanti and the Northern Territories, their dependence on African chiefs became even more marked; meanwhile, chiefs, required by their British masters to carry out unpopular measures, came under pressure themselves. In the Colony in the south, the British administration also relied on Western-educated Africans, such as members of the legislative council, for support (as well as advice). At the same time, Africans involved in running the colonial administration were adversely affected by the wartime rise in the cost of living. These clerks or African "officials" were aware that their request for a war bonus was regarded as secondary to that of the European officers, but they pressed their claims in the war period with new vigor and success. Generally, African grievances grew, were articulated in the local African press—and on occasion led to concessions from the British. For their part, British officials, from the governor downwards, were under strain, but the evidence suggests that their managing of affairs was characterized by short-term, survival-centered pragmatism rather than by any supposed ideology or conspiracy of "divide and rule."

During Clifford's governorship, chiefs were given a greater say in public affairs. As he recognized, the reality of the colonial relationship was that the "natives" were "very largely self governed." The cooperation of the chiefs was essential for the enforcement of legislation passed by the government.[1] With little money and few staff, it had always been in the interest of the British to work through a well-structured "native" administrative system with a clear chain of command, "properly controlled and supervised"—and even more so with staffing cuts during the war.[2] Before the war, he had made a point of visiting almost all the paramount chiefs in the Colony and Ashanti, making it clear that he sought their advice in order to rule the territory effectively through them, and that he was concerned to uphold their authority where he felt it was unjustifiably challenged. During the war, with even fewer officers than usual, such *indirect* rule was, as Clifford observed, the only means possible to carry out the work of the administration.[3]

However, the war hampered Clifford's efforts to improve the colonial government's liaison with chiefs. The normal channel of communication with the local African chief was through the PC or DC, of whom, as we have noted, there were far fewer in post

1. Sir Hugh Clifford, "Recent Developments on the Gold Coast," p. 252.
2. Crowther, *Report on Native Affairs 1915*, Clifford, confid. to Bonar Law, 25/5/16, C096/567.
3. Clifford, confid. to Long, 4/2/18, C096/588.

during the war. The governor had also initiated regular durbars, or district conferences, from 1913—soon after his arrival—to improve consultation with head chiefs. These were then mostly abandoned because of the war, although Clifford remained convinced that the durbar was "a much valued institution" providing an occasion "for the discussion and guidance of native affairs throughout the colony."[4] Occasional meetings of this kind therefore took place despite the war. Opinion in the African press as to the value of such contact varied considerably. Chiefs at a durbar in Cape Coast in 1916 were said to have attended under orders to hear the governor's address. However, Clifford was also given credit for his "sympathetic hearing" and good relations with chiefs, and for issues arising at such durbars being followed up by the relevant PCs or Commissions of Inquiry.[5] Clifford also won praise from Ofori Atta in 1916 for continuing his "sound policy" of "taking the Native Rulers into the confidence of the government."[6] It was obviously in the interests of paramount chiefs that the governor be encouraged to continue to consult them.

Given the British colonial administration's dependence on indirect rule, the erosion of the authority of many African chiefs within their own societies remained a matter of concern to the Gold Coast government throughout the war period. One cause of tension was when a chief, under protection of the often unwitting British colonial government, became autocratic, ignoring traditional constraints such as judgments of the local state council. Much depended on the personality of the chief as to whether he took personal advantage of his position, or was thought to be doing so, to the detriment of his people. The colonial government understood that the main threat to chiefs' authority, as before the war, came from those with new wealth in society, largely from cocoa farming. These were the so-called "young men" who, according to Clifford, threatened to "destroy the tribal constitution."[7] The new wealth could be seen, for example, in Akuepem and Akyem villages, where the wattle and daub hut and grass roof of ten or fifteen years before had often since been replaced by a two-story veranda house of swish brick with corrugated iron roofing.[8] However, "disintegrating forces" appeared to be at work—the result of what the governor sweepingly described as "too much innovation" in society.[9] The economic development the British encouraged was bringing social change and potential political instability.

Meanwhile, the demands made on the population by the wartime colonial administration aggravated tensions within African society. For example, the call for a loyal response to "voluntary" recruitment and government praise for financial donations caused many chiefs, such as those in the Northern Territories (as we saw in the last chapter), to make unpopular demands of their people for men and money.[10] After his 1917 recruiting tour of Eastern Province, Slater reported on the chiefs' "eager and manifestly sincere desire" to help British officers. Their "only lament" was that they did not possess "the old authority"

4. Clifford to Bonar Law, 22/9/16, C096/571/683.

5. E.g., contrast *The Gold Coast Nation*, 23/3/16 with *The African Mail*, 21/4/16, 28/4/16.

6. Address, *Omanhene Akyem Abuakwa and Chiefs*, Visit of Sir Clifford and Lady Clifford to Kyebi, 22/9/16, Enclosure, Clifford to Bonar Law, 22/9/16, CO96/571/683.

7. *Report on Native Affairs, 1915*, Clifford, confid. to Long, 25/5/16, CO96/567.

8. Crowther, *Report on Native Affairs 1916*, quoted by Furley, *Report on Native Affairs 1917*, Clifford, confid. to Long, 9/10/18, CO96/593.

9. Clifford to Long, 10/12/17, C096/583/787.

10. Cf. forced recruitment methods used by chiefs in Nigeria, J. Matthews, "Reluctant Allies: Nigerian Responses to Military Recruitment 1914–18," in M. Page, *Africa and the First World War*, pp. 95–114.

of their fathers, who would have had no problem calling out as many young men as the government might require.[11] Not surprisingly, many chiefs were anxious to be judged "loyal" by the British, but they also wanted to avoid having to impose forcible conscription for fear of endangering their position with their own people. Furley (the new secretary for native affairs following Crowther's death from yellow fever) believed that it was the recruitment campaign of 1917 that for the first time brought home the impact of the war to every inhabitant of the colony. Some chiefs even suggested at this time that the British government officers should relieve them of the responsibility and unpopularity of obtaining recruits by simply taking those they required.[12]

Contributions to Britain's war funds organized by chiefs were not as "voluntary" as the government officially proclaimed. For example, in the state of Akyem Abuakwa in Eastern Province, "general war taxes" were imposed from 1914: some of the money raised was later used for an inducement allowance of £7 to young men volunteering for service in East Africa. The Okeyman Council imposed a tax equivalent to one load of cocoa as a contribution to the Imperial War Fund: 5s for commoners, 8s for stool elders, and £1 for chiefs.[13] In Western Province in 1915, DCs attempted to discourage chiefs from insisting that their subjects give money. But the official British policy of individual voluntary contributions was quite impractical. Most political officers in the colony were aware that, in accordance with custom and practice, the African population looked to their chief and councilors to lead and advise and, if most approved, to impose. "Voluntary" individual wartime contributions were thus usually imposed by the traditional authorities on their peoples.[14] Occasional abuses were dealt with. For example, commoners rebelled against a chief in Kumasi in 1915 partly because it was proved that he had kept for himself money collected for the war fund.[15] By December 1917, contributions across the colony had reached £61,562 with the addition of money for eleven airplanes in response to the appeal for the Royal Flying Corps—by which "the Gold Coast and Ashanti were directly and gloriously represented over the battlefields of Europe."[16] There were also collections by Western-educated individuals and organizations such as the boys at Mfantsipim secondary school, Cape Coast, who donated their school prizes and arranged concerts to raise money for the War Relief Fund.[17] British government officials simply recorded all such collections as proof of "loyalty."

The economic depression in 1917 and 1918 caused further friction between chiefs and people. Challenges to chiefs' jurisdiction had arisen over a long period of time as a result not only of the growth of individual wealth from cash crop farming but also of a more shifting population and the settlement of "aliens." Furthermore, conflict often arose over

---

11. Acting Governor Slater, confid. to Long, 25/1/17, C096/577 and R. Addo-Fening, "Akyem Abuakwa c.1874–1943," p. 486.

12. Furley, *Report on Native Affairs 1917,* Clifford, confid. to Long, 9/10/18, CO96/593.

13. Bye-Laws Akyem Abuakwa, 25/3/18, ADM 11/1/690, PRAAD; and R. Addo-Fening, "Akyem Abuakwa c.1874–1943," pp. 485–486.

14. Letters, J. L. Atterbury and DCs to Secretary of Native Affairs, e.g., 6/10/15, ADM 11/1/611, PRAAD.

15. *Report on Western Province 1914,* 8/4/15, *Supplementary 8, Gazette* 6/9/15, C099/29. Also K. Busia, "Colonial Administration and Social Change in Ghana 1900–1920s" in W. Cartey & M. Kilson (eds.), *The African Reader: Colonial Africa,* (New York, 1970) p. 111.

16. Clifford, secret to Long, 27/12/17, C096/583; also Acting Governor Slater, *Proclamation on the Conclusion of Peace,* 28/6/19, *Gazette* 17/7/19, C099/34/65.

17. F. Bartels, *The Roots of Ghana Methodism,* (London, 1965), pp. 179, 183.

the chief's handling of justice.[18] Fees and fines imposed in the "native" tribunals were, in the absence of any government stipend, a crucial source of stool income. There was clearly an incentive for chiefs and elders to raise charges in times of trade depression when their other sources of revenue, such as profits from cocoa, fell away. Among the extensive literature on the commoner organizations or companies, the *asafo,* are suggestions that they asserted themselves particularly strongly as a political force during periods of economic depression, such as in 1917 and 1918 and later in the 1930s. This was certainly the case during the First World War in Akyem Abuakwa and in Kwahu, where the famous Kwahu charter, forced on the chiefs, or omanhene, by commoners in 1917, included regulations to control judicial fees as well as food prices.[19] Many of the disputes in Ashanti in 1918 also shared the common factor of "young men" complaining at extortionate "oath fees" in "native" tribunals. The amendment to the Native Jurisdiction Ordinance of 1910 had made matters worse by making tribunals compulsory courts of first instance without supervision of fees and fines.[20]

In the war period, the wave of destoolments—successful challenges to the authority of chiefs—caused considerable British concern about the stability of African society throughout the colony. In the event of destoolment, a new chief needed to be chosen by the particular African community and approved by the governor. There was little British analysis as to why such events had taken place. Clifford believed the growing tendency to resort to destoolment was to satisfy "every passing and quite trivial feeling of discontent" rather than being reserved for use as a last resort. He had hoped cases could then be settled less expensively, thus avoiding "ruinous litigation" over, for example, the tribal ownership of land, which placed so many stools in "hopeless financial embarrassment."[21] Destoolments of head chiefs rose from twenty-three in 1909–1913 to thirty-eight in 1914–1918 (of which sixteen took place in 1918 alone) and to forty-one in 1919–24.[22] In 1917, head chiefs called on the government to find some remedy for the frequency with which chiefs were deprived of office "as compared with former days."[23] Fuller judged that the desire to destool chiefs in towns such as Efiduai and Jamasi in 1918 was primarily due to "money matters" such as newly imposed taxes: "Destooling chiefs is becoming infectious in Ashanti."[24]

Apart from challenges of commoners, there was also a tendency for subchiefs to ignore the authority of the omanhene, partly because of the lack of distinction in law between the powers and jurisdiction of chiefs and head chiefs.[25] In the Ayan division near Winneba, in 1917, the population was not prepared to accept a paramount but only local *ohenes.*[26] The instability was such that in March 1918 a delegation of paramounts from Eastern

18. Acting Governor Slater, *LegCo* 25/10/15, *Gazette* 25/11/15, C099/29/101. And see Furley's comments, *Report on Native Affairs 1917,* Clifford, confid. to Long, 9/10/18, CO96/593.

19. E.g., J. Simensen, "Rural Mass Action," pp. 26–30; and "The Asafo of Kwahu, Ghana," pp. 395–406.

20. K. Busia, *The Position of the Chief,* p. 108. See J. Simensen, "Rural Mass Action," p. 29; and Section I, Chapter 3.

21. Clifford, *LegCo* 28/10/18, *Gazette* 9/11/18, C099/33/82.

22. Figures from the *Gazettes* in D. Kimble, *A Political History,* p. 490. See also *Report on Native Affairs 1918,* quoted in Anshan Li, "Social Protest in the Gold Coast," p. 179.

23. Furley, *Report on Native Affairs 1917,* Clifford, confid. to Long, 9/10/18, C096/593.

24. Fuller, diary, 26/7/18, ADM 12/5/160, PRAAD.

25. Harding, PC, *Report on Central Province 1917,* Clifford to Long, 13/6/18, C096/590/331.

26. Harper, quoted by Harding, *Report on Central Province 1917,* Clifford to Bonar Law, 13/6/18, CO96/590/331.

Province led by Ofori Atta called on the governor to guarantee head chiefs greater security of tenure. One complaint was that direct communication between subchiefs and the government had "much increased" and had been "a cause of prejudice" against paramounts.[27] Ofori Atta used government ordinances to counter the wave of destoolments initiated by *asafo* in Akyem Abuakwa between 1913–1918. The wartime economic depression aggravated tensions, which culminated in the attempt to destool the okyenhene himself in November 1918.

Clifford believed the colonial government had to find ways to stabilize the "traditional native" system and the structures of indirect rule. One method was to encourage some local representative government, on traditional lines. British officers were to encourage the admission of leading "young men" or "commoners" to the "native" councils. *Asafoakyefo* (*asafo* officers) were included in divisional chiefs' councils in Akyem Abuakwa in 1918 and in Kwahu after 1920. "Young men" were then incorporated more widely into councils in Akyem Abuakwa in the 1930s—though Clifford's recommendation only became official policy across the colony much later, in the Local Government Ordinance of 1951.[28]

Clifford was convinced that the main solution was to strengthen the legal authority of chiefs, and especially head chiefs, in the native tribunals.[29] The war delayed the new Native Jurisdiction Ordinance, designed to give greater powers to chiefs, until late in 1918. It had been drawn up during 1915 and circulated to principal chiefs in the Colony in a consultation exercise (much approved of by Clifford) prior to being presented to the legislative council. Under Clifford, such consultation prior to legislation had become a matter of course.[30] The draft was only finally forwarded to London in February 1918, but Colonial Office officials were not prepared to be rushed into any measure. The delay meant political officers, PCs and DCs, continued to be overloaded—especially during the war—with court work, including stool disputes, to the neglect of administration. For example, in Eastern Province there were seventy-four appeals from native tribunals to DC courts in 1917.[31]

Clifford and his officials in the Gold Coast, and officials in London, failed to perceive that the concern among a wide range of African opinion was not to promote, but to prevent, any further extension of British involvement in local administration. When the new Native Jurisdiction Bill was finally introduced after the war in February 1919, the colonial government faced unexpectedly widespread African opposition from "traditional" authorities—including head chiefs—as well as from African Western-educated opinion. The law would have given the colonial government new powers, such as defining the jurisdiction of head chiefs. It would have given PCs more control over tribunal proceedings and the governor the right to confirm stool elections.[32] The British were surprised that the bill was now opposed even by some who had long given officers their approval. But

27. *Petition of Paramounts of Eastern Province*, 5/3/18 ADM11/1/684, PRAAD.

28. Clifford, confid. to Bonar Law, 25/5/16, C096/567. And see J. Simensen, "The Asafo of Kwahu, Ghana," pp. 401–402.

29. *The Native Jurisdiction Ordinance* of 1883, amended in 1888, 1904, and 1910. See D. Kimble, *A Political History*, pp. 462–472.

30. Acting Governor Slater, *LegCo* 25/10/15, *Gazette* 25/11/15, C099/29/101. And see D. Kimble, *A Political History*, p. 473 and R. Stone, "Colonial Administration and Rural Politics," p. 88.

31. Clifford, confid. to Long, 4/2/18, C096/588; Ellis, CO Minute, confid. to Long, 472/18, CO96/588; *Report on Eastern Province 1917*, Clifford to Long, 9/7/18, C096/591/389. And see R. Stone, "Colonial Administration and Rural Politics," p. 78.

32. Risley, CO Minute, Clifford to Long, 28/11/18, C096/593/696.

head chiefs had become concerned that the bill would lead to further loss of their authority to the colonial government. They did approve of the exclusion of "native" barristers from chiefs' tribunals: the fewer challenges to their authority the better. Ofori Atta's justification for this exclusion was that such lawyers had studied British law but were not conversant with African customary laws.[33]

The British achieved only a limited perception of the complexities of African political and social relationships. This was despite Clifford's prewar recognition of "curious democratic features" in "native" constitutions in the colony and his advocacy of commoner representation in state councils in 1916. Such features of African society included the popular checks and balances relating to the powers of chiefs and the role of the *asafo*, and how these were affected by cash crop farming, Western education, and now the economic strains of the war.[34] Ironically, any government measure intended to strengthen chiefs' authority was likely to have the opposite effect in the long term by reducing the standing of chiefs among their own peoples.

Urban areas did not easily fit with the British policy of indirect rule. Clifford had decided on a review of town councils just before the outbreak of the war.[35] In April 1915, he presented a detailed case for their abolition, having been convinced by both British and African unofficials that they were not representative institutions, with the African elected members always in a minority. The town councils were, Clifford believed, "uneconomic and inefficient" structures arbitrarily imposed by the colonial government and, in effect, poorly run by a small and constantly changing number of European officers. They had failed to achieve "a municipal spirit" or to prepare "natives" for self government by, for example, accustoming them to direct taxation in the form of rates, as had been the intention. The councils, such as those in Accra, were viewed with a "smouldering discontent" by the population, and the towns were so run down that Cape Coast, according to Clifford, looked in 1915 as if it had "suffered a recent bombardment."[36] While there was considerable sympathy among Colonial Office officials with Clifford's views, it was thought better to delay consideration of town councils until the end of the war. "Natives" were said to have "settled down" to local rates, while towns were continuing to expand.[37] In fact, during the war there was more evidence of urban expansion than of any "settling down" to paying rates.[38] It is thus misleading of Edsman to suggest that there was no effort to tackle the problem of town councils until Guggisberg's period of office in the 1920s.[39] Rather, Clifford's planned overhaul of the administration of the Colony's towns was yet another reform that had to be postponed because of the war.

---

33. For a case of the effective use of British jurisprudence by African lawyers against stool law, see G. Casely Hayford, "The Cape Coast Stool Dispute of 1916," *Paper to African History Seminar,* SOAS, London University, 24/4/91. And Ofori Atta, enclosure, 28/9/18, Clifford to Long, 28/11/18, CO96/593/696.

34. For discussion of the changing relationship between chiefs and British authorities, see H. Kuklick, *The Imperial Bureaucrat,* pp. 52–54.

35. See Chapter 3.

36. Clifford, confid. to Harcourt, 10/4/15, CO96/577.

37. Green, Ellis, Sir John Anderson, CO Minute, Clifford, confid. to Harcourt, 10/4/15. CO96/577.

38. See Table XVII: *Population of the Main Towns 1891–1931* in D. Kimble, *A Political History,* p. 144.

39. B. Edsman, *Lawyers in Gold Coast Politics c.1900–1945,* (Uppsala, 1979), p. 71. And see R. Wraith, *Guggisberg,* p. 207.

From a British perspective, there was no overall cause for concern in the Gold Coast as long as order was largely maintained. Following the news of the outbreak of the war, there were several serious riots between rival *asafo* groups, mostly in the Colony. During the worst of these, at Berraku ("Berracoe") east of Winneba on the coast in Central Province, ninety-three people were reported to have been killed; according to Clifford "war was in the air and firearms were freely used."[40] But none of these incidents was apparently directed against British rule. Occasional disturbances continued, such as the fights between *asafos* in coastal Fante towns (company fights over flags or succession rights or those simply noted as "drunken brawls"), though in 1915 some *asafos* agreed to waive their disputes until the end of the war.[41] The colonial administration sometimes used leniency to help keep the peace. For example, it was thought advisable "for political reasons," in 1916, for the government to lift the heavy court fines imposed for a riot in 1915 over a succession dispute—to the relief and gratitude of the omanhene and councilors of Low Wassaw.[42]

But a lack of order was seen as a problem by many of the local African population who, in this instance, as in the provision of welfare, wanted more (and more efficient) government. Reported crime increased in the war period in the wealthier cocoa districts. Here were good opportunities for theft, with large sums rarely placed in a bank. Immigrants from other West African colonies were often blamed. For example, the increase in theft and assault in Eastern Province in 1914 was said to be largely due to the influx of "alien labourers," such as Krepis from Togo.[43] In 1916 on his visit to Kyebi, Clifford was told of the growing incidence of robbery with violence, perpetrated largely by "unemployed strangers" whose presence reflected the increased mobility as a result of the war.[44] The higher crime rate in Western Province in the war was also believed to be mainly due to foreigners. Men from Lagos were blamed for thefts in Axim. In Ashanti in 1918, the large numbers of unemployed Moshi and Wangara arriving from north of the Northern Territories were held responsible for many cases of highway robbery.[45] The chief commissioner of Ashanti, Fuller, also blamed the Moshis from the north: "They are born thieves and glory in the fact."[46] In contrast, it was demobilized local African carriers (without entitlement to a soldier's pension) who were blamed for rising crime rates at this time in Sierra Leone[47]. In the Gold Coast, there were some instances of soldiers looting and attacking market women on the high roads.[48] Actions concerning debt also seem to have been on the increase. Towards the close of 1915, the chief registrar recorded an increase of almost 50% in debt cases compared with 1912.[49] "Money-doubling" frauds were also becoming more common in Central Province.[50]

40. Clifford, confid. to Bonar Law, 1/5/15, C096/557.

41. Crowther, *Report on Native Affairs 1914,* Clifford, confid to Bonar Law, 8/5/15, C096/557; and *Report on Riots, 1916,* 10/3/16, ADM 11/1/628, PRAAD.

42. PC Western Province Maxwell, to Crowther, 30/10/16, ADM11/1/639, PRAAD.

43. *Report on Eastern Province 1914, Supplementary 8, Gazette* 679/15, C099/29; also *Report on Eastern Province 1915, Supplementary 4, Gazette* 14/7/16, C099/31; and *The African Mail* 5/5/16.

44. Address, Omanhene Akyem Abuakwa, on occasion of Governor's visit, 22nd September 1916. Clifford to Bonar Law, 22/9/16, C096/571/683.

45. *Report on Western Province 1914, Supplementary* 8, Gazette 6/9/15, CO99/29; K. Busia, *The Position of the Chief,* p. 112; and N. van Hear, "Northern Labor," pp. 54–55.

46. Fuller, diary, 13/9/17, ADM 12/5/160, PRAAD.

47. F. Cole, "Sierra Leone and World War I," p. 70.

48. Fuller, diary, 6/4/18, ADM 12/5/160, PRAAD.

49. Acting Governor Slater, *LegCo* 25/10/15, *Gazette* 25/11/15, C099/29/101.

50. E.g., *Police Department Report 1914, Supplementary 5, Gazette* 2/7/15, C099/29.

There were many cases when chiefs called on the government to provide more order during the war, with police being unable to control the situation themselves. For example, Konor Mate Kole asked for police patrols in 1915 to deal with the increasingly frequent "highway robbery" in his division of Eastern Krobo. Representations were also made to the governor by leading chiefs in Eastern Province in March 1918 about the "abnormal increase" in the number of "burglars and highwaymen" and the need for more police.[51] The fact that the police force was not up to strength because of the war was thought to have contributed to this rise in crime. By early 1916, only twelve of the nineteen European police officers were available for duty, and the standard of recruits for the ranks was said to be poor, with low rates of pay still inhibiting recruitment. Pay was so low that almost all members of the force were reported in 1915 and 1916 as illiterate and increasingly "Hauserized," that is, northerners speaking only Hausa, with little or no knowledge of coast languages or English. The situation improved slightly in 1918 (as a result of the severe economic depression) with the recruitment of unemployed factors and clerks.[52] Clifford's plans for improving the police service were postponed because of the war.[53] The result was that the Gold Coast was probably less well policed after World War I than a decade before. Only the unpopular paramilitary escort (or "khaki") police increased in number over the war period.[54] Inspector General Collins's scheme for reorganization, with increases in numbers and pay, was drawn up in 1917. But Collins was drowned shortly afterwards on the *SS Abosso*, and it was left to his successor, Bettington, with Clifford's support, to promote reforms after the war. They were belatedly adopted in 1920.[55]

There were occasional challenges to the authority of the local constabulary in the Colony, as in the Northern Territories (as seen in the last chapter) in 1916 and 1917. Clifford mainly attributed these disturbances to the British drive for army and carrier recruits, but the effects of wartime economic depression and the disruption of an outbreak of bubonic plague in the southeast littoral in March 1917 must also have contributed to new, more serious outbreaks.[56] Trouble was reported at Half Assini in the southwest of the Colony in March 1917, with "gatherings of armed men" and a telegraph line cut, and a more serious challenge to law and order took place at Great Ningo in Eastern Province in May 1917.[57] For a short time it was not safe for a government officer to travel in villages in the Great Ningo district, not far along the coast east of Accra, and a party of police was forced to retreat. A force of ninety men was finally sent under two British officers.[58] Clifford's comments on quelling these "disturbances" are very revealing and run counter to his earlier criticisms of officers in the Northern Territories. Restoring order had been

---

51. Acting Governor Slater to Bonar Law, 5/11/15, CO96/561/894; Clifford to Bonar Law, 8/6/16, CO96/567/411. See also *Representations from Chiefs of Eastern Province*, 5/3/18, Clifford to Long, 4/5/18, CO96/590/254.

52. W. Gillespie, *The Gold Coast Police 1844–1938,* (Accra, 1955), pp. 50–54.

53. Clifford to Long, 10/12/17, C096/583/767; and Clifford, *LegCo* 28/10/18, *Gazette* 9/11/18, C099/33/82.

54. See D. Killingray in D. Anderson & D. Killingray (eds.), *Policing the Empire, Government, Authority and Control 1830–1940,* (Manchester, 1991), p. 120. See Appendix 3, Table B in D. Killingray, "The Colonial Army in the Gold Coast," p. 431.

55. W. Gillespie, *The Gold Coast Police,* pp. 52–53.

56. Clifford to Long, 27/7/17, C096/580/477; also *Report on Native Affairs 1917.* Clifford, confid. to Long, 9/10/18, C096/593; also Clifford to Long, 27/7/17, C096/580/477.

57. *Ibid.*

58. W. Gillespie, *The Gold Coast Police,* p. 52.

handicapped by the fact that "action of a summary and drastic character, such as is possible in an emergency to adopt in a Protectorate, cannot with ease be taken in a District of the Colony."[59] Although the governor did not accept Crowther's advice on punitive measures (such as the destruction of certain evacuated villages), the search for arms and ammunition in the thatch of many houses was said to have rendered them "uninhabitable."[60] The police had difficulty apprehending those said to be the ringleaders, but sixty people were ultimately arrested and charged.[61]

One threat to the stability of the colony that was lifted as a result of the war, to the relief of the Gold Coast government, was a measure devised in London to limit chiefs' control over land use. Land ownership in the colony remained, as it had always been, a highly sensitive issue in British-African relations. In this case, what was involved was the right of the chiefs to alienate land. From the start of the war, the West African Lands Committee in London was provisionally suspended, with the result that the contentious measure of the repeal of the Concessions Ordinance, announced in March 1914, was put "into cold storage."[62] This at least prevented an African outcry on the coast against any interference with land rights, though it did nothing to allay London's concern at what was seen as indiscriminate alienation of land, to the detriment of future generations. There were cases reported by Ofori Atta where land was sold for £60 or less, and then resold for £70 without local consultation. However, as Ellis in the Colonial Office pointed out, although about 2,000 square miles of land had been conceded (out of a total of perhaps 24,200 square miles), "on the greater part of it life goes on as if no grant had been made."[63]

Clifford was very concerned that African land rights should be respected by the British colonial administration. This was for him a duty of trusteeship critical for the local British government's relationship with its African subjects. As governor, he believed himself to be trustee of the land on behalf of African proprietors.[64] When the issue arose in 1917 of the British government paying chiefs for the land that contained bauxite deposits, the Colonial Office proposed that after the war an ordinance be passed enabling the colonial government to take over such areas. The plan was to pay chiefs simply the agricultural value of the land. An editorial in the *Gold Coast Leader* accused the British government of planning a "monopolistic" practice.[65] Clifford agreed. He denounced the plan with "the utmost anxiety and concern" as an unacceptable breach of "definite pledges" given by the British government to the people of the Gold Coast.[66] It raised for him a "vital matter of principle." Any such action would, he argued, gravely damage the "natives' trust and confidence in the government."[67] Fuller, PC for Ashanti, backed Clifford, describing London's proposal as "an immoral bombshell."[68]

---

59. Clifford to Long, 27/7/17, CO96/580/477.
60. *Ibid.*
61. *Report on Native Affairs 1917*, Clifford, confid. to Long 9/10/18, CO96/593.
62. Ellis, Harcourt, CO Minute, 6/10/14, *West African Lands Committee*; also Sir John Anderson to Sir Kenelm Digby, chairman, *West African Lands Committee*, 16/12/14, CO554/21.
63. Sir Kenelm Digby to Sir John Anderson, 18/2/14, C0554/21. R. Addo-Fening, "Akyem Abuakwa c.1874–1943," p. 332; and Ellis, CO Minute, Clifford, confid. to Harcourt, 29/3/15, C096/5565.
64. See discussion of the concept of trusteeship in S. Constantine, *The Making of British Colonial Development Policy*, pp. 18–19.
65. Editorial, *Gold Coast Leader*, 19/1/18.
66. Long, confid. to Clifford, 27/5/17, Clifford, secret to Long, 26/12/17, C096/583.
67. *Ibid.*
68. Fuller, diary 7/4/18, ADM 12/5/160, PRAAD.

This was a case where the determination and forceful character of a governor played an important role in defending local African rights against the British government in London. European trading companies, African unofficials, and the African press were all hostile to the plan, which was likely to stir up considerable trouble. The issue was set aside.[69] For Clifford any government intervention would have been unjust, and a poor return for the support Britain was receiving from African chiefs during the war. It was an example of how the Colonial Office "could not easily override the vested interests of Europeans when these were backed by governors."[70] But the vested interests of Africans were also crucial here, seen in the fierce opposition to interference in land ownership throughout the period of colonial rule, as with the Land Bills of the 1890s. This outcome was also to the advantage of Ofori Atta, who was able, through "astute bargaining," to do well from diamond concessions in 1919, after the war.[71]

One concern among chiefs about maintaining their authority and especially their rights over land at this time related to the published proposals of the Empire Resources Development Committee. The ERDC was a private body formed in London in 1916 with a protectionist economic program to develop and control imperial resources, especially in the tropical colonies, in order to help to reduce Britain's war debt. The ERDC was closely associated with the British South African Company. Members included Lord Milner and a number of Conservative MPs, such as Controller of Oils and Fats Alfred Bigland; and Walter Long, until he became secretary of state for the Colonies in December 1916. Concern about the ERDC among Western-educated Africans in Britain's West African colonies contributed to the political demands of the National Congress of British West Africa (NCBWA) in 1920, after the war.[72] In the context of increasing trade restrictions and regulations, the executive committee of the ARPS, together with seventeen chiefs from Western and Central Provinces and a number of African unofficials, met in Cape Coast in May 1918 and expressed their "grave concern" at the propaganda of the ERDC. They were alarmed at its call for Britain to develop the "estates" of her Empire, including taking control of the "native" oil and cocoa industries. The petitioners demanded protection concerning "the integrity of their immemorial rights to their ancestral land and their economic freedom."[73] They received a categorical assurance, as did the Association of West African Merchants and the Anti-Slavery Society, that, as the secretary of state had made clear in the House of Commons, there was no British government support or sanction for the ERDC. It was "a body with no official standing whatsoever."[74] For the paternalistic Clifford, the ERDC program was "highly mischievous" and "immoral." Lugard, Accra officials, permanent officials at the Colonial Office, and the Association of West African Merchants were all equally hostile. [75] The ERDC plans to develop the empire came to nothing.

69. Ellis, Risley (legal advisor to the CO) Read, CO Minute, Clifford, secret to Long, 26/12/17, CO96/583.

70. A. Roberts, The Imperial Mind," in A. Roberts (ed.), *The Cambridge History of Africa*, p. 30.

71. P. Greenhalgh, *West African Diamonds*, p. 94.

72. See D. Kimble, *A Political History*, p. 53; and D. Killingray, "The Empire Resources Development Committee and West Africa 1916–20," *Journal of Imperial and Commonwealth History*, X, Jan.1982, 2, pp. 194–210.

73. Resolution, in telegram, Clifford to Long, 27/5/18, C096/590.

74. Clifford to Long, 27/5/18, CO96/590. Also West African merchants to Long, 21/1/18 and 1/2/18, C0554/40; and to Milner, 21/3/19, C0554/43; also Anti-Slavery Society to Milner, 20/2/19, C0554/43.

75. Clifford to Lugard, 7/2/18, 1, p. 121, *Lugard Papers*, in A. Osuntokun, *Nigeria in the First World War*, p. 55. See also S. Constantine, *The Making of British Colonial Development Policy*, p. 41.

In fact, the minimal colonial government of the Gold Coast, even more minimal during the war, and even more dependent on the active cooperation and support of African chiefs and their people, was in no position to fully exploit the resources of the "estates" of the Empire, even if it had wanted to. Some officials of the Gold Coast administration were seconded to the military or for administrative work in occupied Togo, from a government that had already been severely short-staffed before August 1914. From the start of the war, most government departments were "depleted of their officers and more or less radically disorganised."[76] As before the war, Clifford was instructed to fill administrative gaps by using medical officers, despite the absence of eleven medical officers already serving with the GCR.[77] In July 1915, a total of seventy-six officers were absent on secondment to the war effort, either in West Africa or in Europe. By October 1915, just under a quarter of the political officers, twenty out of ninety-five, were absent on secondment as a result of the war.[78] This figure remained fairly static over the following two years. The effect of these reductions in numbers was greatly exacerbated by the fact that at any one time approximately a third of all officers were on leave.[79]

In a number of ways, the British administration of the colony became increasingly threadbare during the war period. Temporary shifts in posting to cover for absent colleagues, a feature even before the war, now became "lamentably frequent." For example, three different British officers acted as commissioner of Eastern Province in 1914, and six different officers as DC in Keta in the space of twenty-two months.[80] Administrative reforms that would have reduced workloads had to be postponed, such as plans for a new district inland of Winneba and Saltpond. The failure to appoint a police magistrate for Accra meant the local DC had to continue with extensive judicial duties on top of general administrative work.[81] Maxwell, the commissioner of Western Province, complained that many of his staff were moving two or three times a year to cover for absent colleagues.[82] All ranks were affected. Philbrick, the newly appointed commissioner of Eastern Province, was able to hold his post for only eleven out of every seventeen months, as he was needed to act as chief commissioner of Ashanti when Fuller was away.[83] Good government depended on good knowledge and understanding of local conditions, but constant changes of personnel militated against this.

The result was that there were occasions during the war when the British political administration barely existed in certain areas. Towards the end of 1917, one PC and four

76. Clifford, confid. to Harcourt, 8/9/14, C096/547.

77. Clifford to Harcourt, 20/3/15, C096/556/248; Fiddian, CO Minute. Telegram, Clifford to Harcourt, 7/4/15, C096/557; telegram, Harcourt to Clifford, 10/4/15, C096/557; and see Section I, Chapter 3; and K. D. Patterson, *Health in Colonial Ghana*, p. 12.

78. Lists of officers serving in war operations, *Gazette* 31/7/15, C099/29/60; *Medical and Sanitary Report 1915*, Clifford to Bonar Law, 20/5/16, C096/567/372; Acting Governor Slater, *LegCo* 25/10/15, *Gazette* 25/11/15, C099/29/101.

79. Clifford, *LegCo* 2/11/17, Clifford to Long, 10/12/17, C096/583/767. Acting Governor Slater to Bonar Law, 5/11/15, C096/561/894. And see Table 2, *Administrators on Duty*, in R. Heussler, *Yesterday's Rulers—The Making of the British Colonial Service*, (London, 1963), p. 13.

80. Crowther, *Report of Eastern Province 1914*, 10/6/15, *Supplementary 8*, *Gazette* 6/9/15, C099/29.

81. Acting Governor Slater, *LegCo* 25/10/15, *Gazette* 25/11/15, C099/29/10.

82. PC Western Province Maxwell, *Report on Western Province 1916*, *Supplementary 3*, *Gazette* 29/10/17,C099/32.

83. Calder, CO Minute, Clifford, confid. to Long, 8/1/18, C096/587.

ADCs were in charge of the whole of Central Province. Yet before the war, in 1913, the governor had made a strong case that the provinces were severely undermanned when Central Province had at that time an additional three DCs and another ADC.[84] By January 1918, Clifford was short of a third of his political staff, with only sixty-four officers available for the administration of the whole of the Colony, Ashanti, and the Northern Territories.[85] Fuller was concerned in January 1918 that there was no one to act as commissioner for Ashanti's southern province and declared he was "at his wits' end" to know whom to send to Obuasi.[86] Wraith gave Guggisberg the credit as the first governor of the Gold Coast to deal successfully with the "absurd" system of "general post" of officers constantly on the move.[87] Yet Clifford had raised the issue and obtained permission for extra staff in 1913–1914. Once war intervened, he could do nothing. In such conditions, widespread active African opposition to colonial rule would have had every chance of success.

The war brought worsening conditions of work for both British and African officials.[88] The British officials on the coast were to suffer from the effects of not only severe reductions in their numbers, but also losing their entitlement to leave and the value of their salaries. As elsewhere in British African territories, the war caused a substantial extra burden of work shared out among fewer British staff. For example, from the outbreak of war the printing department was open day and night to cope with the increase in government notices and Reuters telegrams.[89] By mid-1915, officers from the police department were being drafted in to help the "seriously understaffed" secretariat.[90] Like the survey department, the forestry department was effectively closed down for the duration of the war, with most of the personnel seconded to military service and the handful remaining dispersed to help other short-staffed departments. Before the war, in 1907, the Gold Coast survey department had been the largest in Africa, with forty Europeans and 700 Africans engaged in mapping and surveying. Closed in the war, it was not revived until 1921.[91] The customs department had to endure "the strain of an unprecedentedly busy year" in 1916, with nine of its European staff, or 35%, seconded on war service.[92] Staff shortages had become so acute by that year, 1916, that Clifford even suggested that wounded officers from the Western Front be used for "sedentary work" in the secretariat in Accra.[93] A letter was duly sent from the Colonial Office to the War Office, though the London official Flood queried whether any wounded men could be found who would be fit enough to make the long journey out to the tropical climate of West Africa, let alone work in it.[94] Not surprisingly, none was forthcoming.

---

84. *Report on Central Province 1917,* Clifford to Long, 13/6/18, C096/590/331.

85. Telegram, Clifford to Long, 24/1/18, C096/587.

86. Fuller, diary, 31/1/18, and 21/5/18, ADM12/5/160, PRAAD.

87. R. Wraith, *Guggisberg,* p. 218.

88. See E. Wrangham, "The Colonial Service and the First World War: Carrying On, the Service under Strain" in J. Smith (ed.*), Administering Empire. The British Colonial Service in Retrospect,* (London, 1999), pp. 167–181.

89. *Printing Department Report 1914, Supplementary 9, Gazette* 8/9/15, C099/29.

90. Telegram, Acting Governor Slater to Bonar Law, 27/6/15, C096/558.

91. Acting Governor Slater to Bonar Law, 25/6/15, C096/558/528. And L. Gann & P. Duignan, *The Rulers of British Africa,* p. 326.

92. *Customs Department Report 1916,* Acting Governor Slater to Long, 9/7/17, CO96/580/430.

93. Telegram, Clifford to Bonar Law, 21/10/16, C096/571.

94. Flood, CO Minute, Clifford to Bonar Law, 21/10/16, CO96/571.

Morale sagged among many of the British officials who remained in the colony during the war years. Although the journey home became increasingly dangerous as a result of the German U-boat campaign, most married officials, separated from their families by their conditions of service, chose to risk the voyage for as long as they were allowed to. Many who wanted to go back to England to join up and be part of what they saw as the heroic struggle were refused permission to leave and ordered to stay in post. Unable to make an immediate contribution to the world war, they stayed on, often depressed at feeling themselves to be in a tropical backwater. In some areas, as in the Northern Territories where the administration was drastically reduced, officials cracked under the strain. Even the dynamic governor himself showed signs of strain by 1916 with his unbalanced reaction to the disturbances in the north.

With the British so short-staffed, there was an opportunity during the war to appoint Africans to posts in the colonial administration previously reserved for Europeans. But there was strong reluctance among British officials to do so—in contrast with expatriate commercial companies in West Africa, where there tended to be a heavy reliance on African staff during the war.[95] The official grounds were that senior clerks (in the highest administrative post open to an African at this time) did not have the necessary qualities or experience. This was a circular argument, as few clerks had been given substantial responsibility. As Harper acknowledged, if a "native" was able to become a well-to-do barrister, doctor, or trader, it "ought to be possible" to train a "native" as a DC. Harper's admission was an indictment of the very limited role allowed Africans in the colonial administration: "The clerical service does not train or develop comparatively high qualities. It rather stifles them."[96] The application of S. H. Brew (African chief clerk in the medical department) for a political appointment class III was turned down in April 1916. In the Colonial Office, Ellis dismissed the idea of appointing "natives" to DC posts as simply "impracticable."[97] But he did not spell out his grounds, though there was likely to have been Colonial Office suspicion, underpinned by racial prejudice, concerning the loyalty and reliability of "natives" as well as concern at the lack of training. The official British line was that "natives" were not excluded from political service in the colony—since they could take part in local administration as chiefs and elders.

No satisfactory answer was given to the African unofficial, Thomas Hutton Mills, when he asked, in the legislative council in October 1918, why competent "native" officials had not been employed to fill vacancies in either the political service or the PWD.[98] Harper (acting colonial secretary in Accra) replied that it was the government's aim during the war simply to carry on the public service of the colony with a smaller staff "upon the most economic lines that are compatible with efficiency."[99] It is doubtful whether any of the African unofficials believed that economy and efficiency alone came into the calculation concerning the lack of Africanization in the Gold Coast.

Africans had not always been excluded. During the war, in mid-1917, an application for six months' leave in England, including full salary and free passages, was received

95. C. Newbury, "Trade and Technology in West Africa: The Case of the Niger Company 1900–1920," *JAH*, XIX, 4, 1978, pp. 573–574.

96. Acting Colonial Secretary Harper, Acting Governor Slater, confid. to Long, 11/4/17, CO96/579.

97. Ellis, CO Minute, Acting Governor Slater to Long, 11/4/17, CO96/579.

98. Hutton Mills, *LegCo* 29/10/18, *Gazette* 9/11/18, CO99/33/81.

99. Harper, *LegCo* 29/10/18, *Gazette* 9/11/18, CO99/33/81.

from a Mr. J. A. Williams (as recently from a Mr. A. W. Thompson), described as "native District Commissioners" who had served "in a post usually held by Europeans." Both from Accra, they were survivors from an earlier, more liberal, phase of British overrule, having been promoted from the clerical service and appointed DCs in their own right (Williams to Prampram and Thompson to Dixcove). They were two of the three African DCs who had been in post in 1899, before the British colonial administration, including the West African Medical Service, had become increasingly exclusive. They had then been placed under European officers in 1907 before the post of "native commissioner" had finally been abolished in 1910.[100]

Nor was Africanization pursued in the professions or other government services during the war. When African Junior Crown Counsel E. C. Quist resigned in May 1915, officials in the Colonial Office did not recommend his being replaced. "Native" barristers were said to be too much under local African influence to be able to represent the Crown adequately. Clifford believed the experiment had failed, not for lack of ability, but because Quist had feared for his life once his advocacy placed him in conflict with his own people.[101] The governor also added that private practice (as in medicine) was much better remunerated.[102]

There were also very many cases, such as in the Gold Coast railway department, where Africanization was made very difficult by the lack of training schemes instituted before the war. But prejudice also remained a common hindrance.[103] According to Gosling, the postmaster general, "natives" did not have the "stability of character" necessary for the job of district surveyor for the Post Office.[104] These attitudes must have seemed especially absurd to Africans who were aware of the career of men such as James Bannerman, lieutenant governor in 1850–1851, or G. Ekem Ferguson, the well-known surveyor of the late nineteenth century.[105] According to an ironic columnist in the *Gold Coast Leader* in February 1918, England's failure to train Africans was "hardly in accordance with even the ordinary rules of the cricket field."[106]

However, in line with his prewar policy, Clifford drew up a program for Africanization at the end of the war and gave an assurance that opportunities for Africans would be extended far further. He announced plans for opening up a new range of higher appointments to "native" staff in the near future, such as the posts of chief registrar in the supreme court, "native" assistants to DCs, and assistant transport officers and school inspectors.[107] Two appointments made by Clifford in 1919 before he left the colony (C. E. Woolhouse Bannerman as police magistrate and Dr. C. E. Reindorf as a temporary medical officer) were well received by the African press as a sign of things to come.[108] Slater continued to argue Clifford's case to London in the interregnum before Guggisberg's arrival as the new governor. Such appointments should be "the training ground for learning

100. *Regulations Affecting Pay, Conditions and Leave for Native Officials.* Clifford to Long, 17/1/17, CO96/580/450. And also see D. Kimble, *A Political History*, pp. 99–100, 106, and F. Agbodeka, *Ghana in the Twentieth Century*, p. 51.

101. Ribey, CO Minute, Clifford to Bonar Law, 15/5/15, CO96/558/410. Quist was to end his long career as first speaker of Ghana's National Assembly.

102. Clifford, confid. to Bonar Law, 13/7/16, CO96/567.

103. Casely Hayford, *LegCo* 17/5/17, *Gazette* 2/6/17, CO99/32/42.

104. Postmaster General Gosling, Clifford to Harcourt, 24/4/18, CO96/589/245.

105. See, e.g., D. Kimble, *A Political History*, pp. 65–66, 96–97.

106. "Africanus," *Gold Coast Leader*, 2/2/18.

107. *Report of Committee 1919: Condition of Service of Native Clerks, Sessional Papers*, CO98/31.

108. See D. Kimble, *A Political History*, p. 106.

the duties, and appreciating the responsibilities, of posts at present held exclusively by Europeans."[109] Recommendations of the committee under Harper in May 1915 to review conditions for "native" staff included the setting up of institutes in Accra, Sekondi, and Kumasi where clerks could read, be given lectures, and make informal contact with European officials—though Slater believed such contact was best fostered "through the medium of athletics."[110]

Meanwhile, it was now accepted that the wartime rise in the cost of living affected everyone in the colony. The attitude of British officials (and later African officials) became increasingly militant during the war as workloads rose and the value of salaries fell.[111] Early in the war, British officers began to call vociferously for adequate financial remuneration. In March 1915, Clifford expressed "great satisfaction" that he had obtained acknowledgement in the Colonial Office that British salaries were "undeniably poor."[112] The need for a revision of European salaries was therefore accepted in London well before the worst of the rise in the cost of living as a result of the war. But private firms achieved more. By 1916, most mercantile firms and the Bank of British West Africa were giving extra wartime pay to their employees, while the governor, backed by his senior officials, obtained agreement for only a small war bonus in 1916 for the "practically penniless" lowest-paid married British officers. By November 1916, he was warning London of the "very general" discontent throughout the public service as a result of "the great increase in the cost of living since the outbreak of the war."[113] But Clifford was informed by the Colonial Office that a review aligning all official salaries in British West Africa would have to await the end of hostilities.[114]

As Clifford recognized, the grievance was about more than money. British officers became trapped by wartime regulations: unable to resign, unable to join up if they wanted to, and even, finally, unable to go home on leave.[115] Unauthorized resignation would lead to loss of pension and debarment from government employment.[116] As for leave, Clifford pointed out that "The short tour of duty followed by the comparatively long period of leave has always been regarded as the most highly prized privilege and the principal attraction attaching to service in West Africa."[117] Leave was initially reduced during the war from five months to three months and the length of a tour extended from twelve to fifteen and then to eighteen months. During 1917, conditions worsened, with the journey home now extremely dangerous as a result of the German U-boat campaign. In February 1917, women were banned from traveling through the "danger zone," as were all officers

109. Acting Governor Slater, confid. to Milner, 14/8/19, *Sessional Paper l. Conditions of Service of Native Clerks*, CO98/31. Compare with J. Mangan, *The Games Ethic and Imperialism.*

110. *Ibid.*

111. For an earlier version of this, see E. Wrangham, "The Colonial Service and the First World War"; and compare with the colonial service elsewhere in British Africa, e.g., J. Overton, "War and Economic Development: Settlers in Kenya 1914–1918," *JAH*, 27, 1986, pp. 79–103.

112. Clifford to Harcourt, 2/12/14, CO96/550/911; Flood, CO Minute, Clifford to Harcourt, 2/12/14, CO96/550/911; Clifford to Harcourt, 20/3/15, C096/566/247; L. Gann & P. Duignan, *The Rulers of British Africa,* p. 217.

113. Clifford, confid. to Bonar Law, 8/11/16, C096/572. And see Section 2, Chapter 6. re. the rising cost of living.

114. Strachey (head of Nigeria Section) CO Minute, Long to Clifford, 20/2/17, CO96/572.

115. Calder, CO Minute re. telegram, Long to Clifford, 13/2/17; telegram, Long to Clifford, 21/10/17, C096/582.

116. Bonar Law, *Circular 16/7/15, Gazette* 21/8/15, C099/29/64.

117. Clifford to Long, 25/2/18, CO96/588/106.

except invalids by the end of 1917.[118] Women and children were advised to leave instead for the Cape or the United States, or to the relatively high altitude of Buea in British-occupied Cameroon.[119] But junior officers could afford neither leave (except in England) nor the cost of insuring their goods against loss if a ship was torpedoed.[120] London-based officials of the Colonial Office were distinctly unimaginative and unsympathetic. Ellis merely commented that most officers on the coast should be able to survive for as many as two years without any leave at all.[121]

The administration was also affected by the deterioration of working conditions for those who remained in post. In 1915, Slater praised their efforts, due to which "the machinery of government has continued to work smoothly without any perceptible creaking."[122] But the creaking did make itself heard and became louder as the war continued. One sign of strain was the increasing number of days lost as a result of sickness. The official invaliding rate, between 3 and 4% for 1915–1917, remained much the same, but according to Clifford, the unofficial rate was higher, at 5.7% in 1916, as a result of "severe strain" from working longer hours. The additional factor of an unusually wet season was blamed by the governor for the even higher number of working days lost in 1917. The European mortality rate rose from 9.4 per 1,000 in the 1914–1916 period to 11.4 in 1917 and then leaped to 30.7 in 1918 as a result of the influenza epidemic.[123]

As financial conditions worsened, the Colonial Office was forced to take more seriously the growing anger in the service. Clifford believed the "widespread feeling of discontent" justified. The effects of the war were "pressing very severely indeed" on the public officers of the colony. He now calculated that the "necessaries of life" cost at least 75% more than before the war.[124] As Slater argued, withholding a bonus from officials in West Africa, when there had been war grants to home civil servants, would be "indefensible."[125] Yet, although Clifford again argued the case for all European officers, a war bonus was offered from January 1918 only to officers with dependents earning less than £420 a year.[126] The concession did nothing to allay mounting discontent expressed in the sequence of petitions in 1918 that Clifford duly sent on to the Colonial Office. It was finally conceded in London that Sir Alexander Wood Renton, formerly chief justice in Ceylon, be sent out on a special commission to investigate demands of officials in both Nigeria and the Gold Coast.[127] But pressure continued with the announcement of the formation in September 1918 of an

---

118. Telegram, Long to Acting Governor Slater, 3/2/17, C096/578.

119. Ellis, CO Minute, telegram, Acting Governor Slater to Long, 15/3/17, CO96/578; also Acting Colonial Secretary Harper, *Notice* 8/4/17, *Gazette* 21/4/17, C099/32/29.

120. Telegram, Clifford to Long, 10/9/17, C096/582; Telegram, Long to Clifford, 24/12/17; Telegram, Clifford to Long, 30/12/17, C096/583; telegram, Clifford to Long, 23/1/18, C096/587; Clifford, confid. to Long, 23/1/18, CO96/587.

121. Ellis, CO Minute, telegram, Clifford to Long, 10/1/18, C096/587.

122. *Report of Select Committee re. Supply Bill 1916, LegCo* 30/10/15, Acting Governor Slater to Bonar Law, 5/11/15, C096/561/894.

123. *Medical & Sanitary Report 1916,* Clifford to Long, 15/5/17, C096/579/313; *Medical & Sanitary Report 1917,* Clifford to Long, 9/7/18, C096/591/393, see *Medical & Sanitary Report 1918,* C098/30.

124. Clifford to Long, 25/2/18, C096/588/106.

125. Dr. Rice, PMO, Acting Treasurer H. R. Lewis, Enclosure 2, Colonial Secretary Slater, in Clifford to Long, 25/2/18, CO96/588/106.

126. Clifford to Long, 25/2/18, CO96/588/106; Long to Clifford, 16/5/18, Clifford to Long, 25/2/18, C096/588/106.

127. Ellis, CO Minute, telegram, Clifford to Long, 12/8/18, C096/519.

association of all European government officials in British West Africa, which Clifford warned London was very widely supported.[128]

The increasing possibility of a strike by European officials on the West African coast led Ellis, in London, to put forward an unusual rationale for increasing African representation in the colony. He foresaw that it might be difficult to resist the demands of a British Officers' Association used "as a means of extorting higher pay and greater privileges from the government." This prompted him to put forward an interesting financial argument concerning not only trusteeship but the costs and benefits of African representation. Ellis argued that it was the duty of the Colonial Office to protect the general body of African taxpayers from British officials on the coast. The Colonial Office should act as "a sort of trustee" for the "native" taxpayer, who paid the officials' salaries but had no control over them. European officials overseas could not be allowed to form themselves into a "super legislature" through which they granted themselves their own salaries. In the last resort, Ellis suggested, this would have to be countered by granting the "natives" representative institutions, which would in their turn probably want to reduce European salaries.[129] The "colonial system," he admitted, remained "a bureaucracy uncontrolled by a popular legislature."[130] Ellis's novel rationale for African representative government was not discussed further at this time, and the British Officers' Association was simply ignored.[131]

However, two months later, just after the Armistice, with the prospect of higher pay for British officials, Ellis restated his interesting and unusual arguments for cheaper administration in the future: "I think if we are driven to large permanent increases of European salaries, as no doubt we shall be, we shall have to reduce their numbers. I begin to see what I never did before, some merit in the unofficial majorities such as you have in British Guiana and Barbados. They do make for economy in this matter."[132] This relaxed view towards the role of Western-educated Africans was new, but the primacy given to budgetary considerations was entirely typical. This argument, that savings could be made by employing fewer Europeans, with their salaries kept in check by unofficial African majorities, strongly reinforced the case (later reiterated by Guggisberg) in favor of Africanization.[133]

The British officers on the coast finally won their financial case, but only after a tedious and demoralizing struggle with the Colonial Office throughout the war period. The unexpected Armistice in November 1918 spurred Clifford to emphasize to London once more the urgent need for the long-delayed revision of officers' salaries—incorporating a war bonus.[134] The governor was effectively warning that the cooperation of the public service officials should not be taken for granted. Discontent and unrest were "highly infectious." He declared that he personally had "grave apprehensions" if there should be

---

128. Clifford, confid. to Long, 11/9/18, C096/592; Clifford to Long, 18/9/18, C096/592/546. See data re. low paid employees on railways and in post office. General Manager of Railways Bland, to Governor, 17/9/18, Clifford to Long, 10/10/1, C096/593/565. Senior Surveyor Western Postal District Young, 20/8/18, Enclosure 3, Clifford to Long, 18/9/18, C096/592/546.

129. Ellis, CO Minute, Clifford, confid. to Long, 11/9/18, C096/592.

130. A. B. Holmes, "Economic and Political Organizations in the Gold Coast 1920–1945," unpublished PhD thesis, (University of Chicago, 1972), p. 397.

131. Strachey, CO Minute, Clifford, confid. to Long, 11/9/18, CO96/592.

132. Ellis, CO Minute, Clifford, confid. to Long, 25/11/18, CO96/593.

133. See F. Agbodeka, "Sir Gordon Guggisberg's Contribution to the Development of the Gold Coast 1919–1927," *Transactions of the Historical Society of Ghana*, XIII, l, 1972.

134. Telegram, Clifford to Long, 15/11/18, C096/593.

"renewed postponements and disappointments.[135] By late December 1918, the heat had at last been taken out of the war bonus issue. Following an investigation into the cost of living in both Nigeria and the Gold Coast, Sir Alexander Wood Renton's recommendations had, according to Colonial Officials, "forced" them to grant a bonus, retrospectively from January 1, 1917, to all European officers in the West African Service. Leave arrangements returned to normal.[136] During the war itself, Clifford, caught as ever between British officials in London and the interests of British and African officials on the coast, had been unable to give much support to his government officers.

Strains in the service during the war affected British officers' relations with their African subjects. Considering themselves overworked and undervalued, many were less inclined to make contact with the local African population. In their segregated housing, life for many British officers continued in relative isolation. An editorial in the *Gold Coast Leader* complained in 1915: "They live in a ring fence. From the office to the club, with tennis or dinners thrown in, what time or inclination have they for familiarizing themselves with the peoples' point of view or studying their requirements?"[137] Resentment was also expressed that same year in *The Gold Coast Nation* at "the fat salaries and privileges of European civil servants" with their paid passages, pensions, and "expensive and luxuriously furnished residential bungalows."[138]

By 1918, African officials of the Native Subordinate and Clerical Service were vigorously promoting their own claims alongside those of British officers. African clerks reacted to the British officials' salary and war bonus campaign by using similar tactics to set out their own demands. In January 1918, a petition from African officials for a monthly war bonus, citing "the enormously increased cost of living occasioned by the war," was submitted alongside the petition from European officials. Although Clifford supported the application of the African officials, he believed that they did not need the same degree of help as European officers since they were not, in his view, so dependent on imported goods.[139] This was a dubious argument. As Colonial Office officials recognized, both the West Indian staff and "educated natives" were dependent on imported foodstuffs.[140] By February 1918, the governor did acknowledge at last that the "notorious" rise in the cost of locally produced food "hits this class of public servant very hard."[141]

Clifford and his advisors in the colony were now unanimous that the claim of "native officers" could not with justice be put aside if the European officers' claim was to be considered. But there were also crucial practical issues at stake. "Native officers" were Africans who played a vital role at the heart of the colonial administration. Their support and loyalty were essential. Slater's wry comment that "no doubt the average young clerk could economize to a certain extent in the way of clothes" did not deter the coast

135. Clifford, confid. to Long, 25/11/18, CO96/593.

136. The bonus granted from 1 January 1917 was on a scale of between £120 on incomes of up to £500 per annum and £60 on incomes over £700 per annum. Flood, CO Minute, Clifford, confid. to Long, 25/11/18, CO96/593; Harding, CO Minute, telegram, Clifford to Long, 27/12/18, C096/594. See Ellis, Harding, Read, CO Minute, telegram, Clifford to Long, 15/11/18, CO96/593; and telegram, Long to Clifford, 19/11/18, C096/593; Clifford, confid. to Long, 25/11/18, C096/593.

137. Editorial, *Gold Coast Leader* 5/6/15.

138. *The Gold Coast Nation*, 18/11/15.

139. *Petition of Native Subordinate and Clerical Services Staff of the Gold Coast*, 28/1/18, Clifford to Long, 25/2/18, CO96/588/106.

140. Calder, CO Minute, Clifford to Long, 10/12/17, CO96/583/771.

141. Clifford to Long, 25/2/18, CO96/588/106.

government's recommendation of an increase of 5%, with a minimum increase of 3d a day, to all "native" employees and West Indians in government service. This was granted in May 1918.[142]

However, as economic conditions deteriorated during 1918, the benefit of this award was eroded, and the attitude of African officials became more threatening. War conditions encouraged them to organize and to press their case. In September 1918, the governor received a further petition from African officials for an increase of 20% on the war bonus already granted, with a reminder to the government that many firms in West Africa had raised such bonuses to cover the increased cost of living and high rents. As a result, Clifford recommended that the war bonus for "native" employees be included in Sir Alexander Wood Renton's enquiries.[143] An award was finally granted in February 1919, backdated to January 1917, to continue for six months after the war. But this consisted of only half what had been asked for. The rates granted—a bonus of 10% on salaries or a minimum increase of 6d a day—were considered unacceptably little by African officials.[144] Their new petition stated firmly that these salaries were wholly inadequate and should be raised: from a probationer's salary of £48 to a ceiling of £400, as opposed to £300. There should also be a widows and orphans pension fund similar to the one recently introduced for Europeans, as well as advances on houses.[145]

There was a new determination and boldness about these demands from the African officials compared with those presented before the war, as well as a more obvious comparison with conditions enjoyed by European officials. The African unofficials had refused to support salary increases for European officers in 1916.[146] The petition of the African officials in 1919 concluded ominously: they hoped the Secretary of State would give their appeal due consideration in order to spare them "the necessity for taking action which would tend to clog the wheels of the administrative machinery."[147] This appeared to be threatening to strike. The local African press detected "a strike atmosphere in the air." In the light of the recent railway strikes, an editorial in *The Gold Coast Independent*, with some sarcasm, expressed the hope that going on strike would not become as catching as the influenza epidemic.[148]

British officials in London and on the coast had underrated the strength of feeling among African government staff in the colony. The drop in living standards as a result of the war was clearly regarded as intolerable as soon as the war was over. But Colonial Office officials were concerned to not give in to employees' threats. The solution to saving the government's face was the requirement that African officials make a proper case before it could be given due consideration.[149] Clifford was surprised by the strength of

---

142. Colonial Secretary Slater, Enclosure 6, memos, *Members of the Executive Council of the Gold Coast* re. *Petition of Native Officials*, Clifford to Long, 25/2/18; also Long to Clifford, 16/5/18, CO96/588/106.

143. *Further Petition of Native Subordinate and Clerical Services Staff*, 18/9/18, Clifford to Long, 18/9/18, CO96/592/546.

144. Police constables and wardens were given the lower rate of 7d and a halfpenny, and 4d and a halfpenny a day. Colonial Secretary Slater, *LegCo* 19/2/19, Gazette 8/3/19, CO99/34/25.

145. *Ibid.*

146. D. Kimble, *A Political History*, p. 102.

147. *Petition of Native Officials, Accra*, Enclosure 1, 2/1/19, CO98/31.

148. Telegram, Clifford to Milner, 10/2/19, CO96/597. Editorial, *The Gold Coast Independent*, 30/11/18.

149. Flood, Fiddes, CO Minute, Clifford to Milner, 10/2/19, CO96/597.

feeling expressed by African government staff, a disappointing intrusion on his last month as governor. It was easiest to claim that responsibility lay outside the colony. In exaggerated terms, Clifford claimed that this was a "mutiny," possibly influenced by "bolshevism."[150] There was also the embarrassment of the complaints now put forward by African clerks against the Gold Coast's colonial secretary, Slater, who was accused of hostility to African staff and of not supporting their claim to an enhanced war bonus. Neither the governor nor the Colonial Office took the charges against Slater seriously, as he had always vigorously supported Clifford's paternalistic policies. African officials apparently found Slater's constant comparison of the Gold Coast with Ceylon, to the detriment of the Gold Coast, even more irritating than did officials in London. He also had a reputation for being "reserved" and "cold."[151] The attitudes and actions of both British and African officials reflected the tension arising from the worsening economic situation as a result of the war.

African officials were astute in obtaining higher remuneration in the war period by deliberately using the same tactics and many of the same arguments as British officials. By the end of February 1919, there was serious concern in the colonial government that a strike by "natives" might be imminent. Their demands were supported, according to signatures given to the governor, by nearly every clerk in Accra, as well as by the African unofficials in the legislative council and by the local African press.[152] The governor was sufficiently anxious to warn the population that a strike would bring wholesale dismissal, and to order heads of department to stop signing salary increment certificates. He was nevertheless optimistic that Sir Alexander Wood Renton's final recommendations would go beyond the terms of the earlier settlement, and the whole issue would fade away.[153] Clifford's prediction proved correct. A new increased war bonus was granted for the staff of the Native Subordinate and Clerical Service in March 1919. There was to be a 20% increase for those earning not more than £152 a year, 15% for those earning up to £210, and 12.5% for those earning over £210.[154] It was also announced that new government quarters were to be made available for a relatively small rent and that a commission was planned to investigate conditions of service for "native" officials.[155] The agitation died down.

Meanwhile, it was Clifford's belief that the legislative council should also be a focus of political reform. African unofficials, rather than either the colonial administrative service of African officials or the town councils, would, he believed, play the most important educative role in this developing colonial relationship. There was "agitation" for elections among "a few members of the educated community."[156] There were also, as before the war, frequent demands for democratic government and "national suffrage" in the local African press.[157] From Clifford's paternalistic viewpoint, the vast majority of the population had not yet reached sufficient "intellectual development" for the franchise that he believed,

150. Telegram, Clifford to Milner, 11/2/19, CO96/2/19, CO96/597.

151. Telegrams, Clifford to Milner, 18/2/19, 22/2/19, CO96/597; *Petition of Native Clerical Staff,* 18/2/19. Clifford, confid. to Milner, 22/2/19, CO96/597.

152. Telegram, Clifford to Milner, 22/2/19, CO96/597; Flood, CO Minute, Clifford to Milner, 22/2/19, CO96/597. And *Gold Coast Leader,* 29/3–5/4/19, NP 12/9, PRAAD.

153. Clifford, telegram, and confid. to Milner, 23/2/19, CO96/597.

154. Acting Governor Slater, confid. to Milner, 14/8/19, *Sessional Paper 1: Conditions of Service of Native Clerks,* CO98/31.

155. Colonial Secretary Slater, *LegCo* 19/2/19, *Gazette* 8/3/19, CO99/34/25.

156. See discussion in D. Kimble, *A Political History,* pp. 433–435.

157. E. g., editorials, *Gold Coast Leader,* 9/1/15, 10/6/16, 25/11/16; *The Gold Coast Nation,* 2/12/15; "Africanus," *Gold Coast Leader,* 2/2/18.

if granted, might well arouse "racial and tribal animosities."[158] The governor argued that the African population already had local representation through their chiefs and elders. Clifford's views on this remained broadly unchanged throughout his career. His thinking in Trinidad in 1903 and in Ceylon in 1907 closely resembled views expressed in the paper he read to the West African Section of the British Empire Exhibition in Lagos in 1924. In the Gold Coast, he impressed on the members of the legislative council that there could be no institutionalized official opposition in a Crown Colony. In his view, officials and unofficials (all nominated rather than elected) together formed a single corporate body, all of whose members should work together for the prosperity of the Gold Coast colony.[159]

As early as 1915 and despite the disruption of the war, Clifford persistently argued the case to London for a larger and more representative legislative council. It would, he believed, encourage "an intelligent interest" in public affairs and administration, enable information to be passed down through official channels rather than be spread by "false rumours," and give the officials a better insight into "the native point of view."[160] Clifford proposed adding the district manager of the Bank of West Africa to the European unofficials who represented the trading and mining companies and extending African representation of the regions, as there were only two African unofficials at the time (Konor Mate Kole and the lawyer Thomas Hutton Mills), both from Eastern Province. Clifford planned to retain a mixture of paramounts and Western-educated representatives, even though he was prejudiced in favor of chiefs, who he felt "far more accurately represented native public opinion and native aspirations."[161] "Educated natives" should have a place but were only entitled to speak for their own "separate and distinct community." Clifford hoped to be given permission to increase the number of officials from four to ten and the number of unofficials from four to nine, thus retaining an official majority with an overall total of twenty, including the governor.[162] Though this plan was somewhat vague as to who could speak for whom, this was part of Clifford's concept of "partnership with responsible Africans."[163]

In the absence of any definite imperial policy on legislatures before and during the war, the Colonial Office was happy to allow the governor a larger number of appointed African representatives, as the Gold Coast was judged ready for some constitutional development. Such an enlargement of the legislative council was not without precedent in British West Africa. Nigeria had had a twenty-man legislature with six nominated Africans since 1914.[164] The war played its part in making possible this modest concession by London officials. The people of the Gold Coast were thought to have shown themselves to be "intensely loyal" as well as "progressive in economic matters," and with more elementary education than in any other West African colony.[165] There was caution, however, as to what could safely be achieved in wartime without creating an "unsettling effect." As Sir

158. Clifford, confid. to Harcourt, 15/4/15, C096/557. See H. Gailey, *Clifford,* pp. 49–53, 63–64; and J. A. Langley, *Pan Africanism and Nationalism in West Africa 1900–1945,* (London, 1973), p. 131.

159. Clifford, confid to Harcourt, 17/3/15, C096/556; Clifford, *LegCo* 25/9/16, quoted in M. Wight, *The Gold Coast Legislative Council,* (London, 1964), p. 77.

160. Clifford, confid. to Harcourt, 10/4/15 and 15/4/15, C096/577; and to Bonar Law, 25/11/15, C096/561.

161. Clifford to Harcourt, 15/4/15, CO96/577.

162. *Ibid.*

163. H. Gailey, *Clifford,* p. 136.

164. L. Gann & P. Duignan, *The Rulers of British Africa,* p. 165.

165. Green, CO Minute, Clifford to Harcourt, 15/4/15, CO96/577.

John Anderson advised cynically in 1915: "If the Governor wants a big Council to harangue I should let him have it."[166] Permission was finally granted for increasing the number of European unofficials by one (to a total of three) and the number of African unofficials by four (to a total of six).[167] The governor was well satisfied, believing that this was "the most far reaching reform which has been instituted in the colony for many years."[168]

It was certainly true that Clifford's modest reform transformed the legislative council into a much more lively forum from September 1916. The three chiefs' representatives, Nana Ofori Atta, the most prominent Western-educated chief in Eastern Province; the *omanhene* of Anamabu, an educated Fanti; and the *awuna* of Ga, a literate Ewe, gave chiefs a much more substantial representation. This prompted *The Gold Coast Nation* to question whether this was an "innovation," reminding its readers that the Fanti Confederation, drafted as long ago as 1871, had had elected representatives.[169] There were also now three leading Western-educated Africans from the coastal community: the lawyer Thomas Hutton Mills, to represent the Western-educated community of Accra; E. J. P. Brown, the Cape Coast barrister, secretary of the ARPS and close associate of *The Gold Coast Nation;* and J. Casely Hayford, a lawyer with chambers in Sekondi, to represent the interests of the Western Province, as there was no Western-educated paramount chief in that region.[170] An earlier government list had contrasted the figures of one literate chief (the omanhene of Bensu) out of a total of forty-seven chiefs in Western Province, with sixteen literates out of forty-two in Eastern Province, and seven out of thirty in Central Province.[171]

There was some surprise among Colonial Office officials at the inclusion of E. J. P. Brown and Casely Hayford, both of whom had been on the land deputation in 1911 and, it was thought, could give the local British government "great trouble."[172] Clifford, more shrewd than some officials in London, argued that exclusion would only encourage ARPS pretensions as an "extra-constitutional body seeking to act as the accredited spokesman of the chiefs and tribes of the colony."[173] Similarly, the governor believed it preferable if Casely Hayford (recognized as "somewhat given to fomenting agitation") laid his charges against the government from within the legislative council rather than from without. The war had made an impact here too. Clifford had noted Casely Hayford's efforts in organizing the collection of subscriptions for war expenses. As a result, the governor appears to have been reassured that criticisms of government were not necessarily a sign of "disloyalty."[174]

This change in the constitution, the enlargement of the legislative council, was judged by Clifford before he left the coast to be "the most important reform" of his period in office in the colony.[175] It was not the case, as Sampson suggested, that "it became necessary" for Clifford to reconstitute the legislative council.[176] The reform occurred because Clifford

166. Ellis, Sir John Anderson CO Minute, Clifford, confid. to Harcourt, 15/4/15, CO96/557.
167. Hood, CO Minute, Clifford, confid. to Bonar Law, 25/11/15, 0096/561.
168. Clifford, confid to Bonar Law, 19/1/16, C096/567.
169. *The Gold Coast Nation,* 21/7/17.
170. Clifford, confid. to Bonar Law, 17/6/16, C096/567.
171. Minute, 4/4/14, Secretary of Native Affairs to PC of Central Province, ADM 11/1/498, PRAAD.
172. Flood, Ellis, CO Minute, Clifford, confid. to Bonar Law, 17/6/16, CO96/567.
173. Clifford, confid. to Bonar Law, 17/6/16, CO96/567.
174. *Ibid.*
175. Clifford, *LegCo* 28/10/18, *Gazette* 9/11/18, C099/34/82.
176. Secretary of the Joint Council of Chiefs M. Sampson, quoted in D. Apter, *Ghana in Transition,* (Princeton, 1972), p. 138.

judged it both advisable and desirable. It had been very much his own initiative, acceded to by London officials, even though "almost too much for a hesitant Secretary of State."[177]

The success of initiating this change was all the more important to a governor frustrated with so many of his plans blocked by the war. This initiative to strengthen the African voice encouraged growing African demands at the end of the war. These included ever-stronger calls in the African press for elective representation, ARPS demands for its voice to be heard, and the plans of individuals such as Casely Hayford for a West African conference. This was to bring together Western-educated representatives from all four British West African colonies, to establish a constitutional, as well as a development and welfare, program.[178] Clifford contributed, if indirectly, to this later British acceptance of the elective principle, introduced into British West Africa in the mid-1920s and itself a milestone in terms of managing constitutional opposition in the colonies.

The African newspaper response to Clifford's political reform was finely balanced. There was cautious praise for a governor who followed "a policy of trust" towards an ultimate "actual control of affairs" by Africans—even if this was seen as only "a small step," given that the enlarged legislative council remained only an advisory body.[179] Clifford's perspective was different. For him the enlarged council was sufficient at this time. It fitted his vision of the colonial relationship: his aim of governing the colony in closer coordination with those whom he judged to be the leading representatives of the local population—both African traditional authorities and a very limited number of African officials and African unofficials. Guggisberg was to follow Clifford's precedent of not pressing legislation if there were strong unofficial opposition, unless forced to do so by London.[180]

As before the war, Clifford did not believe that the African press represented the views of leaders of the local community. He dismissed the newspapers as "few in number, of a very poor description" and "often deplorably inaccurate," and the proportion of "natives" reading them as very small.[181] Clifford's sweeping dismissal appears to reflect the fact that the Gold Coast government could not influence the press as it might have wished. Yet the tenor of the African newspaper comment in the colony was for the most part remarkably restrained in this period, including the frequent criticism that there was only nominated rather than elected African representation on the legislative council. The press in Nigeria, although similar in calling for elections and Africanization, was markedly more hostile and critical of Lugard's administration.[182] The *Gold Coast Leader* expressed no sorrow at the news of Lugard's resignation as Governor of Nigeria in February 1919, but it did suggest that Lord Milner, now secretary of state for the colonies, change the basis of the colonial administration and create a united British West Africa. Who better, it asked, than Sir Hugh Clifford to be given the post of Governor-General—"since he commands the confidence of entire West Africa"?[183]

---

177. G. Metcalfe, *Great Britain and Ghana, Documents of Ghana History 1807–1957,* p. 549.

178. For discussion of the postwar conference meeting in 1920 in Accra and the formation of the NCBWA, see D. Kimble, *A Political History,* pp. 435–441.

179. Editorials, *The Gold Coast Nation,* 6/5/15; *Gold Coast Leader,* 14/10/16, 4/11/16, 25/11/16.

180. See R. Stone, "Colonial Administration and Rural Politics," p. 87, and D. Kimble, *A Political History*, pp. 435–436.

181. Clifford, confid. to Bonar Law, 25/11/15, CO96/561.

182. F. Omu, *Press and Politics in Nigeria 1880–1937,* (London, 1971), pp. 212–214; and see A. Osuntokun, *Nigeria in the First World War,* pp. 79–88, 92–93; and D. Kimble, A *Political History,* p. 435.

183. *Gold Coast Leader,* 9/2/19.

Much of the African press critique of Crown Colony government in the Gold Coast concentrated on calling for an end to the exclusion of Africans from administrative and professional appointments. The call for acceptance of the elective principle in the colonies was often linked to the well-known demand of the American War of Independence: "no taxation without representation."[184] Given Christian teaching concerning the equality of man, the *Gold Coast Leader* inquired as to what was to be the place of the "negro" after the war.[185] There was hope among Western-educated West Africans that the Gold Coast and the other British West African colonies would, at some time in the not too distant future, attain "wealth, dignity and political freedom" within the British Empire.[186] Clearly, restraint was partly a conscious ploy. It was believed that "loyalty" and a "responsible attitude" during Britain's war were likely to bring British acknowledgement of such rights and an improved status for Africans after the war was over.[187]

As the war progressed, there was increased reference in the local African press to important international events. The reading public could follow reports about, for example, the Indian Congress party seeking autonomy within the Empire and being on the road to self-government following the 1917 Montague Declaration. This included such phrases as "the gradual development of self governing institutions with a view to the progressive realization of responsible government in India as an integral part of the British Empire." There was also awareness of the 1917 revolution in Russia, where "the people are at last to have a voice," as well as of politics within Britain, where the Labour Party manifesto advocated self-determination for British subjects.[188]

Clifford's approach to government in the Gold Coast does not provide evidence of any conscious Machiavellian British purpose of "divide and rule." Neither chiefs nor Western-educated Africans were seen as a threat to be met by playing off the one group against the other. Chiefs remained overwhelmingly dependable, while the increase in the number of Africans in the legislative council was a genuine initiative of Clifford's. But the governor showed some shrewdness in having Casely Hayford voicing his criticisms of, say, government financial matters inside the council rather than outside it. There were chiefs too among the new men in the council—suggesting that Clifford wanted advice from prominent and influential Africans of a range of backgrounds in the one arena. He strongly supported African access to the professions and to training and education on a wide front in his program for the development of the colony. But there was little long-term calculation here—the pressures on Clifford to adapt policy arose from the exigencies of war rather than from new demands of his African subjects—and, as before the war, there were anomalies. His rejection of much educated African opinion in the press (reflecting his dislike of criticism of Crown Colony government) does not neatly square with his advocacy of Africanization.

184. For example, *The Gold Coast Nation*, 9/1/15, 27/3/15, 10/6716, 2/9/16, 2/2/18. *Gold Coast Leader*, 8/4/15, 6/5/15, 20/7/16, 28/12/16, 24/11/17.

185. *Gold Coast Leader*, 27/7/18.

186. Editorial, *Gold Coast Leader*, 21/11/14.

187. Editorial, *The Gold Coast Nation*, 11/3/15.

188. See, e.g., *Gold Coast Leader*, 24/4/15, 5/1/18, 19/5/17, 21/9/18, 28/12/18; *The Gold Coast Independent*, 17/8/18; and *African World*, 19/10/18, and *The Montague Declaration* quoted in D. K. Fieldhouse, *The Colonial Empires. A Comparative Survey from the 18th Century*, (London, 1982), p. 285.

At the strategic level of colonial government, the governor was not alone among his contemporaries in having no clear vision of how to reconcile two different administrative approaches. On the one hand there was the policy from 1916 of including more Western-educated Africans (who did not represent "traditional" African authority) into advising central government as members of the legislative council (even though this had the effect of encouraging their hopes for a wider political responsibility). On the other hand, in local government the governor gave priority to increasing the powers of the traditional native authorities of chiefs and elders, within the practice of indirect rule. The immediate priority, however, was financial rather than political. With members of the Western-educated African elite continuing to argue for reform rather than revolution, Clifford and his government could afford to concentrate less on issues of control and more on restoring the health of the economy and finances as soon as possible, once the war had ended.

Even so, as we have seen, British colonial rule during the war had been even more dependent than before on the support of "native" authorities. Clifford's view, typical of British colonial officers in this period, was that the "real" leaders of African communities were the chiefs. From the time of his arrival in the colony, Clifford had been especially concerned to improve the government's relations with the chiefs and elders in the Gold Coast. As a pragmatic administrator, he was well aware that government priorities were above all to maintain law and order and the revenue. But officials' understanding of what they called "traditional" African society remained limited. Clifford's plans to stabilize "native" administration by reforming the Native Tribunals Ordinance and giving greater powers to head chiefs were, to his surprise, finally rejected by the "traditional" elite of chiefs and elders—as well as by the Westernized African elite. Only the policy of protecting African land rights won popular support.

Clifford and Slater had supervised a paper-thin British supervision during the war years. At this time, as before, they governed Africans who may be said to have wanted *less* government, in terms of less taxation and less interference in trade, land, and "native administration," yet also wanted *more* (if different) government regarding law and order, development, and welfare projects, and effective administration of towns. In this unfavorable wartime context, the governor and his colleagues relied heavily on the "loyal" support of the "native" administration. Clifford had tried to divert the mounting frustration in the colonial service among both British and African officials by his promises of improved pay in the near future and by arguing their case strongly with London. He had put Africanization firmly on the agenda even though relatively little was achieved during the war. He had also sought to extend government consultation with Africans. This had been more successful in central government, with the increase in the number of African unofficials in the enlarged legislative council, than in the differing forms of local government. His hopes of reforming municipal administration, for example, were frustrated by the war. Nevertheless, the general principle of increased consultation (seeking to improve the government's relationship with its subjects) had won acceptance in the Colonial Office—as well as raising expectations for future reforms in colonial rule in the near future.

Section III

Postwar

Chapter 10

After the War: Conclusions

The impact of the war continued to be felt in the colony long after the cease-fire of November 1918. In the trading boom of 1919 and 1920, the release of shipping after the Armistice "created feverish activity in the trade of the colony and revived hopes for the future that a few months before had seemed depressingly remote."[1] But after the boom came the sudden slump of 1921. It was well into the 1920s before the end of the dramatic fluctuations in supply and demand that the war had initiated, and before economic conditions seemed to settle into anything like a predictable pattern. However, appearances were deceptive. No simple return to prewar conditions was possible. The war had brought significant changes. For Africans in the colonial economy, for example, trading conditions remained less favorable, and the cost of living continued to be substantially higher, than before the war. The war had interrupted British plans for development. Improved public services and welfare reforms were postponed. African protests, some through newly formed unions, became more widespread. There was a new intensity in African expectations and demands.

In relation to the main export crop of the Gold Coast, cocoa, the British government backtracked, adopting a "hands-off" approach in the light of African realities—while the very much more favorable conditions during the boom of 1919 made wartime plans for government interference seem inappropriate. For example, a committee set up in 1919 (on Clifford's advice before he left for his new post as governor in Nigeria) to consider Tudhope's wartime recommendations to enforce good cocoa husbandry had come to the conclusion that the plans were unworkable. Without the cooperation of the chiefs, there could be no effective colonial administration, let alone enforceable legislation. The committee took the easy way out. Chiefs were now merely "instructed to do what they could" to protect forests, prevent cocoa farmers from extending their farms beyond what they could easily tend, and regulate the quality of beans put up for sale by using bylaws under the Native Jurisdiction Ordinance. It was also hoped that they would recommend the use of recognized markets and weighing scales.[2] But the idea of compulsory licenses for buyers would, it was now thought, run counter to free trade and be impossible to administer.

Nor was inspection at the port of shipment (with eleven ports in all) considered practicable, partly because of the difficulty at this time of obtaining "suitable and reliable inspectors."[3] The committee recommended that manufacturers in Great Britain be contacted to find out what quality of cocoa they desired and whether they would be prepared to include the cost of such inspection. In fact, inspection was too labor-intensive—though sampling would perhaps have been practicable.[4] Only one of Tudhope's proposals was

1. *Trade Report 1918*, CO98/30.
2. *Report of the Committee Concerning the Cocoa Industry of the Gold Coast*, 30/10/19, CO98/31.
3. *Ibid.*
4. R. Southall, "Cadbury on the Gold Coast," p. 61.

therefore at first officially accepted after the end of the war: that farmers should be liable to be taken before a DC court and fined if they failed to take "elementary" precautions against disease and pests. But even this suggestion was put aside by the new postwar governor, Guggisberg, in his concern to maintain good relations with Gold Coast farmers. He sought to reassure them that rumors of government plans to limit cocoa production were false.[5] With no sure method of increasing yields per acre, any report that the British colonial government was considering restrictions on extending planting was bound to be met with alarm. Guggisberg was also careful to restate the government's firm commitment to a policy of preserving the land for the people and supporting the administration of chiefs and their councilors.

Overall, many features of the Gold Coast cocoa trade remained as before the war—as did British officials' concerns about cocoa's vulnerability to disease. Whether there was widespread long-term damage to the cocoa crop as a result of wartime neglect remains difficult to estimate. Certainly British officers were unable to institute the precautions they believed necessary to protect cacao trees against the spread of disease or to protect the beans against decay from poor fermentation practices. The official contemporary view was that the "natural remedy" for diseased farms was for African farmers to leave them alone to recover for a year or two.[6] This, however, normally produced a lower yield. Whether recovery was guaranteed or whether disease would one day spread unchecked across the whole colony was not known.[7] Capsids were already identified as a serious threat in this period and not, as Green and Hymer suggest, only in the mid-1920s. They also, surprisingly, omit fungoid diseases altogether from their "serious" category of cacao diseases.[8] The effect of a new disease attacking the whole tree rather than just the fruit, observed in Eastern Province in the early 1920s, appears to be the first recorded instance of the swollen shoot virus. Leaving farms fallow did not prevent the spread of swollen shoot in the decades that followed. The first agricultural research station opened only much later, in 1936, but it is a mistake to claim that no research took place before this. Keeping records and collecting data by British officials, before and during the period of the First World War, was to provide "a vital research service" for government officers after the Second World War.[9]

Another prewar feature, linked to fears for the health of the cacao trees and the colony's export trade in the long term, was the continuing government attempt to persuade local cocoa farmers to diversify. British government officials were never able to persuade the majority of cash crop farmers to reduce the colony's dependence on a single cash crop. Despite the considerable upheavals of the war period, cocoa became even more predominant. Other vegetable exports, such as palm products, were not maintained at their higher wartime level once cocoa prices stabilized after the war. Output and value of both palm oil and palm kernels rose in the boom of 1919, only to fall heavily in the slump of 1921 and to settle back to a low level of relative insignificance by 1923. In 1918, Clifford had noted the extraordinary overall rate of decline in the twenty-seven years since 1891,

---

5. Guggisberg, *Governor's Annual Address, LegCo* 1923–4, in G. B. Kay, *Political Economy*, p. 240.

6. Clifford, quoted by Colonial Secretary Slater, to *LegCo* 23/10/16, *Sessional Papers on the Gold Coast Cocoa Industry*, CO98/27.

7. E.g., R. Green & S. Hymer, "Cocoa in the Gold Coast," p. 309. Also see the serious threat to cacao cultivation from pests and pathogens in Ghana in the 1990s in F. Danquah, "The Capsid, Black Pod, and Swollen Shoot Cacao Diseases," pp. 1–2.

8. R. Green & S. Hymer, "Cocoa in the Gold Coast," p. 309.

9. F. Danquah, "Capsid, Black Pod and Swollen Shoot Cacao Diseases," pp. 283–287.

with exports of palm oil down nearly four million gallons and exports of palm kernels more than halved.[10] The reasons for the postwar decline were the same as for the prewar period: cocoa was easier to manage and, above all, made more profit for the producer. There was also growing world competition from palm oil plantations in the Dutch East Indies, Malaya, and the Belgian Congo, which affected West African production.[11]

There was also continuity in the pattern of exports, with minerals remaining second in value to cocoa both during and immediately after the war. However, trade patterns remained unpredictable. The decline in gold was somewhat compensated for by the rise in manganese, but the relative value of cocoa greatly increased. Cocoa exports were worth over £300,000 more than mineral exports in 1918, and by 1923 had risen to well over £4m more. The trend towards ever greater dependence of the colony's economy on cocoa continued at this time, with the government able to do little more than record the statistics. Only in the 1930s, with the effects of the Depression and Britain's leaving the gold standard, did the mining sector of the economy more than recover its position. In 1929 cocoa accounted for 79% of all exports, but this fell to 56% in 1935. By 1938 the value of gold exports once more exceeded cocoa.[12]

There were marked changes, too, arising from the disruption caused by the war. One very important discontinuity was that the previous uninterrupted rise in profits for the major export, cocoa, was not replicated in the postwar period. Sharp fluctuations in demand and price continued into the 1920s. Initially, to the great relief of all concerned—both African farmers and British officials—cocoa exports picked up very rapidly once the war ended. From their lowest point in 1918, they reached record levels in quantity and price in the postwar boom of 1919. The local price, as low as 2s a sixty lb. load shot up to 10s immediately after the Armistice, to reach 40s by December 1919.[13] Cocoa enjoyed a remarkably quick recovery as traders competed to ship and sell the huge stocks that had accumulated during the war. "The new office blocks and automobiles, the din of busy lorries, the aroma of cigars smoked by African and European alike, were manifest in Accra and other centres. A permanent spring was in the air. Germany was to be made to pay, and so apparently were the customers."[14] The price per ton in Liverpool, £34 at the end of the war, rose to £82 in June 1919, reaching £122 in February 1920, but then collapsed in the postwar slump to £39 by December 1920.[15] Cocoa proved vulnerable in international markets—as was seen again very soon, at the end of the 1920s, with the onset of the Depression. Apart from these extreme fluctuations, another change as a result of the war was that the balance of controlling interests in the trade shifted. In contrast with 1913, it was the United States rather than Germany that by 1922 accounted for nearly half the Gold Coast's trade with foreign countries, while New York replaced Hamburg as the center of the world cocoa trade.[16]

The severe fluctuations in the price of cocoa in the war period brought damaging long-term effects for many African farmers. For example, it appears that much of the indebtedness

10. Clifford to Long, re. 1918 Estimates, 10/12/17, CO96//583/767.
11. *The Gold Coast Independent*, 13/7/18. For the similar postwar decline in Nigeria, see D. Meredith, "Government and the Decline of the Nigerian Oil Palm Export Industry 1919–1939," *JAH*, 25, 3, 1984.
12. Lord Hailey, *An African Survey*, p. 327.
13. *Report on Blue Book 1919*, CO98/32.
14. N. Edwards, *Cadbury on the Gold Coast*, p. 20.
15. *Blue Book 1923*, CO100/73. See N. Cox-George, *Studies in Finance and Development*, p. 66.
16. *Trade Report 1922–23*, CO98/38; and R. Southall, "Cadbury on the Gold Coast," p. 300.

among farmers in the 1930s had its roots in the debts incurred during the war years.[17] A complex network of African cocoa brokers, from the smallest trader or trader-farmer to much larger scale produce buyers, were all vulnerable when prices collapsed. However, the financial uncertainties that persisted after the war, as well as the improvements in road transport, provided incentives for expatriate firms to penetrate inland and bypass the older generation of African middlemen involved in the overseas trade. Some African traders, squeezed out of the export sector, also took up opportunities in the expanding domestic trade (such as in local food) at a time, in the early 1920s, when it was stimulated by the spread of motorized transport.[18]

A significant postwar feature of the colony's cocoa export trade—arising from the experience of wartime conditions—was the spread of farmers' cooperatives. These arose partly as a result of government attempts to encourage cooperatives from above, and partly as a result of African hold-up initiatives from below. A large organization, the Gold Coast Farmers' Association (formed in 1922) discussed prices, hold-ups, and storage with the governor and was successful in shipping cocoa direct to the United States (until funds were misappropriated in the mid-1920s). Also in 1922 the agricultural department started cocoa growers' associations in the divisions of Ashanti, Mampong, Bompata, and Tasamanso. These organizations were an important background to later cooperative ventures such as the formation of the Gold Coast and Ashanti Cocoa Federation during the Depression, which organized the successful hold-up in 1930–1931.[19] By 1935, with twenty-nine societies closely attached to the agricultural department combining credit and marketing facilities, Lord Hailey estimated that cooperative farming societies had developed on a larger scale in the Gold Coast than in any other British territory in Africa.[20] But they still accounted for only about 2.8% of the total crop.[21] By the 1940s, local societies were reorganized at a national level in the Gold Coast Marketing Association, and by the mid-1950s cooperative societies handled about one-fifth or more of all cocoa in the Gold Coast.[22]

African workers reacted to government labor policies and the continuing low labor rates with new solidarity and organized action after the war. Governor Guggisberg continued the usual British practice of putting pressure on chiefs to provide "communal labour" for government projects, with a "determined effort" to obtain labor justified as being in the long term interest of the inhabitants.[23] There was no mention of pay. Guggisberg complained of the drain from the colony of skilled artisans such as carpenters and fitters, though he acknowledged that every steamer carried away one or more who "were sometimes tempted

17. C. Gunnarsson, *The Gold Coast Cocoa Industry*, p. 93.

18. As in Nigeria, see J. G. Deutsch, "Educating the Middlemen," pp. 31–41; A. Nwabughuogu, "From Wealthy Entrepreneurs to Petty Traders," p. 374. And P. H. Drummond-Thompson, "The Impact of Motorised Road Transport Upon the Organization of Internal Trade in Nigeria: 1919–45," unpublished MA thesis, (SOAS, London University, 1983), p. 50.

19. *Ibid.*

20. Lord Hailey, *An African Survey*, p. 475.

21. W. Hancock, *Survey of British Commonwealth Affairs Volume II: Problems of Economic Policy 1918–1919*, (London, 1942), p. 227 quoted in A. Phillips, *The Enigma of Colonialism*, p. 90.

22. See, e.g., Introduction, P. Hill, *The Gold Coast Farmer;* and M. Kilson, "The Emergent Elites," p. 358.

23. Guggisberg, LegCo 26/11/19, *Gazette* 8/12/19, CO99/34/100. And see also R. Thomas, "Forced Labor in West Africa," pp. 94–97.

by higher wages."[24] He had no solution other than to ask the African unofficials and "influential members of the Native Community" to appeal to these men on patriotic grounds: with the "active campaign of work ahead of us," the "necessities of our own country come first."[25]

As with farmers' cooperatives, so with labor trade unions. To the surprise of British officials, the immediate postwar period saw the beginnings of the formation of African trade unions and strike action. African railway workers and artisans led the way. Minimal concessions were made to railway workers when strikes occurred in February, March, and June 1919 at Sekondi and Accra. The committee appointed by the governor to investigate the claims concluded in July 1919 that pay should not be raised, railway pay rates being comparable with those prevailing in the mines. However, it did advise that the previous schedule of working hours be restored, and it recommended a range of improved benefits, such as disability payments, pensionable senior posts, and provision of cheap accommodation in Sekondi. These were clearly popular measures, though it was bound to take time and money to implement them, with some 600 men to be housed.[26] The lack of a pay raise led to railway workers' strikes spreading to Accra. A final agreement to raise the basic manual wage from 1s to 1s 9d a day was reached in 1920. The strikes then subsided after 1921, partly as a result of the disappearance of acute inflation, as well as the lowered demand for labor as an impact of the slump.[27]

That the issue of pay across the colony could not continue to be ignored by British officials also became clear with the formation of an Artisans' and Laborers' Union in Accra in 1920. The union rejected the government's new schedule of rates of pay, which had been agreed with the large employers of labor at a conference in May 1920. Although conditions of free trade were normally applauded, both government and European trading companies agreed at this time, when strikes were feared, that pay rates should be "stabilised" to avoid disputes, stoppages, and "unhealthy competition." [28] Unhealthy for whom? Competition was clearly in the interest of African workers in the postwar conditions of a severe shortage of both skilled and unskilled labor. This was recognized by the first-ever strike of artisans in government service in the Gold Coast in April and May 1921. African artisans succeeded in stopping the government from reducing their wages in the slump, even if they did not immediately succeed in obtaining a raise.[29]

There had also been unprecedented solidarity and determination among African government clerks in the Gold Coast concerning the delay in being granted a satisfactory war bonus. The campaign bore fruit. A committee appointed by Clifford before he left the colony in 1919 reported in May 1919 with detailed proposals for improved pay, promotion, and conditions of work for all the 1,616 clerks in government departments in the colony. The new scales raised initial pay for clerks and teachers to £48, as the petitioners had requested, with the possibility of accelerated promotion up the salary scales.[30] These

---

24. *Ibid.*
25. *Ibid.*
26. Acting Governor Slater to Long, 19/7/17. *Sessional Papers on Gold Coast Government Railway Workers' Pay 1919,* CO98/31.
27. See C. Tsey, "Gold Coast Railways," pp. 222–223.
28. *Artisans' and Laborers' Accra Schedule of Rates of Pay,* 20/5/20, ADM 11/778, PRAAD; and *Reports of the PWD 1920,* C098/34; 1921, CO98/38.
29. *Ibid.*
30. *Report of Committee: Conditions of Service of Native Clerks, Sessional Papers,* CO98/31.

proposals were finally approved by Milner, now the British imperial secretary of state, in November 1919, a month after Guggisberg's arrival as governor in Accra.

Thus an important feature of the war and immediate postwar period was the emergence into the spotlight of a range of Africans involved in their own increasingly vocal protest against deteriorating economic conditions in the colony. These included clerks, farmers, traders, brokers, and skilled workers. Such actions were not orchestrated or led by either the "traditional" African elite of chiefs and elders, or the Westernized African elite of lawyers, academics, and businessmen, many of whom lived in the coastal towns. This wider spectrum of African occupational groups was also involved in later protest at the effects of the Depression in the 1930s, and subsequently formed the core of the mass nationalist movement that arose largely as a result of economic conditions after the Second World War. By then a large proportion of the African population of the colony backed the view of Nkrumah and the other leaders of the Convention Peoples' Party that the time had come for Africans to run their own administration. The First World War proved a turning point in this respect.

After the First World War, the colonial government continued to make greater financial demands on all its subjects. Tax increases of the war period, such as higher *ad valorem* rates and specific import duties, were retained. By the end of 1919, as a result of the high rates of taxation as well as the trade boom, the revenue had risen to over £2.5m, more than double that of 1918. Most of the wartime taxation was then retained, in the sudden slump of 1921. One reason for the colonial administration in the Gold Coast continuing with the high levels of wartime taxation was a new British policy: the postwar imperial ban on trade spirits and the restrictions on imports of other spirits. This had a serious impact on the government's revenue. Before he left the colony in March 1919, Clifford had been concerned at the damaging effects of the ban which had been adopted, according to Flood in the Colonial Office, to impress the allies at the peace conference and to satisfy "the temperance crowd."[31] Clifford had hoped that there would be no impediment to financing the colony's development plans so long delayed by the war; now there would have to be a period of major fiscal readjustment as a result of the loss of customs revenue from trade spirits.[32] In the legislative council in July 1919, the newly appointed African unofficial, Casely Hayford, was told that taxation raised in the war had to be retained because of the "financial position" of the colony.[33]

Thus for Africans dependent on international trade, the ending of the war did not bring a return to prewar prosperity. Rather, it led to a significant and sustained rise in their cost of living. High import prices amid fluctuating supplies of imports remained important new features of the immediate postwar period in the Gold Coast. For example, in 1919, the value of flour imports rose tenfold, general food and tobacco fivefold.[34] Meanwhile, African farmers received lower prices for their agricultural exports. For example, the price paid for cocoa in Liverpool fell from £122 per ton in February 1920 to £39 in December of that same year.[35] The colonial economic equation had tipped against the

31. Flood, Colonial Office memo 8/4/19, CO554/43.

32. Telegram, Clifford to Long, 26/1/18, CO554/41; also Clifford, confid. to Milner, 6/3/19, CO99/34/64.

33. Casely Hayford, *LegCo* 30/6/19, *Gazette* 19/7/19, CO99/34/64.

34. *Report on the Blue Book 1919*, CO98/32.

35. See Cox-George, *Studies in Finance and Development*, p. 66.

local population. Imported food was in short supply, which badly affected those of the local population who had come to depend on a whole range of international imports, while prices remained very high in local markets. Restrictions on foodstuffs to West Africa from Britain began to be lifted by the Ministry of Food in December 1918, but many products such as sugar, butter, and cheese were still in short supply during the first half of 1919. There was no equivalent to the 1919 rice riots in Freetown, largely due to the absence of the same dependence on a single staple food import in the Gold Coast colony. Syrian or Lebanese traders, a target in the Sierra Leone riots, were not singled out in the same way in the Gold Coast.[36] Even so, the new governor of the Gold Coast colony, Guggisberg, reported in May 1920 that "all the big towns in the south are short of food."[37]

In this situation, British officials had recourse to asking for assistance from African retailers. Fuller arranged a mass meeting with market women in Ashanti in August 1919 as a result of concerns at the continuing high prices and food shortages. He found the women in the main market "quite reasonable" over not raising prices further.[38] Although the international trade did eventually stabilize after the substantial disruptions of the long war period, conditions for African producers were never again as favorable as before the war. It seems that real income in the British West African colonies declined from this period.[39] The cost of European goods continued to be higher after the war, while prices for African exports (as for primary products worldwide) remained lower. The barter terms of trade did not recover over the next decade and had not reached their prewar levels by the time of the Great Depression.[40] It is true that the income terms of trade did recover between 1922 and 1927, though this was due to the growth in the volume of exports. Farmers were able to increase production (helped by cocoa trees planted before the war now coming into maturation) to compensate in part for the increased price of imports.[41] But this recovery in incomes, made possible by farmers, especially in Ashanti, simply producing more, came to an end with the collapse in demand and prices in the late 1920s and early 1930s. The term "the long depression" may give a misleading impression of economic uniformity across the interwar period, but the First World War did undoubtedly break the steady rise in real incomes that had been a feature of the prewar cocoa boom.[42]

Another cause of the less favorable trading relationship for Africans after the war was the greater government acceptance (the British imperial government in London as well as the colony's government on the coast) of monopolistic practices by expatriate companies. The colonial administration had failed, for example, to prevent the shipping company Elder Dempster and the "Combine" of large expatriate trading firms from gaining during

36. See T. Falola, "The Lebanese in West Africa," in J. F. A. Ajayi & J. D. Y Peel (eds.), *People and Empires.*

37. Quoted in R. Addo-Fening, *Akyem Abuakwa c.1874–1943*, p. 347.

38. Fuller, diary 9/8/19, 13/8/19, ADM 12/5/160, PRAAD.

39. See B. Ingham & C. Simmons, *Development Studies and Colonial Policy,* pp. 230–233. See, for example, Freund's conclusion that the Nigerian tin miners' real wages never returned to prewar levels. W. Freund, "Labor Migration to the Northern Nigerian Tin Mines 1903–1945," *JAH,* 22, 1, 1981, p. 82.

40. A. G. Hopkins, *An Economic History of West Africa*, p. 184.

41. See C. Gunnarsson, *The Gold Coast Cocoa Industry,* pp. 87–91.

42. See Susan Martin, "The Long Depression: West African Export Producers and the World Economy, 1914–45" in I. Brown (ed.), *The Economies of Africa and Asia in the Interwar Depression,* (London, 1989), and review, J. Forbes Munro, "Rethinking the Thirties," in *JAH* 31, 2, 1990.

the war at the expense of small shippers (both African and European) and African farmers. The bigger companies could survive wartime conditions: fluctuating demand; periods of low profit margins or losses; the new trading restrictions; and the increasing overhead costs including insurance, freight rates, and government taxes. These difficulties led to further combinations of the major trading firms involved with both buying exports and selling imports, such as the amalgamation in 1919 of the three companies of the "Combine" (the African Association, Swanzy, and Millers) into the "Africa and Eastern Trading Corporation" (AETC).[43] Such a combination of relatively large companies was able to benefit in the war and immediate postwar period by gaining a bigger share of the market and accumulating capital as a result of the increases in the value of imports—even though quantities of imports fell.[44]

Companies involved only in exports had to be of a certain size to have sufficient capital to withstand long periods of loss. For example, Cadbury had exceptional amounts of cocoa awaiting shipment during the last two years of the war.[45] However, other companies were unable to withstand the effects of the 1917–1918 downturn in trade, or the later postwar slump. Many small African firms, such as the Tarquah Trading company, were finally "incorporated into the oligopolistic structure," in its case by being taken over in 1920 by the AETC. Some large companies in British West Africa also failed to survive the slump: for example, the Niger Company, taken over by Lever in 1920. Trading amalgamations were to culminate in the formation of the giant UAC (United Africa Company) in 1929.[46]

It was the ever-larger expatriate trading firms—as opposed to shipping companies—that came to dominate the trade of Britain's West African colonies after the war, in the 1920s. But in the case of the shipping company Elder Dempster, near monopoly of the war years was to work against its dominance in the long term. The major European traders became determined to reduce their dependence on any single shipping company. Elder Dempster's exceptionally advantageous position continued for three years after the war while shipping was still in short supply. But then new Dutch competition emerged in 1920 with the Holland Steamship Company, German ships reappeared in 1921, and American and French shipping stayed at much higher levels than before the war. This new competition coincided with the slump, surplus shipping, a new rate war, and finally the re-establishment of a West African Shipping Conference in 1924. Elder Dempster initially dominated this shipping cartel, to an even greater extent than before the war (the other members being Woermann and the Holland West Africa Line). However, the big merchant firms, such as the AETC, were also developing monopolistic muscle in the 1920s and increasingly able to ship independently of the Shipping Conference and its high rates. Their attitude was affected by the extent of their former dependence on the Elder Dempster line during the war as well as its continuing dominance over conference shipping once the war ended.[47] The battle was ultimately won by the new trading giant UAC in 1929

43. A. G. Hopkins, "Big Business in African Studies," p. 121; and J. G. Deutsch, "Educating the Middlemen," p. 30. Also P. Jones, "The United Africa Company in the Gold Coast/Ghana: 1920–1965," unpublished PhD thesis, (London, 1983), pp. 38–53.

44. Cf. Francophone Africa, see C. Coquery Vidrovitch, "L'Impact des Interets Coloniaux: SCOA et CFAO dans l'Ouest Africain, 1910–1965," *JAH*, XVI, 4, 1975, p. 599.

45. R. Southall, "Cadbury on the Gold Coast," pp. 134–136.

46. R. Howard, *Colonialism and Underdevelopment,* pp. 99–100.

47. Percentage of tonnage by national registration: British: 59.5% in 1913; 75.1% in 1920; 59.3% in 1925; percentage of conference tonnage; Elder Dempster 75% in 1913–1914; 80% in 1924–1925. C. Leubuscher, *The West Africa Shipping Trade,* Tables 1 & 34, pp. 31–53.

when Elder Dempster lost 40% of its West African trade. The initial reason for UAC maintaining their own oceangoing ships was as a security against excessive freight charges by the Shipping Conference and the advantage it gave the company in negotiating lower rates on Conference ships. It soon proved to be markedly cheaper.[48] But none of these monopolistic developments and trends favored African producers or middlemen.

The British colonial government, as we have seen, strove during the war to establish a universally accepted currency in the Gold Coast as a means of stabilizing the economy and stimulating trade. Its continuing struggles in this regard after the war typify a situation in which British officials found themselves located uncomfortably among forces beyond their control. Africans had suffered from the fall in the value of sterling as a result of the war. The lack of an adequate currency had created uncertainty and insecurity, contributing to fluctuations in the colony's trade. Shortage of coin was still a major problem in the Gold Coast immediately after the war ended, although the colonial government made sustained efforts to improve provision. In February 1919, the African unofficial E. J. P. Brown referred to the lack of small coins as "becoming acute" and making the sale of fish, farm provisions, and general foodstuffs in local markets especially difficult.[49] Some silver and nickel coins had just been received and more were expected in mail steamers, but Clifford continued to press for yet more coin to be shipped, both low denomination coins and as much silver as possible.[50] He was convinced that the local population would put more silver (much still hoarded) into general circulation only if they had the confidence that there would no longer be a shortage of coin.[51] But hoarding seems to have continued, as a result of the intrinsic value of silver and nickel coins as well as the economic instability of the times. There was clearly also an important African calculation that the British would continue to provide currency to replace what was taken out of circulation. As with the harbor works at Accra, money was continually poured in by the government, only to disappear.

There was also still a problem of persuading the population to accept paper notes at face value. In June 1919, Nana Ofori Atta drew the government's attention to the serious difference in value between silver and paper currency as a result of the widespread preference for silver coin. He reported that at Nsawam it required 34s 6d in notes to match 25s in silver. Clearly the government ordinance regarding the official value of the paper currency was "not functioning." Farmers detested the notes, and the only solution, Ofori Atta believed, was for the government to obtain more silver currency.[52] The Liverpool Chamber of Commerce complained of the same problem. Farmers, especially up-country, were said to be "very much averse to accepting notes for their produce."[53] There were also reports of paper money being rejected by food sellers in the markets.[54] Fuller, illustrating the relatively benign and practical administration of the time, also condemned "the glaring

48. See D. K. Fieldhouse, *Merchant Capital and Economic Decolonization. The United Africa Company 1929–1987,* (Oxford, 1994), p. 177.

49. E. J. P. Brown, *LegCo* 19/2/19, *Gazette* 8/3/19, CO99/34/25.

50. Acting Colonial Secretary, *LegCo* 19/2/19, *Gazette* 8/3/19, CO99/34/25. Also *West African Currency Board Report for year ending 30/6/19,* CO554/42; and telegram, Clifford to Milner, 24/4/19, CO554/41.

51. Clifford to Sir William Mercer, West African Currency Board, 5/7/19, CO554/41.

52. Nana Ofori Atta, *LegCo* 30/6/19, *Gazette* 19/7/19, CO99/34/64.

53. Liverpool Chamber of Commerce to Milner, 4/4/19, CO554/42.

54. *The Gold Coast Nation,* 31/5–7/19 and 7/6/19.

injustice" of making "natives" accept notes from the government while European firms were refusing paper money over the counter.[55] The Gold Coast government could do no more than give the reassurance that the Currency Board in London was making every effort to obtain metal currency and have it shipped. The worldwide shortage of silver, a result of the Great War, was beyond the colonial government's control, and therefore only a limited supply was available for coinage. However, by June 1919, more than £350,000 of silver coin had been imported into the colony since the end of the war, and practically all of it was apparently in circulation. Consignments of nickel-bronze coinage, unobtainable at the end of the war, were now said to be arriving by every mail boat. But currency notes were also still needed. They might be unpopular, but over £1m in value were now circulating in the colony, including, from June 1919, some £5 notes.[56]

Another important eventual outcome for the British West African colonies of the upheavals of the war period was yet another currency: this time, an effective new coinage. Although the currency situation in the Gold Coast had eased by October 1919, Slater informed Milner that there was still "the very real requirement of a very much larger circulation of coin in the colony."[57] According to the district manager of the Bank of West Africa, nothing short of £4m in silver would relieve the situation "in the slightest degree."[58] However, there was likely to be a shortage of silver for at least three or four years as a result of the war. The solution devised by the West Africa Currency Board in 1919 was a cheaper metal currency, an improvement on the previous idea of a coin coated with zinc or tin, which could wear away. The new coins were an improved alloy of spelter, copper, and aluminum, which would take a good impression for printing, had no intrinsic value, would not tarnish, and would be practically indestructible.[59] Guggisberg was able to inform London officials in November 1919 that the suggestion of a new alloy coinage had been generally favorably received in the Gold Coast, provided it could be sent out in sufficiently large quantities of £1m or possibly £2m.[60]

As a result of the introduction of the new mixed-metal coinage in September 1920, the currency problem was finally judged to be "less acute" in the Gold Coast Colony—after a prolonged period of disruption. The coins were of the same size, weight, and denominations as the silver coins, £5m worth of which remained in circulation. Although the alloy was said not to be so popular as silver, there was the advantage for the government that it was not hoarded. Over £0.5m worth of alloy coins were imported in 1920, and as much again in 1921, and over £1.5m in 1922. A small number of low denomination nickel-bronze coins were still in circulation, but they did not now play such a crucial role as when they had been brought in to help ease the critical shortage of silver.[61]

The war had exposed even more sharply the limitations of the colonial administration.[62] The economic uncertainties of the period, including fluctuations in trade and the un-

55. Fuller, diary 24/9/19, ADM 12/5/160, PRAAD.

56. Acting Colonial Secretary, *LegCo* 30/6/19, *Gazette* 19/7/19, CO99/34/64.

57. Acting Governor Slater to Milner, 3/10/19, CO554/41/795.

58. District Manager Talland, Bank of West Africa, 26/9/19, Enclosure 1, Acting Governor Slater to Milner, 3/10/19, CO554/41/795.

59. *Report of Meeting of Joint West Africa Committee,* House of Commons, 23/5/19, CO554/41.

60. Telegram, Guggisberg to Milner, 13/11/19, CO554/41.

61. *Treasury Report 1920,* CO98/34; also *Blue Book 1922,* CO100/72.

62. Elsewhere in Africa, world wars highlighted the shortcomings of British administrations. See, for example, Gardner Thompson, *Governing Uganda. British Colonial Rule and its Legacy*, Part 2,

precedented depression and slump, left British officials even less freedom of maneuver than before the war. With plans shelved and projects curtailed, the colonial government, exceptionally short-staffed, had stumbled uncertainly through the war. The impact of the British colonial government on the Gold Coast remained, in many respects, slight. Yet not all the consequences of war were negative. The survival of the colony's trade was largely due to the opening of new markets, especially in the United States, to compensate for those lost as a result of the war. The government had had no powers to summon shipping or finance to help the colony through the severe economic depression of 1917 and 1918. It had been dependent on the major expatriate companies to keep the economy, and therefore government revenue, afloat.

Despite these constraints, two governors of the Gold Coast, Clifford (1912–1919) and Guggisberg (1919–1927), were able to influence decisions made in Whitehall concerning financial policy and construction projects. To the extent that it was possible in the war period and its aftermath, they were both to have a personal impact on the colony. Before the war, Clifford had won over London officials to the financial principle of using the colony's surplus balances to increase capital expenditure. This was all the more important given that the limited supply of capital remained a key constraint on British colonial rule.[63] The war then stopped the policy of drawing on colony funds at a time when external loans were still unobtainable. The Gold Coast government maintained the revenue during the war only by raising taxes. In the immediate postwar years, government construction plans were still hampered by continuing shortages of funds and of African skilled and unskilled labor. In addition, the administration struggled with the delayed leave and retirements of officials and with the difficulty of finding trained European staff to fill vacancies.[64]

However, consciously following in the footsteps of his predecessor and well aware that the war had drastically slowed down progress, the next governor, Guggisberg, successfully pressed London to continue Clifford's ambitious program of public works. This was to be started in the immediate postwar period. During the war, African enterprise had built roads and extended their use, while British initiatives for the railways had stalled. For Guggisberg, as for Clifford, capital was especially needed for railways—which had already dramatically cut the cost of transport compared with rates of human porterage, estimated as thirty times more expensive per ton mile.[65] Guggisberg's aim, again like his predecessor, was to tap the agricultural and mineral wealth of the colony for more money to be available to spend on educational and medical provision. As we have seen, railway construction had continued sporadically in the early war period for as long as Clifford could push for it. Although it was restarted as soon as possible after the war ended, much extra work on the railways had accumulated in terms of long overdue maintenance. Supplies remained very short, even after the Armistice. Engine spares and permanent way materials were practically unobtainable in the immediate postwar period, and except for cement, prices showed no sign of falling. None of the locomotives and rolling stock ordered in July 1918 were delivered during 1919, partly as a result of strikes in England.[66] So while the Gold Coast government continued after the war to believe that railway transport was the priority,

---

(Kampala, 2003), for the limitations of colonial rule exposed by the Second World War in that East African territory.

63. See P. J. Cain & A. G. Hopkins, *British Imperialism, Volume II: Crisis and Deconstruction, 1914–1990,* (London, 1993).

64. *PWD Report 1919,* CO98/32, and see Fuller's diary, 30/7/19, ADM 12/5/160, PRAAD.

65. J. Hogendorn in L. Gann & P. Duignan, *Colonialism in Africa 1870–1960, IV,* p. 296.

66. *Railway Reports 1918*: CO98/32; 1919: CO98/33.

it took time for repairs to be undertaken, let alone construction works to be restarted. Early in 1919, trading companies were urging the Colonial Office to take West African railways in hand, as they were "all run down."[67]

Notwithstanding the governors' efforts, the African population expressed impatience and frustration at the impact of the war on the railways in the Gold Coast and the slowness of recovery. For example, in June 1919, the government was pressed by Nana Ofori Atta for a date for the resumption of work on the Accra-Kumasi railway. Only in December 1919 did work restart on realigning the Sekondi-Kumasi railway. Construction of the northern extension of the Accra railway, delayed by the shortage of labor, was only finally resumed in April 1920. The total number of derailments in 1921 had reached the unprecedented figure of 140 within the year. The number of engine failures, at fifty-four, was more than double that of 1918.[68] In November 1919, Guggisberg succinctly summed up the effects of the war on the Gold Coast railway: "We have lost four years of work."[69] Given the reduced spending from the start of the war, well before all work stopped at the beginning of 1917, as well as the deterioration of the railway stock, this was an understatement. The war had been a substantial setback for the colonial government's plans for railway construction.

Other development schemes had also been shelved as a result of the war. The disruption to the government's road building programs continued in the postwar period. It was well into 1919 before the PWD collected the necessary funds, labor, and concrete to begin undertaking repairs and improvements once more. By the end of that year, a five-year program of road construction had been drawn up under the aegis of the new governor—although, like his predecessor, Guggisberg overrated the importance of railways and underrated roads in his development plans for the Gold Coast. Work was also hampered by the difficulty of obtaining labor, both as a result of high wages being paid on cocoa farms during the postwar boom and because the local population disliked receiving wages in paper money.[70]

Nonetheless, as we have seen, just before and during the war, and quite unexpectedly, a revolution in road transport had begun in the Gold Coast, very largely due to African initiative. This was to herald a major change for the colony. During the war, when the Gold Coast government had neither funds nor London's permission to provide for the new motor traffic, African producers had seized trading opportunities and provided much of the necessary road network. The scale of the African road system constructed in the Gold Coast during the war period encouraged the steep rise in the number of motorcars and light trucks transported to the colony for commercial use by African, European, and American trading companies. A former Cadbury agent recalled that immediately after the end of hostilities, truck traffic was "very heavy" in cocoa areas without access to a railway, such as on the Winneba—Swedru and Cape Coast—Saltpond roads in Central Province, and that by 1919 many of the trading firms had their own fleets of trucks "which sought cocoa anywhere it was to be found, even along the most primitive paths. Head carriage and cask-rolling were becoming things of the past."[71] The numbers of motor

67. Manchester Chamber of Commerce to Milner, 19/3/19, CO554/42.

68. Nana Ofori Atta, *LegCo* 30/6/19, *Gazette* 19/7/19, C099/34/64. *Railways Report 1919,* C098/32. The railway capital account was increased by £780,799 in 1920 and went up again by £1,883,201 in 1921. *Railways Report 1920,* CO98/34; *Railways Report 1921,* CO98/38.

69. Guggisberg, *LegCo* 26/11/19, *Gazette* 8/12/19, C099/34/100.

70. Director of PWD reply to Casely Hayford, *LegCo* 30/6/19, *Gazette* 19/7/19, C099/34/64.

71. N. Edwards, *Cadbury on the Gold Coast,* p. 20.

vehicles rose rapidly. Decorated cars and motorcycles were prominent in the great procession through Accra for the peace celebrations of August 1919.[72] New vehicle registrations numbered 1,084 in 1920 alone, by which time the PWD had a fleet of fifty-two cars and 125 trucks.[73] As early as 1921, the description of traffic in the territory, often apparently short of a lamp or a horn, was becoming increasingly familiar to later travellers: "Excessive speeding is so common that a short journey on any of the motor roads is always in the nature of an adventure."[74]

The remarkable transformation of road transport in the Gold Coast colony during the war years was exceptional in British West Africa. Motor vehicle transport in Nigeria, though also now featuring African enterprise, with cocoa farmers and traders contributing to the construction of roads, was on a smaller scale relative to the size of the two colonies. The manager of the Nigerian railways, E. M. Bland, was sufficiently impressed by the Ford motor vehicles he had seen in the Gold Coast in 1919 to order an initial six Ford trucks for Nigeria.[75] And in *The Red Book of West Africa* of 1920, Alistair Macmillan described the conditions in Accra as unique in the region: "Innumerable motor lorries with trailers attached, laden to the utmost with bags of the precious beans, roar, rattle, and rush, interrupted with equally numerous motor cars in the feverish haste of the cocoa season, and provide a spectacle of activity such as cannot be seen elsewhere in West Africa." [76]

Contemporary photographs show the extent of the new motor traffic in the Gold Coast colony by 1920. European companies and African agents can be seen with large numbers of vehicles, such as Ford motorcars just landed on the beach at Accra (imported by W. Bartholomew & Co. Motor Engineers) and some of the "forty strong motor lorries" used by the Anglo-Guinea Produce Co. Ltd. for transporting cocoa to Accra. Meanwhile, African trading companies like Ocansey acted as agents to American motor companies. Other African firms, for example, R. L. Cofie Allotey and the Colonial Motor Company (sole agents for Dodge Motors), provided a vehicle repair service in the streets of Accra where, by 1920, "numerous motor cars menace life and limb in the narrow thoroughfares."[77] Britain's African subjects in the Gold Coast can be seen here for what they were: not passive and indifferent but enterprising and active in seizing any opportunities that arose in the context of international trade.

African frustration at the overall impact of the war on the colony served to stiffen Guggisberg's resolve in 1919 to try to complete the full range of his predecessor's construction projects. Clifford had raised local African expectations of what would be provided soon after the war. When he left in 1919, Guggisberg, in a more favorable climate of opinion, was able very quickly, in 1920, to launch a development plan for the Gold Coast, with the blessing of the Colonial Office.[78] One effect of the war regarding development and welfare plans was to halt progress in the short term—but subsequently to accelerate the

72. Government poster, 14/8/19, ADM 11/1/758, PRAAD.

73. P. Jones, "The United Africa Company," p. 74; *also PWD Report 1920*, CO98/34.

74. J. Atterbury, PC Central Province, *Report on Central Province 1921*, C098/36.

75. E. M. Bland, "The Nigerian News and Notes XV(11)1928," in O. Oshin, "Road Transport and Declining Fortunes of the Nigerian Railway 1901–1959," *Journal of Transport History*, 12,1, March 1991, 19.

76. A. Macmillan, *The Red Book of West Africa,* (London, 1920), p. 173.

77. N. Edwards, *Cadbury on the Gold Coast*, pp. 20–21; and see photographs in A. Macmillan, *The Red Book of West Africa.*

78. Contrast with Lugard's legacy in Nigeria; see L. Nicolson, *The Administration of Nigeria 1900–1960,* (London, 1969), pp. 217–218.

pace of change. In paternalistic terms reminiscent of Clifford, Guggisberg described the role of governor in the colonial relationship as "the head of a family."[79] There was, as Slater described, considerable optimism in the colony at what lay ahead, now "the dark days" of the war had finally passed. The colony could "look forward with a good conscience to the enjoyment of a new prosperity."[80] The Ten Year Development Plan of 1920, to be paid for out of the balances accumulated in and just after the war as well as by loans, was announced by Guggisberg as a joint venture between Britain and the "native community" of the colony.[81] The war thus had the effect of postponing rather than sabotaging Governor Clifford's development program.

The leap in available funds that allowed PWD work to begin in earnest after the war only occurred in 1920. The "native" hospital for Accra, so long delayed, headed the list of priorities for public buildings. Other "native" hospitals were to follow, as well as secondary and technical schools. There were also plans for the construction of, for example, town halls and post offices; courts of justice, prisons, and police barracks; and town improvements to relieve congestion, as in Accra and Cape Coast.[82] Another delayed development was the installation of a telephone system, though the breakthrough came only when funds and the necessary materials at last became available.[83] A substantial amount was therefore achieved before the onset of the Depression at the end of the decade again stopped all such construction works.

Governor Guggisberg appreciated the need for a massive injection of funds if a deepwater harbor (now likely to be at Sekondi-Takoradi), was ever to be built in the Gold Coast.[84] In 1919 he received the report of the inquiry set up by Clifford in February 1918 to investigate whether Sekondi was the best site. In the 1920 estimates of Guggisberg's development program, the largest single sum set aside from loan funds, £2m, was to be for harbor works. Preliminary work was well under way at Sekondi-Takoradi by 1922. The wartime fiasco of money lost on Accra harbor—ignored in Kimble's brief description—helps to explain the strength of local African opposition in the 1920s to the expenditure proposed for the Takoradi works.[85] A deepwater harbor near Accra had to wait another forty years, when construction began in 1954 at Tema.

For both Clifford and Guggisberg, improvements in transport and communications were a means to provide resources for financing welfare projects. Clifford's ambition, that after the war the benefits of European medical science would be spread to the rural population of the colony and would involve "numbers of native medical men," was to be echoed by his successor.[86] Although Guggisberg recognized that reforms would take some time to implement in what were still "abnormal circumstances" immediately after the long war, he agreed that there needed to be opportunities for "native" medical officers and medical training on the coast. Progress had been "seriously retarded" by the war as

79. Guggisberg, *LegCo* 9/10/19, *Gazette* 13/10/19, CO99/34/86.

80. Acting Governor Slater, *Proclamation to the Chiefs and People of Gold Coast on the Conclusion of Peace 28th June 1919, Gazette* 19/7/19, C099/34/65.

81. Guggisberg, *LegCo* 9/10/19, *Gazette* 13/10/19, CO99/34/86.

82. Guggisberg, *LegCo* 26/11/19, *Gazette* 8/12/19, CO99/34/100.

83. Of the Post & Telegraph extraordinary budget, £22,000 was spent on telephone trunk lines and exchanges in 1920. *Blue Books: 1920, CO100/70; 1921, CO100/71; 1922, CO100/72.*

84. Guggisberg, *LegCo* 29/11/19, *Gazette* 8/12/19, CO99/34/100; R. Wraith, *Guggisberg,* (London, 1967), p. 82; and *PWD Report 1922/23,* CO98/38.

85. D. Kimble, *A Political History of Ghana,* p. 57.

86. Clifford, *LegCo* re. 1919 Estimates 28/10/18, *Gazette* 9/11/18, CO99/33/82.

well as by prejudiced officials before the outbreak of war, as we have seen. Some of the substantial loan of £4m of Guggisberg's Ten Year Plan was to finance construction of hospitals and dispensaries, as well as water supplies and drainage schemes. The prewar figure of between fifty and sixty medical officers was only matched finally in the mid-1920s.[87]

But local African medical needs were not immediately met. That the war had been remote and yet had a substantial impact on the colony is seen in the reaction of the Fia of Awuna in 1919. One year after the end of the war, conditions had by no means returned to normal. In November 1919, the Fia was urging that, once the war was over, a medical officer be posted to Keta, as there had been no permanent doctor there for three years.[88] He was told that the war had in fact been over for a year—but that the medical department was still not up to full strength. Meanwhile Keta would continue to be visited by a medical officer stationed in Lome, Togo. The Fia firmly stated his people's priorities: their own government doctor and hospital, pumps for wells, a proper drainage system, and help with guarding against further erosion by the sea. The official British response was simply that it was impossible to carry out simultaneously all work postponed by the war.[89] Though true, this was hardly a response designed to satisfy local demand, which was, again, for more colonial provision.

African priorities could be very different from those of the British administrators. For example, Keta was judged by British officers to be in more urgent need of a post office than a hospital. Ofori Atta was told in June 1919 that it was not yet possible to fill the vacant medical posts in what the okyenhene called "the long isolated places" in Eastern Province. Ofori Atta also asked if the medical department was prepared to consider examining "native" medicines, with a view to licensing "native" medicine men. The government response was that this was not practical, on account of the "secret processes" used by such medicine men. Greater government interest in African herbal remedies was only expressed much later, in the early 1930s, when Ofori Atta was finally asked by the government to provide specimens of plants with medicinal properties. The colonial administration sought to give reassurance in 1919, immediately after the war, that more Africans were now being included in the existing medical service with, for example, twenty-eight African nurses on probation and twenty-two African dispensers in training.[90] This response, however, exposed how minimal medical provision and training still were in the colony.

Further epidemics after the war, such as the outbreak of smallpox in Accra in 1920, gave extra urgency to government measures to improve sanitary conditions and public health. The most serious epidemic of the immediate postwar period, following hard on the heels of the terrible effects of the influenza pandemic, was the outbreak of cerebrospinal meningitis in the Northern Territories and Northern Ashanti in 1919 and 1920. It began in February 1919 in the northwestern province of the Northern Territories at the time of a severe drought. With no farm work available, northerners congregated in overcrowded

---

87. Guggisberg, *LegCo* 9/10/19, *Gazette* 13/10/19, CO99/34/86; *LegCo* re. 1920 Estimates 26/11/19, *Gazette* 8/12/19, CO99/34/100. See Table 2: *Government Physicians 1906–54,* in D. K. Patterson, *Health in Colonial Ghana,* p. 110.

88. *Fia* of Awuna, *LegCo* 17/11/19, *Gazette* 6/12/19, CO99/34/99

89. *Ibid.*

90. Nana Ofori Atta, and Acting PMO, *LegCo* 30/6/19, *Gazette* 19/7/19, CO99/34/64. K. D. Patterson, *Health in Colonial Ghana,* pp. 28–30.

conditions to drink *peto* (beer made from guinea corn), which unfortunately helped spread the infection. The outbreak extended across the sudanic belt of West Africa, including Northern Nigeria, aided, as were other epidemics, by the mobility of population in this hinterland region, especially in wartime.[91]

The evidence does not support Wraith's criticism that, in contrast with Guggisberg, Clifford was "inordinately concerned with the European population" in health matters.[92] Guggisberg was, rather, determined to carry on the progressive measures that Clifford had proposed. An important further step was achieved in 1924 with the acceptance of a new class of "junior" African medical officers, who could now become full medical officers after sufficient hospital experience. At last, during the 1920s, the West African Medical Service began to treat larger numbers of Africans. But the regional imbalance continued: in 1927–1928, twenty-eight of the thirty-nine hospitals and all four dispensaries were sited in the Colony, with only eleven spread across the whole of Ashanti and the Northern Territories.[93]

As with health programs (and as in the other British territories in West Africa), provision of education also suffered during the war in the Gold Coast. Problems continued into the postwar period: shortages of staff and materials took time to remedy. The staffing situation was not helped by British officials taking long-delayed leave. The director of education in the Gold Coast went on leave in March 1919 for five and a half months after a tour of nearly twenty-five months—double the length of a normal tour before the war. Few school inspections took place, either during or immediately after the war, with administrative officers not available. There was also little building because of the high cost of imports and shortage of labor and the fact that lime, tar, and cement were still practically unobtainable in 1919. Many schools in the coastal towns were described as little more than large ill-ventilated halls: noisy, dusty, and overcrowded, with inadequate sanitary accommodation and no playgrounds. There was some improvement in the supply of books in 1919 after a period of a serious paper shortage during the war. But there were not enough desks, and still too few teachers, as a result of insufficient pay. Salaries had changed little if at all since before the war. In 1919 many students attending the Accra Training College were reported as completing, or planning to complete, the statutory five years as a teacher—before leaving the profession.[94] And the contrast in regional provision remained stark. In that same year, 1919, there were 15,000 pupils in government or government-assisted mission schools in Eastern Region but only 211 school pupils in the Northern Territories, where there were no assisted mission schools—because it was government policy, as in northern Nigeria, to discourage missions in Muslim or thinly "Islamized" areas.[95]

However, from 1919, Guggisberg began to build on the educational reforms set up by his predecessor. The report of the educational committee set up by Clifford was

---

91. *Medical and Sanitary Report 1920,* CO98/34, see, e.g., D .C. Dorward, in A. Roberts (ed.), *The Cambridge History of Africa,* pp. 441–442. For previous periodic outbreaks, as in 1906–8, see R. Thomas, "Forced Labor in British West Africa," pp. 79–103; and R. Dumett, "Campaign Against Malaria," pp. 173–174.

92. R. Wraith, *Guggisberg,* p. 83.

93. See D. Kimble, *A Political History,* p. 109; and D. K. Patterson, *Health in Colonial Ghana,* pp. 13–18.

94. *Education Report 1919,* CO98/32; *Education Report 1920,* CO98/34.

95. *Report of Special Committee, Sessional Paper XVII, 1918–19,* CO98/31 in R. Thomas, "Education in Northern Ghana, 1906–1940. A Study in Colonial Paradox." *The International Journal of African Historical Studies,* VII, 3,1975, p. 439.

published in October 1919, after he had left the coast. The main proposal was for a government secondary school in or near Accra, long called for by the African educated elite. There was also to be increased provision for girls, with a girls' primary school in Sekondi, a girls' boarding school in Accra, and a Women Teachers' Training College. Increased funding would also support a raise in teachers' salaries; provide grants to assisted schools; and extend technical education, with the enlargement of Accra technical school and also additional technical, or industrial, schools at Cape Coast, Sekondi, and Kumasi.[96] The trade school at Kyebi, opened by Clifford just after the war in January 1919, was to become something of a showpiece. It was later visited by the Prince of Wales on his visit to the colony in 1925. In 1922, three similar trade schools were opened in Yendi, Mampong, and Assuantsi, with courses on agriculture, carpentry, and bricklaying.[97] Clifford's contribution in putting technical education high on the Gold Coast agenda has not been adequately recognized. Again, Guggisberg has been seen as the driving force for this development and has even, erroneously, been given the sole credit, as by Foster and Wraith, for the "innovation" of trade or "industrial" schools in the 1920s.[98]

Guggisberg shared Clifford's strong belief that greater government provision of education was essential. Given that more funds were now forthcoming in the postwar years, Guggisberg ordered a second, much more extensive, report on education in the colony. Its fifty recommendations, presented in May 1920, enlarged on the previous recommendations of the committee commissioned by Clifford.[99] It was now suggested that the proposed government secondary school should be sited at Achimota. Details were also given of increased teachers' pay, including equal pay for women teachers, and greater provision of technical education. Guggisberg's aim was to see 50% of European staff in technical departments replaced by "natives," more government teacher training colleges and girls' schools, an increased number of education officers and inspectors, and the formation of provincial education committees. A program of works was also included for the period 1920–1930.[100] In 1925, an Education Ordinance with new pay scales sought belatedly to address the problem of how to raise the status of the teaching profession, which had fallen to a low level during the war.[101]

Guggisberg's well-known emphasis on education as "the keystone of progress" has tended to put the groundwork achieved by his predecessor into shadow.[102] Clifford's educational reform program for the colony had largely been a casualty of the war, but the disruption strengthened Guggisberg's determination to respond to a "desire for Education which is now widespread and growing."[103] For Guggisberg, "the worst blow" to education in the colony had been the closure of the Basel mission, and "the greatest evil of the war"

---

96. *Report of Special Committee on Education,* 8/10/19, *Sessional Papers,* CO98/31.

97. See R. Addo-Fening, *Akyem Abuakwa 1874–1943,* p. 271; and M. Kilson, "The Emergent Elites of Black Africa," p. 371.

98. P. Foster, *Education and Social Change in Ghana,* (London, 1965), p. 150; and R. Wraith, *Guggisberg,* pp. 135–140.

99. Guggisberg, *LegCo* 9/10/19, *Gazette* 13/10/19, CO99/34/86.

100. Guggisberg, *LegCo* re 1920 Estimates 26/11/19, *Gazette* 8/12/1, CO99/34/100; *Report on Education 1920, Sessional Paper,* CO98/33.

101. H. McWilliam, *Development of Education in Ghana,* (London, 1959), pp. 55–56.

102. Guggisberg, *LegCo* 1/3/23, *Gazette* 17/3/23, quoted in F Bourret, *Ghana. The Road to Independence 1919–1957,* (London, 1960), p. 27. See also Brigadier General Sir F. G. Guggisberg, extract from *The Keystone,* (London, 1924), in R. O. Collins (ed.), *Western African History, Volume 1,* (New York, 1990), pp. 225–228.

103. *Education Report 1920,* CO98/34.

the enforced delay in extending the education system.[104] Like his predecessor, he realized just how important was provision of education for the development, and meeting the expectations, of Britain's African subjects.

Guggisberg's record in the Northern Territories is also very instructive: it shows how far one governor's aspirations could differ from another's yet also how huge the obstacles could be to their realization. "Uneven development"—a reality by default, whatever Clifford's prejudices before and during the war—was to continue despite Guggisberg's best efforts to reverse it. His stated hopes were unambiguous. In 1919 he announced: "The career of the Northern Territories as the Cinderella of the Gold Coast is nearing its end: as Cinderella she has done good and unobtrusive work. Her reward for that, and for the gallantry of her soldiers, is in sight."[105] Here was recognition by the coastal government of the southerners' dependence on the north's recent provision of soldiers and carriers—as well as on peacetime northern labor for mines and farms in the colony and Ashanti. Guggisberg's vision of the future integration of the north included "trains heavily laden with groundnuts, shea butter, corn and cattle steaming across the Volta."[106] He was firmly optimistic that "there can be no doubt that at some future time the produce of the Northern Territories will be a considerable factor in the trade of the whole country."[107]

Thus, in the 1920s, the Northern Territories did receive more attention and money than previously. It was spent, for example, on the colony's infrastructure, including an extension of the telegraph and telephone systems. A Kumasi-Tamale road suitable for motor traffic was completed in April 1920 and used by Guggisberg himself the following year.[108] There were other postwar government initiatives to boost internal trade: the war had delayed plans to promote cattle breeding in the north to supply meat for the whole colony and to end reliance on cattle from French territory. The straight-backed Dagomba cattle of the Northern Territories were reckoned to be better meat producers than the humpbacked Moshi cattle from across the French border to the north (though Moshi cattle had the advantage of traveling better). A significant indication of commitment to the northern trade came when the veterinary department was finally reorganized and moved from Kumasi to Tamale in 1922, and a junior trade school was opened at Yendi in 1922.

But for the most part, the Northern Territories were to remain remote, arid, and poor, without commercial crops, mines, or a cheap transport system. Welfare provision, or the lack of it, tells a similar story here—again in spite of, rather than because of, British official intentions. A separate department of education for the north was set up in 1926, but funds and educational provision remained extremely limited. There was no secondary school in the Northern Territories until 1951, and only one graduate in 1957.[109] Inadequacies in health provision were more striking still. The effects of the influenza and other epidemics

---

104. Guggisberg, *LegCo* 26/11/19, *Gazette*, 8/12/19, CO99/34/100; and *LegCo* 21/1/21, quoted in D. Kimble, *A Political History*, p. 79.

105. Guggisberg, *LegCo* 9/10/19, *Gazette* 13/10/19, CO99/34/86.

106. *Ibid.*

107. Guggisberg, *Minutes of the Tamale Conference*, 11/3/21, in M. Staniland, *The Lions of Dagbon*, p. 53.

108. Guggisberg, *The Gold Coast. A Review of the Events of 1920–1926 and The Prospects of 1927–1928*, (Accra, 1927), p. 108.

109. R. Bening, "Colonial Development Policy," pp. 67–68; and R. Thomas, "Education in Northern Ghana," p. 427.

on a subsistence society that was already under unusual war-related strain from exceptionally high rates of labor recruitment were crippling. There was famine at the end of 1922, with people in Zuarungu and northern Mamprusi reduced to eating grass and weeds.[110] Reports from the later interwar period, too, continued to give a picture of a region where the population suffered from regular food shortages and ill health. Contagious diseases such as sleeping sickness spread along the main roads as a result of the mobility of labor. "Kumasi sickness" was the local name for syphilis brought up from the south by returning migrant laborers.[111] Only in the early 1930s did the agricultural department turn its attention to trying to improve and increase the production of food crops in the north, as opposed to searching for possible crops for export.[112] Meanwhile, no railway was ever constructed in the north. The plans for a northern line to link Kumasi with Tamale sank in the postwar slump. The north continued to participate in the colonial economy, primarily as a source of labor for the south. Though Guggisberg had set out to reverse previous neglect, the Northern Territories remained a hinterland backwater: an important and damaging legacy of colonial rule.

Governor Clifford had felt "uneasiness" about the underlying instability of "native" society in all regions of the Gold Coast colony, and not just in the north. Under Clifford, the government became more closely associated with chiefs and, especially when it was itself short-staffed during the war period, more dependent on them. Guggisberg in turn accepted his predecessor's policy that legislation should not be passed if opposed by chiefs in the legislative council. Although Clifford had improved communication and consultation with chiefs, he had been disappointed that the proposed new Native Jurisdiction Ordinance was not supported by "native" authorities. So no effective action was taken either to strengthen the authority of head chiefs or to check the "irresponsibility" of the increasing number of popular challenges to chiefs' authority.[113] Indeed, nothing had been agreed before Clifford left the coast in 1919. Guggisberg's attempt to pass a modified version of this bill in 1922 also failed. Thereafter, as Kimble noted, British government interest was to shift in the interwar period towards methods of improving "native" administration as a whole, rather than concentrating solely on "native" justice.[114]

Furthermore, Guggisberg inherited from Clifford the problems and contradictions that were inherent in a policy that sought to combine indirect rule with modernization and development.[115] There was a mixture of paternalism and lack of perception in the views of these two governors (and their officials) concerning African society. The point has been made that such "feeble alien bureaucracies" were "always handicapped by their ignorance of the societies they sought to direct."[116] As we have seen, Clifford had continued

110. See G. Chada, "*The Radical Railway Workers,*" p. 95; and J. Tosh, "The Cash Crop Revolution in Tropical Africa: An Agricultural Reappraisal," *Journal of African Affairs,* 79, 3, 14, 1980, pp. 79–84.

111. *Report on Ashanti 1930–1931,* K. D. Patterson, *Health in Colonial Ghana,* p. 6; "Report on Nutrition for the Colonial Empire 1939," in F. Bourret, *Ghana. The Road to Independence,* pp. 124–125; and "Report 1913" in C. Tsey, "Gold Coast Railways," p. 330.

112. R. Bening, "Colonial Development Policy," pp. 73–74.

113. Clifford, *LegCo* 28/10/18, *Gazette* 9/11/18, CO99/33/82.

114. See D. Kimble, *A Political History,* pp. 474–479.

115. See M. Crowder, *West Africa Under Colonial Rule,* pp. 217–221; and R. Stone, "Colonial Administration and Rural Politics," pp. 62–102.

116. D. H. Jones, *Review* of M. Crowder & O. Ikime (eds.), *West African Chiefs: Their Changing Status under Colonial Ride and Independence,(Ife, 1970), JAH,* XVI, 1, 1975.

to follow a dual—apparently contradictory, though not unusual—British colonial path. He favored indirect rule in local government through the "traditional" elites of chiefs and elders, while at the same time, at the level of central government, he supported Africanization and an increase in the number of Western-educated African representatives in the legislative council. Clifford gave African unofficials a greater voice in the legislative council as part of his determination to link British rule more closely with local African society.

But Western-educated Africans continued to be viewed with suspicion by local colonial officials: hence the reassurance publicly given by some of their number in the National Congress of British West Africa at this time: "We do not believe in unconstitutional principles or the principles of bolshevism."[117] The early domination of the NCBWA by Western-educated Africans from the Gold Coast was a measure of their increasing initiative and confidence in this period.[118] The founding of the Congress was postponed by the war until 1920, the year after Clifford's departure from the Gold Coast.[119] The importance of prominent individuals from the Gold Coast is striking: its co-founders included Thomas Hutton-Mills and J. E. Caseley Hayford, who became its first president and vice president, respectively. The organization aspired to unite all four British territories in the region. As Kimble discusses at some length, "The political horizons" of the Congress were wider than those of the ARPS; the NCBWA was "working towards a fundamental change in the colonial relationship."[120]

In this context, and with the advantage of the more favorable postwar conditions (including the chance to take out large new loans), Guggisberg was determined not only to continue a program of Africanization but to increase the pace. As Kimble perceived, "Guggisberg simply added his own characteristic drive to the policy initiated by Clifford, but his approach captured the public imagination in a way his predecessor's had never done."[121] The relative freedom of maneuver following the war also encouraged the change of mood. But Guggisberg's goal—50% of European staff in technical departments replaced by "natives"—would take some time, as he recognized. It would be possible only when the new secondary schools and technical colleges now planned for the colony provided the necessary training. One example of this was the opening in 1919 of the new survey school to train surveyors for the PWD and railway department. Meanwhile, it was to be government policy "to employ every suitably qualified 'native' we can."[122]

This was soon to be echoed in the postwar demands of the NCBWA for the eradication of discrimination in the professions and the administration. Yet Africans were hardly encouraged into government service by conditions of work. For example, "native" officials in Ashanti and the Northern Territories could be required to serve three years continuously without any vacation at all. This ruling must help explain "the great difficulty in finding

117. Meeting, NCBWA and League of Nations Union, 8/10/20, ADM 5/4/10. PRAAD.

118. See, e.g., pp. 204–205 above regarding their criticisms in the legislative council of government policy towards the outbreak of influenza.

119. See, e.g., Eluwa G. I. C., "Background to the Emergence of the National Congress of British West Africa," *African Studies Review,* 14, 2, September, 1971.

120. D. Kimble, *A Political History*, p. 375.

121. *Ibid.*, pp. 105–106.

122. Guggisberg, *LegCo* 26/11/19, *Gazette* 8/12/19, C099/34/100. In 1919 there were three, and by 1927 there were thirty-eight Africans in posts previously reserved for Europeans. See R. Wraith, *Guggisberg*, p. 231.

clerks who willingly accept transfer to the Northern Territories."[123] Guggisberg nevertheless expressed the hope in October 1919 that more and more "natives" would feel encouraged to help with the administration of the colony and join the ranks of officials.[124] The staff shortages of the war period confirmed the strength of Clifford's prewar arguments concerning the need for further Africanization.

However, it was the policy of supporting chiefs, seen by the British as the main bulwark of the "native" administration, that was given priority. British officials continued after the immediate war period with their efforts to try to strengthen "traditional" authorities. The channels of communication developed under Clifford were the background to the Provincial Councils of Chiefs introduced in the constitution of 1925 under Guggisberg and given wider functions in 1927.[125] The period of Clifford's governorship and the war, followed by Guggisberg's efforts of the 1920s, can be seen as a period of transition in the British-African colonial relationship from "noninterventionist" to a more active "interventionist" indirect rule in the interwar period. As pragmatic administrators, Clifford and Guggisberg could see it was essential to uphold the "traditional" powers of chiefs on which the colonial administration relied. The irony was that chiefs' authority was in the long run undermined within African society by its close association with British rule. Meanwhile, Guggisberg, like Clifford, found the problem of town councils intractable, and declared in 1927 that his failure to achieve substantial reforms in African municipal self-government was his only real disappointment as governor.[126] Overall, the British continued to rule the Gold Coast, pragmatically and piecemeal, as before—so that what began as short-term convenience grew into long-term contradiction.

British colonial rule in the Gold Coast was circumscribed and faced innumerable, sometimes insuperable, obstacles, especially during the war. Nevertheless, one argument of this study has been that the personality, character, and aspirations of a governor—an autocrat, after all, in his own territory—could have a traceable impact. Was Clifford's contribution to the Gold Coast in the end more one of style and intention than substantial achievement? British colonial administrators have been labeled as either "developers" or "conservationists"—but Clifford was both.[127] He saw himself as a "builder," even though he was forced, to his frustration, into the role of "caretaker" because of the war. Yet the war stoppages in the long term gave extra muscle to postwar reform, even if the original intention had not been *reculer pour mieux sauter* ("to draw back in order to make a better jump.") Clifford's achievement, though relatively small, was to have obtained Colonial Office support for extending the role of government, including increased responsibility for the welfare of the African population. London officials, won around by Clifford to new levels of spending before the war, were sympathetic with his frustration at wartime delays. So much of Clifford's "building" (construction projects and reforms) was ultimately achieved, even though often delayed by the war into the interwar period.

---

123. Acting Governor Slater, confid. to Milner, 14/8/19, *Sessional paper l. Conditions of Service of Native Clerks,* CO98/31; and M. Staniland, *The Lions of Dagbon,* p. 50.

124. Guggisberg, *LegCo* 9/10/19, *Gazette* 13/10/19, CO99/34/86.

125. See D. Kimble, A *Political History,* p. 440; and R. Stone, "Colonial Administration and Rural Politics," p. 88.

126. R. Wraith, *Guggisberg,* p. 207

127. C. Erlich, "Building and Caretaking: Economic Policy in British Tropical Africa 1890–1960," *Economic History Review, xxvi* , 4, 1973.

While Western-educated Africans in the Gold Coast complained in this period about crown colony status and the slow pace of political reform, they nonetheless had a high regard for Sir Hugh Clifford. The local press exercised its freedom to criticize policies, yet repeatedly made this distinction between the man and the system in which he served. When there was—in 1916, during the war—a threefold increase in the number of Africans to serve as unofficials on the legislative council, this constitutional change received, at best, lukewarm support. It could be acknowledged as an important step "towards actual control of affairs," but it was not to be regarded as a "gift" from the British but as a "right" of the people.[128] And the press insisted that it did not go far enough. The four new men were, like those already sitting, merely nominated, not elected. Already there had been general criticism of the Gold Coast's system of government: "The people are not consulted."[129] Now there was particular criticism that three of the four new nominees were chiefs: such a move had been anticipated—and condemned as a British ploy to divide chiefs from the people, and thus to gain "absolute control of our land."[130] News of what was happening in the wider world fueled opposition: from 1916 it was clear that the people of India could expect elected representation after the war, while the March 1917 Revolution in Russia was hailed as "a wave of democracy," since "the people at last have a voice."[131] By the end of 1918, the *Gold Coast Leader* was in no doubt that, through having been cooperative and having contributed to the British war effort, the people of the Gold Coast had "shown we are worthy of some recognition."[132]

Yet such wartime expressions of frustration and aspiration were, throughout, tempered by acknowledgement of the personal merits of the governor. After his speech to the newly enlarged legislative council in 1916, Clifford's government and administration were lauded as "the most eventful, the most efficient and the most distinguished since Downing Street assumed responsibility for our affairs."[133] Clifford had already been approvingly described as a "man of remarkable personality" and "a centre of energy."[134] By 1918, he could be credited as the governor under whom the gulf between black and white in the Gold Coast had been "gradually, permanently, bridged."[135] The press could describe Clifford as "our popular governor" and as having "a real and genuine interest in the welfare of the people."[136] He had "steadily worked to bring all classes together," and the fact that "all now meet on common ground in affairs" was "largely due to his initiative."[137] Style and sensitivity were also important. Sir Hugh's and Lady Clifford's sincerity and respect for Africans and African societies were often remarked on by the local African press. Thus the *Gold Coast Leader* praised the Cliffords in 1915 for "the very courteous observance of native etiquette" and again for the manner in which "all was said and done" at a conference in Sekondi, just a month before they finally left the colony in March 1919.[138] Clearly there were other British officials in West Africa, including governors, who did not match up to these standards. By his personality as well as his policies, Governor Clifford may be said to have

128. *Gold Coast Leader*, 14/10/16; *The Gold Coast Nation*, 28/7/17, 17/8/17.
129. *Gold Coast Leader*, 9/1/15.
130. *Gold Coast Leader*, 15–22/4/16.
131. *Gold Coast Leader*, 5–12/8/16; 19/5/17.
132. *Gold Coast Leader*, 14–21/12/18.
133. Editorial, *Gold Coast Leader*, 4/11/16.
134. *Gold Coast Leader*, 2/1/15.
135. *Gold Coast Leader*, 26/1/18.
136. *Gold Coast Leader,* 6–13/7/18.
137. *Gold Coast Leader,* 12/1/18.
138. *Gold Coast Leader* 9/9/15, NP 16/4, and 22/2/19, NP 12/9, PRAAD.

improved British-African colonial relations during this period—despite the intrusion of the First World War.

Guggisberg, similarly a paternalist administrator, was determined to continue Clifford's work. In his first speech to the Gold Coast legislative council in October 1919, Guggisberg paid generous tribute to his predecessor—a tribute that was all the more generous in that Clifford had made it clear that he was unhappy about being succeeded by an engineer who lacked administrative experience (and Clifford was not alone in his view that Guggisberg owed his elevation to governor to an ambitious wife as well as his distinguished war service). Guggisberg declared: "In his plans for the progress of the great races of his country, and for the development of its natural wealth for the benefit of those races, Sir Hugh Clifford has given me a start such as I venture to think no Governor has had before. I sincerely trust that whatever disappointment Sir Hugh may have felt in not seeing all his plans mature will be greatly exceeded by his satisfaction at the edifice rising from the foundations so surely laid by him." Guggisberg then emphasized (recorded in capital letters when this speech was published in *The Government Gazette*) that the aim of the administration of the Gold Coast colony now in his care would continue to be "THE PROGRESS OF THE PEOPLE."[139]

A forceful governor could wield influence in determining policy. As in other British tropical Crown Colonies, he was preeminent locally—even if he was, of course, expected to fulfill metropolitan goals—while working with local interests that included commercial companies as well as the African population. Anne Phillips has complained that the history of British colonialism sometimes reads as "a history of eccentric individuals" with "variations between individual administrators" assumed to be of great significance.[140] But this complaint seems to arise from a reluctance to accept the evidence. Indeed, the Colonial Office, to the chagrin of some MPs, normally negotiated with (rather than dictated to) governors in the colonies. As has been said, London officials were "always jealous of Governors' pretensions."[141]

Despite the obvious limitations of his paternalism, Clifford often vigorously defended African interests. This rests uneasily with any presumption of cynicism. His actions and correspondence do not suggest that issues of how Africans should be treated arose simply out of an administrative requirement for African acquiescence in colonial rule (even if, as governor, Clifford had the prime responsibility to provide order). There was unquestionably for Clifford a moral dimension to imperialism. Livingstone's nineteenth-century call for the civilizing mission of white rule, with Christianity hand in hand with commerce, has echoes here. The acceptance of an obligation to provide welfare services in the colonies developed only slowly in Britain.[142] Clifford made a contribution to this process.

The war had shown just how fragile was the administration, and how vulnerable was the economy, of a remote corner of the seaborne British Empire—especially one with an export trade dominated by a single cash crop. The overall cost of the war to the Gold

139. Guggisberg, *LegCo* 9/10/19, *Gazette* 13/10/19, C099/34/86. And see R. Wraith, *Guggisberg*, pp. 74–75.

140. A. Phillips, *The Enigma of Colonialism*, p. 157

141. M. Havinden & D. Meredith, *Colonialism and Development*, p. 313. And see D. J. Morgan, *The Official History of Colonial Development*, 5, pp. 299–300.

142. M. Havinden & D. Meredith, *Colonialism and Development*, p. 6.

Coast colony is difficult to compute. Figures are available for wartime expenditure such as the Togo campaign (the £60,000 cost was charged to the Gold Coast colony) or the contributions to the Imperial Exchequer (initially £500,000, then an additional £200,000). But the cost of much of the impact of the war on the African population and the colonial administration of the Gold Coast is impossible to assess. This includes the sudden collapse of the prewar boom in the cocoa trade and the reduction in returns for agricultural produce, the diversion of manpower, the damage to the neglected infrastructure, and the postponement of development and welfare projects (with the additional expense of taking over the Basel and Bremen schools).

The First World War was a decisive period—as has been pointed out, at the halfway point in the Gold Coast's colonial history. There was no return, in 1919, to the relative prosperity and promise of 1913. These were years of dislocation and hardship for all people of the territory (in varying degrees), but above all they showed the inadequacy of colonial rule. This in turn led to African frustration and disillusionment and, increasingly, impatience, criticism, and organized protest. By 1919, there was a new reality: worse trade conditions and a higher cost of living—yet little of the promised development and welfare that rendered the colonial presence more acceptable. The war had wrecked Clifford's immediate plans and dashed African hopes. Because of the war, the balance of cost and benefit shifted decisively: hence the need for Guggisberg to satisfy the expectations of his African subjects of the Gold Coast in the years that followed the Great War, if he was to retain a continuing acquiescence in colonial rule. For as Akurang-Parry has put it, in retrospect the First World War had acted as an "agency for the advancement of African social consciousness and a sense of political empowerment."[143]

British optimism at the ending of the war was overshadowed—despite Guggisberg's efforts—by "a period of gradual disillusion" among Africans in the 1920s, before the sharp effects of the Depression in the 1930s.[144] Emphasis is usually placed on the "adverse economic trends" of the 1930s and 1940s as giving rise to a movement that eventually brought colonial rule to an end. But it seems more appropriate to see the "long period of economic hardship" as extending back further, even if unevenly, to the period of the First World War and its aftermath.[145] The fall in the price of exports and rise in the price of imports (in reduced supply) that occurred again at the beginning of the Second World War produced sharp questioning from African spokesmen. So, for example, the initial unenthusiastic response of the paramount of the Ga people to the colonial government's appeal for support in 1939 gave voice to familiar economic grievances. He announced to an approving audience in Accra that the British and Germans were related and that this was, once again, their fight.[146] The implication was clear: this second twentieth-century European war was not the business of Africans, who knew from experience how damaging such a war could be to their trade and standard of living.

The strengths and weaknesses of the British administration of the Gold Coast during the First World War reveal colonial rule as too complex for simple characterization. British

143. Akurang-Parry, "Africa and World War I," in T. Falola (ed.), *Colonial Africa 1885–1939*, 3, p. 67.

144. R. W. July, *The Origins of Modern African Thought*, (London, 1968), p. 456.

145. A. G. Hopkins, *An Economic History of West Africa*, pp. 184–185.

146. W. P. Holbrook, "British Propaganda and the Mobilization of the Gold Coast War Effort 1939–1945," *JAH*, 26, 4, 1985, p. 353. See also adverse economic conditions and widespread resistance to recruitment in D. Killingray, "Military and Labor Recruitment in the Gold Coast During the Second World War," *JAH*, 23,1, 1982, pp. 92–94.

officials had struggled through the war years. Like Clifford before him, Guggisberg praised them for having played their part in "the great chain of Empire" across the world.[147] But the survival of the Gold Coast colony had, at one level, been "touch and go"—though what threatened it was a loss of financial viability rather than concerted opposition from its subject peoples when it was at its most vulnerable. This had been shoestring colonial administration, especially in terms of money and manpower. Yet Clifford's ambitions, albeit frustrated by war, were ultimately achievable. Meanwhile, the governor and his officials retained authority as local agents of the metropolitan government and as arbiters among competing groups in the territory. Order was, if imperfectly, maintained.

Here in the Gold Coast colony was a light form of colonial rule, with interdependence manifest between British and African. If laissez-faire describes a necessary British approach to international trade throughout this period, it was exemplified too in the postwar approach to the all-important production of cocoa. African farmers were largely left alone, leaving British officials still worrying about the vulnerability of cocoa to disease and also about the reliance on a single cash crop. As with continuing "uneven development"—the deepening differences between the north of the country on the one hand and the center and south on the other—so with the drift towards monoculture: these were trends which British officials, at different times and in different ways, tried to halt but were powerless to prevent. While clearly capable of maintaining general control in difficult circumstances and of launching a considerable development and welfare program, the administration was makeshift and, in a number of respects, remarkably weak. When faced by difficulties, it chose, because it had to, dialogue with its African subjects: whether women in the markets, or chiefs, or Western-educated unofficials in the legislative council. The latter groups, meanwhile, represented a potential difficulty in terms of the coherent evolution of colonial rule and eventual transition of power. But again we see here not the "divide and rule" manipulation of a cynical colonial power but rather the unintended consequence of short-term political choices made by an administration hard put to sustain, let alone reinforce, its own position.

Finally, the chronicle of the Gold Coast currency—presented in each section of this study—tells us much about the colonial relationship. The British colonial government had played an intermediary role during the war. Clifford found himself caught, as so often, between London officials; European trading, shipping, and mining companies; and African farmers and traders. There were on the one hand, in London, the constraints on providing sufficient coin and a lack of concern about the problems of introducing paper money rapidly as a wartime emergency measure. On the other hand, on the West African coast, there were the problems of coin being hoarded and the widespread African suspicion and distrust of paper currency. The governor had taken every opportunity to try to spur the Colonial Office and the Currency Board into action to produce coin, while cautioning against the overhasty introduction of notes. At the same time he had tried to maintain the confidence of the African population with his calls for calm and patience and his reassurance regarding the value of paper money. Clifford's prewar hopes of stimulating the money economy and reducing hoarding had been dashed by wartime economic instability. But the upheavals and the increasing value and scarcity of silver and the nickel-bronze currency had led to the introduction of a more effective coinage by the end of the war period, which, in the longer term, met the needs of all parties and helped

147. Guggisberg, *LegCo* 9/10/19, *Gazette* 13/10/19, C099/34/86. And see also Clifford, *LegCo* 28/10/18, *Gazette* 9/11/18, C099/33/82.

to stabilize the colony's trade. Here as elsewhere, no British colonial policy succeeded in providing the solution to a problem unless it was acceptable to the mass of the African population.

Analysis of this period reveals a much more intricate and variegated picture of colonial rule than that of an all-powerful British imperial policy being imposed on the Gold Coast. British officials in London or on the West African coast did not necessarily agree with each other, or with African producers, or with expatriate European interest groups, on issues that preoccupied them. But it was not merely a question of agreement. A study of the colony and the governorship of Sir Hugh Clifford in this period reveals the *limits* of the power of the colonial government. Problems and conditions thrown up by the First World War sharply exposed such limitations. From now on, Africans in the Gold Coast were to be more demanding of British colonial rule.

Sources

A. Primary Sources

1. Official Unpublished

- **Public Records and Archive Department (PRAAD), Accra, Ghana**

Administration: Series: 1913–1920: "Native Affairs" and Officers' Diaries:

ADM 11/1/501—ADM 12/5/150; ADM 56/1/165—56/1/213, PRAAD

- **Colonial Office Records, The National Archive (UK),** formerly the Public Record Office, Kew

Series CO 96. Original Correspondence, the Gold Coast. (Accra-London)

1912. Vols. 515–526	1915. Vols. 555–564	1918. Vols. 587–596
1913. Vols. 527–540	1916. Vols. 565–576	1919. Vols. 597–601
1914. Vols. 541–554	1917. Vols. 577–586	

Series CO 343. Gold Coast Register of Correspondence

1911–1919. Vols. 23–26

Series CO 879. Confidential Print

Vols. 108–114

Series C0 554. Original Correspondence, West Africa

1912–1919. Vols. 16–44

Series CO 555. Register Correspondence, West Africa

Series CO 537. Civil Defence: Secret

1919–1921. Vols. 720–721

- **Records of the Royal Botanic Gardens, Kew**

Miscellaneous Reports, Royal Botanic Gardens, Kew. 1910–1926: 10.32. Gold Coast Cocoa

Miscellaneous Reports, Royal Botanic Gardens, Kew. 1907–1928: 10.32. Gold Coast Agricultural Department

Miscellaneous Reports, Royal Botanic Gardens, Kew: 1916–1928: 10.2. Oil Palm. No. 913: The Gold Coast

Miscellaneous Reports, Royal Botanic Gardens, Kew: 1905–1921: 10.2. West Tropical Africa—Forests, including Liberia

Miscellaneous Reports, Royal Botanic Gardens, Kew: 1892–1914: Gold Coast Forest Exploration

- **Records of the Ashanti Goldfields Corporation Ltd., Guildhall Library, City of London**

AGC Journals Ms 14168. Vol. 6. 1913–1917; Vol. 7. 1917–1922.

AGC Bullion Books 1897–1936. Ms 14169. Vol. 2. 1908–1919; Vol. 3. 1919–1935.

AGC Mines Correspondence Outwards: London Office to Obuasi, Gold Coast. Ms 14170. 1914–1918: Vols. 27–36.

AGC Mines Correspondence Inwards: Obuasi Office to London. Ms 14171.1914–1918: Vols. 36–46.

GC "Private" Letter Book. Ms 14172. Copy Letters of Chairman, Secretary and General Manager. 1901–1921.

AGC Reports to Annual General Meeting. Ms 24661.1913–1916 Vol. 4; 1916–1921 Vol. 5.

2. Official Published (Colonial Office, London)

- ***CO 97. Acts, The Gold Coast Colony.*** Vols. 5-7.

- ***CO 98. Sessional Papers, The Gold Coast***

Proceedings of the Executive Council: 1912–1919: Vol. 22

Proceedings of the Legislative Council: 1912–1919: Vols. 19, 27, 29, 31, 33

Administrative (Departmental) Reports: 1912–1922/23: Vols. 21, 23–26, 28, 30, 32, 34, 36, 38

Tudhope's *Interim Enquiry* and *Final Report on the Cocoa Industry 1918–1919, CO98/27, CO98/31*

Education Committee Reports: Report on Secondary Education 1915, CO98/27; Report of Special Committee on Education 1919, CO98/31.

- ***CO 99. The Gold Coast Government Gazette***

1912–1920. Vols. 24–35. Includes alternative source for: *Addresses of the Governor* to the Legislative Council; *Legislative Council Debates, Administrative (Departmental) Annual Reports*: Agriculture, Audit, Customs, Education, Forestry, Harbour Works, Railways, Roads, Medical and Sanitary, Mines, Native Affairs, Police, Post and Telegraph, Printing, Prisons, Public Works, Survey, Trade, Transport, Treasury, Veterinary, Water Works and the regions: Eastern, Central and Western Provinces, Ashanti and the Northern Territories.

- ***CO 100. Blue Books of Statistics, the Gold Coast***

1912–1922. Vols. 62–72

- ***Colonial Office Lists: 1912–1919***

3. Unofficial Unpublished

• *Manuscript Collection, Rhodes House, Oxford*

T. E. Fell, Letters from the Gold Coast 1897–1915. Mss Afr. 315–318. Fell was Assistant Commissioner, Ashanti.

Harper Papers, Mss. s. 344. Commissioner for Eastern Province. Unofficial diaries from 1914.

John Holt Papers (shipper) Mss. Afr. 1525. Letters 1911–1919 Box 13. File 5.

Harry Martin, Reminiscences 1902–1931. Mss Afr. 610. Swanzy Trading Firm.

Sir John Maxwell, Diaries from 1909. Mss. Afr. s. 2133. Commissioner of Western Province in the war; and acting colonial secretary, Accra, in 1916.

Miss E. McKillican, Notes. Mss. Afr. 854. Headmistress of Girls' School, Aburi, 1923.

Alexander Ross, Diaries 1905–1913. Mss Afr. s. 469–475. Wioso, Sefwi station.

J. E. Symonds, Royal Engineers-Senior Inspector, Telegraphs. Diaries: 1909–1918. Mss. Afr. r. 163 Book 2 1912-1916; Mss. r. 164 Book 3 1917-1918; Mss. Afr. r. 165 Book 4 1918.

• *Sir Hugh Clifford Papers [private collection, Mrs. Clifford Holmes].*

4. Unofficial Published

• *Public Records and Archive Department of Ghana*

Newspapers: *Gold Coast Leader*, *The Gold Coast Nation*

NP 12/9–NP 16/4, miscellaneous 1915–1919, PRAAD.

• **The British Museum Newspaper Library, Colindale, London**

1. *Gold Coast Leader*: 1914–1918, Accra

The largest weekly average circulation for a Gold Coast African newspaper (1912–1914: 57,200. (*Government Gazette*: 65,350). Circulation fell during the war. By 1922, the paper had been overtaken by *The Gold Coast Independent.* Publication was interrupted during the last quarter of 1917 as a result of the wartime lack of paper. Issues were produced monthly rather than weekly in 1918. (For information on press, see Blue Books, CO100, 62–71)

2. *The Gold Coast Nation*: 1914–1918, Cape Coast

The average weekly circulation rose steeply from the official record of only 520 in 1912–1914, to 38,400 in 1915. But by 1921 circulation was right down to 9024.

3. *The Gold Coast Independent: 1918, Accra*

First published June 1918, it became the premier paper in the colony by 1921, with over twice the circulation of its nearest rival, the *Gold Coast Leader.*

4. *The African Telegraph & Gold Coast Mirror: 14/11/14 to 25/2/15*

Not then published for the rest of the war.

5. *African Times and Orient Review: 1918 only*

Publication had stopped in 1914 as a result of bankruptcy. (Owner: Duse Mohammed.)

6. *African World*: 1914–1918

Main focus on South and East Africa, but occasional articles and supplements on West Africa, often reproducing articles from the local press, such as *The Sierra Leone Weekly News*, 30/11/18.

7. *The African Mail*: 8/14–5/1/17, Liverpool

Edited by E. D. Morel. Also included articles from the local West African press, e.g., *The Lagos Standard*. The end of publication coincided with the launch of the new weekly journal, *West Africa*.

8. *West Africa*: *3/2/17–11/18*

B. Secondary Sources

1. Books and Articles

Abaka, E. *"Kola is God's Gift": Agricultural Production, Export Initiatives and the Kola Industry of Asante and the Gold Coast, c. 1820–1950.* (Athens, Oxford, Accra, 2005).

Agbodeka, F. *Ghana in the Twentieth Century.* (Accra, 1972).

Agbodeka, F. "Sir Gordon Guggisberg's Contribution to the Development of the Gold Coast 1919–1927," *Transactions of the Historical Society of Ghana,* XIII, 1, 1972.

Ajayi, J. F. A., & Crowder, M. (eds.), *History of West Africa,* Vol. 2. (London, 1987).

Ajayi, J. F. A., & Peel, J. D. Y. (eds.), *People and Empires in African History: Essays in Memory of Michael Crowder.* (London, 1992).

Akurang-Parry, K. O. "Colonial Forced Labour Policies for Road-building in Southern Ghana and International Anti-forced Labour Pressures, 1900–1940," *African Economic History 28,* 2000.

Akurang-Parry, K. O. "Africa and World War I," in Falola. T. (ed.), *Colonial Africa 1885–1939,* Vol. 3. (Carolina, 2002).

Akurang-Parry, K. O. "African Agency and Cultural Initiatives in the British Imperial Military and Labour Recruitment Drives in the Gold Coast (Colonial Ghana) during the First World War," *African Identities,* 4, 2, 2006.

Akurang-Parry, K. O. "Disrespect and Contempt for Our Natural Rulers: The African Intelligentsia and the Effects of British Indirect Rule on Indigenous Rulers in the Gold Coast, c. 1912–1920," *The International Journal of Regional and Local Studies,* 2, series 2, 1, 2006.

Allen, C. *Tales from the Dark Continent: Images of British Colonial Africa in the Twentieth Century.* (London, 1979).

Allman, J., Geiger, S., & Musisi, N. (eds.), *Women in African Colonial Histories.* (Indiana UP, 2002).

Allman, J., & Parker, J. *Tongnaab: The History of a West African God.* (Bloomington, IN, 2005).

Amin, S. "Underdevelopment and Dependence in Black Africa—Origins and Contemporary Forms," *Journal of African Studies*, 4, 1992.

Anderson, D., & Killingray, D. (eds.), *Policing the Empire: Government, Authority, and Control, 1830–1940.* (Manchester, 1991).

Andrew, C. M., & Kanya-Forstner, A. S. "France, Africa, and the First World War," *Journal of African History*, XIX, 1, 1978.

Anin, T. E. *Gold in Ghana.* (London, 1990).

Apter, D. *Ghana in Transition.* (Princeton, 1972).

Arhin, K, "The Pressure of Cash and the Political Consequences in Asante in the Colonial Period," *Journal of African Studies*, 3,1976.

Arhin, K. *West African Traders in the Nineteenth and Twentieth Centuries.* (London, 1979).

Asiwaju, A. "Migration as a Revolt: the Example of the Ivory Coast and the Upper Volta before 1945," *Journal of African History*, XVII, 1976.

Austin, G. "The Emergence of Capitalist Relations in South Asante Cocoa Farming c.1916–33," *Journal of African History*, 28, 1987.

Austin, G. *Labour, Land and Capital in Ghana: from Slavery to Free Labour in Asante, 1807–1956.* (Rochester, 2005)

Austin, R. *African Economic History. Internal Development and External Dependency.* (London, 1987).

Awolowo, O. *Awo: The Autobiography of Chief Awolowo.* (London, 1960).

Bartels, F. *The Roots of Ghana Methodism.* (Cambridge, 1965).

Bassett, T. "The Development of Cotton in Northern Ivory Coast, 1910–1965," *Journal of African History*, 29, 1988.

Bauer, P. *West African Trade.* (Cambridge, 1954).

Bayart, J-F. *The State in Africa. The Politics of the Belly.* (London/New York, 1993).

Becker, D. G., & Sklar, R. L. (eds.), *Post Imperialism and World Politics.* (Westport, 1999).

Beckman, B. *Organizing the Farmers. Cocoa Politics and National Development in Ghana.* (Uppsala, 1976).

Bening, R. B. "Colonial Development Policy in Northern Ghana 1898–1950," *Bulletin of the Ghana Geographical Association*, 17, 1975.

Berridge, R. *The Politics of the South African Run. European Shipping and Pretoria.* (London, 1987).

Boahen, A. A. *Ghana: Evolution and Change in the Nineteenth and Twentieth Centuries.* (London, 1975).

Boahen, A. A. (ed.), *General History of Africa, Volume 7, UNESCO.* (New York, London, 1985).

Boahen, A. A. *African Perspectives on Colonialism.* (Baltimore, 1987).

Boakye-Boaten, A. "Indigenous Retail Trade and Markets in Ashanti during the Colonial Era, 1902–1945," *Bulletin of the Geographical Association*, 17, 1975.

Boateng, E. *A Geography of Ghana.* (Cambridge, 1959).

Bourret, F. *Ghana—The Road to Independence 1919–1957.* (Oxford, 1952).

Brown, I. (ed.), *The Economies of Africa and Asia in the Inter-War Depression.* (London, 1989).

Bush, B. *Imperialism, Race and Resistance.* (London, 1999).

Busia, K. *The Position of Chief in the Modern Political System of Ashanti.* (London, 1951).

Busia, K. "Colonial Administration and Social Change in Ghana 1900–1920s," in Cartey, W., & Kilson, M. (eds.), *The African Reader: Colonial Africa.* (New York, 1970).

Cain, P., & Hopkins, A. *British Imperialism. Crisis and Deconstruction 1914–1990.* (London, 1993).

Cardinall, A. W. *The Natives of the Northern Territories of the Gold Coast.* (London, 1920).

Cartey, W., & Kilson, M. (eds.), *The African Reader: Colonial Africa.* (New York, 1970).

Cary, J. *Mister Johnson.* (London, 1939).

Casely Hayford, G. "The Cape Coast Stool Dispute of 1916." Paper given to the African History Seminar, School of Oriental and African Studies, London University, 24/4/91.

Casely Hayford, J. *The Truth About the West African Land Question.* (London, 1913).

Casely Hayford, A., & Rathbone, R. "Politics, Families, and Freemasons in the Colonial Gold Coast," in Ajayi, J. F. A. & Peel, J. D. Y. (eds.), *People and Empires in History. Essays in Memory of Michael Crowder.* (London, 1992).

Clarke, P. B. *West Africans at War 1914–1918, 1939–1945. Colonial Propaganda and its Cultural Aftermath.* (London, 1986).

Clayton, A., & Killingray, D. *Khaki and Blue. Military Police in British Colonial Africa.* (Ohio, 1989).

Clifford, Sir H. Introduction to Claridge, W.W., *A History of the Gold Coast and Ashanti.* (London, 1915).

Clifford, Sir H. "Recent Developments in the Gold Coast," Address to the Africa Society, 17/6/19, in *The Journal of the Africa Society*, XVIII, lxxii, 1919.

Clifford, Sir H. *The Gold Coast Regiment in the East Africa Campaign.* (London, 1920).

Clifford, Lady. *Our Days on the Gold Coast.* (London, 1919).

Collins, R. O. (ed.), *Western African History, Volume I.* (New York, 1990).

Constantine, S. *The Making of British Colonial Development Policy 1914–1940.* (London, 1984).

Coquery Vidrovitch, C. "L'Impact des Interets Coloniaux: S.C.O.A. et C.F.A.O. dans l'Ouest Africain 1910–1965," *Journal of African History*, XVI, 1975.

Coquery-Vidrovitch, C. *African Women. A Modern History.* (Boulder, CO, 1997).

Cordell, D., & Gregory, J. "Labour Reservoirs and Population: French Colonial Strategies in Koudougou, Upper Volta 1914–1939," *Journal of African History*, 23, 1982.

Cox-George, N. *Studies in Finance and Development, The Gold Coast (Ghana) Experience 1914–1950*. (London, 1973).

Crisp, J. *The Story of an African Working Class. Ghanaian Miners' Struggle 1870–1980.* (London, 1984).

Crowder, M. *West Africa Under Colonial Rule.* (London, 1968).

Crowder, M. "The First World War and Its Consequences," in Boahen, A. A. (ed.), *General History of Africa,Volume 7, UNESCO.* (London, 1985).

Crowder, M., & Osuntokun, J. "The First World War and West Africa," in Ajayi, J. F. A., & Crowder, M. (eds.), *History of West Africa,*Volume 2. (London, 1987).

Danquah, F. *Cocoa Diseases and Politics in Ghana 1909–1966.* (New York, 1995).

Datta, A., & Porter, R. "The Asafo System in Historical Perspective. An Enquiry into the Origin and Development of a Ghanaian Institution," *Journal of African History*, XII, 1971.

Davies, P. N. *The Trade Makers. Elder Dempster in West Africa 1852–1972.* (London, 1973).

Davies, P. N. *Trading in West Africa 1840–1920.* (London, 1976).

Debrunner, H. W. *A History of Christianity in Ghana.* (Accra, 1967).

Dewey, C., & Hopkins, A. G. (eds.), *The Imperial Impact: Studies in the Economic History of Africa and India.* (London, 1978).

Dickson, K. B. "The Development of Road Transport in Southern Ghana and Ashanti Since About 1850," *Transactions of the Historical Society of Ghana*, 5, 1, 1961.

Dickson, K. B. "Evolution of Sea Ports in Ghana 1800–1928," *Annals of the Association of American Geographers,* 55, 1965.

Dickson, K. B. *A Historical Geography of Ghana.* (Cambridge, 1969).

Digre, B. *Imperialism's New Clothes. The Repartition of Tropical Africa 1914–1919.* (New York, 1990).

Dorward, D. C. "British West Africa and Liberia," in Roberts, A. D. (ed.), *The Cambridge History of Africa, Volume 7. From 1905 to 1940.* (Cambridge, 1986).

Dumett, R. "The Campaign Against Malaria and the Expansion of Scientific and Sanitary Medical and Sanitary Services in British West Africa 1898–1910," *African Historical Studies,* 1, 2, 1968.

Dumett, R. "Africa's Strategic Minerals during the Second World War," *Journal of African History,* 26, 1985.

Dumett, R. "Disease and Mortality Among Gold Miners of Ghana: Colonial Government and Mining Company Attitudes and Policies 1900–1938," paper given to the African History Seminar, School of Oriental and African Studies, London University, October 1992.

Dunn, J., & Robertson, A. F. *Dependence and Opportunity. Political Change in Ahafo.* (Cambridge, 1973).

Edsman, B. J. *Lawyers in Gold Coast Politics 1900–1945.* (Uppsala, 1979).

Edwards, N. *Cadbury on the Gold Coast: A Brief Survey of the Commercial and Social Activities of Cadbury Brothers Limited in that Colony 1900–1945.* (Bournville, 1955).

Ehrlich, C. "Building and Caretaking: Economic Policy in British Tropical Africa 1890–1960," *Economic History Review*, XXVI, 1973.

Fage, J. D. *A History of West Africa.* (Cambridge, 1969).

Falola, T. "The Lebanese in Colonial West Africa," in Ajayi, J. F. A., & Peel, J. Y. D. (eds.), *People and Empires in African History: Essays in Memory of Michael Crowder.* (London, 1992).

Falola, T. (ed.), *Colonial Africa 1885–1939*, Vol. 3. (Carolina, 2002).

Falola, T. *The Power of African Cultures.* (Rochester, NY, 2003).

Falola, T. *Economic Reform and Modernisation in Nigeria, 1945–1965.* (Kent State University Press, 2004).

Falola, T. *The Dark Webs: Perspectives on Colonialism in Africa.* (Carolina, 2005).

Falola, T. *A History of Nigeria.* (Cambridge, 2008).

Farwell, B. *The Great War in Tropical Africa 1914–1918.* (New York, 1986).

Field, M. J. *Search for Security. An Ethno-Psychiatric Study of Rural Ghana.* (London, 1960).

Fieldhouse, D. K. The *Colonial Empires. A Comparative Survey from the 18th Century.* (London, 1982).

Fieldhouse, D. K. *Merchant Capital and Economic Decolonization. The United Africa Company, 1929–1987.* (Oxford, 1994).

Forbes Munro, J. "Monopoly & Speculators: British Investment in West African Rubber 1905–1914," *Journal of African History*, 22, 1981.

Forbes Munro, J. *Britain in Tropical Africa 1880–1960. Economic Relations and Impact.* (London, 1984).

Forbes Munro, J. Review, "Rethinking the Thirties," *Journal of African History*, 31, 2, 1990.

Foster, P. *Education and Social Change in Ghana.* (London, 1965).

Freund, W. M. "Labour Migration to the Northern Nigerian Tin Mines 1903–1945," *Journal of African History*, 22, 1, 1981.

Fry, R. *Bankers in West Africa. The Story of the Bank of West Africa Ltd.* (London, 1976).

Fuller, Sir F. *A Vanished Dynasty—Ashanti.* (London, 1921).

Gailey, H. A. *Clifford: Imperial Proconsul.* (London, 1982).

Gann, L. H., & Duignan, P. *Colonialism in Africa,* Volume 2, (Cambridge, 1970); and Volume 4, (Cambridge, 1975).

Gann, L. H., & Duignan, P. (eds.), *African Proconsuls—European Governors in Africa.* (New York, 1978).

Gann, L. H., & Duignan, P. *The Rulers of British Africa 1870–1914.* (London, 1978).

Gannon, M. "The Basle Mission Trading Company and British Colonial Policy in the Gold Coast," *Journal of African History*, 24, 1983.

Gaunt, M. *Alone in West Africa.* (London, 1912).

Gillespie, W. H. *The Gold Coast Police 1844–1938.* (Accra, 1955).

Gocking, R. S. "British Justice and the Native Tribunals of the Southern Gold Coast Colony," *Journal of African History*, 34,1993.

Gocking, R. S. *The History of Ghana.* (Westport, 2005).

Gorges, Brigadier General E. H. *The Great War in Africa.* (London, 1930).

Graham, C. K. *The History of Education in Ghana from the Earliest Times to the Declaration of Independence.* (London, 1971).

Green, R. H., & Hymer, S. H. "Cocoa in the Gold Coast: A Study in the Relationship between African Farmers and Agricultural Experts," *Journal of African History*, XXVI, 1966.

Greenhalgh, P. *West African Diamonds 1919–1983. An Economic History.* (Manchester, 1985).

Gregory, J. Review of J. Marchal, "Chronique d'un Cercle de L'AOF Recueil D'Archives du Poste de Ouahiougya (Haute Volta) 1908–1941 (Paris 1980)," *Journal of African History*, 24, 3, 1983.

Guggisberg, Brigadier General Sir F. G. *The Gold Coast. A Review of the Events of 1920–1927 and the Prospects for 1927–1928.* (Accra, 1927).

Guggisberg, Brigadier General Sir F. G. "The Keystone (London, 1924)," in Collins, R. O. (ed.), *Western African History*, Volume I. (New York, 1990).

Gunnarsson, C. *The Gold Coast Cocoa Industry 1900–1939. Production, Prices, and Structural Change.* (Lund, 1978).

Guyer, J. (ed.), *Money Matters. Instability, Values and Social Payments in the Modern History of West African Communities.* (London, 1995).

Hailey, Lord. *An African Survey.* (Oxford, 1938).

Haliburton, G. M. "The Anglican Church in Ghana and the Harris Movement in 1914," *Bulletin of the Society for Anglican Church History*, 4,1963.

Haliburton, G. M. *The Prophet Harris.* (London, 1971).

Hancock, W. H. *Survey of British Commonwealth Affairs, Volume II, Problems of Economic Policy 1918–1939, Part I.* (Oxford, 1964).

Hasty, J. *The Press and Political Culture in Ghana.* (Indiana UP, 2005).

Hatton, P. H. S. "The Gambia, the Colonial Office, and the Opening Months of the First World War," *Journal of African History*, VII, 1966.

Havinden, M., & Meredith, D. *Colonialism and Development, Britain and Its Tropical Colonies 1850–1960.* (London/New York, 1993).

Haywood, Colonel A. S., & Clarke, Brigadier. F. A. S., *The History of the Royal West African Frontier Force.* (London, 1964).

Henige, D. *Colonial Governors from the Fifteenth Century to the Present.* (Wisconsin, 1970).

Henige, D. "Akan Stool Succession Under Colonial Rule—Continuity or Change," *Journal of African History*, XVI, 1975.

Henige. D. *Historical Evidence and Argument.* (Wisconsin, 2005).

Herbst, J. *States and Power in Africa, Comparative Lessons in Authority and Control.* (Princeton, 2000).

Hetherington, P. *British Paternalism and Africa 1920–1940.* (London, 1978).

Heussler, R. *Yesterday's Rulers. The Making of the British Colonial Service.* (Oxford, 1963).

Hill, P. *The Gold Coast Farmer. A Preliminary Survey.* (London, 1956).

Hill, P. *Studies in Rural Capitalism in West Africa.* (Cambridge, 1970).

Hodges, G. *The Carrier Corps. Military Labor in the East African Campaign 1914–1918.* (New York, 1988).

Hogendorn, J., & Johnson, M. *The Shell Money of the Slave Trade.* (Cambridge, 1986).

Holbrook, W. P. "British Propaganda and the Mobilization of the Gold Coast War Effort 1939–1945," *Journal of African History*, 26,1985.

Hopkins, A. G. "Economic Aspects of Political Movements in Nigeria and the Gold Coast 1918–1939," *Journal of African History*, VII, 1966.

Hopkins, A. G. *An Economic History of West Africa.* (London, 1973).

Hopkins, A. G., Review of P. N. Davies, "The Trade Makers: Elder Dempster in West Africa 1852–1972 (London, 1973)." *Journal of African History*, XV, 3, 1974.

Hopkins, A. G. "Imperial Business in Africa. Part I, Sources," *Journal of African History*, XVII, 1, 1976.

Hopkins, A. G. "Imperial Business in Africa, Part II, Interpretations," *Journal of African History*, XVII, 2, 1976.

Hopkins, A. G. "Big Business in African Studies," *Journal of African History*, 28, 1987.

Hopkins, A. G. "Back to the Future: From National History to Imperial History," *Past and Present*, 164, 1999.

Hopkins, A. G. "Making Poverty History," *International Journal of African Historical Studies* 38, 3, 2005.

Hopkins, A. G. (ed.), *Global History.* (London, 2006).

Howard, M. "Structure and Process in History," *The Times Literary Supplement*, 23–29/6/89.

Howard, R. *Colonialism and Underdevelopment in Ghana.* (London, 1978).

Ilegbune, C. "Concessions, Scramble and Land Alienation in British South Central Ghana 1885–1915," *African Studies Review*, 19, 1976.

Iliffe, J. *The African Poor: A History.* (Cambridge, 1988).

Ingham, B. *Tropical Exports and Economic Development. New Perspectives on Producer Response in Three Low Income Countries.* (London, 1981).

Ingham, B., & Simmons, C. *Development Studies and Colonial Policy.* (London, 1986).

Isaacman, A., & Isaacman, B. "Resistance and Collaboration in Southern and Central Africa c. 1850–1920," *The International Journal of African and Historical Studies*, X,1977.

Jeffries, R. *Class, Power and Ideology in Ghana: The Railwaymen of Sekondi.* (Cambridge, 1978).

Jenkins, P. "The Anglican Church in Ghana 1905–24," *Transactions of the Historical Society in Ghana*, XV, i, 1974.

Johnson, T. "Protest, Tradition and Change. An Analysis of Southern Gold Coast Riots 1890–1920," *Economy and Society*, 1, 1972.

Johnson, T. "Protest: Tradition and Change," *Economy & Society*, 3, 1974.

Jones, D. H., Review of Crowder, M., & Ikime, O., "West African Chiefs: Their Changing Status Under Colonial Rule and Independence (Ife, 1970)," in *Journal of African History*, VI, 1975.

July, R. *The Origins of Modern African Thought*. (London, 1968).

Kay, G. B. *The Political Economy of Colonialism in Ghana 1900–1960*. (Cambridge, 1972).

Kennedy, D. "Imperial History and Post Colonial Theory," *Journal of Imperial and Commonwealth History*, 24, 3, 1996.

Kesner, R. M. "Builders of Empire: The Role of Crown Agents in Imperial Development 1880–1914," *Journal of Imperial and Commonwealth History*, V, 1977.

Killingray, D. "Repercussions of World War I in the Gold Coast," *Journal of African History*, XIX, 1978.

Killingray, D., & Matthews, J. "Beasts of Burden: British West African Carriers in the First World War," *Canadian Journal of African Studies*, 13, 1979.

Killingray, D. "The Empire Resources Committee and West Africa 1916–1920," *Journal of Imperial and Commonwealth Studies*, X, 1982.

Killingray, D. "Military and Labour Recruitment in the Gold Coast during the Second World War," *Journal of African History*, 23, 1, 1982.

Killingray, D. "Military and Labour Policies in the Gold Coast during the First World War," in Page, M. E. (ed.), *Africa and the First World War*. (London, 1987).

Killingray, D. "War & Society in Africa, 1914–20," paper given to the African History Seminar, School of Oriental and African Studies, London University, November 1989.

Kilson, M. "The Emergent Elites of Black Africa 1900–1960," in Gann, L. H., & Duignan, P. (eds.), *Colonialism in Africa 1870–1960*, Volume 2. (Cambridge, 1970).

Kimble, D. A. *Political History of Ghana 1850–1928*. (London, 1963).

Konings, P. *The State and Rural Class Formation in Ghana: A Comparative Analysis*. (London, 1986).

Kuklick, H. *The Imperial Bureaucrat. The Colonial Administrative Service in the Gold Coast 1920–1939*. (Stanford, 1979).

Ladouceur, P. A. *Chiefs and Politicians: the Politics of Regionalism in Northern Ghana*. (London, 1979).

Langley, J. A. *Pan Africanism and Nationalism in West Africa 1900–1945*. (Oxford, 1973).

Leith Ross, S. *Stepping Stones. Memoirs of Colonial Nigeria 1907–1960*. (London, 1983).

Leubuscher, C. *The West African Shipping Trade 1909–1959*. (Leiden, 1963).

Lewis, P. (ed.), *Africa. Dilemmas of Development and Change*. (West View, CO, 1998).

Leys, C. *The Rise and Fall of Development Theory*. (Oxford, 1977/96).

Lonsdale, J., & Berman, B. "Coping with the Contradictions: The Development of the Colonial State in Kenya 1895–1914," *Journal of African History*, 20, 1979.

Loomba, A. *Colonialism/PostColonialism*, 2nd ed. (London, 2005).

Lovejoy, P. E., & Falola, T. (eds.), *Pawnship, Slavery and Colonialism in Africa*. (Trenton, NJ, 2003).

Louis, W. R. *Great Britain and Germany's Lost Colonies 1914–1919.* (Oxford, 1967).

Lucas, Sir Charles. *The Gold Coast and the War.* (London, 1920).

Lucas, Sir Charles. *The Partition and Colonization of Africa.* (Oxford, 1922).

Lunn, J. *Memoirs of the Maelstrom. A Senegalese History of the First World War.* (London, 1999).

MacMillan, A. *The Red Book of West Africa.* (London, 1920).

Mangan, J. *The Games Ethic and Imperialism: Aspects of the Diffusion of an African Ideal.* (London, 1986).

Martin, S. "The Long Depression: West African Export Producers and the World Economy 1914–45," in Brown, I. (ed.), *The Economies of Africa and Asia in the Inter-War Depression.* (London, 1989).

Matthews, J. K. "World War I and the Rise of African Nationalism. Nigerian Veterans as Catalysts of Change," *The Journal of Modern African Studies*, 20, 3, 1982.

Matthews, J. K. "Reluctant Allies: Nigerian Responses to Military Recruitment 1914–1918," in Page, M. E. (ed.), *Africa and the First World War.* (London, 1987).

McCaskie, T. C. "Anti-Witchcraft Cults in Asante: An Essay in the Social History of an African People," *History in Africa*, 8, 1981.

McPhee, A. *The Economic Revolution in British West* Africa. (London, 1926).

McWilliam, H. A. O. *Development of Education in Ghana.* (London, 1959).

Meredith, D. "Government and the Decline of the Nigerian Oil Palm Export Industry 1919–1939," *Journal of African History*, 25, 3, 1984.

Metcalfe, G. E. *Great Britain and Ghana. Documents of Ghana History 1807–1957.* (London, 1964).

Mikell, G. *Cocoa and Chaos in Ghana.* (New York, 1989).

Miles, J. "Rural Protest in the Gold Coast: The Cocoa Hold-Ups 1908–1938," in Dewey, C., & Hopkins, A.G. (eds.), *The Imperial Impact: Studies in the Economic History of Africa and India.* (London, 1978).

Moore, D., & Guggisberg, F. G. *We Two in West Africa.* (London, 1909).

Morgan, D J. *The Official History of Colonial Development*, Volume I. (London, 1986).

Naanen, B. "Economy within an Economy: The Manilla Currency, Exchange Rate Stability and Social Conditions in S.E. Nigeria 1900–1948," *Journal of African History*, XIX, 1978.

Newbury, C. *Selected Documents. British West Africa.* (Oxford, 1971).

Newbury, C. "Trade and Technology in West Africa: The Case of the Niger Company 1900–1920," *Journal of Imperial and Commonwealth Studies*, IV, 1977.

Nicolson, I. F. *The Administration of Nigeria 1900–1960.* (Oxford, 1969).

Nicolson, I. F., & Hughes, C.A. "A Provenance of Pro-consuls: British Colonial Governors 1900–1960," *Journal of Imperial And Commonwealth Studies*, IV, 1977.

Nwabughuogu, A. I. "From Wealthy Entrepreneurs to Petty Traders: The Decline of African Middlemen in Eastern Nigeria 1900–1950," *Journal of African History*, 23, 1982.

Ohadike, D. C. "The Influenza Pandemic of 1918–1919 and the Spread of Cassava Cultivation in the Lower Niger, A Study of Historical Linkages," *Journal of African History*, 22, 1981.

Oldham, J. H. (ed.), *The International Review of Missions,* VI, 21, 1917.

Oliver, R., & Atmore, A. *Africa Since 1800.* (London, 1972).

Olukoju, A. "Elder Dempster and the Shipping Trade of Nigeria during the First World War," *Journal of African History*, 33, 1992.

Omu, F. I. A. *Press and Politics in Nigeria 1880–1937.* (London, 1978).

Osuntokun, A. "Disaffection and Revolts in Nigeria During the First World War, 1914–1918," *Canadian Journal of African Studies*, V, ii, 1971.

Osuntokun, A. *Nigeria in the First World War.* (London, 1979).

Overton, J. "War and Economic Development: Settlers in Kenya 1914–1918," *Journal of African History,* 27, 1986.

Owusu, M. *Uses and Abuses of Political Power. A Case Study of Continuity and Change in the Politics of Ghana.* (Chicago, 1970).

Page, M. E. (ed.), *Africa and the First World War.* (London, 1979).

Parker, J. *Making the Town, Ga State and Society in Early Colonial Accra.* (Oxford, 2000).

Parsons, R. T. *The Churches and Ghana Society 1918–1955.* (Leiden, 1963).

Patterson, K. D. *Health in Colonial Ghana: Disease, Medicine, and Economic Change 1900–1955.* (London, 1981).

Patterson, K. D. "The Influenza Epidemic of 1918–1919 in the Gold Coast," *Journal of African History*, 24, 1983.

Perrings, C. "Good Lawyers But Poor Workers": Recruited Angolan Labour in the Copper Mines of Katanga 1917–1921," *Journal of African History*, XVIII, 1977.

Phillips, A. *The Enigma of Colonialism. British Policy in West Africa.* (Indiana, 1989).

Phillips, H. *Black October. The Impact of the Spanish Influenza Epidemic of 1918 on South Africa.* (Pretoria, 1990).

Popper, K. *The Poverty of Historicism.* (London, 1957).

Rathbone, R. "World War I and Africa: Introduction," *Journal of African History*, XIX, 1978.

Rathbone, R. "Murder and Politics in Colonial Ghana: Law and Politics in the 1940s," *Journal of African History*, 30, 1989.

Rathbone, R. *Murder and Politics in Colonial Ghana.* (New Haven & London, 1993).

Rathbone, R. *Nkrumah and the Chiefs.* (Oxford, Accra, Athens, 2000).

Rattray, R. S. *Ashanti.* (Oxford, 1923).

Rhodie, S. "The Gold Coast Cocoa Hold-Up of 1930–31," *Transactions of the Historical Society of Ghana*, IX, 1965–68.

Richardson, P. "The Recruiting of Chinese Indentured Labour for the South African Gold Mines 1903–1908," *Journal of African History*, XVIII, 1977.

Richardson, P. *Chinese Mine Labour in the Transvaal.* (London, 1982).

Roberts, A. (ed.), *Cambridge History of Africa,* Volume 7. (Cambridge, 1986).

Roberts, A. (ed.), *The Colonial Moment in Africa: Essays in the Movement of Minds and Materials 1900–1940.* (Cambridge, 1990).

Robertson, A. F. *The Dynamics of Productive Relationships: African Share Contracts in a Comparative Perspective.* (Cambridge, 1987).

Rodney, W. *How Europe Underdeveloped Africa.* (London, 1972).

Sampson, M. *The Makers of Modern Ghana*, Volume I. (Accra, 1969).

Seers, D. "The Stages of Economic Development of a Primary Producer in the Middle of the Twentieth Century," *Economic Bulletin of Ghana*, 7, 1963.

Silver, J. "The Failure of European Mining Companies in the 19th Century Gold Coast," *Journal of African History*, 22, 1981.

Simensen, J. "Rural Mass Action in the Context of Anti-colonial Protest: The Asafo Movement of Akim Abuakwa, Ghana," *Canadian Journal of African Studies*, VIII, 1975.

Simensen, J. "The Asafo of Kwahu, Ghana: A Mass Movement for Local Reform Under Colonial Rule," *International Journal of African Historical Studies*, VIII, 1975.

Smith, J. (ed.), *Administering Empire. The British Colonial Service in Retrospect.* (London, 1999).

Smith, N. *The Presbyterian Church of Ghana 1835–1960.* (Accra, 1966).

Staniland, M. *The Lions of Dagbon: Political Change in Northern Ghana.* (Cambridge, 1975).

Stone, R. "Protest, Tradition and Change—Critique," *Economy and Society*, 3, 1974.

Strachan, H. *The First World War in Africa.* (Oxford, 2004).

Summers, A., & Johnson, R. W. "World War I Conscription and Social Change in Guinea," *Journal of African History*, XIX, 1978.

Sutton, I. "The Volta River Salt Trade: The Survival of an Indigenous Industry," *Journal of African History*, 22, 1981.

Sutton, I. "Labour in Commercial Agriculture in Ghana in the Late 19th and Early 20th Centuries," *Journal of African History*, 24, 1983.

Szereszewski, R. *Structural Changes in the Economy of Ghana 1891–1911.* (London, 1965).

Thomas, R. "Forced Labour in British West Africa: The Case of the Northern Territories of the Gold Coast 1906–1927," *Journal of African History*, XIV, 1, 1973.

Thomas, R. "Education in Northern Ghana 1900–1940. A Study in Colonial Paradox," *The International Journal of African Historical Studies*, VII, 3, 1975.

Thomas, R. "Military Recruitment in the Gold Coast during the First World War," *Cahiers d'Etudes Africaines*, 15, 1975.

Thomas, R. "The Bongo 'Riots' and Their Background: Aspects of Colonial Administration and African Response in Eastern Upper Ghana," *Journal of African History*, 24, 1983.

Thompson, G. *Governing Uganda. British Colonial Rule and Its Legacy.* (Kampala, 2003).

Tomkins, S. M. "Colonial Administration in British Africa during the Influenza Epidemic of 1918–19," *Canadian Journal of African Studies*, 28, 1, 1994.

Tordoff, W. *Ashanti Under the Prempehs 1888–1935.* (Wisconsin, 1959).

Tosh, J. "The Cash Crop Revolution in Tropical Africa: An Agricultural Reappraisal," *African Affairs*, 79, 1980.

Van Onselen, C. "Worker Consciousness in Black Mines: Southern Rhodesia 1900–1920," *Journal of African History*, XIV, 1972.

Von Troil, M. *Changing Paradigms in Development: South, East and West—A Meeting of Minds in Africa.* (Upsala, 1993).

Ward, W. E. F. *A History of Ghana.* (London, 1958).

Webster, J. B., Boahen, A. A., & Idowu, H. O. *The Revolutionary Years: West Africa Since 1800.* (London, 1980).

Wight, M. *The Gold Coast Legislative Council.* (London, 1946).

Williamson, T., & Kirk-Greene, T. *Gold Coast Diaries: Chronicles of Political Officers in West Africa, 1900–1919.* (London, NY, 2000).

Wraith, R. E. *Guggisberg.* (London, 1967).

Wrangham, E. "The Colonial Service and the First World War: 'Carrying On,' The Service under Strain," in Smith, J., *Administering Empire. The British Colonial Service in Retrospect.* (London, 1999).

Wrangham, E. "An African Road Revolution: The Gold Coast in the Period of the Great War," *Journal of Imperial and Commonwealth History*, 32, 1, 2004.

Wrigley, C. C. "Aspects of Economic History," in Roberts, A. D. (ed.), *The Cambridge History of Africa, Volume 7, From 1905 to 1940.* (Cambridge, 1986).

Wolfson, F. *Pageant of Ghana.* (London, 1958).

2. Unpublished PhD Theses

Addo-Fening, R. "Akyem Abuakwa c. 1874–1943: A Study of the Impact of Missionary Activities and Colonial Rule on a Traditional State." (University of Legon, Accra, 1980).

Bush, R. C. "The Colonial Factor and the Social Transformation on the Gold Coast to 1930." (University of Leeds, 1984).

Chada, G. T. Z. "Labour Protest, Group Consciousness and Trade Unionism in West Africa: the Radical Railway Workers of Colonial Ghana 1900–1950." (University of Toronto, 1981).

Cole, F. "Sierra Leone and World War I." (University of London, 1994).

Danquah, F. "The Capsid, Black Pod and Swollen Shoot Cacao Diseases in Ghana, 1910–1966." (Iowa State University, 1991).

Deutsch, J. G. "Educating the Middlemen: A Political and Economic History of Statutory Cocoa Marketing in Nigeria, 1936–1947." (University of London, 1990).

Grau, E. E. "The Evangelical Presbyterian Church (Ghana and Togo) 1914–1946. A Study in European Mission Relations Affecting the Beginning of an Indigenous Church." (University of Hartford, 1964).

Holmes, A. B. "Economic and Political Organizations in the Gold Coast, 1920–1965." (University of Chicago, 1972).

Jones, P. "The United Africa Company in the Gold Coast/Ghana 1920–1965." (University of London, 1983).

Killingray, D. "The Colonial Army in the Gold Coast: Official Policy and Local Response 1890–1947." (University of London, 1982).

Li, A. "Social Protest in the Gold Coast. A Study of the Eastern Province in the Colonial Period." (University of Toronto, 1993).

Prempeh, S. "The Bremen and Basle Missions and Their Successors in the Gold Coast." (University of Aberdeen, 1977).

Simensen, J. "Commoners, Chiefs and Colonial Government. British Policy and Local Politics in Akim Abuakwa, Ghana, under Colonial Rule." (University of Trondheim, 1975).

Southall, R. J. "Cadbury on the Gold Coast 1907–1938: The Dilemma of the Model Firm in a Colonial Economy." (University of Birmingham, 1975).

Stone, R. "Colonial Administration and Rural Politics in South Central Ghana 1919–1951." (University of Cambridge, 1974).

Tsey, C. E. "Gold Coast Railways. The Making of a Colonial Economy 1879–1929." (University of Glasgow, 1986).

Van Hear, N. "Northern Labour and the Development of Capitalist Agriculture in Ghana." (University of Birmingham, 1982).

Wrangham, E. "The Gold Coast and the First World War: The Colonial Economy and Clifford's Administration." (University of London, 1999).

3. Unpublished MA Theses

Drummond-Thompson, P. H. "The Impact of Motorized Road Transport upon the Organization of Internal Trade in Nigeria, 1919–1945." (School of Oriental and African Studies, London University, 1983).

Mickelsen, K. "Yellow Fever, Sanitation, Mining Labour in the Gold Coast. 1900–1913." (School of Oriental and African Studies, London University, 1973).

Wrangham, E. "The British Occupation and Early Administration of the Northern Territories of the Gold Coast 1897–1907." (School of Oriental and African Studies, London University, 1973).

Principal Officials

A. Secretaries of State for the Colonies, 1910-1921:

Nov. 1910	Lewis (later Viscount) Harcourt
May 1915	Andrew Bonar Law
Dec. 1916	Walter (later Viscount) Long
Jan. 1919	Viscount Milner
Feb. 1921	Winston Churchill

B. Under-Secretaries & Other Principal Officials at the Colonial Office:

Sir John Anderson	Permanent Under-Secretary of State (1911-1916)
W. D. Ellis	Head of the West Africa & Mediterranean Department (renamed in 1918: The Gold Coast & Mediterranean Department)
A. J. Fiddian	Spokesman for Tropical Africa Medical Work, CO
J. E. W. Flood	Principal Clerk, West African Section, CO
Sir George Fiddes	Assistant Under-Secretary of State. March 1916: Permanent Under-Secretary of State
J. F. N. Green	Deputy Head, West African Department, CO
H. J. Read	March 1916: promoted from Principal Clerk to Assistant Under-Secretary of State (as Sir Herbert Read)
A. D. Steel-Maitland	May 1915: Parliamentary Under-Secretary of State

C. Governors of the Gold Coast Colony, 1910-1919:

March 1904	Sir John P. Rodger
Nov. 1910	Sir James J. Thorburn
Dec. 1912	Sir Hugh C. Clifford
Oct. 1919 (-1927)	Brigadier-General Sir Frederick G. Guggisberg

Appendix I

The Gold Coast in 1916

Map by A. E. Kitson, Gold Coast government surveyor, Royal Geographical Society, London: Ghana S/G3.

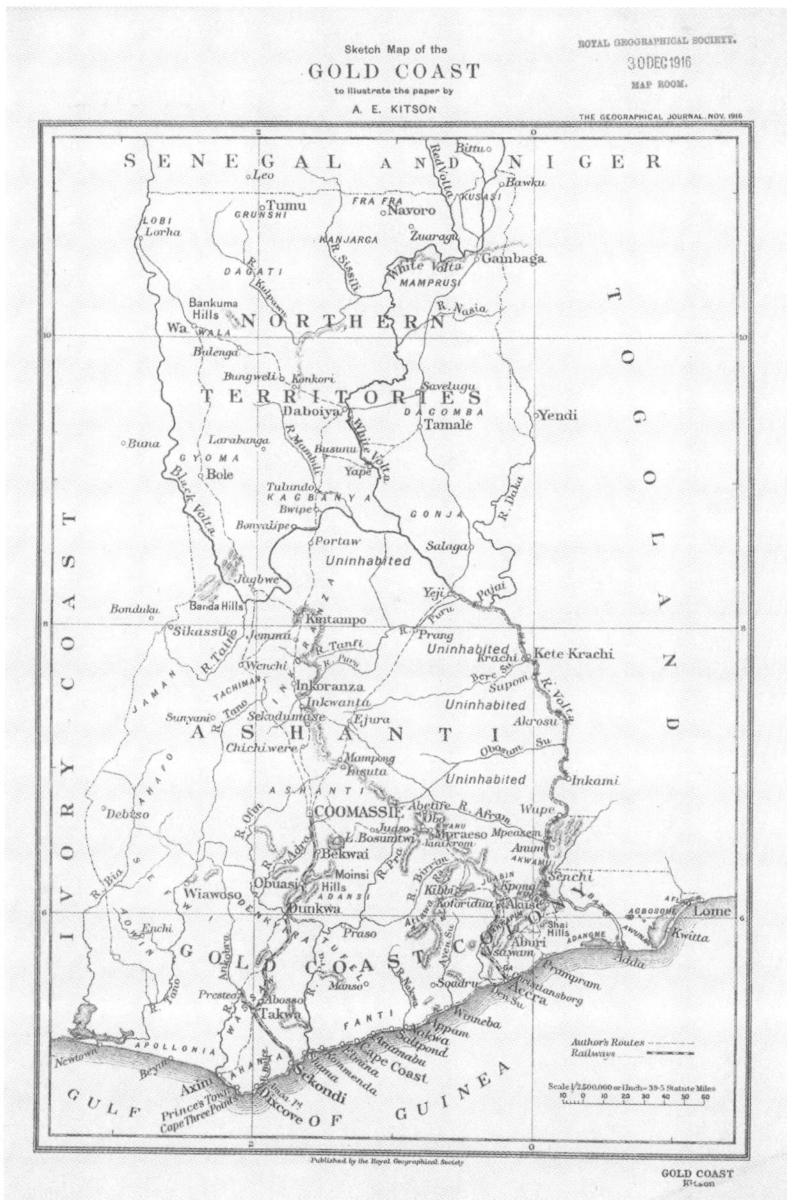

Appendix II

Principal Exports from the Gold Coast 1905–1914

National Archive, Kew, London CO 99/29

APPENDIX M.

VALUE AND QUANTITY OF THE PRINCIPAL VEGETABLE PRODUCTS EXPORTED FROM THE COLONY DURING THE LAST TEN YEARS.

Year.	Cocoa.		Cola-Nuts.		Guinea Grains.		Gum Copal.		Lumber, (Native Timber.)		Palm Kernels.	
	Lbs.	Value. £	Pkgs.	Value. £	Lbs.	Value. £	Lbs.	Value. £	Feet.	Value. £	Tons.	Value. £
1905	11,407,608	186,809	4,342	60,110	18,581	164	29,212	406	8,363,362	84,428	9,781	78,625
1906	20 104,504	336,268	1,703	73,632	46,769	516	194,162	2,215	7,795,922	80,012	9,355	80,833
1907	20,956,400	515 089	6,278	78,901	87,074	1,127	398,363	5,134	18,528,348	169,458	9,753	101,822
1908	28,545,910	540,821	4,484	84,362	21,317	282	380,951	4,759	19,009,963	158,305	8,956	77,821
1909	45,277,606	755,347	* 6,615	93,850	57,754	862	62,042	762	9,838,959	82,937	11,598	112,425
1910	50,692,949	866,671	5,156,500 lbs.	77,716	48,645	882	53,847	647	14,935,935	148,077	14,182	185,058
1911	88 987,324	1,613,468	5,791,931 ,,	93,099	99,386	2,099	80,042	1,110	13,973,396	138,821	13,254	175,891
1912	86,568,481	1,642,733	7,133,165 ,,	134,231	158,488	3,304	67,133	1,077	23,573,651	228,745	14,628	205,365
1913	113,239,980	2,489,218	7,024,868 ,,	144,705	41,036	706	38,205	555	37,391,848	366,094	9,744	159,128
1914	52,888 tons.	2,193,749	7,862,414 ,,	142,190	18,894	319	18,549	265	24,587,217	240,878	5,633	88,671

Year.	Palm Oil.		Rubber.		Cotton.		Copra.	
	Gallons.	Value. £	Lbs.	Value £	Lbs.	Value £	Tons.	Val £
1905	1,598,272	88,359	3,633,106	323,774	29,124	516	251	3,158
1906	2,143,118	125,008	3,649,668	334,504	92,886	1,021	327	4,290
1907	1,867,945	119,468	3,549,548	333,120	56,088	966	386	6,186
1908	2,253,371	129,534	1,773,248	168,142	51,480	1,171	612	6,489
1909	2,007,296	102,978	2,764,190	263,694	31,290	790	809	10,451
1910	2,044,945	161,388	3,223,265	358,876	11,421	263	755	13,032
1911	1,610,209	128,916	2,668,667	219,447	9,701	238	779	13,259
1912	1,444,432	112,885	1,990,699	168,729	20,395	506	620	11,841
1913	860,155	65,652	1,317,369	87,915	27,497	688	629	14,292
1914	495,763	37,646	654,133	21,631	23,514	588	656	11,825

* Equal to 4,888,208 lbs.

Appendix III

Gold Coast Imports and Exports 1910–1919

National Archive, Kew, London CO 98/32

TABLE SHOWING CUSTOMS DUTIES (IMPORT, EXPORT & TOTAL DUTIES)

FOR THE YEARS 1910-1919.

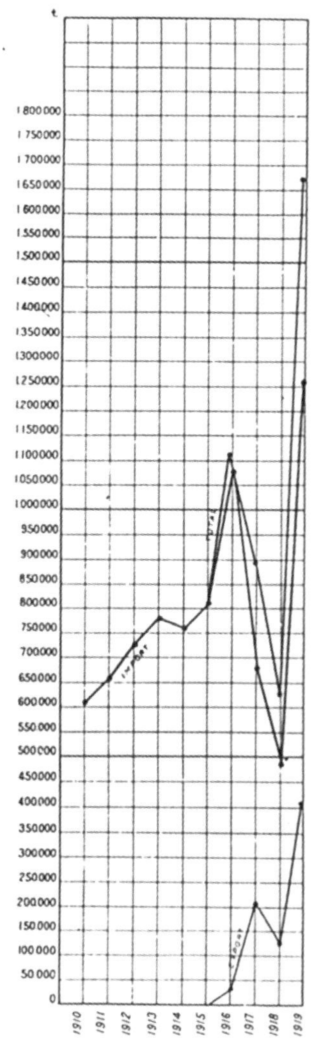

Index

D

E

F

H

N

O

P

Q

R

S

U

Y

Z